SECOND EDITION

Introduction to Estates and Trusts

SECOND EDITION

Introduction to Estates and Trusts

By

The Philadelphia Institute

Susan J. G. Shrader, Editor

West Publishing Company
St. Paul New York Los Angeles San Francisco

PRODUCTION CREDITS
Text Design David Farr, ImageSmythe, Inc.
Copyedit Barbara Bergstrom
Composition Northwestern Printcrafters
Index Patricia Lewis

WEST'S COMMITMENT TO THE ENVIRONMENT

In 1906, West Publishing Company began recycling materials left over from the production of books. This began a tradition of efficient and responsible use of resources. Today, up to 95 percent of our legal books and 70 percent of our college texts are printed on recycled, acid-free stock. West also recycles nearly 22 million pounds of scrap paper annually—the equivalent of 181,717 trees. Since the 1960s, West has devised ways to capture and recycle waste inks, solvents, oils, and vapors created in the printing process. We also recycle plastics of all kinds, wood, glass, corrugated cardboard, and batteries, and have eliminated the use of styrofoam book packaging. We at West are proud of the longevity and the scope of our commitment to our environment.

Production, Prepress, Printing, and Binding by West Publishing Company.

610 Opperman Drive
P.O. Box 64526
St. Paul, MN 55164-0526

Printed in the United States of America

99 98 97 96 95 94 93 92 8 7 6 5 4 3 2 1 0

Library of Congress Cataloging-in-Publication Data

Introduction to estates and trusts / The Philadelphia Institute : Susan J. G. Shrader, editor. — 2nd ed.
p. cm.
Includes index.
ISBN 0-314-93379-4 (hard)
1. Decedents' estates—United States. 2. Trusts and trustees—United States. 3. Inheritance and transfer tax—Law and legislation—United States. 4. Probate law and practice—United States. I. Shrader, Susan J. G. II. Philadelphia Institute.
KF778.I57 1992
346-7305'2—dc20
[347.30652] 92-25
CIP

ACKNOWLEDGMENTS

The Philadelphia Institute in Philadelphia, Pennsylvania was established in 1970 to train college graduates as paralegals to work with attorneys in various areas of the law. The school offers courses in specialized areas of the law such as Corporate Finance and Business Law, Litigation Management, Real Estate, Employee Benefit Plans, Administrative and Public Law, International Trade Law and Business, and Fiduciary Management. There is also a General Practice course. This book will be used as the required text for the Fiduciary Management course.

The book was written as an introductory-level book to teach students the basic concepts of estate and trust administration and estate planning. The original version of this book was published in 1979. Because of sweeping tax law changes, this book has been completely revised. All forms and tax examples shown in the book have been updated. Although the book was written primarily for the paralegal student, it is also a useful reference for the lay person faced with settling a family estate or trust.

I would like to thank the text reviewers whose careful reading of the first edition and revised manuscript provided invaluable suggestions: Anna Durham, Athens Area Technical College; Bernard Helldorfer, St. John's University; Michael Kosh, Marywood College; Michael Lampert, Florida Atlantic University; Lennart Larson, Southern Methodist University; Dianna Murphy, Sullivan College; Bob Rosplock, Lakeland Community College; Margaret T. Campbell, University of Maine; Donna Donathon, Marshall University Community College; and Deborah Green, Henry Ford Community College.

I would also like to thank my father, Guy George Gabrielson, Esquire, for his many hours of helpful lawyer to paralegal "brainstorming"; my husband Craig C. Shrader for helping me with the technical aspects of producing the text on the computer; and the staff at West Publishing Company, especially Mary Verrill and Elizabeth Hannan. In addition, I would like to thank Jess Leventhal, Esquire, for his advice and for providing some of the Pennsylvania forms found in the book. Ann Cook, a fellow paralegal at Pepper, Hamilton & Scheetz and part-time accounting instructor at The Philadelphia Institute, provided valuable advice on the accounting chapter. I would especially like to thank Arnold Rosenberg at The Philadelphia Institute for his many hours of review. I could not have covered a subject of this magnitude without the help of all of these individuals.

Philadelphia, Pennsylvania
January, 1992

SUSAN J. G. SHRADER
THE PHILADELPHIA INSTITUTE

PREFACE

This book was designed as an introductory level text for paralegal students studying estate and trust administration and planning. The settlement of an estate is covered chronologically from the decedent's death to the final accounting and distribution of the assets of the estate. The last chapter discusses some basic estate planning considerations.

The study of law is primarily the process of learning a new language. This text uses layperson's language, gradually introducing students to new terms used in the field of fiduciary law. The student is gradually introduced to new terms and concepts so that he or she becomes comfortable in using them and is not overwhelmed.

Forms and letters used during the estate and trust administration process are illustrated throughout the book. Their purpose is to familiarize the student with the basic forms required for probating a will, qualifying as the personal representative, and collecting the assets in the estate or for the benefit of the decedent's family such as veteran, Social Security, and employee benefits. The probate forms illustrated in the text are from Pennsylvania and may be different than forms used in other states. However, they are very useful in learning the basic concepts of estate and trust administration. Since most states use the Uniform Probate Code, these forms follow the UPC format.

The field of fiduciary management can be pursued in a bank trust department as well as a law firm. Because of my experience in both areas as well as in independent practice, I have illustrated how these skills can be used in more than one employment situation.

Examples, problems, and questions are given in each chapter to promote class discussion. Often there are no black and white answers in law. Thus the teacher can use the questions as a catalyst to class discussion. There may be several correct answers to them.

This book will provide a solid foundation for the paralegal to start a career in estate and trust administration and planning. Competence in the field can only be accomplished through actual job experience, but a basic knowledge of the concepts is essential before that job experience can be attained. This book can provide that foundation for the student interested in becoming an estate and trust paralegal.

Contents in Brief

Preface vii

Chapter One
Introduction to Estates and Trusts 1

Chapter Two
Probate 9

Chapter Three
Valuation of Assets, Filing an Inventory, and Payment of Debts 29

Chapter Four
Gift Tax 99

Chapter Five
The Federal Estate Tax and the Federal Estate Tax Return 131

Chapter Six
State Taxation of Estates and Trusts 297

Chapter Seven
Formal Accounting 309

Chapter Eight
Settlement by Agreement 359

Chapter Nine
Distribution of Assets 373

Chapter Ten
Estate Planning and Drafting 389

Appendix
Uniform Probate Code 463

Glossary 601

Subject Index 617

Forms Index 635

CONTENTS

Preface vii

CHAPTER ONE

Introduction to Estates and Trusts 1

The Role of Law in Governing Estates and Trusts 1

Methods of Transfer of Assets 1
Lifetime Transfers 1
Outright Gift 1
Gifts in Trust 1

Gifts upon Death 2
Wills 2
Intestacy 3
The Personal Representative 5

The Estate Plan 6

The Role of the Paralegal 6
Checklists and Procedures 7
Confidentiality 8
Dealing with Clients 8
Letters 8

CHAPTER TWO

Probate 9

Formal and Informal Probate 10

Preliminary Information 11
Decedent's Name 11
Death Information 12
Decedent's Domicile 14
Decedent's Assets 15
Will Search 15

If No Will Is Found 16
Administrator 16
Petition for Administration 17
Renunciation 17
Administrator D.B.N. 18
Fees 18
Bond 18
Short Certificate 19

If a Will Is Found 20
Executor 20
Petition for Probate and Letters Testamentary 20
Renunciation 21
Administrator C.T.A. 21
Administrator D.B.N.C.T.A. 21
Fees 21
Bond 21
Witnesses 22
Short Certificates 22

After Appointment of Personal Representative 23
Legal Advertising 23
Filing System 23
Reminder Systems 24
Estate Checking Account 25
Notifying Beneficiaries 25
Application for Employer Identification Number 26
Ancillary Letters 26

CHAPTER THREE **Valuation of Assets, Filing an Inventory, and Payment of Debts 29**

Duties of the Personal Representative 29
Discovery 30
Possession 30
Valuation 30
Liquidation 30
Payment of Debts 30
Opening Estate Bank Account 30

Discovery of Assets 31
Safe Deposit Boxes 33

Acquiring, Valuating, and Liquidating Assets 34
Intangible Personal Property 35
Cash 35
Bank Accounts 36
Life Insurance 40
Corporate and Governmental Securities 43
Other Business Interests 56
Claims and Contracts 57

Tangible Personal Property 67
Definitions 67
Security of Tangible Personal Property 67

Valuation of Tangible Personal Property 72
Sale of Tangible Personal Property 72

Real Estate 73
Interests in Real Estate 73
Physical Control 74
Mortgage Payments 77
Treatment of Property Leased to Others 77
Decedent's Obligations as a Tenant 77
Valuation of Real Estate 78
Sale of Real Estate 79

Payment of Debts 84
Priority of Payment 84
Payment of Bona Fide Claims 85
Treatment of Doubtful Claims 85

Estate Bank Accounts 85
Interest-Bearing Accounts 85
Checking Accounts 86
Balancing the Checkbook 86
Using a Journal System 88

Investment Problems 91
Legal Restraints 91
Common Investments of Estates 91
Savings Accounts and Certificates of Deposit 91
United States Treasury Bills 92
Commercial Paper 92

Preparing and Filing an Inventory of Decedent's Property 93

Acquiring Possession of Assets without Letters 96

CHAPTER FOUR

Gift Tax 99

Legal Elements of a Gift 99
Transfer for Less Than Adequate and Full Consideration 99
Donative Intent 99
Delivery 100
Acceptance 102

Federal Taxation of Gifts 102
Taxable Transfers 103
Transfers into Joint Names 103
Transfers in Trust 104

Valuation 104

Nontaxable Transfers 105
Marital Deduction 105
Disclaimers 106

Annual Exclusion 106
Present Interests 106
Future Interests 107

Unified Credit 108
Charitable and Educational Exclusion 109
Cumulative and Progressive Rates 109
Relationship to Federal Estate Tax 110
Deductions 111
Preparing the Federal Gift Tax Return 111
Gift Splitting Between Spouses 122
Generation-Skipping Transfer Tax 123
Computation of the Tax 123

CHAPTER FIVE **The Federal Estate Tax and the Federal Estate Tax Return 131**

Preliminary Step—The Application for the Federal Employer Identification Number 133
Assembling Facts 134
Estate Checkbook, Journal, and Ledger 135
Review of File 135
Analysis of Decedent's Lifetime Papers 135

Preparing the Return 135

Schedule A—Real Estate 141
Forms of Ownership of Real Property 141
Method of Reporting Real Estate 144
Valuation of Real Estate 144

Schedule A-1, Section 2032A Valuation 150
Schedule B—Stocks and Bonds 151
Valuation of Stocks and Bonds 151
Types of Stocks and Bonds 158
Accrued Interest and Dividends 167
Alternate Valuation 170
Operation of § 2032 171

Schedule C—Mortgages, Notes, and Cash 177

Bank Accounts 177
Notes and Mortgages 179
Cash 179

Schedule D—Proceeds of Life Insurance 179
Types of Insurance 181
Including Proceeds of Life Insurance in the Gross Estate 182
Inclusion in the Gross Estate of Insurance Proceeds Payable to Beneficiaries Other Than the Estate 183

Schedule E—Jointly Owned Property 185
Forms of Ownership of Property 185
Federal Estate Tax Treatment of Joint Property 187

Schedule F—Other Miscellaneous Property Not Reportable on Any Other Schedule 192
Noncorporate Business Interests 192
Tangible Personal Property 195
Interests in Trusts 197
Pensions and Death Benefits 198
Insurance on the Life of Others 199
Miscellaneous Property 199

Schedule G—Transfers During Decedent's Life 201
Reporting of Transfers on the Return 202

Schedule H—Powers of Appointment 205
Distinction between General and Special Powers 207
General Powers Created before October 22, 1942 209
General Powers Created after October 21, 1942 211

Schedule I—Annuities 213
Types of Annuities 215
Federal Estate Taxation of Annuities 217
Annuity Payments under Approved Plans 217

Schedule J—Funeral and Administration Expenses 220
Funeral Expenses 220
Deductions from Funeral Expenses 220
Executors' Commissions 221
Attorneys' Fees 223
Accountants' Fees 223
Miscellaneous Expenses 223
Election to Deduct Administration Expenses on the Fiduciary Income Tax Return 224
Double Deductions on Form 706 and Form 1041 226
Expenses Relating to Tax Exempt Income 227
Community Property Considerations 228

Schedule K—Debts, Mortgages, and Liens 228
Debts 228
Contingent Liabilities 232
Mortgages and Liens 233

Schedule L—Net Losses During Administration and Costs of Administering Property Not Subject to Claims 234
Net Losses During Administration 234
Expenses Incurred in Administering Property Not Subject to Claims 237

Schedule M—Marital Deduction 237
Unlimited Marital Deduction 239
Form of Marital Share 240
Size of Marital Share 242
Election against Will or Exercise of Dower or Curtesy Rights 243
Disclaimer of Interest under Will 243
Simultaneous Death 244

Schedule N—Qualified ESOP Sales (Under Section 2057) 248
Schedule O—Charitable Bequests 248
Types of Qualifying Recipients 248
Types of Gifts 252
Gifts in Trust 252
Unitrusts and Annuity Trusts 253
Valuation of Charitable Gifts 253
Preparation of Schedule O 254

Schedule P—Credit for Foreign Death Taxes 255
Schedule Q—Credit for Tax on Prior Transfers 257
Schedule R—Generation–Skipping Transfer Tax 258
Schedule S—Excise Tax on Excess Pension Distributions 260
Continuation Schedules 263
Recapitulation Schedule 263
Computation of Tax 266
Calculation of Taxable Estate 266
Attachments 267
Peter Chessman Estate 267

Return Procedures 268
Filing the Return with the Internal Revenue Service 268
Payment of the Tax 268
Signatures on the Return 287
Exhibits To Be Submitted 288

Filing the Return with the State 293
Audit of the Federal Estate Tax Return 293

Post-Audit Review and Litigation 294

CHAPTER SIX

State Taxation of Estates and Trusts 297

State Death Taxes 297
Estate versus Inheritance Tax 299
Specific Exemptions 299
Deductions 299
Charitable Bequests 300
Progressive versus Flat Tax Rates 300
Residency and Location of Property 302
Gifts in Contemplation of Death 303
Pre-1977 Law 303

Jointly Owned Property 304
Between Husband and Wife 304
Other Joint Property 304

Tax Waivers 305
Community Property States 305

CHAPTER SEVEN

Formal Accounting 309

Assembling the Necessary Facts 311
Checkbook 311
Capital Transactions 312
Dividends and Interest 313
Non-Cash Distributions 315

Principal and Income 315
Problem Areas 324
Stock Dividends 325
Capital Gains Distributions from Mutual Funds 325
Expenses for Repairs to Trust or Estate Assets 325
Depreciation 326

Disbursements and Distributions 326
Disbursements 326
Administrative Expenses 326
Payments to Family Members 327
Funeral Expenses 327
Other Debts and Taxes 327

Distributions 328

Balancing an Account and Reconciling It with Assets on Hand 330

Waiver of Income Accounting 331

Examination of Fiduciary Accounts 332
Preparation of an Accounting 341
Cover Page 341
Composition of Net Balances 342
Receipts of Principal 342
Gains and Losses on Sales or Other Dispositions 342
Disbursements of Principal 342
Principal Distributions to Beneficiaries 343
Principal Balance on Hand 343
Information Schedules—Principal Investments Made 344
Changes in Investment Holdings—Capital Changes 344
Receipts of Income 344
Disbursements of Income 344
Income Distributions to Beneficiaries 344
Proposed Distributions to Beneficiaries 345
Signature and Affidavit 345

Procedures of Notice and Audit 348
Notice to Interested Parties 348
Court Audit 349
Adjudication 350

CHAPTER EIGHT

Settlement by Agreement 359

Drafting the Agreement 360
Elements of the Agreement 360
Caption 360
Title 361
Salutation 361
Recital of Background 361
Account 361
Approval of Account 361
Receipt 361
Release 362
Waive Filing, Etc. 362
Future Audit 362
Indemnification 363
Refunding Provision 363
Succession 363
Governing Law 363
Signing and Sealing 363

Acknowledgment 364

Examples of Agreements 364

CHAPTER NINE

Distribution of Assets 371

Determining the Distributive Shares 371
Intestate Distribution 371
The Typical Patterns of Distribution in a Will 373
Types of Bequests 373

Statutory Modifications of Will Provisions 374
Election by Surviving Spouse 374
Mortmain 375
Abatement, Ademption, and Lapse 375

The Problem of Whether to Distribute in Cash or in Kind 376

Obtaining Court Approval of Distribution 378
The Schedule of Distribution 378
Deciding Whether or Not a Schedule of Distribution Is Necessary 378
Techniques Used in Preparing the Schedule of Distribution 382
Accounting for Receipts during the Interim and Reappraisal of Assets 382
Special Problems If There Is a Marital Deduction Gift or Trust 383
Designation of Exact Dollar Amounts and Earmarking of Specific Legacies for Distributees 384

Approval of a Schedule of Distribution 384

Physical Distribution 384
General Problems of Distribution 384
Distribution to a Minor or Incompetent 384
Distribution to a Foreign Fiduciary 385

Distribution of Real Estate 385
Distribution When Real Estate Is Listed in a Schedule of Distribution Filed with the Court 385
Distribution of Real Estate Where No Schedule Is Prepared or Where a Schedule of Distribution Is Prepared but Is Not Filed 386
The Problem of Whether or Not to Transfer Real Estate on the Record Where No Schedule Is Filed 386
Cancellation of Fire and Liability Insurance 386

Distribution of Tangible Personal Property 386
Distribution of Intangible Personal Property 387
Distributing Cash 387
Distributing Stocks and Bonds 387

Satisfaction of Award 388

Discharge of Fiduciary 388

CHAPTER TEN

Estate Planning and Drafting 389

The Initial Client Interview 390
Information Needed 390
Assets and Liabilities 395
Likely Appraisers and Markets for Sale 396
Agreements 396
Dispositive Wishes 397

Discussion of Fees 398

The Techniques of Planning 399
Liquidity 399
Life Insurance 400
Acquiring More Liquid Asset 400

Prompt Disposal of Assets 401
Reduction of Tax Bite 403
Lifetime Gifts 403
The Marital Deduction 405
The Use of Trusts to Prevent Repeated Taxation 406
Using Charitable Gifts 408

Estate Planning Computations 409

The Anatomy of a Will 411
The Component Parts 412
Preamble 414
Payment of Funeral Expenses and Expenses of Last Illness 414
Funeral and Burial Instructions 414
Preresiduary Gifts 415
Residuary Clause 426
Standard "Boilerplate" Provisions 430
Appointment of Fiduciaries 434
Signature of Testator 436

Codicils 437

The Anatomy of a Trust 437
Types of Trusts 439
Testamentary 439
Inter Vivos 440

Typical Trust Provisions 450
Preamble 450
Dispositive Provisions 450
Standard "Boilerplate" Provisions 455
Trustees 459
Schedule of Property 459
Compensation Agreement 460
Execution 460

Amendment and Revocation 460

Procedures after Execution of Wills and Trusts 461
Location of Originals 461
Related Documents 461
Periodic Review of Estate Plans 462

APPENDIX **Uniform Probate Code 463**

Glossary 601

Subject Index 617

Forms Index 635

SECOND EDITION

Introduction to Estates and Trusts

CHAPTER ONE

Introduction to Estates and Trusts

THE ROLE OF LAW IN GOVERNING ESTATES AND TRUSTS

We live in a society that permits private ownership of property.[1] One of the rights of private ownership is the ability to transfer property from one person to another during life or upon one's death. These transfers are normally subject to taxes by the federal government and/or by the states. The right to transfer property may be conditioned on the payment of taxes.[2]

Aside from taxes, society has established certain other laws that may prohibit or modify the objectives of a transferor of property. For example, the laws of most states do not allow a person to bypass a spouse completely in making distributions of assets after death.

The remainder of this chapter will give you an overview of the methods of transmission of wealth and the legal restraints that our society has imposed on such transfers.

METHODS OF TRANSFER OF ASSETS

Lifetime Transfers

Outright Gift A gift is the transfer of property from one person to another without any exchange of property or money requested in return. There are few restraints placed on a living person's right to make a gift to another living person with no strings attached. This is not to say that such gifts are free of tax. They are not. There is a federal gift tax that will be discussed later on in this book.[3]

Gifts in Trust Sometimes a person wants to make a gift of property to another without giving the recipient full power to treat

1. Throughout this book the word "property" refers to tangible things like real estate, jewelry, or paintings, as well as intangible things like stocks or money.

2. The tax aspects of transfers will be discussed in Chapters Five and Six.

3. See Chapter Four.

the property as his or her own. For example, a grandparent may want to provide funds for a grandchild's college education. If the money is given outright to the grandchild, or even to the grandchild's parents, there is no absolute assurance that the money will be used for college tuition. To assure the use of the money in the manner intended by the grandparent, a "trust" may be created.

A trust is a legal device whereby one person (the "trustee") holds legal ownership of property for the benefit of another (the "beneficiary"). The creator of the trust (the "transferor" or "settlor") may specify the terms and conditions under which the trustee is to provide the benefits of the property held in trust for the beneficiary. In the example above, the grandparent could create a trust, naming a bank or an individual as trustee, and place $20,000 in the trust. The trust document (sometimes called a "deed of trust") might provide that the money is to be held by the bank until the grandchild is admitted to college and then be paid out periodically to meet the costs of tuition. In the meantime the money in the trust is invested and will earn income, thus increasing the value of the trust.

Trusts may be set up during one's lifetime or at death. A trust created during lifetime is known as an "inter vivos" trust. One created at death (through the use of a will) is called a "testamentary" trust.

Gifts upon Death

Wills When a person dies owning property, it is possible to convey that property to others. The written instructions concerning the disposition of the decedent's assets after death are known as a "will." The laws of the various states (but not any federal law) determine the requirements that allow a writing to be considered a valid will. In addition, state law will set forth which of a group of seemingly valid writings is the one to be considered the will of the decedent.

The Characteristics of a Will Each state has its own law concerning the form that a will must take to be valid. The basic requirements common to most states are:

1. The will must be in writing.
2. The will must be signed by the "testator".[4]
3. The testator must be of legal age.
4. The will must be dated.
5. The will must be witnessed.

4. That is, the person whose will the writing purports to be.

Codicils A will may be amended by a later writing that meets the requirements of a will. The amendment is called a "codicil." In common usage, a codicil only changes part of a will, leaving the majority of it intact.[5] If a testator wants to make significant changes in a will, it is best to draft an entirely new document as the will rather than have a long, complicated codicil.

The Governing Will Occasionally after someone's death, more than one document is discovered each appearing to be a will. Often such documents are contradictory in their provisions. Only one, however, may be considered the "will" of the testator. The most recently dated will is the one recognized as determinative by virtually all states. All earlier wills and codicils that are not in accord with the last document will be disregarded.

Testamentary Capacity In order to issue a valid will, the testator must be acting knowingly. That is, he or she must have the mental capabilities to understand what property is owned and to whom it shall be given by the will. This requires a lesser degree of mental facilities than might be necessary for other legal encounters, such as being a party to a contract. When a person does have these capabilities, it is said that he possesses "testamentary capacity." This is commonly called "being of sound mind."

Further, a will must be the free act of the testator. The will is not valid if it was the result of someone forcing the testator to sign. This is known as "duress" and invalidates the document. For example, suppose it could be proven that a threat was made against the life of the testator unless a particular will was signed. The law would not allow such a will to have any effect.

Other examples of conduct on the part of other parties that invalidate a will are "fraud" and "undue influence." Fraud is using trickery to prompt the signing of a document. Undue influence is using one's position of trust to take advantage of another.

Intestacy A person who dies without having left a valid will is said to have died "intestate." The law of every states makes provision for who is to receive the assets of the decedent in such circumstances. Not surprisingly, those who are favored by the law are the surviving spouse, children, grandchildren, parents (or grandparents), brothers and sisters. When there is an intestacy, the law of a state will provide not only the order in which surviving relatives shall share in the estate of the decedent but also the percentage of the estate that will go to each class of surviving relatives.

5. A codicil is usually labeled as such, referring specifically to the will which it is amending.

EXAMPLE
A Father's Intestacy

> The law of state X provides that in the case of intestacy the estate shall be distributed entirely to the surviving spouse if no children were born to the decedent. If there were children, then one-half of the estate goes to the children, in equal shares, and one-half to the surviving spouse. If there is no surviving spouse, then the estate will pass to the surviving issue of the decedent in equal shares.
>
> Vern Mills dies without a will and is survived by his wife Verna and his children Felix, Wanda, and Ferris. How much of Vern's estates does each of these survivors receive?
>
> Under the law of state X, Verna as the surviving spouse gets one-half and each of the children gets one-sixth (one-third of the one-half remaining).

Intestate laws typically provide that when a person who is in a class that is to receive a share of the decedent's estate has died before the decedent,[6] that person's children will take the place of the predeceasing person. This is called a "per stirpes" distribution. For example, if Felix Mills had died before his father and been survived by two children, what share of Vern's estate would each of Felix's children receive? They would each receive one-twelfth (one-half of the one-sixth due to their father).

PROBLEM

Doris Binkle died intestate survived by only two children, Edna and Frieda. Both Edna and Frieda have two children. In addition, Doris is survived by Bob, Leo, and Helen Binkle, the children of Doris's son Ned, who died a year before Doris.

The relevant state intestate law provides for the following order of distribution:

1. If no children survive, to the surviving spouse;
2. If children survive, one-third to the surviving spouse and two-thirds to the surviving children;
3. If no children or spouse survives, to surviving parents;
4. If no parents survive, to surviving brothers and sisters.

If a member of one of the above classes predeceases the decedent, his or her share shall go to their surviving issue.[7]

Who receives Doris's assets? What proportion does each receive?

---

6. This is known as "predeceasing."

7. Issue is a legal term referring to descendants; children, grandchildren, great-grandchildren, etc.

The Personal Representative

Appointment Once a valid will has been shown to exist, or it has been established that the decedent died intestate, it is necessary for the court having authority over the decedent's estate[8] to appoint someone to be the representative of the estate. This person is responsible to supervise the collection, preservation, and ultimate distribution of the decedent's property. The person so appointed is commonly called a "personal representative" or "fiduciary." Banks or trust companies frequently serve as personal representatives. When they do, they are often referred to as "corporate fiduciaries." A personal representative who has been named in the will may be named as an "executor," if he is a man, or "executrix" if she is a woman. One who is named by the court is known as an "administrator" or "administratrix." In most states today the feminine term is rarely used, and once a person is appointed to serve as personal representative, he or she is simply referred to as executor or administrator.

The law of every state has special provisions governing the manner in which a fiduciary[9] must deal with property entrusted to him. The fiduciary must keep the property separate from other property; must exercise prudent judgment in preserving, selling, investing, and otherwise dealing with the property; and must also be faithful to the interests of those to whom the property will ultimately be distributed.

Collection and Distribution of the Estate The aggregate wealth of a decedent is referred to as an "estate." The process of collecting the assets that comprise the estate, paying all of the decedent's debts, paying the death taxes, and distributing the balance of the assets to the beneficiaries or heirs[10] is referred to as "administration of the estate."

Distribution of the assets will normally be in strict accordance with the directions of the testator contained in the will. For example, the testator may have stated that the house will go to son John, a car to nephew Harry, and the remainder of the estate to the surviving spouse. In that simple case the personal representative would follow the instructions in the will by preparing a deed for the house in favor of John, a transfer of the motor vehicle title to

8. Most states have specialized courts to administer decedents' estates. The names of such courts vary. It may be a "Probate" Court, "Surrogate's" Court, or "Orphans' " Court, or some other name depending on the state. As soon as possible, you should learn the name of the court in your state that has authority over decedents' estates.

9. A trustee is also a fiduciary.

10. A beneficiary is someone named in a will. An heir inherits property based on his or her relationship to the decedent, because there is no will. The property is divided according to intestate law.

the nephew Harry, and whatever documents are necessary to transfer the remaining property to the spouse.

In certain situations the decedent will have left a will that, in part, may not be followed for purposes of distribution. In most jurisdictions a spouse has the power to disregard the deceased spouse's will and receive that share of property that would have been received had the spouse died intestate. The exercise of this right by the spouse is referred to as "an election to take against the will." The method of carrying out such an election is governed by the law of the state in which the estate is probated. Wills are probated in the state where the decedent resides or is "domiciled."

Accounting State law requires fiduciaries to disclose all transactions that have occurred during the administration of the estate or trust. After some time has elapsed since the beginning of the administration of the estate or trust, or when final distribution of the property is about to take place, the fiduciary is required to "account" for the property which he has administered. A statement must be prepared showing the property that came into the fiduciary's possession, the income from that property during the period of administration, any changes in the content of the property (for example, a sale or purchase of an asset), payments of debts and expenses, distributions to the beneficiaries, and any balance remaining. In most circumstances, the fiduciary's account must be approved by the appropriate court.

The Estate Plan

One of the roles of the lawyer in the area of estates and trusts is to explain to the client the interrelationship between the general body of law relating to transfer of wealth (state law) and the federal and state laws imposing taxes on those transfers. The lawyer's initial job is to suggest a plan for transmitting wealth that fulfills the transferor's desires concerning how the property should ultimately be transmitted and minimizes taxes, thereby maximizing the wealth actually transmitted. That plan, which is a game plan for the transmission of wealth, is referred to by lawyers as an "estate plan."

The estate plan will call for a certain plan of distribution of property at death that is set forth in a will. Often the estate plan will also call for inter vivos gifts of property, either outright or in trust.

THE ROLE OF THE PARALEGAL

Fiduciaries usually engage the services of an attorney, not only for legal advice, but also for the day-to-day administration of the estate or trust. This is true of both individual and corporate fiduciaries. In addition, corporate fiduciaries usually have departments that administer trusts and estates. It is the attorney or the corporate fiduciary who hires the paralegal. Throughout this book, whenever reference is made to the duties of the fiduciary (except for matters of policy), such duties or activities should be understood to mean those of the paralegal as well.

Indeed, from the time that a client first visits a lawyer for the purpose of discussing an estate plan, through the time that the client chooses to make lifetime gifts of property, until finally the client dies and there is an estate to administer, the lawyer's assistant may be called upon to perform or assist in the performance of many of the services rendered to the client. This includes drafting the will and/or trust, ascertaining important information, filing papers with the court, preparing tax returns and accounts, and generally keeping track of the assets entrusted to the fiduciary.

Many of the concepts discussed in this book will be entirely new to you. Some extremely technical material is reviewed. You should not expect to become an expert from this book alone. A great deal of time and effort must be devoted to that end—and this is only the beginning. Concepts are to be understood, not memorized. As you read through this book, take time out to think about the areas discussed. Make sure you understand each new concept before moving on to the next. To this end, your instructor should be available to answer those questions that you may find unanswered in the text.

Checklists and Procedures

Any law office that handles a large amount of estate and trust work will probably have its own forms and methods of doing things. Repetition of the same problems encountered with different clients leads to standardization. One of the functions that a paralegal may perform as an invaluable aid in the law office or corporate fiduciary is to develop checklists and standard procedures to help carry out the tasks at hand in an orderly way. Having a checklist of items needed for a particular matter often prevents the omission of a crucial document or bit of information.

Outlining procedures in advance so that the necessary steps can be followed when a particular situation arises saves time and avoids errors. Most law offices, banks, and trust companies are very aware that their costs are directly related to the time it takes to perform certain tasks. When matters can be attended to quickly and efficiently, the paralegal becomes of crucial importance to the law firm or corporate fiduciary.

Throughout this book checklists and procedures will be suggested. You should understand that they are just that—

suggestions—not dictates. Anything may be tailored to the particular requirements of the law and customs of the locale in which they will be used. On your own, you may think of better, more complete, or different types of checklists that lend themselves to the kind of work you will be doing as a paralegal.

Confidentiality

As a paralegal you will learn a great deal of confidential information. Clients discussing their financial and family affairs with their bank or attorney do so in the most private way. Clients take these matters extremely seriously. It will not always be easy to distinguish confidential from nonconfidential information. Clients will be offended if their affairs are discussed in public. Therefore, it is best never to discuss a client's business (or your firm's or bank's business) with any outsider. Nor should you have such a discussion with someone from your office in a public place.

Dealing with Clients

You will be a newcomer to the law office or bank in which you will be working. The clients are not used to you and, especially in a law firm setting, may have reservations about dealing with you because you are not a lawyer. All of this should be overcome in time. It is very important that you not call or write a client unless you have the permission of a lawyer or, in the case of a bank, your supervisor. Once rapport has been established, many clients find it preferable to talk with the paralegal rather than an attorney. You must wait, however, for this to be indicated to you. When in doubt about the propriety of any action which you are about to take, check with the lawyer or other person who is supervising you.

Letters

Obviously, you may not in any way hold yourself out to the public as a lawyer. A letter signed by you on law firm stationery could mislead the recipient into believing you are a lawyer. Therefore, promptly after you begin work, ask one of the lawyers who is supervising you how you should sign letters that you write.

CHAPTER TWO

Probate

The word "probate" is used in several ways both in general practice and in the course of these materials. When a lawyer says, "I must probate Mr. Modest's will," he is using the word as a verb meaning to prove the authenticity of the will after Mr. Modest has died. When a will is "submitted for a probate," the words mean not only the actual proof of the will's authenticity, but also in general refers to the judicial procedure by which the authenticity of the will is proven and a personal representative is appointed. The word "probate" is used to refer to the judicial procedure by which an administrator is appointed even where there is no will to be proven. In addition, the term "probate" is used when referring to the actual administration of the estate from qualification of the personal representative to final settlement. In all cases the term "probate" refers to assets directly under the control of the personal representative, hence under the will. Life insurance payable to someone other than the estate, jointly owned property, annuities, pensions, and other assets that automatically pass to a beneficiary are not "probate" assets.

Probate has several purposes. First, if there is a will, probate provides a means of proving the authenticity of the will and publicly recording it. This provides legal recognition of the fact that the decedent has left instructions for the disposition of his property. If no such instructions had been given the property would be disposed of under the state laws of intestate distribution.

In addition, probate imposes upon the personal representative the responsibility for liquidating and distributing the decedent's property. By placing the entire responsibility on one or more designated parties probate serves to maintain harmony among the members of the decedent's family and the beneficiaries of the estate.

Further, by means of probate the personal representative becomes entitled to take legal actions on behalf of the decedent. For example, if it becomes advisable to sell the shares of General Motors stock belonging to the decedent, the stock transfer agent will require proof that the person selling the stock is the legal representative of the decedent. Upon receiving this proof, the stock transfer agent will proceed to transfer the shares of General Motors without worrying whether the person who ordered the sale of the stock has the actual authority to do so. Thus, the proof of the court's designation of the personal representative facilitates the transaction of business.

FORMAL AND INFORMAL PROBATE

There are essentially two different methods in use among the various states by which a will may be probated. "Formal" probate requires that the person who is offering the will for probate (the "proponent") give advance notice to all those who may have an interest in the estate of the offering of the will. This allows the interested parties to appear at a hearing to contest the validity of the will if they wish, or to contest appointment of the personal representative.

Informal probate is a simpler procedure dispensing with the requirement to notify all interested parties. The personal representative produces the will before an officer of the court.[1] The witnesses to the will must accompany the personal representative to attest to their signatures. After the witnesses have given an oath that they did see the testator sign (or that this is, in fact, the true signature of the testator), the will is considered proven. No notice is sent to any interested parties. If someone wishes to contest the validity of the will, affirmative action must be taken to have the Registrar hold a formal hearing inquiring into the validity of the will.

In many cases, if the will was recently executed (signed by the testator), it usually contains a "self-proving" clause. This is a notarized statement that is usually accepted by the court so that the witness does not have to appear personally. This self-proving clause is helpful because so often witnesses to wills are secretaries or other office personnel who work with the attorney who prepared the document. At the time of the testator's death, they may have moved away or died themselves. It is important for the paralegal to check for the self-proving clause in a will. Where there is no such clause, the witnesses must be located.

The Uniform Probate Code (U.P.C.) is a proposal adopted by the National Conference of Commissioners on Uniform State Laws and the American Bar Association. The code has been adopted in one form or another in fifteen states.[2]

1. This officer may be known as the Register of Wills, or Surrogate, or some other name depending upon the state designation. For simplicity, we will refer to the officer as the "Registrar," as is the case under the Uniform Probate Code §§ 1–201(36).

2. Alaska, Arizona, Colorado, Idaho, Maine, Michigan, Minnesota, Montana, Nebraska, New Jersey, New Mexico, North Dakota, Pennsylvania, South Carolina, and Utah. Source: Commission on Uniform State Laws National Organization. Excerpts from the official text of the Uniform Probate Code (1990 ed.) are reproduced as the Appendix in this book.

PRELIMINARY INFORMATION

It is necessary to have certain basic items of information to complete the probate procedure regardless of the specific provisions of the probate law in a given state. This information may be grouped into general categories of personal information about the decedent, information about the will, and information concerning the decedent's assets.

Decedent's Name It is not uncommon to find that the decedent may have used more than one name. Very often people are not consistent in the way they sign their name to a document. In a letter to a friend one might sign with a nickname. On a driver's license one might use a middle initial. On a diploma one might prefer to have his or her full name shown, including the middle name. In this way it happens that assets of a decedent may have been registered using a middle initial, and the will may have been signed with the decedent's middle name fully written.

The customary way of showing more than one name for the same individual is the abbreviation "a/k/a" which stands for "also known as." For example, "Martin Moore, a/k/a Martin M. Moore, a/k/a Martin Milton Moore."

Because the assets registered in the name of the decedent are the subject matter of the administration of the estate, it is the name or names by which the decedent's assets are registered that should be used for the estate proceedings, in addition to the decedent's name as shown on the will. The name shown on the decedent's birth certificate or driver's license may be immaterial. Even the name by which the decedent was generally known may be immaterial unless it happens to be the name registered on an asset or used in the will. The only purpose of including a name in addition to the name of the decedent shown in the will is to be able to transfer the decedent's assets to the personal representative or beneficiary, and it will be difficult to transfer an asset registered in a name you have not included.

Not all assets are "registered" in a person's name. For example, a table or chair or other items of tangible personal property are not registered in the owner's name. Ownerships of such items is determined by possession and, possibly, by a bill of sale.

Common examples of assets whose ownership is registered by name are:

Asset	Registration
Real estate	Deed
Automobile	Certificate of Title
Security	Certificate
Savings account	Passbook

The name of the estate of the decedent usually takes the form "Estate of . . . , Deceased." It is important to include the word "Deceased" so as to distinguish the estate from an incompetent's estate or minor's estate.[3]

CHECKLIST

Procedure to Determine Name of Estate

1. Examine the will (if any) and certificates of stock, bank accounts, savings passbooks, and other registered assets.
2. Use the name of the decedent as it appears in the will (if any).
3. Also use any name of the decedent that appears on any asset registered in the decedent's name alone.
4. When using more than one name, place a/k/a between one name and the next.

PROBLEMS

What name or names should be used for the estate proceedings of the following decedents:

1. Lawrence Alan Lowell II, died leaving a will signed "Lawrence A. Lowell." His checking account was in the name of "Lawrence A. Lowell," and his friends and family always called him "Larry." He had no other assets.
2. Peg Mayer owned a parcel of real estate. The deed shows her name as Margaret Mayer. She died without a will, and the only other asset found among her possession was a savings account passbook in the name of Peg I. Mayer.

Death Information Information concerning the place, time, date, and cause of the decedent's death is also necessary. This information is usually shown on the "death certificate." A death certificate is a document prepared by a physician to record the significant facts surrounding the death of each human being and to declare the human being legally dead. Except in unusual circumstances that may require an autopsy or other postmortem investigation, a death certificate is prepared immediately after death. Usually there is a space on the death certificate for the funeral director to indicate the date and place of interment. Copies of the death certificate can be obtained either from the funeral director or from the county recorder of vital statistics. Frequently there is a charge for each copy of a certificate issued. In some jurisdictions an official copy of the death certificate must be produced at probate. Information concerning the funeral is generally not necessary for purposes of probate. In many places, however, it is customary not

3. Courts also appoint representatives to attend to the affairs of minors and legally incompetent persons.

to begin the probate process until after the decedent's funeral, unless it is important to preserve the assets, or if the funeral cannot take place for several days after the decedent's death.

The funeral director will usually provide several copies of the death certificate to the decedent's family or directly to the attorney. The paralegal should make certain that at least one copy of the certificate will be available for the initial conference with the client.

EXAMPLE
Estate Binder Index

One copy of the death certificate should be permanently retained in an index binder for the estate. An index binder can be made in several ways and sizes but probably the most convenient type is the 8½″ x 14″ cardboard binder with a fastener at the top and numbered tabs along the right side. The numbers on the tabs correspond to the numbers of the items as shown in the index.

Estate of Lillian Furlin, Deceased

1. Last Will (dated: July 6, 1987)
2. Death Certificate (Date of Death: December 21, 1990)
3. Petition for Probate and Letters Testamentary
4. Letters Testamentary (granted: December 27, 1990)
5. Personal Property Tax Return for 1990
6. Proofs of Advertising of the Grant of Letters Testamentary
7. Notice of Taxpayer Identification Number (23-648795)
8. Lifetime Federal Income Tax Return for 1990
9. Receipt for Preliminary Payment of Inheritance Tax
10. Appraisal of Personal Property
11. Appraisal of Real Estate
12. Inventory (dated: April 10, 1991)
13. Fiduciary Income Tax Return for Fiscal Year Ending July 31, 1991
14. Personal Property Tax Return for 1989
15. Inheritance Tax Return (filed: September 10, 1991)
16. Federal Estate Tax Return (filed: September 10, 1991)
17. Receipt for Inheritance Tax
18. Notice of filing of an Appraisement for Inheritance Tax
19. Inheritance Tax Appraisement
20. Fiduciary Income Tax Return for Fiscal Year Ending July 31, 1992

It is advisable to place item number one at the bottom of the binder to make it easier to add subsequent items as they are acquired. If the binder being used requires that holes be punched in the papers, it should be remembered that certain items (such as original tax receipts) should not be mutilated. Such items can be added to a binder by fastening an envelope to a binder page and placing the item in the envelope.

Experience is probably the best teacher of what kinds of papers should go into the binder. The object is to be able to pick up the binder and very quickly have (i) a good idea of where the estate proceedings stand at any moment and (ii) ready access to any of the most important papers. Certainly the binder should start with a copy of the will or trust instrument. It should contain a copy of each tax return (with a covering letter for each, stamped to show the date of receipt by the taxing authority). Each paper prepared for filing with a court such as an inventory, an account, or a schedule of distribution should be included. Many lawyers find it helpful to include a few other items that may be referred to frequently, such as a memorandum prepared early in the administration of an estate intended to guide the timing of various steps. Selectivity is necessary to prevent the binder from containing the whole file, but no arbitrary rule is likely to be useful in determining what should be in the binder and what should not. In addition, the paralegal responsible for many estates in the office should develop his or her own tickler system to flag important dates before the deadlines.

Decedent's Domicile A person's domicile is his regular and permanent home. The place of the domicile of the decedent is of considerable importance because the court having authority over a decedent's estate is the court of the county and state in which the decedent was domiciled at the time of death. Since some states have markedly different death taxes, the tax liability of the estate may vary substantially depending upon the state of domicile at the time of death. There may also be a question as to whether the executor named in the decedent's will may serve in the state in which the decedent was domiciled. For example, a corporate executor may not be qualified to transact business in the state in which the decedent was domiciled at death. Also, some states do not allow out-of-state residents to qualify as the sole executor. In such cases, a resident co-executor must be appointed to serve.

Determining Place of Domicile Most people have only one place where they have a home and no question of domicile would arise. Others may have more than one home, such as a house or apartment in the city and a house at the seashore or mountains. Many college students away at school have a residence on campus but they think of their family house in their hometown as home. It is in such circumstances that the questions of domicile arise. The general rule is that a person changes domicile only when that person has a fixed intention to establish a new domicile at a certain place and actually leaves the old domicile and arrives at the new place. The person's fixed intention or state of mind may be determined by evaluating the facts and circumstances. The following facts are helpful in determining domicile of a decedent, if there is any doubt:

2. The place where the decedent resided.
3. The place where the decedent last voted.
4. The place from which the decedent filed tax returns.
5. The address shown on the decedent's driver's license and auto registration.
6. The address used for the decedent's bank accounts.

PROBLEM

Mr. Good owned a large and attractive home known as "Hilltop," on several acres of ground in Richville, Pennsylvania. He maintained there a staff consisting of a butler, housekeeper, cook, maid, and gardener. Every Friday after work he would be driven by his chauffeur from his offices in Prairieland, Maryland, to Hilltop and on Monday morning he would be returned to Prairieland. During the week he resided in a modest but comfortable home in Prairieland so as to be near his offices. His automobile was owned by his business and registered in Maryland. He had no driver's license, but his chauffeur was licensed in Maryland. He had a savings account at the branch of The Bank and Trust Company of Old Park Road near Hilltop, and he had a checking account at a commercial bank in Prairieland, Maryland. He filed his federal income tax return showing his Maryland home address and he filed a Pennsylvania state income tax return showing the Hilltop address. Whenever he would have parties for friends he would use Hilltop, but occasionally he would entertain a few people in his Maryland house. He voted in Maryland because election day falls on a Tuesday. Decide where Mr. Good's domicile was located and indicate what factors led you to your conclusion.

Decedent's Assets Another initial step in the administration of an estate should be an inquiry into the general nature and approximate total value of the decedent's assets. In many jurisdictions some asset information must be disclosed at the commencement of the estate proceedings. After the administration of estate has begun, a much more detailed list of all assets must be prepared and the assets accumulated.

Will Search One of the initial inquiries of the paralegal after learning of the death of the decedent is the determination of the existence of a will. The administration of an estate where there is a will may have a vastly different result than the administration of the same estate when there is no will. As soon as possible following death, a search should be made for a will (and codicils, if any).

There are four likely places to find a will:

1. In the office of the lawyer who prepared the will.
2. In the vault of the bank or trust company named in the will as executor.
3. In a safe deposit box owned by the decedent.
4. In the decedent's home.

If No Will Is Found

Administrator The decedent is considered to have died *intestate* if no will is found. It should then be determined if the appointment of a personal representative (administrator) is necessary. If the decedent's assets can be transferred without such an appointment, it might be advisable to dispense with the appointment since this should result in avoidance of additional costs. If it is decided that a personal representative should be appointed, the paralegal should consult the law of the jurisdiction where the decedent was domiciled to find who has the right to administer the estate. For example, under the Uniform Probate Code[4] the following persons have priority for appointment in the following order where there is no will:

a. The surviving spouse of the decedent;
b. The issue (lineal descendants) of the decedent (except minors);
c. The parent or parents of the decedent;
d. The brothers and sisters of the decedent;
e. and so on through the decedent's heirs-at-law (or next-of-kin).

Factual information concerning names, addresses, ages, and relationships of the close relatives of the decedent should be gathered from the family members. The law should then be applied to the facts to determine who are the heirs of the decedent, and who has the right to administer the estate.

PROBLEM

Assume that under the law of the state in which an unmarried decedent was domiciled at death the persons entitled to administer the estate are those entitled under the intestate law to the

4. Section 3–203(a).

decedent's estate according to the sizes of their shares. The intestate law provided that the following would share in the estate:

1. Son: one-half (½)
2. Grandson: one-quarter (¼)
3. Granddaughter: one-quarter (¼)

Who has the right to administer the estate?

Petition for Administration After it has been determined who shall administer the estate, appropriate steps should be taken to have the administrator duly appointed. Normally, the initial step is the filing of a "Petition for Administration" or a "Petition for Letters of Administration." In some jurisdictions printed forms are available to be completed and filed; in other places the petitions are entirely typewritten by the lawyer; and in still other jurisdictions the forms are prepared by the Registrar. In any event, the proposed administrator will have to appear in person to be sworn to carry out the duties of his office faithfully.

Regardless of the form the request to be appointed administrator takes, it is reasonably certain that the following information will be required. It may be helpful to set this up in the form of a checklist so that no essential fact is overlooked when speaking with the prospective administrator.

CHECKLIST
Information Generally Required for Petition for Administration

1. Name and address of the administrator.
2. Name or names of the decedent.
3. Decedent's address (domicile).
4. Date of death.
5. Place of death.
6. Name and address of the surviving spouse, if any.
7. Names and addresses of the decedent's heirs-at-law.
8. An estimate of the value of the decedent's personal property.
9. An estimate of the value and location of any real estate in the decedent's own name.

A copy of the Petition in the form it is actually filed should be inserted in the permanent index binder of the estate.

Renunciation Any party having the right to administer the estate who does not wish to serve may renounce such right by filing with the court the appropriate form of renunciation. In some jurisdictions the party renouncing may suggest the appointment of a substitute. Whether the suggestion will be honored depends upon local law and custom. A renunciation is commonly used when several persons of equal degree of relationship with the decedent jointly have the right to administer the estate. It becomes unwieldy to have more than two or three personal representatives serving at the same time. In such circumstances those entitled to serve might agree among themselves as to which ones will act and which will renounce.

Like the Petition for Appointment of an Administrator, the renunciation may be made on a form provided by the Registrar or prepared solely by the attorney. The renunciation is very simple in style, stating the name of the decedent, the name of the person renouncing (and perhaps that person's relationship to the decedent), and the fact that the right to administer is being relinquished.

Administrator D.B.N. If an administrator appointed by the Registrar resigns, dies, or is removed after taking office, the Registrar will appoint a successor, known as an administrator D.B.N. (de bonis non; literally: of no goods). The concept is that the first administrator collected the assets and the successor is merely taking over.

Fees Fees are usually required to be paid at the time of filing the Petition with the Registrar. Often, the attorney will advance the necessary costs and be reimbursed from the estate funds after they are collected. Generally, the fees are modest, varying according to the size of the estate. Even in the largest estates, the filing fees would not be more than several hundred dollars.

In many states, the administrator initially makes a declaration concerning the expected value of the assets in the estate. If the value is greater as shown by the filing of the death tax return, a supplemented filing fee may have to be paid to accord with what should have been paid originally.

Bond In many jurisdictions a fidelity bond is required to be posted by the administrator before assuming the duties of office. The bond is a promise by the bonding company ("surety") to pay to the state ("obligee") for the benefit of persons interested in the estate (such as the heirs) up to a certain amount in the event of default by the administrator. If the administrator faithfully discharges his duties according to law, then the bond will not have to be paid. The bonding company will charge a premium based on the amount of the bond, which is set by the court according to the value of the assets that will be administered.

The following is a sample of the text of a typical fidelity bond:

KNOW ALL MEN BY THESE PRESENTS, That we Leonard D. Smith as Principal and Insurance Co. of North America are held and firmly bound unto the Commonwealth of Pennsylvania in the sum of Ten thousand ($10,000.00) dollars, to be paid to the said Commonwealth: To which payment well and truly to be made we bind ourselves, jointly and severally, for and in the whole, our heirs, executors and administrators, and each and every of them, firmly by these presents.

Sealed with our seals. Dated the 28th day of October in the year of our Lord One Thousand Nine Hundred and Ninety-two (1992).

The Condition of this Obligation is, That if the above bounden Leonard D. Smith Administrator of all and singular the assets of Susan F. Smith, Deceased, of any of them, shall well and truly administer the estate of said decedent according to law, then this obligation to be void as to the administrator or administrators who shall so administer the estate; otherwise it shall remain in force and effect.

Signed, sealed and delivered ______________________ [*Seal*]

in presence of ______________________ [*Seal*]

Short Certificate One of the purposes of having a personal representative appointed is to obtain the power and authority to transfer assets and otherwise administer the estate. This power and authority is demonstrated to the world by the document appointing the personal representative, sometimes known as a decree or Letters of Administration. The personal representative can give evidence of the grant of the decree or the grant of Letters by giving certified copies thereof or "short certificates" issued by the court or Registrar evidencing the appointment of the personal representative. The paralegal should determine how many short certificates will be required for the estate administration. Generally one will be needed for:

1. Each asset to be transferred.
2. Entry into decedent's safe deposit box.
3. The opening of a safe deposit box for the estate.
4. The opening of a bank account for the estate.
5. The forwarding of the decedent's mail to the law office (where appropriate).

Most businesses require that the short certificates have a raised seal and be dated within 60 days of the date of the request. The legal assistant should order only the number of certificates currently needed. Additional certificates can be ordered as needed at a later date.

CHECKLIST
Procedures for Filing Petition for Administration with Registrar

With a review of the previous discussion it should now be possible for you to prepare a checklist or standard procedure to be followed in your state whenever an estate requires that an administrator be appointed.

1. Gather information necessary for completing the Petition and complete the Petition.
2. Arrange for administrator to be present.
3. Obtain any necessary renunciations.
4. Take check for filing fees.
5. Take death certificate (if required).
6. Arrange for a representative of the bonding company to be available.
7. Ascertain the number of short certificates needed.

If a Will Is Found

Executor When the decedent has left a will that meets the requirements of the state, it may be offered for probate. Before offering the will to the Registrar it will first be necessary to locate the executor, if one has been named in the will.

The person named as executor should be contacted to make certain that he (or the bank or trust company) is willing to serve in that capacity. If so, the name, address, and telephone number of the executor should be recorded and arrangements should be made for that person to meet with the paralegal to discuss the estate proceedings and to be officially appointed by the Registrar.

Petition for Probate and Letters Testamentary The appointment of the executor by the Registrar is accomplished by the filing of a Petition for Probate and Letters Testamentary. The word "probate" comes from the Latin root which means "to prove," and the probate procedures is for the purpose of "proving" the will. The will is reviewed by the Registrar to make certain that it meets the requirements of a valid will and the signature of the testator is verified by the witnesses to the will. In some jurisdictions printed forms are available to be completed and filed; in other places the petitions are entirely typewritten by the lawyer; and in still other jurisdictions the forms are prepared by the Registrar. In any event, the executor will have to appear in person to be sworn to carry out the duties of his or her office faithfully.

CHECKLIST
Information Generally Required for Probate and Letters Testamentary

1. Name and address of the executor.
2. Name or names of the decedent.
3. Decedent's address (domicile).
4. Date of death.
5. Place of death.
6. Date of will and codicils, if any.

7. A statement as to whether the decedent has married or has had children born after the signing of the will.
8. An estimate of the value of the decedent's personal property.
9. An estimate of the value and location of any real estate in the decedent's own name.

The paralegal should make several photocopies of the original will and codicils, if any, for many uses during the administration of the estate. The original will must be filed with the Registrar. One photocopy should be placed in the permanent index binder of the estate.

If possible, a copy of the Petition in the form it is actually filed should be inserted in the permanent index binder of the estate.

Renunciation Any executor named in the will does not have to administer the estate but may renounce such right by filing the appropriate form of renunciation.

Administrator C.T.A. If an executor named in the will predeceases the testator or renounces *before* taking office, the will should be examined to see if a substitute executor has been named by the testator. If a substitute has been named he may be appointed by the Registrar to administer the estate. If no substitute has been named, or if the will fails to name an executor, then an administrator C.T.A. (cum testamento annexo; literally: "with will attached") will be appointed by the Registrar by the filing of a Petition for Probate and Letters of Administration C.T.A.

Administrator D.B.N.C.T.A. If an executor appointed by the Registrar resigns, dies, or is removed *after* taking office, the will should be examined to see if a successor is named, in which case he may be appointed by the Registrar to take over the administration. If no successor has been named, then an administrator D.B.N.C.T.A. (de bonis non cum testamento annexo; literally: "of no goods, with will attached") will be appointed by the filing of a Petition for Letters of Administration D.B.N.C.T.A.

Fees It is usually required that filing fees be paid at the time of filing the Petition. These may be advanced by the attorney and reimbursed by the estate. Filing fees when there is a will should be identical or very close in amount to those paid when there is no will.

Bond Normally no bond will be required of an executor who is a resident of the state where the estate is being administered. If the executor is not a resident of the state, no bond will be required if the testator has so provided in the will unless the Registrar deems it necessary. In some states the will must specifically waive surety on the bond, whether or not the executor is a resident. This alone can be an important reason to have a will.

A corporate fiduciary (commercial bank or trust company) is rarely required to post bond.

Witnesses The present whereabouts of the witnesses to the signing of the will should be ascertained. The witnesses should be contacted to see if they will be available at the time of probating the will. A record should be made of their names, current addresses, and telephone numbers when the will is executed to make it easier to find them when the will is offered for probate. In some jurisdictions it is customary to pay a witness fee to the witnesses for attending the probate.

If the witnesses can't be located, the personal representative appointed under the will must prove the validity of the testator's signature. This can be done in some states by a bank or other institution acknowledging the testator's signature if they had a good business relationship with the decedent. In some states, if the will was drafted according to local law, the signature does not have to be proven unless there is some doubt as to the authenticity of the signature.

Short Certificates The same procedure for short certificates is followed as when there is no will.[5]

CHECKLIST

Filing Petition for Probate and Letters Testamentary

The procedure for filing for Probate and Letters Testamentary is as follows:

1. Gather information necessary for completing the Petition and complete the Petition.
2. Arrange for the executor and witnesses to be present.
3. Take original will and codicils, if any.
4. Take check for filing fees.
5. Take death certificate (if required).
6. If necessary, arrange for a representative of the bonding company to be available.
7. Compute the number of short certificates needed.

---

5. See "Short Certificate" above in this chapter, under "No Will Is Found."

After Appointment of Personal Representative

Legal Advertising In most jurisdictions the grant of Letters of Administration or Letters Testamentary must be advertised in accordance with law to foreclose the claims of creditors. The Uniform Probate Code provides:

§ 3–801. [Notice to Creditors.]

Unless notice has already been given under this section, a personal representative upon his appointment shall publish a notice once a week for 3 successive weeks in a newspaper of general circulation in the [county] announcing his appointment and address and notifying creditors of the estate to present their claims within 4 months after the date of the first publication of the notice or be forever barred.

The paralegal should arrange for the advertising to appear and to be paid for. The proofs of advertising[6] should be retained in the records of the estate. In some jurisdictions the court clerk will arrange for this advertisement.

Filing System One of the most essential features of the administration of an estate is the filing system employed for the documents and data collected.

The purpose of the filing system is threefold:

1. to provide an organized method of segregating the data.
2. to facilitate the quick retrieval of the data.
3. to provide a permanent record for the important documents.

The permanent record is the index binder that has been discussed earlier. Further suggestions for the binder will be made throughout.

The need to separate the data in an organized matter and to enable the quick retrieval of information that is required is clearly a prerequisite for any worthwhile filing system. There are many types of systems that could be employed, and the paralegal should arrive at a system that serves the purposes intended.

The following is one filing system that has been used with considerable frequency and has many advantages. Separate file folders are assigned to each part of an estate's administration as follows:

1. Correspondence.
2. Documents (will, Petition, etc.).

6. The newspaper in which the advertising appears will supply an affidavit that includes a copy of the notice as it appeared in the newspaper. The "proof of advertising" may have to be submitted to the court in the future.

3. Bills and receipts.
4. Estate checking account.
5. Inventory.
6. State Inheritance Tax.
7. Federal Estate Tax.
8. U.S. Lifetime Income Tax.
9. State Lifetime Income Tax.
10. U.S. Fiduciary Income Tax.
11. Local taxes.
12. Investments.
13. Account and distribution.

There should also be separate folders tailor-made to the needs of the particular estate, such as claims by or against the estate, or the sale of a parcel of real estate.

This system permits quick retrieval of information because each item is compartmentalized. The system also allows cross-referencing of material. For example, if while working on a tax return one wanted to make note of some fact for use in preparing the Account, a memorandum of that fact could be placed in the account folder.

Reminder Systems In the administration of estates numerous dead lines must be met. For example, tax returns must be filed by a certain date. Systems must be designed and followed in order to assist the paralegal in seeing that the deadlines are met. As soon as the personal representative has been appointed, the reminder system or systems for that estate should be placed in operation. It would also be wise to use a combination of systems in case one fails.

Reminder Cards At the time the estate is started a set of 3″ x 5″ index cards may be made for the important due dates of estate items. The cards will be filed in a card file box with dividers by the month or by the month and day. The cards should be inserted well in advance of the due date so that sufficient time will be available for preparation of the document.

Calendar The dates on which certain items are due in an estate may be noted on the desk calendar of the paralegal. It is suggested that the notations be inserted at dates well in advance of the actual due dates to leave time for preparation.

Control List A chronological list of the due dates of federal estate tax returns, for example, for all estates being handled by the paralegal should be made. This will show at a glance what return is due next.

Computer Tickler Systems There are many computer tickler systems used in law offices and trust departments. If your office has a master system, the paralegal should be certain to put all his or her accounts on the system. If there is no such system, the paralegal may wish to use a program such as "Estate Administrator."[7]

Estate Checking Account Unless a bank or trust company is serving as the personal representative, the estate should have its own checking account. The paralegal should arrange for the opening of the account for which the following will be needed:

1. Short Certificate.
2. Check for initial deposit.
3. The personal representative in person or signature cards signed by the representative.

All cash transaction of the estate should go through the estate's checking account.[8] All dividends, cash, and other receipts should be deposited in the account and all disbursements and distributions should be made from the account by check signed by the personal representative. For example, some of the initial disbursements might be the witness fees, if any; reimbursement of the attorneys for filing fees for Petition for appointment of personal representative; legal advertising; funeral expenses; and the like.

Notifying Beneficiaries After appointment of the personal representative, those entitled to share in the distribution of the estate should be notified in writing of the appointment of the personal representative and of their respective interests in the estate. Some states mandate such notice.

The Uniform Probate Code[9] requires that notice be sent to the heirs and devisees within thirty days of the appointment of the personal representative.[10] The notice need only be sent by ordinary mail; convey the name and address of the personal representative; indicate that it is being sent to persons who have, or may have, some interest in the estate; reveal whether bond has been posted; and describe the court where papers relating to the estate are on file.

The notice to the beneficiaries would be an appropriate method by which the paralegal could request the social security

7. "Estate Administrator" is owned by the Philadelphia Institute and it and the Fiduciary Accountant program is often used (this will be mentioned in Chapter Seven in greater detail).

8. The importance of this will be seen in Chapter Seven, concerning filing Accounts with the court.

9. Section 3–705.

10. A devisee is a person specifically named in the will to receive property or cash. Heirs are the decedent's blood relations. An heir may or may not receive a bequest under the will. If there is no will, the heirs will automatically inherit the property through intestate succession.

number of the individual beneficiaries and, in the case of charitable beneficiaries, a copy of their exemption letter,[11] if any.

Application for Employer Identification Number Shortly after the appointment of the personal representative, every estate should have an employer identification number assigned to it by the Internal Revenue Service. This number will be used in identifying the estate for tax purposes, like the income tax return that is filed by the personal representative on the income received by the estate during its administration. The number may be obtained by filing Form SS-4 with the District Director of Internal Revenue (shown in the following Example).

Ancillary Letters Frequently, a decedent leaves property in more than one state. The will is probated in the state where the decedent resided. When property is located in states other than the state of residence, it may be necessary, depending on the law of the state in which the property is located, to have a personal representative appointed in those other states. The letters issued to the personal representative acting outside the state of the decedent's residence are called "ancillary letters."

For example, if decedent's will was probated in California but contained real estate located in Oregon, the personal representative would need to be appointed by the court in Oregon in order to sell or lease the real estate there. Therefore, a petition for ancillary letters (either testamentary or of administration) would have to be filed in Oregon.

CHECKLIST
Estate Settlement

The value of checklists and the function of paralegals with respect to creating checklists have been discussed above. From the matters discussed above in this chapter the development of a checklist for the settlement of an estate could be started:

1. Open file folder.
2. Prepare reminder system.
3. Petition for Letters.
4. Advertise Grant of Letters.
5. Apply for identification number.
6. Notify beneficiaries.
7. Determine if ancillary letters will be necessary and apply for them.

---

11. An exemption letter is the formal notice from the federal government indicating that the charity is tax exempt and that contributions to it are tax deductible.

EXAMPLE *Form SS-4*

Form **SS-4**
(Rev. April 1991)
Department of the Treasury
Internal Revenue Service

Application for Employer Identification Number

(For use by employers and others. Please read the attached instructions before completing this form.)

EIN

OMB No. 1545-0003
Expires 4-30-94

Please type or print clearly.

1 Name of applicant (True legal name) (See instructions.)

2 Trade name of business, if different from name in line 1	3 Executor, trustee, "care of" name
4a Mailing address (street address) (room, apt., or suite no.)	5a Address of business (See instructions.)
4b City, state, and ZIP code	5b City, state, and ZIP code

6 County and state where principal business is located

7 Name of principal officer, grantor, or general partner (See instructions.) ▶

8a Type of entity (Check only one box.) (See instructions.)
☐ Estate ☐ Trust
☐ Individual SSN ______ ☐ Plan administrator SSN ______ ☐ Partnership
☐ REMIC ☐ Personal service corp. ☐ Other corporation (specify) ______ ☐ Farmers' cooperative
☐ State/local government ☐ National guard ☐ Federal government/military ☐ Church or church controlled organization
☐ Other nonprofit organization (specify) ______ If nonprofit organization enter GEN (if applicable) ______
☐ Other (specify) ▶ ______

8b If a corporation, give name of foreign country (if applicable) or state in the U.S. where incorporated ▶	Foreign country	State

9 Reason for applying (Check only one box.)
☐ Changed type of organization (specify) ▶ ______
☐ Started new business
☐ Purchased going business
☐ Hired employees
☐ Created a trust (specify) ▶ ______
☐ Created a pension plan (specify type) ▶ ______
☐ Banking purpose (specify) ▶
☐ Other (specify) ▶

10 Date business started or acquired (Mo., day, year) (See instructions.)	11 Enter closing month of accounting year. (See instructions.)

12 First date wages or annuities were paid or will be paid (Mo., day, year). **Note:** *If applicant is a withholding agent, enter date income will first be paid to nonresident alien. (Mo., day, year)* . . . . ▶

13 Enter highest number of employees expected in the next 12 months. **Note:** *If the applicant does not expect to have any employees during the period, enter "0."* . . . . ▶	Nonagricultural	Agricultural	Household

14 Principal activity (See instructions.) ▶

15 Is the principal business activity manufacturing? . . . . ☐ **Yes** ☐ **No**
If "Yes," principal product and raw material used ▶

16 To whom are most of the products or services sold? Please check the appropriate box. ☐ Business (wholesale)
☐ Public (retail) ☐ Other (specify) ▶ ☐ N/A

17a Has the applicant ever applied for an identification number for this or any other business? . . . . ☐ **Yes** ☐ **No**
Note: *If "Yes," please complete lines 17b and 17c.*

17b If you checked the "Yes" box in line 17a, give applicant's true name and trade name, if different than name shown on prior application.

True name ▶ Trade name ▶

17c Enter approximate date, city, and state where the application was filed and the previous employer identification number if known.

Approximate date when filed (Mo., day, year)	City and state where filed	Previous EIN

Under penalties of perjury, I declare that I have examined this application, and to the best of my knowledge and belief, it is true, correct, and complete	Telephone number (include area code)

Name and title (Please type or print clearly.) ▶

Signature ▶ Date ▶

Note: *Do not write below this line. For official use only.*

Please leave blank ▶	Geo.	Ind.	Class	Size	Reason for applying

For Paperwork Reduction Act Notice, see attached instructions. Cat. No. 16055N Form **SS-4** (Rev. 4-91)

CHAPTER THREE

Valuation of Assets, Filing an Inventory, and Payment of Debts

This chapter concerns the duties of the personal representative of the estate to accumulate all of the assets that the decedent owned, to prepare and file an inventory[1] of those assets, and to pay debts of the decedent. These functions are frequently performed by the paralegal working for the estate's attorney.

DUTIES OF THE PERSONAL REPRESENTATIVE

The obligation of the personal representative to begin the process of conserving the decedent's assets actually begins at the date of death, even though no authorization to act has yet been issued by a court. In most situations, however, no action is necessary until after grant of letters by the court unless there is some obvious danger that the assets may be destroyed or stolen in the interim.

The legal obligation of the personal representative is to protect and to preserve the assets of the estate. Quick action should be taken to gather assets and secure their safety. Although a person may decide to squander assets during life, after death the personal representative is charged with administering the estate of the decedent in an orderly, prompt, and economical fashion. If this is accomplished, it will result in expediting the preparation of the inventory, the death tax returns, and the account[2] of the personal representative. Furthermore, with prompt action, the assets will more likely be preserved for the benefit of the intestate heirs or beneficiaries under the will.

The duties of the personal representative that we are concerned with in this chapter may be categorized as follows:

1. An inventory is the formal listing of all assets of the estate that pass through the hands of the personal representative.

2. In most estates, a formal document is filed with the court showing all receipts and disbursements by the personal representative. This is known as an "account" and will be discussed in Chapter Seven.

Discovery

The personal representative must seek out every item of value owned by the decedent.

Possession

The personal representative must take possession of all of the discovered items so they will be available for payment of claims and distribution to the proper beneficiaries.

Valuation

The personal representative must determine the dollar value of each asset as of the time of death.

Liquidation[3]

In general, the personal representative is under an obligation to convert assets to cash, to preserve their value as of the date of death. If there is a risk that the assets, such as long-term bonds or stocks in a depressed market, may decline in value due to liquidation, selling may not be advisable. A professional investment advisor should be consulted before any sales are made. This, of course, does not include assets specifically given in kind to the beneficiaries under the will.

Payment of Debts

To the extent that the assets of the estate are sufficient to do so, it is the duty of the personal representative to pay the debts of the decedent. If there are insufficient assets, there is a priority schedule established by state law that will guide the personal representative in deciding which debts to pay first.

Opening Estate Bank Account

In the administration of virtually every estate it will be necessary for the personal representative to have a distinct bank account into which funds may be deposited and from which debts may be paid. This account (usually a checking account) is opened in the name of the estate with the personal representative having authority to make withdrawals or write checks. As a general rule, the estate account may be opened by presenting a short certificate to the bank along with filling out the other normal papers to open an account (e.g., signature card, initial deposit slip, etc.).

3. Liquidation is the sale of property for cash.

DISCOVERY OF ASSETS

The process of discovering assets is not something done by rote. While there are great benefits to approaching this job in a mechanical way by using a checklist, it is always necessary to exercise careful thought and imagination to do the job properly.

In most estates, the paralegal will have no familiarity with the decedent's assets unless the will was prepared by the paralegal's employer. As a normal part of preparing a will, the drafter will get as much information as possible about the testator's assets to make administration of the estate easier. Not being able to speak with decedents, you will have to consult people who knew them. Frequently you will find that there is no one person who has all the answers about the decedent's assets. Relatives and close friends, business associates, accountants, bankers, stockbrokers, attorneys, and insurance agents may all have some helpful information. If all the information is not available from relatives, you may have to contact nonrelatives, and you should explain to them why you are making the inquiry. It may be necessary to provide either a short certificate or letter of authorization from a surviving spouse or child to the person from whom you are seeking the information. Here is an example of such a letter, which will be prepared in the attorney's office, although signed by the relative.

EXAMPLE
Letter of Authorization

Mr. Noel Larson
Vice-President
Bank of Old Lancaster
492 Ford Street
Bismarck, ND 58501

March 3, 1991

Re:[4] Estate of Percy James

Dear Mr. Larson:

I know that my husband placed great confidence in you in handling his financial affairs. Since his death, we have not been able to locate all of the assets that I believed he had.

Would you be so kind as to speak with our attorney, Rhonda Blount, and supply her with any information you may have regarding my husband's various investments. I am sure that your help will ease our difficulty considerably. Thank you for your kindness and courtesy.

Very truly yours,

/s/ Mary Belle James

Mary Belle James

4. In regard to; with reference to. A term frequently used by lawyers.

In this chapter we will consider the characteristics of many different kinds of assets. The initial concern in all cases, however, is learning whether the decedent owned any such assets. In a very real sense, the paralegal may become involved in a treasure hunt, never knowing exactly where the next clue may lead.

The place to start is usually the decedent's home. In the usual case, the spouse or some other family member will go through the decedent's belongings at home and call the important documents to your attention. Papers and objects such as jewelry, bank books, or the like, may be important in themselves. These may also lead you to additional items located elsewhere. For example, there may be a receipt from a stock brokerage for the purchase of shares in a company.

Since family members may not be sure of what is important and what is not, you may ask that they look for certain things. The following checklist is intended to suggest those kinds of things you should remind the family members, or others making the search, to look for. The list is not meant to be exhaustive.

CHECKLIST
Locating Assets

1. Wills, codicils, and trust documents.
2. Stock certificates.
3. Bonds.
4. Checkbooks and bank books (and cancelled checks).
5. Insurance policies.
6. Safe deposit box keys.
7. Charge account cards or plates.
8. Cards or correspondence concerning Social Security, Medicare, or veterans' benefits.
9. Deeds for real estate.
10. Title documents for cars, trailers, boats, or airplanes.
11. Old tax returns.
12. Statements or correspondence from banks, brokers, accountants, or attorneys.
13. Storage company receipts.

QUESTION

Can you think of other items that you would want to add to this list?

Your ability to discover assets quickly and efficiently will increase as you learn more about the nature of each type of asset that a decedent may have possessed.[5] To carry out this process of discovery you will find it helpful to develop your own checklist. No checklist, however, will accomplish the job of discovery by itself. It

5. See "Acquiring, Valuating, and Liquidating Assets" in this chapter for a discussion of various types of assets.

can only serve to remind you of types of assets you may not yet have looked for. Your success in discovery will depend upon your skill at recognizing and following clues. Sometimes the clues will be as obvious as a check drawn to a stockbroker. Other times the clue may be as obscure as the inclusion of a dividend on an income tax return or an off-hand comment in a letter.

To be certain that the personal representative has made a diligent search for all the decedent's bank accounts, a form letter should be sent to all the banks or savings and loans in the area where the decedent lived and worked. The letter should ask the institution to inform you if it has any record of any loans or assets owned by the decedent, including a safe deposit box or joint accounts. It is always very helpful if the paralegal has personal contact with each bank.

Safe Deposit Boxes

Many people keep their valuables in locked boxes in bank vaults. These safe deposit boxes may contain, or lead to the discovery of, the principal assets of the estate. Obviously, if you find a safe deposit box key at the decedent's home or if a family member knows that the decedent had such a box, you will know that the box itself must be examined. Even if no key is found and no one knows of a safe deposit box, you should write to all banks at which the decedent had an account to determine if he did rent such a box. An example of a letter to banks requesting this information follows. It should not be necessary to send a short certificate merely to get this information.

EXAMPLE

Letter Requesting Safe Deposit Box Information

[*Letterhead*]

Grand Bank
Broad and Wide Streets
Bigtown, CO 80225

November 17, 1991

Re: A. F. Allen

Dear Sir/Madam:

This office represents the executrix of the Estate of A. F. Allen.

Please advise us if Mr. Allen held a safe deposit box at your bank at the time of his death on October 14, 1991. If he did, would you please letus know the number of the box and the branch at which the box is located. Thank you for your attention in this matter.

Very truly yours,

/s/Joan Bayley

Joan Bayley
Legal Assistant

Once the safe deposit box or boxes are located it will be necessary to gain access to them. In most states procedures have been developed to protect against the possibility that the personal representative or some other party might try to empty the safe deposit box and fail to include its contents in his records or tax returns. Therefore, in most states a representative of the state or the bank in which the box is located must accompany the personal representative when the box is first opened following the death of the decedent.

In order to have the safe deposit box opened it will be necessary to arrange for a meeting at the bank with the appropriate state official or bank officer. At this meeting it will normally be necessary to show a short certificate. In most states the personal representative must be present and sign the bank record showing access to the safe deposit box. A complete list is then made of all the items found in the box. Once this is done, the box may be emptied and its contents kept by the attorney for the estate. An alternative, at the option of the personal representative and attorney, is to have the safe deposit box transferred to the name of the personal representative.

In many states, it is possible to gain immediate entry to the safe deposit box for purposes of searching for the decedent's will only. The formalities mentioned above are not followed, but no property other than the will may be removed from the safe deposit box.

ACQUIRING, VALUATING, AND LIQUIDATING ASSETS

All of the assets that a person owns may be categorized as either real property or personal property. Real property is land and those buildings or other things permanently on the land, like trees, water, etc. The terms real estate or realty are also frequently used to describe this kind of property.

Personal property (or personalty) is all property aside from real property. This type of property may be further divided into two groups—tangible and intangible. The distinction between tangible and intangible depends upon whether or not you can touch the thing of value. If you can, it is tangible; if not, intangible. Clearly an automobile and a television set are tangible personal property. Just as clearly a claim for personal injuries is intangible personal property.

The difference might be illustrated by considering two stock certificates. One certificate is for 100 shares of General Motors common stock. You can certainly touch that certificate, but it is not the certificate that is valuable. It is the ownership interest in the company that has value. You cannot touch that ownership interest. If the certificate is lost it can be replaced without substantial expense. The other stock certificate (hypothetically) is for 100 shares of Gutenberg Press, Inc. The company has been defunct since 1520. Since Gutenberg Press, Inc., was the first printer of the Bible, the certificate itself has a unique value. From these examples you can see that 100 shares of General Motors is intangible personal property while the certificate for 100 shares of Gutenberg Press, Inc., is tangible personal property.

PROBLEM

Group the following items into one of three categories: real property, tangible personal property, or intangible personal property.

1. Television set.
2. House and lot at 1615 McDermott Blvd., Littletown.
3. United States Series EE Bonds.
4. Check representing a refund on an insurance policy.
5. Stamp collection.
6. A one-half interest in a partnership owning 200 acres of undeveloped land.
7. Household furnishings.
8. 50 shares of United Utility Company.
9. A five-year lease, fully paid in advance, for an apartment at Royal Arms House, Miami, Florida.
10. One-half of the outstanding stock in A & B Realty Corporation (whose sole asset is ownership of five stores on Sunny Avenue, Los Angeles, California).
11. A wardrobe of 125 suits.
12. $5,000 in cash.
13. An 1862 five-dollar bill.

In most estates the bulk of the assets will consist of intangible personal property—cash, bank deposits, life insurance policies, and securities (i.e., stocks and bonds). Each type of asset requires different techniques to collect, value, and liquidate. Paralegals play a vital role in this area, often being given complete charge of these matters.

Intangible Personal Property

Cash Cash is the easiest asset of an estate to collect and value.[6] Most people do not keep large amounts of cash. It is just too risky.

6. No liquidation is necessary, or possible, as cash is absolutely liquid, capable of purchasing assets or simply being placed on deposit in a bank.

Many people do, however, have large amounts of money in safe deposit boxes or even at home. Once cash is located, it should immediately be placed into the estate bank account. If it is inconvenient to quickly get it to the bank where the estate account is kept, it should be changed into the form of a bank check or money order at the nearest bank. This is an easy procedure. Any bank will issue its check or money order in exchange for cash. The check or money order should be drawn payable to the estate. It may then be deposited only in the estate bank account. This should be done promptly even though the danger of loss or theft of the cash has been eliminated.[7]

Bank Accounts Bank accounts may be held in the name of one or several individuals. There may be different tax consequences depending on the way in which the account is held[8] and, more importantly for our present purposes, different ways of dealing with a bank account in joint names as opposed to one in the the name of the decedent alone. Some states require that a tax waiver be presented before the asset will be released.

Accounts in the Name of Decedent Alone Each bank account in the name of the decedent should be closed and the funds should be transferred to an account in the name of the estate. It is customary for the bank to require an order signed by the personal representative (either on its own forms or in a letter) directing that the account be closed and the funds be delivered in some specified way. The bank will also require a short certificate or its equivalent as proof of the authority of the personal representative, and in the case of savings accounts it will require surrender of the bank book as well.

For tax purposes it is important to obtain a letter from each bank confirming certain facts about each account in which the decedent had an interest.[9] For checking accounts the requested information should include the balance as of the date of death and a list of any checks honored subsequent to death and prior to the bank's receipt of notice of death.[10] A sample letter designed to obtain that information as well as to transfer the remaining balance to the estate bank account follows.

7. If the bank check or money order is lost it can be replaced by the bank. Cash, of course, cannot be unless there is some insurance coverage protecting against its theft.

8. See Chapter Five for a discussion of tax on a bank account held by more than one person.

9. The date of death value will be includible in the valuing of the estate for purposes of determining the death taxes due.

10. In most states a bank is permitted to honor, for a very limited period after death, checks drawn by the decedent. Upon receiving notice of death or upon expiration of that limited period, the bank should decline to pay checks. The person to whom such a check was written then becomes a creditor of the estate when the check is not honored by the bank.

EXAMPLE
Letter Requesting Bank Account Information

[*Letterhead*]

The Franklin Bank
One Bankers Plaza
New York, NY 10000

August 1, 1991

Re: Estate of Celia Alexander
Checking Account No. 3271941

Dear Sir/Madam:

This office represents Olivia Alexander, administrator of the Estate of Celia Alexander. Ms. Celia Alexander maintained the above-captioned checking account at your bank up until the time of her death on July 21, 1991.

Please confirm in writing to this office the balance standing to the credit of the decedent's account as of the date of her death. Would you also please supply us with a record of any checks honored by the bank after her death and prior to receiving this notice? If the account is interest bearing, please give us the amount of accrued interest earned in the account up until Ms. Alexander's death.

Finally, please close out the account by sending your check payable to the estate. Enclosed herewith is a short certificate evidencing the grant of letters of administration to Ms. Olivia Alexander.

Thank you for your attention to this matter.

Very truly yours,

/s/Walter J. Sloan

Walter J. Sloan[11]

If the account involved is a savings account or an interest-bearing checking account, it is necessary to determine both the balance on the date of death and the amount of any interest accrued as of that date. A sample letter for that purpose follows.

EXAMPLE
Letter Requesting Savings Account Information

[*Letterhead*]

The Hartford Bank
52 Heinz Road
New York, NY 10000

August 1, 1991

Re: Estate of Celia Alexander
Savings Account No. 157,766

Dear Sir/Madam:

This office represents Olivia Alexander, the administratrix of the Estate of Celia Alexander. Ms. Celia Alexander maintained the above-captioned savings account at your bank up until the time of her death on

11. Technically, letters requesting information from banks and orders to close accounts should come from the personal representative. Requests are, however, usually honored when they come from the attorney representing the personal representative. You should determine if this procedure applies in the area where you will be working.

July 21, 1991. A short certificate evidencing the grant of letters of administration to Ms. Olivia Alexander, the account book itself, and a withdrawal slip for the entire balance in the account (including accrued interest) are enclosed herewith.

Please confirm in writing the balance in the account as of the decedent's date of death, including interest accrued to that time. Also, please send your check, made payable to the estate, for the balance with interest to the date the account is closed, to me at the letterhead address.

Very truly yours,

/s/Walter J. Sloan

Walter J. Sloan

Accounts in the Name of the Decedent and Another Person Bank accounts may be owned jointly by more than one person. As a general rule when such joint accounts exist, each named individual has the right to withdraw the full amount on deposit. Similarly, when one owner of the joint account dies, the balance in the account usually passes automatically to the survivor(s). Some accounts are held in joint names for "convenience only," such as in the case of an elderly parent and a responsible son or daughter who is named on the account so that the son or daughter can pay the parent's bills if necessary. When the account is opened, the bank will request that both parties sign the "signature card" stating that the account is to be held jointly "for convenience only" and will remain in the estate of the parent.

The personal representative has no right to take possession of a joint account unless it is a "convenience account," as it never becomes a part of the probate estate.[12] The personal representative must, however, obtain information about the joint account similar to that for a solely owned account. This is so because there may be death taxes due on all or a portion of the joint account.[13] In addition, it will be important to know the date on which the account was placed in joint names as this will have death tax consequences. A request for this information should be included in the letter to the bank along with the request for date of death value.

Accounts in the Name of Decedent "In Trust" for Another Person Some states recognize what are called "tentative trusts" or "Totten trusts."[14] Generally, these are savings accounts opened in the name of the decedent "in trust for X." During the lifetime of the decedent

12. The probate estate is all those assets that pass under the will of the decedent.

13. See Chapter Five for a discussion of the taxation of joint bank accounts.

14. The name "Totten" comes from a famous New York court case that established some of the legal principles involved in such accounts.

he has full control over that account and can make withdrawals whenever desired for any purpose. The balance remaining in such an account at the decedent's death passes automatically to the named beneficiary. The personal representative cannot control the funds but again must obtain information about the account for tax purposes, including the date the account was opened.

Accounts under the Uniform Gifts to Minors Act Many states have adopted the Uniform Gift to Minors Act. Under this law a bank account may be opened on behalf of a minor with a custodian[15] named for the account. Unlike a tentative trust, this type of account is never at the complete discretion of the custodian. Instead, the funds on deposit may only be withdrawn for the benefit of the minor named in the account. The person who made the gift may not get the money back.

With this type of account it will be important to determine when the account was opened because this will have tax significance. The money in the account, however, does not come into the possession of the personal representative. A letter should be written to the bank in which the account is maintained in the same fashion as a letter involving a joint account or tentative trust.

Information about bank accounts will be important in filing the death tax returns as well as the inventory. It will be very helpful in preparing these documents if information about all bank accounts is kept in one convenient place. For this purpose, some sort of "spread sheet" or ledger system may be used. The manner in which the information is kept is not as important as the fact that all the pertinent facts are included. Here is an example of a form which might be used.

EXAMPLE
Ledger Sheet

Name of Bank	Account No. and Type	Title of Account	Date Account Opened	Date of Death Balance (& Accumulated Interest)
Fourth Federal Savings & Loan Association	Savings # 36–204	Name of Decedent	February 23, 1986	$ 1,014.38 9.87 (acc. int.) $ 1,024.25
Jerrold Trust Bank	Checking # 116–362–1	Name of Decedent and Spouse	April 9, 1987	$ 328.55
Finkman Bank	Checking # 0003–2–17	Name of Decedent and Conrad Frillth	September 22, 1987	10,399.46
Beneficient Savings Bank	Savings # H 42–337	Name of Decedent and Spouse	May 27, 1988	21,476.00 794.63 (acc. int.) 22,270.63

15. A person who holds title to the account, much like a trustee would.

Life Insurance The term "life insurance" applies to contracts issued by life insurance companies under which, in return for certain premiums, the company agrees to pay to designated beneficiaries an agreed amount at a time in the future (usually, but not always, fixed by the death of a certain person). The contract itself is often referred to as a "life insurance policy." The person whose death causes payment by the insurance company is known as the "insured." The insured is in many cases, but not all, the "owner" of the policy. It is generally the obligation of the owner to pay the necessary premiums to the insurance company. The owner usually has the right to name the beneficiaries, to pledge the policy as collateral for a loan, or to terminate the policy and receive its realizable value. The value realizable upon termination of a policy before it matures is often referred to as the "cash value" of the policy. When a policy matures (by the death of the insured or in some cases by the passage of the requisite number of years), the "face value" or full contract amount is paid to the beneficiaries. It is worth the effort to become familiar with these terms because they will be used in later sections of the book.

Collection of Insurance Proceeds The personal representative (or attorney for the personal representative) may be asked to assist in collecting the proceeds of a life insurance policy even if all of the proceeds go to named beneficiaries. If the policy is payable to the estate it is definitely the personal representative's duty to collect the policy. The paralegal should collect all policies, if possible, so that he or she can have access to the information on federal form number 712 that shows the amount to be reported on the death tax returns. The paralegal should request that Form 712 (issued in triplicate) be sent to the attorney's office when the claim for the proceeds of the policy is being made.

To collect the proceeds of a policy, each life insurance company insists on receiving an official claim on its own form. To obtain this form it is customary to send the company a letter identifying the insured, giving the policy number and stating the date of death. The insurance company will also require a copy of the death certificate of the insured and the policy itself.[16] Surrender of the policy itself is not an absolute requirement but does speed the application. If the policy has been lost, payment of the insurance proceeds will normally be somewhat delayed.

A sample letter to an insurance company requesting a claim form and enclosing the relevant documents follows.

16. Frequently, a helpful insurance agent will already have filled out the claim form for the beneficiary but may still need a copy of the death certificate if it has not already been supplied.

EXAMPLE
Letter Requesting Insurance Proceeds

[*Letterhead*]

August 20, 1991

Morse Insurance Company
123 Oakmont Street
Morse, IA 52106

Re: Estate of James Donahue
Policy No. 54–019102

Dear Sir/Madam:

This office represents Marcy Clark, the executrix of the Estate of James Donahue who died on August 8, 1991. Enclosed herewith are the following papers for the purpose of making a claim for the proceeds, which are payable to Marcy Clark:

1. Death certificate
2. Policy no. 54–019102.

Please send me the appropriate claim form for completion and return, if necessary.

Very truly yours,

/s/John Olsen
John Olsen

In some cases, documentation in addition to the completed claim form may be necessary to establish the identity of the beneficiary and to prove that he survived the decedent.

It is a standard provision of most life insurance policies that the proceeds are to be paid to the estate of the insured if none of the named beneficiaries survives the insured. If this is the case, the insurance company will require proof of the authority of the personal representative. This is accomplished by enclosing a short certificate in the letter to the company or attaching it to the claim form.

Amount of Proceeds Payable For several reasons the precise amount payable by the insurance company is often more than the face value of the policy.

Return of Unearned Premium Premiums are generally paid in advance of the period during which coverage is in effect. That portion of the premium attributable to the balance of the period still remaining at the time of the insured's death has not yet been earned by the insurance company and it may be payable to the beneficiaries.

Postdeath Interest Many companies pay interest on the face value of the policy from the date of death until actual payment is made.

"Dividends" on Policies Issued by Mutual Insurance Companies Some insurance companies are owned by stockholders who share in the profits of the company. Others are mutual companies technically owned by the policyholders. The profits of mutual companies are paid to the policyholders in the form of annual "dividends"[17] which may be (1) taken in cash, (2) applied to reduce the next year's premium, (3) left with the company to earn interest, or (4) used to purchase additional life insurance.

At the time of death, in addition to the face value of the policy and any unearned premium, the beneficiary may be entitled to certain payments relating to the dividends. The form of payment would vary with the different treatment of dividends prior to death. Briefly, the following types of payments might apply:

1. Dividend taken in cash. If the dividend is taken each year in cash, it is possible that the policy will provide for payment of a partial dividend in the year the insured died.
2. Dividend applied to reduce the next year's premium. In this case if the premium payable for year two of the policy is $200 and the dividend for year one is $10, the dividend for year one will be applied to the premium for year two and the policyholder will have to pay a premium of only $190 for year two. If the insured dies during year two, the beneficiary is entitled to a return of the unearned premium calculated on the basis of $200. In addition, as to the dividend which would be paid at the end of year two, the discussion in "Dividend Taken in Cash" would apply.
3. Dividend left with the company to earn interest. If the dividends had been left with the company to earn interest, the beneficiary will be entitled to the aggregate dividends paid prior to death plus the interest they earned to the date of death. As to payment of a portion of the dividend for the year of death the discussion in "Dividend Taken in Cash" would apply.
4. Dividend used to purchase additional life insurance. Where the dividend has been used to purchase additional insurance, the beneficiary will be entitled to receive the proceeds of that insurance. In addition, as in other cases a partial dividend for the year of death may be payable as set forth in subsection "Dividend Taken in Cash."

Under most life insurance policies the beneficiary has a number of options available relating to the form in which he will receive the

17. The word "dividend" is in quotation marks so you will not confuse this for tax purposes with dividends paid to corporate stockholders.

proceeds. Typical options would be (1) a lump sum payment, (2) interest payments on the proceeds that will be left with the company or (3) an annuity. An annuity is essentially a periodic payment in a fixed amount to continue for a term of years or until the death of a beneficiary. The choice among such options should not be made lightly. The circumstances of the beneficiaries as well as the specific terms of the policy must be considered carefully. In most cases the lump sum option is preferable, as historically a life insurance company does not pay as high an interest rate on the money as other investments. In addition the beneficiary may need a lump sum payment to pay expenses. The option to take a lump sum distribution usually expires after a certain period of time after death, normally 60 days. Thus these options should be considered immediately.

Valuation of Life Insurance All information concerning the proceeds of each life insurance policy is shown, broken down, on federal Form 712. An example of Form 712 follows.

QUESTIONS

Form 712 requires the insurance company to supply a great deal of information about the policy and its value at the date of death.

What other information is called for in the form? Why do you think that is done?

Copies of Form 712 must be filed with the federal Estate Tax Return for each life insurance policy on the life of the decedent.

Corporate and Governmental Securities

Definitions The word "securities" is not subject to a single definition that would be accurate in all circumstances. We will use the word security to mean a written document that gives evidence of either a debt obligation or participation in the ownership of an enterprise. The classic example of a debt security is a bond. The classic example of a security that represents a participation in the ownership of an enterprise is a share of common stock. Forms of securities are not by any means limited to these two classic types. The combinations of interests that may be included in a single security are almost endless. We will therefore discuss only these two most common types—stock and bonds.

Stocks A share of common stock in a corporation represents a proportionate interest in the property (often referred to as "net assets") and profits of the corporation. A corporation is a form of representative democracy. The stockholders elect a Board of Directors that runs the corporation. Of all the people who may invest money in a corporation, (e.g. by lending money to it or buying a

EXAMPLE *Treasury Form 712*

Form **712** (Rev. October 1990) Department of the Treasury Internal Revenue Service

Life Insurance Statement

OMB No. 1545-0022
Expires 2-29-92

Part I Decedent—Insured (To Be Filed With United States Estate Tax Return, Form 706)

1 Decedent's first name and middle initial	2 Decedent's last name	3 Decedent's social security number (if known)	4 Date of death
Craig C.	Cornell	142-42-4222	6/21/91

5 Name and address of insurance company

The Metropolitan Life Insurance Co., Philadelphia, PA 19000

6 Kind of policy	7 Policy number
Whole Life	175-22-75001

8 Owner's name. If decedent is not owner, please attach copy of application.	9 Date issued	10 Assignor's name. Please attach copy of assignment.	11 Date assigned
	7/5/62		

12 Value of the policy at the time of assignment	13 Amount of premium (see instructions)	14 Name of beneficiaries
		Estate of Craig C. Cornell

15	Face amount of policy	$ 100,000.00
16	Indemnity benefits	$
17	Additional insurance	$
18	Other benefits	$
19	Principal of any indebtedness to the company that is deductible in determining net proceeds	$
20	Interest on indebtedness (item 19) accrued to date of death	$
21	Amount of accumulated dividends	$ 375.00
22	Amount of post-mortem dividends	$ 1,072.00
23	Amount of returned premium	$
24	Amount of proceeds if payable in one sum	$ 101,447.00
25	Value of proceeds as of date of death (if not payable in one sum)	$

26 Policy provisions concerning deferred payments or installments.

Note: *If other than lump-sum settlement is authorized for a surviving spouse, please attach a copy of the insurance policy.*

27 Amount of installments $

28 Date of birth, sex, and name of any person the duration of whose life may measure the number of payments.

29 Amount applied by the insurance company as a single premium representing the purchase of installment benefits $

30 Basis (mortality table and rate of interest) used by insurer in valuing installment benefits.

31 Was the insured the annuitant or beneficiary of any annuity contract issued by the company? ☐ Yes ☒ No

32 Names of companies with which decedent carried other policies and amount of such policies if this information is disclosed by your records.

The undersigned officer of the above-named insurance company hereby certifies that this statement sets forth true and correct information.

Signature ▶ /s/ John Smith Title ▶ Secretary Date of Certification ▶ 8/2/91

Instructions

Paperwork Reduction Act Notice.—We ask for the information on this form to carry out the Internal Revenue laws of the United States. You are required to give us this information. We need it to ensure that you are complying with these laws and to allow us to figure and collect the right amount of tax.

The time needed to complete and file this form will vary depending on individual circumstances. The estimated average time is:

Form	Recordkeeping	Preparing the form
712	18 hrs., 25 min.	18 min.

If you have comments concerning the accuracy of these time estimates or suggestions for making this form more simple, we would be happy to hear from you. You can write to both the IRS and the Office of Management and Budget at the addresses listed in the instructions of the tax return with which this form is filed. **DO NOT** send the tax form to either of these offices. Instead, return it to the executor or representative who requested it.

Statement of Insurer.—This statement must be made, on behalf of the insurance company which issued the policy, by an officer of the company having access to the records of the company. For purposes of this statement, a facsimile signature may be used in lieu of a manual signature and if used, shall be binding as a manual signature.

Separate Statements.—A separate statement must be filed for each policy.

Line 13.—Report on line 13 the annual premium, not the cumulative premium to date of death. If death occurred after the end of the premium period, report the last annual premium.

Form **712** (Rev. 10-90)

EXAMPLE *Treasury Form 712, continued*

Form 712 (Rev. 10-90) Page **2**

Part II **Living Insured**

(File With United States Gift Tax Return, Form 709. May Be Filed With United States Estate Tax Return, Form 706, Where Decedent Owned Insurance on Life of Another)

SECTION A.—General Information

33 First name and middle initial of donor (or decedent)	34 Last name	35 **Social security number**

36 Date of gift for which valuation data submitted . . . ▶

37 Date of decedent's death for which valuation data submitted . . . ▶

SECTION B.—Policy Information

38 Name of insured	39 Sex	40 Date of birth
41 Name and address of insurance company		

42 Kind of policy	43 Policy number	44 Face amount	45 Issue date
46 Gross premium		47 Frequency of payment	
48 Assignee's name			49 Date assigned
50 If irrevocable designation of beneficiary made, name of beneficiary	51 Sex	52 Date of birth, if known	53 Date designated

54 If other than simple designation, quote in full. (Attach additional sheets if necessary.)

55 If policy is not paid up:

a Interpolated terminal reserve on date of death, assignment, or irrevocable designation of beneficiary . . .

b Add proportion of gross premium paid beyond date of death, assignment, or irrevocable designation of beneficiary . . .

c Add adjustment on account of dividends to credit of policy . . .

d Total (add amounts on lines a, b, and c) . . .

e Outstanding indebtedness against policy . . .

f Net total value of the policy (for gift or estate tax purposes) (subtract amount on line e from amount on line d) .

56 If policy is either paid up or a single premium:

a Total cost, on date of death, assignment, or irrevocable designation of beneficiary, of a single-premium policy on life of insured at attained age, for original face amount plus any additional paid-up insurance (additional face amount $ __________) . . . .
(If a single-premium policy for the total face amount would not have been issued on the life of the insured as of the date specified, nevertheless, assume that such a policy could then have been purchased by the insured and state the cost thereof, using for such purpose the same formula and basis employed, on the date specified, by the company in calculating single premiums.)

b Adjustment on account of dividends to credit of policy . . .

c Total (add amounts on line a and line b) . . .

d Outstanding indebtedness against policy . . .

e Net total value of policy (for gift or estate tax purposes) (subtract amount on line d from amount on line c) . . .

The undersigned officer of the above-named insurance company hereby certifies that this statement sets forth true and correct information.

Signature ▶ /s/ John Smith Title ▶ Secretary Date of Certification ▶ 8/2/91

★ U.S. GPO:1990-518-279/20298

portion of the corporation) the holders of common stock run the highest risk of losing their investment and generally enjoy the possibility of the largest gain thereon. They are the last investors to be paid in the event the corporation goes out of business. On the other hand, there is no upper limit to the value they may realize if the enterprise is successful.

Some corporations issue one or more types of preferred stock in addition to common stock. Preferred stock differs from common stock in that both the risk of loss and the possibility of large gain are more limited. Such stock is said to be "preferred" because owners of this type of stock have the right to receive dividends before the holders of common stock receive dividends. Also, preferred stockholders receive preferential treatment in the event the corporation goes out of business.

Bonds Bonds and other debt instruments are obligations to pay a fixed sum of money at a specified date in the future and to pay interest on the sum until that date. They may be issued by private corporations, governments, or semi-governmental agencies. Characteristically, they call for interest at a fixed rate to be paid periodically either to the registered owner or to the person who presents a coupon that is physically clipped from the bond. If a corporation goes out of business all bonds are debts of that corporation that must be paid in full before any distribution can be made to the stockholders. Therefore, bondholders characteristically have the lowest risk of loss. Similarly, they have little opportunity for gain in the value of their security.

Physical Control Upon discovering that a decedent owned securities, the personal representative must give high priority to obtaining possession of those securities. Precise records must be kept of each certificate and its whereabouts. When a certificate first comes into the hands of the personal representative, a complete record should be made of its important terms: the name and address of the registered owner or owners, the name of the corporation or other issuing organization, the certificate number, the number of shares (or face value, interest rate, and maturity date in the case of bonds) represented by the certificate, the type of security, the par value[18] of shares, the issue date, and any restrictions on transfer that might appear on the certificate.

The necessary information on all securities should be centrally located in the same way that a "spread sheet" for bank accounts is kept. Information for both bank accounts and securities may be combined in one "spread sheet." Here is an example of recording the desired information about securities.

18. Par value is the stated value of a stock declared for purposes of paying certain types of state taxes. It does not really bear on the value of the stock.

EXAMPLE *Spread-Sheet Securities*

Number of Shares	Type of Stock	Name of Corporation	Registration	Certificate #	Issue Date	Par Value	Date of Death Value[19]
100	Common	Glib and Wild Corporation	Decedent and Spouse, jointly	Q763984	June 17, 1984	$1.00	62.375/share = $6237.50
25	Preferred	Outright Boatwrights, Inc.	Decedent alone	A–1024	December 13, 1986	None	No Market
10	Common	A.E.L.L., Inc.	Decedent and daughter, Sue Ella, jointly	K–296391	October 20, 1985	$.06	$500/share = $5,000

Once the securities have been examined, they should be placed in a safe deposit box or bank vault to avoid loss or theft. Some people prefer to examine securities in the bank and have Xerox copies made of them for any future reference, when necessary. Securities should only be removed from their place of safe keeping when it is necessary to deliver them for sale or re-registration.

A sample stock certificate and corporate bond are reproduced on the following pages.

Registration Securities, like bank accounts, may be owned individually by the decedent or with other people. If they are owned jointly with others, the securities will automatically go to the survivor. The same information is kept on such jointly owned securities for tax purposes as is for individually owned securities. They do not, however, become part of the probate estate.

Securities registered in the name of the decedent alone should be re-registered in the name of the estate. Re-registration eases problems relating to theft or loss and places the securities in the form required to sell them.

In the event a security is sold the estate will have five market days (days on which the stock markets are open) to deliver those securities in "negotiable form." Negotiable form means a form whereby they may readily be transferred to the buyer. A security listed in the decedent's name, rather than in the name of the estate of the decedent, is not considered to be in negotiable form, and delivery of a security in such form will not be "good delivery." If the estate is put to the task of re-registering securities after they are sold, the process may take more than a month, and the estate will be deemed to have "failed" to deliver and the sale may be negated. During the period that the stock must be re-registered, the estate may lose an advantageous sale if the market should decline.

The following steps must be taken to re-register securities. First, the personal representative must ascertain the transfer agent for the particular stock of the company. A transfer agent is one who

EXAMPLE *A Sample of a Certificate (front and back)*

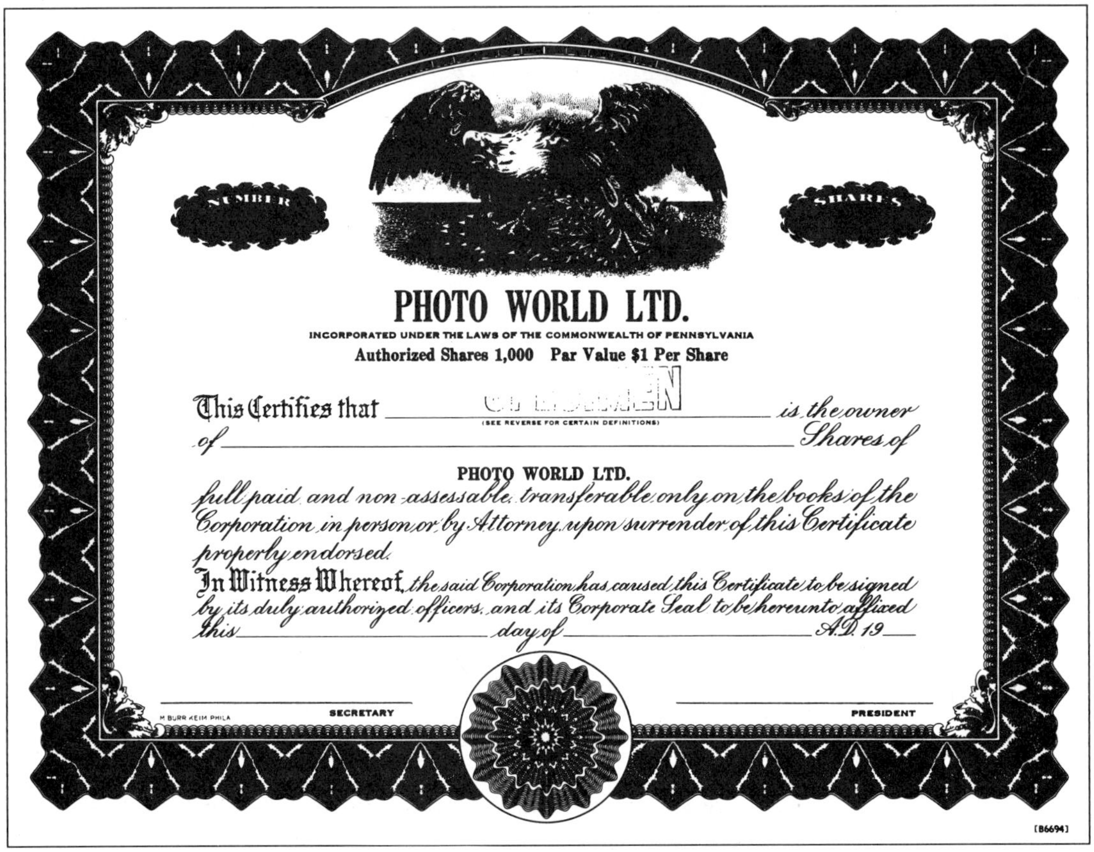

NUMBER SHARES

PHOTO WORLD LTD.

INCORPORATED UNDER THE LAWS OF THE COMMONWEALTH OF PENNSYLVANIA

Authorized Shares 1,000 Par Value $1 Per Share

This Certifies that ____ SPECIMEN ____ is the owner

(SEE REVERSE FOR CERTAIN DEFINITIONS)

of ____ Shares of

PHOTO WORLD LTD.

full paid and non-assessable transferable only on the books of the Corporation in person or by Attorney upon surrender of this Certificate properly endorsed.

In Witness Whereof, the said Corporation has caused this Certificate to be signed by its duly authorized officers, and its Corporate Seal to be hereunto affixed this ____ day of ____ A.D. 19__

H BURR KEIM PHILA

SECRETARY PRESIDENT

[B6694]

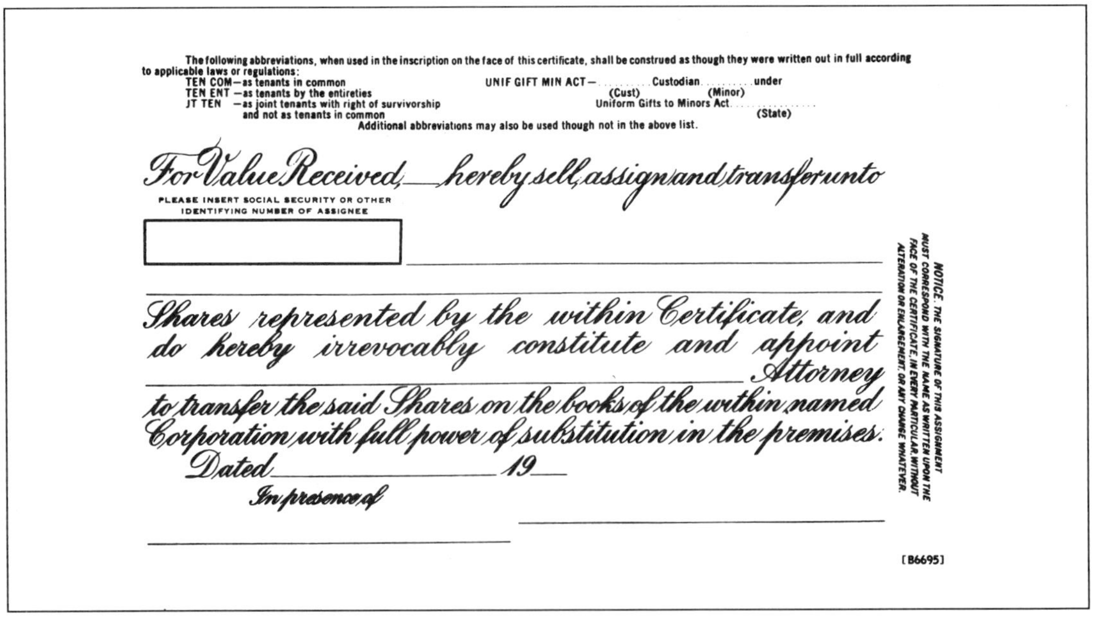

The following abbreviations, when used in the inscription on the face of this certificate, shall be construed as though they were written out in full according to applicable laws or regulations:

TEN COM—as tenants in common
TEN ENT—as tenants by the entireties
JT TEN—as joint tenants with right of survivorship and not as tenants in common

UNIF GIFT MIN ACT—.......... Custodian .... under
(Cust) (Minor)
Uniform Gifts to Minors Act ....
(State)

Additional abbreviations may also be used though not in the above list.

For Value Received, ____ hereby sell, assign and transfer unto

PLEASE INSERT SOCIAL SECURITY OR OTHER IDENTIFYING NUMBER OF ASSIGNEE

____

Shares represented by the within Certificate, and do hereby irrevocably constitute and appoint ____ Attorney to transfer the said Shares on the books of the within named Corporation with full power of substitution in the premises.

Dated ____ 19__

In presence of

____

NOTICE: THE SIGNATURE OF THIS ASSIGNMENT MUST CORRESPOND WITH THE NAME AS WRITTEN UPON THE FACE OF THE CERTIFICATE, IN EVERY PARTICULAR WITHOUT ALTERATION OR ENLARGEMENT, OR ANY CHANGE WHATEVER.

[B6695]

EXAMPLE *Corporate Bond (front)*

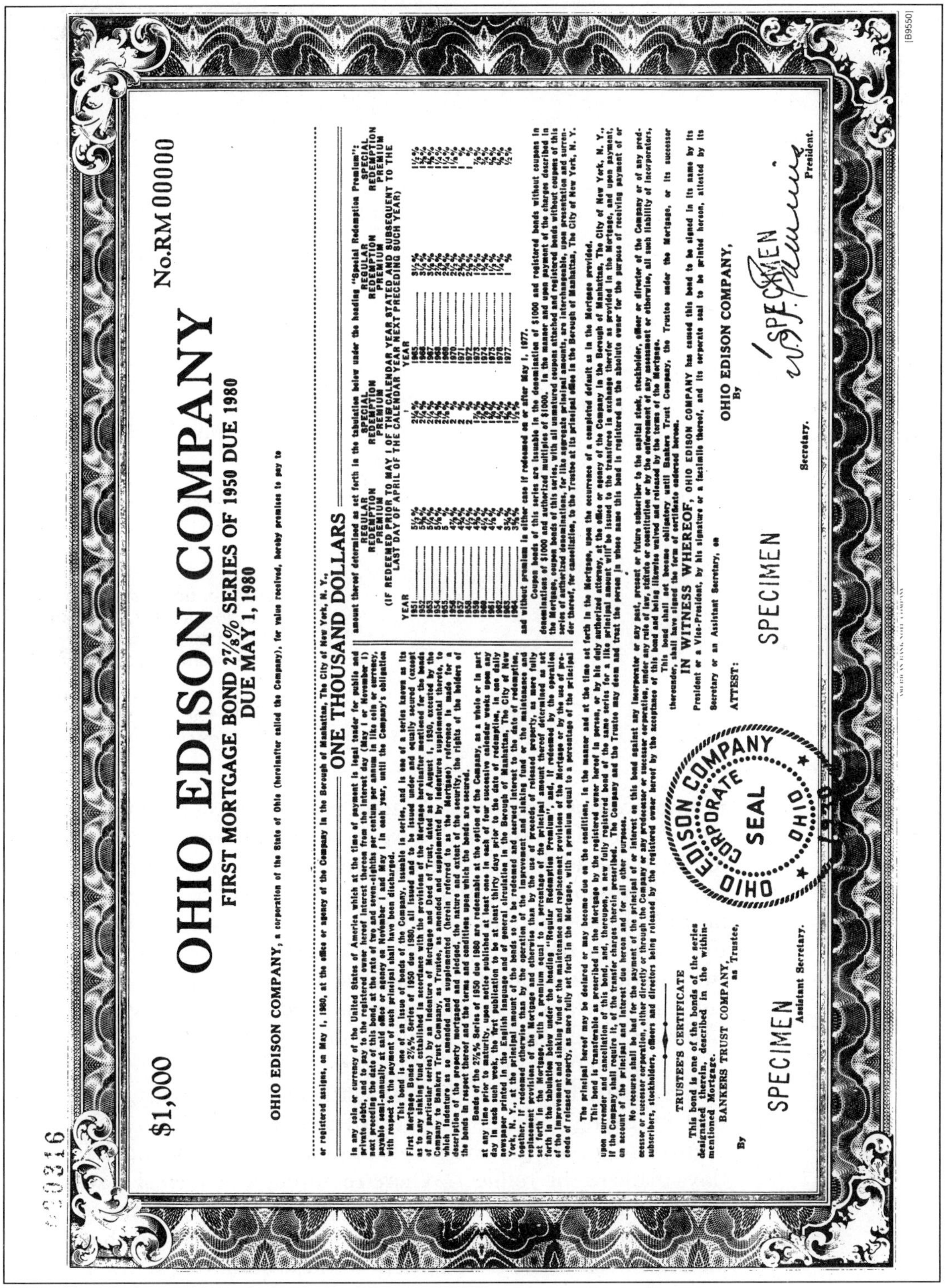

020316

$1,000 No.RM 00000

OHIO EDISON COMPANY

FIRST MORTGAGE BOND 2⅞% SERIES OF 1950 DUE 1980
DUE MAY 1, 1980

OHIO EDISON COMPANY, a corporation of the State of Ohio (hereinafter called the Company), for value received, hereby promises to pay to

....

or registered assigns, on May 1, 1980, at the office or agency of the Company in the Borough of Manhattan, The City of New York, N. Y.,

ONE THOUSAND DOLLARS

in any coin or currency of the United States of America which at the time of payment is legal tender for public and private debts, and to pay to the registered owner hereof interest thereon from the interest day (May 1 or November 1) next preceding the date of this bond, at the rate of two and seven-eighths per centum per annum in like coin or currency, payable semi-annually at said office or agency on November 1 and May 1 in each year, until the Company's obligation with respect to the payment of such principal shall have been discharged.

This bond is one of an issue of bonds of the Company, issuable in series, and is one of a series known as its First Mortgage Bonds 2⅞% Series of 1950 due 1980, all issued and to be issued under and equally secured (except as to any sinking fund established in accordance with the provisions of the Mortgage hereinafter mentioned for the bonds of any particular series) by an Indenture of Mortgage and Deed of Trust, dated as of August 1, 1930, executed by the Company to Bankers Trust Company, as Trustee, as amended and supplemented by indentures supplemental thereto, to which Indenture as so amended and supplemented (herein referred to as the Mortgage) reference is made for a description of the property mortgaged and pledged, the nature and extent of the security, the rights of the holders of the bonds in respect thereof and the terms and conditions upon which the bonds are secured.

Bonds of the 2⅞% Series of 1950 due 1980 are redeemable at the option of the Company, as a whole or in part at any time prior to maturity, upon notice published at least once in each of four successive calendar weeks upon any day in each such week, the first publication to be at least thirty days prior to the date of redemption, in one daily newspaper printed in the English language and of general circulation in the Borough of Manhattan, The City of New York, N. Y., at the principal amount of the bonds so to be redeemed and accrued interest to the date of redemption, together, if redeemed otherwise than by the operation of the improvement and sinking fund or the maintenance and replacement provisions of the Mortgage and otherwise than by the use of proceeds of released property, as more fully set forth in the Mortgage, with a premium equal to a percentage of the principal amount thereof determined as set forth in the tabulation below under the heading "Regular Redemption Premium", and, if redeemed by the operation of the improvement and sinking fund or the maintenance and replacement provisions of the Mortgage or by the use of proceeds of released property, as more fully set forth in the Mortgage, with a premium equal to a percentage of the principal amount thereof determined as set forth in the tabulation below under the heading "Special Redemption Premium":

(IF REDEEMED PRIOR TO MAY 1 OF THE CALENDAR YEAR STATED AND SUBSEQUENT TO THE LAST DAY OF APRIL OF THE CALENDAR YEAR NEXT PRECEDING SUCH YEAR)

YEAR	REGULAR REDEMPTION PREMIUM	SPECIAL REDEMPTION PREMIUM	YEAR	REGULAR REDEMPTION PREMIUM	SPECIAL REDEMPTION PREMIUM
1951	5½%	2¼%	1965	3½%	1½%
1952	5⅜%	2¼%	1966	3¼%	1⅜%
1953	5¼%	2¼%	1967	3⅛%	1⅜%
1954	5⅛%	2⅛%	1968	2⅞%	1¼%
1955	5 %	2⅛%	1969	2¾%	1¼%
1956	4⅞%	2 %	1970	2½%	1⅛%
1957	4¾%	2 %	1971	2⅜%	1 %
1958	4½%	2 %	1972	2⅛%	1 %
1959	4⅜%	1⅞%	1973	1⅞%	⅞%
1960	4¼%	1⅞%	1974	1¾%	¾%
1961	4⅛%	1¾%	1975	1½%	⅝%
1962	4 %	1¾%	1976	1¼%	⅝%
1963	3¾%	1⅝%	1977	1 %	½%
1964	3⅝%	1½%			

and without premium in either case if redeemed on or after May 1, 1977.

Coupon bonds of this series are issuable in the denomination of $1000 and registered bonds without coupons in denominations of $1000 and authorized multiples of $1000. In the manner and upon payment of the charges described in the Mortgage, coupon bonds of this series, with all unmatured coupons attached and registered bonds without coupons of this series of authorized denominations, for like aggregate principal amounts, are interchangeable, upon presentation and surrender thereof, for cancellation, to the Trustee at its principal office in the Borough of Manhattan, The City of New York, N. Y.

The principal hereof may be declared or may become due on the conditions, in the manner and at the time set forth in the Mortgage, upon the occurrence of a completed default as in the Mortgage provided.

This bond is transferable as prescribed in the Mortgage by the registered owner hereof in person, or by his duly authorized attorney, at the office or agency of the Company in the Borough of Manhattan, The City of New York, N. Y., upon surrender and cancellation of this bond, and, thereupon, a new fully registered bond of the same series for a like principal amount will be issued to the transferee in exchange therefor as provided in the Mortgage, and upon payment, if the Company shall require it, of the transfer charges therein prescribed. The Company and the Trustee may deem and treat the person in whose name this bond is registered as the absolute owner for the purpose of receiving payment of or on account of the principal and interest due hereon and for all other purposes.

No recourse shall be had for the payment of the principal of or interest on this bond against any incorporator or any past, present or future subscriber to the capital stock, stockholder, officer or director of the Company or of any predecessor or successor corporation, either directly or through the Company or any predecessor or successor corporation, under any rule of law, statute or constitution or by the enforcement of any assessment or otherwise, all such liability of incorporators, subscribers, stockholders, officers and directors being released by the registered owner hereof by the acceptance of this bond and being likewise waived and released by the terms of the Mortgage.

This bond shall not become obligatory until Bankers Trust Company, the Trustee under the Mortgage, or its successor thereunder, shall have signed the form of certificate endorsed hereon.

IN WITNESS WHEREOF, OHIO EDISON COMPANY has caused this bond to be signed in its name by its President or a Vice-President, by his signature or a facsimile thereof, and its corporate seal to be printed hereon, attested by its Secretary or an Assistant Secretary, on

TRUSTEE'S CERTIFICATE

This bond is one of the bonds of the series designated therein, described in the within-mentioned Mortgage.

BANKERS TRUST COMPANY, as Trustee,

By SPECIMEN Assistant Secretary.

OHIO EDISON COMPANY CORPORATE SEAL OHIO

ATTEST: SPECIMEN Secretary.

OHIO EDISON COMPANY,
By SPECIMEN President.

[B9550]

EXAMPLE ***Corporate Bond (back)***

For Value Received .... hereby sell, assign and transfer unto .... of.. the within-mentioned bond of the OHIO EDISON COMPANY and hereby irrevocably authorize said Company to transfer said bond on the books of said Company. Dated:.............................. .... Witness:	OHIO EDISON COMPANY REGISTERED FIRST MORTGAGE BOND 2⅞% SERIES OF 1950 DUE 1980 $1,000 DUE MAY 1, 1980 INTEREST PAYABLE MAY 1 and NOVEMBER 1 PRINCIPAL AND INTEREST PAYABLE IN THE BOROUGH OF MANHATTAN, THE CITY OF NEW YORK, NEW YORK United States Internal Revenue stamps required by law have been affixed to the within-mentioned Mortgage and Deed of Trust, and cancelled. (B9551)

is employed by a corporation to attend to transfers of its stock. In the case of relatively small corporations, the company may transfer its own stock on its books. However, with medium size and large companies, the stock is usually transferred by a transfer agent (normally a bank). The name of the transfer agent is usually disclosed on the face of the stock certificate, but if up-to-date information is required, it may be necessary to check with the company itself or to consult a service such as that provided by the Commerce Clearing House "Corporation Directory."

A written request to make the transfer into the name of the estate should be sent to the transfer agent or company, as the case may be, along with the stock certificate(s) themselves and a short certificate, or its equivalent, that bear a date not more than 60 days prior to the request. Where required, a waiver of state death taxes or an affidavit of domicile must also be submitted. The waiver of state inheritance tax shows the corporation that provision has been made for payment of these state taxes. Such a form will normally be required when the corporation was incorporated in the same state as decedent's residence.

Generally the affidavit of domicile is needed if the corporation was incorporated in some state other than the state in which the decedent was domiciled. An example of such a form follows.

EXAMPLE
Affidavit of Individual Executrix

STATE OF PENNSYLVANIA }
County of Philadelphia } ss.

Prudence Holloway, being duly sworn, deposes and says that she resides at c/o 13th Floor, 401 Walnut Street, Philadelphia, Pennsylvania 19106, State of Pennsylvania, and is executrix of the estate of Lawrence Dain, deceased, who died on the 25th day of November 1989; that at the time of his death the domicile, legal residence, of said decedent was at 1234 Lancaster Pike, Wayne, County of Delaware, State of Pennsylvania;

That the said decedent was not a resident of the State of New York and did not reside, dwell, or lodge in the said State for the greater part of any twelve consecutive months during the twenty-four months immediately preceding his death and did not by any formal instrument executed within one year of his death, or by his Last Will and Testament declare himself to be a resident of the said State;

That this affidavit is made for the purpose of securing the transfer or delivery of the following described property owned by said decedent at the time of his death:

400 shares of the common A stock of New York Times, a New York Corporation.

That all debts of decedent and all estate, inheritance taxes, prior legacies, and administration expenses of the estate have been paid or are adequately provided for.

That said certificates were physically located in the County of Philadelphia, State of Pennsylvania, at the time of decedent's death and had no business status in any other state.

Sworn to before me
this 26th day of
December, 1991

/s/**Prudence Holloway**
Executrix

/s/**Ronald Cresswell**
Notary Public

When transferring stocks or bonds it is necessary either to endorse the back of the stock certificate or bond or to attach a separate form to it, known as a stock power (or bond power). This form serves the same purpose as an endorsement—it allows the stock or bond to be transferred. The reason for using such a form is to prevent the stock or bond from being transferred improperly, as after a loss or theft. An endorsement on the stock or bond makes it

EXAMPLE *Stock Power*

ASSIGNMENT SEPARATE FROM CERTIFICATE 123A — Printed for and Sold by John C. Clark Co., 1326 Walnut St., Phila.

For Value Received, I, Prudence Holloway, Executor of the Will of Lawrence Dain, Deceased,

hereby sell, assign and transfer unto Estate of Lawrence Dain

PLEASE INSERT SOCIAL SECURITY OR OTHER IDENTIFYING NUMBER OF ASSIGNEE

One thousand (1,000) *Shares of the* common $1 par

Capital Stock of the Sun Oil Company

standing in Lawrence Dain *name on the books of said* Company *represented by*

Certificate No. 7663, 52745, 7111 *herewith and do hereby irrevocably constitute and appoint*

The Fidelity Bank, by *attorney to*

transfer the said stock on the books of the within named Company with full power of substitution in the premises.

Dated December 26, 1991 /s/ Prudence Holloway

In presence of

S/E Barrett Barton

Signature Guaranteed

/s/ S. Frederick Blair

United National Bank

fully transferable. By sending the power to the transfer agent separately, the stock or bond is not transferable unless and until the power is received also.

The signature of the personal representative on the stock power or bond power must always be witnessed, and usually its authenticity must be guaranteed by a commercial bank or stockbroker. That guarantee is made by means of a rubber stamp on the face of the power plus the signature of an authorized officer of a commercial bank or brokerage house. A filled-in sample of a stock power is shown on this page. A bond power is virtually the same.

Sometimes the personal representative will find that the decedent has maintained an investment account with a stockbroker under the terms of which the broker retained the securities for the account of the decedent. In such situations the broker holds securities in "street name" or "nominee name," which is generally a fictitious name used by that broker for ease in conducting transfers. The courses of action open to the personal representative in such a case are (1) to change the name of the broker's account to the name of the estate, (2) to demand delivery of the securities, or (3) to demand transfer of the securities to a bank or other broker as agent for the personal representative. Any of these may be accomplished by delivery to the broker of a short certificate or its equivalent along with written instructions signed by the personal representative.

In recent years many brokerage houses have had difficulty keeping up with the volume of transactions they are called upon to make. Partly because of a fear of errors and partly because of a fear of loss, most experienced fiduciaries prefer to place the securities either in the hands of a bank as custodian or in a safe deposit box rather than keeping them in street name.

United States Savings Bonds Many people own U.S. Savings Bonds. The most common types are Series E and Series EE Bonds. These are issued with face values in multiples of twenty-five dollars and accrue interest until cashed in. There are also Series H Bonds that are issues in denominations of $500 and larger and pay out interest every six months.

After death, it is common practice to redeem U.S. bonds, although they may be re-registered in the name of the estate. To cash in U.S. bonds is a simple matter. The personal representative should endorse the bonds, have the signature guaranteed, and give the bonds to a Federal Reserve Bank or to any bank authorized to act as an agent for the federal government[19] along with a death certificate and short certificate. Values of U.S. bonds may be determined from tables put out by the federal government (and available at most banks).

If the U.S. bond was held jointly and the survivor wants to continue to hold the bond, it may be re-registered in the survivor's name alone. In addition to the bond, Treasury Form PD 1787 must be given to the bank along with a death certificate for the decedent. Treasury Form PD 1787 is shown in the next Example.

Sale of Securities

Marketability Virtually any asset may be sold as long as you can find someone to buy it. That may not only be time-consuming but may also result in receiving a price that is below what the personal representative believes it is worth. One of the great advantages of investing in corporate securities is that they may be easily "marketable," thereby doing away with problems of finding a willing buyer.

19. This will include commercial banks, savings banks, and savings and loan associations that are insured by the Federal Deposit Insurance Corporation or Federal Savings and Loan Insurance Corporation.

EXAMPLE *Treasury Form PD 1787*

PD F 4000
Department of the Treasury
Bureau of the Public Debt
(Revised May 1989)

REQUEST BY OWNER FOR REISSUE OF UNITED STATES SAVINGS BONDS/NOTES TO ADD BENEFICIARY OR COOWNER, ELIMINATE BENEFICIARY OR DECEDENT, SHOW CHANGE OF NAME, AND/OR CORRECT ERROR IN REGISTRATION

OMB No. 1535-0023
Expires 2/29/92

IMPORTANT: Follow instructions on the reverse in filling out this form. Any person who makes a statement on this form knowing it to be false, fictitious or fraudulent may be fined $10,000 or imprisoned for five years, or both.
PRINT IN INK OR TYPE ALL INFORMATION.

PAPERWORK REDUCTION STATEMENT: The completion of this form by any member of the public is voluntary. However, if completion of the transaction named below is desired, the information on this form must be provided.

To: Federal Reserve Bank
The undersigned hereby presents and surrenders for reissue the following-described United States Savings Bonds.
Total face amount ________________

ISSUE DATE	DENOMINATION (FACE AMOUNT)	SERIAL NUMBER	INSCRIPTION (Please type or print names, including middle names or initials, social security account number, if any, and addresses as inscribed on the bonds.)

(If space is insufficient use continuation sheet on page 4, sign it and refer to it above -- or use Form PD 3500 for this purpose.)

I hereby certify that ____________________ (Name of coowner) is the principal coowner of any bonds registered in coownership form submitted herewith and is responsible for any federal tax liability arising from this transaction (SEE TAX LIABILITY NOTICE), and I hereby request that said bonds be reissued in the following form of registration:

Mr. ☐ Mrs. ☐ Miss ☐ ____
(First name) (Middle name or initial) (Last name)

Address ____
(Number and street or rural route) (City or town) (State) (ZIP Code)

If a coowner or beneficiary is desired, complete the following line:

With Mr. ☐ Mrs. ☐ Miss ☐ ________________________________ as ☐ coowner ☐ beneficiary
(First name) (Middle name or initial) (Last name)

TAXPAYER IDENTIFYING NUMBERS (See General Instructions, page 3)

☐☐☐-☐☐-☐☐☐☐ (S.S. No. - Owner or first coowner)   ☐☐☐-☐☐-☐☐☐☐ (S.S. No. - Second coowner or beneficiary)   ☐☐-☐☐☐☐☐☐☐ (Employer Identification Number)

If new bonds are not to be delivered to address shown thereon, give delivery instructions here.
Name ________________________________
Address ________________________________
(Number and street or rural route) (City or town) (State) (ZIP Code)

Reissue is requested for the reason(s) shown below:

IN ALL CASES THIS FORM MUST BE SIGNED ON THE REVERSE SIDE

1. ☐ To add a coowner or beneficiary.
2. ☐ To change present beneficiary to coowner.
3. ☐ To eliminate a living beneficiary and reissue the bonds in either single ownership form or with another person as coowner or beneficiary. (For Series E and H bonds and savings notes, the present beneficiary must consent on page 2.)
4. ☐ To reissue in the name of a surviving owner, coowner, or beneficiary or in his/her name and that of another person as coowner or beneficiary. (Proof of death of owner, coowner, or beneficiary named on Series E or H bonds or savings notes, and owner or coowner named on Series EE or HH bonds, must be furnished.)
5. ☐ Change of name by: (a) ☐ marriage (b) ☐ divorce (c) ☐ court order (d) ☐ naturalization (e) ☐ otherwise if (e) is checked , furnish explanation: ________________
6. ☐ Correct error in registration. (See specific instruction No. 6) Provide following information:
   (a) The bonds were purchased by: ________________
   (b) The funds belonged to: ________________
   (c) Explanation of error ________________

EXAMPLE *Treasury Form PD 1787, continued*

COMPLETE ITEMS 1. AND/OR 2., IF APPLICABLE

1. My present legal name was changed from the name shown on the bonds by reason of ☐ marriage or ☐ ____________ (Specify nature of action, e.g., divorce decree, court order, naturalization, etc.) on ____________ (Date) in proceedings before ____________ (Name of court or other authority, including address, city and state);

2. I certify under penalty of perjury, that the number shown on the form is my correct taxpayer identification number; and that I am not subject to backup withholding either (i) because I have not been notified that I am subject to backup withholding (as a result of a failure to report all interest or dividends), or (ii) because I have been notified by the Internal Revenue Service that I am no longer subject to backup withholding.
(Please refer to instructions on Page 3.)

THIS FORM MUST BE
3. **SIGNED HERE X** ____________________ (Owner's present legal name)

☐☐☐-☐☐-☐☐☐☐ (Social Security Account Number) ____________________ (Home Address)

I CERTIFY that ____________________, whose identity is well-known or proved to me, signed this request for reissue, in my presence, acknowledging the same to be a free act and deed and affirming the statements therein to be true and correct on ____________ (Date).

(OFFICIAL STAMP OR SEAL)

____________________ (Signature and title of certifying officer)

____________________ (Address)

CONSENT OF BENEFICIARY

(NOTE: The beneficiary named on Series E or H bonds or savings notes must consent to elimination of his or her name from the registration.)

I am the designated beneficiary on the bonds described herein, including any continuation sheets, and consent to the elimination of my name from said bonds. ____________________ (Signature of beneficiary)

____________________ (Home Address) ☐☐☐-☐☐-☐☐☐☐ (Social Security Account Number)

I CERTIFY that ____________________, whose identity is well-known or proved to me, signed the above consent, in my presence, acknowledging the same to be a free act and deed on ____________ (Date).

(OFFICIAL STAMP OR SEAL)

____________________ (Signature and title of certifying officer)

____________________ (Address)

INSTRUCTIONS TO CERTIFYING OFFICER

Each person appearing before you must establish identification by positive and reliable evidence before this form is signed, unless he or she is personally well-known to you. You should place an adequate notation on this form, or on a separate record, showing exactly how identification was established. A notation is adequate if it is sufficiently detailed to permit, at a later date, a determination of the exact identification actually used. You and, if you are an officer or employee of an organization, the organization, will be held fully responsible for the adequacy of the identification.

The signature to the request must be executed in your presence. Then you should fully complete and sign the certification form provided for your use for each signature you witness.

If you are an employer (rather than an officer) authorized to certify signatures, insert the words "Authorized Signature" in the space provided for the title. Insert the place and date, as required on the form. Impress the seal of your organization or, if the seal is not available to you and your organization is an authorized issuing agent for Series EE savings bonds, imprint the Issuing Agent's Validating Stamp in the space provided.

RESERVED FOR IDENTIFICATION NOTATIONS

☐ Customer Account Number and Date Established: ☐ Document(s) -- Description(s):

☐ Identified by (Signature and Address):

FOR FEDERAL RESERVE BANK USE ONLY

☐ This transaction was a taxable event

$ ____________ was reported under ____________ (Social Security Account Number) for ____________ (Year)

☐ This transaction was not a taxable event. No interest was reported

(2)

Securities for which a ready and willing group of buyers and sellers exist are said to be "marketable" because they may be sold readily. Those for which there are no ascertainable buyers are said to be "nonmarketable." For example, securities traded on a national exchange such as the New York Stock Exchange or the American Stock Exchange are likely to be very "marketable." Trading goes on in the securities listed on such exchanges on a reasonably regular basis, probably daily. On the other hand, securities in a corporation that has been owned by one family or small group of individuals for a long period of time are "nonmarketable" because no regular purchases or sales occur.

When a security is publicly traded it becomes a much more salable item than securities that are not traded publicly. Furthermore, it is much easier to value stocks or bonds in public companies than those in closely held[20] companies.

Selling the Securities The general duty of a personal representative is to liquidate the assets of the estate except for those given specifically to beneficiaries by the terms of the will. Unless all those people who have an interest in the estate consent to retaining a given security, a prudent personal representative should sell all securities except in states utilizing the Uniform Probate Code (§ 3–906) that requires distribution in kind. By retaining securities without consent, the personal representative takes the risk that the security will decline in value and he will be charged with paying to the estate the amount of loss incurred by delaying the sale. (This is frequently referred to as a "surcharge.")

The processes of sale vary greatly depending on the marketability of the securities. Small holdings of publicly traded securities may be disposed of through a stockbroker. The sale of securities for which there is no established market may depend upon extensive negotiations with people interested in purchasing them. The process of such negotiation, the factors that go into it, and the legal steps necessary to conclude such a sale are beyond the scope of this book.

Other Business Interests Not all ownership interests in business are in the form of securities. The decedent may have operated a business as a sole proprietor or may have been a general partner or a limited partner in a partnership. A general partner is a partner who shares in the assets, profits, and losses of a partnership in the proportion to his interest. A limited partner has a limited share of the responsibility for losses and generally also has only a limited share of the opportunity for profit.

20. Another term used for corporations having a small number of shareholders and for which there is no public trading.

Because of the special risks involved in being a sole proprietor or a general partner, most states restrict the power of a personal representative to act with regard to such assets. The extent of such restrictions goes beyond the scope of this book. The basic duties of the personal representative to discover assets, take possession of them, value them, and liquidate them apply in these situations but the acts necessary to accomplish each step may be quite different from dealing with marketable securities.

Claims and Contracts The decedent's papers, family members, or the circumstances surrounding his death may indicate the existence of other types of intangible personal property. Among these may be promissory notes (an obligation by someone to pay money to the decedent), claims, or contracts. In general, these should be reviewed by an attorney promptly upon being discovered, but the valuation and safe-keeping problems should not be overlooked by the personal representative.

If the decedent had a claim against another person, either because of that person's failure to perform on a contract or because the other person caused injury to the decedent, prompt steps must be taken by the personal representative to preserve the claim. The laws of the state in which the decedent resided, or where the claim arose will provide that lawsuits on such claims must be brought within a specified time (the statute of limitations) that may be as short as one or two years.

Where the decedent held a judgment[21] against another person or entity, but less than all of the amount or amounts due were collected at the time of his death, the personal representative should take whatever steps are necessary to enforce the judgment.

Several particular types of claims deserve special attention because of the frequency with which they occur.

Social Security Benefits Any monthly benefit that the decedent was receiving prior to death, whether because of old age or disability, end with his or her death. The estate is entitled only to the payment due for the month before the month in which death occurs. Any Social Security checks relating to months after that, which are received by the personal representative or family, must be returned to the local office of the Social Security Administration and a receipt should be obtained. If the decedent and spouse were receiving old age or disability payments by means of a joint check, any such checks containing a payment to which the decedent is no longer entitled must also be returned, a receipt obtained,

21. A judgment is an order by a court directing a party (the judgment debtor) to pay money to another party (the judgment creditor).

and a request presented for reissuance of the check payable to the surviving spouse alone.

The decedent's estate, or in lieu of the decedent's estate the person furnishing proof that he or she paid for the decedent's burial, is eligible to claim the Social Security lump-sum death benefit. The amount of the benefit is three times the decedent's monthly annuity, subject to a maximum limit of $255. Only the estates of those classified as Social Security "workers," that is, those who had contributed to the Social Security System through their earnings, as contrasted to a person receiving benefits as a surviving dependent of a deceased "worker," are entitled to the burial benefit. The claim for the payment must be made on Form SSA–8–F4 accompanied by a receipted copy of the funeral bill. If the funeral bill has not been paid, the lump-sum death benefit will be made directly to the funeral director. Before the estate makes a claim for the lump sum death benefit, the paralegal should check with the funeral home to see if they have initiated the claim as part of their services (refer to Form SSA–8–F4 in the Example).

The surviving dependents of a deceased worker should be referred to the local Social Security Administration office, so that they may make claims for survivors' benefits in the event that they have not already done so. In general, widows or widowers over sixty years of age, children under eighteen (or if attending school between ages eighteen and twenty-three), and certain other people, including certain disabled persons regardless of age, may qualify for monthly benefits. The monthly benefits are calculated in accordance with a formula on the basis of the worker's rates of contribution to the Social Security Insurance System during his or her lifetime. The claim for the survivors benefits should be made on Social Security Form SSA-24 (see page 63). Additional information on Social Security benefits is available in the *Social Security Handbook,* Department of Health, Education and Welfare, Social Security Administration, published by the Superintendent of Documents, U.S. Government Printing Office, Washington, D.C. 20402.

Veterans' Benefits If a decedent was a veteran of any war, the estate and surviving dependents and parents (in some cases) may be entitled to any or all of a number of benefits. These include insurance, burial, pension, and miscellaneous benefits that arise both through the Veterans' Administration and under state law. In the event that it appears that one or more of the decedent's surviving dependents or parents is entitled to federal benefits, that person should contact the Veterans' Administration. To find out about the availability of state benefits for veterans a person should contact an organization like the American Legion or the Veterans of Foreign Wars. Illustrative federal forms concerning the burial

EXAMPLE *Social Security Form SSA–8–F4*

TOE 120/145/155

DEPARTMENT OF HEALTH AND HUMAN SERVICES
Social Security Administration

Form Approved
OMB No. 0960-0013

APPLICATION FOR LUMP-SUM DEATH PAYMENT*

I apply for all insurance benefits for which I am eligible under Title II (Federal Old-Age, Survivors, and Disability Insurance) of the Social Security Act, as presently amended, on the named deceased's Social Security record. (This application must be filed within 2 years after the date of death of the wage earner or self-employed person.)

*This may also be considered an application for insurance benefits payable under the Railroad Retirement Act.

1.	(a) PRINT name of Deceased Wage Earner or Self-Employed Person → (herein referred to as the "deceased")	FIRST NAME, MIDDLE INITIAL, LAST NAME
	(b) Check (✓) one for the deceased →	☐ Male ☐ Female
	(c) Enter deceased's Social Security Number →	___ ___ ___ / ___ ___ / ___ ___ ___ ___
2.	PRINT your name →	FIRST NAME, MIDDLE INITIAL, LAST NAME
3.	Enter date of birth of deceased *(Month, day, year)* →	
4.	(a) Enter date of death *(Month, day, year)* →	
	(b) Enter place of death *(City and State)* →	
5.	(a) Did the deceased ever file an application for Social Security benefits, a period of disability under Social Security, supplemental security income, or hospital or medical insurance under Medicare? →	☐ Yes *(If "Yes," answer (b) and (c).)* ☐ No ☐ Unknown *(If "No" or "Unknown," go on to item 6.)*
	(b) Enter name(s) of person(s) on whose Social Security record(s) other application was filed. →	FIRST NAME, MIDDLE INITIAL, LAST NAME
	(c) Enter Social Security Number(s) of person(s) named in (b). (If unknown, so indicate) →	___ ___ ___ / ___ ___ / ___ ___ ___ ___
6.	ANSWER ITEM 6 **ONLY** IF THE DECEASED WORKED WITHIN THE PAST 2 YEARS.	
	(a) About how much did the deceased earn from employment and self-employment during the year of death? →	AMOUNT $
	(b) About how much did the deceased earn the year before death? →	AMOUNT $
7.	ANSWER ITEM 7 **ONLY** IF THE DECEASED DIED PRIOR TO AGE 66 AND WITHIN THE PAST 4 MONTHS.	
	(a) Was the deceased unable to work because of a disabling condition at the time of death? →	☐ Yes *(If "Yes," answer (b).)* ☐ No *(If "No," go on to item 8.)*
	(b) Enter date disability began *(Month, day, year)* →	
8.	(a) Was the deceased in the active military or naval service (including Reserve or National Guard *active* duty or active duty for training) after September 7, 1939 and before 1968? →	☐ Yes *(If "Yes," answer (b) and (c).)* ☐ No *(If "No," go on to item 9.)*
	(b) Enter dates of service. →	From: *(Month, Year)* To: *(Month, Year)*
	(c) Has anyone (including the deceased) received, or does anyone expect to receive, a benefit from any other Federal agency? →	☐ Yes ☐ No
9.	Did the deceased work in the railroad industry for 7 years or more? →	☐ Yes ☐ No

Form **SSA-8-F4** (7/89) Destroy prior editions — Page 1

EXAMPLE *Social Security Form SSA–8–F4, continued*

10. (a) Did the deceased ever engage in work that was covered under the social security system of a country other than the United States? → ☐ Yes ☐ No *(If "Yes," answer (b).) (If "No," go on to item 11.)*

(b) If "Yes," list the country(ies). →

11. Is the deceased survived by a spouse or ex-spouse? (If "No," go on to item 12. If "Yes," give the following information about all marriages of the deceased including marriage in effect at time of death.) (If you need more space, use "Remarks" section on back page or attach a separate sheet.) ☐ Yes ☐ No

Last marriage of the deceased			
To whom married *(Name at Birth)*		When *(Month, day, year)*	Where *(Enter name of City and State)*
	How marriage ended	When *(Month, day, year)*	Where *(Enter name of City and State)*
	Marriage performed by: ☐ Clergyman or public official ☐ Other *(Explain in Remarks)*	Spouse's date of birth (or age)	
	Spouse's Social Security Number *(If none or unknown, so indicate)* ___ ___ ___/___ ___/___ ___ ___ ___		

Previous marriage of the deceased If none, write "None."			
To whom married		When *(Month, day, year)*	Where *(Enter name of City and State)*
	How marriage ended	When *(Month, day, year)*	Where *(Enter name of City and State)*
	Marriage performed by: ☐ Clergyman or public official ☐ Other *(Explain in Remarks)*	Spouse's date of birth (or age)	If spouse deceased, give date of death
	Spouse's Social Security Number *(If none or unknown, so indicate)* ___ ___ ___/___ ___/___ ___ ___ ___		

12. The deceased's surviving children (including natural children, adopted children, and stepchildren) or dependent grandchildren (including stepgrandchildren) may be eligible for benefits based on the earnings record of the deceased.

List below ALL such children who are now or were in the past 12 months UNMARRIED and:

- UNDER AGE 18
- AGE 18 TO 19 AND ATTENDING SECONDARY SCHOOL
- DISABLED OR HANDICAPPED (age 18 or over and disability began before age 22)

(If none, write "None.")

Full Name of Child	Full Name of Child

13. Is there a surviving parent (or parents) of the deceased who was receiving support from the deceased either at the time the deceased became disabled under the Social Security law or at the time of death? → ☐ Yes ☐ No (If "Yes," enter the name and address of the parent(s) in "Remarks".)

14. Have you filed for any Social Security benefits on the deceased's earnings record before? → ☐ Yes ☐ No

NOTE: If there is a surviving spouse, continue with item 15. If not, skip items 15 through 18.

15. If you are not the surviving spouse, enter the surviving spouse's name and address here

16. (a) Were the deceased and the surviving spouse living together at the same address when the deceased died? ☐ Yes ☐ No (If "Yes," go on to item 17.) (If "No," answer (b).)

(b) If either the deceased or surviving spouse was away from home (whether or not temporarily) when the deceased died, give the following:

Who was away? → ☐ Deceased ☐ Surviving spouse

Date last home	Reason absence began	Reason they were apart at time of death

If separated because of illness, enter nature of illness or disabling condition.

Form **SSA-8-F4** (7/89) Page 2

EXAMPLE *Social Security Form SSA–8–F4, continued*

If you are the surviving spouse, and if you are under age 66, answer 17.

17.	(a) Are you so disabled that you cannot work or was there some period during the last 14 months when you were so disabled that you could not work? →	☐ Yes ☐ No
	(b) If "Yes," enter the date you became disabled. →	*(Month, day, year)*

Answer 18 ONLY if you are the surviving spouse.

18.	Were you married before your marriage to the deceased? *(If "Yes," give the following about each of your previous marriages. If you need more space, use "Remarks" section on back page or attach a separate sheet.)* →	☐ Yes ☐ No

To whom married		When *(Month, day, year)*	Where *(Enter name of City and State)*
Your previous marriage	How marriage ended	When *(Month, day, year)*	Where *(Enter name of City and State)*
	Marriage performed by: ☐ Clergyman or public official ☐ Other *(Explain in Remarks)*	Spouse's date of birth (or age)	If spouse deceased, give date of death
	Spouse's Social Security Number *(If none or unknown, so indicate)* ___ ___ ___/___ ___/___ ___ ___ ___		

Remarks: *(You may use this space for any explanation. If you need more space, attach a separate sheet.)*

I know that anyone who makes or causes to be made a false statement or representation of material fact in an application or for use in determining a right to payment under the Social Security Act commits a crime punishable under Federal law by fine, imprisonment or both. I affirm that all information I have given in this document is true.

SIGNATURE OF APPLICANT Signature *(First name, middle initial, last name) (Write in ink)* ▶	Date *(Month, day, year)*
	Telephone Number(s) at which you may be contacted during the day Area Code

Mailing Address *(Number and street, Apt. No., P.O. Box, or Rural Route)*

City and State	ZIP Code	Enter Name of County (if any) in which you now live

Witnesses are required ONLY if this application has been signed by mark (X) above. If signed by mark (X), two witnesses to the signing who know the applicant must sign below, giving their full addresses.

1. Signature of Witness	2. Signature of Witness
Address *(Number and street, City, State, and ZIP Code)*	Address *(Number and street, City, State, and ZIP Code)*

Form **SSA-8-F4** (7/89) Page 3

EXAMPLE *Social Security Form SSA-8-F4, continued*

RECEIPT FOR YOUR CLAIM FOR THE SOCIAL SECURITY LUMP-SUM DEATH PAYMENT

TELEPHONE NUMBER TO CALL IF YOU HAVE A QUESTION OR SOMETHING TO REPORT	SSA OFFICE	DATE CLAIM RECEIVED
TELEPHONE NUMBER		

RECEIPT FOR YOUR CLAIM

Your application for the lump-sum death payment has been received and will be processed as quickly as possible.

You should hear from us within________days after you have given us all the information we requested. Some claims may take longer if additional information is needed.

In the meantime, if you change your mailing address, you should report the change.

Always give us your claim number when writing or telephoning about your claim.

If you have any questions about your claim, we will be glad to help you.

CLAIMANT	SOCIAL SECURITY CLAIM NUMBER

DECEASED'S NAME (If surname differs from claimant's name)

COLLECTION AND USE OF INFORMATION FROM YOUR APPLICATION — PRIVACY ACT/PAPERWORK ACT NOTICE

I. The Social Security Administration is authorized to collect the information on this form under sections 202(i) and 205(a) of the Social Security Act, as amended (42 U.S.C. 402(i) and 405(a)).

II. While it is voluntary, except in the circumstances explained below, for you to furnish the information on this form to Social Security, no lump-sum death payment may be paid unless an application has been received by a Social Security office. Your response is mandatory where the refusal to disclose certain information affecting your right to payment would reflect a fraudulent intent to secure payment not authorized by the Social Security Act.

III. The information on this form is needed to enable Social Security to determine if you are entitled to the lump-sum death payment. It will also enable us to determine if there are any survivors of the deceased who may qualify for monthly Social Security benefits as dependents of the deceased.

IV. Failure to provide all or part of this information could prevent an accurate and timely decision on your claim, and could result in the loss of some benefits for eligible dependents of the deceased.

V. Although the information you furnish on this form is almost never used for any other purpose than stated in Part III, above, there is a possibility that in the administration of the Social Security programs or for the administration of programs requiring coordination with the Social Security Administration, information may be disclosed to another person or to another government agency as follows:

1. To enable a third party or an agency to assist Social Security in establishing rights to Social Security benefits and/or coverage.
2. To comply with Federal laws requiring the release of information from Social Security records (e.g., to the General Accounting Office and the Veterans Administration).
3. To facilitate statistical research and audit activities necessary to assure the integrity and improvement of the Social Security programs (e.g., to the Bureau of the Census and private concerns under contract to Social Security.)

VI. The information you provide may also be used without your consent in automated matching programs. These matching programs are computer comparisons of Social Security Administration records with records kept by other Federal agencies or State and local government agencies. Information from these matching programs can be used to establish or verify a person's eligibility for Federally funded or administered benefit programs and for repayment of payments or delinquent debts under these programs.

These and other reasons why information about you may be used or given out are explained in the Federal Register. If you would like more information about this, get in touch with any Social Security office.

TIME IT TAKES TO COMPLETE THIS FORM

We estimate that it will take you about 10 minutes to complete this form. This includes the time it will take to read the instructions, gather the necessary facts and fill out the form. If you have comments or suggestions on how long it takes to complete this form or on any other aspect of this form, write to the Social Security Administration, ATTN: Reports Clearance Officer, 1-A-21 Operations Bldg., Baltimore, MD 21235, and to the Office of Management and Budget, Paperwork Reduction Project (0960-0013), Washington, D.C. 20503.

Form **SSA-8-F4** (7/89) Page 4

☆U.S. Government Printing Office: 1989-241-312/80089

EXAMPLE *Social Security Form SSA–24*

Form Approved
OMB No. 0960-0062

DEPARTMENT OF HEALTH AND HUMAN SERVICES	SOCIAL SECURITY ADMINISTRATION APPLICATION FOR SURVIVORS BENEFITS (PAYABLE UNDER TITLE II OF THE SOCIAL SECURITY ACT) *IMPORTANT – Read instructions before completing form. Detach and retain ONLY the instruction sheet.*	(DO NOT WRITE IN THIS SPACE) VA DATE STAMP

1. FIRST NAME – MIDDLE NAME – LAST NAME OF VETERAN *(Type or print)*
2. DATE OF DEATH

NOTE: If the veteran's Social Security No. is unknown, complete Items 4, 5, 6 and 7 about veteran.

3. SOCIAL SECURITY NO. OF VETERAN
4. DATE OF BIRTH
5. PLACE OF BIRTH
6. NAME OF FATHER
7. MAIDEN NAME OF MOTHER
8. DID THE VETERAN WORK IN THE RAILROAD INDUSTRY AT ANY TIME AFTER 1936? ☐ YES ☐ NO

NOTE: The following information should be furnished for each period of the veteran's active service (regular or reserves) after September 7, 1939, in the military service of the United States or service as a commissioned officer in the Public Health Service or the National Oceanic and Atmospheric Administration or during WWII, Philippine or Filipino or Allied country military service. If additional space is needed, attach a spearate sheet.

9A. DATE ENTERED ACTIVE SERVICE	9B. SERVICE NO.	9C. DATE SEPARATED FROM ACTIVE SERVICE	9D. GRADE, RANK, OR RATING, ORGANIZATION AND BRANCH OF SERVICE

10. RELATIONSHIP OF APPLICANT TO VETERAN ☐ SURVIVING SPOUSE ☐ CHILD ☐ PARENT
11. DATE OF BIRTH OF APPLICANT
12. VETERANS ADMINISTRATION FILE NO.

CHILDREN: Show names of surviving children (including natural children, adopted children, and stepchildren) or dependent grandchildren (including stepgrandchildren) who at any time since the veteran died, were unmarried and (a) under age 18; (b) age 18 to 19 and attending Secondary school; (c) disabled or handicapped (18 or over and disability began before age 22).

13A.	13B.
13C.	13D.

I know that anyone who makes or causes to be made a false statement or representation of material fact in an application or for use in determining a right to payment under the Social Security Act commits a crime punishable under Federal law by fine, imprisonment, or both. I affirm that all information I have given in this document is true.

14. DATE *(Month, day, year)*
15. SIGNATURE OF APPLICANT *(First name, middle initial, last name) (Sign in ink)* SIGN HERE ➡
16. MAILING ADDRESS OF APPLICANT *(No. and street or rural route, city or P.O., State and ZIP Code)*
17. TELEPHONE NO. *(Include Area Code)*

WITNESSES REQUIRED ONLY IF SIGNATURE OF APPLICANT IS MADE BY "X" MARK ABOVE

18A. SIGNATURE OF WITNESS	18B. ADDRESS OF WITNESS *(No. and street, city, State and ZIP Code)*
19A. SIGNATURE OF WITNESS	19B. ADDRESS OF WITNESS *(No. and street, city, State and ZIP Code)*

ITEMS BELOW TO BE COMPLETED BY THE VETERANS ADMINISTRATION *(Use reverse for "Remarks")*

20. PROOFS RECEIVED *(Check)*	21. PROOFS REQUESTED FROM CLAIMANT OR OTHER *(Specify)*
☐ DEATH ☐ MARRIAGE	☐ DEATH ☐ MARRIAGE
☐ AGE ________ (NAME)	☐ AGE ________ (NAME)
________ (NAME)	________ (NAME)
________ (NAME)	________ (NAME)
☐ OTHER *(Specify)*	☐ OTHER *(Specify)*

22. DATE
23. NAME AND ADDRESS OF TRANSMITTING VA OFFICE

VA FORM APR 1987 **SSA-24** EXISTING STOCKS OF VA FORM SSA-24, SEP 1985, WILL BE USED. ★U.S.GPO:1988-0-219-528 013577 allowance, claim for life insurance, and widow's or orphan's benefits follow within the next pages.

Company Benefits The personal representative should contact the decedent's last employer and former employers to inquire about any benefits payable either to the decedent, the estate, or to beneficiaries. There are a number of types of such benefits, any or all of which may pertain to the particular decedent's situation.

Retirement Plans—Pension, Profit-Sharing The decedent and possibly the decedent's spouse or other beneficiaries may have been receiving a benefit under a pension or profit-sharing retirement plan. The terms of such plans should be reviewed by the personal representative to determine whether or not the decedent, the estate, or a beneficiary is entitled to any additional benefits. The personal representative should ascertain whether or not any death benefits are payable either to the decedent's estate or a named beneficiary.

Thrift Plans Should the employer have a thrift plan[22] available for its employees, the personal representative should inquire whether the decedent's estate or any beneficiary is entitled to payments under such a plan. Such plans usually involve an incentive from the employer to save money out of each paycheck.

Deferred Compensation Plans Where an employee is in a relatively high income tax bracket, the employee may have elected to defer payment of a portion of his compensation until later years, typically retirement years, to take advantage of the lower income tax rates at such time. In the event that all such deferred compensation has not been paid out at the time of the employee's death, the personal representative should ascertain whether or not the portion unpaid is due to the estate or a named beneficiary.

Employee Credit Unions The decedent may have been a member of and have made deposits in an employee credit union. As in the case of a bank account, the account that the employee had may have been in his or her own name or joint names. Any such property should be treated in the same manner as any other solely owned or jointly owned property.

Group Insurance The decedent may have been insured under a group life insurance contract provided by the employer. A claim under such group insurance would normally be made in the same manner as claims for other life insurance benefits.

22. Essentially, a savings plan.

EXAMPLE *Application for Burial Benefits*

OMB Approved No. 2900-0003
Respondent Burden: 1/3 Hour

Department of Veterans Affairs

(DO NOT WRITE IN THIS SPACE)
VA DATE STAMP

APPLICATION FOR BURIAL BENEFITS

(Under 38 U.S.C., Chapter 23)

IMPORTANT – Read instructions carefully before completing form. YOUR COMPLIANCE WITH ALL INSTRUCTIONS WILL AVOID DELAY. Type or print all information.

1. FIRST, MIDDLE, LAST NAME OF DECEASED VETERAN

2. SOCIAL SECURITY NO. OF VETERAN

3. VA FILE NO.
C–

4A. FIRST, MIDDLE, LAST NAME OF CLAIMANT

4B. MAILING ADDRESS OF CLAIMANT *(Number and street or rural route, city or P.O., State and ZIP Code)*

PART I – INFORMATION REGARDING VETERAN

5A. DATE OF BIRTH

5B. PLACE OF BIRTH

6A. DATE OF DEATH

6B. PLACE OF DEATH

6C. DATE OF BURIAL

SERVICE INFORMATION *(The following information should be furnished for the periods of the VETERAN'S ACTIVE SERVICE)*

7A. ENTERED SERVICE		7B. SERVICE NO.	7C. SEPARATED FROM SERVICE		7D. GRADE, RANK OR RATING, ORGANIZATION AND BRANCH OF SERVICE
DATE	PLACE		DATE	PLACE	

8. IF VETERAN SERVED UNDER NAME OTHER THAN THAT SHOWN IN ITEM I, GIVE FULL NAME AND SERVICE RENDERED UNDER THAT NAME

9. ARE YOU CLAIMING THAT THE CAUSE OF DEATH WAS DUE TO SERVICE?

☐ YES ☐ NO

PART II – CLAIM FOR BURIAL BENEFITS AND/OR INTERMENT ALLOWANCE IF PAID BY CLAIMANT

NOTE – If claiming Plot Allowance Only, do not complete Part II, but complete Parts III and IV on reverse.

10. PLACE OF BURIAL OR LOCATION OF CREMAINS

11. WAS BURIAL (WITHOUT CHARGE FOR PLOT OR INTERMENT) IN A STATE OWNED CEMETERY, OR SECTION THEREOF, USED SOLELY FOR PERSONS ELIGIBLE FOR BURIAL IN A NATIONAL CEMETERY?

☐ YES ☐ NO *(If "NO," complete Items 13 and 14)*

12. WAS BURIAL IN A NATIONAL CEMETERY OR CEMETERY OWNED BY THE FEDERAL GOVERNMENT?

☐ YES ☐ NO *(If "NO," complete Items 13 and 14)*

13. BURIAL PLOT, MAUSOLEUM VAULT, COLUMBARIUM NICHE, ETC. COST IS: *(CHECK ONE)*

☐ PAID BY ANOTHER PERSON(S)
☐ PAID BY CLAIMANT FOR BURIAL
☐ DUE FUNERAL DIRECTOR
☐ NONE
☐ DUE CEMETERY OWNER

14. IF PLOT/INTERMENT EXPENSES ARE UNPAID, WHO WILL FILE CLAIM FOR EXPENSES? *(Name and Address)*

15. TOTAL EXPENSE OF BURIAL, FUNERAL, TRANSPORTATION AND IF CLAIMED, BURIAL PLOT *(This includes cremation, cost of burial urn, and placement of cremains)*
$

16. AMOUNT PAID
$

17. WHOSE FUNDS WERE USED?

18A. HAS PERSON WHOSE FUNDS WERE USED BEEN REIMBURSED?

☐ YES ☐ NO *(If "YES," complete Items 18B and 18C)*

18B. AMOUNT OF REIMBURSEMENT
$

18C. SOURCE OF REIMBURSEMENT

19A. HAS OR WILL ANY AMOUNT BE ALLOWED ON EXPENSES BY LOCAL, STATE OR FEDERAL AGENCY?

☐ YES ☐ NO *(If "YES," complete Items 19B and 19C)*

19B. AMOUNT
$

19C. SOURCE

20. WAS THE VETERAN A MEMBER OF A BURIAL ASSOCIATION OR COVERED BY BURIAL INSURANCE?

☐ YES ☐ NO *(Before answering, read and comply with Instruction 11)*

VA FORM FEB 1991 **21-530**

SUPERSEDES VA 21–530, FEB 1990, WHICH WILL NOT BE USED.

EXAMPLE *Application for Burial Benefits, continued*

PART III – CLAIM FOR PLOT COST ALLOWANCE

IMPORTANT – Complete only if burial was NOT in a national cemetery or cemetery owned by the Federal Government.

21. WAS BURIAL (WITHOUT CHARGE FOR PLOT OR INTERMENT) IN A STATE OWNED CEMETERY, OR SECTION THEREOF, USED SOLELY FOR PERSONS ELIGIBLE FOR BURIAL IN A NATIONAL CEMETERY	22. PLACE OF BURIAL OR LOCATION OF CREMAINS	
23A. COST OF BURIAL PLOT *(Individual Grave Site, Mausoleum Vault, or Columbarium Niche)* $	23B. DATE OF PURCHASE	23C. DATE OF PAYMENT
24A. HAVE BILLS BEEN PAID IN FULL? ☐ YES ☐ NO *(If "NO," complete Item 24B)*	24B. AMOUNT PAID $	25. WHOSE FUNDS WERE USED?
26A. HAS PERSON WHOSE FUNDS WERE USED BEEN REIMBURSED? ☐ YES ☐ NO *(If "YES," complete Items 26B and 26C)*	26B. AMOUNT OF REIMBURSEMENT $	26C. SOURCE OF REIMBURSEMENT
27A. HAS OR WILL ANY AMOUNT BE ALLOWED ON EXPENSES BY STATE OR FEDERAL AGENCY? ☐ YES ☐ NO *(If "YES," complete Items 27B and 27C)*	27B. AMOUNT $	27C. SOURCE

PART IV – CERTIFICATION AND SIGNATURE

I CERTIFY THAT the foregoing statements made in connection with this application on account of the named veteran are true and correct to the best of my knowledge and belief.

28A. SIGNATURE OF CLAIMANT *(If signed by mark, complete Items 34A. thru 35B) (If signing for firm, corporation, or State agency, complete Items 28B thru 29)*	28B. OFFICIAL POSITION OF PERSON SIGNING ON BEHALF OF FIRM, CORPORATION OR STATE AGENCY
29 FULL NAME AND ADDRESS OF THE FIRM, CORPORATION, OR STATE AGENCY FILING AS CLAIMANT	

NOTE – Where the claimant is a firm or other unpaid creditor, Items 30A thru 33 MUST be completed by the individual who authorized services.

I CERTIFY THAT the foregoing statements made by the claimant are correct to the best of my knowledge and belief.

30A. SIGNATURE OF PERSON WHO AUTHORIZED SERVICES *(If signed by mark, complete Items 34A thru 35B)*	30B. NAME OF PERSON AUTHORIZING SERVICES *(Type or Print)*
31. ADDRESS *(Number and street or rural route, City or P.O., State and Zip Code)*	
32. DATE	33. RELATIONSHIP TO VETERAN

WITNESS TO SIGNATURE IF MADE BY "X" MARK

NOTE: Signature made by mark must be witnessed by two persons to whom the person making the statement is personally known, and the signatures and addresses of such witnesses must be shown below.

34A. SIGNATURE OF WITNESS	34B. ADDRESS OF WITNESS
35A. SIGNATURE OF WITNESS	35B. ADDRESS OF WITNESS

PENALTY – The law provides severe penalties which include fine or imprisonment, or both, for the willful submission of any statement or evidence of a material fact, knowing it to be false.

DEPARTMENT OF VETERANS AFFAIRS HEADSTONES AND MARKERS

The Department of Veterans Affairs will furnish, upon request, a Government headstone or marker at the expense of the United States for the unmarked graves of certain individuals eligible for burial in a national cemetery, but not buried there. These individuals include any veteran with an other than dishonorable discharge who dies after service or any serviceman or servicewoman who dies on active duty. Certain other individuals may also be eligible for the headstone or marker. Headstones or markers for all individuals in a national or post cemetery are furnished automatically without request from the family.

The Department of Veterans Affairs may make a limited reimbursement for the cost of a privately purchased headstone or marker, or for additional engraving on a headstone or marker purchased prior to the veteran's death. If a veteran is buried in a national cemetery, or is provided a Government headstone or marker, this benefit is not payable. The amount of reimbursement is payable to the purchaser but not the seller and the amount payable will not exceed the actual average cost of a Government headstone or marker.

For additional information and an application, contact the nearest VA office. Please state whether you wish to apply for a Government headstone or marker or whether you wish to apply for limited reimbursement for costs incurred in acquiring a non-Government headstone or marker.

*U.S. Government Printing Office: 1991 — 282-804/46133

EXAMPLE *Claim for Life Insurance*

Form Approved
OMB No. 2900-0060

Veterans Administration

CLAIM FOR ONE SUM PAYMENT
GOVERNMENT LIFE INSURANCE
ALL PREFIXES

1. INSURANCE FILE NO. *(Include prefix)* F

2. INSURANCE POLICY NO. *(Include prefix)*

3. NET AMOUNT OF INSURANCE $

4. CLAIMANT'S SHARE *(In fractions)*

PRIVACY ACT INFORMATION – No proceeds may be paid unless a completed claim form has been received (38 U.S.C. 717 and 752). The information provided, on a voluntary basis, will be used by VA employees and your authorized representative in the maintenance of Government insurance records. Responses may be disclosed outside the VA only if the disclosure is authorized under the Privacy Act, including the routine uses identified in VA system of records, 36VAOO, Veterans and Armed Forces Personnel U.S. Government In-Force Life Insurance Records, published in the Federal Register.

IMPORTANT INSTRUCTIONS

BENEFICIARY - This form may be used only when the insured has authorized payment under Option 1 (ONE SUM). Upon receipt of this completed claim form, the insurance proceeds will be paid as authorized by the insured. DO NOT USE THIS FORM IF YOU PREFER MONTHLY PAYMENTS. Notify the office that maintains the insured's records and information will be sent about other options available.

Complete all items, if known, and ATTACH PROOF OF DEATH. Type or print in ink. DO NOT DELAY filing application. The VA does not pay interest on delayed payments.

NOTE - If the beneficiary is a minor or incompetent, the person having custody of the beneficiary should complete the form and give his/her address in Item 11.

The law limits to $10.00 the fee payable to any attorney for the preparation, presentation and prosecution of claims for benefits under laws administered by the Veterans Administration.

When the claim form is completed, send it to the VA office that maintains the insured's records. The addresses of the Veterans Administration offices that maintain insurance records are:

Veterans Administration
Regional Office and Insurance Center
P.O. Box 8079
Philadelphia, PA 19101

Veterans Administration
Regional Office and Insurance Center
Federal Building, Fort Snelling
St. Paul, MN 55111

5. FIRST, MIDDLE AND LAST NAME OF INSURED VETERAN	6. DATE OF DEATH	7. PLACE OF DEATH
8. FIRST, MIDDLE AND LAST NAME OF BENEFICIARY	9. RELATIONSHIP TO INSURED	10. BENEFICIARY'S DATE OF BIRTH

11. ADDRESS OF BENEFICIARY *(Or address where check is to be mailed)*

12. CLAIMANTS TELEPHONE NUMBER *(Include Area Code) (Will only be used if additional information is required)*
A. HOME NUMBER | B. WORK NUMBER

I certify that the foregoing entries are true and correct to the best of my knowledge and belief.

13. SIGNATURE OF BENEFICIARY OR PERSON HAVING CUSTODY *(Do not print)*	14. DATE SIGNED

PENALTY - The law provides severe penalties which include fine or imprisonment, or both, for the willful submission of any statement or evidence of a material fact, knowing it to be false, or for the fraudulent acceptance of any payment to which you are not entitled.

VA FORM DEC 1983 **29-4125** EXISTING STOCKS OF VA FORM 29-4125, MAY 1982, WILL BE USED. ☆ U.S.G.P.O.: 1986 - 491-867/56185

Tangible Personal Property

Definitions The distinction between tangible and intangible personal property has already been discussed. The most common types of tangible personal property in an estate are automobiles, home furnishings, antiques, objects of art, collections of stamps, or coins and jewelry. Each requires special treatment by the personal representative.

Security of Tangible Personal Property It is the responsibility of the personal representative to take control of the tangible personalty to preserve its value for the estate. This may mean changing locks on the decedent's home. Extremely valuable items of tangible personal property might be placed in storage or in a bank vault. The personal representative may want to obtain or continue

EXAMPLE *Application for Dependency and Indemnity Compensation or Death Pension by a Surviving Spouse or Child*

Form Approved
OMB No. 2900-0004

Veterans Administration

(DO NOT WRITE IN THIS SPACE)
VA DATE STAMP

APPLICATION FOR DEPENDENCY AND INDEMNITY COMPENSATION OR DEATH PENSION BY A SURVIVING SPOUSE OR CHILD (INCLUDING ACCRUED BENEFITS AND DEATH COMPENSATION, WHERE APPLICABLE)

IMPORTANT – Read instructions carefully before completing this form. Answer all items fully. Detach and retain ONLY the instruction sheet. If more space is required, attach additional sheets and identify each answer by item number. Type or print the answers.

1. NAME OF DECEASED VETERAN *(First, middle, last)*		2. SOCIAL SECURITY NO.
3. IF VETERAN PREVIOUSLY APPLIED TO THE VETERANS ADMINISTRATION FOR ANY BENEFIT, INSERT VA FILE NUMBER, IF KNOWN. C–	4. RAILROAD RETIREMENT NO.	5. VETERANS ADMINISTRATION FILE NO. XC–
6A. NAME OF CLAIMANT *(First, middle, last)*		6B. TELEPHONE NO. *(Include Area Code)*
6C. MAILING ADDRESS OF CLAIMANT *(No. and street or rural route, City or P.O., State and ZIP Code)*		6D. RELATIONSHIP TO VETERAN *(Check one)* ☐ SURVIVING SPOUSE ☐ CHILD
		6E. SOCIAL SECURITY NO. OF SURVIVING SPOUSE

PART I – IDENTIFICATION AND SERVICE INFORMATION OF VETERAN *(See Instructions, Paragraph H)*

7. DATE OF BIRTH	8. DATE OF DEATH	9. PLACE OF DEATH

10. ARE YOU CLAIMING THAT THE CAUSE OF DEATH WAS DUE TO SERVICE?
☐ YES ☐ NO

11A. ENTERED ACTIVE SERVICE		11B. SERVICE NO.	11C. SEPARATED FROM ACTIVE SERVICE		11D. GRADE, RANK OR RATING, ORGANIZATION AND BRANCH OF SERVICE
DATE	PLACE		DATE	PLACE	

12. IF VETERAN SERVED UNDER A NAME OTHER THAN THAT SHOWN IN ITEM 1, GIVE FULL NAME AND SERVICE RENDERED UNDER THAT NAME

PART II – INFORMATION RELATING TO MARRIAGE *(See Instructions, Paragraph I)*

INFORMATION RELATING TO VETERAN

13. HOW MANY TIMES WAS VETERAN MARRIED?

14A. MARRIAGE		14B. TO WHOM MARRIED	14C. HOW MARRIAGE ENDED *(Death, divorce, etc.)*	14D. MARRIAGE ENDED	
DATE	PLACE			DATE	PLACE

INFORMATION RELATING TO SURVIVING SPOUSE

NOTE: If claimant is not veteran's surviving spouse, omit Items 15 to 21 inclusive.

15. HOW MANY TIMES HAS SURVIVING SPOUSE BEEN MARRIED?	16. HAS SURVIVING SPOUSE REMARRIED SINCE DEATH OF VETERAN?

17A. MARRIAGE		17B. TO WHOM MARRIED	17C. HOW MARRIAGE ENDED *(Death, divorce, etc.)*	17D. MARRIAGE ENDED	
DATE	PLACE			DATE	PLACE

VA FORM APR 1987 **21-534** EXISTING STOCKS OF VA FORM 21-534, SEP 1985, WILL BE USED. 665287

EXAMPLE *Application for Dependency and Indemnity, continued*

PART II – INFORMATION RELATING TO MARRIAGE *(Continued)*

18. DATE OF BIRTH	19. WAS A CHILD BORN OF SURVIVING SPOUSE'S MARRIAGE TO VETERAN? *(Complete only if the surviving spouse was married to the veteran for less than one year)*

20. DID SURVIVING SPOUSE LIVE CONTINUOUSLY WITH THE VETERAN FROM DATE OF MARRIAGE TO DATE OF DEATH?

☐ YES ☐ NO *(If "No," complete Item 21)*

21. CAUSE OF SEPARATION *(Explain fully, giving reason, date of separation, duration, etc. If separation was by court order, attach a certified copy of such order)*

PART III – INFORMATION CONCERNING CHILDREN *(See Instructions, Paragraph J)*

IDENTIFICATION OF CHILDREN AND INFORMATION RELATIVE TO CUSTODY

NOTE – List below the name of each child of the veteran who is (1) under 18 years of age (or under 23 years of age if attending school) or (2) of any age if permanently incapable of self-support by reason of mental or physical defect. The term "child" includes an illegitimate, adopted, or step child of the veteran as well as any child whose marriage has been terminated by divorce, annulment, or death of a spouse. If the birth of a child of a veteran is expected, that fact should be stated.

22A. NAME OF CHILD *(First, middle initial, last)*	22B. DATE OF BIRTH *(Mo., day, yr.)*	22C. SOCIAL SECURITY NO. OF CHILD	22D. IDENTIFY *(Check each applicable category)*				
			MARRIED PREVI-OUSLY	STEPCHILD OR ADOPTED	ILLEGI-TIMATE	OVER 18 ATTENDING SCHOOL	SERIOUSLY DISABLED

23. NAME(S) OF ANY CHILD(REN) NOT IN YOUR CUSTODY	24. MONTHLY AMOUNT YOU CONTRIBUTE TO CHILD'S SUPPORT
	$

NOTE: If you are only applying for Dependency and Indemnity Compensation, do not complete Parts IV, V or VI. For example, if the veteran died while on active duty or died due to a service-connected condition.

PART IV – NET WORTH OF SURVIVING SPOUSE AND/OR CHILD/REN *(See Instructions, Paragraph K)*

ITEM NO.	SOURCE	AMOUNTS				
		SURVIVING SPOUSE OR CUSTODIAN OF CHILD/REN	NAME OF CHILD/REN			
25A.	STOCKS, BONDS, BANK DEPOSITS .	$	$	$	$	$
25B.	REAL ESTATE *(Do not include residence)*					
25C.	OTHER PROPERTY					
25D.	NET WORTH	$	$	$	$	$

EXAMPLE *Application for Dependency and Indemnity, continued*

PART V – INCOME OF SURVIVING SPOUSE AND/OR CHILDREN AND CUSTODIAN OF CHILD/REN
(Important – Carefully read paragraph L of Instructions before completing this section)

26. SOCIAL SECURITY INFORMATION

A. HAVE YOU APPLIED FOR OR ARE YOU RECEIVING OR ENTITLED TO RECEIVE BENEFITS FROM THE SOCIAL SECURITY ADMINISTRATION ON YOUR OWN BEHALF OR ON BEHALF OF A CHILD/REN IN YOUR CUSTODY? ☐ YES ☐ NO	B. BEGINNING DATE *(Month, year)*

MONTHLY BENEFIT(S)	SURVIVING SPOUSE OR CUSTODIAN OF CHILDREN	EACH CHILD'S SHARE
C. AMOUNT OF MONTHLY SOCIAL SECURITY CHECK	$	$
D. ADDITIONAL MEDICARE DEDUCTION		
E. TOTAL MONTHLY BENEFITS *(Sum of 26C and 26D)*	$	$

F. IS SOCIAL SECURITY BASED ON YOUR OWN EMPLOYMENT?

☐ YES ☐ NO

REPORT GROSS MONTHLY INCOME, BY SOURCE, INCLUDING ANY MONTHLY DEDUCTIONS FOR EACH FAMILY MEMBER

ITEM NO.	SOURCE (A)	SURVIVING SPOUSE OR CUSTODIAN OF CHILD/REN (B)	AMOUNT OF INCOME — NAME OF CHILD/REN (C)	(D)	(E)	BEGINNING DATE — MONTH/YEAR (F)
27A.	U.S. CIVIL SERVICE					
27B.	U.S. RAILROAD RETIREMENT					
27C.	MILITARY RETIREMENT					
27D.	BLACK LUNG BENEFIT					
27E.	SUPPLEMENTAL SECURITY INCOME/PUBLIC ASSISTANCE					
27F.	ALL OTHER INCOME *(Specify source) (USE ITEM 36, "Remarks" for additional space)*					

REPORT EXPECTED GROSS ANNUAL INCOME *(OR ONE-TIME INCOME)* FOR THE 12 MONTH PERIOD FROM DATE OF VETERAN'S DEATH OR, IF CLAIM IS FILED MORE THAN 45 DAYS AFTER THE VETERAN DIED, THE 12 MONTH PERIOD FROM THE DATE THE CLAIM IS SIGNED.

ITEM NO.	SOURCE	(B)	(C)	(D)	(E)	(F)
28A.	EARNINGS					
28B.	DIVIDENDS, INTEREST, ETC.					
28C.	LIFE INSURANCE					
28D.	ALL OTHER INCOME *(Specify Source (for additional space, use Item 36, "Remarks")*					

EXAMPLE *Application for Dependency and Indemnity, continued*

PART VI – DEDUCTIBLE EXPENSES

NOTE: Your income may be reduced by the amount of unreimbursed expenses of the veteran's or his/her child's last illness and burial and the veteran's just debts which were paid by you. Be sure to include as income in Items 27F and 28D any reimbursement received on these expenses or debts. See paragraph N of Instructions for reporting payments and reimbursements made after filing of your claim.

29A. NAME AND ADDRESS OF PERSON TO WHOM PAID	29B. TOTAL AMT. OF EXPENSE OR DEBT	29C. NATURE OF EXPENSE OR DEBT	29D. DATE PAID	29E. AMOUNT PAID BY YOU
	$			$

PART VII – MISCELLANEOUS INFORMATION

30. HAS A SURVIVING SPOUSE OR CHILD FILED CLAIM FOR COMPENSATION FROM THE OFFICE OF WORKERS' COMPENSATION PROGRAMS BECAUSE OF DEATH OF VETERAN ON WHOSE SERVICE THIS CLAIM IS FILED?

☐ YES ☐ NO

31. IS A CLAIM OR COURT ACTION PENDING, OR HAS A COURT DECREE AWARDING DAMAGES ON A SETTLEMENT OR COMPROMISE OF A CLAIM BASED ON THE DEATH OF THE VETERAN BEEN MADE?

☐ YES ☐ NO *(If "Yes," explain in Item 36, "Remarks")*

32. IS A CLAIM FOR SURVIVOR BENEFIT PLAN (SBP) ANNUITY FROM A SERVICE DEPARTMENT PENDING OR AN AWARD OF THE SBP ANNUITY BEEN MADE BASED ON THE DEATH OF THE VETERAN?

☐ YES ☐ NO *(If "Yes," explain in Item 36, "Remarks")*

33A. HAS THE SURVIVING SPOUSE OR CHILD FILED CLAIM PREVIOUSLY WITH THE VETERANS ADMINISTRATION? ☐ YES ☐ NO *(If "Yes," complete Items 33B through 35 inclusive)*	33B. NAME OF PERSON ON WHOSE SERVICE CLAIM WAS MADE	33C. RELATIONSHIP TO CLAIMANT
34. VA FILE NO.	35. OFFICE WHERE CLAIM WAS FILED *(City and State)*	

PART VIII – CERTIFICATION AND ADDITIONAL COMMENTS

36. REMARKS *(If additional space is needed, attach separate sheet)*

CERTIFICATION: I CERTIFY THAT the foregoing statements are true and correct to the best of my knowledge and belief.

37. DATE SIGNED	38. SIGNATURE OF CLAIMANT, CUSTODIAN OR GUARDIAN

WITNESSES – If you sign by (X), it must be witnessed by two persons who know you personally and the signatures and addresses of such witnesses must be shown.

39A. SIGNATURE OF WITNESS	39B. ADDRESS OF WITNESS
40A. SIGNATURE OF WITNESS	40B. ADDRESS OF WITNESS

PENALTY – The law provides severe penalties which include fine or imprisonment, or both, for the willful submission of any statement or evidence of a material fact, knowing it to be false, or for fraudulent acceptance of any payment to which you are not entitled.

casualty insurance on the tangible property. When automobiles or other mobile equipment is involved the personal representative should be certain that the property is not used unless adequate liability insurance coverage has been obtained.

Valuation of Tangible Personal Property Items of tangible personal property should be valued by experts from appraisal companies or auctioneers. Such experts should certify to the values given. It is often helpful to have these valuations completed at an early date, so that the personal representative has a working list of the property for which he is responsible. The paralegal will frequently be called upon to locate and contact appropriate experts.

Where there are items of particularly high value, such as jewelry, objects of art, and antiques, special appraisers may have to be found. With such items, it is usually a good idea to secure at least two independent appraisals.

Estate appraisers tend to set conservative figures on tangible personal property items in anticipation of the values being used later for death tax purposes. Therefore, if there is no specific direction in the decedent's will for the disposition of tangible personal property and the personal representative decides to sell it, care should be exercised to see that the property is sold for its fair market value.

A similar caution should be stated with regard to the amount of casualty insurance to be carried. Insurable value may be much higher than the value shown in appraisals prepared for death tax returns. This is not a reflection of dishonesty on the part of appraisers. It is a recognition that most insurance is meant to cover replacement cost while death tax values are generally a low estimate of what could have been realized if the object had been sold at the time of death.

Sale of Tangible Personal Property In the event that items of tangible personal property are not specifically devised and the personal representative decides to sell them, he may proceed in several ways. If the property has considerable value, the personal representative may wish to submit it for auction. Auctioneers generally charge a 10% to 15% commission on the gross selling price, except where unusual items are involved, in which case the auctioneer and the personal representative may enter into a negotiated agreement.

Where the property is ordinary furniture and furnishings, the personal representative may solicit bids from dealers who generally will remove the property from the premises. In such situations, the personal representative should be guided by the appraisal values previously secured.

Automobiles and other such property (boats, airplanes, expensive appliances) may generally be sold either by private advertising or through dealers. Automobile dealers purchasing for their own account will generally only be willing to pay the wholesale value listed in the "Blue Book," an automobile trade publication. Private individuals will usually be willing to pay the higher retail price for automobiles. The "Blue Book" values for automobiles are changed every three months to reflect the fact of regular depreciation. Therefore, it is important to refer to the most recent edition when assessing the fairness of the price offered. Most banks and automobile dealers keep copies of the "Blue Book," and some are willing to quote from it on the telephone. Perhaps in your practice you will be able to establish a working relationship with a bank loan officer or automobile dealer whom you will be able to rely on for quoting prices.

After the sale of the tangible personal property, the personal representative should cancel any insurance on it and request a rebate of the unused premium.

Real Estate

Interests in Real Estate Real estate is land and those buildings or other things (e.g., trees, water, etc.) that are permanently a part of the land. Unimproved real estate is a phrase frequently used to describe land alone. Improved real estate is land on which buildings have been constructed.

The law recognizes a wide variety of ways of dividing the right to use and enjoy real estate among different parties. The owner of real estate has the right to do as he sees fit—live on the land, build on it, farm, etc. The owner may grant someone else the right to occupy the land or buildings for a fixed period of time by "leasing" or "renting." The owner then becomes a landlord or lessor and the person temporarily occupying the premises is known as a tenant or lessee.

Ownership or possession of real estate may be shared by a number of people. For example, a person may give a house to two sisters. Each sister then has the right to share the entire house, as each is an owner. There are basically two ways in which more than one person may own real estate; as "tenants[23] in common" or "joint tenants with the right of survivorship."

Tenants in common have a fractional share of the ownership of the whole property that may be sold or otherwise disposed of (as by will). Each tenant in common may be said to own an "undivided" interest. It is "undivided" because the whole property can

23. In this sense, "tenant" does not refer to one who is renting the real estate but one who shares in the complete ownership with one or more other people.

not be cut up into shares. When one of the tenants in common dies, the portion owned by that person passes to his heirs or beneficiaries. The surviving tenant(s) in common then must share the property to the same extent they did when the original tenant in common was still living.

A joint tenancy with right of survivorship is one in which the surviving co-tenant(s) have a right to the entire property on the death of the other co-tenant(s). A joint tenant may convey ownership of his portion of the property without the consent of the other joint tenants. This is not a joint "tenancy by the entireties." A tenancy by the entireties is only shared by a husband and wife. During their lifetimes, neither spouse may sell the real estate unless the other also agrees to sell and signs the deed conveying the property. On the death of one spouse, the survivor automatically becomes the sole owner of the real estate. The paralegal should be aware that some states have abolished ownership as tenants by the entireties.

In many states, a spouse has certain rights in real estate even though not listed as an owner of it. This is because a spouse has the right to take a certain portion of the deceased spouse's estate, regardless of what the decedent's will may provide. Therefore, even though only one spouse may own real estate, if there are dower rights attached the real estate may not be properly transferred during life unless the other spouse agrees to the transfer.

A personal representative may, therefore, have to deal with real estate in a variety of ways, according to the interest that the decedent had in it (e.g., landlord, co-owner, tenant). You should also be aware that there are other types of interests in real estate, such as oil rights, water rights, or rights to travel on land, which will not be discussed.

To be certain of the manner in which the decedent owned real estate it will be necessary to see the deed to the property (if the decedent was an owner) and/or the lease (if the decedent was renting from the owner or renting to other people). If the family does not have the original or copies of these documents, the paralegal may be asked to obtain them. Every state has a system of recording sales of real estate. These records will be kept in an office known as the Recorder of Deeds, Recorder of Documents, or some similar title. How to go about finding a particular document is a matter that will vary from state to state. You may find it useful to go to your local courthouse and learn the system used in your area.

Most leases for real estate are not recorded. Obtaining a copy will probably require requesting it from the other party to the lease.

Physical Control Assuming that real estate has not passed directly to the heirs (which will be so in many cases), the personal representative will be charged with properly attending to real estate that is part of the probate estate.

Security of Premises The obligation of the personal representative to provide adequate security for buildings and other improvements on real estate will differ in every case. Depending upon the circumstances, the attorney for the estate and paralegal should consider whether or not adequate provision has been made or should be made for (1) changing the locks on the buildings to prevent entry by persons having keys; (2) retaining answering services for telephones still in use and security services (particularly where the buildings are vacant); (3) alerting the local police that the property is vacant; (4) discontinuing or curtailing such services as newspaper, milk and bread deliveries, telephone service, fuel oil deliveries, and the like.

The condition of the premises may require the personal representative to make repairs in order to secure the property properly. For instance, there may be evidence of severe roof leakage that could cause damage to both the building and any contents. The same may be true with regard to broken glass or plumbing. The paralegal may be given the responsibility of seeing that these matters are property attended to.

Casualty and Liability Insurance Casualty insurance insures the property itself against various kinds of physical damages, such as fire, vandalism, or flooding. For example, if a house is destroyed by fire, casualty insurance would pay the owner the amount for which the house was insured.

Liability insurance insures against injuries that may be sustained by people on the property. For example, a person walking on the sidewalk may fall because of a defect and sue the property owner. Liability insurance would pay whatever amount the injured party might be awarded in the lawsuit.

Frequently the insurance coverage on a residential property will be in the form of a "homeowner's policy" that includes both casualty and liability insurance. The paralegal may have to determine if such coverage exists on the property and, if not, to obtain both types of insurance. Some companies are reluctant to insure vacant property because it is a higher risk for the company. However, they will usually continue coverage for a period of time, giving the personal representative time to either sell or lease the property.

If insurance is already in existence on the real estate, the insurance carrier should be given written notice of the death of the property owner (the insured). A type of letter that may be used for this purpose follows:

EXAMPLE
Letter Notice of the Death of Homeowner

[*Letterhead*]

December 30, 1991

Insurance Company of New Caledonia
16th Street & Frank Parkway
Philadelphia, PA 19102

RE: Estate of Lawrence Dain
Homeowner's Policy No. 931940

Dear Sir:

I am the attorney for the personal representative of the Estate of Lawrence Dain, who died on November 25, 1991, and who was the owner of the above-captioned homeowner's policy with your company.

I understand the policy insured the premises the decedent owned with his surviving spouse, Letitia Dain, at 1234 Lancaster Pike, Wayne, Pennsylvania 19087, for a value of $75,000, the contents for a value of $40,000, and the owners' liability for up to $100,000.

Please confirm in writing to me at the letterhead address that the policy with limits as described is in force; and let me know the date the policy must be renewed. Future premium notices should be sent to Mrs. Lawrence Dain, at 1234 Lancaster Pike, Wayne, Pennsylvania 19087.

Sincerely,

The paralegal should ascertain if the coverage afforded by the insurance in effect is adequate in view of the current value of the real estate. This may require that an insurance appraisal be made.[24] Once this is done, the new insurance should be ordered. When the policy is obtained the paralegal should keep it with the other important documents of the estate.

If the premises contain valuable tangible personal property, the insurance policy should also insure its value. Also, if the property is vacant because of the death of the decedent, that fact should be brought to the attention of the insurance company so that property coverage will be issued.

Maintenance The personal representative is responsible for the maintenance of any real estate prior to its distribution or sale. Physical maintenance of the property will require some care. For example, while the personal representative may wish to decrease expenditures by reducing the heating of vacant property during the winter months, if the heat is turned off completely the water pipes may freeze and burst causing damage far in excess of any fuel savings. Thus, the cost savings of such measures should always be weighed against the possibility of damaging the property. These

24. An appraisal of the value of the real estate for death tax purpose should also be obtained. See Chapter Five, "Valuation of Real Estate." These two appraisals may not be the same.

facts should be pointed out to the personal representative by the attorney or paralegal.

Mortgage Payments It is rare to find a piece of real estate that does not have a mortgage on it. The paralegal should immediately obtain information about the name of the mortgage holder (mortgagee), the amount of monthly payment on the mortgage, and whether taxes must be paid along with the mortgage payment to the mortgagee. Like deeds, mortgages are recorded and a copy may be obtained from the appropriate office in your locale if no evidence of the mortgage is found among the decedent's papers and the family has no information about it.

In some cases the decedent may have had mortgage life insurance. This is insurance that will pay off the balance due on the mortgage at the time of the decedent's death. This could be an important asset of the estate. Conversely the decedent may have a "home equity loan" whereby he borrowed additional money using his home as collateral. This would be another debt for the estate to pay.

The reason attending to the mortgage is urgent is that if there is a default in payments on the mortgage, the mortgagee may foreclose.[25] on the property. If this is done, the estate may be put to considerable expense and even face the loss of the real estate subject to the mortgage.

Treatment of Property Leased to Others If the decedent owned real property that is leased to others, the attorney or paralegal should immediately review the terms of any written lease. If there is no written lease, the term of the lease is considered to be equal to the period for which rent is paid. For example, if rent is paid monthly, it is a "month-to-month" lease. In such circumstances, after proper notice, the lease may be terminated at the end of the period for which rent has been paid.

The terms of the lease should be reviewed to determine its length and ascertain the extent of the decedent's obligation to maintain the premises. In addition, the tenant should be notified of the decedent's death and told to make all future rental payments to the estate of the decedent. That instruction should be accompanied by a short certificate (or its equivalent) as the tenant is entitled to assurance of the personal representative's authority.

Decedent's Obligations as a Tenant In the event that the decedent was renting property from another at the time of death (in other words was a tenant or lessee), the attorney or paralegal should

25. When payments on the mortgage are in arrears, the mortgagee may obtain possession of the real estate or have it sold through the court and obtain the proceeds of the sale.

review the lease. The lease may or may not have a provision with regard to the death of the lessee. If the decedent was an elderly person, the lease may have been drafted with the possibility in mind that the lessee would die during the term of the lease. Typically, such leases will contain a so-called "liquidated damages" or "death" clause by which the lessor and lessee agree that in the event the lessee dies during the term of the lease, the lessee's estate will be obligated to pay to the lessor rent for a limited number of months after the premises have been vacated, rather than for the remaining term of the lease as would otherwise be the case. The paralegal should inform the lessor or lessor's rental agent of the decedent's death and verify the terms of the lease.

Most leases do not have liquidated damages provisions. In the normal situation, the decedent's estate has the obligation to pay rent for the balance of the term of the lease. There is a corresponding duty upon the lessor in such a case to try to reduce the damages that may be due the lessor by re-leasing the premises. It is common practice in such situations to negotiate with the landlord and reach a figure to settle the decedent's liability under the lease. This negotiation is probably best conducted by an attorney rather than a paralegal. Do not, as a paralegal, enter such negotiations with the landlord without the knowledge and approval of your supervising attorney.

Regardless of when the premises are to be vacated, the paralegal should check the limits of any tenant's insurance policy to see that they are adequate to cover the contents of the leased premises, as well as any possible liability. The paralegal should also consider whether the lock on an apartment should be changed and whether any other security or maintenance measures should be taken.

Most leases provide for the payment of a security deposit and/or escrow moneys. The security deposit protects the landlord from any damage to the premises done by the tenant. Escrow money is in essence pre-payment of rent. Both security and escrow deposits are refundable to the tenant on termination of the lease (provided the property has not been damaged and all rent paid). The paralegal should determine whether or not any security deposit or escrow of rent is properly due the estate (which stands in place of the decedent).

Valuation of Real Estate The best method of arriving at a true value of real estate is by selling it. Often, however, a sale is not going to occur, as when the real estate is distributed to the heirs or beneficiaries of a will. Even when a sale is anticipated, the personal representative may not know what the property is worth and, therefore, what price should be asked for it.

In cases when the real estate is not sold or when an estimate of its value is necessary prior to putting it up for sale, the estate retains an appraiser. Appraisers usually charge fees based on the value of the real estate. The burden of these fees is lightened by the fact that they are proper administration expenses of the estate and are deductible for death tax purposes.

The appraiser must certify to the fair market value of the property at the time of the decedent's death. The "fair market value" of the property is supposed to be the price at which the property would change hands between a willing seller and a willing buyer. In actual fact, the appraisal is often conservative, in contemplation of the figure being included in the death tax returns. If a sale of the property is contemplated, the appraiser should be told so that this fact may be taken into account in estimating the value.

As an aid to the appraiser, the paralegal may wish to provide a copy of the most recent deed, if one is available. The last sale price is a strong indicator of present value. In addition, if the property is leased, the appraiser will want a copy of the lease. The appraiser will have to consider the return on investment that a potential purchaser would receive. The terms of the lease will be critical for this.

Sale of Real Estate Pursuant to the general duty to liquidate estate assets the personal representative may wish to sell real estate. In addition, the personal representative may have to sell a particular parcel of real estate when, prior to death, the decedent entered into a binding contract for its sale in the future. It is particularly important to consult the lawyer in charge of the estate when real estate transactions are involved. The paralegal should be sure that the personal representative has legal authority to make such a sale and that at each step the documents being executed are proper.

Method of Sale The two basic methods of selling real estate are a public auction or a privately negotiated transaction. While a sale may be personally negotiated between a personal representative and a buyer, it is customary in either the auction or private sale situation for the personal representative to engage the professional assistance of an auctioneer in the former case or real estate broker in the latter. If the sale is a large or unusual one the terms of an agreement with an auctioneer or real estate broker may be negotiable. In most situations, however, those terms are fixed by custom in the local area.

Agreement of Sale Once the personal representative and a buyer have come to some understanding on the essential terms concerning the sale of a parcel of real estate, a contract, frequently referred

EXAMPLE *Agreement of Sale*

AGREEMENT FOR THE SALE OF REAL ESTATE
This form recommended and approved for, but not restricted to,
use by members of the Pennsylvania Association of REALTORS®
COPYRIGHT PENNSYLVANIA ASSOCIATION OF REALTORS® 1973

S & C 1969B
(Rev. 3-85)
(Mod. 1-86)

COPIES	
1. White	Seller
2. Yellow	Agent
3. Pink	Buyer
4. Blue	Mortgagee
5. Gold	
6. Green	Buyer's copy at time of signing.

AGENT FOR THE SELLER
Main Line Board of Realtors
PA. LICENSED BROKER

SUB AGENT FOR SELLER

PA. LICENSED BROKER

This Agreement, this 7th day of February A.D. 19 92

1. **PRINCIPALS (1-78) Between** Prudence Holloway, Executor of the Estate of Lawrence Dain

(residing at .... **Zip** .... **) hereinafter called Seller,**
and Norman Arthur and Frances Arthur, his wife

(residing at .... **Zip** .... **) hereinafter called Buyer.**

2. **PROPERTY (3-85) Seller hereby agrees to sell and convey to Buyer, who hereby agrees to purchase:**
ALL THAT CERTAIN lot or piece of ground with buildings and improvements thereon erected, if any, known as:
1234 Arch Street, City of Philadelphia, County of Philadelphia, Pennsylvania
(Legal description to be furnished.)
in the .... **of** .... **County of** ....
State of .... **, Zip** ....
Zoned ....

3. **TERMS (3-85) (a) Purchase Price** One Hundred Seventy-Five Thousand ($175,000) **Dollars**
which shall be paid to the Seller by the Buyer as follows:
(b) Cash or check at signing this agreement: $ 1,750.00
(c) Cash or check to be paid on or before: March 7th 1992 $ 33,250.00
(d) .... $ ....
(e) Cash or certified check at time of settlement: $ 140,000.00
TOTAL $ 175,000.00
(f) Written approval of Seller to be on or before: March 7th 1992
(g) Settlement to be made on or before: May 17th 1992
(h) Conveyance from Seller will be by fee simple deed of special warranty.
(i) Payment of transfer taxes will be divided equally between Buyer and Seller.
(j) The following shall be apportioned pro-rata as of and at time of settlement: Taxes as levied and assessed, rents, interest on mortgage assumptions, condominium fees and homeowner association fees if any, water and or sewer rents if any, together with any other lienable municipal services.

to as an Agreement of Sale, may be executed. A standard form of such an agreement is shown on this page and the next three pages.

Real estate practices may vary from place to place and this form is suppled as an example only and not as a model to be followed in other jurisdictions.

The basic terms of any agreement of sale are as follows: names of the parties, legal description[26] of the property, price and manner of payment, settlement or closing date,[27] the kind of deed to be given, the state of the title to be transferred, whether possession will be given, and the apportionment between buyer

26. A legal description is reciting in words the directions and distances of a piece of real estate, beginning from a certain, fixed point.

27. The "settlement" is the meeting at which the money agreed upon as the sales price is exchanged for the deed to the property. This is also referred to as the "closing."

EXAMPLE *Agreement of Sale, continued*

4. **MORTGAGE CONTINGENCY (3-85)** This sale is NOT contingent upon any mortgage financing except as hereinafter provided.
5. **SPECIAL CLAUSES**
   (a) This sale is NOT contingent in any manner upon the sale or settlement of any other real estate except as may be hereinafter provided.

MORTGAGE CONTINGENCY - Term and amount of mortgage required by Buyer: 30 years, $140,000.00; Interest and type mortgage required by Buyer: market rate %, type: fixed; Commitment date for approval of the mortgage: April 30, 1992; Mortgage application to be made through the office of: Mellon Bank, and if said mortgage cannot be obtained, this agreement shall be null and void and all deposit monies returned to the Buyer on or before date for settlement as provided herein.

TERMITE INSPECTION - Purchasers at their own expense shall have the right to cause a termite inspection to be made of the premises within seven days of the signing of this contract by the party to sign last. In the event such inspection reveals termite infestation or damage or damage or infestation by other wood-destroying insects, Sellers shall then at Sellers' own expense prior to the date of closing eliminate said termite infestation, repair structural damage caused thereby and furnish Purchaser with a one-year guarantee from said termite control company against further termite infestation or Sellers shall forthwith tender or cause to be tendered to Purchasers all money paid hereunder. Purchasers, however, at their own option, may refuse tender, waive the results of the termite inspection report and thereupon this contingency shall be deemed satisfied.

RADON GAS INSPECTION - Buyer may, at his option and expense, have the property inspected for the presence of radon gas. If Buyer chooses to have this inspection, the inspection must be completed and the Seller notified of the results within fourteen days of Buyers receipt of a fully executed copy of this Contract. If radon gas is found to be present in levels that exceed the acceptable level established by the Pennsylvania Department of Environmental Protection, the Seller may correct the condition and furnish the Buyer with a certification demonstrating that the condition has been remedied. If the Seller refuses to remedy the condition, the Buyer may terminate this Contract or waive this contingency. In the event the Contract is terminated, all deposit monies shall be returned to the Buyer.

and seller of costs involved in the sale, such as transfer or deed taxes, real estate taxes, and water and sewer rents. In addition to these terms, the parties may agree to include specialized provisions regarding, for example, the sale of items located on the premises as appliances, rugs, draperies, etc., or making the agreement contingent on the buyer's being able to secure a mortgage to cover part of the purchase price. The date for settlement or closing, which is when the property actually changes hands, is typically set 30 or 120 days after the date of the agreement in order to give the parties time to make financial and other necessary arrangements.

Settlement or Closing The terms "settlement" and "closing" are synonymous. In different parts of the country one or the other will be favored. The word "settlement" is used in this book although

EXAMPLE *Agreement of Sale, continued*

6. NOTICES & ASSESSMENTS (3-85)

(a) Seller represents as of the approval date of this agreement, that no public improvement, condominium or homeowner association assessments have been made against the premises which remain unpaid and that no notice by any government or public authority has been served upon the Seller or anyone on the Seller's behalf, including notices relating to violations of zoning, housing, building, safety or fire ordinances which remain uncorrected unless otherwise specified herein.

(b) If required by law, Seller shall deliver to Buyer on or before settlement, a certification from the appropriate municipal department or departments disclosing notice of any uncorrected violation of zoning, housing, building, safety or fire ordinances.

(c) Seller will be responsible for any notice of improvements or assessments received on or before the date of Sellers approval of this agreement, unless improvements consist of sewer or water lines not in use.

(d) Buyer will be responsible for any notice served upon Seller after the approval date of this agreement and for the payment thereafter of any public improvement, condominium or homeowner association assessments.

7. TITLE AND COSTS (1-86)

(a) The premises are to be conveyed free and clear of all liens, encumbrances, and easements, EXCEPTING HOWEVER, the following: existing building restrictions, ordinances, easements of roads, easements visible upon the ground, privileges or rights of public service companies, if any; otherwise the title to the above described real estate shall be good and marketable and such as will be insured by a reputable Title Insurance Company at the regular rates.

(b) In the event the Seller is unable to give a good and marketable title and such as will be insured by a reputable Title Company, subject to aforesaid, Buyer shall have the option of taking such title as the Seller can give without abatement of price or of being repaid all monies paid by Buyer to the Seller on account of the purchase price and the Seller will reimburse the Buyer for any costs incurred by the Buyer for those items specified in paragraph 7(c) items (1), (2), (3), and in paragraph 7(d); and in the latter event there shall be no further liability or obligation on either of the parties hereto and this agreement shall become NULL AND VOID and all copies will be returned to Seller's agent for cancellation.

(c) The Buyer will pay for the following:

(1) The premium for mechanics lien insurance and/or title search, or fee for cancellation of same, if any.
(2) The premiums for flood insurance and/or fire insurance with extended coverage, insurance binder charges or cancellation fee, if any.
(3) Appraisal fees and charges paid in advance to mortgagee if any.
(4) Buyer's normal settlement costs and accruals.

(d) Any survey or surveys which may be required by the Title Insurance Company or the abstracting attorney, for the preparation of an adequate legal description of the premises (or the correction thereof), shall be secured and paid for by the Seller. However, any survey or surveys desired by the Buyer or required by his/her mortgagee shall be secured and paid for by the Buyer.

8. FIXTURES, TREES, SHRUBBERY, ETC. (1-81) All existing plumbing, heating and lighting fixtures (including chandeliers) and systems appurtenant thereto and forming a part thereof, and other permanent fixtures, as well as all ranges, laundry tubs, T.V. antennas, masts and rotor systems, together with wall to wall carpeting, screens, storm sash and/or doors,shades, awnings, venetian blinds, couplings for automatic washers and dryers, etc., radiator covers, cornices, kitchen cabinets, drapery rods, drapery rod hardware, curtain rods, curtain rod hardware, all trees, shrubbery, plantings now in or on property, if any, unless specifically excepted in this agreement, are included in the sale and purchase price. None of the above mentioned items shall be removed by the Seller from the premises after the date of this agreement.; Any remaining heating and/or cooking fuels stored on the premises at time of settlement are also included under this agreement. Seller hereby warrants that he will deliver good title to all of the articles described in this paragraph, and any other fixtures or items of personalty specifically scheduled and to be included in this sale.

9. DEPOSIT AND RECOVERY FUND (5-85) Deposits or hand monies shall be paid to agent for Seller, who shall retain the same until consummation or termination of this agreement in conformity with all applicable laws and regulations. Agent for the Seller may, at his/her sole option, hold any uncashed check tendered as deposit or hand monies, pending the acceptance of this offer.

A real estate recovery fund exists to reimburse persons who have suffered monetary loss and have obtained an uncollectable judgment due to fraud, misrepresentation or deceit in a real estate transaction by a Pennsylvania licensee. For complete details, call 717-783-3658.

10. POSSESSION AND TENDER (3-85)

(a) Possession is to be delivered by deed, keys and physical possession to a vacant building (if any) broom clean, free of debris at day and time of settlement, or by deed and assignment of existing lease(s) at time of settlement if premises is tenant occupied at the signing of this agreement, unless otherwise specified herein. Buyer will acknowledge existing lease(s) by initialing said lease(s) at time of signing of this agreement of sale if tenant occupied.

(b) Seller will not enter into any new leases, written extension of existing leases, if any, or additional leases for the premises without expressed written consent of the Buyer.

(c) Formal tender of an executed deed and purchase money is hereby waived.

(d) Buyer reserves the right to make a pre-settlement inspection of the subject premises.

11. MAINTENANCE AND RISK OF LOSS (3-85)

(a) Seller shall maintain the property (including all items mentioned in paragraph #8 herein) and any personal property specifically scheduled herein in its present condition, normal wear and tear excepted.

(b) Seller shall bear risk of loss from fire or other casualties until time of settlement. In the event of damage to any property included in this sale by fire or other casualties, not repaired or replaced prior to settlement, Buyer shall have the option of rescinding this agreement and receiving all monies paid on account or of accepting the property in its then condition together with the proceeds of any insurance recovery obtainable by Seller. Buyer is hereby notified that he may insure his equitable interest in this property as of the time of the acceptance of this agreement.

"closing" is equally applicable. The purpose of the settlement is to fulfill at one time and place all of the obligations of the parties to the agreement of sale. Settlement is generally held at a place chosen by the buyer or the buyer's attorney. The paralegal must assemble the following list of documents because the personal representative will typically be required to submit them at the time of settlement in order to document the transaction properly: death certificate, short certificate of the granting of letters, proof of payment of real estate tax and water and sewer rent for the three years immediately preceding the year in which settlement takes place (either receipts or certifications from the various taxing authorities are used), real estate tax and water and sewer bills for the current year (or receipts for payment), receipts for payment or proof that adequate provision has been made for state and federal

EXAMPLE *Agreement of Sale, continued*

12. **RECORDING (3-85)** This agreement shall not be recorded in the Office for the Recording of Deeds or in any other office or place of public record and if Buyer causes or permits this agreement to be recorded, Seller may elect to treat such act as a breach of this agreement.
13. **ASSIGNMENT (3-85)** This agreement shall be binding upon the parties, their respective heirs, personal representatives, guardians and successors, and to the extent assignable, on the assigns of the parties hereto, it being expressly understood, however, that the Buyer shall not transfer or assign this agreement without the written consent of the Seller.
14. **DEFAULT-TIME OF THE ESSENCE (1-79)** The said time for settlement and all other times referred to for the performance of any of the obligations of this agreement are hereby agreed to be of the essence of this agreement. Should the Buyer:
    (a) Fail to make any additional payments as specified in paragraph #3, or
    (b) Furnish false or incomplete information to the Seller, the Seller's agent, or the mortgage lender, concerning the Buyer's legal or financial status, or fail to cooperate in the processing of the mortgage loan application, which acts would result in the failure to obtain the approval of a mortgage loan commitment, or
    (c) Violate or fail to fulfill and perform any other terms or conditions of this agreement,
    then in such case, all deposit money and other sums paid by the Buyer on account of the purchase price, whether required by this agreement or not, may be retained by the Seller:
    (1) On account of the purchase, or
    (2) As monies to be applied to the Seller's damages, or
    (3) As liquidated damages for such breach,
    as the Seller may elect, and in the event that the Seller elects to retain the monies as liquidated damages in accordance with paragraph #14(3), the Seller shall be released from all liability or obligations and this agreement shall be NULL AND VOID and all copies will be returned to the Seller's agent for cancellation.
15. **AGENT(S) (3-85)** It is expressly understood and agreed between the parties that the named Agent, Broker, and any Sub Agent, Broker and their salespeople, employees, officers and or partners, are Agent(s) for the Seller, not the Buyer, however, the Agent(s) may perform services for the Buyer in connection with financing, insurance and document preparation.
16. **REPRESENTATIONS (3-85)** It is understood that Buyer has inspected the property, or hereby waives the right to do so and has agreed to purchase it as a result of such inspection and not because of or in reliance upon any representation made by the Seller or any other officer, partner or employee of Seller, or by the Agent, Sub Agent, if any, of the Seller, their salespeople and employees, officers and or partners.
    The Buyer has agreed to purchase it in its present condition unless otherwise specified herein. It is further understood that this agreement contains the whole agreement between the Seller and the Buyer and there are no other terms, obligations, covenants, representations, statements or conditions, oral or otherwise of any kind whatsoever concerning this sale. Furthermore, this agreement shall not be altered, amended, changed or modified except in writing executed by the parties.

APPROVAL BY BUYER — BUYER /s/ Norman Arthur (SEAL)
WITNESS AS TO BUYER .... — BUYER /s/ Frances Arthur (SEAL)
WITNESS AS TO BUYER .... — BUYER .... (SEAL)

APPROVAL BY SELLER
Seller hereby approves the above contract this .... day of .... A.D. 19 ....
and in consideration of the services rendered in procuring the Buyer, Seller agrees to pay the named Agent a fee of 6% (six) ....
of/from the herein specified sale price. In the event Buyer defaults hereunder, any monies paid on account shall be divided ...., Seller, ..., Agent, but in no event will the sum paid to the Agent be in excess of the above specified Agent's fee.
WITNESS AS TO SELLER .... — SELLER /s/ Prudence Holloway (SEAL)
WITNESS AS TO SELLER .... — SELLER .... (SEAL)
AGENT BY: .... — SELLER .... (SEAL)

TO: .... (Agent) Date February 2 19 92

In conjunction with the purchase of the premises described in this agreement of sale attached hereto, I/We hereby authorize your firm to perform the services as indicated below by my/our initials.
A. Order Title insurance in any reputable title insurance company .... (INITIALS)
B. Order insurance in the amount of $ .... ☐ Homeowners ☐ Fire & Extended Coverage ☐ Flood .... (INITIALS)
C. .... (INITIALS)

taxes due from the estate (typically satisfied with a waiver from the taxing authorities), and a deed from the executor or administrator to the buyer.

At the settlement a sheet is prepared by the title clerk[28] showing the agreed purchase price, tax apportionment and adjustments, the amount due to the seller, and amount necessary to be paid by buyer.

A copy of the settlement sheet on the sale of real estate should be kept in the file of estate documents. Another copy of it should be kept with tax records of the estate as certain items paid at the

28. Most sales of real estate are insured by title insurance to protect the purchaser. This insurance guarantees that the buyer is getting the absolute title to the real estate. The title insurance company has one of its employees, a title clerk, prepare the necessary papers at the settlement.

settlement may be deductible from either death taxes or income taxes of the estate.

Following settlement, the paralegal should cancel any insurance that was carried on the real estate and request that a rebate of any unearned premiums be paid to the estate.

PAYMENT OF DEBTS

The extent of the decedent's debts will be discovered in the course of the initial steps of administration or will be formally presented as a result of advertising the grant of letters.[29] The personal representative should make sure that the estate is solvent before any creditor is paid. An estate is solvent if it has sufficient assets to pay all debts. If not, the estate is said to be insolvent. If the estate is insolvent and a creditor is paid more than his share of the assets, the personal representative may be personally responsible to the extent of the overpayment.

Priority of Payment

In the event that the decedent's estate is insufficient to pay all creditors, the following is a common order of priorities for payment, subject to claims due the United States and to the claims of certain secured creditors:[30]

1. Administration costs, including court costs, compensation of the personal representative, attorney fees, expenses of litigation by the estate, the cost of preserving property (e.g., for carpenters, painters, maintenance, and insurance), travel, telephone and miscellaneous expenses of the personal representative;
2. The cost of decedent's funeral and burial, and the cost of the final illness; and
3. All other claims, including generally the claims of the State for death taxes.

Secured creditors, that is those who have had assets pledged by the decedent during lifetime, are entitled to have their claims satisfied from the pledged assets. To the extent that the pledged assets are not adequate to pay off the entire secured claim, the secured creditor becomes a general creditor with the same rights as other

29. In order to have the court discharge the personal representative, proof of advertising that the decedent has died and notifying creditors where to present claims must be presented.

30. A secured creditor is one who has been pledged certain assets. A pledge is a device of giving someone an interest in a certain asset that allows the creditor to take possession and ownership of that asset if the debtor does not pay the debt owed.

general creditors (i.e., the claim for the balance of the money due will be placed in category 3 above).

Priorities of creditors vary from state to state. Some states have "family exemptions" or "homestead rights" that allow surviving members of the family to take priority over creditors in regard to certain specific assets or limited sums of money. The attorney in charge of the estate should be consulted for detailed instructions wherever there is a chance the estate will not have sufficient assets to pay all claims in full.

Payment of Bona Fide Claims

If the decedent's estate is clearly solvent the personal representative should promptly pay those debts that are known to be obligations of the decedent's estate. Payment of such bona fide claims should be made from the estate checkbook. If a bill has been received, it, together with the estate's check, should be sent to the creditor with a letter requesting a receipt. Receipts together with the cancelled check should be kept in the estate's records as proof of payment.

In some states where the probate procedure is informal, the personal representative will rarely be requested to produce the receipts at the audit or for death tax purposes. However, in many states where probate procedures are relatively formal, prior to permitting an expense to be used as a deduction for state death tax, the Registrar requires that every administration expense be "proven" by the personal representative submitting a receipted copy of every bill.

Treatment of Doubtful Claims

If the validity of a claim made against the estate is in doubt, no payment should be made until the court has had an opportunity to hear the matter and decide the merit of the claim. The danger in paying doubtful claims prior to being directed to do so by the court is that heirs or beneficiaries may be able to hold the personal representative personally liable for paying claims that later prove to be invalid. It is the job of the estate's attorney and paralegal to see that nothing is done to put the personal representative in a position of jeopardy. It is therefore wise to look at claims made against the estate with a careful eye.

ESTATE BANK ACCOUNTS

Interest-Bearing Accounts

If the estate has a great deal of cash, either initially or as a result of the sale of assets, an interest-bearing account, such as a savings account or an interest-bearing checking account, should be opened.

The advantage of having an interest-bearing account is that it allows money to earn interest until it is distributed to the heirs or beneficiaries. In most estates of any significant size, it is likely that it will be a minimum of eighteen months to two years before complete distributions may be made. Furthermore, if investments are to be made by the personal representative, the interest-bearing account will be a convenient place to deposit the proceeds from the sale of such investments. For simplicity, it is recommended that the personal representative keep only one bank account for all estate transactions.

Checking Accounts

The checking account of an estate serves a vital function in keeping trace of all receipts and disbursements. The checkbook records will be helpful, if not crucial, to the preparation of the death tax returns and the filing of the formal account with the court. The checks themselves act as a record of the disbursements, and the endorsements on the checks by the creditors serve as acknowledgements of receipt of payment. Cancelled checks may be used as proof of payment for tax and account purposes.

Estate checkbooks usually come three checks to a page, with an end stub on which to fill in the relevant information about the check at the time the check is written. The stub serves the purpose of providing information until the cancelled check is returned. The following Example shows a filled-in estate check and its stub. Note that there is a space available on each stub for recording deposits in the checking account. It will also be helpful to record on the reverse side of the stub the receipt (e.g., proceeds from sale of stock, proceeds from sale of automobile, redemption of U.S. Series E Bonds, etc.) from which the deposit was made. Doing this will make it easier to compile a list of receipts and disbursements for the formal account.[31]

Balancing the Checkbook As each bank statement for the checking account is received,[32] the checkbook should be balanced to see that the checks and deposits have been entered correctly and that the bank's records are reconciled with the records of the estate. You all have probably had experience in balancing your own checking accounts. The following is one of several methods that may be used:

31. Since the account distinguishes items of principal and income, it will be additionally helpful to note on the reverse of the stub whether the receipt is principal or income.

32. Active accounts will get monthly statements. Less active accounts may receive statements once every two or three months.

EXAMPLE *Estate Check and Stub*

NAME NO. 007

Estate of Delbert Mason, Jr.

Sept. 5 19 91 55-1/212

PAY TO THE ORDER OF Dietrich Funeral Home, Inc. $ 1,512.00

One thousand five hundred twelve and 00/100 DOLLARS

MIDLANTIC
Midlantic National Bank
EDISON, NJ 08818

MEMO Funeral Expenses /s/ Delbert Mason, III
Executor

⑆021200012⑆ SAMPLE

$ 1,512.00
No. 007
Sept. 5 19 91
TO Dietrich Funeral Home

	DOLLARS	CENTS
BAL. FOR'D	2327	11
DEPOSIT/ CREDIT		
TOTAL		
THIS PAYMENT	1512	00
OTHER DEDUCTIONS		
BAL. FOR'D	815	11

01 CHKG 0086

NAME NO.

19 55-1/212

PAY TO THE ORDER OF $

DOLLARS

MIDLANTIC
Midlantic National Bank
EDISON, NJ 08818

MEMO

⑆021200012⑆ SAMPLE

Step 1 Take the balance as shown on the bank statement and add to it any deposits made since the closing date on the statement (verifying that all deposits made during the time of the statement have been shown on the statement).

Step 2 Arrange the checks returned with the statement in numerical order and list all outstanding checks by number and amount.

Step 3 Total the amount of outstanding checks (including those that have been written since the closing date of the statement).

Step 4 Subtract the total from Step 3 from the total obtained in Step 1.

Step 5 Subtract from the figure reached in Step 4 the amount of any bank charges shown on the statement.

Step 6 The answer obtained in Step 5 should agree with the balance in the checkbook. Any discrepancy must be pursued until the error is found.

If in Step 6, the answer does not agree with the checkbook, a myriad of things could be wrong. Here are a few suggestions for hunting down the mistake:

1. Check over your work done in the six steps outlined above.
2. Compare the amounts shown on the returned checks with the amounts shown on the statement.
3. Compare the deposits as entered in the checkbook with those shown on the statement.
4. Check the mathematics of the subtraction of the amounts of the checks in the checkbook and the addition of deposits in the checkbook.

Using a Journal System Checkbooks have limited space to make all the notations which may be necessary in an estate. It may be utilized as a brief record of deposits and checks without much detail and is always a way of determining the current bank balance. In estates where there will be numerous transactions it will be helpful to keep a running account of receipts and disbursements in addition to the checkbook. This may serve to verify the checkbook and also to give the additional detail which may be necessary. The running account may be kept in a cash journal, of which there are basically two types—the two-column journal and the four-column journal. At its simplest, a journal is a chronological record of each transaction.

In a two-column journal system the first column has a dollar entry for each incoming item and the second column has a dollar entry for each outgoing item. In the four-column system, receipts and disbursements are itemized separately under both the principal and income columns.

EXAMPLE
Journal Systems

Two-Column Journal

1991		Receipts	Disbursements
Feb. 23	Balance forward	2,100.00	
23	Dividend, $.10/sh. 250 shs. Goren Machines	25.00	
24	Dividend, $1.50/sh. 100 shs. Fanciful Foods	150.00	
24	Proceeds of sale, 46 shs. IBN	4,350.00	
25	Internal Revenue Service 1990 fiduciary income tax		420.00
Mar. 5	Purchase of 200 shs. Horner, Ltd.		3,750.00

Four-Column Journal

1991		Principal Rec.	Principal Disb.	Income Rec.	Income Disb.
Feb. 23	Balance forward	1,300.00		800.00	
23	Dividend, $.10/sh. 250 shs. Goren Machines			25.00	
24	Dividend, $1.50/sh. 100 shs. Fanciful Foods			150.00	
24	Proceeds of sale, 46 shs. IBN	4,350.00			
25	Internal Revenue Service, 1990 fiduciary income tax				
	—attributable to ordinary income				320.00
	—attributable to capital gain		100.00		
Mar. 5	Purchase of 220 shs Horner, Ltd.		3,750.00		

In effect, the two-column journal is merely a statement of transactions in the checking account. The receipts column is equivalent to a list of the deposits made, and the disbursements column is equivalent to a list of the checks drawn. Obviously, the journal has considerably more space available for giving greater detail to all entries, and you could indicate in the journal whether the entry is a principal or income item. Except for space considerations, the two-column journal serves as little more than the checkbook.

The four-column journal serves as a running account (with respect to cash items only) for court accounting purposes. When the formal accounting is prepared, one can almost run down each of the four columns to obtain the entries needed for Principal Receipts, Principal Disbursements, Income Receipts, and Income Disbursements. Of course, such items as stock splits, conversions, and distributions of tangible personal property (noncash items) will not appear in the journal. But the basic information needed to prepare the accounting is there.

Balancing the Journal The journal should be balanced periodically and compared with the balance shown in the checkbook. This may be most conveniently done when each bank statement is received, and also at reaching the bottom of each page in the journal. It is also a good idea to draw a line across the journal page that bears the last entry for a particular year. A double line should also be drawn after the last transaction shown on the accounting. This alerts the person examining the account to the fact that the account is balanced.

When the estate is concluded, the principal receipts column should be totalled and should equal the total of principal disbursements. (Distributions to heirs or beneficiaries are considered disbursements.)

Paralegals are often given the job of keeping and balancing the estate checkbook and journal.

PROBLEM

Your office represents the executrix of the estate of Arnold Boyd and you are responsible for maintaining the checking account and journal. Please prepare a simulated checkbook and four-column journal for the following transactions. Assume all cancelled checks have been returned with the last bank statement except those indicated with an asterisk. The balance shown on the bank statement, with a closing date of April 29, 1991, is $972.34. At what figure should the account balance on May 7, 1991?

1. Initial opening deposit of $1,000.00, advanced by the principal beneficiary of the estate on March 27, 1991.
2. Check for $700.00 to James Nils for retail estate appraisal fee; April 1, 1991.
3. Deposit from proceeds of redemption of U.S. Series E Bonds of $1,203.60; April 2, 1991.
4. Check to Chatsworth Bank in amount of $2.20 for stock transfer fee on 100 shares of United Corrugated Co., Inc., stock; April 1, 1991.
5. Check to Internal Revenue Service for Mr. Boyd's 1990 income taxes (he died January 8, 1991) in amount of $500.00; April 2, 1991.
6. Deposit of $1,316.00 in proceeds from sale of the decedent's home furnishings; April 13, 1991.
7. Check to Worthington Monuments, Inc., in amount of $950.00 for grave stone; April 13, 1991.
8. Check to John Easton, M.D., in amount of $108.00 for services to decedent during last illness; April 18, 1991.
9. Check to Register of Wills in amount of $9.00 for additional short certificates; April 18, 1991.
10. Deposit of $600.00 from dividends on I. B. Meats, Inc., stock; April 15, 1991.
11. Deposit of $22.09 from refund on medical insurance policy; April 14, 1991.
12. Deposit of $200.00 on collection of debt owing to decedent; April 16, 1991.
13. Check to State Income Tax Bureau in the amount of $100.15 for decedent's 1990 state income taxes; April 14, 1991.
14. Check to Louis Gain in amount of $600.00 for real estate appraisal; April 27, 1991.
15. Deposit of $200.00 from refund on life insurance policy; May 3, 1991.

16. Check to James Nil in amount of $400.00 for real estate appraisal; May 3, 1991.
17. Check to Recorder of Deeds in amount of $5.30 for copy of deed; May 4, 1991.
18. Check to Freedley Insurance Company in amount of $10.50 for balance due on homeowner's policy on decedent's residence; May 6, 1991.

INVESTMENT PROBLEMS

The personal representative has the duty to liquidate the assets of the estate so that all valid debts may be paid and a prompt distribution made to the heirs or beneficiaries. Nevertheless, in many instances, once assets are liquidated, or if there are large amounts of cash in the estate, it may become necessary for the personal representative to invest the estate assets pending final distribution. Not to invest the assets would be to cause a loss to the estate. Money may be put to work earning more money for the heirs or beneficiaries, even if it is by simply opening an estate savings account.

Legal Restraints

Most states have laws regarding the manner in which assets of an estate may be invested. These restraints may be circumvented by provisions in the decedent's will that give the personal re presentative the right to invest in areas that may not be allowed under the state law in the absence of an enabling provision in the will.

It should be no surprise to you that state law imposes restrictions that allow investments only of the most conservative nature. Some of the more common types of investments are discussed in the next section.

Common Investments of Estates

Savings Accounts and Certificates of Deposit We have already discussed the estate savings account. In opening such an account the personal representative should be made aware of the differences in interest paid by commercial banks, savings banks, and savings and loan associations. As a general rule, savings and loan associations will pay the highest interest on regular savings accounts. Savings banks will pay somewhat less than savings and loan associations (perhaps ¼%), but more than commercial banks do on regular savings accounts.

Another way of depositing money with a bank, and having it insured by the federal government for up to $100,000,[33] is through certificates of deposit. These deposits are for a minimum period of time—perhaps as short as ninety days, or as long as six years. Interest paid on the "CD" (certificate of deposit) will be higher than on regular savings accounts because the bank knows that it will have the use of the depositor's money for a certain period. There may be minimum amounts such as $500 or $1000 required to buy a CD. Banks compete to attract deposits and the paralegal may be asked to ascertain where the highest interest is paid on a fixed-time deposit. (Note that if funds are withdrawn prior to the date fixed in the CD, a penalty is paid with the depositor losing some interest, although none of the principal amount deposited is ever forfeited.)

United States Treasury Bills Where relatively large sums are involved, the personal representative may consider investing in United States Treasury Bills through the bond investment department of a bank. For a modest fee, the bond investment department will purchase bills being sold by the U.S. Treasury at auction on most Mondays of the year. An order to purchase must be placed on the Friday morning immediately prior to the Monday auction. Investment in Treasury bills are made in multiples of $1,000. Treasury bills are a safe investment, and there is also a secondary market in bills, which gives the estate the ability to sell them prior to their maturity date. The personal representative will have paid something less than the face amount for their purchase, but at their maturity, the bills are worth their face amount, the difference being the interest earned. Treasury bills may be purchased for relatively short periods (less than 30 days) as well as for longer periods (usually up to 180 days).

Commercial Paper Commercial paper is a slightly more risky investment for a personal representative than Treasury bills. Commercial paper is an unsecured obligation of a corporation to pay back the amount invested (actually a loan to the corporation), plus interest, at a certain date in the future. The rates of interest paid on commercial paper are almost always higher than those paid on treasury bills. The difference reflects the greater risk involved.

High-grade commercial paper[34] may be purchased through the bond investment department of many commercial banks or

33. The Federal Deposit Insurance Corporation and Federal Savings and Loan Insurance Corporation guarantee the depositor that regardless of what happens to the particular bank in which the funds are placed, the federal government will make good on all accounts for up to $100,000. This insurance protection is free of charge and is automatic at most banks in this country. The paralegal should be certain that he or she is dealing with an insured institution.

34. That is, the obligation of a corporation that certain financial institutions have rated as a good risk.

through a stockbroker. The minimum investment in commercial paper may be very high—perhaps up to $50,000. As with the purchase of Treasury bills there will be a service charge by the bank or commission payable to the stockbroker.

The personal representative should be extremely cautious before committing sizable amounts of the estate's money for investment in commercial paper. The length of time the money will be tied up is also an important factor to consider. In making such investments, the personal representative must keep in mind the goals of protecting the assets invested and keeping them in near-liquid form so that they may be used to pay debts and taxes and ultimately be distributed without having to wait for maturity dates in the future. For the personal representative's peace of mind as well as the protection of the estate's heirs or beneficiaries, it is better to have a sure, conservative rate of return than an insecure, higher rate of return on the estate's assets. The lawyer or paralegal may have to verbalize this constraint to the personal representative.

PREPARING AND FILING AN INVENTORY OF DECEDENT'S PROPERTY

In many states the personal representative is obligated to file an Inventory with the probate court, listing all of the decedent's assets for which the personal representative is responsible. Since property passing by operation of law or pursuant to a contract (such as jointly owned property or life insurance, etc.) is not part of the decedent's estate and, therefore, not subject to the control of the personal representative, it is not reported on the Inventory. Only so-called "probate" assets are included.

Generally the Inventory must contain a list of all real and personal property of the decedent, except real estate located outside of the state in which the inventory is filed. Where there is real estate located outside the state, the personal representative may elect to include a list of it in a memorandum at the end of the Inventory. The Inventory should include the values of each particular item as of the decedent's date of death.

The local rules of the Registrar of the county where the decedent was domiciled as well as the state law govern such things as the style of the Inventory, the number of copies to be filed, and the filing fees. A typical example of a Pennsylvania Inventory follows.

Whenever the personal representative learns of the existence of property that has not been included in the original inventory, it will be necessary to disclose this information in a Supplemental Inventory or on the estate accounting.

Not all states require the filing of an Inventory. The filing of the state death tax return serves essentially the same purpose. In

EXAMPLE *Inventory*

FILE IN DUPLICATE
COPY NEED NOT BE SWORN TO

Will
Adm. No. ______________ 19 ____ Filed ______________

REGISTER OF WILLS

COMMONWEALTH OF PENNSYLVANIA
COUNTY OF PHILADELPHIA } ss.

INVENTORY

Prudence Holloway

Personal Representative(s) of the Estate of Lawrence Dain

deceased, being duly sworn according to law, depose and say that the items appearing in the following inventory include all of the personal assets wherever situate and all of the real estate in the Commonwealth of Pennsylvania of said decedent, that the valuation placed opposite each item of said inventory represents its fair value as of the date of the decedent's death, and that decedent owned no real estate outside of the Commonwealth of Pennsylvania except that which appears in a memorandum at the end of this inventory.

Sworn to and subscribed before me this
Eighth day of
August A.D. 19 91

/s/ Prudence Holloway
Prudence Holloway

Attorney – *(Name)* Ronald Cresswell *(Sup. Ct. I.D. No.)*

(Address) 15 Pine Street, Philadelphia, PA 19000

DATE OF DEATH	LAST RESIDENCE	DECEDENT'S SOCIAL SECURITY NO.
4/15/91	Philadelphia, PA	123-000-444

REAL ESTATE - Situate at 1234 Arch Street, City of Philadelphia, Pennsylvania	$ 75,000.00
TANGIBLE PERSONAL PROPERTY - As per appraisal of Henry Myers, Appraiser, (copy attached)	6,000.00
SECURITIES - 4000 shares Dain Enterprises, Inc. (Pa.) com., par value $1 @ 150	600,000.00
$1,000 City of New York, New York, 7-1/4 due 9/1/96 @ 92	920.00
1000 shares Sun Oil Company (Pa.) com., par value $1 @ 50	50,000.00
(NYSE) .25; dividend payable 4/26/91	250.00
Note due from Leonard Dain for $10,000.00 due 3/31/86 with interest @ 5% per year (uncollectible)	-0-
LIFE INSURANCE - Metropolitan Life Insurance Company - Policy #54019102, payable to decendent's estate	25,000.00
BANK ACCOUNTS - Bowery Savings Bank, New York, New York - Account No. 8766 (includes accrued interest of $102.97)	4,102.97
TOTAL	$ 761,272.97

Memorandum: The decedent owned real estate situate at Ocean View Drive, Seal Harbor, Maine, having a fair market value of $40,000 at the date of his death.

NOTE: *The Memorandum of real estate outside the Commonwealth of Pennsylvania may, at the election of the personal representative include the value of each item, but such figures should not be extended into the total of the Inventory. (See Section 3301 (b) of PEF Code of 1972.)*

This form to be used only in estates of persons dying on or after February 23, 1956.

10-24 (Rev. 7/81)

some states, even though the filing of an Inventory is required at an early date, nothing compels the personal representative to file within that time unless one of the parties in interest petitions the court to force such a filing. Therefore, it has become common practice in such states to file the Inventory along with the state death tax return.

PROBLEM

TO: LAWYER'S ASSISTANT
FROM: Charles Denis

The following is a list of all of the property we have gathered in connection with the estate of Ernest Mann, a Pennsylvania decedent who died in an airplane crash on July 29, 1991, and was survived by his wife and one of their two children. The decedent's wife is named Gloria Mann, and his surviving child, Boyd Mann.

The following items were found in the decedent's safe deposit box:

- –Certificate No. 30761 for 150 shares of Huppmobile $1 par common stock, name of Ernest Mann.
- –One five-dollar ($5) gold piece dated 1878.
- –Certificates #71111 and 71112 for 350 shares and 100 shares, respectively, of Chrysler Corporation no-par common stock, name of Ernest Mann, issued July 1, 1972.
- –Certificates #871966 and 871967 for 200 shares and 100 shares respectively of IBM Corporation no-par common stock, the first in name of Ernest Mann, the second in the names of "Ernest Mann and Gloria Mann, joint tenants with right of survivorship."
- –Northwestern Mutual Life Insurance Policy No. 60121, owned by Ernest Mann, insuring life of Ernest Mann for $25,000, and naming "Al Mann, insured's son, if he survives insured," as beneficiary.
- –Deed dated September 3, 1940, for real estate situate at 473 West Mole Street, Philadelphia, Pennsylvania (decedent's residence), name of decedent and Gloria Mann as tenants by entireties, grantees—purchased for $35,000.
- –Deed dated June 21, 1968, for real estate situate at Lot No. 3, Pocono Road, Mt. Pocono, Paradise Township, Monroe County, Pennsylvania, name of decedent alone—purchased for $5,000.
- –U.S. Savings Bond No. 60793412Y, $25, Series "E" issued January 1942, name of Ernest Mann (priced at $37.62 on July 29, 1991).

The following items were found in the decedent's desk at his home:

(a) Checkbook for Account No. 4351–6 at Girard Trust Bank; the checks bear the following information.
"Ernest Mann
Gloria Mann
473 West Mole Street
Philadelphia, Pa. 19104"

(b) The last entry in the checkbook shows a check was drawn payable to "Gloria Mann" for household expenses; the amount of the check was $975.00, and the check was dated July 16, 1991; there is no record the check was cashed; the balance on the decedent's records as of July 17, 1991, shows as $3,671.56.

(c) Letter from R. J. Holmes, president of Asamera Oil Co., dated July 3, 1991, welcoming Ernest Mann as a new stockholder.

(d) Uncashed check from Social Security Administration, payable to "Ernest Mann", in the amount of $116.00, shows as "Soc. Sec. for June."

(e) One man's gold watch, inscribed "To Ernest Mann, for 25 years of faithful service—International Business Machines Corporation—March 1, 1991."

Please prepare the initial draft of an Inventory to be filed in the Philadelphia Orphan's Court. I am attaching the appropriate form for that purpose. Insert a question mark where the form requires information that you do not have. However, indicate on a separate sheet what additional information you require.

What steps do you think should be taken to complete the job of accumulating assets?

ACQUIRING POSSESSION OF ASSETS WITHOUT LETTERS

Up to this point in this chapter we have assumed that probate was completed and letters testamentary or letters of administration had been granted. In certain limited situations, however, it is possible for members of the decedent's family or other interested parties (including the named executor under the decedent's will or those who would inherit from the decedent) to dispense with probate and accumulate assets without having letters granted. Where all the interested parties are agreeable and adequate provision is made for the payment of death taxes and the decedent's debts, a simple procedure may be used.

Where the decedent's assets consist entirely of life insurance proceeds payable to named beneficiaries, real and personal property held jointly with a survivor, or claims under an employee's pension, profit-sharing or other benefit plan, the property passes automatically without the need for intervention by a personal representative. There may be a responsibility on the part of the transferees (those who receive the money or property) to make provision for the payment of death taxes. There is no need, however, to proceed through probate.

Even in the case where certain of the decedent's assets are in the decedent's name alone or are payable to the estate, it is conceivable to dispose of the assets without letters having to be issued. For example, banks or persons owing money to the decedent may refuse to pay anyone other than the personal representative (in order to protect themselves and be assured that the obligation to the decedent has been discharged). If the sums involved are relatively small, however, it may be possible for the interested parties to enter into an agreement[35] by which the debtor or obligor agrees to make payment to the family in return for an agreement by the members of the family to indemnify[36] the obligor in the event that a personal representative is later appointed or taxes are unpaid and the taxing authorities assess the obligor.

State law may also provide for the disposition of the decedent's assets without any administration or with an abbreviated form of administration where the amounts involved are small (e.g., \$5,000 or \$10,000). Titles to motor vehicles may frequently be transferred to the persons entitled to receive them without a personal representative being appointed. In states that allow this, it would be normal to provide the Division of Motor Vehicles with a copy of the death certificate and an affidavit that all debts of the decedent have been paid.

The United States government will permit savings bonds of a decedent to be paid or reissued in the names of the persons entitled to them, pursuant to an agreement between all the interested parties entitled to share in the estate.

While it is important for you to know of the possibility of collecting assets without the grant of letters, most attorneys have found that it is often cheaper and easier in the long run to obtain letters even in very small estates. By doing so, the court provides for the protection of interested parties by certifying what has been done by the personal representative.

35. Settlements by Agreement are the subject of Chapter Eight.

36. That is, to return the sums paid.

CHAPTER FOUR

Gift Tax

To someone who thinks of gifts as neatly wrapped packages to be opened on one's birthday, this chapter may come as a surprise. There is a considerable body of law concerning such questions as what is a gift, when is a gift made, and whether the gift-giver (donor) retains any rights in the gift. This chapter will briefly discuss those questions and then turn to the taxation of gifts by the federal government and by some states.

LEGAL ELEMENTS OF A GIFT

A gift can be analyzed in terms of four separate elements:

1. A gift is a transfer of property for less than an adequate and full consideration in money or money's worth.
2. A gift is a transfer of property made with a donative intent.
3. The property that is the subject of a gift must be delivered to the recipient (donee).
4. The donee must accept the gift.

Each of these elements deserves some discussion.

Transfer for Less Than Adequate and Full Consideration

The classic birthday gift is a transfer of property with no "consideration." "Consideration" in this context means "return payment" or "reciprocal obligation." Most gifts are made in that manner. A few gifts, however, are made in a form that might at first glance appear to be a sale. If the sale price is less than the value of the property, the difference between the value and the price may be a gift from the "seller" to the "buyer."

Donative Intent

"Donative intent" is a wish to enrich the recipient by a present gift of property. A used car salesman may sell a car for "much less than it is really worth," but he has not made a gift to the purchaser because the salesman has no donative intent. A commercial transaction—even one conducted at a loss—is not a gift.

Delivery

Delivery of property to the donee may be accomplished in a variety of ways. It is customary when making a gift of a portable, tangible object to physically place the object in the hands of the donee or an agent of the donee, such as his lawyer. It is obvious that the same technique of delivery could not be used for a piece of real estate or for certain other kinds of property. A symbolic delivery is sufficient in many cases.

Sometimes a "deed of gift" is used to accomplish symbolic delivery. A "deed of gift" is a writing signed by the donor describing the property and stating the donor's intention to make a present gift of that property to the donee by delivery of the deed of gift. Frequently, the donor will write a letter to the donee to disclose the gift and fix the date on which it was made. Examples of both such methods follow.

EXAMPLE
Methods of Symbolic Delivery of Gift

Deed of Gift

I, LETITIA DAIN, hereby irrevocably give, transfer, and convey to my son, LEMUEL DAIN, all of my right, title, and interest in the oil painting known as *The Bathers* by Toulouse-Lautrec, which is presently on a two-month loan to the Chicago Art Institute.

INTENDING TO BE LEGALLY BOUND HEREBY, I have hereunto set my hand and seal this 8th day of February, 1991.

/s/Letitia Dain [Seal]
Letitia Dain

Accepted:
February 8, 1991

/s/Lemuel Dain
Lemuel Dain

Letter Informing Donee of Gift

S. Throckmorton Jones
46 Waverly Place
Rumson, NJ 07760

August 26, 1991

Dear Sam:

As an expression of my love and affection, I have today transferred to your name as a gift 100 shares of the common stock of International Business Machines, Inc. My certificate for those shares has been sent to the transfer agent along with an executed stock power on which my signature has been guaranteed by Merrill, Lynch, Pierce, Fenner, and Smith, Inc. The transfer agent has been instructed to deliver the shares directly to you.

Sincerely,

/s/ Dad

S. Throckmorton Jones

The letter informs the donee of a gift of stock and a stock transfer power will be used to carry out the gift.[1]

Incomplete or ambiguous acts of delivery form the basis for much of the litigation concerning gifts that occurs. Consider the case of a mother who opens a safe deposit box in the joint names of herself and her daughter. Assume that the mother places jewelry and cash in the box but the daughter never enters the box during her mother's lifetime because the mother retained all of the keys. Upon the death of the mother, who is entitled to the jewelry and cash? The daughter may claim it as a gift to her. The personal representative of the mother may claim it as part of the mother's estate. In many instances, it may be necessary to have a court resolve these questions.

One function of a lawyer and of a lawyer's assistant is to prevent such litigation by helping clients avoid ambiguous or incomplete acts of delivery. When a gift is intended, all of the technicalities of transferring the property should be accomplished promptly. When no gift is intended the form in which property is held should not be ambiguous.

The banks have attempted to avoid potential litigation by requiring that both parties sign a signature card clearly instructing what is to become of the funds at the death of either joint owner when the account is first opened. If the account is established for convenience only, it is stated on the signature card or other document provided by the bank. Rather than setting up a joint account for convenience, it is more appropriate to have one party open an account (or box) in his or her own name and grant to the other party a power of attorney[2] to use the funds (or open the box). That would make it clear that no gift of property was intended. Rather, for reasons such as convenience, a second party was merely granted access to the property.

1. Examples of stock power are shown in Chapter Three under "Corporate and Governmental Securities."

2. A power of attorney is a grant to another, in writing, allowing that person to act on behalf of the person who has granted the right so to act.

Acceptance

A prospective donee always has the legal right to decline a gift. That seldom happens. It happens so seldom that acceptance is generally presumed unless the donee takes reasonable prompt action in refusing the gift.

Where there is reason to doubt that any of the four elements of a gift is present, the facts should promptly be discussed with the lawyer in charge.

FEDERAL TAXATION OF GIFTS

As you may suspect, the federal estate tax and the state death taxes would raise considerably less revenue if people were able to make tax-free inter vivos transfers of property. In 1924 the early gift tax statute was enacted. This was designed to tax inter vivos (during lifetime) transfers. Under present law every donor (the person making the gift) may give $10,000 (in cash or property in kind) to as many donees (persons receiving the gift) during one year, as he wishes. If he gives more than $10,000 per year to a donee, he must report the gift and file a Gift Tax Return (Form 709).

Presently the gift tax return is an annual return. From 1976 to 1982 the return was a quarterly return. The return was required to be filed if the gifts for the quarter or the year exceeded $25,000. The present annual return is required to be filed on April 15 of the year following the gift or the due date of the donor's personal income tax return.

In addition to the $10,000 per year annual exclusion, each donor is entitled to use all or a portion of his unified credit. The amount of the credit, after 1987, is $192,800. This is equivalent to the $600,000 exemption on the Federal Estate Tax Return (Form 706). When the donor makes a taxable gift, the IRS has ruled that it is mandatory that he use his unified credit. When he uses a portion or all of his credit (depending on the amount of the gift) for inter vivos gifts, the credit available at his death will be reduced. Thus if Mr. Jones gives a gift of $202,800 to his son during his lifetime using his entire unified credit and his $10,000 per donee annual exclusion, he will have no gift tax to pay at the time of the gift. However at his death, he will have no effective unified credit to offset his federal estate tax. It is thus important for the legal assistant to check the decedent's records for any lifetime gifts when calculating the Federal Estate Tax Return. Even a small estate may have federal estate taxes to pay if the decedent made substantial gifts during his or her lifetime, thus using the unified credit.

Gift taxes are cumulative. Thus all taxable gifts ever made by the donor must be reported on his or her 709 on Schedule B.

Because the tax is cumulative, the student should have some familiarity with prior gift tax laws. These will be briefly summarized in this chapter.

From 1976 to 1981, all transfers made within three years of death were included in the decedent's gross estate. Prior to 1977, the gifts were included only if the decedent had made the gift "in contemplation of death." There was a great deal of litigation surrounding whether the gift was in contemplation of death or not. Now under code § 2035, outright transfers, not including life insurance and transfers from certain trusts, made within three years of death are not included in the decedent's gross estate unless the decedent retains some powers over the property. There are a few exceptions to this rule, such as when the executor is determining if the estate qualifies for the special use valuation, deferral of estate taxes, or stock redemptions under code § 303.

Generally the federal gift tax exclusions and the unified credit are sufficiently large that the average person never pays a federal gift tax or even considers federal gift tax problems. Federal gift taxes are, however, an important consideration for many individuals. This section of the text will consider the federal taxation of gifts.

Taxable Transfers

Any gift over the $10,000 annual exclusion must be reported on the federal gift tax Form 709. However, not every gift results in a gift tax being due. Nevertheless, each gift should be considered potentially taxable. As a practical matter, small gifts are usually not reported or taxed. A $20 birthday gift does not have to be reported to the IRS. When a return is being prepared for a larger gift, it is usually wise to report the smaller gifts on the return so that a full disclosure is made.

Transfers into Joint Names When the sole owner of property transfers the property into the names of the owner and another as tenants in common, the owner has made an apparent gift of one-half the value of the property unless the other tenant can show contribution to the property. More difficult situations arise when the owners transfer property to themselves and another as joint tenants with right of survivorship.

The valuation of a gift made by placing property in joint names depends on state law. If the joint tenants can be severed by any joint tenant without consent of the others, the transaction is treated for federal gift tax purposes as if it were the creation of a tenancy in common. The value of the right of survivorship inherent in a joint tenancy would be disregarded.

EXAMPLE
Joint Tenancy and Right of Survivorship

> A and B purchase securities worth $30,000, taking title as "A and B as joint tenants with right of survivorship." A contributes $10,000 and B contributes $20,000 of the purchase price. B has made a gift of $5,000 to A (A's half interest in the securities: $15,000 minus funds provided by A, or half of $10,000).

If the joint tenancy cannot be severed by one joint tenant acting alone, the value of the right of survivorship must be considered. This is normally the situation in a tenancy by the entireties or other joint tenancies between husband and wife. Under present gift tax law, assuming that both spouses are U.S. citizens, a husband and wife can make unlimited gifts to each other with no tax liability incurred.

The date of the gift is important. In most cases the date of the gift is obvious: the date of the check or the trade date of a security gifted to the donee. However, in the case of a joint bank account, the gift is made at the time when one of the parties makes the first withdrawal from the account in an amount in excess of his contribution to the account plus the interest attributable to that contribution. Thus if A and B establish a joint account, each contributing $10,000, when A withdraws $11,000 a gift has been made to A from B. If the money simply sits in the account then no gift has been made.

Transfers in Trust Gifts may be made outright or in trust. The form of the trust has an important effect on the federal gift tax consequences. The creation of a revocable trust—a trust that the settlor can revoke at will—is not a completed gift. The creation of an irrevocable trust (or the addition of property to such a trust) constitutes a gift to the extent interests in the trust pass to persons other than the settlor. Under some circumstances, a gift in trust may be made by someone other than the settlor. For instance, the renunciation by an income beneficiary of a power to withdraw corpus may be a gift to the person or persons who have the remainder interest in the trust. A gift to a trust is an indirect gift. It is treated as a gift of separate interests to the beneficiaries, and not to the trust itself as an entity.

Valuation Except in the case of life insurance, there are no new valuation problems to be considered with regard to the federal gift tax. The valuation concepts and techniques discussed in connection with the federal estate tax are applicable to gifts. The relevant valuation date is the date of transfer.

To obtain the value of a life insurance policy that is the subject of a gift, it is necessary to write to the issuing insurance company requesting a Form 938 as of the date of transfer. This will establish the value of the policy as of that date. The regulations are quite complex, but the best shorthand approximation of the value of a life insurance policy for federal gift tax purposes is the cost as of the transfer date of a single premium that would result in the issuance of a new policy affording identical coverage and identical future premiums.

Nontaxable Transfers

Marital Deduction The unlimited marital deduction resulted from the inequities caused by community property tax law. As described earlier in the text, eight states (Arizona, California, Idaho, Louisiana, Nevada, New Mexico, Texas, and Washington) have community property systems. Under those systems property acquired by the effort of either spouse during the marriage is deemed to belong one-half to the husband and one-half to the wife. Accordingly, if community property is given to a third person, such as a child of the husband and wife, that gift is deemed to be given one-half by the husband and one-half by the wife. Since the federal gift tax rates are progressive, donors in community property states would have a tax advantage over donors in states that do not have community property if the tax law ignored the difference.

EXAMPLE
The Gift Tax Law Prior to 1977

In order to understand the history of the gift tax law it is necessary to cite an example prior to 1977. If a husband and wife in a community property state made a taxable gift from community property of $100,000 to their son in 1976, that gift under community property law would have been a gift from the mother of $50,000 to the son and a gift from the father of $50,000 to the son. Assuming that gift was the first taxable gift made by either spouse and that all exclusions and credits were exhausted, the mother would have paid a federal gift tax of $10,600 and the father would have paid a similar federal gift tax. Thus the total tax would have been $21,200. By contrast, had the parties lived in a non–community property state and had all the property been acquired by the husband's efforts, he would have made a $100,000 gift to his son and his wife would have made no gift. If there was no legislation to correct this inequity, the total federal gift tax would have $23,800 or approximately 12% more than if the parties lived in a community property state.

Once this concept is understood, it is easy to understand gift splitting, because it is a device to make the impact of the federal gift tax similar in both the community property and non–community property states.

Gift splitting simply means that a gift of non–community property made by a husband or a wife to a third party may be treated for federal gift tax purposes as being made one-half by each, if both husband and wife agree to treat the gift that way. To so agree, they must both sign the federal gift tax return. Because of gift splitting the taxpayers in the preceding illustration would pay the exact same tax regardless of whether they are in a community property jurisdiction or not.

The marital deduction for gift tax purposes is analogous to the marital deduction for federal estate tax purposes. There is an unlimited marital deduction to a spouse no matter what the amount of the gift, unless the spouse is not a U.S. citizen. If the spouse is not a citizen, then there is a $100,000 exemption available. Any amount over $100,000 would be subject to tax.

The rationale behind the federal gift tax marital deduction is that the property that qualifies for the deduction will be taxed when the wife transfers it by gift or upon her death. That is the same rationale underlying the federal estate tax marital deduction. Property that qualifies for the marital deduction will be taxable in the donee spouse's estate and vice versa.

Disclaimers A person who makes a "qualified disclaimer" of property is not treated as having made a gift. Thus if Mrs. Jones, as the spouse and beneficiary under Mr. Jones's will, wishes to disclaim property received under her husband's will, she may do so without incurring a gift tax. This is a very good way for Mrs. Jones to (1) keep the property out of her estate and (2) to make tax-free gifts to her children (presuming that her children are also Mr. Jones's issue). She does not have to use any of her unified credit or her annual exemption to make these gifts.

Annual Exclusion

Present Interests A donor is entitled, each year, to make a $10,000 gift per donee to as many donees as he wishes, without having to file a federal gift tax return. Thus if Mr. Jones wishes to give each of his 10 children $10,000 a year, he can give away $100,000 without incurring a gift tax. A federal gift tax return must be filed only if the annual exclusion is exceeded. For all gifts made prior to 1982, there was a $3,000 per year exclusion available. This exclusion is available only for gifts of present interest. Thus if you wish to give a gift of future interest to a donee, the gift will not qualify for the exclusion.

In addition to the $10,000 exclusion a donor may "split" the gift to any donee with his spouse. The spouse may also use her annual exclusion to give property to the same donee. Thus if Mr.

and Mrs. Jones wish to give their son cash to purchase a new home, they may each give him $10,000, for a total of $20,000. In addition they can likewise give their daughter-in-law and their three grand children each $20,000. Thus they can actually give the family $100,000 each year tax-free, without having to use any portion of their unified credit. The funds do not have to come from each spouse's own assets. The funds may all come from Mrs. Jones' assets. Thus, the actual source of the contribution is irrelevant when spouses are involved. Gift splitting is only available between spouses.

Future Interests A future interest is a gift of property that the recipient will not come into possession of or enjoyment of until some time in the future. On the other hand, a present interest is one in which the donee has a present unrestricted right to the property. An example of a future interest is a remainder of a trust subject to a preceding life estate.

EXAMPLE
Present and Future Interests

A creates a $50,000 trust to pay the income to B for life and the principal to B's children on B's death. B has a present interest, so the gift to him (the value of his right to receive income for life) qualifies for the $10,000 annual exclusion. B's children have future interests; the value of the gift to them does not qualify for the annual exclusion.

A common desire of many persons is to make gifts to minor children. However, not trusting the child's judgment the donor may not wish a child to have the property until he or she reaches age 21. At the same time, the donor will desire to take advantage of the annual exclusion.

If property is transferred to an irrevocable trust to accumulate the income and to pay it and the principal to the child on his twenty-first birthday, a future interest is created because the child is not able to enjoy the property until sometime in the future. It follows that under the general rule the $10,000 annual exclusion is not available. However, the Internal Revenue Code provides for special federal gift tax treatment of such future interests under certain conditions. If the trust provides (1) that income and principal may be used for the minor's benefit, and (2) that any income and principal not distributed during minority shall be paid to the minor at age 21 (or to his or her estate or as he or she may appoint if he or she dies before age 21), then the gift qualifies for the annual exclusion as a present interest. The terms of many trusts have been tailored to accomplish this result. They are sometimes referred to as "Section 2503(c) trusts" in honor of the

Internal Revenue Code section that creates this exception to the present interest rule.

The above exception to the general rule that future interests do not qualify for the annual exclusion also permits gifts made under the Uniform Gifts to Minors Acts to qualify for the annual exclusion. Uniform Gifts to Minors Acts are in force in virtually all states. They permit securities and bank accounts and other property to be registered in the name of A, custodian for B, a minor, under the (name of state) "Uniform Gifts to Minors Act." Such a registration constitutes a completed gift from the donor to the minor. The custodian, A, manages the property and decides when and how much of it to distribute to the minor, except that he must give it all to the minor on attaining age 21, or 18, depending upon state law.

Unified Credit

Gifts made prior to 1977 had a $30,000 lifetime exemption, analogous to the $60,000 federal estate tax specific exemption that existed at that time. If the total amount of gifts made by a taxpayer over his lifetime, in excess of the available annual exclusions, was not more than $30,000, no federal gift tax was due.

Under the Tax Reform Act of 1976 the unified credit is allowed in place of both the former federal gift and estate tax exemptions. Whatever unified credit is not used up in being applied against the federal gift tax is available for application against the estate tax at death.

The unified credit is a credit against the tax payable and reduces, dollar for dollar, the federal gift taxes computed under the new rates. In effect, a $192,800 credit (after 1989) is the equivalent of a $600,000 exemption. To illustrate the difference between the credit and the exemption, presume a donor makes a gift of $700,000. An "exemption" of $600,000 would reduce the taxable gift to $100,000, which would be subject to a federal gift tax of $23,000 under the gift tax laws. With a "credit" of $192,800 the taxable gift is $700,000, on which the gift tax is $229,800. The tax due is reduced by the $192,800 credit, leaving a gift tax due of $37,000.

Unified Credits and Exemption Equivalents
(Phase-in from 1978 to 1987)

Year	Unified Credit	Exemption Equivalent
January 1, 1977–June 30, 1977	$ 6,000	
July 1, 1977–December 31, 1977	30,000	$120,666
1978	34,000	134,000
1979	38,000	147,333
1980	42,500	161,563
1981	47,000	175,225
1982	62,800	225,000

1983	79,300	275,000
1984	96,300	325,000
1985	121,800	400,000
1986	155,800	500,000
1987 and thereafter	192,800	600,000

Charitable and Educational Exclusion

There is an unlimited educational and medical expense exclusion available. The educational expense must be paid directly to the educational institution and must be for tuition only. Room, board, and books do not qualify for the exclusion.

Qualifying medical expenses are defined by Internal Revenue Code § 213 (for income taxes), but generally most normal medical expenses, such as doctor bills, hospital expenses, and drug expenses qualify. If the donee is reimbursed by medical insurance, that amount would not qualify.

The educational exclusion was very important for people who established trusts for their children's college education. Most college tuitions are now more than $10,000 per year. Parents might have been burdened by having to pay a gift tax on a portion of the money required for tuition. The exclusions are subtracted from the total gifts and split gifts on the gift tax return.

Cumulative and Progressive Rates

To compute the federal gift tax rate on a particular gift, it is necessary to know all the gifts that the taxpayers made in preceding years. The federal gift tax rate for any year's gifts is based upon the total taxable gifts made since June 6, 1932, when the federal gift tax was enacted. The rate is both cumulative and progressive.

The effect of cumulative rates is to remove any advantage (except the annual exclusion) from spreading gifts over a period of years. The applicable tax bracket is calculated by adding the taxable gifts of the current year to all previous taxable gifts of the donor. Without cumulative rates, the total federal gift tax on gifts of $100,000 in each of five years would be less than the gift tax on a $500,000 gift in one year. With cumulative rates, the two taxes are the same. The operation of cumulative rates is best understood by the following example.

EXAMPLE
Cumulative Rates on Taxable Gifts

In year 1 taxpayer makes $20,000 of taxable gifts. The tax rate table (see below) indicates that the tax is $3,800. In year 2 taxpayer makes taxable gifts of another $20,000. The tax in year 2 is not $3,800. It is $4,400, computed as follows:

1. Amount of taxable gifts for year 2	$20,000
2. Total amount of taxable gifts for preceding years (year 1)	+20,000
3. Total taxable gifts	40,000
4. Tax computed on # 3 (from tax rate table)	8,200
5. Tax computed on # 2 (from tax rate table)	−3,800
6. Gift tax on gifts in year 2	$ 4,400

The credit which remains to the donor for the year the taxable gifts are made is applied to offset the tax liability thus ascertained.

EXAMPLE
Gift Tax Rate Table under the Tax Reform Act of 1986

Table A
Unified Rate Schedule

Column A Taxable amount over	Column B Taxable amount not over	Column C Tax on amount in column A	Column D Rate of tax on excess over amount in column A (Percent)
0	$10,000	0	18
$10,000	20,000	$1,800	20
20,000	40,000	3,800	22
40,000	60,000	8,200	24
60,000	80,000	13,000	26
80,000	100,000	18,200	28
100,000	150,000	23,800	30
150,000	250,000	38,800	32
250,000	500,000	70,800	34
500,000	750,000	155,800	37
750,000	1,000,000	248,300	39
1,000,000	1,250,000	345,800	41
1,250,000	1,500,000	448,300	43
1,500,000	2,000,000	555,800	45
2,000,000	2,500,000	780,800	49
2,500,000	3,000,000	1,025,800	53
3,000,000	-------------	1,290,800	55

Relationship to Federal Estate Tax

Prior to 1977, the federal gift tax rates were three-quarters of the federal estate tax rates. Therefore, there was an obvious advantage in making gifts. However, the Tax Reform Act of 1976 unified the federal estate and federal gift tax so the rates are now identical.

Deductions

In addition to the exclusions discussed above, there are deductions to the taxable gift allowed. These are the charitable deduction, deductions for gifts to political organizations, gifts to other qualified community organizations, and the marital deduction. In some cases there are split-interest gifts, for example, where the son receives income for life from a trust, and the remainder passes to charity. Only the remainder interest (the amount actually going to charity) would qualify for the charitable deduction.

The marital deduction for gifts made after 1981 is unlimited. Thus spouses may transfer any amount of gifts to each other without incurring a gift tax on the transfer. Generally most transfers of terminable interests (such as life estates or annuities with a specific termination date or time) do not qualify for the marital deduction. The only exception to this is "qualified terminable interest property" (QTIP). The spouse's entire interest in this type of property will qualify for the gift tax marital deduction. (See Chapter Five for more details concerning QTIP.)

For gifts made after 1976 and before 1982, a $100,000 marital deduction was available. The next $100,000 of gifts was fully taxable. For gifts over $200,000 a 50% deduction was available. The spouse was also entitled to the $3,000 annual exclusion. For gifts prior to 1977 there was a 50% marital deduction available for all gifts. The spouse must have been a U.S. resident in order to qualify for the marital deduction.

All jointly owned property qualifies for the unlimited marital deduction after 1981.

Preparing the Federal Gift Tax Return

The operation of the annual exclusion, the unified credit, the marital deduction, gift-splitting, and cumulative rates in combination may now be illustrated. Suppose in June 1989 Tom Saylor, a bachelor, made a gift of $10,000 to his sister, Patsy Smith. The gift tax would have been zero and no gift tax return would have been due because the gift did not exceed the annual exclusion.

In December 1990, Tom made a gift of $15,000 to Patsy. A federal gift tax return would have to be filed since the gift is greater than the annual exclusion. The gift would qualify for the $10,000 annual exclusion (Tom's only gift to Patsy in 1990). The remaining $5,000 would generate a gift tax of $900.00. The unified credit must be utilized so that no tax would be due. The credit applies to the amount of tax, not the value of the gift. Tom's remaining unified credit would be reduced to $191,900 ($192,800 less $900). The federal gift tax return would have been filed to show that the unified credit was being partially utilized. This of course reduces the amount of credit available to Tom's estate at the time of his death.

In November 1991, Tom married the former Miss Lynne Elayne Jones and on December 30, 1991, gave an additional $20,000 to his sister, Patsy. If Lynne consents to gift-splitting (and there is no good reason not to consent), the situation would be regarded as if there was a $10,000 gift by the husband and a similar gift by the wife. Each of these gifts is less than the annual exclusion. However, a federal gift tax return would have been filed, to indicate that the spouses elected to split the gift.

In June 1992 Tom makes a gift of $50,000 to his sister. If the spouses elect to split the gift to Patsy, it would be treated as a $25,000 gift from each. Each spouse would have to file a federal gift tax return to report the $15,000 gift ($25,000 less the $10,000 annual exclusion) and utilize a portion of each of their unified credit. When Lynne uses her unified credit to offset the tax due on the $15,000 gift, her credit would be reduced by $2,800 (the tax due on a $15,000 gift). Tom's unified credit was previously reduced by $900 when he made the gift to his sister Patsy in 1990.

Because the gift tax is cumulative, the previous taxable gift of $5,000 (recall the amount of the gift was $15,000 but Tom was able to reduce it to $5,000 by using $10,000 annual exclusion) will have to be included on his 1992 gift tax return. The previous $5,000 gift is thus added to the 1992 $15,000 gift resulting in total taxable gifts of $20,000. The tax is computed on the total taxable gifts of $20,000 ($3,800 tax) and then the tax is reduced by the amount of tax paid (or unified credit used) on the previous gift ($900). The balance ($3,800 less $900) is the tax due on the 1990 return. In effect, by adding all the previous gifts together the donor is placed in a higher tax bracket. Tom will be liable for a gift tax of $2,900 for his $15,000 gift to his sister, where Lynne will only be liable for a gift tax of $2,800 for the same gift. To illustrate this example, two completed gift tax returns are shown on the following pages. In addition, a short Form 709-A is also illustrated. The short-form federal gift tax return is used only in the case where spouses are reporting nontaxable gifts that they have consented to split.

Both the marital and charitable deductions are computed after the annual exclusions are deducted. Thus if a donor made a $19,000 gift to charity, the entire amount would qualify for the charitable deduction. However, the $10,000 annual exclusion is deducted first; therefore only $9,000 is included in the total amount of the gifts. The charitable deduction is limited to $9,000.

Prior to 1977 a $30,000 lifetime exemption was allowed for gifts. It could be taken at one time or a portion could be taken each quarter or year.

EXAMPLE *Husband's Federal Gift Tax Return—Form 709*

Form **709** (Rev. October 1990) Department of the Treasury Internal Revenue Service

United States Gift (and Generation-Skipping Transfer) Tax Return

(Section 6019 of the Internal Revenue Code) (For gifts made after December 31, 1989, and before January 1, 1993)

Calendar year 19 92

▶ **See separate instructions. For Privacy Act Notice, see the instructions for Form 1040.**

OMB No. 1545-0020 Expires 8-31-93

Part 1.—General Information

1 Donor's first name and middle initial	2 Donor's last name	3 **Social security number**
Tom R.	Saylor	100: 34 :2743
4 Address (number, street, and apartment number)		5 Domicile
4732 Elm Street		Pennsylvania
6 City, state, and ZIP code		7 Citizenship
Pleasantville, PA 16341		USA

	Yes	No
8 If the donor died during the year, check here ▶ ☐ and enter date of death ______, 19 ____		
9 If you received an extension of time to file this Form 709, check here ▶ ☐ and attach the Form 4868, 2688, 2350, or extension letter.		
10 Enter the total number of separate donees listed on Schedule A—count each person only once . . . 1		
11 If you (the donor) filed a previous Form 709 (or 709-A), has your address changed since the last Form 709 (or 709-A) was filed?		X
12 Gifts by husband or wife to third parties.—Do you consent to have the gifts (including generation-skipping transfers) made by you and by your spouse to third parties during the calendar year considered as made one-half by each of you? (See instructions.) (If the answer is "Yes," the following information must be furnished and your spouse is to sign the consent shown below. If the answer is "No," skip lines 13–18 and go to Schedule A.)	X	
13 Name of consenting spouse Lynne E. Saylor — 14 SSN 123-45-6888		
15 Were you married to one another during the entire calendar year? (See instructions.)	X	
16 If the answer to 15 is "No," check whether ☐ married ☐ divorced or ☐ widowed, and give date (see instructions) ▶		
17 Will a gift tax return for this calendar year be filed by your spouse?	X	

18 **Consent of Spouse**—I consent to have the gifts (and generation-skipping transfers) made by me and by my spouse to third parties during the calendar year considered as made one-half by each of us. We are both aware of the joint and several liability for tax created by the execution of this consent.

Consenting spouse's signature ▶ /s/ Lynne E. Saylor **Date** ▶ 4/3/93

Part 2.—Tax Computation

1	Enter the amount from Schedule A, Part 3, line 15	1	15,000 00
2	Enter the amount from Schedule B, line 3	2	5,000 00
3	Total taxable gifts (add lines 1 and 2)	3	20,000 00
4	Tax computed on amount on line 3 (see Table for Computing Tax in separate instructions)	4	3,800 00
5	Tax computed on amount on line 2 (see Table for Computing Tax in separate instructions)	5	900 00
6	Balance (subtract line 5 from line 4)	6	2,900 00
7	Maximum unified credit (nonresident aliens, see instructions)	7	192,800 00
8	Enter the unified credit against tax allowable for all prior periods (from Sch. B, line 1, col. C)	8	900 00
9	Balance (subtract line 8 from line 7)	9	191,900 00
10	Enter 20% (.20) of the amount allowed as a specific exemption for gifts made after September 8, 1976, and before January 1, 1977 (see instructions)	10	-0-
11	Balance (subtract line 10 from line 9)	11	191,900 00
12	Unified credit (enter the smaller of line 6 or line 11)	12	2,900 00
13	Credit for foreign gift taxes (see instructions)	13	-0-
14	Total credits (add lines 12 and 13)	14	2,900 00
15	Balance (subtract line 14 from line 6) (do not enter less than zero)	15	-0-
16	Generation-skipping transfer taxes (from Schedule C, Part 3, col. H, total)	16	-0-
17	Total tax (add lines 15 and 16)	17	-0-
18	Gift and generation-skipping transfer taxes prepaid with extension of time to file	18	-0-
19	If line 18 is less than line 17, enter BALANCE DUE (see instructions)	19	-0-
20	If line 18 is greater than line 17, enter AMOUNT TO BE REFUNDED	20	-0-

Please attach check or money order here

Under penalties of perjury, I declare that I have examined this return, including any accompanying schedules and statements, and to the best of my knowledge and belief it is true, correct, and complete. Declaration of preparer (other than donor) is based on all information of which preparer has any knowledge.

Donor's signature ▶ /s/ Tom R. Saylor Date ▶ 4/3/93

Preparer's signature (other than donor) ▶ Date ▶

Preparer's address (other than donor) ▶

For Paperwork Reduction Act Notice, see page 1 of the separate instructions for this form. Form **709** (Rev. 10-90)

EXAMPLE *Husband's Federal Gift Tax Return—Form 709, continued*

Form 709 (Rev. 10-90) Page 2

SCHEDULE A Computation of Taxable Gifts

Part 1.—Gifts Subject Only to Gift Tax. *Gifts less political organization, medical, and educational exclusions—see instructions*

A Item number	B Donee's name, relationship to donor (if any), and address and description of gift. If the gift was made by means of a trust, enter trust's identifying number below and attach a copy of the trust instrument. If the gift was securities, enter the CUSIP number(s), if available.	C Donor's adjusted basis of gift	D Date of gift	E Value at date of gift
1	Patsy Smith (sister) 14 South Street Cheyenne, WY 82001 Cash		6/15/92	$50,000

Part 2.—Gifts Which are Direct Skips and are Subject to Both Gift Tax and Generation-Skipping Transfer Tax. You must list the gifts in chronological order. *Gifts less political organization, medical, and educational exclusions—see instructions. (Also list here direct skips that are subject only to the GST tax at this time as the result of the termination of an "estate tax inclusion period." See instructions.)*

A Item number	B Donee's name, relationship to donor (if any), and address and description of gift. If the gift was made by means of a trust, enter trust's identifying number below and attach a copy of the trust instrument. If the gift was securities, enter the CUSIP number(s), if available.	C Donor's adjusted basis of gift	D Date of gift	E Value at date of gift
1	None			

Part 3.—Gift Tax Reconciliation

1	Total value of gifts of donor (add column E of Parts 1 and 2)		1	50,000 00
2	One-half of items 1 attributable to spouse (see instructions)		2	25,000 00
3	Balance (subtract line 2 from line 1)		3	25,000 00
4	Gifts of spouse to be included (from Schedule A, Part 3, line 2 of spouse's return—see instructions) If any of the gifts included on this line are also subject to the generation-skipping transfer tax, check here ▶ ☐ and enter those gifts also on Schedule C, Part 1.		4	
5	Total gifts (add lines 3 and 4)		5	25,000 00
6	Total annual exclusions for gifts listed on Schedule A (including line 4, above) (see instructions)		6	10,000 00
7	Total included amount of gifts (subtract line 6 from line 5)		7	15,000 00
Deductions (see instructions)				
8	Gifts of interests to spouse for which a marital deduction will be claimed, based on items ______ of Schedule A	8		
9	Exclusions attributable to gifts on line 8	9		
10	Marital deduction—subtract line 9 from line 8	10		
11	Charitable deduction, based on items ______ to ______ less exclusions	11		
12	Total deductions—add lines 10 and 11		12	-0-
13	Subtract line 12 from line 7		13	15,000 00
14	Generation-skipping transfer taxes payable with this Form 709 (from Schedule C, Part 3, col. H, Total)		14	
15	Taxable gifts (add lines 13 and 14). Enter here and on line 1 of the Tax Computation on page 1		15	15,000 00

(If more space is needed, attach additional sheets of same size.)

EXAMPLE *Husband's Federal Gift Tax Return—Form 709, continued*

Form 709 (Rev. 10-90) Page **3**

SCHEDULE A **Computation of Taxable Gifts** (continued)

16 Terminable Interest (QTIP) Marital Deduction. (See instructions.)

☐ ◄ Check here if you elected, under the rules of section 2523(f), to include gifts of qualified terminable interest property on line 8, on page 2. Enter the item numbers (from Schedule A) of the gifts for which you made this election ►

17 Election out of QTIP Treatment of Annuities

☐ ◄ Check here if you elect under section 2523(f)(6) to **NOT** treat as qualified terminable interest property any joint and survivor annuities that are reported on Schedule A and would otherwise be treated as qualified terminable interest property under section 2523(f). (See instructions.) Enter the item numbers (from Schedule A) for the annuities for which you are making this election ►

SCHEDULE B **Gifts From Prior Periods**

Did you (the donor) file gift tax returns for prior periods? (If "Yes," see instructions for completing Schedule B below.) . . . . ☒ **Yes** ☐ **No**

A Calendar year or calendar quarter (see instructions)	B Internal Revenue office where prior return was filed	C Amount of unified credit against gift tax for periods after December 31, 1976	D Amount of specific exemption for prior periods ending before January 1, 1977	E Amount of taxable gifts
Dec. 1990	Philadelphia, PA	900		5,000
Dec. 1991	Philadelphia, PA	-0-		-0-

1 Totals for prior periods (without adjustment for reduced specific exemption)	1	C: 900 / E: 5,000
2 Amount, if any, by which total specific exemption, line 1, column D, is more than $30,000	2	
3 Total amount of taxable gifts for prior periods (add amount, column E, line 1, and amount, if any, on line 2) (Enter here and on line 2 of the Tax Computation on page 1.)	3	5,000

SCHEDULE C **Computation of Generation-Skipping Transfer Tax**

Note: *Inter vivos direct skips which are completely excluded by the GST exemption must still be fully reported (including value and exemptions claimed) on Schedule C.*

Part 1.—Generation-Skipping Transfers

A Item No. (from Schedule A, Part 2, col. A)	B Value (from Schedule A, Part 2, col. E)	C Split Gifts (enter ½ of col. B) (see instructions)	D Subtract col. C from col. B	E Nontaxable portion of transfer	F Net Transfer (subtract col. E from col. D)
1					
2					
3					
4					
5					
6					

	Split gifts from spouse's Form 709 (enter item number)	Value included from spouse's Form 709		
If you elected gift splitting and your spouse was required to file a separate Form 709 (see the instructions for "Split Gifts"), you must enter all of the gifts shown on Schedule A, Part 2, of your spouse's Form 709 here. In column C, enter the item number of each gift in the order it appears in column A of your spouse's Schedule A, Part 2. We have preprinted the prefix "S-" to distinguish your spouse's item numbers from your own when you complete column A of Schedule C, Part 3. In column D, for each gift, enter the amount reported in column C, Schedule C, Part 1, of your spouse's Form 709.	S-			
	S-			
	S-			
	S-			
	S-			
	S-			
	S-			
	S-			

(If more space is needed, attach additional sheets of same size.)

EXAMPLE Husband's Federal Gift Tax Return—Form 709, continued

Form 709 (Rev. 10-90) Page **4**

Part 2.—GST Exemption Reconciliation (Code section 2631) and Section 2652(a)(3) Election

Check box ▶ ☐ if you are making a section 2652(a)(3) (special QTIP) election (see instructions)

Enter the item numbers (from Schedule A) of the gifts for which you are making this election ▶ ....

1	Maximum allowable exemption	1	$1,000,000
2	Total exemption used for periods before filing this return	2	
3	Exemption available for this return (subtract line 2 from line 1)	3	
4	Exemption claimed on this return (from Part 3, col. C total, below)	4	
5	Exemption allocated to transfers not shown on Part 3, below. You must attach a Notice of Allocation. (See instructions.)	5	
6	Add lines 4 and 5	6	
7	Exemption available for future transfers (subtract line 6 from line 3)	7	

Part 3.—Tax Computation

A Item No. (from Schedule C, Part 1)	B Net transfer (from Schedule C, Part 1, col. F)	C GST Exemption Allocated	D Divide col. C by col. B	E Inclusion Ratio (subtract col. D from 1.000)	F Maximum Estate Tax Rate	G Applicable Rate (multiply col. E by col. F)	H Generation-Skipping Transfer Tax (multiply col. B by col. G)
1					55% (.55)		
2					55% (.55)		
3					55% (.55)		
4					55% (.55)		
5					55% (.55)		
6					55% (.55)		
7					55% (.55)		
8					55% (.55)		
					55% (.55)		
					55% (.55)		
					55% (.55)		
					55% (.55)		
					55% (.55)		
					55% (.55)		
					55% (.55)		
					55% (.55)		
Total exemption claimed. Enter here and on line 4, Part 2, above. May not exceed line 3, Part 2, above			**Total generation-skipping transfer tax.** Enter here, on line 14 of Schedule A, Part 3, and on line 16 of the Tax Computation on page 1				

(If more space is needed, attach additional sheets of same size.)

*U.S. GPO:1991-518-940/20362

EXAMPLE *Wife's Federal Gift Tax Return—Form 709*

Form **709** (Rev. October 1990) Department of the Treasury Internal Revenue Service

United States Gift (and Generation-Skipping Transfer) Tax Return

(Section 6019 of the Internal Revenue Code) (For gifts made after December 31, 1989, and before January 1, 1993)

Calendar year 19 92

▶ **See separate instructions. For Privacy Act Notice, see the instructions for Form 1040.**

OMB No. 1545-0020 Expires 8-31-93

Part 1.—General Information

1 Donor's first name and middle initial: Lynne E.	2 Donor's last name: Saylor	3 **Social security number**: 123 : 34 : 2743
4 Address (number, street, and apartment number): 4732 Elm Street		5 Domicile: Pennsylvania
6 City, state, and ZIP code: Pleasantville, PA 16341		7 Citizenship: USA

		Yes	No
8	If the donor died during the year, check here ▶ ☐ and enter date of death ______________, 19 ___		
9	If you received an extension of time to file this Form 709, check here ▶ ☐ and attach the Form 4868, 2688, 2350, or extension letter.		
10	Enter the total number of separate donees listed on Schedule A—count each person only once . . . ☐		
11	If you (the donor) filed a previous Form 709 (or 709-A), has your address changed since the last Form 709 (or 709-A) was filed?		X
12	Gifts by husband or wife to third parties.—Do you consent to have the gifts (including generation-skipping transfers) made by you and by your spouse to third parties during the calendar year considered as made one-half by each of you? (See instructions.) (If the answer is "Yes," the following information must be furnished and your spouse is to sign the consent shown below. If the answer is "No," skip lines 13–18 and go to Schedule A.)	X	
13	Name of consenting spouse Tom R. Saylor — 14 SSN 100-34-2743		
15	Were you married to one another during the entire calendar year? (See instructions.)	X	
16	If the answer to 15 is "No," check whether ☐ married ☐ divorced or ☐ widowed, and give date (see instructions) ▶		
17	Will a gift tax return for this calendar year be filed by your spouse?	X	

18 Consent of Spouse—I consent to have the gifts (and generation-skipping transfers) made by me and by my spouse to third parties during the calendar year considered as made one-half by each of us. We are both aware of the joint and several liability for tax created by the execution of this consent.

Consenting spouse's signature ▶ /s/ Tom R. Saylor **Date** ▶ 4/3/93

Part 2.—Tax Computation

		Line	Amount	
1	Enter the amount from Schedule A, Part 3, line 15	1	15,000	00
2	Enter the amount from Schedule B, line 3	2	-0-	
3	Total taxable gifts (add lines 1 and 2)	3	15,000	00
4	Tax computed on amount on line 3 (see Table for Computing Tax in separate instructions)	4	2,800	00
5	Tax computed on amount on line 2 (see Table for Computing Tax in separate instructions)	5	-0-	
6	Balance (subtract line 5 from line 4)	6	2,800	00
7	Maximum unified credit (nonresident aliens, see instructions)	7	192,800	00
8	Enter the unified credit against tax allowable for all prior periods (from Sch. B, line 1, col. C)	8	-0-	
9	Balance (subtract line 8 from line 7)	9	192,800	00
10	Enter 20% (.20) of the amount allowed as a specific exemption for gifts made after September 8, 1976, and before January 1, 1977 (see instructions)	10	-0-	
11	Balance (subtract line 10 from line 9)	11	192,800	00
12	Unified credit (enter the smaller of line 6 or line 11)	12	2,800	00
13	Credit for foreign gift taxes (see instructions)	13	-0-	
14	Total credits (add lines 12 and 13)	14	2,800	00
15	Balance (subtract line 14 from line 6) (do not enter less than zero)	15	-0-	
16	Generation-skipping transfer taxes (from Schedule C, Part 3, col. H, total)	16	-0-	
17	Total tax (add lines 15 and 16)	17	-0-	
18	Gift and generation-skipping transfer taxes prepaid with extension of time to file	18	-0-	
19	If line 18 is less than line 17, enter BALANCE DUE (see instructions)	19	-0-	
20	If line 18 is greater than line 17, enter AMOUNT TO BE REFUNDED	20	-0-	

Please attach check or money order here

Under penalties of perjury, I declare that I have examined this return, including any accompanying schedules and statements, and to the best of my knowledge and belief it is true, correct, and complete. Declaration of preparer (other than donor) is based on all information of which preparer has any knowledge.

Donor's signature ▶ /s/ Lynne E. Saylor Date ▶ 4/3/93

Preparer's signature (other than donor) ▶ Date ▶

Preparer's address (other than donor) ▶

For Paperwork Reduction Act Notice, see page 1 of the separate instructions for this form. Form **709** (Rev. 10-90)

EXAMPLE *Wife's Federal Gift Tax Return—Form 709, continued*

Form 709 (Rev. 10-90) Page 2

SCHEDULE A Computation of Taxable Gifts

Part 1.—Gifts Subject Only to Gift Tax. *Gifts less political organization, medical, and educational exclusions—see instructions*

A Item number	B Donee's name, relationship to donor (if any), and address and description of gift. If the gift was made by means of a trust, enter trust's identifying number below and attach a copy of the trust instrument. If the gift was securities, enter the CUSIP number(s), if available.	C Donor's adjusted basis of gift	D Date of gift	E Value at date of gift
1	Patsy Smith 14 South Street Cheyenne, WY 82001 Cash		6/15/92	50,000

Part 2.—Gifts Which are Direct Skips and are Subject to Both Gift Tax and Generation-Skipping Transfer Tax. You must list the gifts in chronological order. *Gifts less political organization, medical, and educational exclusions—see instructions. (Also list here direct skips that are subject only to the GST tax at this time as the result of the termination of an "estate tax inclusion period." See instructions.)*

A Item number	B Donee's name, relationship to donor (if any), and address and description of gift. If the gift was made by means of a trust, enter trust's identifying number below and attach a copy of the trust instrument. If the gift was securities, enter the CUSIP number(s), if available.	C Donor's adjusted basis of gift	D Date of gift	E Value at date of gift
1	None			

Part 3.—Gift Tax Reconciliation

1	Total value of gifts of donor (add column E of Parts 1 and 2)	1	50,000 00
2	One-half of items 1 attributable to spouse (see instructions)	2	25,000 00
3	Balance (subtract line 2 from line 1)	3	25,000 00
4	Gifts of spouse to be included (from Schedule A, Part 3, line 2 of spouse's return—see instructions). If any of the gifts included on this line are also subject to the generation-skipping transfer tax, check here ▶ ☐ and enter those gifts also on Schedule C, Part 1.	4	
5	Total gifts (add lines 3 and 4)	5	25,000 00
6	Total annual exclusions for gifts listed on Schedule A (including line 4, above) (see instructions)	6	10,000 00
7	Total included amount of gifts (subtract line 6 from line 5)	7	15,000 00
	Deductions (see instructions)		
8	Gifts of interests to spouse for which a marital deduction will be claimed, based on items ______ of Schedule A . . . 8		
9	Exclusions attributable to gifts on line 8 . . . 9		
10	Marital deduction—subtract line 9 from line 8 . . . 10		
11	Charitable deduction, based on items ______ to ______ less exclusions . 11		
12	Total deductions—add lines 10 and 11	12	-0-
13	Subtract line 12 from line 7	13	15,000 00
14	Generation-skipping transfer taxes payable with this Form 709 (from Schedule C, Part 3, col. H, Total)	14	
15	Taxable gifts (add lines 13 and 14). Enter here and on line 1 of the Tax Computation on page 1	15	15,000 00

(If more space is needed, attach additional sheets of same size.)

EXAMPLE *Wife's Federal Gift Tax Return—Form 709, continued*

Form 709 (Rev. 10-90) Page 3

SCHEDULE A Computation of Taxable Gifts (continued)

16 Terminable Interest (QTIP) Marital Deduction. (See instructions.)

☐ ◀ Check here if you elected, under the rules of section 2523(f), to include gifts of qualified terminable interest property on line 8, on page 2. Enter the item numbers (from Schedule A) of the gifts for which you made this election ▶

17 Election out of QTIP Treatment of Annuities

☐ ◀ Check here if you elect under section 2523(f)(6) to **NOT** treat as qualified terminable interest property any joint and survivor annuities that are reported on Schedule A and would otherwise be treated as qualified terminable interest property under section 2523(f). (See instructions.) Enter the item numbers (from Schedule A) for the annuities for which you are making this election ▶

SCHEDULE B Gifts From Prior Periods

Did you (the donor) file gift tax returns for prior periods? (If "Yes," see instructions for completing Schedule B below.) ☐ Yes ☒ No

A Calendar year or calendar quarter (see instructions)	B Internal Revenue office where prior return was filed	C Amount of unified credit against gift tax for periods after December 31, 1976	D Amount of specific exemption for prior periods ending before January 1, 1977	E Amount of taxable gifts
	None			
1 Totals for prior periods (without adjustment for reduced specific exemption)	1			−0−

2 Amount, if any, by which total specific exemption, line 1, column D, is more than $30,000	2	
3 Total amount of taxable gifts for prior periods (add amount, column E, line 1, and amount, if any, on line 2) (Enter here and on line 2 of the Tax Computation on page 1.)	3	−0−

SCHEDULE C Computation of Generation-Skipping Transfer Tax

Note: *Inter vivos direct skips which are completely excluded by the GST exemption must still be fully reported (including value and exemptions claimed) on Schedule C.*

Part 1.—Generation-Skipping Transfers

A Item No. (from Schedule A, Part 2, col. A)	B Value (from Schedule A, Part 2, col. E)	C Split Gifts (enter ½ of col. B) (see instructions)	D Subtract col. C from col. B	E Nontaxable portion of transfer	F Net Transfer (subtract col. E from col. D)
1					
2					
3					
4					
5					
6					

	Split gifts from spouse's Form 709 (enter item number)	Value included from spouse's Form 709		
If you elected gift splitting and your spouse was required to file a separate Form 709 (see the instructions for "Split Gifts"), you must enter all of the gifts shown on Schedule A, Part 2, of your spouse's Form 709 here.	S-			
In column C, enter the item number of each gift in the order it appears in column A of your spouse's Schedule A, Part 2. We have preprinted the prefix "S-" to distinguish your spouse's item numbers from your own when you complete column A of Schedule C, Part 3.	S-			
In column D, for each gift, enter the amount reported in column C, Schedule C, Part 1, of your spouse's Form 709.	S-			
	S-			
	S-			
	S-			
	S-			
	S-			

(If more space is needed, attach additional sheets of same size.)

EXAMPLE *Wife's Federal Gift Tax Return—Form 709, continued*

Form 709 (Rev. 10-90) Page **4**

Part 2.—GST Exemption Reconciliation (Code section 2631) and Section 2652(a)(3) Election

Check box ▶ ☐ if you are making a section 2652(a)(3) (special QTIP) election (see instructions)

Enter the item numbers (from Schedule A) of the gifts for which you are making this election ▶ ....

1	Maximum allowable exemption	1	$1,000,000
2	Total exemption used for periods before filing this return	2	
3	Exemption available for this return (subtract line 2 from line 1)	3	
4	Exemption claimed on this return (from Part 3, col. C total, below)	4	
5	Exemption allocated to transfers not shown on Part 3, below. You must attach a Notice of Allocation. (See instructions.)	5	
6	Add lines 4 and 5	6	
7	Exemption available for future transfers (subtract line 6 from line 3)	7	

Part 3.—Tax Computation

A Item No. (from Schedule C, Part 1)	B Net transfer (from Schedule C, Part 1, col. F)	C GST Exemption Allocated	D Divide col. C by col. B	E Inclusion Ratio (subtract col. D from 1.000)	F Maximum Estate Tax Rate	G Applicable Rate (multiply col. E by col. F)	H Generation-Skipping Transfer Tax (multiply col. B by col. G)
1					55% (.55)		
2					55% (.55)		
3					55% (.55)		
4					55% (.55)		
5					55% (.55)		
6					55% (.55)		
7					55% (.55)		
8					55% (.55)		
					55% (.55)		
					55% (.55)		
					55% (.55)		
					55% (.55)		
					55% (.55)		
					55% (.55)		
					55% (.55)		
					55% (.55)		

Total exemption claimed. Enter here and on line 4, Part 2, above. May not exceed line 3, Part 2, above		**Total generation-skipping transfer tax.** Enter here, on line 14 of Schedule A, Part 3, and on line 16 of the Tax Computation on page 1	

(If more space is needed, attach additional sheets of same size.)

*U.S. GPO:1991-518-940/20362

EXAMPLE *The Federal Gift Tax Return—Short Form 709-A*

Form **709-A** (Rev. November 1990) Department of the Treasury Internal Revenue Service

United States Short Form Gift Tax Return

(For "Privacy Act" notice, see the Form 1040 Instructions)

Calendar year 19 91

OMB No. 1545-0021 Expires 10-31-93

1 Donor's first name and middle initial Tom R.	2 Donor's last name Saylor	3 **Donor's social security number** 100 : 34 : 2743
4 Address (number, street, and apartment number) 4732 Elm Street		5 Legal residence (domicile) Pennsylvania
6 City, state, and ZIP code Pleasantville, PA 16341		7 Citizenship USA

8 Did you file any gift tax returns for prior periods? . . . . ☒ **Yes** ☐ **No**
If "Yes," state when and where earlier returns were filed ▶ December 1988 – Philadelphia

9 Name of consenting spouse Lynne E. Saylor	10 **Consenting spouse's social security number** 123 : 45 : 6888

Note: Do not use this form to report gifts of closely held stock. Instead, use Form 709.

List of Gifts

Donee's name and address and description of gift (a)	Donor's adjusted basis of gift (b)	Date of gift (c)	Value at date of gift (d)
Patsy Smith 14 South Street Cheyenne, WY 82001 Cash		12/30/91	20,000

Consent

I consent to have the gifts made by my spouse to third parties during the calendar year considered as made one-half by each of us.

Consenting spouse's signature ▶ /s/ Lynne E. Saylor **Date** ▶ 4/5/92

Under penalties of perjury, I declare that I have examined this return, and to the best of my knowledge and belief it is true, correct, and complete. Declaration of preparer (other than donor) is based on all information of which preparer has any knowledge.

Donor's signature ▶ /s/ Tom R. Saylor **Date** ▶ 4/5/92

Preparer's signature (other than donor's) ▶ **Date** ▶

Preparer's address (other than donor's) ▶

For Paperwork Reduction Act Notice, see the instructions on the reverse of this form. Form **709-A** (Rev. 11-90)

Gift Splitting Between Spouses

If spouses have elected gift splitting, they should each file separate federal gift tax returns showing the split gift on Schedule A, part 3, line 2, and each should, depending upon the amount of the split gift, sign the "Consent of Spouse" on the other's return. By consenting to the gift the donor and spouse each become jointly liable for the gift tax for that calendar year. If the donor and spouse elect to split gifts of not more than $20,000 ($6,000 for pre-1982 gifts) per year per donee, they may file a Form 709-A (short form gift tax return). If the spouse elects gift splitting, the spouse not actually making the gift does not need to file a separate federal gift tax return if the gifts to which he or she is consenting do not require the filing of a federal gift tax return, i.e., do not exceed the annual exclusion. As mentioned previously, spouses may in effect double their tax-free gifts by gift splitting. Each spouse may give any number of donees $10,000 each annually, as well as utilizing their unified credits of $192,800 each. If the spouses wish to give their son $40,000, they can do so by each giving him $20,000 in December and $20,000 in January and generate no gift tax.

EXAMPLES

Requirement to File the Gift Tax Return (with Gift Splitting)

1. A husband made gifts of $25,000 in 1989 to a third-party donee. His wife made no gifts. Each spouse is required to file a 1989 Form 709. He made a gift that exceeded the $10,000 exemption by $15,000. She is required to file because she is considered to have made a gift of $12,500 when she signed her consent to gift splitting.
2. A wife made a gift valued at $18,000. Her husband made no gifts. He is not required to file a return because his portion of the gift (through gift splitting) is only $9,000, less than the $10,000 exclusion. She is required to file because her gift exceeded the annual exclusion by $8,000.
3. Both spouses must consent to the gifts on their own returns. The gift splitting does not apply to gifts of community property. Community property gifts are automatically treated as being one-half from each. The consent to the gift must be made by the due date of the return (April 15 for calendar year returns.)
4. In 1991, Gerry gave his son Andrew $3,000 on February 3; $3,000 on May 10; and $4,000 on December 5. On December 5 he gave an additional $30,000 to Sally. No federal gift tax return is due for the gifts to his son because they total $10,000 (the annual exclusion). However he will have to file a federal gift tax return for the gift made to Sally, and it would be wise to report the other gifts to his son on the same return even though no tax is due.

Generation-Skipping Transfer Tax

The generation-skipping transfer tax is a tax separate from the gift tax. In 1986 a new generation-skipping transfer tax (GST) was introduced, replacing the original GST tax enacted by the 1976 Tax Reform Act. The 1986 GST tax was an attempt to simplify the tax by applying the tax to direct beneficial interests. The prior law was extremely complex and required many difficult projections and calculations.

The tax applies to direct skips (such as property transferred from grandfather to grandchild) as well as taxable distributions and terminations of trust property. A "direct skip" is a transfer either outright or in trust for the benefit of a person at least two generations below the transferor. This person is called the "skip" person. Any person who is a spouse of the transferor is considered to be in the same generation as the transferor, regardless of his or her age. If a transferor's child is deceased, the transfer to his grandchild is not considered a skip. Everyone is "moved up" a generation if there is a deceased descendant of the transferor. Thus if X makes a gift to his grandson and X's son is deceased, there is no GST tax. If X makes a gift to his great-grandson the transfer may be subject to the GST tax.

Each transferor has a $1 million lifetime exemption to be used for all transfers. In addition, up until 1990 there was a $2 million exemption available per grandchild.

A "taxable termination" occurs upon the termination of an interest in a GST trust. The termination usually occurs at the death of a person with a life interest or at a point of time directed by the grantor when the trust was established.

The GST tax rules are applied to transfers made after October 22, 1986. Inter vivos transfers made between September 25, 1985, and prior to October 22, 1986 are treated with a few exceptions as having been made on October 23, 1986.

Direct skips occurring at death are reported on Form 706, not Form 709. Unlike the estate tax, which is imposed on the entire estate regardless of who the distributees are, the GST tax is imposed upon the value of the property interests that actually pass to skip persons. Schedule R (Form 706) is used to report the GST tax payable by the estate and Schedule R-1 (706) is used to compute the GST tax payable by any trusts included in the gross estate. (See Chapter 5 for further details.)

Computation of the Tax The method of determining the taxable amount for the GST tax depends on whether the transfer is a taxable distribution, a taxable termination, or a direct skip.

Taxable Distributions The amount subject to the transfer tax is the amount received by the transferee. This amount is reduced by any expenses incurred in determination or collection of the tax.

Taxable Terminations The amount subject to tax is the value of the property in which the interest terminates. This is also reduced by any expenses attributable to termination.

Direct Skips The amount subject to tax is the value of the property received by the transferee.

After the value of the transfer has been determined, the amount may be reduced by the $1 million exemption of the transferor. This exemption may be allocated by the transferor or in the case of his death, by his executor. It must be made by the due date of Form 706, whether or not a Form 706 is required to be filed. The exemption may be applied to gifts in different years until the amount is completely used.

If a transferor places assets in a trust, uses his entire exemption, and the assets appreciate, the appreciation is not subject to tax. If on the other hand only a portion of the exemption is used, the portion not exempted would be subject to tax if the assets appreciate.

EXAMPLE
Computing the GST

X establishes a $1 million trust for the benefit of her grandchildren and great grandchildren. X uses her entire $1 million exemption. The assets appreciate to $10 million. None of the appreciation is subject to tax.

X established a $5 million trust and uses $500,000 of his exemption. The value of the trust appreciates to $10 million. Only one-tenth ($1 million) of the appreciation would be exempt because at the time of the transfer only one-tenth of the property qualified as exempt.

If a decedent dies having used only a portion of his exemption, his estate may use the balance of the exemption on his Form 706.

In general, the rate of the GST tax is the same as the maximum rate for Form 706, currently 55% (scheduled to be reduced to 50% in 1993) and the "inclusion ratio." The inclusion ratio can best be explained by the following example.

EXAMPLE
Computing the Inclusion Rate

Robert Jones, a widower, transfers $2 million to a trust for the benefit of his grandchildren in January 1991. The $1 million exemption is allocated to his trust, assuming no other deductions the GST tax would be calculated as follows:

1. The $1 million exemption divided by the total value of the trust ($2 million) is .5;
2. The .5 is subtracted from 1. The inclusion ratio is 1 minus .5, or .5.

The tax is the maximum federal estate tax rate (in 1987, 55%) multiplied by the inclusion ratio (.5). The tax would thus be 27.5%.

Due to the complexity of the calculation and the fact that the legal assistant will rarely encounter a GST tax situation where a donor is gifting more than $1 million, this book will not go into any more detail on the calculation. However it is important for the legal assistant to be aware of what the generation-skipping transfer tax is and to see an example because it is referred to frequently. The tax may have to be calculated either on Form 706 or 709.

A completed Form 709 for Mr. Jones' $2 million gift follows. In addition to the above information, the student should be aware that Mr. Jones did elect to use his entire unified credit; the gift made to the trust was of future interest so no annual exclusions were available; and the $2 million grandchild exclusion expired on January 1, 1990, so that was not available. The gift is subject to both gift and GST taxes. The combined taxes on the $2 million gift would be $1,409,500 or 70% of the gift.

EXAMPLE *Grandparent's Gift to Grandchildren—Form 709*

Form **709** (Rev. October 1990)
Department of the Treasury
Internal Revenue Service

United States Gift (and Generation-Skipping Transfer) Tax Return

(Section 6019 of the Internal Revenue Code) (For gifts made after December 31, 1989, and before January 1, 1993)

Calendar year 19 91

▶ See separate instructions. For Privacy Act Notice, see the Instructions for Form 1040.

OMB No. 1545-0020
Expires 8-31-93

Part 1.—General Information

1 Donor's first name and middle initial	2 Donor's last name	3 Social security number
Robert	Jones	172 : 30 : 7333
4 Address (number, street, and apartment number)		5 Domicile
23 Winding Way		Pennsylvania
6 City, state, and ZIP code		7 Citizenship
Philadelphia, PA 19087		USA

		Yes	No
8	If the donor died during the year, check here ▶ ☐ and enter date of death ______, 19 ___.		
9	If you received an extension of time to file this Form 709, check here ▶ ☐ and attach the Form 4868, 2688, 2350, or extension letter.		
10	Enter the total number of separate donees listed on Schedule A—count each person only once. ☐		
11	If you (the donor) filed a previous Form 709 (or 709-A), has your address changed since the last Form 709 (or 709-A) was filed?		X
12	Gifts by husband or wife to third parties.—Do you consent to have the gifts (including generation-skipping transfers) made by you and by your spouse to third parties during the calendar year considered as made one-half by each of you? (See instructions.) (If the answer is "Yes," the following information must be furnished and your spouse is to sign the consent shown below. If the answer is "No," skip lines 13–18 and go to Schedule A.)		
13	Name of consenting spouse — 14 SSN		
15	Were you married to one another during the entire calendar year? (See instructions.)		
16	If the answer to 15 is "No," check whether ☐ married ☐ divorced or ☐ widowed, and give date (see instructions) ▶		
17	Will a gift tax return for this calendar year be filed by your spouse?		

18 Consent of Spouse—I consent to have the gifts (and generation-skipping transfers) made by me and by my spouse to third parties during the calendar year considered as made one-half by each of us. We are both aware of the joint and several liability for tax created by the execution of this consent.

Consenting spouse's signature ▶ **Date ▶**

Part 2.—Tax Computation

		Line	Amount
1	Enter the amount from Schedule A, Part 3, line 15	1	2,550,000 00
2	Enter the amount from Schedule B, line 3	2	-0-
3	Total taxable gifts (add lines 1 and 2)	3	2,550,000 00
4	Tax computed on amount on line 3 (see Table for Computing Tax in separate instructions)	4	1,052,300 00
5	Tax computed on amount on line 2 (see Table for Computing Tax in separate instructions)	5	-0-
6	Balance (subtract line 5 from line 4)	6	1,052,300 00
7	Maximum unified credit (nonresident aliens, see instructions)	7	192,800 00
8	Enter the unified credit against tax allowable for all prior periods (from Sch. B, line 1, col. C)	8	-0-
9	Balance (subtract line 8 from line 7)	9	192,800 00
10	Enter 20% (.20) of the amount allowed as a specific exemption for gifts made after September 8, 1976, and before January 1, 1977 (see instructions)	10	-0-
11	Balance (subtract line 10 from line 9)	11	192,800 00
12	Unified credit (enter the smaller of line 6 or line 11)	12	192,800 00
13	Credit for foreign gift taxes (see instructions)	13	-0-
14	Total credits (add lines 12 and 13)	14	192,800 00
15	Balance (subtract line 14 from line 6) (do not enter less than zero)	15	859,500 00
16	Generation-skipping transfer taxes (from Schedule C, Part 3, col. H, total)	16	550,000 00
17	Total tax (add lines 15 and 16)	17	1,409,500 00
18	Gift and generation-skipping transfer taxes prepaid with extension of time to file	18	-0-
19	If line 18 is less than line 17, enter BALANCE DUE (see instructions)	19	1,409,500 00
20	If line 18 is greater than line 17, enter AMOUNT TO BE REFUNDED	20	

Please attach check or money order here

Under penalties of perjury, I declare that I have examined this return, including any accompanying schedules and statements, and to the best of my knowledge and belief it is true, correct, and complete. Declaration of preparer (other than donor) is based on all information of which preparer has any knowledge.

Donor's signature ▶ /s/ Robert Jones Date ▶ 3/22/92

Preparer's signature (other than donor) ▶ Date ▶

Preparer's address (other than donor) ▶

For Paperwork Reduction Act Notice, see page 1 of the separate instructions for this form. Form **709** (Rev. 10-90)

EXAMPLE *Grandparent's Gift to Grandchildren—Form 709, continued*

Form 709 (Rev. 10-90) Page 2

SCHEDULE A Computation of Taxable Gifts

Part 1.—Gifts Subject Only to Gift Tax. *Gifts less political organization, medical, and educational exclusions—see instructions*

A Item number	B Donee's name, relationship to donor (if any), and address and description of gift. If the gift was made by means of a trust, enter trust's identifying number below and attach a copy of the trust instrument. If the gift was securities, enter the CUSIP number(s), if available.	C Donor's adjusted basis of gift	D Date of gift	E Value at date of gift
1	None			

Part 2.—Gifts Which are Direct Skips and are Subject to Both Gift Tax and Generation-Skipping Transfer Tax. You must list the gifts in chronological order. *Gifts less political organization, medical, and educational exclusions—see instructions. (Also list here direct skips that are subject only to the GST tax at this time as the result of the termination of an "estate tax inclusion period." See instructions.)*

A Item number	B Donee's name, relationship to donor (if any), and address and description of gift. If the gift was made by means of a trust, enter trust's identifying number below and attach a copy of the trust instrument. If the gift was securities, enter the CUSIP number(s), if available.	C Donor's adjusted basis of gift	D Date of gift	E Value at date of gift
1	Trust under agreement of Robert Jones and First National Trust Bank, Philadelphia, PA for the benefit of Paulette Jones, Perry Jones and Jerry Jones (grandchildren)	1,000,000	1/91	2,000,000

Part 3.—Gift Tax Reconciliation

1	Total value of gifts of donor (add column E of Parts 1 and 2)	1	2,000,000	00
2	One-half of items ______ attributable to spouse (see instructions)	2	-0-	
3	Balance (subtract line 2 from line 1)	3	2,000,000	00
4	Gifts of spouse to be included (from Schedule A, Part 3, line 2 of spouse's return—see instructions). If any of the gifts included on this line are also subject to the generation-skipping transfer tax, check here ▶ ☐ and enter those gifts also on Schedule C, Part 1.	4		
5	Total gifts (add lines 3 and 4)	5	2,000,000	00
6	Total annual exclusions for gifts listed on Schedule A (including line 4, above) (see instructions)	6	-0-	
7	Total included amount of gifts (subtract line 6 from line 5)	7	2,000,000	00
	Deductions (see instructions)			
8	Gifts of interests to spouse for which a marital deduction will be claimed, based on items ______ of Schedule A ... 8			
9	Exclusions attributable to gifts on line 8 ... 9			
10	Marital deduction—subtract line 9 from line 8 ... 10			
11	Charitable deduction, based on items ______ to ______ less exclusions ... 11			
12	Total deductions—add lines 10 and 11	12	-0-	
13	Subtract line 12 from line 7	13	2,000,000	00
14	Generation-skipping transfer taxes payable with this Form 709 (from Schedule C, Part 3, col. H, Total)	14	550,000	00
15	Taxable gifts (add lines 13 and 14). Enter here and on line 1 of the Tax Computation on page 1	15	2,550,000	00

(If more space is needed, attach additional sheets of same size.)

EXAMPLE Grandparent's Gift to Grandchildren—Form 709, continued

Form 709 (Rev. 10-90) Page 3

SCHEDULE A Computation of Taxable Gifts (continued)

16 Terminable Interest (QTIP) Marital Deduction. (See instructions.)

☐ ◄ Check here if you elected, under the rules of section 2523(f), to include gifts of qualified terminable interest property on line 8, on page 2. Enter the item numbers (from Schedule A) of the gifts for which you made this election ► ________________

17 Election out of QTIP Treatment of Annuities

☐ ◄ Check here if you elect under section 2523(f)(6) to **NOT** treat as qualified terminable interest property any joint and survivor annuities that are reported on Schedule A and would otherwise be treated as qualified terminable interest property under section 2523(f). (See instructions.) Enter the item numbers (from Schedule A) for the annuities for which you are making this election ►

SCHEDULE B Gifts From Prior Periods

Did you (the donor) file gift tax returns for prior periods? (If "Yes," see instructions for completing Schedule B below.) . . . . ☐ Yes ☒ No

A Calendar year or calendar quarter (see instructions)	B Internal Revenue office where prior return was filed	C Amount of unified credit against gift tax for periods after December 31, 1976	D Amount of specific exemption for prior periods ending before January 1, 1977	E Amount of taxable gifts
	None			

1 Totals for prior periods (without adjustment for reduced specific exemption)	1	
2 Amount, if any, by which total specific exemption, line 1, column D, is more than $30,000	2	
3 Total amount of taxable gifts for prior periods (add amount, column E, line 1, and amount, if any, on line 2) (Enter here and on line 2 of the Tax Computation on page 1.)	3	-0-

SCHEDULE C Computation of Generation-Skipping Transfer Tax

Note: *Inter vivos direct skips which are completely excluded by the GST exemption must still be fully reported (including value and exemptions claimed) on Schedule C.*

Part 1.—Generation-Skipping Transfers

A Item No. (from Schedule A, Part 2, col. A)	B Value (from Schedule A, Part 2, col. E)	C Split Gifts (enter ½ of col. B) (see instructions)	D Subtract col. C from col. B	E Nontaxable portion of transfer	F Net Transfer (subtract col. E from col. D)
1	2,000,000				2,000,000
2					
3					
4					
5					
6					
If you elected gift splitting and your spouse was required to file a separate Form 709 (see the instructions for "Split Gifts"), you must enter all of the gifts shown on Schedule A, Part 2, of your spouse's Form 709 here. In column C, enter the item number of each gift in the order it appears in column A of your spouse's Schedule A, Part 2. We have preprinted the prefix "S-" to distinguish your spouse's item numbers from your own when you complete column A of Schedule C, Part 3. In column D, for each gift, enter the amount reported in column C, Schedule C, Part 1, of your spouse's Form 709.		Split gifts from spouse's Form 709 (enter item number)	Value included from spouse's Form 709		
		S-			
		S-			
		S-			
		S-			
		S-			
		S-			
		S-			
		S-			

(If more space is needed, attach additional sheets of same size.)

EXAMPLE Grandparent's Gift to Grandchildren—Form 709, continued

Form 709 (Rev. 10-90) Page 4

Part 2.—GST Exemption Reconciliation (Code section 2631) and Section 2652(a)(3) Election

Check box ▶ ☐ if you are making a section 2652(a)(3) (special QTIP) election (see instructions)

Enter the item numbers (from Schedule A) of the gifts for which you are making this election ▶

1	Maximum allowable exemption	1	$1,000,000
2	Total exemption used for periods before filing this return	2	-0-
3	Exemption available for this return (subtract line 2 from line 1)	3	1,000,000
4	Exemption claimed on this return (from Part 3, col. C total, below)	4	1,000,000
5	Exemption allocated to transfers not shown on Part 3, below. You must attach a Notice of Allocation. (See instructions.)	5	-0-
6	Add lines 4 and 5	6	1,000,000
7	Exemption available for future transfers (subtract line 6 from line 3)	7	-0-

Part 3.—Tax Computation

A Item No. (from Schedule C, Part 1)	B Net transfer (from Schedule C, Part 1, col. F)	C GST Exemption Allocated	D Divide col. C by col. B	E Inclusion Ratio (subtract col. D from 1.000)	F Maximum Estate Tax Rate	G Applicable Rate (multiply col. E by col. F)	H Generation-Skipping Transfer Tax (multiply col. B by col. G)
1	2,000,000	1,000,000	.5	.5	55% (.55)	27.5	550,000
2					55% (.55)		
3					55% (.55)		
4					55% (.55)		
5					55% (.55)		
6					55% (.55)		
7					55% (.55)		
8					55% (.55)		
					55% (.55)		
					55% (.55)		
					55% (.55)		
					55% (.55)		
					55% (.55)		
					55% (.55)		
					55% (.55)		
					55% (.55)		
Total exemption claimed. Enter here and on line 4, Part 2, above. May not exceed line 3, Part 2, above		1,000,000	**Total generation-skipping transfer tax.** Enter here, on line 14 of Schedule A, Part 3, and on line 16 of the Tax Computation on page 1				550,000

(If more space is needed, attach additional sheets of same size.)

*U.S. GPO:1991-518-940/20362

CHAPTER FIVE

The Federal Estate Tax and the Federal Estate Tax Return

On October 4, 1976, President Gerald R. Ford approved the Estate and Gift Tax Reform Act of 1976. That act made comprehensive, complex, and significant changes in the federal estate tax provisions of the Internal Revenue Code of 1954. Since the 1976 Tax Reform Act, the Internal Revenue Code and Treasury Regulations have been revised several times. The most recent tax law changes were made in 1986, 1988, 1989, and 1990. These changes have forced everyone in tax-related fields to study the most recent regulations constantly. It is strongly recommended that the legal assistant practicing in this field attend tax seminars and read pertinent literature as often as possible. This chapter is written pursuant to the tax laws in effect in 1990. It is intended to be a lesson in basic tax concepts, although many specific examples are used to teach these concepts.

The federal estate tax is imposed upon all property owned at the time of death as well as all property in which the decedent had an interest or over which he or she maintained some control at the time of death. Whereas most state death taxes are determined to a certain extent by the relationship of the beneficiary to the decedent or the amount the beneficiary is to receive, the federal estate tax looks directly to the decedent's total estate itself and begins the determination of the amount of tax due from there.

The decedent's total estate is known as the total gross estate and comprises the following:[1] all property in which the decedent

1. The categories of property and property interests set forth above have their origins in various sections of the Internal Revenue Code and are in turn reported at various schedules of the Form 706, United States Estate Tax Return, and references to each have been provided. Although the format of the Form 706 may change from time to time, the changes are most often of form and not of substance as the underlying principles of taxation, as represented by the pertinent sections of the Internal Revenue Code, remain the same. The actual format of the Form 706, United States Estate Tax Return, which is commonly referred to as the federal estate tax return, is of secondary importance so long as the intricacies of the federal estate tax are fully understood. However, as an illustrative aid, throughout this chapter reference will be made to the various schedules of the federal estate tax return that appear throughout the chapter, so that the student will have an opportunity to better apply some of the concepts discussed and presented.

had an interest;[2] dower or curtesy interests;[3] adjustments for gifts made within three years of decedent's death;[4] transfers with retained life estates;[5] transfers taking effect at death;[6] revocable transfers;[7] annuities;[8] joint interests;[9] powers of appointment;[10] and proceeds of life insurance.[11]

After all of the categories enumerated above are totaled to compute the total gross estate, the decedent's taxable estate,[12] is computed by subtracting from the gross estate the various items that are permitted as deductions. These are areas of permissible deductions: funeral expenses and administration expenses;[13] claims against the estate, indebtedness, and mortgages;[14] casualty losses;[15] transfers for public, charitable, and religious uses;[16] and bequests to the surviving spouse (marital deduction).[17]

Next, all gifts made after December 31, 1976, are added to the taxable estate. On this total amount a tentative tax is computed. The tentative tax less the aggregate gift taxes payable on post December 31, 1976, gifts is the basis against which the "unified credit" is applied. After allowance for the unified credit additional credits may be taken for state death taxes, as computed from the table provided in separate instructions to Form 706; for federal gift taxes paid in certain cases; for foreign death taxes; and for taxes paid as a result of prior transfers.

Under the unified tax system (unifying estate and gift taxes so that both tax rates are the same) a unified credit of $192,800 applies to estates of decedents, and gifts made during and after 1988. This credit was phased in as follows:

Year of Death	Unified Credit	Exemption Equivalent
1982	$ 62,800	$ 225,000
1983	79,300	275,000
1984	96,300	325,000
1985	121,800	400,000

2. Internal Revenue Code (IRC) § 2033, Form 706 Schedules A (Real Estate), A-1 2032A valuation (Special Use Valuation), B (Stocks and Bonds), C (Mortgages, Notes, and Cash), and F (Other Miscellaneous Property).
3. IRC § 2034, Form 706 Schedule M.
4. IRC § 2035, Form 706 Schedule G.
5. IRC § 2036, Form 706 Schedule G.
6. IRC § 2037, Form 706 Schedule G.
7. IRC § 2038, Form 706 Schedule G.
8. IRC § 2039, Form 706 Schedule I.
9. IRC § 2040, Form 706 Schedule E.
10. IRC § 2041, Form 706 Schedule H.
11. IRC § 2042, Form 706 Schedule D.
12. Defined by § 2051 of the Internal Revenue Code.
13. IRC § 2053, Form 706 Schedule J.
14. IRC § 2053, Form 706 Schedule K.
15. IRC § 2054, Form 706 Schedule L.
16. IRC § 2055, Form 706 Schedule O.
17. IRC § 2056, Form 706 Schedule M.

Year of Death	Unified Credit	Exemption Equivalent
1986	155,800	500,000
1987	192,800	600,000

Thus if the gross estate and the adjusted taxable gifts (made after 12/31/78) are less than $600,000, the executor is not required to file a federal estate tax return. If the decedent, however, made gifts prior to death and used some or all of his unified credit against the gift tax (this applies to gifts made after 1977), decedent's unified credit may, in effect, be reduced or completely exhausted.

The federal estate tax rates are severe. The tax rates, for a taxable estate, start at 37% and increase to 55% for estates or gifts in excess of three million dollars. For estates over ten million dollars, there is an additional tax of 5% for the amount in excess of ten million dollars. This additional tax on very large estates effectively takes away the $600,000 exemption. Because the tax rates are so severe, it is important to offer clients effective estate planning for their individual estates prior to their deaths.

Federal estate tax returns must be filed within nine months after the date of the decedent's death.[18] In most cases, and for virtually all large estates, the federal estate tax return will not be prepared in final form and filed until shortly before it is due. However, several steps that relate directly and indirectly to the federal estate tax return will have been taken during the early period of the administration of the estate.

Preliminary Step—The Application for the Federal Employer Identification Number

Early in the period of the administration of every estate, a form called an "Application for Federal Employer Identification Number" should be processed.[19] The only purpose in filing this printed form is to obtain a federal taxpayer identification ("FEIN") for the estate. Although the decedent's social security number will appear on the federal estate tax return when it is filed, the taxpayer identification number will appear on any fiduciary income tax returns that may be filed by the estate during the period of administration and is utilized by the payors of dividends, interest, and other income items in the same manner as an individual's social security number.

In filing this document with the Internal Revenue Service (and, as a general rule, in filing any document with any taxing authority), it is advisable to obtain a receipt that will serve as evidence that the necessary documents have been filed.

18. IRC § 6075(a).

19. See Chapter Two, "Application for Employer Identification Number."

EXAMPLE
Cover Letter for Documents Filed with the Internal Revenue Service

District Director of Internal Revenue
6th & Arch Streets
Philadelphia, PA 19106

Re: Estate of Lawrence Dain, Deceased

Dear Sir:

Enclosed herewith please find an Application for Federal Employer Identification Number that has been signed by one of the Executors of the above-captioned estate.

Kindly acknowledge receipt of this document by signing the enclosed copy of this letter and returning it to the undersigned in the self-addressed, stamped envelope that is enclosed for your convenience.

Very truly yours,
/s/Prudence Holloway
Prudence Holloway

Assembling Facts

The preparation of a federal estate tax return requires a careful analysis of all of the records and documents relating to the estate, as well as the records and documents relating to the financial activities of the decedent during lifetime that may have an effect on the size of his estate for federal estate tax purposes. It cannot be emphasized enough that no short-cuts to thorough examination should be taken. Without exaggeration, the preparer of the federal estate tax return will be as familiar, for all practical purposes, with the decedent's asset-and-liability situation as the decedent himself.[20]

The estate tax return itself, as previously mentioned, is a very extensive and detailed document. Of even greater significance, however, is the fact that all federal estate tax returns are, at minimum, reviewed by the Internal Revenue Service to determine whether a more detailed "field audit" is required. Virtually all large estates and many modest estates undergo such a "field audit," which involves a detailed examination by an estate tax agent who will require the representative of the estate to substantiate all of the information set forth on the return. The examining agents, all of whom are lawyers, are generally highly skilled. Careful and complete preparation of the federal estate tax return is essential in order to be adequately prepared for an audit.

20. See Chapter Three for a more complete treatment of this matter.

Three major sources of information are useful in assembling the facts necessary for the preparation of the federal estate tax return.

Estate Checkbook, Journal, and Ledger A review of the financial records of the estate will disclose much of the information that will ultimately be required. Chapter Two, which includes a discussion of record keeping, presents the proper manner of recording an estate's financial transactions. If the records have been kept accurately, they will disclose many of the estate's assets. The estate checkbook should also directly reflect most of the decedent's debts and the expenses of the administration of the estate, at least to the extent that these items have been paid out of the estate checking account prior to the time the federal estate tax return is prepared.

Review of File The most important source of information will be the file that was opened at the time the estate came into existence. In reviewing the file, each and every letter and all memoranda and other documents should be read. Frequently the existence of an asset or liability will be reflected only in one letter or one memorandum in the file. Painstaking review of every document is a necessity.

Analysis of Decedent's Lifetime Papers In addition to reviewing all documentation relating to the estate, it is important to review any wills or trusts established by other persons in which the decedent possessed any interest at the time of death, as well as to review any trusts that may have been created by the decedent during lifetime. In addition, any gift tax returns that were filed by the decedent during lifetime, the decedent's federal income tax returns for the three years preceding death, and all of the cancelled checks from the decedent's checking accounts for the three years preceding death should be carefully analyzed. Subsequent portions of this chapter will discuss the importance of these documents.

It is suggested that the easiest way to collate the data that will be collected from the foregoing sources is on a rough copy of the actual estate tax return. After preparing several returns, the lawyer's assistant will become quite familiar with the tax return and will be able to place items immediately on the appropriate schedule of the return as they are discovered.

PREPARING THE RETURN

A completed federal estate tax return reflects a comprehensive understanding of federal estate tax law. The following discussions will attempt to analyze and present the various federal estate tax law provisions as they relate to the actual financial data disclosed on the federal estate tax return. In this fashion the student will be exposed to the federal estate tax theory as well as the very practical consideration of how this is reflected on the document actually filed with and examined by the Internal Revenue Service.

With the exception of the portion of page one that relates to the final computation of tax and cannot be completed until the entire return has been filled out, the initial pages of the federal estate tax return request background information. Please refer to the reproduction of page one of the estate tax return (Form 706) which follows, with the upper portion completed.

The decedent's Social Security number may be obtained most easily from the death certificate or from copies of lifetime federal income tax returns. The address of the executor, which is shown on page one of Form 706, will determine the address to which all communications will be forwarded by the Internal Revenue Service, and for this reason it might be advisable to utilize the attorney's address to avoid the possibility that a document forwarded to the executor might not reach the attorney. If there is no corporate executor, the address of the lawyer representing the executors should be inserted as shown in the Example so that all communications will be sent directly to the lawyer. To eliminate any delay in receipt of correspondence, a power of attorney Form 2848, allowing the attorney to represent the estate in its dealings with the IRS, should be filed at the time of filing the federal estate tax return.[21]

A reproduction of page two of the estate tax return relating to general information about the decedent appears along with a brief discussion of its elements.

The Elections by the Executor (Part 3, Form 706) are a summary of information contained in the return. Typically, these elections are made after the return is complete and the estate assets have been thoroughly investigated. All boxes should be checked. If the answer is "yes," a separate schedule is often required to be attached to the return. We will briefly review the elections as shown on the return. These concepts will be discussed in more detail in other sections of the chapter.

The first election in Part 3 concerns alternate valuation. The executor of the estate may elect to value all of the property included in the decedent's gross estate as of six months after the decedent's date of death where the property still exists as of that date, or as of the date of distribution, sale, or exchange of such property as it is distributed, sold, exchanged, or otherwise dis-

21. See sample Form 2848 under "Exhibits to Be Submitted," later in this chapter.

EXAMPLE *Form 706, United States Estate (and Generation-Skipping Transfer) Tax Return, Page One*

Form **706** (Rev. July 1990) Department of the Treasury Internal Revenue Service

United States Estate (and Generation-Skipping Transfer) Tax Return

Estate of a citizen or resident of the United States (see separate instructions). To be filed for decedents dying after December 31, 1989, and before January 1, 1993.
For Paperwork Reduction Act Notice, see page 1 of the instructions.

OMB No. 1545-0015 Expires 6-30-93

Part 1.—Decedent and Executor

1a Decedent's first name and middle initial (and maiden name, if any): Peter	1b Decedent's last name: Chessman		2 Decedent's social security no.: 045 : 96 : 2487
3a Domicile at time of death (county and state): Philadelphia, PA	3b Year domicile established: 1950	4 Date of birth: 8/1/1905	5 Date of death: May 3, 1991
6a Name of executor (see instructions): Sandra Chessman, Michael Scott, Esq.	6b Executor's address (number and street including apartment number or rural route; city, town, or post office; state; and ZIP code): c/o Michael Scott, Esq., 401 Walnut Street, 20th Floor, Philadelphia, PA 19106		
6c Executor's social security number (see instructions): 123 : 45 : 6789			
7a Name and location of court where will was probated or estate administered: Register of Wills, Philadelphia County, Philadelphia, PA			7b Case number: 15623 of 1991
8 If decedent died testate, check here ▶ [X] and attach a certified copy of the will.		9 If Form 4768 is attached, check here ▶ [ ]	
10 If Schedule R-1 is attached, check here ▶ [ ]			

Part 2.—Tax Computation

1	Total gross estate (from Part 5, Recapitulation, page 3, item 10)		1
2	Total allowable deductions (from Part 5, Recapitulation, page 3, item 20)		2
3	Taxable estate (subtract line 2 from line 1)		3
4	Adjusted taxable gifts (total taxable gifts (within the meaning of section 2503) made by the decedent after December 31, 1976, other than gifts that are includible in decedent's gross estate (section 2001(b))		4
5	Add lines 3 and 4		5
6	Tentative tax on the amount on line 5 from Table A in the instructions		6
7a	If line 5 exceeds $10,000,000, enter the lesser of line 5 or $21,040,000. If line 5 is $10,000,000 or less, skip lines 7a and 7b and enter zero on line 7c	7a	
b	Subtract $10,000,000 from line 7a	7b	
c	Enter 5% (.05) of line 7b		7c
8	Total tentative tax (add lines 6 and 7c)		8
9	Total gift tax payable with respect to gifts made by the decedent after December 31, 1976. Include gift taxes paid by the decedent's spouse for such spouse's share of split gifts (section 2513) only if the decedent was the donor of these gifts and they are includible in the decedent's gross estate (see instructions)		9
10	Gross estate tax (subtract line 9 from line 8)		10
11	Unified credit against estate tax from Table B in the instructions	11	
12	Adjustment to unified credit. (This adjustment may not exceed $6,000. See instructions.)	12	
13	Allowable unified credit (subtract line 12 from line 11)		13
14	Subtract line 13 from line 10 (but do not enter less than zero)		14
15	Credit for state death taxes. Do not enter more than line 14. Compute credit by using amount on line 3 less $60,000. See Table C in the instructions and **attach credit evidence** (see instructions)		15
16	Subtract line 15 from line 14		16
17	Credit for Federal gift taxes on pre-1977 gifts (section 2012)(attach computation)	17	
18	Credit for foreign death taxes (from Schedule(s) P). (Attach Form(s) 706CE)	18	
19	Credit for tax on prior transfers (from Schedule Q)	19	
20	Total (add lines 17, 18, and 19)		20
21	Net estate tax (subtract line 20 from line 16)		21
22	Generation-skipping transfer taxes (from Schedule R, Part 2, line 10)		22
23	Section 4980A increased estate tax (from Schedule S, Part I, line 17) (see instructions)		23
24	Total transfer taxes (add lines 21, 22, and 23)		24
25	Prior payments. Explain in an attached statement	25	
26	United States Treasury bonds redeemed in payment of estate tax	26	
27	Total (add lines 25 and 26)		27
28	Balance due (or overpayment) (subtract line 27 from line 24)		28

Under penalties of perjury, I declare that I have examined this return, including accompanying schedules and statements, and to the best of my knowledge and belief, it is true, correct, and complete. Declaration of preparer other than the executor is based on all information of which preparer has any knowledge.

Signature(s) of executor(s) ______ Date ______

Signature of preparer other than executor ______ Address (and ZIP code) ______ Date ______

EXAMPLE Form 706, Page Two

Form 706 (Rev. 7-90)

Estate of: Peter Chessman

Part 3.—Elections by the Executor

Please check the "Yes" or "No" box for each question.	Yes	No
1 Do you elect alternate valuation?	X	
2 Do you elect special use valuation? If "Yes," you must complete and attach Schedule A-1		X
3 Do you elect to pay the taxes in installments as described in section 6166? If "Yes," you must attach the additional information described in the instructions.		X
4 Do you elect to postpone the part of the taxes attributable to a reversionary or remainder interest as described in section 6163?		X

Part 4.—General Information (Note: *Please attach the necessary supplemental documents.* **You must attach the death certificate.**)

Authorization to receive confidential tax information under Regulations section 601.502(c)(3)(ii), to act as the estate's representative before the Internal Revenue Service, and to make written or oral presentations on behalf of the estate if return prepared by an attorney, accountant, or enrolled agent for the executor:

Name of representative (print or type)	State	Address (number, street, and room or suite no., city, state, and ZIP code)
Michael Scott	PA	401 Walnut Street, 20th Floor Philadelphia, PA 19106

I declare that I am the ☒ attorney ☐ accountant ☐ enrolled agent **(you must check the applicable box)** for the executor and prepared this return for the executor. I am not under suspension or disbarment from practice before the Internal Revenue Service and am qualified to practice in the state shown above.

Signature	CAF number	Date	Telephone number

1 Death certificate number and issuing authority (attach a copy of the death certificate to this return).
#

2 Decedent's business or occupation. If retired, check here ▶ ☐ and state decedent's former business or occupation.
Executive

3 Marital status of the decedent at time of death:
☒ Married
☐ Widow or widower—Name, SSN and date of death of deceased spouse ▶
☐ Single
☐ Legally separated
☐ Divorced—Date divorce decree became final ▶

4a Surviving spouse's name	4b Social security number	4c Amount received (see instructions)
Sandra Chessman	123 ⋮ 45 ⋮ 6789	$277,265.31

5 Individuals (other than the surviving spouse), trusts, or other estates who receive benefits from the estate (do not include charitable beneficiaries shown in Schedule O) (see instructions). For Privacy Act Notice (applicable to individual beneficiaries only), see the Instructions for Form 1040.

Name of individual, trust, or estate receiving $5,000 or more	Identifying number	Relationship to decedent	Amount (see instructions)
Linda Chessman	123-67-9177	daughter	22,734.69
		50% Residue of the estate	305,000.00
Laura Chessman	123-67-9778	daughter	20,000.00
		50% Residue of the estate	305,000.00
Peter Chessman Parrot Foundation	54-22179	(None) Charitable Bequest	10,000.00
All unascertainable beneficiaries and those who receive less than $5,000 ▶			
Total			940,000.00

(Continued on next page) **Page 2**

posed of within six months of the decedent's date of death.[22] The purpose of alternate valuation is to give the executor the option of revaluing the assets in case they have declined in value during the six months. It is important to note here that you may not elect alternate valuation unless the election will decrease both the value of the gross estate and the net estate. It may sound strange to want a higher valuation, but consider the case where there is a nontaxable estate, or an estate with a small tax due, and the property is passing to beneficiaries with much larger estates. The property that they are receiving from the first estate will be eventually valued in the beneficiaries' estates or sold during their lifetime. They will want the basis of that property to be as high as possible, in order to realize less capital gain or estate taxes. The IRS did not want taxpayers to use this "loophole" and thus established the regulation that the valuation must result in a decrease of the size of the gross estate.

The second election concerns special-use valuation. The box will be checked "yes" if Schedule A-1 is attached to the return. This is when the executor may elect to value property at its present use rather than its highest and best use. For example, a family farm may have a much higher value if it is sold to a developer who intends to build a shopping center on the land. However, if the family wishes to continue farming, it would not be fair to have to pay taxes on the higher value. There are several restrictions to using the special-use valuation: the property must continue its present use for ten years and be owned and managed by a qualified heir. The value may not be reduced by more than $750,000.

The third election concerns deferred/installment payments (IRC § 6166). The executor may elect to defer the Form 706 tax attributable to a closely held business for up to 5 years and then pay in ten installments. The interest rate is only 4% for the first million dollars in value. Again, there are many restrictions to qualifying for this election.

The fourth election, postponing the tax on reversions and remainders per § 6163, allows the estate to postpone the payment of the 706 tax until six months after the property comes into the possession of the estate. Interest still accrues on the tax so unless there is a cash flow problem for the estate, there is no advantage in deferring the tax payment.

Election number five, transferring the tax liability for certain employee stock-ownership plans, allows the executor to transfer the liability while preserving the § 6166 election (to pay the tax in installments).

The General Information (Part 4, Form 706) concerns personal information about the decedent (see next Example). There is

22. IRC § 2032.

EXAMPLE *Form 706, Page Three*

Form 706 (Rev. 7-90)

Part 4.—General Information *(continued)*

	Please check the "Yes" or "No" box for each question.	Yes	No
6	Does the gross estate contain any section 2044 property (qualified terminable interest property (QTIP) from a prior gift or estate)(see instructions)? (Q. Tip.)		X
7a	Have Federal gift tax returns ever been filed? If "Yes," please attach copies of the returns, if available, and furnish the following information:		X
7b	Period(s) covered — 7c Internal Revenue office(s) where filed		
	If you answer "Yes" to any of questions 8–16, you must attach additional information as described in the instructions.		
8a	Was there any insurance on the decedent's life that is not included on the return as part of the gross estate?		X
b	Did the decedent own any insurance on the life of another that is not included in the gross estate?		X
9	Did the decedent at the time of death own any property as a joint tenant with right of survivorship in which (1) one or more of the other joint tenants was someone other than the decedent's spouse, and (2) less than the full value of the property is included on the return as part of the gross estate? If "Yes," you must complete and attach Schedule E		X
10	Did the decedent, at the time of death, own any interest in a partnership or unincorporated business or any stock in an inactive or closely held corporation?		X
11a	Did the decedent make any transfer described in section 2035, 2036, 2037, or 2038 (see the instructions for Schedule G)? If "Yes," you must complete and attach Schedule G	X	
b	If "Yes," was it a valuation freeze subject to section 2036(c)?		X
12	Were there in existence at the time of the decedent's death:		
a	Any trusts created by the decedent during his or her lifetime?		X
b	Any trusts not created by the decedent under which the decedent possessed any power, beneficial interest, or trusteeship?	X	
13	Did the decedent ever possess, exercise, or release any general power of appointment? If "Yes," you must complete and attach Schedule H.		X
14	Was the marital deduction computed under the transitional rule of Public Law 97-34, section 403(e)(3) (Economic Recovery Tax Act of 1981)? If "Yes," attach a separate computation of the marital deduction, enter the amount on item 18 of the Recapitulation, and note on item 18 "computation attached."		X
15	Was the decedent, immediately before death, receiving an annuity described in the "General" paragraph of the instructions for Schedule I? If "Yes," you must complete and attach Schedule I.		X
16	Did the decedent have a total "excess retirement accumulation" (as defined in section 4980A(d)) in qualified employer plans and individual retirement plans? If "Yes," you must complete and attach Schedule S.		X

Part 5.—Recapitulation

Item number	Gross estate	Alternate value	Value at date of death
1	Schedule A—Real Estate		
2	Schedule B—Stocks and Bonds		
3	Schedule C—Mortgages, Notes, and Cash		
4	Schedule D—Insurance on the Decedent's Life (attach Form(s) 712)		
5	Schedule E—Jointly Owned Property (attach Form(s) 712 for life insurance)		
6	Schedule F—Other Miscellaneous Property (attach Form(s) 712 for life insurance)		
7	Schedule G—Transfers During Decedent's Life (attach Form(s) 712 for life insurance)		
8	Schedule H—Powers of Appointment		
9	Schedule I—Annuities		
10	Total gross estate (add items 1 through 9). Enter here and on line 1 of the Tax Computation.		

Item number	Deductions	Amount
11	Schedule J—Funeral Expenses and Expenses Incurred in Administering Property Subject to Claims	
12	Schedule K—Debts of the Decedent	
13	Schedule K—Mortgages and Liens	
14	Total of items 11 through 13	
15	Allowable amount of deductions from item 14 (see the instructions for item 15 of the Recapitulation)	
16	Schedule L—Net Losses During Administration	
17	Schedule L—Expenses Incurred in Administering Property Not Subject to Claims	
18	Schedule M—Bequests, etc., to Surviving Spouse	
19	Schedule O—Charitable, Public, and Similar Gifts and Bequests	
20	Total allowable deductions (add items 15 through 19). Enter here and on line 2 of the Tax Computation	

Page 3

a portion at the bottom of the page showing the amount received by the spouse and all other beneficiaries receiving $5,000 or more. If the beneficiaries are receiving a specific bequest, it is relatively easy to calculate the amounts they will be receiving. If they are residuary beneficiaries or receiving a percentage of the estate, it will be more difficult. Generally, if the exact amount of the beneficiary's interest cannot be ascertained, a brief description of that interest, stated in terms of a fractional portion of the net estate, is satisfactory. The questions continue on page three of the tax return. These are generally answered after the preparer has completed the majority of the return and has a thorough knowledge of the assets in the estate.

The last section is the recapitulation. This is a summary of all the schedules and is completed after all the information has been entered on the return. The first page of the return, showing the tax computation, is completed last.

Schedule A—Real Estate[23]

Having completed the preliminary information, we turn to the first of many schedules contained in the estate tax return. The first of these is Schedule A.

Forms of Ownership of Real Property The decedent's ownership interest in real property may take any one of several forms.

Outright Ownership If the real property in question is owned solely by the decedent, the property will be listed on Schedule A and its full value as of the date of death will be set forth in the right-hand column.

Tenancy in Common A tenancy in common exists where two or more persons each own an undivided interest in the entire property. This means that while there is more than one owner of the property, the interests are not physically distinct but are fractional interests in the whole.

Under the law of most states, a tenancy in common exists when two or more persons own an interest in property and the deed or other document conveying the ownership interest to them does not clearly indicate the form of ownership. Thus, if the property were owned by "Lawrence Dain and Martin Murray" without any additional words indicating the type of interest owned by the parties, they would be deemed to be tenants in common in most states. If the deed does not specifically indicate the form of

23. IRC § 2033.

EXAMPLE *Form 706, Schedule A—Real Estate*

Form 706 (Rev. 7-90)

Estate of: Peter Chessman

SCHEDULE A—Real Estate

(For jointly owned property that must be disclosed on Schedule E, see the Instructions for Schedule E.)
(Real estate that is part of a sole proprietorship should be shown on Schedule F. Real estate that is included in the gross estate under section 2035, 2036, 2037, or 2038 should be shown on Schedule G. Real estate that is included in the gross estate under section 2041 should be shown on Schedule H.)
(If you elect section 2032A valuation, you must complete Schedule A and Schedule A-1.)

Item number	Description	Alternate valuation date	Alternate value	Value at date of death
1	Apartment building, 1598 Boat Street, Philadelphia, PA, per appraisal of Samuelson Realtors, copy of which is attached			40,000
	Not disposed of within six months following death	11/3/91	50,000	
	Rent payable on first day of each month at $245 per month per tenant			
	Rent due and payable at date of death	11/3/91	735	735
2	Agreement to purchase lot, 1203 Loyola Avenue, Philadelphia, PA. Agreement of sale dated April 20, 1991, by Stanley Brown and the decedent; settlement date May 29, 1991. Valued at purchase price			10,000
	Not disposed of within six months following death	11/3/91	10,000	
3	House and lot, 135 Shoreline Drive, Ocean City, NJ, valued per appraisal of Beach Realty, which is attached. Owned by decedent and his brother, Robert Chessman, as tenants in common, total value $50,000			34,000
	Not disposed of within six months following death	11/3/91	34,340	
	Total from continuation schedule(s) (or additional sheet(s)) attached to this schedule			
	TOTAL. (Also enter on Part 5, Recapitulation, page 3, at item 1.)		95,075	84,735

(If more space is needed, attach the continuation schedule from the end of this package or additional sheets of the same size.)

Schedule A—Page 4

ownership, the attorney handling the estate should be consulted, as a matter of precaution, for a determination of whether the interest is a tenancy in common or a joint tenancy under the law of the state in which the property is located.

A tenancy in common interest in real property would be reported on Schedule A. Thus, for example, if a property where owned by the decedent and some other person as "tenants in common," the federal estate tax return for the decedent's estate would report a percentage interest (whether one-half or any other percentage specified in the deed) in the property and would list this interest on Schedule A, with the value of the decedent's share being shown in the right-hand column. In some cases it is significant to know that the value of such an interest for federal estate tax purposes may be less than a straight mathematical division of the market value of the whole piece of real estate. This reflects the difficulty of selling a fractional interest in a tenancy in common.

Joint Tenancy A joint tenancy is similar to a tenancy in common in that two or more owners possess an undivided interest in the property. The primary distinction between a tenancy in common and a joint tenancy, at least with respect to the preparation of the federal estate tax return, is that a joint tenancy involves a right of survivorship. This means that if one of the joint tenants dies, the ownership of the entire property automatically passes to the surviving joint tenant or tenants without the necessity of any payment to the estate of the decedent by the surviving joint tenant. Because of the survivorship feature, as stated above, a joint tenancy will not be presumed. The joint tenancy must be specifically spelled out in the deed or other instrument conveying the property. Thus, the deed for a property that was owned jointly by to or more persons would indicate that the property had been conveyed to "Lawrence Dain and Martin Murray, as joint tenants with right of survivorship."

Although the estate of the deceased joint tenant has no interest in the property following his death, the deceased joint tenant's interest in the property prior to death will be subject to tax and reported under Schedule E, which relates to jointly owned property. A more detailed discussion of jointly owned property will be set forth in the section of this chapter relating to § 2040 of the Internal Revenue Code (Joint Interests) and Schedule E.

Tenancy by the Entireties In essence, a tenancy by the entireties is a joint tenancy where the owners of the property are husband and wife. Although there are distinctions between joint tenancies and tenancies by the entireties in terms of the rights of the owners during their lifetimes, these differences are largely irrelevant for the purpose of this text. Unlike the situation existing with joint ownership between unmarried individuals, any property that was titled in the names of the decedent and his wife would, under the law of most jurisdictions, be considered to be owned by them jointly with a right of survivorship, i.e., as tenants by the entireties. Property owned in this manner by husband and wife is also reportable in the estate of the deceased spouse on Schedule E of the federal estate tax return even though the interest of the deceased spouse passes at death to the surviving spouse.

Method of Reporting Real Estate The method by which property to be reported on Schedule A should be listed and described is set forth in the Internal Revenue Service Form 706 instructions with two examples, one assuming date of death valuation and the other assuming alternate valuation. The example relating to alternate valuation should not be reviewed until after the discussion of alternate valuation that appears in the next section of this chapter. In regard to the date of death valuation example, it should be noted that rent that is due on the real property but uncollected at the date of death, as well as rent accrued to that time but not yet due, is properly reported with the real property to which it relates. If the value set forth on the federal estate tax return for a parcel of real estate is based on an appraisal, a copy of the appraisal and an explanation of the basis of the appraisal should be attached to the return. A professionally prepared appraisal will contain its own statement of the basis on which value was set.

Methods of describing real estate vary from place to place. The type of description appropriate for the federal estate tax return is one that makes it relatively easy for the auditing agent to check the precise form of ownership from the public records. Because of the real property–recording system in use, in some areas it is most helpful to give lot and block numbers while in others it is customary to give the book and page numbers of the last recorded deed. It is usually not necessary to provide a surveyor's description of the land in the federal estate tax return. Until you are certain of the method in use in the area in which you work, guidance should be sought from the lawyer for whom you are working.

Valuation of Real Estate Valuation of real estate is largely a matter of expert judgment, and no attempt should be made to ascribe a value to any particular parcel without consultation with the attorney who represents the estate. Under certain circumstances, a value reported on the federal estate tax return may not be supported by any appraisal. The assessed value of real property for local real estate tax purposes may, in some instances and in some localities, be helpful if the assessed value is based on the market value of the property or some percentage thereof. Furthermore, if the property is a residential property in a neighborhood that contains many similar, if not identical, homes, the value may be determined on the basis of recent sales of similar properties, thereby eliminating the expense of an appraisal. Generally speaking, however, for commercial real estate and for high-priced residential real estate an appraisal of some sort will be necessary to satisfy the examining agent that the value returned is fair and reasonable. Such an appraisal may merely be a simple letter prepared by a neighborhood real estate broker, in the case of residential real estate. Normally, in the case of commercial property one would obtain an elaborate, indexed appraisal from a qualified appraiser or commercial broker who will consider, among other factors, the physical condition of any buildings erected on the property, the history and future of the neighborhood, the rental income that the property produces, and the costs of ordinary maintenance and repair. An example of a residential appraisal and a commercial property appraisal follows.

EXAMPLE
Appraisals

RESIDENTIAL APPRAISAL

Appraisal of Premises

2451 Dabney Drive, Merion
Lower Merion Township
Montgomery County, Pennsylvania
Made for Estate of Martin Murray
July 18, 1991

LOT SIZE: 127 ft. frontage x 114 ft. rear; 275 ft. left line depth and 250 ft. right line depth, minus recently conveyed portion of rear.

ASSESSMENT: 14.1

IMPROVEMENTS: 60-year-old 3-story residence of granite construction, with slate roof. 2-car detached garage of same construction.

CONTENTS: *1st floor:* Huge entrance hall with beamed ceiling and fireplace; parlor with fireplace and built-ins; French doors to screened porch; dining room with beamed ceiling and fireplace; cloak room, powder room; butler's pantry with built-ins; breakfast room off dining room; original white-tile kitchen; pantry; lavatory; laundry; back stairs and rear porch.

2nd floor: Master bedroom with fireplace, sitting room with fireplace and build-ins, and master bath of color red ceramic tile, plus three large bedrooms and additional ceramic tile bath, rear hall with linen closets.

3rd floor: 3 bedrooms, 1 white-tile bath and storeroom.

Basement: Full, with outside entrance.

EQUIPMENT: Mostly copper plumbing; has a modern oil-fired hot water boiler, summer/winter hookup; new electric service (circuit breaker).

REMARKS: Excellent residential area, service by good schools and within walking distance of P.C.R. and shopping.

VALUATION: The plot of ground I value at $100,000
The improvements I value at 250,000
$350,000

Certification of Valuation
I hereby certify that I have personally examined the above property; that I have no personal interest therein; that my employment in making this valuation is in no way contingent on the amount of my calculation, and that I therefore set forth a value for estate purposes of

THREE HUNDRED FIFTY THOUSAND ($350,000) DOLLARS

____
Realtor

COMMERCIAL APPRAISAL

MARKET VALUATION REPORT

2560 EAST MAIN STREET,
INCLUDING
3463 BROAD STREET,

PHILADELPHIA, PENNSYLVANIA

Index **Page**

Letter of Transmittal . . . .
Summary . . . .

Appraisal Report

1. Location . . . .
2. Registered Owner . . . .
3. Purpose of Appraisal . . . .
4. The Property:
   (1) Land Area . . . .
   (2) Building Area . . . .
   (3) Description of Improvements . . . .
      (A) First Floor . . . .
      (B) Second Floor . . . .
      (C) Heating . . . .
      (D) Air-Conditioning . . . .
      (E) Electric . . . .
      (F) Rail . . . .
      (G) Gas . . . .
      (H) Water and Sewer . . . .
   (4) Real Estate Assessment . . . .
   (5) Zoning . . . .
5. Underlying Assumptions and Limiting Conditions . . . .
6. Certification of Value . . . .

Exhibits

1. Map of Area Showing Block and Lot of Property . . . .

2. Photographs of Subject Property.................................
3. Qualifications of Appraiser (Summary) ....

Index

Letter of Transmittal

December 18, 1991

Philadelphia, PA 19106

Attention Mr. Martin
Re: Market Valuation Report
2560 East Main Street
Philadelphia, Pennsylvania

Gentlemen:

In accordance with your request, I have personally inspected the above-captioned premises and made a study of matters pertinent to its value, as outlined in the attached Report.

After an analysis and a comprehensive study of the property, it is my opinion that the Market Value of this property, as of December 9, 1991, is:

FIVE HUNDRED THOUSAND DOLLARS—($500,000)

I certify that I have no financial or other interest in the said property; that my employment in the capacity of Appraiser is in no way contingent upon the amount of this appraisement, and that I have based the value of the real estate upon a study of conditions pertinent to its value and my knowledge of real estate.

Respectfully submitted,

____

Appraiser

Summary

LOCATION: 2560 East Main Street, including 3463 Broad Street
Philadelphia, Pennsylvania
REGISTERED OWNER: Lawrence Smith (2560 East Main Street)
Jane Smith (3463 Broad Street)
SIZE OF SITE: 25,332 Square Feet (approximate)
BUILDING AREA: 25,046 Square Feet (approximate)
REAL ESTATE ASSESSMENT: $275,900
ZONING: "G-2 Industrial"
STREET IMPROVEMENTS & PUBLIC UTILITIES:
Main Street: Cobblestone cartway, rail, concrete sidewalk, granite curbs
Almond Street: Macadam cartway, concrete sidewalk, concrete curbs
Broad Street: Macadam cartway, concrete sidewalk, concrete curbs
City Water and Sewer
Gas and Electric
Railroad
Telephone
Police and Fire Protection
MARKET VALUE: $500,000

Appraisal Report

1. LOCATION: 2560 East Main Street, including 3463 Broad Street
   Philadelphia, Pennsylvania
2. REGISTERED OWNER: Lawrence Smith (2560 East Main Street)
   Jane Smith (3463 Broad Street)
3. PURPOSE OF APPRAISAL: The purpose of this appraisal is to determine the Fair Market Value of the subject property. The value given represents "Market Value," which is the price a willing and informed seller, without compulsion, will accept and a willing and informed buyer, without compulsion, will pay.
4. THE PROPERTY:
   (1) LAND AREA:
   2560 E. Main Street
   120′ x 204′8″—24,560 Square Feet
   3463 Broad Street
   14′ x 55′2″—772 " "
   Total Land Area
   (approximate) —25,332 Square Feet
   (2) BUILDING AREA:
   One-story—
   120′ x 204′ —24,480 Square Feet
   Second Floor—
   22′ x 18′
   17′ x 10′ —566 " "
   Total Building Area
   (approximate) —25,046 Square Feet
   (3) DESCRIPTION OF IMPROVEMENTS: The subject property comprises a tract of land containing approximately 24,560 square feet with a 120′ frontage on Main Street and a 204′8″ frontage on Almond Street and Broad Street. Included with the property is premises Broad Street, improved with a two-story row dwelling on a lot measuring 14′ x 55′2″. The improvements consist of a one-story, part two-story, industrial building, brick construction, part corrugated steel in the rear wall, concrete foundation, steel beams and columns, high bay in the center with monitor-type skylights, wood roof deck, built-up composition roofing, steel casement sash, and part glass block windows. Small basement area under the office section is reached by an inside stairway. Walk-in entrance to the office section from Tioga Street; walk-in entrance to the shop area from Livingston Street. Rail siding into the building from Tioga Street through an 18′ x 14′ double-wood door. Two loading doors on Almond Street. Inside stairway to the second floor. 14′ to 20′ clearance under the beam.
      (A) FIRST FLOOR: Office and manufacturing areas. Office area with a walk-in entrance from Tioga Street consists of an entrance lobby, four private offices with a connecting hallway, two toilet rooms. Brick tile floor, painted plaster walls and ceiling, fluorescent lights. Heated and air-conditioned. Men's toilet room containing two toilets and one wash stand; women's toilet room containing one toilet and one wash stand. Manufacturing area with two rows of steel columns, high bay in the center with an approximate 20′ clearance under the hook of the crane, approximately 14′ clearance

under the beam in the two side bays, concrete floor, exposed wood ceiling, factory-type lighting. The center bay is serviced by a traveling crane on a runway. Northern Engineering cab crane, 50-ton capacity, cab operated. The easterly bay is serviced by a traveling craneway with two hoists (6-ton total capacity); the westerly bay is serviced by two traveling craneways, each with a 4-ton hoist. Radiant-gas–fired heaters throughout the shop area. Tool room enclosed by wire mesh and wood partition walls with an inside stairway to the second-floor offices. Toilet room containing one toilet and one outside wash stand. Rail siding from Tioga Street into the building. The manufacturing area connects with the first floor of premises 3463 Livingston Street to the rear, improved with a shop locker and toilet room; toilet room containing two toilets, one urinal, one Bradley basin. Heated by an oil-fired unit in the basement, duct system.

(B) SECOND FLOOR: Reached by two inside stairways. Consists of three offices, one of which is an upper level. Painted plastered walls and ceilings, wood floors, fluorescent lights. Radiation. Window unit air-conditioner. Storage room.

(C) HEATING: The office section is heated by radiation, furnished by an American Standard oil-fired, hot-water system. Manufacturing area heated by individual gas-fired radiant-heating units. Ruud gas-fired hot water heater. International oil-fired, low-pressure steam boiler in the basement (not in operation).

(D) AIR-CONDITIONING: The office areas are air-conditioned; the first floor from a Worthington unit through a duct system. Individual units in the second-floor offices.

(E) ELECTRIC: 600 amp service. 220-volt/3-phase, 440-volt/3-phase. Power distribution throughout the manufacturing area.

(F) RAIL: Available. Penn Central siding from Tioga Street into the building.

(G) GAS: Available. Furnished by the Philadelphia Gas Works.

(H) WATER AND SEWER: Available. Furnished by the City of Philadelphia.

(4) REAL ESTATE ASSESSMENT: $275,900—2560 E. Main Street
$13,600—3463 Broad Street

(5) ZONING: "G-2 Industrial"

5. UNDERLYING ASSUMPTIONS AND LIMITING CONDITIONS: Certain information contained in this Report was obtained from sources believed to be reliable, but is in no sense guaranteed. It is assumed that title to the property is good and marketable and that there are no encumbrances that cannot be cleared through regular processes; that no responsibility is assumed by the Appraiser for legal matters, especially those affecting title to the property; that the plans and other allied information furnished to the Appraiser are correct.

   No right is given to publish this Report, or any part of it, without the consent of the Appraiser.

6. CERTIFICATION OF VALUE: I hereby certify that the property was personally inspected and a comprehensive study made to appraise the property; that I have no financial or other interest in the property; that my employment as Appraiser is in no way contingent upon the

> amount of the appraisement and that, in my opinion, the Market Value of the subject property, as of December 9, 1991, is
>
> FIVE HUNDRED THOUSAND DOLLARS
>
> ($500,000)
>
> Commercial appraisals also contain a section for "exhibits" that includes a map of the area with the block and lot of property indicated, photographs of the property at issue, and a summary of the appraiser's qualifications.

SCHEDULE A–1, SECTION 2032A VALUATION

The Tax Reform Act of 1976 and the Revenue Act of 1978 provide that if certain conditions are met, the executor may elect to value real property included in the decedent's estate, which is devoted to farming or closely held business use, on the basis of that property's value as a farm or closely held business. In other words, a farm may be included for estate tax purposes at its value as a farm, rather than what its value *might* be if sold to a developer for home sites or a shopping center.[24] Use of the special valuation, however, may not reduce the gross estate by more than $750,000. Detailed information must be provided if the special valuation is elected by the executor and a special tax lien is created until the termination of the liability.[25]

Special Use Valuation was intended to soften the tax bite for family businesses such as farms and closely held corporations. These businesses usually have the majority of their liquid funds (cash) invested in the land or equipment. In order to pay the taxes due the business may have to be sold. The IRS permits two ways by which businesses may be preserved: (1) payment of taxes by installment (6166), and (2) special-use valuation. To qualify for the Special Use Valuation (possibly decreasing the value of the business for tax purposes by as much as $750,000) several conditions must be met. The business must continue in its present use for at least ten years after the decedent's death (the family cannot take the lower value and then sell the farm to a developer a year or two later). The business must be owned and operated by a "qualified" heir (a family member). The value of the business must represent at least one-half of the value of the adjusted gross estate. And, the decedent must have owned the business for at least five years prior to death.

24. Valuing real estate in this manner is termed appraising a piece of property at its "highest and best use."

25. See IRC 2032A and 6324B.

Schedule A-1 will usually not be prepared by the legal assistant; therefore, it is not included in Peter Chessman's estate. However Schedule A-1 is provided for illustrative purposes on the next page.

PROBLEM

The office for which you work represents the estate of Hugo Furst. At the time of his death Mr. Furst owned the following real estate:

1. A residence at 1023 Shady Street, Harrisburg, Pennsylvania, valued at $150,000.
2. A townhouse with three apartments at 1125 Knotty Street, Harrisburg, Pennsylvania, valued at $175,000 that carries a $100,000 mortgage for which Mr. Furst's estate is liable.
3. A one-half interest as a tenant in common in a beach house at 1615 Beach Lane, Oceanville, New Jersey, (his brother owns the other half interest). The beach house was worth $127,000 at the date of death.

Please prepare a Schedule A for Mr. Furst's 706 return.

Schedule B—Stocks and Bonds[26]

Since most persons with large estates have substantial portfolios of marketable stocks and bonds, Schedule B of the estate tax return will frequently be the longest and most difficult to prepare. All stocks and bonds that are owned solely by the decedent are to be reported on this schedule. Stocks and bonds that are owned of record by the decedent who is merely holding title for another should not be included.

Valuation of Stocks and Bonds The general rule enunciated in the Regulations promulgated by the Treasury Department is that stocks and bonds are to be valued at their fair market value. The method of valuing stocks and bonds that are actively traded is set forth in § 20.2032–2 of the Regulations, as follows:

> (b) *Based on selling prices.* If there is a market for stocks or bonds, on a stock exchange, in an over-the-counter market, or otherwise, the mean between the highest and lowest quoted selling prices on the valuation date is the fair market value per share or bond. If there were no sales on the valuation date, but there were sales on dates within a reasonable period both before and after the valuation date, the fair market value is determined by taking a weighted average of the means between the highest and lowest sales on the nearest date before and the nearest date after the valuation date. The average is to be weighed inversely by the respective numbers of trading days between

26. IRC § 2033.

EXAMPLE *Form 706, Schedule A-1—Section 2032A Valuation*

Form 706 (Rev. 7-90)

Estate of: Peter Chessman

Decedent's Social Security Number 045 : 96 : 2487

SCHEDULE A-1—Section 2032A Valuation

Part 1.—Type of Election:

☐ **Protective election (Regulations section 20.2032A-8(b)).**—Complete Part 2, line 1, and column A of lines 3 and 4. (See instructions.)
☐ **Regular election.**—Complete all of Part 2 (including line 11, if applicable) and Part 3. (See instructions.)

Part 2.—Notice of Election (Regulations section 20.2032A-8(a)(3))

Note: *All real property entered on lines 2 and 3 must also be entered on Schedules A, E, F, G, or H, as applicable.*

1 Qualified use—check one ▶ ☐ Farm used for farming, *or*
▶ ☐ Trade or business other than farming

2 Real property used in a qualified use, passing to qualified heirs, and to be specially valued on this Form 706.

A Schedule and item number from Form 706	B Full value (without section 2032A(b)(3)(B) adjustment)	C Adjusted value (with section 2032A(b)(3)(B) adjustment)	D Value based on qualified use (without section 2032A(b)(3)(B) adjustment)
None			
Totals			

Attach a legal description of all property listed on line 2.
Attach copies of appraisals showing the column B values for all property listed on line 2.

3 Real property used in a qualified use, passing to qualified heirs, but not specially valued on this Form 706.

A Schedule and item number from Form 706	B Full value (without section 2032A(b)(3)(B) adjustment)	C Adjusted value (with section 2032A(b)(3)(B) adjustment)	D Value based on qualified use (without section 2032A(b)(3)(B) adjustment)
None			
Totals			

If you checked "Regular election," you must attach copies of appraisals showing the column B values for all property listed on line 3.

(Continued on next page) **Schedule A-1—Page 6**

EXAMPLE *Form 706, Schedule A-1—Section 2032A Valuation, continued*

Form 706 (Rev. 7-90)

4 Personal property used in a qualified use and passing to qualified heirs.

A Schedule and item number from Form 706	B Adjusted value (with section 2032A(b)(3)(B) adjustment)	A (continued) Schedule and item number from Form 706	B (continued) Adjusted value (with section 2032A(b)(3)(B) adjustment)
		"Subtotal" from Col. B, below left	
Subtotal		**Total adjusted value**	

5 Enter the value of the total gross estate as adjusted under section 2032A(b)(3)(A). ▶

6 Attach a description of the method used to determine the special value based on qualified use.

7 Did the decedent and/or a member of his or her family own all property listed on line 2 for at least 5 of the 8 years immediately preceding the date of the decedent's death? ☐ **Yes** ☐ **No**

8 Were there any periods during the 8-year period preceding the date of the decedent's death during which the decedent or a member of his or her family:

	Yes	No
a Did not own the property listed on line 2 above?		
b Did not use the property listed on line 2 above in a qualified use?		
c Did not materially participate in the operation of the farm or other business within the meaning of section 2032A(e)(6)?		

If "Yes" to any of the above, you must attach a statement listing the periods. If applicable, describe whether the exceptions of sections 2032A(b)(4) or (5) are met.

9 Attach affidavits describing the activities constituting material participation and the identity and relationship to the decedent of the material participants.

10 Persons holding interests. Enter the requested information for each party who received any interest in the specially valued property.

	Name	Address
A		
B		
C		
D		
E		
F		
G		
H		

	Identifying number	Relationship to decedent	Fair market value	Special use value
A				
B				
C				
D				
E				
F				
G				
H				

You must attach a computation of the GST tax savings attributable to direct skips for each person listed above who is a skip person. (See instructions.)

11 Woodlands election.—Check here ▶ ☐ if you wish to make a woodlands election as described in section 2032A(e)(13). Enter the Schedule and item numbers from Form 706 of the property for which you are making this election ▶

You must attach a statement explaining why you are entitled to make this election. The IRS may issue regulations that require more information to substantiate this election. You will be notified by IRS if you must supply further information.

Schedule A-1—Page 7

EXAMPLE Form 706, Schedule A-1—Section 2032A Valuation, continued

Form 706 (Rev. 7-90)

Part 3.—Agreement to Special Valuation Under Section 2032A

Estate of: Peter Chessman	Date of Death 5/3/91	Decedent's Social Security Number 045 : 96 : 2487

We (list all qualified heirs and other persons having an interest in the property required to sign this agreement) ______________________________ ,

being all the qualified heirs and ______________________________ ,

being all other parties having interests in the property which is qualified real property and which is valued under section 2032A of the Internal Revenue Code, do hereby approve of the election made by ______________________________ ,
Executor/Administrator of the estate of ______________________________ ,
pursuant to section 2032A to value said property on the basis of the qualified use to which the property is devoted and do hereby enter into this agreement pursuant to section 2032A(d).

The undersigned agree and consent to the application of subsection (c) of section 2032A of the Code with respect to all the property described on line 2 of Part 2 of Schedule A-1 of Form 706, attached to this agreement. More specifically, the undersigned heirs expressly agree and consent to personal liability under subsection (c) of 2032A for the additional estate and GST taxes imposed by that subsection with respect to their respective interests in the above-described property in the event of certain early dispositions of the property or early cessation of the qualified use of the property. It is understood that if a qualified heir disposes of any interest in qualified real property to any member of his or her family, such member may thereafter be treated as the qualified heir with respect to such interest upon filing a Form 706-A and a new agreement.

The undersigned interested parties who are not qualified heirs consent to the collection of any additional estate and GST taxes imposed under section 2032A(c) of the Code from the specially valued property.

If there is a disposition of any interest which passes or has passed to him or her or if there is a cessation of the qualified use of any specially valued property which passes or passed to him or her, each of the undersigned heirs agrees to file a **Form 706-A,** United States Additional Estate Tax Return, and pay any additional estate and GST taxes due within 6 months of the disposition or cessation.

It is understood by all interested parties that this agreement is a condition precedent to the election of special use valuation under section 2032A of the Code and must be executed by every interested party even though that person may not have received the estate (or GST) tax benefits or be in possession of such property.

Each of the undersigned understands that by making this election, a lien will be created and recorded pursuant to section 6324B of the Code on the property referred to in this agreement for the adjusted tax differences with respect to the estate as defined in section 2032A(c)(2)(C).

As the interested parties, the undersigned designate the following individual as their agent for all dealings with the Internal Revenue Service concerning the continued qualification of the specially valued property under section 2032A of the Code and on all issues regarding the special lien under section 6324B. The agent is authorized to act for the parties with respect to all dealings with the Service on matters affecting the qualified real property described earlier. This authority includes the following:

- To receive confidential information on all matters relating to continued qualification under section 2032A of the specially valued real property and on all matters relating to the special lien arising under section 6324B.
- To furnish the Service with any requested information concerning the property.
- To notify the Service of any disposition or cessation of qualified use of any part of the property.
- To receive, but not to endorse and collect, checks in payment of any refund of Internal Revenue taxes, penalties, or interest.
- To execute waivers (including offers of waivers) of restrictions on assessment or collection of deficiencies in tax and waivers of notice of disallowance of a claim for credit or refund.
- To execute closing agreements under section 7121.
- Other acts (specify) ▶ ______________________________

By signing this agreement, the agent agrees to provide the Service with any requested information concerning this property and to notify the Service of any disposition or cessation of the qualified use of any part of this property.

Name of Agent	Signature	Address

The property to which this agreement relates is listed in Form 706, United States Estate (and Generation-Skipping Transfer) Tax Return, and in the Notice of Election, along with its fair market value according to section 2031 of the Code and its special use value according to section 2032A. The name, address, social security number, and interest (including the value) of each of the undersigned in this property are as set forth in the attached Notice of Election.

IN WITNESS WHEREOF, the undersigned have hereunto set their hands at ______________________________ ,
this_________ day of _________ .

Qualified Heirs ______________________________

Other Interested Parties

Schedule A-1—Page 8

the selling dates and the valuation date. For example, assume that sales of stock nearest the valuation date (Friday, June 15) occurred two trading days before (Wednesday, June 13) and three trading days after (Wednesday, June 20) and that on these days the mean sale prices per share were \$10 and \$15, respectively. The price of \$12 is taken as representing the fair market value of a share of the stock as of the valuation date

$$\frac{(3 \times 10) + (2 \times 15)}{5}$$

If, instead, the mean sales prices per share on June 13 and June 20 were \$15 and \$10, respectively, the price of \$13 is taken as representing the fair market value

$$\frac{(3 \times 15) + (2 \times 10)}{5}$$

As a further example, assume that the decedent died on Sunday, October 7, and that Saturday and Sunday were not trading days. If sales of stock occurred on Friday, October 5, at mean sale prices per share of \$20 and on Monday, October 8, at mean sale prices per share of \$23, then the fair market value per share of stock as of the valuation date is \$21.50. If stocks or bonds are listed on more than one exchange, the records of the exchange where the stocks or bonds are principally dealt in should be employed. In valuing listed securities, the executor should be careful to consult accurate records to obtain values as of the applicable valuation date. If quotations of unlisted securities are obtained from brokers, or evidence as to their sale is obtained from officers of the issuing companies, copies of the letters furnishing such quotations or evidence of sale should be attached to the return.

(c) *Based on bid and asked prices.* If the provisions of paragraph (b) of this section are inapplicable because actual sales are not available during a reasonable period beginning before and ending after the valuation date, the fair market value may be determined by taking the mean between the bona fide bid and asked prices on the valuation date, or if none, by taking a weighted average of the means between the bona fide bid and asked prices on the nearest trading date before and the nearest trading date after the valuation date, if both such nearest dates are within a reasonable period. The average is to be determined in the manner described in paragraph (b) of this section.

In most cases, the regulations quoted above will provide the necessary guidance for valuing stocks and bonds owned by a decedent. The required information will normally be obtainable, at least with respect to securities in most publicly held corporations from the *Wall Street Journal* or the financial section of any large newspaper.

The application of the foregoing regulations may be demonstrated by the following examples:

EXAMPLE
Valuation of Stocks and Bonds

Assume that E. Braxton died on Monday, July 11, 1991, and that, at the time of his death, he was the owner of 100 shares of common stock of International Business Machines, Inc., which is traded on the New York Stock Exchange. The quotations for the date of death value of that stock would be found in the *Wall Street Journal* for Tuesday, July 12, 1991, and, the entitled "New York Stock Exchange Transactions" would reveal the following information:

1991 High	1991 Low	Stocks	Div.	Sales in 100s	High	Low	Close	Net Chg.
354½	291¾	IBM	4	294	332	321	321½	−10

The two figures on the left indicate the highest and lowest prices at which IBM had traded during 1991. The names of the corporations, arranged alphabetically, come next along with the dividend paid on the stock. Thus, the "4" next to the name of the company indicates that each share of IBM stock receives dividends of $4 a year. The figure "294" under the "Sales in 100s" column discloses that 29,400 shares of IBM stock changed hands on July 11, 1991. The "high" for the day was also $332 a share; in other words, the stock sold at its highest price for the day in the early morning trading. The "low" for the day was $321, and at the close of the market, the stock had recovered minimally to $321.50 a share. The final column shows the net change for the day and indicates that the stock "lost" $10 a share, compared to the closing price on the previous trading day, Friday, July 8, 1991.

The value of each share of IBM stock in E. Braxton's estate would be $326.50, the mean between the high of $332 and the low of $321, and the 100 shares would thus have a value of $32,650.

If E. Braxton died on Saturday, July 16, 1991, no trading took place on the valuation date. To value the IBM stock, it would be necessary to obtain figures for Friday, July 15, 1991, the previous trading day, as well as Monday, July 18, 1991, the following trading day. The *Wall Street Journal* is published five days a week and the figures for Friday, July 15, can be obtained from the paper published on Monday, July 18, 1991, that would indicate the following:

1991 High	1991 Low	Stocks	Div.	Sales in 100s	High	Low	Close	Net Chg.
354½	291¾	IBM	4	385	333	326½	331½	+4½

Thus, on Friday, July 15, the stock sold at a high of $333 a share and a low of $326.50 a share, and the mean between high and low was $329.75. By averaging the mean on Friday ($329.75) with the mean on Monday ($326.50), we would arrive at a value per share of $328.125 and the value of the 100 shares in the decedent's estate would thus be $32,812.50.

If E. Braxton had died on Friday, July 15, 1991, owning 100 shares of common stock of the Tasty Baking Company, which is traded on the American Stock Exchange, the necessary information would be found in the *Wall Street Journal* for Monday, July 18, 1991, on the page devoted to "American Stock Exchange Transactions."

1991 High	1991 Low	Stocks	Div.	Sales in 100s	High	Low	Close	Net Chg.
23⅜	18¼	Tasty Bk.	.88	1	19⅝	19⅝	19⅝	—

This would indicate that only 100 shares of this stock traded on the day in question; that the price of the stock for this single transaction was $19.625; and that there was no change for the day, the stock having closed at the same price on Thursday, July 14, 1991. Thus, the value of the 100 shares held in the estate would be $1962.50.

In some cases, an estate will include stocks or bonds of a publicly owned corporation, which are rarely traded. If there are no actual sale prices or bona fide bid and asked prices available on a date within a reasonable period either before the valuation date or within a reasonable period after the valuation date, the mean between the highest and lowest available sale prices or bid and asked prices on any one date that is reasonably close to the valuation date, whether before or after, will normally be acceptable.

In comparatively rare situations, the selling prices or bid-and-asked prices will not be an accurate reflection of the market value of the stock. For example, if sales occurring at or near the date of death are extremely few, such sales may not indicate fair market value. In some exceptional cases, the number of shares of stock held by an estate in relation to the number of shares that are normally traded may be relevant in determining whether the selling price is an accurate reflection of value. For example, if the number of shares held by the estate in a particular company exceeds the number of shares that could be sold over a reasonable period of time without adversely affecting the market price, the executors may take the position that the estate is entitled to some discount from the quoted price in valuing the stock; such discount is commonly referred to as "blockage."

Actual sales may also be an inaccurate reflection of value if the block of stock held by an estate represents a controlling interest in the corporation. In that case, the stock as a block may be worth more than the normal per share price multiplied by the total number of shares.

Situations in which selling prices do not reflect fair market value are fairly unusual and, when they do arise, the attorney who is representing the estate will have to exercise his judgment in fixing a value to be returned on the federal estate tax return.

For purposes of the discussion of stocks and bonds that follows, it may be assumed that there are no unusual circumstances and that the value to be shown on the federal estate tax return represents the mean between the high and low sale prices on the date of death.

Types of Stocks and Bonds

Government Securities in General Government Securities are debt obligations issued by federal, state, or local governmental units as a means of raising funds. The federal government offers securities to raise funds for the general purposes of carrying on the business of government. In addition, numerous federal agencies issue bonds to raise funds for particular activities within their purview.

Most municipal bonds (those issued by state governments or local governmental units within the state) are issued to raise funds for the carrying out of some particular purpose, for example, school improvements, the building of a bridge, or the construction of a turnpike. Bonds issued by state and local governments are often referred to as "tax-free municipal bonds" because interest on them is exempt from federal income tax. However, such bonds are not exempt from federal estate tax.

Bonds provide for the payment of a fixed rate of interest and also provide for eventual repayment of the face amount of the bonds on some fixed date or dates in the future. For example, an estate may hold $10,000 of Pennsylvania Turnpike Bonds, 4.2% due November 1, 1997. The owner of these bonds would be entitled to interest payments of $420 a year (4.2% × $10,000), usually payable semi-annually, and would also be entitled to redeem the bonds for their full face value of $10,000 on the maturity date, November 1, 1997. The value of these bonds at any given time, however, would be affected by a number of factors, including the credit rating of the governmental unit that issued the bonds and interest notes that are currently available on bonds of similar quality. For example, assume that the bonds in question had been issued in 1955, at which time municipal authorities similar to the Pennsylvania Turnpike Commission were required to pay 4.2% in order to borrow money. Presumably, purchasers of these bonds would have paid approximately "par" for the bonds. The par value or face value is the stated value on the bonds and the value at which the bonds can ultimately be redeemed at maturity. Thus, if an individual had purchased these bonds when they were originally issued in 1955, he or she would have paid $10,000 for the bonds with the expectation of receiving $420 of tax-free interest each year and the return of his initial investment of $10,000 in 1997 when the bonds matured.

At the time of the investor's death, however, these bonds may be worth substantially less than their face value. Assume, for purposes of discussion, that at the time of the decedent's death, the Pennsylvania Turnpike Commission would be required to pay 6% to borrow money, and assume further that, at or near the time of the decedent's death, the same municipal authority had issued bonds that were also payable in 1997 but which involved an annual return of 6%. An investor purchasing these bonds would be required to buy only $7,000 face value of such bonds in order to receive interest of $420 a year ($7,000 × 6%). In such a case, it is likely that the decedent's bonds that were purchased in 1955 would be worth substantially less than $10,000 on the open market. If the credit of the borrower was good, however, the bonds would probably be worth more than $7,000 since they could be redeemed for $10,000 in 1997, and this expectation of gain would push their price to a higher level, even though, as a result, the rate of return in the form of interest would be pushed below 6%. The value of government bonds at the time of the decedent's death may be obtained from the financial section of a newspaper (the most reliable source again being the *Wall Street Journal*). If the bonds were not traded actively and if their values are not reported in any such newspaper, the value may be obtained from a brokerage house that may have access to other trading records. It is customary to ask the decedent's broker either to provide the original information concerning the value of bonds or to confirm the information taken from other sources. In part this reflects the fact that people inexperienced at valuing bonds may misinterpret the information printed in newspapers. The method of valuation employed should be carefully recorded in writing so that it will be available for reference when the return is audited.

In the example we have been using, information may be obtained that indicates that on the date of death, the applicable value, for federal estate tax purposes, was 82, representing the mean between a bid price of 81 and an asked price of 83. In such a case, ownership of these bonds would be reflected on Schedule B of the estate tax return:

$10,000	Pennsylvania Turnpike, 4.2% due 11/1/97. Interest payable semi-annually on May 1 and November 1	82	$8,200.00

In addition to listing the bond itself, it is also necessary to report on Schedule B any accrued interest that may be payable on the bond. The concept of accrued interest may be best explained by examples.

EXAMPLE
Determining Accrued Interest

If interest on the bonds in question is payable on May 1 and November 1 of each year ($210 semiannually), and if the decedent died on February 1, 1991, the federal estate tax return would have to include accrued interest for three months (November, December, and January), and the accrued interest in such a case, would amount to $105.

If the decedent had died on November 10, accrued interest for nine days would be reportable on Schedule B. The amount of the accrued interest could be determined by multiplying the annual interest ($420) by a fraction, the numerator of which would be the number of days elapsed between the date of the decedent's death and the date of the last interest payment, and the denominator of which would be 365. Thus, assuming a date of death of November 10, the accrued interest on the Pennsylvania Turnpike bonds would amount to $10.36, calculated as follows:

$$\frac{9}{365} \times \$420 = \$10.36$$

Accrued interest must be included in every case, except in the rare instance of bonds that sell "flat," i.e., without accrued interest.

United States Savings Bonds These bonds are widely held and many estates will have at least a few, usually Series "E," "EE," and "H." These bonds may be valued by means of a chart that is published monthly by the Treasury Department and can be obtained from most banks. The redemption chart for Series EE bonds follows.[27] It is important to bear in mind that Series "E" Bonds continue to earn interest even after their original maturity date. Therefore, many such bonds have a value, at date of death, that substantially exceeds their face value.

Series H savings bonds are reported at their face value and accrued interest is shown as a separate item on Schedule B.

United States Treasury Bonds Certain Treasury bonds issued by the federal government may be redeemed at par, plus accrued interest, for the payment of federal estate tax, even though the bonds may be selling in the open market at substantially below par on the date of death. Such bonds are sometimes referred to by lawyers and bankers as "flower bonds," "death bonds," or "estate tax bonds." The specific bonds that may be used in this manner may be determined from a current list of eligible issues, which is published in several tax services and may be obtained from any Federal Reserve Bank or branch or from the Public Affairs Office, Bureau of Public Debt (Treasury Dept.), Washington, D.C. 20239-0001. A copy of that list is reprinted here. The Treasury Department is no longer issuing any new "flower bonds." After all the bonds presently issued mature, there will no longer be any "flower" bonds.

Provided that bonds in the estate that are eligible for payment of the federal estate tax have a market value below par it is, of course, advantageous to use the bonds in payment of that tax. In that manner, the full par value rather than the depressed market value will be realized by the estate. In such a case the bonds used

27. These documents are included solely for the purpose of familiarizing the student with their format. The student should be aware that redemption charts for Series EE Bonds and lists of qualified death bonds are revised from time to time, and current copies must be obtained for use on the job.

EXAMPLE *Redemption Chart for U.S. Series EE Savings Bonds*

U.S. SAVINGS BONDS, SERIES EE-REDEMPTION VALUES AND INTEREST EARNED AMOUNTS BY DENOMINATION-DECEMBER 1991

ISSUE YEAR	ISSUE MONTHS	$50		$75		$100		$200		$500		$1,000		$5,000		$10,000	
		REDEMP. VALUE	INTEREST EARNED	REDEMP. VALUE	INTEREST EARNED	REDEMP. VALUE	INTEREST EARNED	REDEMP. VALUE	INTEREST EARNED	REDEMP. VALUE	INTEREST EARNED	REDEMP. VALUE	INTEREST EARNED	REDEMP. VALUE	INTEREST EARNED	REDEMP. VALUE	INTEREST EARNED
1991	July thru Dec.	Not eligible for payment															
	June	25.52	.52	38.28	.78	51.04	1.04	102.08	2.08	255.20	5.20	510.40	10.40	2,552.00	52.00	5,104.00	104.00
	May	25.60	.60	38.40	.90	51.20	1.20	102.40	2.40	256.00	6.00	512.00	12.00	2,560.00	60.00	5,120.00	120.00
	Apr.	25.70	.70	38.55	1.05	51.40	1.40	102.80	2.80	257.00	7.00	514.00	14.00	2,570.00	70.00	5,140.00	140.00
	Mar.	25.78	.78	38.67	1.17	51.56	1.56	103.12	3.12	257.80	7.80	515.60	15.60	2,578.00	78.00	5,156.00	156.00
	Feb.	25.88	.88	38.82	1.32	51.76	1.76	103.52	3.52	258.80	8.80	517.60	17.60	2,588.00	88.00	5,176.00	176.00
	Jan.	25.98	.98	38.97	1.47	51.96	1.96	103.92	3.92	259.80	9.80	519.60	19.60	2,598.00	98.00	5,196.00	196.00
1990	Dec.	26.08	1.08	39.12	1.62	52.16	2.16	104.32	4.32	260.80	10.80	521.60	21.60	2,608.00	108.00	5,216.00	216.00
	Nov.	26.18	1.18	39.27	1.77	52.36	2.36	104.72	4.72	261.80	11.80	523.60	23.60	2,618.00	118.00	5,236.00	236.00
	Oct.	26.28	1.28	39.42	1.92	52.56	2.56	105.12	5.12	262.80	12.80	525.60	25.60	2,628.00	128.00	5,256.00	256.00
	Sep.	26.38	1.38	39.57	2.07	52.76	2.76	105.52	5.52	263.80	13.80	527.60	27.60	2,638.00	138.00	5,276.00	276.00
	Aug.	26.48	1.48	39.72	2.22	52.96	2.96	105.92	5.92	264.80	14.80	529.60	29.60	2,648.00	148.00	5,296.00	296.00
	July	26.58	1.58	39.87	2.37	53.16	3.16	106.32	6.32	265.80	15.80	531.60	31.60	2,658.00	158.00	5,316.00	316.00
	June	26.70	1.70	40.05	2.55	53.40	3.40	106.80	6.80	267.00	17.00	534.00	34.00	2,670.00	170.00	5,340.00	340.00
	May	26.80	1.80	40.20	2.70	53.60	3.60	107.20	7.20	268.00	18.00	536.00	36.00	2,680.00	180.00	5,360.00	360.00
	Apr.	26.92	1.92	40.38	2.88	53.84	3.84	107.68	7.68	269.20	19.20	538.40	38.40	2,692.00	192.00	5,384.00	384.00
	Mar.	27.04	2.04	40.56	3.06	54.08	4.08	108.16	8.16	270.40	20.40	540.80	40.80	2,704.00	204.00	5,408.00	408.00
	Feb.	27.16	2.16	40.74	3.24	54.32	4.32	108.64	8.64	271.60	21.60	543.20	43.20	2,716.00	216.00	5,432.00	432.00
	Jan.	27.28	2.28	40.92	3.42	54.56	4.56	109.12	9.12	272.80	22.80	545.60	45.60	2,728.00	228.00	5,456.00	456.00
	PROCEEDS FROM SERIES EE SAVINGS BONDS WITH ISSUE DATES BEGINNING JANUARY 1990 MAY BE ELIGIBLE FOR SPECIAL TAX EXEMPTION WHEN USED FOR POST SECONDARY EDUCATION - SEE INSIDE FRONT COVER.																
1989	Dec.	27.40	2.40	41.10	3.60	54.80	4.80	109.60	9.60	274.00	24.00	548.00	48.00	2,740.00	240.00	5,480.00	480.00
	Nov.	27.52	2.52	41.28	3.78	55.04	5.04	110.08	10.08	275.20	25.20	550.40	50.40	2,752.00	252.00	5,504.00	504.00
	Oct.	27.64	2.64	41.46	3.96	55.28	5.28	110.56	10.56	276.40	26.40	552.80	52.80	2,764.00	264.00	5,528.00	528.00
	Sep.	27.76	2.76	41.64	4.14	55.52	5.52	111.04	11.04	277.60	27.60	555.20	55.20	2,776.00	276.00	5,552.00	552.00
	Aug.	27.90	2.90	41.85	4.35	55.80	5.80	111.60	11.60	279.00	29.00	558.00	58.00	2,790.00	290.00	5,580.00	580.00
	July	28.02	3.02	42.03	4.53	56.04	6.04	112.08	12.08	280.20	30.20	560.40	60.40	2,802.00	302.00	5,604.00	604.00
	Jan. thru June	28.16	3.16	42.24	4.74	56.32	6.32	112.64	12.64	281.60	31.60	563.20	63.20	2,816.00	316.00	5,632.00	632.00
1988	July thru Dec.	29.00	4.00	43.50	6.00	58.00	8.00	116.00	16.00	290.00	40.00	580.00	80.00	2,900.00	400.00	5,800.00	800.00
	Jan. thru June	29.98	4.98	44.97	7.47	59.96	9.96	119.92	19.92	299.80	49.80	599.60	99.60	2,998.00	498.00	5,996.00	996.00
1987	July thru Dec.	31.06	6.06	46.59	9.09	62.12	12.12	124.24	24.24	310.60	60.60	621.20	121.20	3,106.00	606.00	6,212.00	1,212.00
	Jan. thru June	32.28	7.28	48.42	10.92	64.56	14.56	129.12	29.12	322.80	72.80	645.60	145.60	3,228.00	728.00	6,456.00	1,456.00

INTEREST EARNED:
ELIGIBLE FOR SPECIAL TAX EXEMPTION (BEGINNING 1990)
NOT ELIGIBLE FOR SPECIAL TAX EXEMPTION

DECEMBER 1991
INSIST ON PROPER IDENTIFICATION.

1

in payment of the tax must be valued at par on the federal estate tax return. On the other hand, if such bonds have a market value in excess of par, they would not be used to satisfy the estate tax liability because that would, in effect, be exchanging the bonds for less than they could be sold in the marketplace. In such a case, the bonds would be includible in the estate at their market value. For example, a particular issue of United States bonds may be selling on the open market at approximately 65 (meaning that a $1,000 bond of this issue could be purchased for $650) but it may be one of the bonds eligible for redemption at par in payment of federal estate tax. The estate would use the bond for payment of the estate tax thereby realizing $1,000 rather than the $650 market value. In such a case it follows that the bond would have to be valued at par ($1,000) on the federal estate tax return since the estate would actually be realizing that sum from the redemption of the bond in payment, whether partial or full, of the federal estate tax due. The procedure for redeeming such bonds at par will be discussed in a later section of this chapter.

EXAMPLE

U.S. Treasury Bonds Redeemable at Par in Payment of Federal Estate Tax

Series	Dated	Due
3s 1995	Feb. 15, 1955	Feb. 15, 1995
3½s 1990	Feb. 14, 1958	Feb. 15, 1990
3½s 1998	Oct. 3, 1960	Nov. 15, 1998
4¼s 1987–92	Aug. 15, 1962	Aug. 15, 1992
4s 1988–93	Jan. 17, 1963	Feb. 15, 1993
4⅛s 1989–94	April 18, 1963	May 15, 1994

Corporate Securities An estate will frequently hold corporate securities having significantly different characteristics. The following is a brief discussion of the various types of corporate debt and equity securities that may have to be valued and reported on Schedule B of the tax return.

Common Stock The purchaser of common stock of a corporation acquires a share of the ownership of the corporation. For example, if a corporation has 1,000,000 shares of issued and outstanding common stock and one stockholder owns 10,000 shares of that stock, that stockholder is, in effect, the owner of 1% of the corporation. The holders of common stock customarily elect the members of the Board of Directors that governs the affairs of the corporation and also votes on other matters of great importance to the corporation. Stockholders are entitled to receive dividends on their stock when, as, and if such dividends are declared by the directors of the corporation. If a corporation should go out of business, the common stockholders are entitled to receive their pro rata share of the assets of the corporation remaining after payment of debts and prior obligations to preferred shareholders. The common stock of publicly owned corporations is the security most commonly traded.

Preferred Stock Preferred stock is a class encompassing stock owners who are granted a preference over the holders of common stock as to dividends and, in some instances, a preference in distribution of the assets of the corporation on liquidation. As a general rule, preferred stockholders do not vote, although some corporations do issue voting preferred stock. Preferred stockholders are entitled, however, to receive their dividends before any dividends are paid on common stock. In most cases, preferred stockholders are entitled to a limited amount of dividends, regardless of the profitability of the business for any given year. For example, X Corporation may have two classes of stock, a $4 preferred stock and a common stock. Before any dividends could be paid on the common stock, X Corporation would have to pay $4 on each share of the preferred stock. Unless the preferred stock also had rights to participate with the common stock in dividends in excess of the preference amount (so-called "participating" preferred stock), if X Corporation had an extremely profitable year, the preferred stockholders would receive only $4 per share and would not participate at all in the increased earnings of the corporation.

Some preferred stock is said to be "cumulative preferred" because the rights to the preferred dividend accumulate from year to year if the earnings of the corporation are not sufficient to pay them. Until the cumulated dividends are paid, as well as the dividend for the current year, no dividend may be paid to holders of common stock. If the preferred stock is noncumulative, the right to an unearned dividend would expire at the end of each year.

Many publicly owned corporations have preferred, as well as common, stock and many of the extremely large corporations have more than one class of preferred stock, each class of preferred granting slightly different rights to its holders in terms of dividends and, possibly, in terms of rights to receive distributions in case of liquidation[28] of the corporation.

Bonds and Debentures Business corporations, like governmental units, issue debt securities to raise cash for capital improvements and other business activities. Bonds are distinguished from other common forms of debt securities such as debentures and notes because they are normally secured by a mortgage on certain real property owned by the borrowing corporation. In the event the borrower defaults on its obligation to pay interest or repay prin-

28. "Liquidation" is the sale of all the assets of the corporation when it is going out of business.

cipal, the bondholders may obtain ownership and sell the real property that secured the bond in order to satisfy their claim.

A debenture is similar to a bond except that it is not normally secured by a mortgage on property of the corporation. Although the different features of bonds and debentures are relevant to the investing public in setting a value for a particular security, for the purpose of valuation for Schedule B, where there are available bid-and-asked prices, the differences between bonds and debentures need not concern the lawyer's assistant. On the other hand, if there is no public market for the particular security in question, then the different features of the securities are, of course, relevant in arriving at an appropriate valuation.

The bonds and debentures of many corporations are actively traded and are reported on a daily basis in the *Wall Street Journal* and other large newspapers. Like the government bonds discussed previously, corporate bonds and debentures involve a promise on the part of the borrower to pay the principal back to the lender at some future date and the promise to pay interest at a specified rate until the principal is repaid. The holder of a bond or debenture does not have an interest in the ownership of the corporation although he may have an interest in some of its property. The bond or debenture holder is a creditor of the corporation.

Warrants and Rights Warrants and rights are other forms of securities issued by corporations. Basically, they are the right to buy stock (usually common) or other securities of a corporation some time in the future at a fixed price. Rights are generally of shorter duration than warrants and are typically offered exclusively to existing shareholders. Warrants may be issued to existing shareholders or may be issued in connection with the sale of bonds or other securities by the corporation. For example, a corporation may sell a $1,000 bond bearing interest at 6% with principal due in thirty years and with a warrant attached to purchase in the future at a given price a specified number of shares of the common stock of the corporation. The warrants serve as an added inducement to the lender since, if the corporation prospers and the value of its common stock increases, the ability to purchase the common stock at some future date at a fixed price will be a valuable asset.

Investors frequently trade warrants and rights and their value is determined, at least in part, by the value of the stock to which they relate. For example, an estate may include warrants or rights to purchase 100 shares of the common stock of X Corporation at $20 per share at any time prior to November 1, 1997. If the prospects for X Corporation, in the eyes of the investing public, are good, these warrants or rights may have a significant value even though the present value of the common stock of X Corporation is less than $20. That is, if investors think it is likely that the common stock of X Corporation will be selling at a price in excess of the warrant price on November 1, 1997, they may be willing to buy the warrant at the present time in the hope of realizing a profit at some future date, when the value of the stock of the corporation exceeds the price at which they will be able to purchase the stock. For purposes of the Schedule B, warrants and rights are valued in the same manner as shares of stock, taking the mean between the high and low sale prices for the warrants or rights on the date of death.

Convertible Securities Corporations also frequently issue convertible preferred stock or convertible bonds or debentures. Such securities, in addition to their other attributes, give to their owner the ability to convert the preferred stock or bond into a fixed number of shares of the common stock of the issuing corporation at some time in the future. The value of a convertible preferred stock or bond will depend in part upon the opinion of investors of the prospects for the corporation's common stock. This "expectation" relating to the future value of the common stock will be reflected in the price at which the convertible preferred stock, bonds, or debentures trade in the open market.

Investment Company Shares Investment companies, which are commonly referred to as "mutual funds," are companies whose assets consist solely of cash, bonds, and securities of various corporations. Individuals who invest in mutual funds are thereby, in effect, buying a share in a portfolio of investments. The value of the mutual fund's shares will obviously vary with the value of the securities that it owns. There are two basic types of mutual funds, "closed end funds" and "open end funds."

Open End Funds An open end mutual fund is one in which the investors have the right, at any time, to redeem their shares of the fund for cash or stock equal to their pro rata share of the mutual fund. For example, if a mutual fund has cash, bonds, and securities that, as of January 15, 1991, had a total value of $70,000,000 and if X owned 10 shares of the fund out of a total of 10,000 shares, then on January 15, X could exchange his 10 shares for 10/10,000 of the $70,000,000 or $70,000.

Open end mutual funds are valued in a manner that is basically different from the valuation of other types of securities. Quotations for the bid and asked prices for most of the larger funds may be found in the *Wall Street Journal* and other similar publications. Unlike other securities, where the date of death value is the mean between the high and low or the bid and the asked prices, shares in open end mutual funds are valued at the bid price that equals the shares' pro rata portion of the value of the total portfolio or the redemption price, commonly known as the "Net Asset

Value" or "NAV." The asked price equals the pro rata portion of value plus sales commissions relating to the purchase of shares, if any.

The valuation of these shares involves two unique features. First, the NAV or bid price is used rather than the mean between the bid and asked price, and second, if the date of death occurs on a date on which there is no quoted NAV, the value is based on the NAV price quoted by the company for the first trading day preceding the applicable valuation date. No weight is given to the NAV price on the first trading day following the valuation date, as in the usual situation.

Closed End Funds Unlike the open end fund, the owner of shares of a closed end mutual fund has no right to redeem his or her shares in return for his or her pro rata share of the value of the fund's portfolio. The owner of shares of such a fund may realize cash for his shares only by selling them to another investor. The value of such shares is based on investors' views of the future profits of the fund derived from increases in the value of the securities comprising the portfolio and income generated by those investments in the form of dividends on stock and interest on debt securities. For purposes of Schedule B, the shares of closed end mutual funds are valued in the same manner as shares of stock of business corporations whose stock is traded over the counter, i.e., the value equals the mean between the bid and asked prices on the date of death, and so on.

One may determine whether a particular fund is open end or closed end either by referring to the separate lists for such funds in the financial section of a newspaper such as the *Wall Street Journal* or by conferring with a stockbroker who will easily be able to obtain the information.

Bank Common Trust Funds Many banks operate investment funds similar to mutual funds for the use of the customers of their trust departments. The funds are said to be "commingled" investment funds because investments of many individuals are put into one fund. Units of participation (shares) in such a fund may occasionally be in a trust that must be included in the decedent's gross estate for federal estate tax purposes. The purchase of these units is not unlike the purchase of open end mutual fund shares. However, unlike mutual funds, it is quite possible that the only source for a quotation on the value of the holding in the bank's common trust fund will be the bank itself. The value of funds maintained by banks is not generally reported in any of the financial publications, and if the gross estate does include units in such a fund, the value should be obtained by communication directly with the trust department of the bank involved.

Accrued Interest and Dividends In addition to valuing the securities that are owned by the decedent, it is important to include the value of certain distributions to which the estate may be entitled as a result of its ownership of stocks or bonds.

Accrued Interest The earlier discussion relating to government bonds described the method of reporting accrued interest. That discussion applies not only to government bonds, but to corporate bonds as well. In each case in which a bond is included in the taxable estate, it is necessary to include also the interest that was accrued on that bond or due and not yet paid, as of the date of death.

Accrued Cash Dividends With respect to stocks, whether common, preferred, or convertible preferred, it is also necessary to value, in addition to the actual security, any right to receive dividends that may be outstanding as of the valuation date. If the decedent is entitled to a dividend but has not yet received it as of the date of death, it must be added to the value of his stock. Three significant dates relate to payment of a dividend by a corporation. The "declaration date" is the date on which the Board of Directors of the corporation decides to pay a dividend on the stock and declares that the dividend will be paid. The "record date" is the date that determines the people who will receive the dividend being paid by the company. That is, only people who are shareholders on the records of the corporation on the record date are entitled to receive the dividend. The third date of significance is the "payment date." That is the date on which the dividend is actually distributed to the shareholders.

For example, X Corporation may have declared a dividend of $.25 per share on September 1, payable to all shareholders of record on September 15, with the actual date of payment of the dividend to be September 30. If the decedent died on or after September 15, but prior to the time the dividend was actually paid, his estate would include, in addition to his shares in X Corporation, the value of the right to receive the dividend payable on September 30. This asset would be reflected as an "accrued dividend," and the amount of the dividend would be reported separately on Schedule B, immediately after the particular stock was reported as follows:

100 X Corp., common	10.00	$1,000.00
Dividend of $0.25 per share declared 9/1 to holders of record on 9/15 payable 9/30		25.00

For a period of three or four days prior to the record date, stock in a corporation trades on the open market "ex-dividend." During this period purchasers of the stock will not be entitled to receive the current dividend. Thus, a purchaser of X Corporation's stock on September 14 would purchase the stock "ex-dividend" since processing delays would keep that purchaser from being a shareholder of record on the books of the corporation by September 15. Even though the purchaser would own the stock, the seller would receive the dividend on September 30 when it was paid. During the period of time that a stock sells "ex-dividend," the value of that stock will be reduced by approximately the amount of the declared dividend that is to be paid in the near future. If a decedent dies owning stock that is trading "ex-dividend" on the applicable valuation date because the dividend payment date has not arrived, the amount of the dividend is not included in the gross estate as a separate item and shown as an accrued dividend. Instead, the amount of the dividend is added to the value of the stock in determining fair market value as of the date of death.

For example, if the mean between the high and low prices for X Corporation's stock on the date of death is $10.00 per share, and if the stock is selling ex-dividend on that date with respect to a quarterly dividend of $.25 per share, the appropriate value of each share of stock, for federal estate tax purposes, will be $10.25 and will be shown as follows:

100 shs. X Corp. common, including $.25 per share ex-dividend on date of death	10.25	$1,025.00

In valuing stock for purposes of preparing the federal estate tax return, it is important to determine whether there are any accrued dividends that will be received by the estate. It is a simple matter to determine whether a stock is selling ex-dividend, since the newspaper quotation will show that the stock is selling without the dividend by placing an "X" immediately before the quotations for that day. The newspaper, however, will offer no indication that the record date has passed and that a stock is entitled to an accrued dividend. This can only be determined by referring to one of the dividend record books that are published by several financial services and that report the record dates that public corporations have declared for all dividends. The most widely used of these books is Standard and Poor's *Weekly Dividend Record.* Thus, in valuing the stock in X Corporation, it will be necessary not only to obtain quotations for the valuation date from the newspaper, but also to check the dividend record book to determine if, shortly following the decedent's death, the holder of the stock will be receiving a dividend that was payable to shareholders of record on some date prior to the decedent's death. As a practical matter, it is necessary to check the dividend record book only with respect to stocks on which dividends are paid shortly following the decedent's death. Since the period between the record date and the payment date rarely exceeds a month, if the estate (or the surviving joint owner, in the case of jointly owned stock) receives no dividend for more than a month following the date of death, one may be reasonably certain that the decedent was not entitled to any accrued dividend at the date of death. If, however, a dividend is received by the holder of the stock within approximately a month following the date of death, the dividend record book should be carefully checked to ascertain the record date for that dividend and, consequently, whether or not it is necessary to report an accrued dividend on the federal estate tax return.

Stock Dividends and Stock Splits In addition to cash dividends, many corporations pay dividends in the form of additional stock. To take a well-known example, Georgia Pacific Corporations pays a 1% stock dividend and has done so for many years. This means that the owner of 100 shares of Georgia Pacific stock will receive one share of stock as a stock dividend on the first declared stock dividend payment date after becoming record owner of 100 shares. Thereafter, the stockholder will continue to receive stock dividends equal to 1% of the number of shares that are owned on the record date. Accrued stock dividends, like accrued cash dividends, must be reported and included in the federal estate tax return. Therefore, if the record date for the payment of a stock dividend has passed, but the dividend has not been received prior to the date of death, the tax return should include the accrued dividend of additional stock. This additional stock should be valued in the same manner and on the same date as the shares actually held at the date of death are valued. For example,

100 shs. X Corp., common	10	$1,000.00
1% accrued stock dividend (1 share)	10	10.00

In addition to stock dividends, corporations occasionally split their stock by issuing additional shares to each shareholder of record on a given date. For example, if X Corporation decides to split its stock two for one, the holder of 100 shares of its stock will receive an additional 100 shares from the company. When stock splits become effective, the value of the stock in the corporation, as determined in the open market, will automatically adjust to reflect the additional shares outstanding. Thus, if a stock is selling at approximately $100 a share and "splits two for one," the value of the stock in the market will normally decrease to approximately $50 a share since the total value of the company is now represented by twice as many shares of issued and outstanding stock. A similar adjustment will normally take place in regard to stock dividends, and for this reason the stock dividends are separately valued. In terms of preparing the federal estate tax return, it is important to determine if any splits became effective on or near the applicable valuation date so that no errors will result in the number of shares that are reported on the estate tax return or in their value. The necessary information may be obtained from the Commerce Clearing House "Capital Changes Reporter."

Alternate Valuation All of the discussion to this point dealing with the valuation of stocks and bonds and the valuation of real estate (in the section devoted to Schedule A of the return) has assumed that assets owned by the estate are to be valued as of the date of the decedent's death. It is appropriate at this point to discuss and explain the concept of alternate valuation, which permits the personal representative to value the property as of a date after the date of death.

Section 2032 of the Internal Revenue Code that deals with alternate valuation provides as follows:

(a) GENERAL.—The value of the gross estate may be determined, if the executor so elects, by valuing all the property included in the gross estate as follows:
  (1) In the case of property distributed, sold, exchanged, or otherwise disposed of, within six months after the decedent's death such property shall be valued as of the date of distribution, sale, exchange, or other disposition.
  (2) In the case of property not distributed, sold, exchanged, or otherwise disposed of, within six months after the decedent's death, such property shall be valued as of the date six months after the decedent's death.
  (3) Any interest or estate which is affected by mere lapse of time shall be included at its value as of the time of death (instead of the later date) with adjustment for any difference in its value as of the later date not due to mere lapse of time.

The basic purpose of the alternate valuation provisions is to permit a reduction in the amount of tax that would otherwise be payable if the gross estate had suffered a shrinkage in its aggregate value in the period between the decedent's death and the filing of the estate tax return. For example, an estate may consist largely of marketable stocks and bonds that, at the date of death, have a value of $1,000,000. If the stock market suffers a precipitous decline in the six-months period following death, the value of these assets may depreciate to fifty percent or less of their date-of-death value. Because of the hardship that would result if the estate were required to pay taxes on $1,000,000 worth of assets at a time when the estate consisted of assets with a value of only $500,000 or less, the Internal Revenue Code provides for alternate valuation.

It is important to understand that an election to use the alternate valuation date must apply to *all* assets. The statute does not permit the personal representative to pick some assets to be revalued and leave others at date-of-death value.

Alternate valuation must always be lower than date-of-death value. In the past a higher alternate valuation could have been chosen so that the surviving beneficiaries could receive a "step up in basis" on the property that they were inheriting. This was often used in an estate where there was no tax due on the Form 706 anyway, such as when the estate passed to the surviving spouse. The beneficiaries could thus get the highest possible basis in the property so that when they eventually sold the property, they would not have as much capital gain to report. The IRS saw this "loophole" and qualified the statute in 1985.

Stocks and bonds will be most frequently affected by alternate valuation although real estate and ownership of interests in sole proprietorships, partnerships, or other types of business ventures may also be affected.

Operation of § 2032 As pointed out in the quotation from § 2032, the alternate valuation date for any property that is disposed of in any manner by the estate within six months following the decedent's death is the date of the disposition. Such a disposition could be in the form of a distribution, sale, exchange, or some other form. Where alternate valuation is chosen, all property that is retained by the estate for six months following the decedent's death must be valued as of the date six months after the decedent's death.

The value of any asset that automatically increases or decreases by mere lapse of time will not be changed if alternate valuation is chosen. For example, if an estate elects alternate valuation, the date-of-death value and the alternate value for bank accounts, insurance policies, bank certificates, United States "E," "EE," and "H" bonds and other similar assets will be identical even though interest or income earned between the date of death and the alternate valuation date will have increased the value of the particular asset.

The regulations at § 20.6018–3(c) (6) provide:

> If, pursuant to Section 2032, the executor elects to have the estate valued at a date or dates subsequent to the time of the decedent's death, there must be set forth on the return: (i) An itemized description of all property included in the gross estate on the date of the decedent's death, together with the value of each item as of that date; (ii) An itemized disclosure of all distributions, sales, exchanges, and other dispositions of any property during the six month period after the date of the decedent's death, together with the dates thereof; and (iii) The value of each item of property in accordance with the provisions of Section 2032. Interest and rents accrued at the date of decedent's death and dividends declared to stockholders of record on or before the date of

the decedent's death and not collected at that date are to be shown separately.

The following examples assume alternate valuation.

EXAMPLES

Valuing Shares of Stock

1. The decedent owned 100 shares of X Corporation stock, which had a value of $10 a share on November 1, 1991, the date of death, and was entitled to receive a cash dividend (declared on October 5, 1991, to holders of record on October 20, 1991) of $.25 a share on November 5, 1991. On January 15, 1992, the stock split two for one. None of the stock was sold, distributed, exchanged, or otherwise disposed of within the six months following death and, on the six-month anniversary date of death, the stock was selling at $4.50 a share. This asset would be reported as follows:

Description	Unit Value	Subsequent Valuation Date	Alternate Value	Value at Date of Death
100 shs. X Corp. 100 shs. received as a 2 for 1 split on 1/15/92.	10.00			$1,000.00
200 shs. not disposed of within six months following death	4.50	5/1/92	$900.00	
Dividend declared 10/5/91 to holders of record 10/20/91 payable on 11/5/91			25.00	25.00

2. The decedent owned 216 shares of X Corporation stock, which had a value of $10 a share on November 1, 1991, the date of death. The company paid a 4% stock dividend on March 15, 1992, as a result of which the estate received 8.64 shares (4% × 216). In addition, the estate purchased .36 shares in order to round out its stock dividend to an even 9 shares. The entire 225 shares were retained for six months following death, at which time the stock was selling at $9.50 a share. This asset would be reported as follows:

Description	Unit Value	Subsequent Valuation Date	Alternate Value	Value at Date of Death
216 shs. X Corp. Received 8.64 shs. as a 4% stock dividend on 3/15/92	10.00			
224.64 shs. not disposed of within six months following death	9.50	5/1/92	$2,134.08	

included in the estate since the issuance of this stock to all shareholders would not have resulted in any change in the estate's percentage ownership of the corporation. In other words, for purposes of valuation, a stock dividend is treated like a stock split, not a cash dividend. Note that the fractional share purchased by the estate is not taken into account in calculating declaration and alternate valuation.

3. Assume the same facts as in the preceding example except that the estate elected to sell its fractional share, instead of purchasing a fractional share to round out its holding.

Description	Unit Value	Subsequent Valuation Date	Alternate Value	Value at Date of Death
216 shs. X Corp. Received 8.64 shs. as a 4% stock dividend on 3/15/92	10.00			$2,160.00
Sold .64 shs. on 3/15/92		3/15/92	$ 6.40	
224 shs. not disposed of within six months following death	9.50	5/1/92	$2,128.00	

The preceding examples all involve assets that depreciated in value between the date of death and the alternate valuation date. As previously mentioned, an election of alternate valuation applies to each and every asset in the estate. The executor is not given the option to pick and choose either date-of-death value or alternate value, depending upon the performance of the particular asset. In a typical case, some of the assets in the estate may have increased in value in the six months following death, and other assets may have decreased in value during the same period of time. If alternate valuation is chosen, the alternate valuation date will apply to all of the assets, both those that decreased in value during the six months and those that increased in value during the same period. Thus, to determine whether or not alternate valuation should be elected, it is necessary to revalue *all* of the assets held in an estate to determine whether the aggregate estate has increased or decreased in value.

Any worthless securities should be listed at the bottom of the schedule. A letter from a qualified broker stating that the securities are worthless should be attached to the Form 706.

The next example shows a completed Schedule B on which the alternate valuation date has been used.

EXAMPLE *Form 706, Schedule B—Stocks and Bonds*

Form 706 (Rev. 7-90)

Estate of: Peter Chessman

SCHEDULE B—Stocks and Bonds

(For jointly owned property that must be disclosed on Schedule E, see the Instructions for Schedule E.)

Item number	Description including face amount of bonds or number of shares and par value where needed for identification. Give CUSIP number if available.	Unit value	Alternate valuation date	Alternate value	Value at date of death
1	1000 shs. Allegheny Ludlum Steel Corp. com NYSE CUSIP 142183-7-2	400.00			400,000.00
	Not disposed of within six months following death	317.03625	11/3/91	317,036.25	
2	200 shs. American Telephone & Telegraph Co. com NYSE CUSIP 030117-10-9	50.6875			10,137.50
	Not disposed of within six months following death	53.65625	11/3/91	10,731.25	
	Dividend declared 3/15 to holders of record 4/1 payable 5/5	.85	11/3/91	170.00	170.00
3	500 shs. Chicago, Milwaukee, St. Paul & Pacific Railroad com NYSE	58.625			29,312.50
	250 shs. received as three-for-two split record date 5/3/91 payable 5/23/91	58.625			14,656.25
	750 shs. not disposed of within six months following death CUSIP 378246-10-3	50.25	11/3/91	37,687.50	
4	100 shs. Continental Bank Com OTC	70.00			7,000.00
	100 shs. distributed CUSIP 235174-09-2	55.75	10/20/91	5,575.00	
	Dividend declared 4/15 to holders of record 5/1 payable 5/20	.50	11/3/91	50.00	50.00
5	200 shs. Crown, Cork & Seal Co., Inc., including $0.45 per share ex-dividend com NYSE CUSIP 107302-40-3	74.15			14,830.00
	Not disposed of within six months following death	68.75	11/3/91	13,750.00	
6	$50,000 Illinois State Toll Highway Commission; 4% due 1/1/95; interest paid semi-annually 1/1 and 7/1	86.25			43,125.00
	Not disposed of within six months following death	84.375	11/3/91	42,187.50	
	Accrued interest 11/15 to 5/3			660.00	660.00
	Total from continuation schedule(s) (or additional sheet(s)) attached to this schedule . . .				
	TOTAL. (Also enter on Part 5, Recapitulation, page 3, at item 2.)			385,000.00	519,941.25

(If more space is needed, attach the continuation schedule from the end of this package or additional sheets of the same size.)
(The instructions to Schedule B are in the separate instructions.)

Schedule B—Page 10

PROBLEM

Valuing Stocks in a Decedent's Portfolio

Your office represents the estate of James Joseph Jones. Using quotations that are shown below, prepare a Schedule B for Mr. Jones's 706 return. He died on December 13, 1991. All stocks illustrated here are listed on the New York Stock Exchange. All stocks are common unless otherwise indicated:

1. American Electric Power—750 shares
2. Bank of America—150 shares
3. Tenneco—500 shares*
4. CBS—500 shares
5. Cabot Oil and Gas—725 shares
6. Pacific Telesis—100 shares
7. Bangor Hydrolic Company—2,000 shares
8. Pepsi Company—300 shares
9. Singer—400 shares
10. Sherwin Williams—225 shares
11. Ameritech—1,250 shares
12. Texaco—600 shares
13. Philadelphia Electric preferred series H—1,000 shares

*There was a Tenneco cash dividend in the amount of $.77 per share, payable December 31, 1991 to owners of record December 10, 1991; declared December 1, 1991.

-A-A-A-

	20	16⅝	AmCapBdFd	ACB	1.68	8.8	...	94	19½	19⅛	19⅛	− ⅛
	19⅝	16¼	AmCapCvSec	ACS	1.39e	7.5	...	54	18⅝	18⅜	18½	− ¼
	7⅝	5⅛	AmCapIncTr	ACD	.84	11.4	...	230	7½	7⅜	7⅜	...
	69	48½	AmCyanmd	ACY	1.50	2.6	15	3271	58⅛	56⅜	57¾	+1⅜
	33	26⅝	AmElecPwr	AEP	2.40	7.4	12	2838	32⅞	32⅜	32⅝	− ⅛
	30⅜	18¼	AmExpress	AXP	1.00	5.3	13	12864	18⅞	18½	18¾	+ ⅛
	29⅞	17⅛	AmFamily	AFL	.40	1.4	16	1770	28	27½	28	+ ½
	43⅝	28	AmGenerl	AGC	2.00	4.7	10	1542	42½	42	42⅜	...
	8½	7	AmGvIncFd	AGF	.77a	9.6	...	323	8¼	8	8	− ⅛
	10⅜	9	AmGvIncoP	AAF	1.14	11.1	...	309	10¼	10⅛	10¼	...
	11	9⅞	AmGvTermTr	AGT	.94	8.8	...	57	10⅝	10⅝	10⅝	...
	31⅜	22¾	AmHlthProp	AHE	2.64	8.8	15	289	30⅛	29¾	30⅛	+ ⅜
	32¼	20	AmHeritgLf	AHL	1.08	3.7	12	19	29¾	29½	29½	− ⅜
	79⅛	46½	AmHomePdts	AHP	2.60	3.4	18	4152	77⅜	76½	76¾	− ⅜
	102	72	AmIntGroup	AIG	.50	.6	12	2510	88½	88	88⅛	+ ½
n	10⅜	9½	AmMunTermTr2	BXT	.62	6.4	...	78	9¾	9⅝	9¾	...
n	10⅜	9⅝	AmMunTermTr	AXT	.65e	6.4	...	38	10⅛	10⅛	10⅛	...
	10¾	8⅞	AmOpIncoFd	OIF	.98e	9.4	...	212	10⅜	10¼	10⅜	...
	15⅛	6¼	AmPrecInd	APR	.20	3.1	13	198	6½	6¼	6½	+ ¼
	43⅜	15½	AmPresidnt	APS	.60	1.7	11	737	35¼	34⅞	35¼	+ ⅞
	11½	7⅝	AmRE Ptnrs	ACP	2.00	18.8	9	142	10¾	10½	10⅝	...
	7⅜	5	AmRltyTr	ARB		...	...	9	5¼	5¼	5¼	...
	2½	**⅛**	**AmSvgBk**	**ASB**		**...**	**...**	**223**	**¼**	**⅛**	**5/32**	**+ 1/32**
	3⅝	**¼**	**AmSvgBk pf**			**...**	**...**	**132**	**15/32**	**5/16**	**⅜**	**+ 1/16**
	4½	1⅛	AmShipBldg	ABG		...	...	46	2	1¾	1⅞	...
s	46⅛	25⅝	AmStores	ASC	.70	2.6	7	2608	27½	27	27⅜	+ ¾
	40⅜	29	AmT&T	T	1.32	3.5	60	20287	38⅜	38	38⅛	+ ¼
	14⅞	5⅞	AmWasteSvc	AW		...	24	169	6⅞	6⅝	6⅞	...
	25½	15½	AmWaterWks	AWK	.86	3.6	10	682	24⅛	23½	24⅛	+ ½
	18½	13⅝	AmWaterWks pf		1.25	7.2	...	z140	18	17¼	17¼	− ¼
	6½	2	AmHotel	AHR	3.50c	...	4	10	2¾	2¾	2¾	...
	14½	5⅜	Ameriscribe	ACR		...	21	111	8⅛	7⅝	7¾	− ⅛
	69¾	55¾	Ameritech	AIT	3.40	5.3	13	4005	64¾	63⅞	63⅞	− ⅛

-B-B-B-

	32¾	23⅜	BancoBilV	BBV	1.49e	6.0	6	1	24⅞	24⅞	24⅞	− ⅛
	55⅞	40	BancoSantdr	STD	2.17e	5.4	7	2	40⅛	40⅛	40⅛	− ⅛
s	47¾	27¼	BcpHawii	BOH	1.20	2.9	10	474	40⅞	40½	40¾	+ ½
x	118¼	81½	Bandag	BDG	1.20	1.1	20	x144	113⅝	112	113¼	+ ⅜
	17½	14¼	BangorHyd	BGR	1.28	7.7	11	64	16⅝	16⅝	16⅝	...
	12⅞	3	BankBost	BKB	.20j	...	...	4276	11¾	11⅛	11¼	− ⅛
	33	11¼	BankBost pfA		3.37e	11.3	...	24	29⅞	29½	29⅞	+ ⅝
	32	10¾	BankBost pfB		3.25e	11.0	...	1	29½	29½	29½	+ ⅝
	54	16	BankBost pfC		5.88e	11.3	...	z2350	52	51	52	+1½
	36⅛	16½	BankNY	BK	1.52	5.6	22	1903	27⅞	27¼	27⅜	− ⅛
	98⅜	83⅝	BankNY adj pf		7.94e	8.4	...	422	94¼	94⅛	94¼	−2½
	39	27⅛	BankNY adj pfA		3.29e	8.8	...	80	37¼	37	37¼	+ ¼
	44¾	23⅛	BankAmer	BAC	1.20	3.4	8	17194	35½	34¼	35	+1½
	43½	33⅛	BankAmer pfA		3.28e	7.6	...	108	43	42	43	+ ⅞
	72½	55¼	BankAmer pfB		6.00	8.3	...	100	72¼	71½	72¼	+ ⅞
	28	25	BankAmer pfF		2.41	9.2	...	166	26¼	25½	26⅛	...
	56	45½	BankAmer pfG		3.25	6.7	...	189	49½	48	48½	+1
	68	39½	BankTrst	BT	2.54	4.0	9	2567	64¾	63⅜	64	+ ⅝
n	10¾	6¾	BannerAero	BAR		...	9	494	7¼	7	7⅛	...
	1⅛	5/16	BanyanMtgInv	VMG		...	...	671	9/16	15/32	½	...
	27⅛	22¾	Barclays pr		2.78	10.6	...	130	26⅜	25⅞	26¼	+ ⅜
	27⅛	22¼	Barclays prB		2.72	10.6	...	79	25⅞	25⅝	25¾	+ ¾
	27⅝	22½	Barclays pfC		2.81	10.7	...	116	26½	26⅛	26⅜	− ⅛
	27¾	24¾	Barclays pfD		2.87	10.7	...	118	27	26½	26⅞	+ ¼

continued on next page

Valuing Stocks in a Decedent's Portfolio, continued

-C-C-C-

	31⅞	15	C&S Sovran	CVN	1.56	5.1	93	10875	30¾	30⅜	30¾	+ ¼
s	37⅛	23½	CBI Ind	CBH	.48	1.7	19	1555	27¾	27	27¾	+ ⅞
	188⅜	128⅝	CBS	CBS	1.00	.8	...	339	133⅜	131½	132	...
	2⅜	**¼**	**CCX**	**CCX**		**...**	**...**	**37**	**1⅜**	**1¼**	**1¼**	**− ⅛**
	9¾	5¾	CDI	CDI		...	18	34	7	6⅞	7	...
	2⅛	**5/16**	**CF IncoPtnr**	**CFI**	**.16**	**39.4**	**...**	**304**	**13/32**	**5/16**	**13/32**	**+ 1/16**
	58¾	36	CIGNA	CI	3.04	5.8	8	885	53⅝	52¼	52½	−1
	7⅜	3⅝	CIGNA High	HIS	.90	12.9	...	409	7	6¾	7	+ ⅛
	28⅛	21⅜	CIPSCO	CIP	1.88	7.0	13	330	27⅛	26⅞	27	...
s	31	8⅛	CML	CML	.02e	.1	20	904	30⅛	29½	29⅞	+ ½
	33	16⅝	CMS Engy	CMS	.48	2.7	...	3368	18	17½	17⅞	+ ¼
	5⅛	**1¾**	**CMS Enhanc**	**CME**		**...**	**22**	**125**	**3¼**	**3⅛**	**3⅛**	**− ¼**
	99	60⅜	CNA Fnl	CNA		...	12	183	85½	81½	82¾	−1¾
	11⅝	8½	CNA IncShrs	CNN	1.16a	10.2	...	65	11⅜	11¼	11⅜	+ ⅛
	93½	72	CPCInt	CPC	2.20	2.5	17	535	87	86½	86⅞	+ ¼
	34¾	21¾	CPI Cp	CPY	.56	2.3	12	350	23⅞	23¼	23⅞	+ ½
x	9½	6⅜	CRIIMI	CMM	1.08	12.7	11	x898	8½	8⅜	8½	+ ¼
x	13⅛	10⅞	CRI Liq	CFR	3.15c	28.6	...	x72	11	11	11	...
	16½	8	CRSS	CRX	.12	1.3	15	268	9⅛	8¾	9	+ ¼
	56¾	29¾	CSX	CSX	1.52	3.0	12	1424	51¾	50½	51¼	+ ½
	24	16⅜	CTS	CTS	.75	4.0	19	9	18¾	18⅝	18⅝	− ⅛
s	29⅝	13⅛	CUC Int	CU		...	40	820	28¼	27¼	28¼	+1¼
	7⅜	2½	CV REIT	CVI	.75e	11.8	...	29	6⅜	6¼	6⅜	+ ⅛
▲x	31⅜	24½	CablWirels	CWP	.87e	2.8	19	x924	31½	31	31½	+1⅛
	52⅞	25	CabltrnSys	CS		...	27	1449	46¼	44½	46⅛	+2
	35⅞	26⅝	Cabot Cp	CBT	1.04b	3.6	17	11	28⅞	28¾	28⅞	+ ⅛
	18⅛	11⅜	CabotO&G	COG	.16	1.3	33	63	12½	12¼	12⅜	+ ⅛
	34⅝	14½	CadenceDsgn	CDN		...	27	1280	20⅞	20¼	20⅝	+ ⅝
	34⅛	12⅞	CaesarWld	CAW		...	12	837	30¼	29½	29¾	− ⅛

-P-Q-

	36¾	22½	PHH Cp	PHH	1.20	4.1	11	109	29½	29¼	29½	+ ⅜
	19	8¾	PHM	PHM	.12	.6	27	1299	19	18¾	19	+ ⅛
	47	18⅞	PNC Fnl	PNC	2.12	4.9	36	1699	43⅜	42⅝	43¼	+ ⅝
	36	17⅞	PNC Fnl pfC		1.60	4.5	...	3	35⅝	35⅝	35⅝	+1⅜
	37	17½	PNC Fnl pfD		1.80	5.1	...	1	35⅝	35⅝	35⅝	+ ⅝
	59⅜	41½	PPGInd	PPG	1.84	4.0	18	1740	46⅜	45⅞	46⅛	+ ¼
▼	**72¼**	**32½**	**PS Gp**	**PSG**	**.60**	**1.9**	**...**	**273**	**33⅜**	**30¾**	**31**	**−2⅜**
	18½	15⅜	PSI Res	PIN	1.00	5.9	8	1077	17⅛	16¾	16⅞	− ⅛
▲	16¼	13¼	PacAmShrs	PAI	1.46	8.8	...	88	16½	16⅛	16½	+ ½
	43⅜	23¾	PacEnt	PET	1.76	7.1	10	2408	25	24⅜	24⅝	+ ⅛
	31¾	24	PacGE	PCG	1.64	5.3	14	2459	30¾	30⅜	30¾	+ ¼
	12½	7¼	PacScientif	PSX	.12	1.3	12	132	9⅛	8¾	9⅛	+ ¼
	47	38½	PacTelesis	PAC	2.14	5.1	16	3391	42½	41⅞	42¼	...
	24⅝	20⅜	PacifiCp	PPW	1.50	6.4	13	1622	23⅞	23⅜	23½	− ¼
s	**23¼**	**7¼**	**PaineWebber**	**PWJ**	**.40**	**2.0**	**9**	**4171**	**20**	**19**	**20**	**+1**
▲	6¼	4¼	PnWbrDecr wt			...	...	1447	6⅜	5⅞	6	− ⅛
	23	**11½**	**PaineWebber pf**		**1.37**	**6.6**	**...**	**142**	**20¾**	**20**	**20¾**	**+1**
	16½	9⅞	PanhdlEast	PEL	.80	5.1	...	9573	16	15⅝	15¾	− ⅛
	4½	2⅜	ParTech	PTC		...	15	4	2⅝	2½	2½	− ⅛
	45⅞	35¾	ParCom	PCI	.70	1.8	30	1470	37⅞	37⅜	37⅞	+ ½
	13	10	ParkElchm	PKE	.32	2.5	51	1	12¾	12¾	12¾	...
	9¼	5¼	ParkerDrl	PKD		...	150	1945	6	5¾	6	+ ¼
	31	22¾	ParkerHan	PH	.92	3.3	26	653	28¼	28	28¼	+ ⅜
	4⅛	**1½**	**PatheComm**	**PCC**		**...**	**...**	**38**	**1⅝**	**1½**	**1½**	**− ⅛**
	3¾	2	PatrickPete	PPC		...	...	106	2⅝	2½	2½	− ⅛
	9⅞	7⅜	PatrDivFd	PDF	.80	8.3	...	317	9⅝	9⅜	9⅝	+ ¼
n	11⅛	8⅝	PatrDivFdII	PDT	.90	8.2	...	526	11	10¾	11	+ ⅛
n	16	12⅝	PatrSelDiv	DIV	1.65	10.4	...	177	16	15¾	15⅞	...
	2¼	**⅜**	**Patten**	**PAT**		**...**	**...**	**228**	**1⅛**	**1**	**1**	**− ⅛**
	27	17¾	PennCentral	PC	.68	2.9	14	324	23⅞	23⅜	23½	+ ⅜
	58¼	42⅜	Penney JC	JCP	2.64	5.0	15	1245	53¼	52⅜	52⅞	+ ½
	50⅝	41¾	PennP&L	PPL	3.10	6.2	12	436	49¾	49¼	49¾	+ ⅜
	60½	49½	PennP&L pf		4.50	8.0	...	z200	57	56½	56½	...
	103	91½	PennP&L pf		8.60	8.3	...	z200	103	103	103	+1
	102½	88	PennP&L pr		8.40	8.3	...	z230	101	100¼	100¾	+ ¾
	104	91½	PennP&L pr		8.70	8.4	...	z50	103¼	103¼	103¼	
	76½	54⅜	Pennzoil	PZL	3.00	5.4	23	382	55⅝	55⅛	55⅜	+ ⅛
x	28¼	21¾	PeopEngy	PGL	1.72	6.5	13	x548	26½	26	26⅜	+ ⅛
	19½	8⅜	PepBoys	PBY	.13	.8	27	1247	17⅜	17	17¼	...
	35⅝	23½	PepsiCo	PEP	.48	1.5	23	14568	31⅞	31⅛	31⅛	− ¼
	34⅝	**21⅜**	**PerkElmer**	**PKN**	**.68**	**2.4**	**19**	**1032**	**27⅞**	**26½**	**27⅞**	**+1⅜**
	18⅞	11¾	PerkFamR	PFR	1.30	7.4	13	58	17½	17⅛	17½	+ ¼

	4⅞	3¾	PermRltyTr	PBT	.55e	12.2	8	84	4½	4⅜	4½	+ ⅛
	8⅝	3¾	PerryDrug	PDS		...	283	141	8⅝	8⅜	8½	− ⅛
▲	20⅜	15⅛	Pet Inc	PT	.18e	.9	...	5748	21¼	20½	20¾	+ ⅜
	25⅜	13¾	PetrieStrs	PST	.20	1.0	116	410	19¾	19⅜	19¾	+ ½
	29	24¼	PeteRes	PEO	2.15e	8.6	...	164	25	24⅝	24⅞	...
	19⅛	16¾	PeteRes pf		1.57	8.9	...	14	17¾	17⅝	17⅝	...
s▲	72½	36⅜	Pfizer	PFE	1.32	1.8	28	10226	74¼	72½	73⅝	+1¼
	5⅞	2⅝	PharmRes	PRX		...	...	149	4⅞	4¾	4¾	...
	79¼	52⅜	PhelpsD	PD	3.00	4.7	7	1805	64⅝	64	64⅜	+ ⅜
	24½	17	PhilaElec	PE	1.30	5.3	13	2558	24½	24¼	24⅜	− ⅛
	98⅝	85½	PhilaElec pfG		8.75	8.9	...	z300	98	97⅛	98	+1
	117	109	PhilaElec pfO		14.63	12.6	...	2	116	116	116	...
	93½	77⅝	PhilaElec pfH		7.85	8.7	...	z100	90¼	90¼	90¼	− ¾
	120	107	PhilaElec pfM		15.25	12.7	...	z300	120	119	120	+ ½
	104	92	PhilaElec pfK		9.50	9.2	...	z200	103½	103	103	− ½
	91⅜	77½	PhilaElec pfJ		7.80	8.7	...	z150	89½	89	89½	− ½
	16⅜	11¾	PhilaSub	PSC	1.00	6.4	13	48	15⅞	15⅝	15⅝	− ⅛
	74⅝	48¼	PhilipMor	MO	2.10	3.0	16	16350	70¾	70	70⅝	+1

-S-S-S-

n	12½	11	SeligSelct	SEL	.84	7.0	...	227	12⅛	11⅞	12	...
	27⅛	13¾	SensorElec	SRM	.30	1.2	24	711	25⅛	24⅝	25	+ ⅜
	66⅛	38¾	SequaA	SQAA	.60	1.5	...	81	41¾	41	41	− ½
	73½	47⅛	SequaB	SQAB	.50	1.0	...	315	48½	48	48½	+ ½
	27½	20¼	ServiceCp	SRV	.56	2.4	16	341	23⅝	23⅜	23½	...
s	13½	3⅜	SvcMdse	SME		...	10	1390	10¾	10½	10⅝	+ ¼
	35¾	22	SvcMastr	SVM	1.92	5.5	12	280	35⅜	34⅝	34⅞	− ¼
	38½	17½	ShawInd	SHX	.50	1.8	24	991	28¾	28	28¼	− ¼
	10⅞	2⅞	ShawmutNtl	SNC		...	...	1025	9	8⅞	8⅞	...
	8¾	5⅞	ShelbyWill	SY	.24	4.0	32	5	6	6	6	...
	56⅝	49⅜	ShellTrans	SC	2.85e	5.4	13	186	52¾	52⅜	52⅜	+ ¾
s	27⅛	17⅝	SherwinWill	SHW	.42	1.8	17	1444	23⅝	23	23⅜	+ ½
	22	9⅞	Shoneys	SHN		...	24	583	21⅜	20¾	20⅞	− ½
n	15⅛	11¾	ShopkoStr	SKO		...	...	871	13	12⅝	12⅞	+ ⅛
	11¾	3½	Showboat	SBO	.10	1.3	29	397	8¼	8	8	− ¼
	24¼	20⅛	SierraPac	SRP	1.84	8.0	13	252	23⅜	23⅛	23⅛	− ⅛
	18⅛	8¾	SignlAprl	SIA		...	...	13	17¼	17⅛	17¼	...
	24⅝	7¼	SignetBk	SBK	.80	4.7	14	309	17¼	16⅞	17⅛	− ⅛
	48¾	22¼	SiliconGrph	SGI		...	25	1523	40	39⅝	40	− ¼
	11¼	8⅜	SingaporeFd	SGF	.60e	6.1	...	209	10	9⅝	9⅞	+ ⅜
n	19⅜	13½	Singer	SEW		...	...	400	17¾	17¼	17¼	− ¼
	13	8	SizelerProp	SIZ	1.00	10.5	14	117	9⅝	9½	9½	− ⅛
	18⅞	9⅝	SizzlerInt	SZ	.16	1.5	13	1822	10⅞	10½	10¾	+ ¼
	18¼	13⅞	Skyline	SKY	.48	3.3	36	174	15	14¾	14¾	− ⅛
n	21	15¼	SmartFinal	SMF	.04e	.2	...	20	18	17¾	17⅞	+ ⅛
	11	5¼	SmithCorona	SCO	.20	3.2	11	1367	6½	6	6¼	+ ¼
	17⅛	8¼	SmithInt	SII		...	17	1498	8⅞	8½	8⅝	+ ⅛

-T-T-T-

	30⅞	16	Tektronix	TEK	.60	3.6	11	1108	16¾	16⅝	16¾	+ ⅛
	1⅞	9/16	TelCom	TEL		...	2	13	1⅛	1⅛	1⅛	+ ⅛
n	30⅜	25¼	TelecomNZ	NZT		...	...	1041	28	27½	27⅝	− ⅛
	24⅜	14½	Teledyne	TDY	.80	3.9	28	888	20¾	20¼	20⅜	+ ⅛
	36⅜	24⅝	TeleEspana	TEF	1.62e	4.5	...	1813	36⅜	36¼	36¼	+ ¼
n	46⅛	24¼	TelefMex	TMX	.17e	.4	...	18009	42½	41¼	41¼	+ ⅝
	51½	28½	TempInland	TIN	.88	2.0	15	914	43¾	42¼	43½	+1½
	23¼	11½	TemplMktFd	EMF	4.04e	19.8	...	790	21⅜	20¼	20⅜	− ½
	9⅝	8⅜	TemplGlbGvt	TGG	.84	9.1	...	274	9¼	9⅛	9¼	...
	9⅛	7¾	TemplGlob	GIM	.84	9.6	...	1510	8⅞	8¾	8¾	− ⅛
	52	29¼	Tenneco	TGT	1.60	5.1	...	4560	31⅜	30¾	31¼	+ ⅞
	22¾	16¼	TeppcoPtnrs	TPP	2.20	11.1	11	189	19⅞	19⅝	19¾	...
	17½	7½	TerexCp	TEX	.06	.5	...	77	11½	11½	11½	− ⅛
	16⅞	6⅛	Teradyne	TER		...	...	1783	14⅛	14	14⅛	+ ¼
▼	9⅜	4¾	Tesoro	TSO		...	4	192	4¾	4⅝	4¾	...
	19⅛	10⅞	Tesoro pf		.54k	...	...	13	11	10⅞	11	...
	70	55½	Texaco	TX	3.20	5.5	11	8751	58⅜	57⅝	58	+ ½
	53	49⅝	Texaco pfC		3.94e	7.6	...	1	52⅛	52⅛	52⅛	...
	25	13	TexInd	TXI	.20	1.1	...	66	19⅛	18⅜	19	+ ⅝
	47⅝	26⅝	TexInstr	TXN	.72	2.6	...	2162	28⅝	27¾	28	+ ¼
	33	27½	TexInstr pf		2.26	7.8	...	1104	29½	28⅞	29⅛	+ ½
	28	18¼	TexPacTr	TPL	.40	2.1	23	7	19⅜	19⅛	19⅛	+ ¼
	41¾	34⅛	TexUtil	TXU	3.00	7.5	...	2518	40⅜	40	40	− ⅛
	7⅝	3⅞	TexfiInd	TXF		...	...	106	5	4⅝	5	+ ⅛

Schedule C—Mortgages, Notes, and Cash[29]

It is necessary to report on Schedule C all mortgages and notes owned and possessed by the decedent which reflect promises made by other individuals to pay money to the decedent, as well as contracts into which the decedent entered for the sale of land and all cash of the decedent whether in his or her possession or held in banks.

Bank Accounts Most estates will include one or more bank accounts reportable on Schedule C. This schedule would include checking accounts, savings accounts, and certificates of deposit representing sums held by banks at interest. You will recall from Chapter Three[30] that shortly following the decedent's death, a letter should be written to the bank or banks holding each account or other deposit. The letter should request that the bank issue a statement indicating the exact balance in the account as of the date of death. The bank letter received in response to the Executor's inquiry concerning the accounts at the bank and the exact date of death balances should be attached to the 706 when it is filed. If there is any question concerning the exact manner in which the account was owned (i.e., individually or jointly), the bank should be asked to confirm in writing the exact registration on its records as of the date of death.

Checking Accounts The letter received from the bank indicating the date-of-death balance in the decedent's checking account should not end the inquiry about the size of that account for purposes of preparing the federal estate tax return. The information provided by the bank will simply be the balance in the account as of the date of death. This figure, however, will not take into account any checks that may have been written by the decedent prior to his death but that had not been presented to his bank for payment by the date of death. For example, the reply from the bank may indicate that as of November 1, 1991, the balance in the decedent's checking account was $5,250. However, analysis of the journal maintained for the estate checking account may indicate that when the decedent's checking account was closed and the balance transferred to the checking account that was opened for the estate, the amount transferred was $4,850. This would indicate that checks totaling $400 were honored by the bank following the date of the decedent's death. The regulations provide that outstanding checks that are honored by the bank after the decedent's death and are charged to his account may be deducted from the date-of-death

29. IRC § 2033,
30. See Chapter Three under "Bank Accounts."

balance so long as the checks were "given in discharge of bona fide legal obligations of the decedent incurred for an adequate and full consideration in money or money's worth." Thus, any outstanding check that related to a debt of the decedent would be properly deducted from the date-of-death balance, but a check that represented a gift would not be deductible whether or not the check was honored.

It is important, therefore, to check the figure supplied by the bank, which reflects the date-of-death balance, against the actual cash received from the bank when the checking account is closed. If the figures are not the same, checks must have been outstanding at the date of death. In that event, the decedent's checkbook or the cancelled checks that are returned by the bank with decedent's last statement should be checked carefully to determine which of the items honored after the date of death can be deducted.

Savings Accounts In obtaining from a bank date-of-death balances for savings accounts and/or certificates of deposit, it is important to specifically request that the bank's letter include not only the balance, but also the interest accrued to the date of death. For example, the decedent's savings account may have had a balance of $10,000 as of January 1, 1991, the date on which interest was last added. A letter to the bank that requests only the date-of-death balance (assume November 1, 1991) might fail to elicit information relating to the interest the account had earned from January 1, 1991 through November 1, 1991, the date of death.

Certificates of Deposit As in the case of savings accounts, when dealing with a certificate of deposit, one must obtain not only the face value of the certificate, but also the figure representing accrued interest to the date of death.

There are several types of certificates of deposit that are commonly available, including certificates on which interest is remitted monthly, quarterly, or at some other convenient interval. Where interest is remitted to the owner, the accrued interest at any given time will not be very substantial since, at the most, it will represent only the interest earned on the certificate since the last interest payment date. In many cases in fact, there will be no accrued interest since, under the terms of some certificates of deposit, the holder is not entitled to receive any interest unless he holds the certificate to the designated interest payment date. "Growth certificates" are certificates of deposit in which all interest is added back to the value of the certificate rather than being remitted to the owner. With respect to growth certificates, the interest that has accrued and has been added to the value of the certificate is of great significance since the face value of the certificate may be considerably lower than its present value, depending, of course, upon the length of time it has been held.

Notes and Mortgages In general, a note or mortgage should be returned at the amount of the unpaid principal plus the interest accrued to the date of death (see Internal Revenue Code Regulation 20.2031–4). Generally speaking, if a note or mortgage is payable in a relatively short period following the decedent's death, the note or mortgage will be returnable for estate tax purposes at its face value plus accrued interest. The foregoing would not apply if there is a question about the collectibility of the obligation because of the insolvency of the debtor and because the property pledged or mortgaged as security for the debt, if any, is not of sufficient value to assure the payment of the indebtedness.

With respect to mortgages or notes that are payable at some distant date in the future, however, it should not be assumed that the asset has a value equal to its face amount, even if the ability of the debtor to eventually repay the note in full is clear. The regulations acknowledge that a note may be worth less than the unpaid amount of principal because of the interest rate or the date of maturity. Thus, the same analysis that was discussed in the section dealing with the valuation of governmental bonds might be applicable to the value of a note or mortgage. The value of such an asset might be significantly lower than its face value if the interest rate provided for in the note were less than interest rates generally available at the date of death for similar types of obligations. It should be noted, however, that the Internal Revenue Service will usually resist any reduction in the value of a note or mortgage below its face amount in the absence of evidence that the solvency of the debtor is questionable.

Cash Any cash found in the possession of the decedent should be listed separately. Often a person will keep cash in their home or safe deposit box. If his or her death was sudden, the person may even have cash in his or her wallet. It is all properly reportable on Schedule C (see next Example).

Schedule D—Proceeds of Life Insurance[31]

Schedule D of the federal estate tax return should include all life insurance policies of every description on the decedent's life, regardless of the type of policy. Insurance is includible in the estate if the decedent possessed any "incidents of ownership" at death or assigned all the "incidents of ownership" in the policy within three years of his death. There are numerous forms of life insurance

31. Section 2042.

EXAMPLE *Form 706, Schedule C—Mortgages, Notes, and Cash*

Form 706 (Rev. 7-90)

Estate of: Peter Chessman

SCHEDULE C—Mortgages, Notes, and Cash

(For jointly owned property that must be disclosed on Schedule E, see the Instructions for Schedule E.)

Item number	Description		Alternate valuation date	Alternate value	Value at date of death
1	Loan of $5,000 to Eva Chessman on June 10, 1983, of which $2,800 remains unpaid.		11/3/91	2,800.00	2,800.00
	Interest, payable at rate of 6%, accrued from 6/10/90 to 5/3/91			149.52	149.52
2	Agreement of Sale for lot, 1010 Cypress Street, Philadelphia, PA, dated 4/30/91; settlement 7/1/91				
	Sale Price	5,000			
	Less payment on account 4/30/91	(500)	11/3/91	4,500.00	4,500.00
3	Cash on hand		11/3/91	200.00	200.00
4	Checking Account No. 1-234-567 Provident National Bank:				
	Date-of-death balance	5,250			
	Less outstanding checks	(400)	11/3/91	4,850.00	4,850.00
5	Savings Account No. AX123,456 Philadelphia Saving Fund Society, including interest accrued to date of death		11/3/91	37,405.00	37,405.00
6	Growth Certificate of Deposit No. 987654, Philadelphia Saving Fund Society, including interest accrued to date of death		11/3/91	35,095.48	35,095.48
	Total from continuation schedule(s) (or additional sheet(s)) attached to this schedule . . .				
	TOTAL. (Also enter on Part 5, Recapitulation, page 3, at item 3.)			85,000.00	85,000.00

(If more space is needed, attach the continuation schedule from the end of this package or additional sheets of the same size.)

Schedule C—Page 11

policies that are available. These types of insurance contracts are most frequently encountered.

Types of Insurance

Term Life Insurance A term life insurance policy involves the payment of a fixed sum by the insured to the insurance company, in return for which the insurance company guarantees to pay the face amount of the policy to the beneficiary designated by the insured, if the insured should die during the "term" of the policy. The insurance coverage lasts for a specified period of years and premiums are paid purely for insurance coverage; the policy has no "cash value" (defined under "Whole Life Insurance"). Most term policies provide that the insured shall have the right to convert the policy into some permanent type of coverage. Certain term policies are cancellable by the insurance company at the end of the contract term, and others are guaranteed renewable by the insured. In every case, however, the cost of the insurance increases as the insured grows older.

Term insurance is often used by young people who want to buy a lot of insurance but cannot afford to pay the higher premiums charged for whole life insurance.

Whole Life Insurance Under a whole life policy, in the usual case, the insured pays the same premium from the time the insurance is first purchased until the time of death. That is, the cost of the insurance does not rise as the insured grows older; nor is the policy cancellable by the insurance company. In certain limited-payment policies, premiums are paid for only a specified number of years after which the policy is deemed to be paid up in full. Because the premium is the same for the duration of the policy, whole life insurance is more expensive at earlier ages and less expensive at later ages than term insurance. A young person who decides to take term insurance, rather than whole life insurance, can purchase more dollars of insurance protection for each dollar of premium paid. However, with whole life insurance, in addition to the pure insurance protection, the insured is able to build an asset that will have some value during lifetime, the "cash value" of the policy. Each year only a part of the premium paid for the policy is allocated to the cost of the insurance for that year; the balance of the premium is added to the "cash value" of the policy. The cash value of the policy may be borrowed against by the insured and, if the insured surrenders the policy at some future date, the cash value may be withdrawn or converted into paid-up or term insurance in a lesser amount.

Endowment Life Insurance An endowment policy involves the payment of the same premium over the term of the policy and generally provides that at the expiration of the term of the policy, the face amount of the policy will be distributed to the policyholder (even though he is living) or converted into an "annuity," i.e., a pay-out over a period of years. For example, an insured might purchase a $10,000, 20-year endowment policy that would provide for the payment of the same premium during each of the 20 years of the payment period (or endowment period). Under such a policy, if the insured died prior to the termination date, the sum of $10,000 would be paid to his beneficiary. If the insured lived to the end of the endowment term, the sum of $10,000 would be paid to him at that time or used by him to purchase an annuity that would provide for periodic payments to him for the balance of his life.

Group Life Insurance Group insurance is a form of term insurance that is purchased through an employer or some professional or occupational group. Its basic attributes differ very little from ordinary term insurance. The main virtue of group insurance is its relatively low cost since the insurance company, by being able to sell large numbers of contracts at one time, cuts its costs of administration and sales thereby reducing the cost of the insurance.

Including Proceeds of Life Insurance in the Gross Estate Insurance companies issue two basic kinds of life insurance policies. A "stock company" is a standard corporation owned by its shareholders that issues policies in return for a fixed premium; any profits from the business flow to the stockholders. A "mutual company" is owned by its policyholders and profits are returned to them in the form of dividends. The type of company and the type of policy that insures the decedent's life are irrelevant for purposes of preparing the federal estate tax return except where the death benefit includes accumulated dividends. All types of insurance provide for the payment of a death benefit if the insured dies while the contract is in force. Regardless of the particular kind of insurance, the full proceeds of the insurance policy will be included in the decedent's estate and reportable on Schedule D if (a) the proceeds are payable to the decedent's estate or if (b) the proceeds are payable to the beneficiaries other than the decedent's estate and the decedent possessed "incidents of ownership" in the policy.

Proceeds Payable to Decedent's Estate Section 2042 of the Internal Revenue Code provides that "The value of the gross estate shall include the value of all property—(1). . . To the extent of the amount receivable by the executor as insurance under policies on the life of the decedent."[32]

With respect to insurance on the life of the decedent that is payable to his estate, the proceeds of the policy are includible in the gross estate for federal estate tax purposes. Such proceeds would include not only the face amount of insurance, but, in addition, the amount of any dividends that had accumulated on the policy, any post-mortem dividends, and any premium that may be returned as a result of the decedent's death. The value to be shown on Schedule D of the federal estate tax return would be the net proceeds from all of these sources as enumerated on the Form 712, issued by the insurance company at the time the policy proceeds were collected.[33] The value of the policy, of course, would be reduced by the amount of any outstanding loan payable to the insurance company. Thus, if an insured borrowed from the insurance company against the cash value of his policy, the amount of any indebtedness at the time of his death would be deducted by the company in calculating the proceeds payable to the beneficiary, and only the reduced amount would be includible in the decedent's estate.

Inclusion in the Gross Estate of Insurance Proceeds Payable to Beneficiaries Other Than the Estate When insurance proceeds are payable to beneficiaries other than the estate, they will be includible in the taxable estate only if the decedent possessed "incidents of ownership" in the policy at the time of his death. The "incidents of ownership" are:

1. The right to change beneficiaries or the amounts of their shares.
2. The right to cash the policy or cancel it.
3. The right to borrow against the policy.
4. The right to pledge the policy as collateral.
5. The right to assign the policy or veto the assignment to another person.
6. The right to prevent cancellation of the policy owned by an employer by purchasing the policy for its cash value.
7. A revisionary interest if he may regain the above rights in the event a beneficiary predeceases the insured.

   The Regulations pursuant to § 2042 of the Internal Revenue Code require the inclusion in the gross estate of the proceeds of life insurance on the decedent's life that are "received by beneficiaries other than the estate . . . if the

32. See Internal Revenue Code Regulation 20.2042–1(b).
33. See Chapter Three with respect to the form of and the manner of obtaining a Form 712.

> decedent possessed at the date of his death any of the incidents of ownership in the policy, exercisable either alone or in conjunction with any other person."[34]

The difficult questions arise in cases where the decedent has attempted to transfer ownership of his life insurance policies during his lifetime in order to remove the proceeds from his taxable estate. As a general rule subject to the provisions of the 1976 Tax Reform Act, the transfer of ownership of a life insurance policy will succeed in removing the proceeds from the gross estate only if the transfer is made more than three years prior to the decedent's death and decedent has retained no "incidents of ownership."

If the insured had assigned the ownership of a life insurance policy to his wife but had retained any economic benefits of the policy such as the right to change the beneficiary or to pledge the policy for a loan, the decedent would be considered to have retained "incidents of ownership" and the policy would be includible in his estate for federal estate tax purposes.[35]

Note that question 8a on page 3 of the Form 706 return asks whether there is any policy of insurance on the decedent's life that is not included in the return as a part of the gross estate. If there is such a policy, complete explanation as to any such policy must be given on Schedule D.

If the decedent was insured under any insurance contract that he never owned or if the ownership of the insurance contract had been transferred by him to either an individual or a trust prior to his death, and if no other complicating factors exist that would require inclusion of the policy in the decedent's estate, this question will be answered "Yes" and reference to such insurance will have to be made on Schedule D, although the value of any such policy will not be includible in the estate. This process of making an entry without carrying the value of the item into the applicable column is often referred to as "carrying the item short." It is frequently used to disclose to the taxing authority the existence of an asset that is claimed to be exempt.

Where an insurance policy on the decedent's life is not included in the gross estate, the Internal Revenue Service invariably requires that a photostatic copy of the insurance contract be submitted at the time of the audit so that the estate tax agent can examine the contract to determine whether or not the ownership and all "incidents of ownership" had been validly assigned by the decedent prior to his death. Accordingly, if there is any such insurance policy, before the policy is submitted to the insurance

34. Section 20.2042–1(c)(1).

35. See Internal Revenue Code Regulation 20.2042–1(c)(2).

company for the purpose of collecting the proceeds, it is advisable to make a complete photostatic copy of the insurance contract and all of its riders, particularly the riders that indicate the manner in which the ownership of the policy was assigned, so that these documents will be available for submission to the examining agent at the time the estate tax return is audited.

At this point it is appropriate to mention the relationship of life insurance proceeds to state inheritance taxes. In many states life insurance that is payable directly to beneficiaries other than the insured's estate is not includible for state death tax purposes.[36] Because of the prevalence of this type of provision in the various state statutes relating to inheritance and estate taxes, life insurance proceeds are generally not made payable to the insured's estate or to the executors of the estate, unless there is some compelling reason that requires such a beneficiary designation. Therefore, although the proceeds of any policy that is owned by the insured will be includible in the gross estate for federal estate tax purposes, payment to some designated beneficiary other than the estate will, in many states, avoid the imposition of a state inheritance or estate tax on the proceeds of the policy.

An example of a completed Schedule D follows.

Schedule E—Jointly Owned Property[37]

Forms of Ownership of Property The various ways in which ownership of property can be shared by more than one person were discussed previously.[38] You will recall that we discussed tenancy in common, community property, joint tenancy with right of survivorship, and tenancy by the entirety. The term "joint tenancy" is property used as a shortened form of "joint tenancy with right of survivorship." Sometimes the terms "joint property" or "jointly owned property" are used—even by lawyers—to refer to all of the types of shared ownership. It is important never to be misled by that loose language. For purposes of estate administration and federal estate taxation it is essential to determine the precise form of ownership.

Schedule E includes all property in which the decedent was a tenant by the entirety or a joint tenant with right of survivorship. It does not include any property in which the decedent was a tenant in common, nor does it include community property. The decedent's proportionate interest in a tenancy in common or community property is reported in the appropriate schedule depending upon the nature of the asset: Schedule A for real estate,

36. See Chapter Six.
37. IRC § 2040.
38. See "Forms of Ownership of Real Property" earlier in this chapter.

EXAMPLE *Form 706, Schedule D—Insurance on the Decedent's Life*

Form 706 (Rev.7-90)

Estate of: Peter Chessman

SCHEDULE D—Insurance on the Decedent's Life

You must attach a Form 712 for each policy.

Item number	Description		Alternate valuation date	Alternate value	Value at date of death
1	The Equitable Life Assurance Society, Policy No. 9,872,664		11/3/91	5,465.00	5,465.00
	Premium refund			9.71	9.71
2	The Equitable Life Assurance Society, Policy No. 9,625,421		11/3/91	22,568.39	22,568.39
	Accumulated Dividends			107.52	107.52
3	The Equitable Life Assurance Society - Group Insurance, Certificate No. 16405-136A		11/3/91	40,000.00	40,000.00
4	New York Life Insurance Company, Policy No. 13-642-147	20,000.00	11/3/91		
	Termination Dividends	115.00			
	Post-Mortem Dividends	16.08			
	Premium Adjustment Mortuary	141.12			
		20,272.20		20,272.20	20,272.20
5	The Northwestern Mutual Life Insurance Co., Policy No. 2-421-697	16,201.00	11/3/91		
	Less: Outstanding loan	(4,620.50)			
	Less: Interest on loan	(3.32)			
		11,577.18		11,577.18	11,577.18
	The beneficiary of Items 1 to 5 was the decedent's wife, Sandra Chessman				
	The policies listed as Items 6, 7 and 8 were owned by the decedent's wife, Sandra Chessman, and are not includible in his estate.				
6	The Equitable Life Assurance Society, Policy No. 6,842,721				
7	The Travelers Insurance Company, Policy No. 1794267				
8	The Travelers Insurance Company, Policy No. 1942768				
	FORMS 712 SUBMITTED HEREWITH				
	Total from continuation schedule(s) (or additional sheet(s)) attached to this schedule . . .				
	TOTAL. (Also enter on Part 5, Recapitulation, page 3, at item 4.)			100,000.00	100,000.00

(If more space is needed, attach the continuation schedule from the end of this package or additional sheets of the same size.)

Schedule D—Page 12

Schedule B for stocks and bonds, etc. The reason for giving different treatment to property held in tenancy by the entirety or joint tenancy with right of survivorship will become evident as we discuss the way in which these forms of ownership are taxed for federal estate tax purposes.

Federal Estate Tax Treatment of Joint Property In general, even though title to jointly owned property passes directly to the surviving joint owner without passing through the decedent's probate estate, and even though such property is not administered as a part of the decedent's estate, jointly owned assets are includible in the gross estate for purposes of computing the federal estate tax. This practice may be contrasted with the pattern followed in the inheritance tax laws of many states that exempts such property partially or completely. See Internal Revenue Code § 2040.

Section 20.2040–1(c) of the Internal Revenue Code Regulations explains the application of § 2040 by means of a number of examples.

(1) If the decedent furnished the entire purchase price of the jointly held property, the value of the entire property is included in his gross estate;
(2) If the decedent furnished a part only of the purchase price, only a corresponding portion of that value of the property is so included;

In example (2), the important question is the percentage of the original purchase money that was furnished by the survivor. Thus, if the decedent and the survivor each contributed $10,000 to purchase land for $20,000, exactly one-half of the value of the land would be taxable in the decedent's estate, even if, at the applicable valuation date, the land was worth more (or less) than $20,000.

(3) If the decedent furnished no part of the purchase price, no part of the value of the property is so included;
(4) If the decedent, before the acquisition of the property by himself and the other joint owner, gave the latter a sum of money or other property which thereafter became the other joint owner's entire contribution to the purchase price, then the value of the entire property is so included, notwithstanding the fact that the other property may have appreciated in value due to market conditions between the time of the gift and the time of the acquisition of the jointly held property;

To illustrate example (4), if the decedent gave $10,000 to his daughter that she invested wisely, and if, at the time when her investments were worth $50,000, she used the $50,000 as her share of the purchase price of assets owned jointly by her and the decedent, the entire value of the jointly owned assets would be included in the decedent's estate. That result occurs because the daughter's contribution consisted of appreciated property acquired from the decedent "for less than an adequate and full consideration in money or money's worth."

(5) If the decedent, before the acquisition of the property by himself and the other joint owner, transferred to the latter for less than an adequate and full consideration in money or money's worth other income-producing property, the income from which belonged to and became the other joint owner's entire contribution to the purchase price, then the value of the jointly held property less that portion attributable to the income which the other joint owner did furnish is included in the decedent's gross estate;

To illustrate example (5), if the decedent gave \$20,000 to his daughter that she invested in a bank deposit on which she received interest of \$1,000 a year, and if, at the end of ten years, she had accumulated \$10,000 of income that was then used to purchase a jointly owned asset with her father, the daughter's contribution of \$10,000 would not be attributed to her father and would be considered a separate contribution by her. This result differs from example (4) because the daughter's contribution was derived from income generated by, rather than appreciation of, property given to her by her father.

(6) If the property originally belonged to the other joint owner and the decedent purchased his interest from the other joint owner, only that portion of the value of the property attributable to the consideration paid by the decedent is included;
(7) If the decedent and his spouse acquired the property by will or gift as tenants by the entirety, one-half of the value of the property is included in the decedent's gross estate; and
(8) If the decedent and his two brothers (or any other people) acquired the property by will or gift as joint tenants, one-third of the value of the property is so included.

An important exception to the eight examples listed above was alluded to "Forms of Ownership of Property" in this chapter. Under the provisions of the 1976 Tax Reform Act (Amending §§ 2040 and 2515 of the IRC), Congress attempted to eliminate the difficulty of determining which spouse was responsible for the acquisition of jointly owned property. The new provision applies only to property owned jointly by husband and wife. Under the 1976 Tax Reform Act, one-half of the value of a qualified joint interest is included in the gross estate of the decedent at the date of death, regardless of which joint tenant furnished the consideration. The definition of a "qualified joint interest" requires the following to be present:

(a) The interest must have been created by the decedent or his spouse or both.

(b) As to personal property, the creation of the joint interest must have been a completed gift for purposes of the gift tax provisions.

(c) In the case of real property, the donor must have elected to treat the joint tenancy as a gift at the time of the creation of the joint tenancy.

(d) This provision applies to joint interest created after December 31, 1976.

This amendment to §§ 2040 and 2515 of the code, in effect, recognizes the contribution furnished by a spouse to the accumulation of jointly owned property. If the donor does not elect to treat creation of joint tenancies as gifts, then the interest will be included in the estate tax return as discussed under "Federal Estate Tax Treatment of Joint Property" of this chapter.

Schedule E is divided into two parts. The first section is used to report joint property held with the decedent's spouse. All property and its total value should be listed on this schedule. (Attach an additional sheet if necessary.) Line 1b subtracts one-half of the total so that only one-half of the value will be included in the taxable estate. All other joint interests (other than those owned with the decedent's spouse) will be shown on Part 2 of Schedule E. According to 1988 tax law, if the surviving spouse is not a U.S. citizen, he or she does not qualify for the automatic fifty percent exclusion. All property would have to be included unless contribution could be shown.

Part 2 of Schedule E shows all other joint interests. The full value of the property is reported here unless contribution by the surviving joint owner can be proven. The amount of the consideration paid by the survivor does not include any amount that was originally received from the decedent for less than money or money's worth. In other words, if the decedent gave the survivor a gift, that can not qualify for a contribution. An example of a completed Schedule E is provided.

In preparing Schedule E of the federal estate tax return, a decision frequently must be made about the portion of jointly owned assets to concede as taxable on the tax return as part of the decedent's estate. In many cases, the answer is self-evident. For example, it is not unusual for a decedent to own a number of assets with the surviving spouse as tenants by the entireties. Checking accounts are frequently owned in this manner, as are stocks and bonds. in addition, the family residence will almost invariably be titled in the names of both husband and wife.

Often, however, it is not at all clear how much the decedent contributed to the purchase of a jointly owned asset and how much was contributed by the surviving joint owner or owners. In such a case, the executor will have a difficult burden of proving to the satisfaction of the examining agent that some portion of the

EXAMPLE *Form 706, Schedule E—Jointly Owned Property*

Form 706 (Rev. 7-90)

Estate of: Peter Chessman

SCHEDULE E—Jointly Owned Property

(If you elect section 2032A valuation, you must complete Schedule E and Schedule A-1.)

PART 1.— Qualified Joint Interests—Interests Held by the Decedent and His or Her Spouse as the Only Joint Tenants (Section 2040(b)(2))

Item number	Description For securities, give CUSIP number, if available.	Alternate valuation date	Alternate value	Value at date of death
1	Checking Account No. 1-234-567 Girard Trust Bank	11/3/91	12,245.04	12,245.04
2	Girard Trust Bank, Income Savings Bonds, Nos. 51555 and 62643	11/3/91	40,000.00	40,000.00
3	Fidelity Bank Savings Certificate No. 01-0444243	11/3/91	20,000.00	20,000.00
4	The First Pennsylvania Banking and Trust Company Savings Certificate No. 9912244	11/3/91	30,000.00	30,000.00
5	House and Lot, located 1201 Loyola Avenue, Philadelphia, PA, value per appraisal attached by Strouse, Greenberg & Co.	11/3/91	439,411.58	439,411.58
6	Contents of home, located 1201 Loyola Avenue, Philadelphia, PA, value per appraisal attached by Samuel T. Freeman & Co.	11/3/91	12,874.00	12,874.00
	Total from continuation schedule(s) (or additional sheet(s)) attached to this schedule			
1a	Totals **1a**			554,530.62
1b	Amounts included in gross estate (one-half of line 1a) **1b**			277,265.31

PART 2.—All Other Joint Interests

2a State the name and address of each surviving co-tenant. If there are more than three surviving co-tenants, list the additional co-tenants on an attached sheet.

	Name	Address (number and street, city, state, and ZIP code)
A.	Linda Chessman	1201 Loyola Avenue, Philadelphia, PA
B.		
C.		

Item number	Enter letter for co-tenant	Description (including alternate valuation date if any) For securities, give CUSIP number, if available.	Percentage includible	Includible alternate value	Includible value at date of death
1	A	Savings Account No. C-1462 Western Savings Fund Society, including interest accrued to date of death	100%	100%	4,241.23
2	A	Savings Account No. 4-241462 Beneficial Savings Bank, including interest accrued to date of death	100%	100%	2,841.23
3	A	Savings Account No. E241-442 Philadelphia Savings Fund Society, including interest accrued to date of death	100%	100%	15,652.23
		Total from continuation schedule(s) (or additional sheet(s)) attached to this schedule			
2b		Total other joint interests **2b**			22,734.69
3		**Total includible joint interests** (add lines 1b and 2b). Also enter on Part 5, Recapitulation, page 3, at item 5			300,000.00

(If more space is needed, attach the continuation schedule from the end of this package or additional sheets of the same size.)

Schedule E—Page 14

consideration had been furnished by the surviving joint tenant or joint tenants. The regulations provide as follows:

> The entire value of jointly held property is included in a decedent's gross estate unless the executor submits facts sufficient to show that property was not acquired entirely with consideration furnished by the decedent, or was acquired by the decedent and the other joint owner or owners by gift, bequest, devise, or inheritance. (§ 20.2040–1(a))

As a practical matter, the only evidence that is clearly satisfactory, under all circumstances, is precise documentation that traces the separate property of the surviving joint owner directly into the property that is jointly held at the date of death. For example, if the surviving joint owner received an inheritance of $10,000 from her father, deposited the inheritance in her separate checking account, and thereafter drew a check against that account that was used to furnish a part or all of the consideration for the purchase of an asset jointly held at the date of death, the executor's burden could be easily and conclusively sustained. The executor could prove the facts by demonstrating to the examining agent that the surviving joint owner had received the inheritance and could produce the cancelled check or checks with which she had used that inheritance to purchase the jointly owned property.

In the typical situation, however, such precise evidence is not available, and an estimate must be made of the amount of property that the estate can prove was contributed by the surviving joint tenant. It is the burden of the estate to prove the extent of the survivor's contribution, and when the return is prepared, the lawyer must make a judgment as to the optimum position that should be argued on behalf of the estate. Before such a judgment is made, however, one must gather as much relevant documentation relating to the contributions of the joint owners as possible. Examples of the necessary documentation would be financial records of the decedent and the other joint owner that relate to the purchase of the asset, the tax returns of the decedent and the other joint owner that may be used to establish the fact that the survivor had income from other sources that could have been used for the purchase of the jointly owned asset, and any other documents that may support the position of the estate that some portion of the consideration was furnished by the survivor.

PROBLEMS

1. In 1972 (F) father and (S) son purchased Blackacre for $50,000. F contributed $30,000 and S contributed $20,000 toward the purchase of Blackacre. F died in 1977 and Blackacre was valued at $80,000 on the date of death. What is included in F's gross estate?

2. In 1960 F died leaving Blackacre to H (husband) and (wife) as tenants by entireties. H died in 1978 and W became sole owner. Blackacre was valued at $50,000. What is included in H's gross estate?
3. H and W owned a home as tenants by the entirety. It is worth $100,000. W died. Her executor can show that W contributed one-half of purchase from funds previously received from H for no consideration. What is included in W's gross estate?
4. (F) father and (S) son had a joint savings account in which they deposited only dividends and interest on securities owned by S. F dies. What is included in F's gross estate? If F supplied all the funds for the purchase of securities by S, what is included in F's estate? What if S died first?
5. In 1976 F gave S Blackacre as a gift. F had a $5,000 basis in Blackacre and its value in 1976 was $10,000. In 1982 S sold Blackacre for $20,000 and reported $15,000 gain. In 1983 F and S purchased Greenacre for $40,000. F and S each contributed $20,000. S's contribution came from the proceeds of sale of Blackacre. F dies. What is included in his gross estate?
6. In 1972 F gave Blackacre to S as a gift. It was worth $10,000. In 1976 S had Blackacre titled in his name and F's as joint tenants. At that time Blackacre was worth $20,000. F died in 1976. What is included in F's gross estate?

Schedule F—Other Miscellaneous Property Not Reportable on Any Other Schedule[39]

The federal estate tax return instructions for Schedule F indicate that all assets includible in the gross estate that are not returnable under any other schedule should be shown under Schedule F. The instructions list a number of examples of such "miscellaneous property." The following discussion concerns the types of assets that typically appear on Schedule F and their peculiarities.

Noncorporate Business Interests Any interest a decedent may own in a corporation is returnable under Schedule B. Noncorporate business interests, i.e., sole proprietorships or partnerships, are returnable on Schedule F.

Sole Proprietorship A sole proprietorship is nothing more than a business that is owned by one individual and is not incorporated. One rarely encounters a business of significant size that is operated as a sole proprietorship because the owner of a sole proprietorship

39. IRC § 2033.

is personally and directly responsible for all debts and liabilities of the business, without any limitation. Thus, if a sole proprietor were to incur a liability in connection with the operation of his business, he would be personally liable for whatever judgment might be rendered against him. His liability would not be limited to the value of his business but could be satisfied out of his other personal assets such as his or her home, auto, etc. Because most persons whose businesses have reached a substantial size desire to limit their liability to the value of the business assets, most business ventures of significant size are eventually incorporated.

Partnerships In addition to sole proprietorships, one frequently encounters businesses or commercial activities that are carried on as a partnership. It is beyond the scope of this text to consider in detail the motives that lead to the establishment of a partnership as opposed to a corporation, or vice versa. The factors that are typically taken into account are numerous and, in many cases, income tax considerations are of paramount importance. Because of certain income tax benefits that are lost if the corporate structure is used, many business ventures of substantial size are conducted in a partnership form. All partnership interests are properly reportable under Schedule F.

Valuation Sole proprietorships and partnerships have much in common with closely held corporate businesses because, in most cases, there is no ready market for the sale of the business interest (or the stock in the closely held corporation) that will conclusively establish the value of the business interest as of the date of death. Questions regarding the valuation of sole proprietorships, partnerships, and closely held corporations are often the central issues in the audit of a federal estate tax return. Frequently, the major asset in an estate will consist of the decedent's interest in the business or businesses in which he was engaged during his lifetime. Unless the business has taken the corporate form and has sold its stock to the public, or unless during his or her lifetime the decedent entered into an agreement with the other owners of the business that provided for the purchase of the decedent's interest by the survivors, there may be no ready market for the sale of the estate's interest. The question of its value will involve negotiation with the estate tax agent.

Valuation will typically depend upon many factors. In a ruling issued by the Internal Revenue Service in 1959 dealing with the valuation of the stock in closely held corporations, it was pointed out that the estate tax regulations "define fair market value, in effect, as the price at which the property would change hands between a willing buyer and a willing seller when the former is not under any compulsion to buy and the latter is not under any compulsion to sell, both parties having reasonable knowledge of relevant facts." This Revenue Ruling (Rev. Rul. 59–60) listed a number of factors that require careful analysis in any attempt to value such a business interest. The listed factors were the following:

(a) The nature of the business and the history of the enterprise from its inception.
(b) The economic outlook in general and the condition and outlook of the specific industry in particular.
(c) The book value of the stock (in the case of a closely-held corporation and the balance sheet of the partnership or sole proprietorship in those cases) and the financial condition of the business.
(d) The earning capacity of the business and its ability to distribute those earnings in the form of dividends or other distributions.
(e) Whether or not the enterprise has good will or other intangible value.
(f) The market price of stocks of corporations engaged in the same or a similar line of business which have their stocks actively traded in a free and open market, either on an exchange or over-the-counter.

In preparing a federal estate tax return that includes the stock of a closely held corporation, a sole proprietorship, or an interest in a partnership, all of the aforementioned factors and any others that may be relevant in a particular case must be considered carefully before a decision is made about the value at which the business interest should be returned. In addition to the foregoing, the position of the decedent in the business enterprise is also of importance, and if his death will have an adverse effect on the fortunes of the business because the decedent's experience and know-how are irreplaceable (this is called "good will"), a substantial reduction in the value of the business interest may be warranted.

Obviously, the lawyer's assistant will not be able to arrive at any definitive answer with respect to the valuation to be placed on an estate tax return for a closely held business interest. Such a decision will be based primarily on the judgment of the attorney who represents the estate and may also be based on many factors that are not within the knowledge of his assistant. However, the assistant will be of substantial help in providing the attorney with the basic raw materials needed to arrive at a well-informed decision. The instructions for Schedule B and Schedule F indicate that when the estate includes an interest in a closely held corporation, a partnership, or a sole proprietorship, complete financial data must be provided for a period of five years immediately preceding the valuation date. Before any meaningful decision of value can be made, it will be necessary to review the financial statements, including balance sheets, statements of profit and loss, and, possibly, tax returns, for the business enterprise for that five-year period. This information should be collected in advance of the preparation of the estate tax return. In many cases, such financial data will be found in other files in the office of the attorney. If such data is not available within the office, it may be obtained from the persons who are operating the business or from the accountant who has prepared financial statements and tax returns for the business.

Miscellaneous Business Assets Other business assets that would be properly includible on Schedule F of the tax return would include royalties payable to an author, inventor, or artist. In addition, if the decedent had been an insurance agent, the right to receive policy renewal commissions payable by insurance companies would also be reported on this schedule. The valuation of such assets, which are indefinite in value, will again involve a matter of judgment in many cases.

As an example, renewal commissions are usually paid to an insurance agent for a period of ten years after an insurance policy is sold. This means that each year, as the insured pays the premium, the agent who sold or wrote the policy will receive some portion of the premium in the form of a renewal commission. When an insurance agent dies, his estate or some designated beneficiary acquires the right to receive such commissions. The amount of the commissions, however cannot be determined with precision since it is impossible to predict the number of policies that will lapse prior to their tenth anniversary date, either because of the death of the insured or for a variety of other reasons. Insurance companies have developed a statistical approach to the valuation of the right to receive renewal commissions. Generally, insurance companies will provide a letter setting forth their estimate of the date-of-death value of the decedent's right to receive renewal commissions during the ten-year period following his death. The estimates of the insurance companies will generally be accepted by the Internal Revenue Service.

The estimated value of future royalties can also usually be obtained from the publisher of a book that may have been written by the decedent or, in the event the decedent was a performing artist, from the agency through which royalties were received (for example, ASCAP).

Tangible Personal Property The items of tangible personal property owned by a decedent, such as household goods, furniture and furnishings, jewelry, works of art, books, boats, and automobiles, are also properly reportable on Schedule F of the estate tax return. Unless these items have an extremely nominal value, and this is quite unusual in a large estate, it is advisable to have the items appraised by a reputable appraiser shortly after the decedent's death. Section 20.2031–6(b) of the Regulations requires an appraisal by an expert when the total value of the tangible personal property owned by the decedent exceeds $3,000.

Frequently, the decedent's will specifically bequeaths the items of tangible personal property either to the surviving spouse or to other close members of the family. Because these items are often distributed to the beneficiaries during the early stages of administration of the estate, the appraisal should be obtained promptly. There are numerous companies whose appraisals will generally be accepted by the Internal Revenue Service as a matter of course.

The value of an automobile may be taken from resources such as the "Blue Book." Note that the retail value, not the wholesale value, should be used.[40]

Because, as previously mentioned, items of tangible personal property are usually distributed shortly after the decedent's death, and because some or all of these items may be sold or otherwise disposed of by the beneficiaries prior to the time the federal estate tax return is audited, it is usually advisable to submit to the Internal Revenue Service the written appraisal that has been prepared by the appraiser as soon as it is received. The appraisal should be accompanied by a request that the Internal Revenue Service authorize the release of the items covered by the appraisal so that the personal representative will feel free to distribute them. The appraisal, in addition to a specific enumeration of all of the items of tangible personal property that were owned by the decedent, either individually or jointly with another person, will include an affidavit by the appraiser setting forth: (1) the appraiser's qualifications; (2) that the articles were actually inspected at the time the appraisal was prepared; and (3) that the figures set forth in the appraisal are in the appraiser's opinion the fair value that would have been received had the articles been sold at a public auction at the time of the decedent's death.

It is necessary to submit a copy of the formal appraisal to the District Director of Internal Revenue for the district in which the decedent resided at the time of his death, together with an affidavit of the executor that the appraisal is complete and accurate. An affidavit is shown in the next Example.

In most cases, including large estates, the value of the articles of tangible personal property will be comparatively modest in com-

40. This is true for all assets listed. Appraisers can lose their certification if they try to discount assets to use for "tax purposes."

EXAMPLE
Preliminaries to the Distribution of Tangible Property

Affidavit of Executor re Appraisal

COMMONWEALTH OF PENNSYLVANIA }
County of Philadelphia } ss.

Sandra Chessman, being duly sworn according to law, disposes and says that she is one of the Executors of the Estate of Peter Chessman, Deceased, late of Philadelphia County, Pennsylvania;

That submitted herewith is the appraisal of personal property which was owned by the decedent, located at 1201 Large Avenue, Philadelphia, Pennsylvania, made by Samuel T. Freeman and Company;

That the articles set forth in the said appraisal constitute all articles of the nature described therein that belonged to the decedent, located at 1201 Large Avenue, Philadelphia, Pennsylvania, and

That deponent is informed that the said Samuel T. Freeman and Company is competent to make the said appraisal.

_______________________ [*Seal*]
(Sandra Chessman, Executrix)

Sworn to and subscribed
before me this 12th day
of June, 1991

____
Notary Public
My Commission Expires:

parison to the value of the other assets in the estate. In some cases, however, unusual antiques, works of art, or items of jewelry may have a value that represents a significant portion of the total estate and, particularly in such cases, the procedure described above should be strictly adhered to before any distribution or other disposition of such items is attempted. In cases where the tangible property is of modest value, lawyers frequently permit distribution or sale on the basis of an appraisal without taking the additional step of getting Internal Revenue Service approval.

In the case of special collections or individual items of great value, a separate appraisal should be requested from an expert in that particular field. For example, if the decedent had a valuable coin collection, a coin dealer should be consulted.

Interests in Trusts The federal estate tax return instructions for Schedule F indicate that "shares in trust funds" are to be reported on that schedule. An individual's interest in a trust may take many forms. In some cases an individual's interest in a trust will result in the taxability of the assets held in the trust at the time of death, while in other cases the interest will not result in the imposition of any tax.

To determine whether or not the decedent possessed any interest in a trust at the time of death, it is necessary to carefully review all financial records. A review of the decedent's income tax returns will disclose whether or not he or she had been receiving taxable income from any trust fund during his or her lifetime. However, the review of the decedent's income tax returns should not end the investigation since, in some cases, the decedent who has an interest in a trust may not have received any taxable income from the trust. For example, if the trust only held stock in a closely held family business on which no dividends were paid, or if the trust assets were invested exclusively in tax-free municipal bonds, no taxable income would have resulted from decedent's interest.

The extent of the decedent's interest in any trust can be ascertained only upon a careful review by the attorney of the document or documents that created the trust, and those documents should be obtained for the attorney's review. Regardless of whether an interest in the corpus of a trust is includible in the estate, accumulated but undistributed income may be due the decedent on his date of death. This income should be reported on Schedule F. Whether or not an interest in a trust is includible in the decedent's gross estate for federal estate tax purposes depends upon a number of considerations beyond the scope of this book.

Pensions and Death Benefits Schedule F requests information regarding the payment of bonuses or awards as a result of the decedent's employment or death. Such payments made as a result of a decedent's death will, in most instances, be reportable under Schedule I that deals with annuities. That schedule would include all payments made under plans established by the decedent's employer, which normally include both retirement and death benefits.

The types of benefits that fall within the purview of Schedule F are bonuses or awards made to a designated person or persons after the decedent's death by his or her employer or by some fraternal or other organization to which the decedent may have belonged during lifetime. Whether or not the payment or bonus is taxable as part of the decedent's estate will depend upon whether or not it is deemed to have been an asset that the decedent possessed at the time of his death. For example, if, as part of the package of employee benefits, the decedent's employer provides for the payment upon death of a $5,000 bonus to such beneficiary as may be designated by the decedent during his or her lifetime, the payment of this bonus might be includible in the decedent's gross estate. Its includibility will depend, however, on the type of other benefits that are available and the extent of the employee's control over the disposition of the bonus. No final determination should be made before consulting with the attorney who handles the estate. The lawyer's assistant can be of great help to the attorney by investigating the facts thoroughly and obtaining for the attorney copies of all the relevant papers.

On occasion, the employer will *gratuitously* make a payment to the decedent's surviving spouse or to some other member of the immediate family following the death of the decedent. This is particularly likely to happen in a case where the decedent was one of the important officers and, perhaps, one of the major shareholders of a closely held corporation. In some cases, the Board of Directors of such a corporation will authorize the payment of a bonus or continuation of salary payments to the surviving spouse following the decedent's death in recognition of the decedent's many years of faithful service to the company. In such cases, although disclosure of the payment should be made on Schedule F of the federal estate tax return, the payments should not be included in the gross estate since, at the time of the decedent's death, there was no right to receive them nor was there any binding obligation on the part of the employer to pay them.

Insurance on the Life of Others If the decedent owned any life insurance on the life of another person, the value of such policy on the date of death would be includible on Schedule F. For example, if X assigned the ownership of his life insurance to his wife and she predeceased him, her estate would include the value of those policies as of her date of death. The value of any such policy should be obtained from the insurance company that wrote the policy. That company will provide a Form 938 indicating the value of the policy for estate tax purposes.

Miscellaneous Property Additional property shown on the return could include the following: debts due the decedent not shown on Schedule C; Section 2044 property (qualified terminal interest property—QTIP trusts) in which the decedent possessed a qualifying income interest; claims filed by or on behalf of the decedent; rights, royalties, patents, and copyrights; leaseholds; judgments; reversionary or remainder interests; unpaid commissions, wages, and vacation pay (all employment benefits); and any refunds due the decedent.

A completed Schedule F follows.

EXAMPLE *Form 706, Schedule F—Other Miscellaneous Property*

Form 706 (Rev. 7-90)

Estate of: Peter Chessman

SCHEDULE F—Other Miscellaneous Property Not Reportable Under Any Other Schedule

(For jointly owned property that must be disclosed on Schedule E, see the Instructions for Schedule E.)
(If you elect section 2032A valuation, you must complete Schedule F and Schedule A-1.)

		Yes	No
1	Did the decedent at the time of death own any articles of artistic or collectible value in excess of $3,000 or any collections whose artistic or collectible value combined at date of death exceeded $10,000? . . . . . . If "Yes," full details must be submitted on this schedule.	X	
2	Has the decedent's estate, spouse, or any other person, received (or will receive) any bonus or award as a result of the decedent's employment or death? . . . . . . If "Yes," full details must be submitted on this schedule.	X	
3	Did the decedent at the time of death have, or have access to, a safe deposit box?	X	

If "Yes," state location, and if held in joint names of decedent and another, state name and relationship of joint depositor.

Girard Bank, Broad & Chestnut Streets, Philadelphia, PA
held jointly with decedent's wife, Sandra Chessman.

If any of the contents of the safe deposit box are omitted from the schedules in this return, explain fully why omitted.

Property belonging to Sandra Chessman omitted.

Item number	Description For securities, give CUSIP number, if available.	Alternate valuation date	Alternate value	Value at date of death
1	Refund, University of Pennsylvania Hospital	11/3/91	122.50	122.50
2	Pennsylvania Blue Shield, Medicare payment	11/3/91	112.00	112.00
3	Associated Hospital Service of Philadelphia, recovery under Major Medical policy	11/3/91	912.15	912.15
4	Six percent interest in "Chessman Building" Partnership			4,000.00
	Sold in accordance with provisions of Buy-Sell Agreement of December 12, 1970	8/15/91	4,000.00	
5	Account due, Herman F. Drummond -- the amount owed at date of death was $6,000.00 of which $500.00 has been repaid to the date of the filing of this return. Recovery of any portion of the balance is unlikely.	11/3/91	500.00	500.00
	Total from continuation schedule(s) (or additional sheet(s)) attached to this schedule . . .		24,353.35	24,353.35
	TOTAL. (Also enter on Part 5, Recapitulation, page 3, at item 6.)		30,000.00	30,000.00

(If more space is needed, attach the continuation schedule from the end of this package or additional sheets of the same size.)

Schedule F—Page 16

EXAMPLE *Form 706, Schedule F—Rider*

SCHEDULE F - Form 706 cont.

Item No.	Description	Alternate Valuation Date	Alternate Value	Value at Date of Death
6	Reversionary interest under Indenture of Trust established March 15, 1962, by the decedent for his nephew, Milton Chessman, which provides for termination on September 30, 1991, or upon the beneficiary's prior death, at which time the principal of the trust is distributable to the decedent's estate. The actuarial value of this reversionary interest is .94325, calculated in accordance with Example 12 of Actuarial Values for Estate and Gift Tax (Publication No. 11 of the United States Treasury Department). The assets held in the trust consist of a $20,000 Certificate of Deposit, No. 12446, from the First Pennsylvania Banking and Trust Company on which there was no accrued income at the date of death. Copy of Indenture submitted herewith.	11/3/91	17,162.00	17,162.00
7	Aetna Life Insurance Company Policy 8056021-3 insuring life of Sandra Chessman per Form 938 attached.	11/3/91	569.81	569.81
8	Collection of antique watches, valued per net proceeds of auction conducted by Sotheby-Parke-Bernet.	9/26/91	6,001.54	6,001.54
9	Accrued income, Indenture of Trust of Lemuel Chessman.	11/3/91	620.00	620.00
	For Information Purposes Only: On July 1, 1991, the Board of Directors of Chessman Manufacturing Company, Inc., voted to pay a bonus of $10,000 to the decedent's spouse, Sandra Chessman, "in recognition of Peter Chessman's many years of devoted service to the company." This bonus was paid on July 15, 1991.			
	Page Total		24,353.35	24,353.35

Schedule G—Transfers During Decedent's Life[41]

Except for gifts of life insurance, the transfers reported on Schedule G are those where the decedent continued to control or enjoy the benefit of the property or gave up such control or benefit within three years of his death. This schedule is not used as often under present law; however, it is important to understand how the schedule should be prepared.

41. IRC §§ 2035–38.

The preparation of Schedule G of the federal estate tax return frequently involves extremely complicated questions of law. It must be understood that the gross estate, for federal estate tax purposes, may well include not only property that was owned by the decedent at the time of his death, but also property that was owned by the decedent during his lifetime and transferred by him or her to others prior to his death. Minimizing the federal estate tax is one of the major goals of estate planning. Therefore, particularly in cases where the client's estate is substantial, attempts will often be made to pass assets to objects of the client's bounty (usually his spouse, children, and other members of his immediate family) in a way that will avoid the imposition of federal estate tax on those assets at the date of the decedent's death. An individual's attempts to divest himself or herself of ownership of assets during lifetime, in order to avoid federal estate tax at the time of his death, will, of necessity, involve questions relating to the federal gift tax that is imposed on many inter vivos transfers.

In Chapter Four, gifts and the federal gift tax return were discussed in detail. It is important to recognize that only limited tax-free gifts may be made by a person. Once the limit is exceeded a federal gift tax is imposed. Thus, a person should not divest himself of any material portion of his property, if he has a large estate, without being fully advised of the federal gift tax consequences of his transfers.

In addition to gift tax consequences, other important considerations must be taken into account at the time any gift is made. Certain requirements must be met in order to guarantee that the value of the assets that are the subject of the gift will not be included in the decedent's estate at the time of death. Some assets transferred by a decedent during his or her lifetime are includible in the gross estate at the time of death. These assets, valued as of the date of death (or alternate valuation date, if alternate valuation has been chosen), must be reported on Schedule G. The lawyer's assistant will not make the determination of what interests are includible; however, once the attorney has made that determination, the lawyer's assistant should be knowledgeable on the method of completing Schedule G.

Reporting of Transfers on the Return The description of each item on Schedule G should include the transferee, date of transfer, and a complete description of the property. If only part of the property transferred is includible in the estate, the preparer should show all of the transfer under the description and explain the parts excluded.

Five types of transfers should be included on Schedule G:

1. Certain gift taxes (IRC § 2035(a)). At Item A enter the total

value of gift taxes paid by the decedent or the estate on gifts made by the decedent or the decedent's spouse within three years of death. The date of the gift, not the date the tax was paid, determines whether the gift tax is included in the gross estate.

2. Other transfers within three years before death (IRS § 2035(a)). Transfers of life insurance policies, life estates, reversionary interests, and powers to revoke are includible if these items would have been includible if they had not been transferred by the decedent within the three-year period prior to death.
3. Transfers with retained life estate (IRC § 2036). These are transfers where the decedent retained some rights to property he transferred such as the right to income or the right to designate beneficiaries. A common example would be a gift to a minor where the decedent is the custodian for the minor.
4. Transfers taking effect at death are includible under IRC § 2037. Such transfers include those under which possession or enjoyment takes effect only after the decedent's death. The decedent must retain a reversionary interest in the property that, immediately before the decedent's death, had a value of 5% or more of the value of the transferred property. A deathbed gift paid by check is not a completed gift until it has been processed by the bank.
5. Revocable transfers are included under IRC § 2038. These transfers are those in which the decedent retained a right to alter or veto any portion of the transfer at the time of his death.

Any transfer not discussed above should be included on Schedule G even if it is not includible in the gross estate. It should be reported "for information only."

It is essential that all documents relating to trusts established by the decedent or other transfers made by the decedent during lifetime be reviewed carefully by the attorney in order to determine whether or not they are includible on the return. In many cases, the answer will be obvious. The difficult situations arise when it is not clear whether the Internal Revenue Code sections and the regulations thereunder require includibility. The answer may ultimately depend upon very subtle interpretations of the statutory law and the cases that have considered similar questions in the past.

If any trust was established by the decedent during his lifetime that involved the transfer of assets with a value of $5,000 or more, full and complete information must be given with respect to the trust, even though the executors may take the position that the assets held in the trust are not subject to tax because the decedent retained no powers that would require inclusion in his gross estate under any of the sections we have considered. This information is elicited on Schedule G.

In reviewing the decedent's checkbooks prior to preparing the federal estate tax return, notations should be made of all large checks. In the case of checks that are clearly gifts, and subject to the provisions of § 2035 relating to gifts made prior to January 1, 1977 (for example, a check made payable to a member of the decedent's family that is unrelated to any business transaction), the attorney representing the estate will have to make a decision as to whether or not the federal estate tax return should concede the includibility of the items. In many cases it is not clear from the face of the check itself (or the check stub) whether or not a gift has been made. For example, it is common to find substantial checks drawn against the decedent's account to the order of a stock brokerage firm. Such checks simply indicate that the decedent had purchased marketable securities about the time the check was drawn. The check would not indicate, however, whether the stock that was purchased had been purchased in the decedent's name (in which case, of course, there would have been no gift) or whether the payment made to the broker represented a payment for stock that had been purchased by the decedent in the name of some other person.

The examining agent, in reviewing the decedent's checkbooks, will demand an explanation of all such items. Therefore, before the federal estate tax return is prepared, it is advisable to investigate such items in order to determine whether or not gifts have been made. This may be done by communicating with the broker or other recipient of the questionable check to determine exactly what had been purchased, and, thereafter, by checking through the decedent's financial records to determine whether the asset that had been purchased was either held by the decedent at the date of death or disposed of by the decedent prior thereto. In many cases, particularly where the decedent was extremely active in his stock market transactions, it may be quite difficult to trace from the decedent's checking account through his broker the items purchased within three years prior to the date of death. To do the job adequately, it is usually necessary to obtain copies of the broker's statements for the three-year period. In addition, one must carefully review the decedent's federal income tax returns for that period as they will disclose any sales of stock by the decedent.

Similarly, since the passbooks for savings accounts normally will also be reviewed by the examining agent at the audit, it is advisable to attempt to trace any substantial withdrawals from the accounts, particularly if made within three years of death.

The lawyer's assistant will be of significant help by gathering all of the relevant documents together, by briefly describing their provisions to the attorney, and by reviewing the decedent's financial records and other relevant data in advance. Then decisions may be made on the application of Schedule G and whether or not any transfers made by the decedent during his or her lifetime must be reported on Schedule G and, if reported, included in the taxable estate.

An example of a completed Schedule G follows.

Schedule H—Powers of Appointment[42]

A power of appointment, in the broadest sense, is a power to designate who shall enjoy the use of property. As the term is used in relation to Schedule H and § 2041 of the Internal Revenue Code, it does not relate to property that the decedent owned,[43] but to property with respect to which some other person had granted to decedent the power to designate the beneficiaries.

A power of appointment may be created in many ways and, depending upon the date of its creation and its specific terms, may result in the taxability of the assets subject to the power of appointment in the estate of the person who possesses the power. In most cases, powers of appointment are specifically granted to a beneficiary of a trust pursuant to the terms of the will or inter vivos deed or indenture that established the trust. For example, a will may create a trust for X and provide that all of the income of the trust be distributed to X during lifetime and that, upon X's death, X be given the power to "appoint" the balance remaining in the trust to beneficiaries of X's choice. This power possessed by X would constitute a power of appointment and, depending upon the specific terms of the power and the scope of X's authority in appointing the assets held in the trust at the time of his death, might require inclusion of the assets of the trust in X's estate.

Not all powers of appointment as defined by § 2041 are specifically labeled "powers of appointment" in the instrument that creates them. The regulations under § 2041 of the Internal Revenue Code provide as follows:

> The term "power of appointment" includes all powers which are in substance and effect powers of appointment regardless of the nomenclature used in creating the power and regardless of local property law connotations. For example, if a trust instrument provides that the beneficiary may appropriate or consume the principal of the trust, the

42. IRC § 2041.

43. A power of appointment that is reserved by the settlor would be a retained interest that would be included on Schedule G of the return as a power to alter, amend, or revoke under § 2038 of the Internal Revenue Code.

EXAMPLE *Form 706, Schedule G—Transfers During Decedent's Life*

Form 706 (Rev. 7-90)

Estate of: Peter Chessman

SCHEDULE G—Transfers During Decedent's Life

(If you elect section 2032A valuation, you must complete Schedule G and Schedule A-1.)

Item number	Description For securities, give CUSIP number, if available.	Alternate valuation date	Alternate value	Value at date of death
A.	Gift tax paid by the decedent or the estate for all gifts made by the decedent or his or her spouse within 3 years before the decedent's death (section 2035(c))	X X X X X	- 0 -	- 0 -
B.	Transfers includible under section 2035(a), 2036, 2037, or 2038:			
1	Transfer of Prudential National Bank Account #172-53-967 to Laura Chessman under Uniform Gifts to Minors Act. Lawrence Chessman, guardian. Transfer made 7/2/86. Decedent retained right to receive income.		20,000	20,000
	For Information Only Schedule F Item 6 refers to a reversionary interest under indenture of trust dated 3/15/62 for the benefit of Milton Chessman.			
	Total from continuation schedule(s) (or additional sheet(s)) attached to this schedule			
	TOTAL. (Also enter on Part 5, Recapitulation, page 3, at item 7.)		20,000	20,000

power to consume or appropriate is a power of appointment. Similarly, a power given to a decedent to affect the beneficial enjoyment of trust property or its income by altering, amending, or revoking the trust instrument or terminating the trust is a power of appointment. . . . [A] power to amend only the administrative provisions of a trust instrument, which cannot substantially affect the beneficial enjoyment of the trust property or income, is not a power of appointment. The mere power of management, investment, custody of assets or the power to allocate receipts and disbursements as between income and principal, exercisable in a fiduciary capacity, whereby the holder has no power to enlarge or shift any of the beneficial interests therein except as an incidental consequence of the discharge of such fiduciary duties is not a power of appointment. (Section 20.2041–1(b)(1)).

Section 2041 and the concept of "power of appointment" relate specifically to powers that have been granted to a decedent by someone else, either by will or inter vivos deed or indenture of trust. The preparer should be alert for interests that the decedent may have in such trusts established by another for the decedent's benefit that allow the decedent to appoint the trust property to himself, his estate, his creditors, or the creditors of his estate. If the answer to line 13 of Part 4 under General Information is "yes," Schedule H must be completed.

Distinction between General and Special Powers Some powers of appointment cause property to be included in the gross estate and others do not. While it is an oversimplification, it is essentially correct to say that the more power the decedent had to deal with the property, the more likely it is to be included in his gross estate.

In order to understand the application of § 2041, it is essential to distinguish between "general powers of appointment" and "limited or special powers of appointment." Only general powers of appointment result in inclusion of property in the taxable estate of the person who possesses the power. The Internal Revenue Code in § 2041 (b) (1) defines "general power of appointment" as follows:

> (1) GENERAL POWER OF APPOINTMENT.—The term general power of appointment means a power which is exercisable in favor of the decedent, his estate, his creditors, or the creditors of his estate. . . .

This means, in essence, that only powers of appointment that impose no limitations on their exercise will be considered general powers of appointment. For example, if the will or other instrument that created the power provides that the beneficiary, at his death, shall have the power to appoint the balance remaining in the trust to "such beneficiaries as he may designate in his will or in any other written instrument," such a power would be considered a general power of appointment since, under the instrument creating the power, no limitations were imposed and the beneficiary of the trust would have the power to appoint the property remaining in the trust at the time of his death to his estate, his creditors, or the creditors of his estate. Similarly, if a trust gave the beneficiary the unrestricted right to withdraw all or any part of the principal at any time, such right would be a general power of appointment since the beneficiary of the trust would have the power to appoint the balance remaining in the trust at any time in favor of herself.

To avoid taxation of the assets of a trust in the estate of a beneficiary of the trust, the will or other instrument that creates the trust will frequently limit the right of the beneficiary to appoint the balance remaining. Such "special" or "limited" powers of appointment do not fall within the ambit of § 2041 and do not result in includibility of the trust assets in the gross estate of the beneficiary.

The broadest type of "limited" power of appointment, and one that is frequently encountered in wills and trusts, might read:

> Upon the death of X, my trustees shall distribute the balance of principal and undistributed income, if any, then remaining of this trust to and among such beneficiaries (other than X's estate, his creditors, or the creditors of his estate) as X may designate in his will or other written instrument delivered to my trustees during his lifetime.

Under the power of appointment set forth above, X would be able to appoint the balance remaining in the trust to any beneficiaries other than his estate, his creditors, or the creditors of his estate. Thus, the property could be appointed to his spouse, his issue, or in any other manner he considered appropriate, so long as the limitation was heeded. Notwithstanding this great latitude, X would not be deemed to have possessed a general power of appointment at the time of his death and the assets held in the trust would not be includible in X's estate under § 2041.

Limited powers of appointment are frequently more limited than the example set forth above. For example, the beneficiary of a trust may have the power to appoint the balance remaining at the time of his death "among his wife and issue in such proportions as he may deem advisable," or among some other limited class of beneficiaries. The important point to remember is that a power of appointment will not be considered a "general" power of appointment unless it is exercisable in favor of the decedent, his estate, his creditors, or the creditors of his estate.

Certain powers of appointment that are broader than the type of limited power that we have discussed will, nevertheless, not be considered "general powers of appointment" under § 2041 of the Internal Revenue Code if they fall within one of the three exceptions enumerated in § 2041 (b) (1). The first of these exceptions is

> (A) A power to consume, invade, or appropriate property for the benefit of the decedent which is limited by an ascertainable standard relating to the health, education, support, or maintenance of the decedent shall not be deemed a general power of appointment.

To illustrate this exception, a trust established under a will or deed may provide that X shall be the sole trustee and that all of the income of the trust will be distributed to X during his lifetime and, further, that X, in his discretion, shall have the power to distribute principal to himself during his lifetime for his "health, education, support, or maintenance." Even though X would have a power exercisable in favor of himself, the existence of the "maintenance" limitation would remove this power from the scope of § 2041 and the assets remaining in the trust at the time of X's death would not be includible in his estate.

If, on the other hand, X had the power to distribute principal to himself without any standard at all or if the standard set forth in the instrument was not limited specifically to the items enumerated in § (b) (1) (A) as quoted (health, education, support, and maintenance), the power of appointment would be considered a "general" power and would result in the inclusion of the trust principal in X's estate. For example, if X had the power to distribute principal to himself for his "comfort and general welfare," the language of the quoted exception would not be met and the power would be considered a "general" power. See Internal Revenue Code Regulation 20.2041–1 (c) (2) for a more detailed discussion of the concept of an "ascertainable standard."

General Powers Created before October 22, 1942 With respect to the federal estate tax effects of general powers of appointment, the date October 22, 1942, is of extreme importance and furnishes the basis for the second and third exceptions previously referred to and enumerated in § 2041 (b) (1) of the Internal Revenue Code. Because the law differed prior to that date, § 2041 (a) (1) provides that even though a decedent may possess a general power of appointment, if the power of appointment was created on or before October 21, 1942, the property to which the power relates will be included in the gross estate *only* if the power is in fact exercised by the decedent, either by his will or by a disposition that, if it related to property owned by the decedent, would require inclusion in the decedent's estate under §§ 2035 to 2038. Thus, if a decedent possesses a general power of appointment that was created prior to October 22, 1942, the property subject to that power will not be includible in his gross estate unless he in fact exercises the power by will or other disposition that, under § 2035, is considered to be in contemplation of death. If he leaves it unexercised and permits the property to pass as if he had not had such a power, no part of the property will be included in his gross estate.

Under the code and the regulations, a power of appointment that is created by a will executed on or before October 21, 1942, is considered a power created on or before such date provided the person executing the will shall have died before July 1, 1949, without having republished the will in any manner (including the execution of a codicil) after October 21, 1942. When the law was changed in 1942, exception was made for wills that had been executed prior to the effective date of the change. The testators of such wills were given until July 1, 1949, to change the provisions in their wills. If the testator died before July 1, 1949, and had not republished his will, the pre-1942 law applied.

With respect to inter vivos trusts, the power, under the Internal Revenue Code Regulations, is considered as created on the date the instrument takes effect, and the regulations specifically provide that "such a power is not considered as created at some future date merely because it is not exercisable on the date the instrument takes effect, or because it is revocable, or because the identity of its holders is not ascertainable until after the date the instrument takes effect." In any case in which a power of appointment exists, the document creating the power must be carefully analyzed to determine the date on which the power was created and the type of power that was created. Any will or trust that bears a date of 1942 or earlier deserves special attention.

Other distinctions in the treatment of powers of appointment depend upon the date the power was created. Under § 2041 (b) (1) (B) of the code, a power created on or before October 21, 1942, that is not exercisable by the decedent "except in conjunction with another person" is not deemed to be a general power of appointment. Thus, if the instrument in question permits X and Y, acting together, to distribute the assets in the trust to such beneficiaries as they may designate, and if the power were created on or before October 21, 1942, even though X and Y have no limitations imposed on their exercise of the power, the power is not considered a general power of appointment and will not result in taxation in either of their estates, even if they actually exercise the power.

The Internal Revenue Code also provides, with respect to powers of appointment created before October 22, 1942, that a partial release of the power by the person possessing the power and a subsequent exercise of the partially released power will not be an exercise of a general power of appointment if the partial release occurred before November 1, 1951. It is not unusual to come across a situation that fits within this provision. A trust may have been established for X under the will of her father who died in 1930 and this trust, in addition to providing for the distribution of the income to X during her lifetime, may have given X the power to distribute the balance of principal at the time of her death among an unlimited class of beneficiaries, including her estate. At the time the power was created in the will of X's father, of course, the law did not require taxation of the assets subject to this power. When the law was changed in 1942, persons who possessed such powers of appointment created prior to the effective date of the change were given an opportunity to partially release their powers and, not infrequently, documents will be encountered in which the person possessing a general power of appointment will have indicated his intention that his power of appointment be limited in favor of beneficiaries other than himself, his estate, his creditors, or the creditors of his estate. Such a partial release, to be effective, must have been executed on or before November 1, 1951, and, in such a case, when X subsequently exercises the power of appointment, her exercise will not be considered the exercise of a general power of appointment and will have no adverse tax consequences.

The partial release transformed a general power into a limited power.

General Powers Created after October 21, 1942 General powers of appointment that were created after October 21, 1942, result in the trust assets being included in the estate of the person possessing the power, whether or not the power is exercised, unless the power is exercisable by the decedent only in conjunction with another person and fits into one of the exceptions that are set forth in § 2041 (b) (1) (C) of the code. See Internal Revenue Code § 2041 (b) (1) (C).

With respect to powers created after October 21, 1942, as pointed out earlier, if the decedent possessed the power of appointment at the time of his death, the property subject to the power of appointment is includible in the decedent's estate, whether or not the power is exercised. If the decedent exercised or released the power during his lifetime, the property subject to the power may, nevertheless, be included in his gross estate under certain circumstances.

In any case in which the decedent at any time possessed a general power of appointment created after October 21, 1942, and released or attempted to release that power of appointment prior to his death, careful analysis by the lawyer of the documents relating to the creation of the power and the exercise of the release will be necessary. As a practical matter most lawyers file a simple photocopy of such documents with the federal estate tax return. If any question concerning the correctness of such copies is raised in the audit of the return, you may be asked to obtain from the appropriate court official a certified or verified copy.

The information disclosed on Schedule H will have to be completed by the attorney handling the estate after careful analysis of the relevant documents. The lawyer's assistant will be of help, once again, by being sufficiently familiar with the concepts relating to Schedule H and powers of appointment in general so that all of the relevant documentation may be assembled in a meaningful manner for review by the attorney.

The preparer must not overlook the "five and five" power (§ 2041 (b) (2)) held by the decedent. The estate of a spouse holding such a power at death must include the greater of $5,000 or 5% of the value of the property subject to the power of appointment, less any amount appointed by the surviving spouse in the year of death if the power is exercisable at the time of death.

The preparer should always ascertain the extent of the decedent's interest in the estate of a predeceased spouse and carefully review any trusts the decedent did not create where the decedent possessed any power of beneficial interest.

EXAMPLE Form 706, Schedule H—Powers of Appointment (Peter Chessman Estate)

SCHEDULE H—Powers of Appointment

(If you elect section 2032A valuation, you must complete Schedule H and Schedule A-1.)

Item number	Description	Alternate valuation date	Alternate value	Value at date of death
1	For Information Only Under an inter vivos trust created August 3, 1968, by John Chessman, decedent received the income of the trust for life with the power to appoint the remainder to any person other than decedent, his estate, his creditors, or the creditors of his estate.			
	Total from continuation schedule(s) (or additional sheet(s)) attached to this schedule . . .		0.00	0.00
	TOTAL. (Also enter on Part 5, Recapitulation, page 3, at item 8.)			

(If more space is needed, attach the continuation schedule from the end of this package or additional sheets of the same size.)
(The instructions to Schedules G and H are in the separate instructions.)

Schedules G and H—Page 18

The completed Schedule H on this page demonstrates that the power in this particular case is not subject to tax.

If the estate included taxable powers, the assets subject to tax would be valued and reported on a "rider"[44] to Schedule H in a manner consistent with the valuation and reporting of similar assets owned directly by the decedent, as is illustrated in the Example for the estate of Lucy Long on the next pages.

PROBLEMS

1. A's father, F, died in 1945, leaving his estate in trust to pay the income to A during his lifetime, and on A's death, to distribute the corpus to such of A's issue as A might by will appoint.
   What is included in A's estate?
2. B's husband, H, died in 1947, leaving half his estate in trust to pay the income to B during her lifetime, and on her death, to distribute the corpus to their issue. The trustee was also directed to pay to B from time to time so much of the corpus of the trust as she might request "for her support in reasonable comfort."
   What is included in B's estate?
3. C's father, F, created a trust in 1945 to last until the death of the survivor of C and his brother, D. During the trust's existence, income is to be paid to F's issue. Corpus distributions can also be

44. A rider is simply a separate sheet attached to the form.

EXAMPLE ***Form 706, Schedule H—Powers of Appointment and Riders (Lucy Long Estate)***

SCHEDULE H—Powers of Appointment

(If you elect section 2032A valuation, you must complete Schedule H and Schedule A-1.)

Item number	Description	Alternate valuation date	Alternate value	Value at date of death
1	Decedent possessed a general power of appointment in the Marital Trust created under Item Fifth of her husband's will. The assets of that Trust are fully taxable, as indicated on the attached Rider.	1/16/92	33,397.72	35,819.01
	Total from continuation schedule(s) (or additional sheet(s)) attached to this schedule . . .			
	TOTAL. (Also enter on Part 5, Recapitulation, page 3, at item 8.)		33,397.72	35,819.01*

(If more space is needed, attach the continuation schedule from the end of this package or additional sheets of the same size.)
(The instructions to Schedules G and H are in the separate instructions.)

*This information is not in Peter Chessman's estate.

Schedules G and H—Page 18

made to any of F's issue on the discretion of C and D, or the survivor of them. On termination the trust property is to be distributed to F's issue.

What is included in C's estate?

(a) if C predeceases D?
(b) if D predeceases C?

4. H left property to his two sons, M and N, in trust to pay the income to H's wife, W, during her lifetime, and on her death, to distribute the corpus to H's grandchildren. The trustees were given discretionary power to make corpus distributions to any of H's issue. This power could be exercised only by joint action of M and N, and it would terminate whenever either of them ceased to be a trustee.

   What is in M's estate if M predeceases N?
   What if it didn't terminate on M's death?

Schedule I—Annuities[45]

An annuity, in general terms, is a series of regular payments of money over a period of time measured in years or by the lifetime of the recipient of the payments (the "annuitant").

45. IRC § 2039.

EXAMPLE Form 706, Schedule H—Powers of Appointment and Riders (Lucy Long Estate), continued

RIDER TO SCHEDULE H

Item No.	Description	Unit Value	Alternate Valuation Date	Alternate Value	Value at Date of Death
	Marital Trust of U/W of William Long				
1.	100 shs. Olin Corp. cmn NYSE	37.625			3,762.50
	Not disposed of within six months following death	35.25	1/16/92	3,525.00	
2.	200 shs. Chas. Pfizer & Co. cmn NYSE	69.375			13,875.00
	200 shs. sold		12/20/91	14,020.00	
3.	50 shs. Seven Up Co. cmn OTC	50.875			2,543.75
	50 shs. sold		12/20/91	2,476.00	
4.	200 shs. Signal Companies, Inc. $2.20 Conv. Pfd OTC				
	20 shs. received as 10% stock dividend 11/15/82	79.25			15,850.00
	220 shs. not disposed of within six months following death	62.6875	1/16/91	13,791.25	
5.	269.72 shs. T. Rowe Price Growth Stock Fund	10.25			2,764.63
	Not disposed of within six months following death	9.50	1/16/91	2,562.34	
				36,374.59	38,795.88
	Gross Value of Trust				
	Less: Counsel Fees			(2,500.00)	(2,500.00)
	Trustees' Commissions			(476.87)	(476.87)
	Net Value of Trust			33,397.72	35,819.01

For Information Purposes Only:
Decedent was a co-Trustee of the Residuary Trust under Item Sixth of Will of William Long for the benefit of William Long, Jr. Decedent had no powers or interests which would cause any portion of that Trust to be included in her gross estate.

Section 2039(a) of the Internal Revenue Code provides:

> (a) GENERAL.—The gross estate shall include the value of an annuity or other payment receivable by any beneficiary by reason of surviving the decedent under any form of contract or agreement entered into after March 3, 1931 (other than as insurance under policies on the life of the decedent), if, under such contract or agreement, an annuity or other payment was payable to the decedent, or the decedent possessed the right to receive such annuity or payment, either alone or in conjunction with another for his life or for any period not ascertainable without reference to his death or for any period which does not in fact end before his death.

Annuities may be created by agreement between individuals or by agreement between an individual and an insurance company that is engaged in the business of selling annuities. In addition, certain payments, lump sum or otherwise, made by the decedent's employer, although not generally thought of as annuities, are taxed as annuities under § 2039 of the Internal Revenue Code. Therefore, for purposes of this chapter, such payments will be referred to as annuities.

Types of Annuities

Private Annuities A private annuity may be created by an agreement between two individuals in which one of the individuals transfers certain property to the other in exchange for the other's agreement to make certain specified payments to the person transferring the property for a fixed period of time or for the balance of that person's life and, perhaps, to another individual or individuals after that person's death.

Commercial Annuities Most annuities, in the ordinary sense of the term, arise out of contracts entered into between an individual during his lifetime and a commercial insurance company. Several common types of annuities are provided by insurance companies:

Straight Life Annuity Under a straight life or "pure" annuity, the annuitant enters into an agreement with the insurance company that provides that in exchange for the payment to be made to the insurance company by the annuitant at the time the contract is entered into, the insurance company will make periodic payments to the annuitant for the balance of his lifetime. Under such an arrangement, the payments are made to the annuitant regardless of how long he lives; upon his death, the payments terminate and nothing is paid to any other beneficiary, nor is there any refund to the annuitant's estate. In such a case, of course, no portion of the value of the annuity would be includible in the deceased annuitant's estate, since there would be no payment receivable by any beneficiary as a result of surviving the decedent. Any payment to which the decedent may have been entitled but which he did not receive before his death would, of course, be includible on Schedule F (Miscellaneous Property) of the federal estate tax return.

As a general rule, an individual will purchase a straight life annuity if her primary concern is to provide for a regular income for herself during the later part of her lifetime and if she is not concerned about providing for any other person after her death. For example, X, age 60, may have an estate of $100,000 that, invested conservatively (in order to protect against any substantial loss of principal), will produce income of approximately $5,000 a year. If X were able to purchase an annuity that would pay her $7,500 a year for the balance of her lifetime, in exchange for a lump-sum premium of $100,000, and if X did not have a husband or children to be provided for after her death, she might consider the purchase of a commercial annuity. If the annuity were a straight life annuity, X would pay $100,000 to the insurance company that, in turn, would promise to pay her $7,500 a year, regardless of the number of years she survived. Such a contract, of course, involves a gamble on the part of the annuitant and the insurer in regard to the life expectancy of the annuitant. If X were to die within a relatively short period of time after purchasing the annuity, she would have made an exceedingly bad bargain. On the other hand, if she lives to be 90 years old, she will have received much more than $100,000 plus the income that sum would have generated.

Joint and Survivor Annuity In a joint and survivor annuity, periodic payments are made until the death of the last survivor of two or more persons. As with a straight life annuity, there is no guarantee as to the number of payments that will be made to the annuitants and no refund to the annuitants' estates or to any of the annuitants' survivors. In the example discussed above with respect to straight life annuities, X would probably have chosen a joint and survivor annuity if she were married and if her husband were dependent upon her for support. Under such an arrangement, the insurance company would make payments to X for the balance of her lifetime and, following her death, would continue to make payments to her widower for the balance of his lifetime. If her husband died before her, all payments would terminate at the time of X's death. Under a joint and survivor annuity, of course, the amount of the annuity will be smaller than could be obtained on a straight life annuity since the insurance company will, generally, be making annuity payments for a longer period under a joint and survivor type than under a straight life type, which is measured by only one life. A joint and survivor annuity may provide for the payment of a fixed amount during the lifetime of either of the annuitants or it may provide for the payment of a larger amount (so long as both annuitants are living) and some smaller amount to the survivor.

Joint and survivor annuities in which only the surviving spouse can receive payments before his or her death automatically qualify for the marital deduction under § 2056 (b) (7).

Refund and Cash-Refund Annuities Under this type of annuity contract, the periodic payments continue only during the lifetime of the annuitant. If, however, the annuitant dies before a stipulated sum has been paid out (which sum is usually the purchase price), the periodic payments continue to be made to the beneficiary designated under the contract until an amount equal to the purchase price has been distributed. Such an arrangement would be a "refund annuity." The contract might also provide that the unpaid balance be paid to a designated beneficiary in a lump sum. Such a contract would be referred to as a "cash-refund annuity."

Term Certain Annuity Under this approach, periodic payments continue for the longer of the lifetime of the annuitant or a fixed number of years. If the annuitant had a 10-year certain annuity contract and died at the end of 4 years, the designated beneficiary would receive payments for the next 6 years. If the same annuitant had survived 11 years from the date of the contract, he would have received payments throughout his lifetime but no one would be entitled to payments after his death.

Employer Annuities Many employers create benefit plans under which retired employees or their beneficiaries are entitled to payments. Such plans may be called pension plans, profit-sharing plans, bonus plans, or other names. While these plans may not be within the normal definition of "annuities," the taxability of such plans in the estate of the employee is governed by § 2039 of the Internal Revenue Code, which applies to annuities generally. Any such plan must be disclosed on Schedule I.

Federal Estate Taxation of Annuities Section 2039 (a) of the Internal Revenue Code requires the inclusion of any payments made to a beneficiary under any annuity contract entered into after March 3, 1931, so long as the decedent, under the contract or agreement, was receiving an annuity or other payment or "possessed the right to receive such annuity or payment."

Once the lawyer establishes the existence of an annuity as described in § 2039 (a) of the Internal Revenue Code, the next question becomes the amount includible in the decedent's estate. The value of the annuity is determined by the use of specially designed actuarial tables that are based on an assumed rate of return of 6%. These tables apply to all transfers made and with respect to all decedents dying on or after January 1, 1971, and appear at §§ 20.2031–10 of the regulations. Because of the complexity of the issues involved and the related mathematical calculations, the decisions and valuations should be made by the lawyer administering the estate or a person trained to make these calculations.

Annuity Payments under Approved Plans Recent tax law changes have made major changes in the taxation of annuities, particularly in respect to plans from employers. The entire amount of the annuity owned by the decedent is included in the estate with the exception of estates of decedents dying before 1985, or after 1984 if the decedent was a participant in any plan, was in pay status on

December 31, 1984, or was separated from service before 1985 and had irrevocably elected the form of the benefit before July 18, 1984. Prior law allowed a $100,000 exclusion. (No exclusion was allowed for the portion contributed by the decedent.) Now no exclusion is allowed.

An annuity or portion of an annuity is only included on Schedule I if the annuity payments continue to a beneficiary after the decedent's death, or if the decedent possessed the right to receive such annuity or payment, either alone or in conjunction with another, for his life or some similar period.

The amount of the annuity to be included is the value of the survivors' interest on the date of death or the alternate valuation date. It is not the value immediately prior to death, but rather the value immediately after the death. Section 2039 (b) specifies the amount to be included in the estate to be determined by two factors: (1) the value of what is payable to survivors, and (2) the portion of the purchase price of the annuity or other contract that was paid by the decedent. Thus, the portion contributed to the purchase of the annuity by the decedent is not included. This can be shown by:

$$\frac{\text{amount included (unknown)}}{\text{value of annuity}} = \frac{\text{decedent's contribution}}{\text{purchase price}}$$

or

$$\text{amount included} = \frac{\text{decedent's contribution}}{\text{purchase price}} \times \text{value of annuity}$$

Thus, if a husband and wife have a joint survivor annuity where the husband paid the entire cost of the annuity and the husband dies first, the entire value of the amounts payable to the wife is included. But if the wife dies first, nothing will be included in her estate.

In respect to commercial annuities, the company provides a valuation letter or a Form 712 detailing the annuities current value. For other annuity valuations, including private annuities, or those where the company does not supply a valuation, the amount includible can be found in the Regulations § 20.2039–1 (c).

Decisions about the taxability of annuities and the valuation of any portion of an annuity to be taxed are among the most difficult decisions encountered in the preparation of the federal estate tax return. The lawyer's assistant can be of great value to the lawyer if he or she understands these problems sufficiently to gather the relevant documents and facts.

An example of Schedule I is set forth on the next page.

Up to this point this chapter has dealt with gathering and reporting the assets of the gross estate. The remainder of the

EXAMPLE *Form 706, Schedule I—Annuities*

Form 706 (Rev. 7-90)

Estate of: Peter Chessman

SCHEDULE I—Annuities

Note: *Generally, no exclusion is allowed for the estates of decedents dying after December 31, 1984 (see instructions).*

	Yes	No
A Are you excluding from the decedent's gross estate the value of a lump-sum distribution described in section 2039(f)(2)? If "Yes," you must attach the information required by the instructions.		X

Item number	Description Show the entire value of the annuity before any exclusions.	Alternate valuation date	Includible alternate value	Includible value at date of death
1	None			
	Total from continuation schedule(s) (or additional sheet(s)) attached to this schedule . . .			
	TOTAL. (Also enter on Part 5, Recapitulation, page 3, at item 9.)		– 0 –	– 0 –

(If more space is needed, attach the continuation schedule from the end of this package or additional sheets of the same size.)
(The instructions to Schedule I are in the separate instructions.)

Schedule I—Page 19

chapter deals primarily with the schedule-by-schedule review of the available deductions and credits used in computing the net federal estate tax due.

Schedule J—Funeral and Administration Expenses[46]

Funeral Expenses To the extent that they constitute allowable expenses of an estate pursuant to the law of the jurisdiction where the estate is being administered, the expenses charged by the funeral director and all other related expenses, such as the cost of interment, flowers, funeral acknowledgements, obituary notices, etc., are all deductible, pursuant to § 2053 (a) (1) of the code. These items are set forth in Part A of Schedule J of the federal estate tax return, by naming the person to whom payment is made and setting forth a brief description of the services rendered.

In addition to the funeral itself, expenses related to purchase of a tombstone, a burial lot, and perpetual care of the gravesite are generally deductible items, provided that the expenditures are not unreasonable in relation to the size of the estate.

Thus, the regulations provide as follows:

> A reasonable expenditure for a tombstone, monument, or mausoleum, or for a burial lot, either for the decedent or his family, including a reasonable expenditure for its future care, may be deducted under this heading, provided such an expenditure is allowable by local law. (Section 20.2053–2)

As with other expenditures, the best method of compiling the information for the federal estate tax return is to review the executors' checkbook to determine those amounts that have already been paid for the items noted. It may be necessary, in addition, to ask the executors to obtain a reasonable estimate for the cost of erecting a tombstone, since that may not have been done by the time the federal estate tax return is prepared. To be properly prepared for an audit of the federal estate tax return, receipted bills and cancelled checks relating to funeral expenses should be retained for possible inspection by the examining agent.

Deductions from Funeral Expenses

Lump-Sum Death Benefit If there is no surviving spouse to receive the lump-sum death benefit payable by the Social Security Administration, the payment must be deducted from the amount of the funeral bill. Presently the maximum death benefit payment is $255. Even if social security does not make the payment directly to

46. IRC § 2053.

the funeral director, as long as there is no spouse who survives the decedent, the amount of the payment must be deducted from the funeral expenses on Schedule J. This rule applies even where the death benefit does not come into the estate but is paid, as is sometimes the case, to a surviving child.

Veterans' Death Benefits The death benefits payable by the Veterans Administration must be deducted from the funeral bill whether or not there is a surviving spouse. The current maximum benefit payable to a veteran receiving a pension is up to $300. If the veteran is not receiving a pension, he may receive $150 for his burial plot (unless he is interred in a national cemetery). If the veteran dies of a service-related injury, the maximum payment is $1,500. In some cases there may also be a county veterans' death benefit payable and this, too, would be deducted from the funeral bill on Schedule J.

Executors' Commissions Part B of Schedule J calls for the amount of the commissions either paid or to be paid to the executors. These commissions are the compensation that the executors are paid for the services that they perform in gathering the assets, preparing the tax returns, and assuming the investment and other responsibilities for the estate. The Internal Revenue Code provides here, as in the case of funeral expenses, that the commissions are deductible for federal estate tax purposes to the extent that they are allowable under the applicable local law. Accordingly, if the local probate court would, in an estate of a given size and complexity, allow a commission not in excess of $10,000, that would be the limit of the deduction on Schedule J.

The commission need not have been paid at the time the federal estate tax return is filed to be deducted. The regulations require only that the commissions set forth be the amount the executors reasonably expected to be paid. In setting forth the amount of the commissions, the return must disclose whether the amount set forth is an estimate, has been finally agreed upon, or has already been paid. The words that are not applicable should be crossed out.

Normally it is not possible to ascertain the amount of the executors' commissions by merely reviewing the checking account records because they will probably not have been paid in full at the time the information is being compiled for preparation of the federal estate tax return. Where there is a corporate executor, there may be either a signed agreement setting the fee or else reference may be made to the bank's published schedule of rates, which would determine the fee. In some jurisdictions the maximum fee allowable may be determined by reference to a schedule of commissions for estates of a given size. In other jurisdictions there is no such schedule, but there is a general rule, as developed by case law, of what would constitute maximum allowable commissions for estates of various sizes.

If the executor is an individual, he may for a number of reasons not wish to claim any commission for acting as executor. If, for example, the executor were the residuary legatee of the estate, he must consider that any commission that he receives would constitute taxable income to him on his individual income tax return, whereas he would otherwise receive this same amount free of income tax as a distribution from the estate. If the individual's income tax bracket is higher than the net effective federal estate tax bracket, he would thus be disadvantaged by taking commissions and would undoubtedly wish to waive them.[47] Such a waiver should be made within six months of the individual's becoming an executor, to be sure the waiver will be considered timely. Where a timely waiver is not made, the executor may become involved in a tax controversy in which the Internal Revenue Service asserts that commissions should be imputed to him as income (and taxed as such) and that the executor's failure to take commissions results in his or her having made a taxable gift to the estate in the amount of the appropriate commissions. An effective waiver avoids both such contentions. The waiver may simply take the form of a letter from the executor to the attorney for the estate advising the attorney that all commissions will be waived.

It should be noted that a bequest or devise in a will to the executor in lieu of commissions is not deductible under Schedule J. However, if the decedent has, in his will, fixed the amount of commissions to be paid the executor, a deduction will still be allowed to the extent that the amount so fixed does not exceed the compensation permissible under local law.

On the audit of the federal estate tax return, the agent will normally require that any amount that has not already been paid to the executor and that is being claimed as a federal estate tax deduction must be supported by an affidavit executed by the executor stating (a) that he will be paid and (b) the amount that he will be paid. An example of an executor's affidavit is shown here.

EXAMPLE
Affidavit of Executor/ Administrator

STATE OF____________________ }
COUNTY OF__________________ } SS.

Before me, the undersigned authority, personally appeared _____, Executor/Administrator for the Estate of _______________, who being

47. The foregoing statement is not always accurate because even if the net federal estate tax bracket is lower than the income tax rate, it may still pay to take the commissions because of the additional advantage of securing a deduction on the state death tax return.

duly sworn did depose and say that executors/administrators' commissions in the sum of $__________ have been agreed upon. If the amount is reduced, the Internal Revenue Service will be notified.

The above commissions have been (or will be) paid as follows:

Date	Amount paid (or to be paid)
	____________________
	____________________

Sworn to and subscribed before me
this ______________ day of_____
A.D. 19_____.

____

Attorneys' Fees Fees paid to counsel for the executors are deductible and are also set forth at Part B of Schedule J. The deductibility of these fees is conditioned upon the same requirements that apply to deductibility of executors' commissions. Thus, the fees deducted must be reasonable in amount, allowable under local law, and either must have been paid or must eventually be paid. In the latter case the discussion relating to executors' fees not yet paid at the time of filing the return is equally applicable to the attorney fee. It should be noted that even though the fiduciary fees are allowed under local law, the IRS is not bound to accept the stated amounts as fully deductible in the 706. Again, the estate checkbook will not be a sufficient source of information to determine the amount of the fees to be claimed on the return. The maximum allowable deduction in a given jurisdiction may often be determined by reference to any applicable statutory schedule or schedule developed by case law of fees for acting as counsel to executors. Of course, only fees incurred on behalf of the estate are deductible.

Accountants' Fees In some estates, particularly larger estates, an accountant may be retained to prepare the decedent's final income tax return, to assist with listing all the assets, and to prepare the 706. These fees would be deductible on Schedule J of the 706. The expense of preparing the estate income tax returns is also deductible, although the deduction is usually taken on the estate's income tax return (the 1041).

Miscellaneous Expenses Part B of Schedule J also provides for the deduction of miscellaneous expenses that are allowable under local law and that are actually incurred as necessary expenses of administering the estate. A necessary expense has been defined as one incurred "in the collection of assets, payment of debts, and distribution of property to the persons entitled to it." These items include probate court costs, accountants' fees, cost of obtaining appraisals, legal advertisements, etc.

For example, a brokerage fee incurred in selling property of the estate is deductible if the sale is necessary in order to (1) pay the decedent's debts, expenses of administration or taxes; (2) preserve the estate; or (3) effect distribution.[48] Most of the selling expenses for real estate may normally be found on the settlement or closing sheet. Such deductible expenses would include brokerage commissions, title insurance company charges, local transfer and deed taxes, and all other charges reasonably necessary to effect the sale. Selling expenses for securities will be found by reviewing the broker's confirmations of sale. Note, though, that the same item cannot be deducted as an administration expense on the federal estate tax return and as a selling expense on the fiduciary income tax return.

The balance of the miscellaneous administration expenses already paid can be compiled by reviewing the checking account records of the executors. The list of expenses should always include the names of the payees and a brief description of the services rendered or to be rendered. However, some of the expenses may not have been paid as yet. For example, often the costs of filing the executors' official court accounting will not have been incurred at the time the federal estate tax return is prepared. These unpaid costs should be computed and set forth as part of a reasonable estimate of additional expenses of administration. The miscellaneous expenses are totaled separately and added together with the executors' commissions, attorneys' fees, and funeral expenses, to arrive at the total of the deductions on Schedule J (see accompanying Example).

Election to Deduct Administration Expenses on the Fiduciary Income Tax Return With the exception of the funeral expenses, which are regarded as personal expenses and are never deductible for fiduciary income tax purposes, the various fees, commissions, and miscellaneous expenses mentioned earlier may all be deductible, in whole or in part, on either the federal estate tax return or on the estate's fiduciary income tax return for the year in which the particular item is paid. Medical expenses of the decedent's last illness can be claimed on the decedent's final 1040 in lieu of the 706. A special rule allows medical expenses paid by the decedent's estate to be deducted on his final 1040 even though the expenses were paid after death (IRC § 213 (c)). The executors may elect to take such deductions for either income tax or federal estate tax

48. Often tangible items of property that cannot be easily divided are given to more than one person. In order to effect proper distribution of such property, it may be necessary to sell the property and distribute the proceeds.

EXAMPLE *Form 706, Schedule J—Funeral and Administration Expenses*

Form 706 (Rev. 7-90)

Estate of: Peter Chessman

SCHEDULE J—Funeral Expenses and Expenses Incurred in Administering Property Subject to Claims

Note: *Do not list on this schedule expenses of administering property not subject to claims. For those expenses, see the Instructions for Schedule L.*

If executors' commissions, attorney fees, etc., are claimed and allowed as a deduction for estate tax purposes, they are not allowable as a deduction in computing the taxable income of the estate for Federal income tax purposes. They are allowable as an income tax deduction on Form 1041 if a waiver is filed to waive the deduction on Form 706 (see the Form 1041 instructions).

Item number	Description	Expense amount	Total Amount
	A. Funeral expenses:		
1	J. R. Matthews & Sons, Funeral Bill	2,800.00	
	Pine Haven, Interment	400.00	
	J. J. Kokes, Inc., Memorial Stone	300.00	
	Total funeral expenses		3,500.00
	B. Administration expenses:		
1	Executors' commissions—amount estimated/agreed upon/paid. (Strike out the words that do not apply.)		
2	Attorney fees—amount estimated/~~agreed upon/paid~~. (Strike out the words that do not apply.)		34,000.00
3	Accountant fees—amount estimated/agreed upon/paid. (Strike out the words that do not apply.)		- 0 -
4	Miscellaneous expenses:	Expense amount	
	Register of Wills, Probate Costs	100.00	
	The Legal Intelligencer, Legal Advertising	12.00	
	Wm. J. Mansfield, Legal Advertising	13.00	
	Continental Bank, Safe Deposit Box Rental	12.00	
	Samuel T. Freeman & Co., Appraisal of Personal Property	77.00	
	Strouse, Greenberg & Co., Real Estate Appraisal	536.00	
	Estimated Additional Administration Expenses	250.00	
	Total miscellaneous expenses from continuation schedule(s) (or additional sheet(s)) attached to this schedule		
	Total miscellaneous expenses		1,000.00
	TOTAL. (Also enter on Part 5, Recapitulation, page 3, at item 11.)		63,500.00

(If more space is needed, attach the continuation schedule from the end of this package or additional sheets of the same size.)

Schedule J—Page 20

purposes on either an item-by-item basis or on a dollar-by-dollar basis (for example, of a single $10,000 counsel fee paid in one year, the estate may deduct $3,000 on the fiduciary income tax return and the balance of $7,000 on the estate tax return).

The choice of where to take a deduction will be a mathematical determination based on where the deduction will yield the greatest tax saving. Generally, deductions used on the fiduciary income tax return cannot be used on the federal estate tax return.

Because of incomplete information in regard to the income tax return, it is often unclear whether an item should be deducted on that return at the time the federal estate tax return is being prepared and filed. In such cases, it is advisable to deduct the Schedule J items on the federal estate tax return as a protective measure, even if the same item is also being taken as a deduction on the fiduciary income tax return. Under § 642 (g) of the code, in order to deduct an administration expense for income tax purposes, the executor will eventually have to file an election within the period of the statute of limitations (3 years from the due date) for that income tax return, declaring that the particular item will not be taken as a deduction for federal estate tax purposes. Until that election is filed with the Internal Revenue Service, the executor is free to wait and see on which tax return the expense item yielded the greater benefit. No such election need ever be filed with the federal estate tax return.

If, after the federal estate tax return has been filed, the choice is made to elect the deduction for income tax purposes, the federal estate tax return will have to be changed. This change may either be communicated to the estate tax–examining agent at the time of the estate tax audit or, if there is no such audit or the audit has already been completed, a letter can be sent to the office of the District Director for the district in which the federal estate tax return was filed, waiving the deduction previously taken on Schedule J, setting forth the additional tax due because of the disallowed deduction, and enclosing a check in payment of that tax. If the eventual decision is to take the deduction on the federal estate tax return, an amended fiduciary income tax return will have to be filed.

If there is no 706 tax due, certain administration expenses deductible on the fiduciary income tax return (Form 1041) may be justifiable and could be "passed through" to the beneficiaries as an "excess deduction" on their personal 1040s on Schedule A.

Double Deductions on Form 706 and Form 1041 As stated in the preceding section "Miscellaneous Expenses," the general rule is that administration expenses may be deducted on *either* the estate tax return *or* the income tax return. There is one basic exception to this rule: *Expenses relating to income in respect of decedents.*

In determining where to claim the deductions, consider the following. (1) The 706 tax rates start at 37% and go as high as 55% (60% on estates over ten million); thus it is usually wise to take the deductions on the 706. (2) Medical expenses can be taken on either the 1040 or the 706. If there is no 706 tax due and the expenses exceed 7.5% of the decedent's adjusted gross income, it may be better to take them on the final 1040.

Section 642(g) of the code, which generally prohibits the taking of double deductions for income and federal estate tax purposes, contains an exception for deductions relating to "income in respect of decedents." This, by the way, is the only clear statutory exception to the double deduction rule.

The double deductions specifically authorized by § 642(g) can really only be appreciated when the term "income in respect of a decedent" is understood. Although it is an income tax concept, it should be mentioned at this point. Examples of "income with respect to a decedent" are income that is earned by the decedent during lifetime but is paid after death—e.g., a last salary payment that is made to the executors and accrued dividends and interest paid after the death of a decedent. Another type of income in respect of a decedent would be renewal commissions paid to the estate or other beneficiaries of a deceased insurance agent on policies written by her during her lifetime. The reason such items are not included as income on a final lifetime return of the decedent is that they were not received prior to death. Individuals normally are not taxed on income until the time of receipt.

Section 691(b) of the code allows certain deductions to be applied against the income in respect of a decedent; such deductions as accrued business expenses, accrued interest payable, and accrued taxes would belong in this category. Since the above items are accrued at the date of death they are due on that date but not yet paid. It is these § 691(b) deductions that may be taken on *both* the estate tax return and the fiduciary income tax returns. These deductions will ordinarily constitute deductible *debts* of the decedent and will therefore appear on the estate tax return on Schedule K that will be discussed in detail later in this chapter.

Expenses Relating to Tax Exempt Income In the unusual estates that produce large amounts of tax exempt income there is one hybrid item of miscellaneous expense. When executors' commissions and attorneys' fees or any of the miscellaneous administration expenses are used as deductions on the fiduciary income tax returns, the income tax regulations require that any portion of those expenses that is attributable to income that is exempt from taxation cannot be taken as a deduction for income tax purposes. Thus, if $10,000 of administration expenses are paid in one year and $2,500 of these expenses are deemed apportionable to tax-exempt income, only $7,500 can be allowed as a deduction on the estate's income tax return. At least the other $2,500 of disallowed expenses should then be deducted on Schedule J of the federal estate tax return, which is the only place the deduction can be utilized. The problem with taking this particular administration expense deduction on the federal estate tax return is that it will generally involve a rather difficult estimate; a guess must be made as to the amount of administration expenses that will be disallowed for fiduciary income tax purposes during the entire course of the estate administration. Therefore, it is necessary to estimate the amount of disallowed expenses on tax returns that have not as yet been prepared. As with all such estimates, the most reasonable estimate possible should be made at the time the federal estate tax return is filed, and any necessary adjustments can be made either at the time of the audit of the return or in a subsequent letter to the District Director.

In setting forth the estimate, the return should always disclose that the figure used is, indeed, an estimate.

Community Property Considerations The deductibility of expenses and claims, as we have pointed out in the preceding paragraphs, depends in part upon their allowability under local law. Where husband and wife owned property as community property, the special rules in those states that have community property may affect the allowable deductions.

Generally, expenses and claims chargeable against the entire community property are deductible only in proportion to the decedent's interest in the property. Thus, in a state where the funeral expenses of the deceased spouse are a charge against the whole community property, only one-half of such funeral expenses will be deductible. Further, in some jurisdictions the entire community property is subject to an estate administration upon the death of one of the spouses and, in such case, only one-half of the administration expenses will be deductible. The other half will be lost.

Schedule K—Debts, Mortgages, and Liens[49]

Debts The usual list of deductible claims against the estate will consist of the unpaid debts of the decedent for purchases made and contracts entered into before his death, the last illness expenses, accrued taxes, and unsecured notes. The elements of a deductible claim are

1. It must have been a personal obligation of the decedent.

49. IRC § 2053.

2. It must have been in existence at the time of his death.
3. It must be enforceable against his estate.
4. If the claim is based upon a promise or agreement, it may be deducted only to the extent that the liability was contracted in good faith and for an adequate and full consideration in money or money's worth.

The above elements will be discussed below as they relate to particular types of claims against the estate.

If the amount of the debt is disputed, deduct only the amount the estate concedes to be a valid claim. If the claim is contested, enter the amount in contest in the column provided.

The place to start when compiling a list of items to appear on Schedule K is the executor's checkbook. Normally, all, or nearly all, of the debts that will appear on the schedule will have been paid by the time the return is being prepared. Schedule K should be filled out by showing the name of the payee and giving a brief description of the nature of the bill. Where debts relate to particular assets, cross-reference should be made to the asset schedules. As in the case with administration expenses and funeral expenses, the cancelled checks and the receipted bills should be retained for possible reference during the audit of the federal estate tax return.

Obligation for Rent Where the decedent lived in an apartment and his or her estate is legally obligated to pay the rent beyond the date of death, the amount of the rental obligation of the estate will generally be deductible. If, by the time the federal estate tax return is prepared, the lease has been terminated and the balance of rent has been paid to the lessor by the estate, the full amount of such payment would be claimed as a debt. (The return of any security deposit held by the lessor should be shown as a miscellaneous asset on Schedule F.)

Medical Expenses As was the case with administration expenses, there is an election available with respect to medical expenses that are unpaid at the time of decedent's death. In preparing the final lifetime income tax return (i.e., the return for the year of death), the executors may elect to deduct on that return those medical expenses that are, in fact, paid by the estate within one year after the date of death, provided that the executors file an election with the District Director of Internal Revenue stating that such expenses will not also be taken as deductions for federal estate tax purposes. As with the election to deduct administration expenses on either the fiduciary income tax or federal estate tax returns, if the executors are uncertain as to whether the tax brackets after final audit of the particular tax returns will be lower for federal estate tax purposes or for purposes of the final lifetime income tax return, the deduction should initially be claimed in both returns. Eventually (if the choice is to take the deduction for income tax purposes) the executors must file the election before the statute of limitations (3 years from due date) runs out with respect to that income tax return. Any change in the federal estate tax return can be accomplished by notifying the examining agent or by writing to the government. If the choice is to take the deduction on the federal estate tax return, that change in the final lifetime return would require the filing of an amended return.

As with the administration expense election, medical expenses may be taken in whole or item-by-item on either tax return. Although it is usually done, neither the Internal Revenue Code nor the regulations would seem to preclude the executors from taking a single medical expense item and deducting part of it on each return. The considerations in choosing where to take these expenses as deductions are the same as discussed under Schedule J; that is, the net effective federal estate tax bracket must be compared with the top bracket on the final lifetime income tax return. The expenses would then be used as deductions on the return that shows the higher rate of tax.

Property Taxes Property taxes are not deductible unless they have accrued[50] prior to the date of death. This does not mean that they must have accrued in the normal accounting sense, but rather that they must have been an enforceable obligation of the decedent at the time of his death. To be deductible, therefore, real estate taxes must generally have become a lien on the property before the date of death. This determination would, of course, depend upon the local law of the jurisdiction in which the taxes are assessed.

Income Tax As previously mentioned, one of the elements of a deductible claim is that the claim must have been in existence at the time of the decedent's death. Therefore, the tax on income of the decedent received after the date of death is not deductible since it was not a claim against the decedent at the time of his death. The tax on income received prior to death is deductible. The rule may be applied very mechanically: any tax paid with respect to a Form 1040 return, which covers the lifetime income of the decedent, is deductible; any tax paid with respect to a Form 1041, the fiduciary income tax return, is not deductible.

It is possible that the amount of the income tax liability for the year of death will not yet be fixed when the federal estate tax return is being prepared. For instance, the due date for a 1991 income tax return is April 15, 1992. If the decedent died on July 15,

50. An accounting term meaning that a debt has become due but has not yet been paid.

1991 (and he had earned sufficient income to incur a tax liability for 1991), the due date for the 1991 income tax return will be the same as the federal estate tax return. Particularly if the final lifetime return is a joint return, the income tax information may not be available in time for preparation of Schedule K of the estate tax return. Either an estimate of the income tax liability will have to be made or, in some cases, it may be in order to request an extension of time to file the federal estate tax return. If an audit of any of the lifetime income tax returns results in additional tax being assessed, the amount of such additional tax, which is properly attributable to the decedent, may be deducted on the federal estate tax return. That deduction can be communicated to the examining agent at the federal estate tax audit, or the estate can make a claim for a refund.

Where a joint income tax return has been filed with the decedent's spouse, there is a Schedule K problem concerning the amount of tax properly attributable to the decedent and, therefore, deductible by the estate. The amount allowed by the Internal Revenue Service in such a case is generally governed by state law. The regulations generally presume that the estate's share of the joint tax liability is an amount that bears the same ratio to the total joint tax liability (for the period covered by the return) as the amount of income tax for which the decedent would have been liable if separate returns had been filed bears to the total of the amount for which the decedent and his spouse each would have been liable if they had filed separate returns. For example, suppose that the tax liability shown on a joint return that has been filed by decedent and his spouse is $16,000. Assume that on the basis of separate returns the income tax liability of a decedent on income prior to the date of death would have been $5,000 and the income tax liability of the surviving spouse on income for the entire year would have been $15,000. The decedent's share of the $16,000 tax shown on the joint return is $4,000, computed as follows:

$$\frac{\text{decedent's separate tax}}{\text{both separate taxes}} \times \text{joint tax}$$

OR

$$\frac{\$5{,}000}{\$20{,}000} \times \$16{,}000 = \$4{,}000$$

Claims Based upon a Promise or Agreement As stated above, one of the elements of a deductible claim is that it must have been contracted for in good faith and for an adequate and full consideration in money or money's worth. Thus, if the decedent had issued a promissory note to his daughter as evidence of his intention to make a gift to her, the amount of such note would not be deductible against the estate because the decedent had received no monetary consideration in return for the note.

Another instance of a nondeductible claim arises where, in consideration for some fixed dollar claim against the estate, the decedent's spouse relinquished her right of dower[51] or other marital rights in the decedent's property or estate. This claim would not be deductible because § 2043(b) of the code specifically provides that such consideration does not constitute the requisite consideration in money or money's worth.

The one exception to the monetary consideration requirement is the category of charitable pledges. A pledge or subscription made during the lifetime, if enforceable against the estate (and in most jurisdictions a pledge card will contain the type of language that will have the effect of making the pledge enforceable against the estate), may be deducted provided, however, that the payment had been in the form of a bequest to charity. For example, if the decedent, during his lifetime, made an enforceable pledge of $5,000 to the Heart Association, this sum would be a deductible claim on Schedule K because a bequest of $5,000 to the Heart Fund would have qualified as a charitable deduction under § 2055 of the code. When the federal estate tax return is audited, the examining agent will generally require the executors to produce the pledge card, or a copy thereof, before he will allow the deduction. Therefore, an effort should be made to obtain the card or a copy when the return is being prepared.

Interest Just as the asset schedules must include interest on bank accounts and other assets owned by the decedent up to the date of death, likewise the estate is entitled to a deduction for any interest owed by the decedent, accrued to the date of death. Thus, if the decedent had a bank loan, the amount of interest due to the date of death should be calculated and added to the principal of the debt set forth in Schedule K. Whenever possible, the interest and principal due as of the date of death should be confirmed in writing with the creditor.

Although there are some rare exceptions developed in recent cases, as a general proposition interest may and should only be deducted up to the date of death.

Contingent Liabilities If the decedent had entered into any transaction that could result in liability at a later date, a deduction for that liability will be allowable only if the circumstances have become such that the amount of the liability has become ascer-

51. In many states each spouse has certain rights to part of the property of the other spouse. The extent of such rights vary greatly from one state to another. Characteristically such rights are enforceable only upon the death of one spouse. Such marital rights are sometimes referred to as "dower" rights of a widow or "curtesy" rights of a widower.

tainable with reasonable certainty. If the amount is not so determinable at the time the return is filed, a notation may be made on Schedule K setting forth the facts and circumstances under which the claim could arise. For example, if there is a federal income tax examination of one of the decedent's lifetime returns in progress when the federal estate tax return is being prepared, it may be advisable to insert a notation, such as the following:

> NOTE: A federal income tax audit of the decedent's 1978 income tax return is currently in progress, but no deficiency assessment has as yet been made.

If by the time the federal estate tax return is audited the amount is still not ascertainable, it might eventually become necessary to file a claim for refund at the time the amount of the liability is eventually determined. In some cases it may even be necessary to file that claim before there is a final determination, so that the estate does not find itself in a position in which the statute of limitations has run out with respect to the filing of such claims.[52]

Mortgages and Liens Only obligations secured by mortgages or other liens on property included in the gross estate are deductible in the second section of Schedule K. If the decedent owned real property listed on Schedule A of the federal estate tax return that was subject to a mortgage, this schedule should cross-reference the appropriate Schedule A item. All of the relevant information relating to the mortgage balance, and any deduction for interest that may have accrued to the date of death, should be set forth on Schedule K, as in the following example:

Amount due First National Bank on mortgage secured by premises 100 Elm Street (see Schedule A, Item 1)	$15,000.00
Interest accrued from date of last payment 12/1/90 to date of death, at 7½%	100.00

The amount of the mortgage should be confirmed not only through the decedent's records, but also by correspondence with the mortgagee, who should be asked to supply the outstanding balance and accrued interest as of the date of death. This letter from the mortgagee, which is commonly referred to as a "pay-off statement," will normally be requested for inspection upon audit of the federal estate tax return.

52. This often happens because the income tax case against the estate may be delayed many times. There is no great hurry to proceed in that case because the income tax statute of limitations can be extended by agreement of the parties. The federal estate tax statute of limitations (three years from the due date of the return), on the other hand, cannot be waived by either the government or the executors.

If the property on which the mortgage is secured is not included in the gross estate because, for example, the property is jointly owned and the surviving spouse has contributed the entire purchase price, no portion of the mortgage owed would ordinarily be deductible on the return, even if the decedent was a signatory to the bond and mortgage. If one-half (or some other percentage) of the property is included in the gross estate, after giving effect to the contribution made by the surviving joint owner, a similar percentage of the mortgage balance and accrued interest will be deductible on Schedule K.

Only interest accrued to the date of death on the decedent's debts is deductible if the § 2032 Alternate Valuation election is made (Treasury Regulation § 20.2053.4). Post-death interest incurred by the executor for a proper purpose, i.e., to protect the estate, is also deductible (Treas. Reg. § 20.2053–3 (d)).

A note payable by the decedent that is secured by collateral appearing on the asset schedules of the federal estate tax return should be listed in this second section of Schedule K. A cross-reference should be made to the asset schedule on which the collateral securing the note appears. An unsecured note would be listed in the first part of Schedule K under "Debts of Decedent." Whether the note is secured or unsecured, complete information concerning the obligee and the interest rate should be given as indicated by the mortgage-payable example under "Mortgages and Liens."

A completed Schedule K showing examples of the foregoing items follows.

Schedule L—Net Losses During Administration and Costs of Administering Property Not Subject to Claims

Net Losses During Administration[53] Schedule L is a rarely used section of the federal estate tax return. The first part of Schedule L is used for allowable deductions for losses incurred during the settlement of the estate. Section 2054 defines such losses as those " . . . arising from fires, storms, shipwrecks, or other casualties, or from theft, when such losses are not compensated for by insurance or otherwise." The regulations make clear that if the estate is partially compensated for a loss, by insurance, or by a third party responsible for the loss, the excess of the loss over the compensation may be deducted. If property worth $1,000 were destroyed and $800 of insurance proceeds were received, the Schedule L deduction would be $200.

53. IRC § 2054.

EXAMPLE Form 706, Schedule K—Debts of the Decedent

Form 706 (Rev. 7-90)

Estate of: Peter Chessman

SCHEDULE K—Debts of the Decedent, and Mortgages and Liens

Item number	Debts of the Decedent—Creditor and nature of claim, and allowable death taxes	Amount unpaid to date	Amount in contest	Amount claimed as a deduction
1	John Wanamaker, Bill for Merchandise	15.00		15.00
2	Bell Telephone Co., September Bill	8.00		8.00
3	1991 Income Tax	3,987.00		3,987.00
4	1991 School Tax	65.00		65.00
	Total from continuation schedule(s) (or additional sheet(s)) attached to this schedule			
	TOTAL. (Also enter on Part 5, Recapitulation, page 3, at item 12.)			4,075.00

Item number	Mortgages and Liens—Description	Amount
1	First Federal Saving and Loan Association, Mortgage Balance on 1201 Loyola Avenue, Philadelphia, PA (Schedule A, Item 1)	4,350.00
	Interest accrued from 1/1/91 to date of death	50.00
2	Acme Loan Co., Balance due on Collateral Note (collateral listed on Schedule B, Items 3-7)	3,000.00
	Interest accrued from 2/15/91 to date of death at 8½%	100.00
	Total from continuation schedule(s) (or additional sheet(s)) attached to this schedule	
	TOTAL. (Also enter on Part 5, Recapitulation, page 3, at item 13.)	7,500.00

(If more space is needed, attach the continuation schedule from the end of this package or additional sheets of the same size.)

(The instructions to Schedule K are in the separate instructions.) **Schedule K —Page 22**

Losses deducted on the first part of Schedule L must relate to events that occurred after the decedent's death and before the damaged property was distributed by the personal representative. Therefore, if the executor deeds a house to a beneficiary and the house subsequently is destroyed in a fire, because the fire occurred after the executor distributed the property, no deduction would be allowed on Schedule L, even if the insurance proceeds did not fully compensate for the loss. Progressive deterioration of property and damage from a normal process are not casualty losses. Thus the steady weakening of a foundation caused by normal or usual wind and weather conditions is not a casualty loss.

The losses described above are generally called "casualty losses." A casualty loss is the complete or partial destruction of property resulting from an identifiable event of a sudden, unexpected, or unusual destructive force, such as an automobile collision, a fire, flood, storm, drought, hurricane, or other similar event.

Uncompensated casualty or theft losses during the period of the estate administration may be taken as deductions on the federal estate tax return or the fiduciary income tax return (but not both) at the election of the personal representative. The election is made in the same manner as the election to deduct administration expenses of the estate. See the discussion under "Election to Deduct Administration Expenses on the Fiduciary Tax Return" in this chapter concerning Schedule J, the timing of the election, and the elements to be considered in making the election.

The deduction for a loss on Schedule L is limited to the value of the asset as it was included in the gross estate. Therefore, if an uninsured painting listed on Schedule F of the return and valued at $5,000 is stolen, the amount of the deduction is limited to $5,000 even if it was worth $6,000 when stolen. In effect, Schedule L can be viewed as an adjustment to the valuation of an asset rather than as a deduction. The $1,000 loss over and above gross estate valuation may, however, be deducted as a theft loss on the fiduciary income tax return. Of course, in such a case, the personal representative must be able to prove the increased value of the painting.

Where alternate valuation is employed and there is a casualty or theft loss that is prior to the alternate valuation date and is either partially or wholly uncompensated, the Internal Revenue Service takes the position that no Schedule L deduction may be taken. Since, as stated above, Schedule L is really adjusting the value of an estate to its post-theft or post-casualty value, no deduction is needed in this case because the asset will not be valued until the alternate valuation date, which will be after the loss. To take the example of the stolen painting, if date-of-death valuation is used there will be a $5,000 asset shown on Schedule F and a $5,000 deduction on Schedule L, and the two entries cancel each other out. (Lawyers and accountants typically refer to such a situation as a "wash," e.g., one entry washes out the other). If alternate valuation is employed there is no entry in any asset schedule, since the asset was not present on the valuation date, and there is no deduction. The net result, as it should be, is the same in either case.

Expenses Incurred in Administering Property Not Subject to Claims[54] The second section of Schedule L is used for deductions relating to expenses of administering property that, while part of the taxable estate, is not part of the probate estate. The phrase "not subject to claims" (which appears at the head of this section of the schedule) refers to the fact that creditors of the decedent can make no claim on such property since it is not part of the probate estate.

The types of property generating a Schedule L expense will normally be trust property that is included as an asset on Schedule G or joint property that is reported on Schedule E. Certain commissions of the personal representative and counsel fees paid with respect to such trust property or joint property are allowable deductions under this schedule. Expenses incurred in connection with property not subject to claims may be deducted on Schedule L only to the extent that they are in fact paid before the expiration of the statute of limitations for the federal estate tax return. In filling out the schedule, a cross-reference should be made to the related asset schedule, as in the sample Schedule L that follows.

Schedule M—Marital Deduction[55]

Where the decedent is survived by a spouse, a deduction is available on the federal estate tax return for the value of the property passing to the surviving spouse. Under present law, there is no limit to the amount that can pass tax free from one spouse to another by means of the estate tax marital deduction, with the exception of certain gifts of terminable interests and gifts to noncitizen spouses (see the following for additional explanation). The nature, availability, and valuation of the marital deduction is the subject of this section of the text.

For purposes of the marital deduction, an interest in property is considered as passing from the decedent to his spouse if

1. The interest is left to the spouse under the will.
2. The interest is inherited (no will) by the spouse.

54. IRC § 2053(b).
55. IRC § 2056.

EXAMPLE *Form 706, Schedule L—Net Losses*

Form 706 (Rev. 7-90)

Estate of: Peter Chessman

SCHEDULE L—Net Losses During Administration and Expenses Incurred in Administering Property Not Subject to Claims

Item number	Net losses during administration (**Note:** *Do not deduct losses claimed on a Federal income tax return.*)	Amount
1	Unreimbursed casualty loss resulting from fire in premises 100 Elm Street, Philadelphia, PA, (Schedule A, Item 1): Value of Property at date of death $17,500.00 Value of Property after fire loss 5,000.00 Amount of fire loss $12,500.00 Less: Insurance recovered 10,000.00	2,500.00
	Total from continuation schedule(s) (or additional sheet(s)) attached to this schedule	
	TOTAL. (Also enter on Part 5, Recapitulation, page 3, at item 16.)	2,500.00*

Item number	Expenses incurred in administering property not subject to claims (Indicate whether estimated, agreed upon, or paid.)	Amount
1	Expenses re Deed of Trust dated 1/7/60 (Schedule G, Item 1)	
	Trustees' Commissions	2,500.00
	Counsel Fee	2,500.00
	Cost of Filing Account	250.00
	Total from continuation schedule(s) (or additional sheet(s)) attached to this schedule	
	TOTAL. (Also enter on Part 5, Recapitulation, page 3, at item 17.)	5,250.00*

(If more space is needed, attach the continuation schedule from the end of this package or additional sheets of the same size.)
(The instructions to Schedule L are in the separate instructions.)

Schedule L —Page 23

*Not included in Peter Chessman's estate.

3. The interest is a dower or curtesy interest of the surviving spouse.
4. The interest was transferred to the spouse by the decedent at any time.
5. The interest was held jointly with right of survivorship.
6. The decedent had a power of appointment over the property and exercised it in favor of the spouse, or if the spouse takes the property in default of the decedent, exercising the power of appointment.
7. The interest is proceeds of a life insurance policy payable to the spouse.

In most jurisdictions where the testator is survived by a spouse, the law gives the spouse the right to elect to receive his or her statutory share of the estate in lieu of the bequests made under the will.[56] This occurs when there is no will or if the spouse is dissatisfied with his or her portion of the estate. If the interest awarded by the state of the decedent's domicile is a life estate or if the interest does not vest at the date of the decedent's death, it does not qualify for the marital deduction under the terminable interest rule.[57] If the surviving spouse obtains a fixed right to a portion of the estate, the dower rights qualify for the marital deduction. In most states, in order to elect to take against a will, the spouse must file the necessary documentation effecting the election within a certain period following the Grant of Letters. Where such a time limit applies, the election will generally have been filed with the local probate court before the time the federal estate tax return is being prepared for actual filing.

Unlimited Marital Deduction The marital deduction is authorized by IRC § 2056. Generally, all property bequeathed to the spouse and all gifts to the spouse made after 1981, will qualify for the marital deduction. Under prior law there were limitations to the marital deduction. Prior to 1982 the deduction was limited to the greater of $250,000 or one-half of the adjusted gross estate. Presently all jointly owned property (owned with the spouse only), life insurance policies payable to the spouse, powers of appointment, and property passing to the surviving spouse in a will contest qualifies for the unlimited marital deduction (Treasury Regulation § 20.2056 (e)-2 (d)). The property must be included in the decedent's gross estate to qualify for the deduction.

56. For the remainder of this section, we will be assuming that the husband has died—the rules are equally applicable if a wife predeceases her husband.

57. "A surviving spouse's interest in property does not qualify for the marital deduction if another person has a contingent interest in the property at the decedent's death." See also "QTIP."

The unlimited marital deduction does not apply to estates of decedents dying before 1982 or to gifts made prior to 1982. It does not apply to transfers resulting from a will executed or trust created prior to September 12, 1981, if the bequest to the surviving spouse is referred to as a "formula" marital clause. (This is the language of prior law, where the marital deduction was computed as a percentage of the estate.) A "transitional rule" referring the "formula" clause applies to the old wills.

Form of Marital Share The types of property interests that qualify for the marital deduction are set forth on Schedule M. As the area is quite complex, the discussion that follows is only intended to provide a general background and to illustrate the types of interests that do qualify. The discussion will also be useful in understanding the estate planning chapter of the text, as one of the goals of planning is likely to be securing the most advantageous tax situation for the estates of both the decedent and the surviving spouse.

Outright Gift The simplest case of property qualifying for the marital deduction is where it is devised or bequeathed to the surviving spouse by outright gift. For example the decedent's will may provide as follows:

> "I give and devise my home, located at 100 Elm Street, to my wife, provided she survives me."

There is no limitation on this gift other than the survival of the wife. If the wife, in fact, outlives her husband, she will inherit the real estate absolutely, and no other person will have any interest in the property. Therefore, the value of the house qualifies for the marital deduction.

Jointly Owned and Other Nonprobate Property Certain property may pass to the surviving spouse either by operation of law or by some other means outside the control of the will. For example, even though the testator's will leaves his entire estate to his son, if all of his property was owned jointly by the testator and his wife (i.e., as entireties property), by operation of law it would all pass to the surviving wife.

Life insurance is another example of property that passes outside the will. If the spouse is the beneficiary of a life insurance policy, the proceeds payable to her may qualify for the marital deduction, even though the insurance proceeds will not form a part of the probate estate (see discussion under "Insurance Proceeds").

Gift in Trust Up to this point our illustrations of property qualifying for the marital deduction have been concerned with property that either passes outright to the spouse under the will or that passes to her outright by operation of law or otherwise. Property may also be placed in trust for the benefit of the spouse. Often the decedent will establish a "marital trust" under his will. The trust normally gives the spouse a terminable interest in the property. The regulations define a "terminable interest" as follows:

> A "terminable interest" in property is an interest which will terminate or fail on the lapse of time or on the occurrence or the failure to occur of some contingency. Life estates, terms for years [and] annuities ... are therefore terminable interests. ... (Section 20.2056 (b) (1))

Perhaps the best way to understand a "terminable interest" is by an example. Assume the testator leaves his property in trust with the income therefrom to be paid to his wife for her life and upon her death the principal to be distributed to his children. The life interest in the property passing to the wife is terminable (upon her death). Such an interest, which is called a "life estate," is an example of a "terminable interest." The property will qualify for the marital deduction unless someone else will receive the property after the spouse's interest terminates. The exception to this is the QTIP election that can be taken by the executor of the estate.[58]

Power of Appointment Trust Section 2056 (b) (5) of the Internal Revenue Code sets forth the criteria that must be met if the testator wishes to create a trust that gives the spouse a life estate and qualifies for the marital deduction by also giving the spouse a general power of appointment over the principal of the trust.[59]

If the decedent gives his spouse a general power of appointment over property held in trust, the property will qualify for the marital deduction. As you will recall, a general power appointment is where a person can appoint the property to anyone, including his own estate or the creditors of his estate, without limitation.

Insurance Proceeds Life insurance proceeds payable in a lump sum to the surviving spouse qualify for the marital deduction. If the proceeds are payable in installments, the method of payment should be as follows:

58. See "Filling out Schedule M" later in this chapter for additional information on QTIP elections.

59. While we are using the term "trust" in this case because in the overwhelming majority of instances that is the form used for this type of transfer, the Internal Revenue Code does provide that the transfer need not be in trust and that the spouse could be given a legal (as opposed to an equitable) life estate as long as the spouse is given the power to appoint the principal or some specific portion of the principal.

1. The proceeds of the policy, or at least a specific portion of the proceeds, must be held by the insurer subject to an agreement (referred to as a "settlement option") to pay the proceeds to the spouse only in installments,
2. The surviving spouse alone must have the power to appoint all or a specific portion of the proceeds to herself or her estate (and no one else may have any power to appoint the proceeds to anyone other than the surviving spouse), and
3. Under the chosen settlement option, the installments to be paid by the insurer to the spouse must be payable annually or more frequently and they must commence not later than 13 months after the date of death. The 13 month requirement is the only important difference between the requirements relating to this special life insurance situation and those relating to ordinary power of appointment trusts. With a trust there is no specific time requirement with regard to income payments. However, they may not be delayed beyond a reasonable period for administration and distribution of the estate.

Size of Marital Share As is indicated by the preceding discussion, there are innumerable ways of obtaining a marital deduction. If the sum of $10,000 is bequeathed, free of tax, to the surviving spouse, that fixed amount will be set forth on Schedule M as the amount of the marital deduction. Such an outright legacy may also take the form of a gift of a particular piece of property rather than cash. In that event the value of the particular property as shown in the appropriate asset schedule of the return will be carried to Schedule M and will be the amount of the marital deduction. As an illustration of the treatment of a legacy of particular property, assume the decedent bequeathed 100 shares of General Motors stock to a surviving spouse. The figure at which this stock would be valued on Schedule B of the return would be the same as that used on Schedule M. If alternate valuation were elected, the value of the stock on the alternate valuation date would be used on Schedule M.

Instead of giving a particular item of property or a specific sum of cash to the spouse, the testator may wish to bequeath a certain percentage of his residuary estate to his wife. Such a gift, which may be either outright or in trust, will qualify for the marital deduction so long as it does not constitute a nondeductible terminable interest.

The marital deduction should be integrated with the new unified credit so that the amount passing to the surviving spouse will be that amount that, after utilization of the unified credit, reduces the estate to its lowest possible amount. Such planning, of course, must be done prior to death when wills are being written and revised.[60] Although such estate planning should be done by the attorney involved, it is advantageous and important for the legal assistant to understand the reasoning behind the clauses he or she will be asked to interpret for purposes of completing the federal estate tax return.

Election against Will or Exercise of Dower or Curtesy Rights For any number of reasons, as has been noted earlier, a surviving spouse may elect to take against the will and receive her statutory share, if there is such a statute, or her common-law right of dower (or curtesy in the case of a surviving husband) in lieu of what was to have passed to her under the will. This action may be taken for a variety of reasons. A will may have provided a trust for a spouse who may wish to get the property outright. There may not have been any provision at all for the husband in the will and by electing he can obtain a portion of the estate. By filing an election to take against the will, the portion that will now be received outright will qualify for the marital deduction.

The rules for determining whether the portion of the estate received by an election qualifies for the marital deduction are the same as for any other property passing to the surviving spouse. In some states where the state law gives the surviving spouse only a life interest in the estate where an election is made, the elective interest would not qualify for the marital deduction. In other states, as the elective share is distributable outright, the amount so passing to the surviving spouse qualifies for the marital deduction just as if the property had passed by outright gift in the will.

Disclaimer of Interest under Will Any beneficiary under a will has the power to say that he or she does not wish to receive the property given provided all four conditions for a "qualified disclaimer" established by the Tax Reform Act of 1976 are met.

- **a.** The refusal must be in writing.
- **b.** The refusal must be received by the transferor of the interest, his legal representative, or holder of the legal title to the property, not later than nine months after the day on which the transfer creating the interest is made, or after the death of the grantor, or the day on which such person attains age 21. The nine-month period for making a disclaimer is to be determined in reference to each taxable transfer.

60. See Chapter Ten with regard to having such provisions in the will.

c. The donee must not have accepted the interest of any of its benefits before making a disclaimer, and

d. The interest must pass to a person other than the person making the disclaimer as a result of the refusal to accept the property. The person making the disclaimer cannot have the authority to direct the redistribution or transfer of the property to another person, if there is to be a qualified disclaimer.

If a surviving spouse disclaims the interest given to him under a will, the property subject to the disclaimer would no longer be deemed to have passed to the surviving spouse for purposes of computing the marital deduction. Conversely, if the testator left property to someone, perhaps her children, who disclaimed their interest in favor of their father, the property would then be deemed to have passed from the decedent to the surviving spouse (the father), and if it met all of the other tests described above, it would qualify for the marital deduction. Such a disclaimer must be made before the due date for filing the federal estate tax return in order to be deemed timely for purposes of securing the marital deduction for the disclaimed property now passing to the surviving spouse. It should also be noted that the Revenue Act of 1978, in an attempt to clarify the qualified disclaimer provisions of the Tax Reform Act of 1976, provides that a disclaimer by the surviving spouse will still be valid if as a result of the disclaimer the property is distributed to a trust in which the surviving spouse has been given an income interest.[61]

Simultaneous Death One of the conditions of obtaining the marital deduction is that the spouse receiving property that qualifies for the deduction must survive the decedent. If a married couple should die under such circumstances that the order of their deaths cannot be established (i.e., if they die in the same airplane crash), a marital deduction may or may not be allowable, depending upon the ownership of the property, the applicable local law, and the terms of the decedent's will.

Property Owned Individually If the decedent owns property in his own name and dies simultaneously with his spouse, the Uniform Simultaneous Death Act, which has been adopted in nearly every state, provides that such property shall be disposed of as if the decedent had survived his spouse, i.e., the order of death was spouse first, then decedent. Following that rule the property would be distributed in accordance with that section of the husband's

61. See the section "Filling Out Schedule Schedule M" for additional information on "qualified disclaimers."

will that sets forth the scheme of distribution where his wife predeceases him because the spouse would be presumed not to have been alive to receive his property at the time of decedent's death. However, the act also states that its terms shall not apply if the decedent has provided for a contrary presumption relating to order of death in his will, trust instrument, or life insurance policy. If the decedent specifically provided that in the case of a simultaneous death, his wife is presumed to have survived him, the presumption would not only be effective for purposes of the Simultaneous Death Act (which would result in property passing from the husband's estate to the wife's, where it would be distributed under the terms of her will), but also for purposes of the marital deduction.

Property Owned Jointly If the decedent and his spouse owned property jointly with a right of survivorship and it is determined that they died simultaneously, the Uniform Simultaneous Death Act provides that one-half of such joint property shall be distributed as if the decedent had survived (i.e., pursuant to the decedent's will) and one-half as if the spouse had survived (i.e., pursuant to the spouse's will). This rule, too, can be varied if the decedent specifically provides otherwise in his will or other testamentary document.

Accordingly, absent a declaration by the decedent that his wife is presumed to have survived him, even though the full value of the property held jointly by the decedent and his wife will be includible in the gross estate of the husband (assuming he has furnished the consideration and no gift was made), only one-half of such property will be deemed to pass to the wife (and through the estate) and the marital deduction will be available only for such one-half interest.

In cases where it is advisable to obtain the maximum marital deduction for the estate of the husband, most wills, trusts, and life insurance policies should provide that in the case of simultaneous death the wife shall be presumed to have survived the husband. Such a provision will enable the husband's estate to obtain a full marital deduction for all of the property which the decedent's will left to his wife.

Filling Out Schedule M Each property interest passing to the surviving spouse and qualifying for the marital deduction should be listed on Schedule M, giving a full description of the property and/or interest and the clause of the will that leaves that property or interest to the spouse. There should also be a cross-reference to the asset schedule and item number of each asset passing to the spouse.

The values to be used for purposes of Schedule M are the values used in the asset schedules. If the property is included in the gross estate at the alternate value, then that value will be used for the marital deduction. If property is subject to an encumbrance—for example, real estate subject to a mortgage—only the net value, in this case the value of the real estate less the outstanding mortgage, qualifies for the deduction and can be listed on Schedule M. In showing the gift of encumbered property on Schedule M, it would be best to show the gift of the asset at the full value shown on Schedule A and then to reduce that valuation by the amount of the mortgage set forth on Schedule K, therefore indicating the computation of the net value passing to the spouse. For example:

Item No.	Description		Amount
1.	Premises 100 Elm Street, Phila., Pa. (Schedule A, Item 1) per Item FIRST of Will	$10,000.00	
	Less: Outstanding mortgage (Schedule K, Item 1)	−5,000.00	
			$5,000.00

If a residuary gift is made to the surviving spouse, Schedule M should show the computation that determined the value of the residuary interest. The computation should, as indicated by the instructions for Schedule M, include a statement containing the following:

1. The value of the nonprobate assets that are part of the gross estate;
2. The values of all legacies under the will (and a reference to the applicable item number of the will); and
3. Dates of birth of anyone whose life span may affect the values of the residuary interests passing to the spouse.[62]

At the top of Schedule M there are four questions to be answered by the preparer of the return. Question 1 of the return refers to a qualified disclaimer. In some cases the surviving spouse does not wish to receive property from the estate. This would occur if the surviving spouse had substantial assets of his or her own. The spouse would then attach a copy of the written qualified disclaimer required by § 2518 (b).

The unlimited marital deduction has the advantage of avoiding any federal estate tax in the first estate. However the second estate may have substantial property and thus have to pay a very large tax. For example:

62. For example, if the wife receives a residuary interest in a trust, the value of that interest is determined by reference to the life expectancy of the life tenant.

Mr. Jones dies with a $1,000,000 estate. After the payment of estate expenses he leaves the entire estate to his wife. There is no tax to pay at Mr. Jones's death. After using his unified credit (equivalent to a $600,000 exemption), the balance qualifies for the marital deduction.

Mrs. Jones has assets of $2,000,000. At her death (presuming she does not remarry) her estate will consist of almost $3,000,000 (her $2,000,000 plus Mr. Jones's $1,000,000). She has her unified credit (equivalent to a $600,000 exemption), but the balance of her estate (after expenses) will be subject to the full estate tax of approximately $1,400,000. (The tax was calculated by using a $3,000,000 estate and deducting $192,800 for the unified credit and $70,000 for state death tax credit. The estate is in the 50% tax bracket.)

Mrs. Jones may elect to "disclaim" her share or a portion of her share of Mr. Jones's estate. This would result in the property passing to Mr. Jones's beneficiaries as if Mrs. Jones had predeceased Mr. Jones. In most cases the property would pass to their children. The taxes should be computed for both situations to see if it is advantageous to file a disclaimer. The disclaimer must be executed within nine months of death.

An example of a disclaimer is attached to Schedule M for the Peter Chessman Estate. A separate disclaimer must be sent to each person or institution holding the particular assets to be disclaimed. This allows the person or institution to release the funds to the next beneficiary. If the asset has already been collected by the executor, such as in the case of cash held in a bank, the disclaimer would be directed to the executor. Thus, in the case where the beneficiary is simply disclaiming a bequest of cash bequeathed to him/her under the will, a letter would be written to the executor citing the article in the will where the bequest was made and disclaiming the bequest. All disclaimers made would be attached to the 706.

Question 2 asks if the spouse is a U.S. citizen. This will affect the amount of the allowable marital deduction. Section 2 of Schedule M refers to a Qualified Terminal Interest Property (QTIP), the terminal interest property that qualifies for the marital deduction. This would be property that the decedent gave to his or her spouse during his or her lifetime, either by outright gift or in trust. The election on Schedule M gives the decedent's executor (the person responsible for preparing the return) the option of electing to bring that property back into the decedent's estate so that it can be used for the marital deduction. This is a complex tax-planning issue that requires a thorough knowledge of the decedent's assets as well as the surviving spouse's assets. Most tax planning, due to the unlimited marital deduction, involves both spouse's estates.

To qualify for the marital deduction the QTIP property must pass from the decedent to the surviving spouse, giving the spouse an income interest for life. The election is irrevocable once the 706 is filed. The qualified terminable interest property will be included in the surviving spouse's estate.

A QTIP transfer must (1) give all income payable at least annually to the surviving spouse during his/her life, (2) ensure that during the surviving spouse's lifetime no one can appoint the property to anyone but the spouse. Most QTIP transfers will be in the form of a trust. However, the bequest of a personal residence or a family farm should qualify for the QTIP election. This election is a post-death tax-planning tool that the executor can use to determine whether it would be more advantageous for the surviving spouse to take the marital deduction in the first spouse's estate, and thus tax the property in the first spouse's estate, or whether the property should be taxed in the second estate. Other than QTIP property, terminal interest property does not qualify for the marital deduction. A completed Schedule M follows.

Schedule N—Qualified ESOP Sales (Under Section 2057)

The deduction allowed on schedule N was repealed for estates of decedents dying after December 19, 1989. It allowed a 50% deduction for Qualified ESOP sales under Section 2057. Prior to the ESOP sales deduction, Schedule N was used for the Orphans' Exclusion. Because this schedule is not presently in use, it will not be illustrated.

Schedule O—Charitable Bequests[63]

A deduction is allowed from the gross estate for the value of property that has been included in the gross estate and that is given to charity. The transfer may have been made by the decedent during his lifetime to take effect at death or by his will. There is no percentage limitation on the amount of the deduction, so that if the entire estate were given to charity, there would be a deduction for the entire net value of the property so passing and the taxable estate would be reduced to zero.

Types of Qualifying Recipients As stated in § 2055(a) of the Internal Revenue Code, for the transfer to be deductible it must be for a public, charitable, or religious use. The organizations may not participate or intervene in a political campaign. If the gift is made to a charitable organization whose name is unfamiliar to you, it is generally easy to check to see if the organization is a qualified

63. IRC § 2055.

EXAMPLE *Form 706, Schedule M—Bequests, etc., to Surviving Spouse and Disclaimer*

Form 706 (Rev. 7-90)

Estate of: Peter Chessman

SCHEDULE M—Bequests, etc., to Surviving Spouse

Terminable Interest (QTIP) Marital Deduction.—If you elect to claim a marital deduction for qualified terminable interest property (QTIP) under section 2056(b)(7), you MUST list on Part 2 of Schedule M all of the property for which you are making the election. Listing property on Part 2 constitutes the making of the QTIP election. No marital deduction will be allowed for any terminable interest property that is listed on Part 1 of Schedule M.

		Yes	No
1	Did any property pass to the surviving spouse as a result of a qualified disclaimer? . . . . *If "Yes," attach a copy of the written disclaimer required by section 2518(b).*		X
2	Is the surviving spouse a U.S. citizen?	X	
3	**Qualified Domestic Trust.**—Do you elect under section 2056A(d) to treat any trusts reported on Schedule M as qualified domestic trusts? (see instructions)		X
4	**Election out of QTIP Treatment of Annuities.**—Do you elect under section 2056(b)(7)(C)(ii) to not treat as qualified terminable interest property any joint and survivor annuities that are included in the gross estate and would otherwise be treated as qualified terminable interest property under section 2056(b)(7)(C)? (see instructions)		X

Part 1.—Property Interests Which Are Not Subject to a QTIP Election

(Note: *A marital deduction will NOT be allowed for any terminable interest property (QTIP) that is listed on Part 1 of Schedule M.)*

Item number	Description of property interests passing to surviving spouse	Value
1	Schedule A, Items 1-3	95,075.00*
2	Schedule B, Items 1-6	375,000.00**
3	Schedule C, Items 1-6	85,000.00*
4	Schedule D, Items 1-5	100,000.00*
5	Schedule E, Items 1-6	277,265.31
6	Schedule F, Items 1-9	30,000.00*
	* Spouse disclaiming all bequests and life insurance. A copy of a signed disclaimer is attached hereto. Jointly owned property is not disclaimed.	
	** Ten thousand dollars from the sale of stock reported on Schedule B was directly bequeathed to the Peter Chessman Parrot Foundation pursuant to Article 5 in the Will. Thus, only $375,000.00 from Schedule B is shown on Schedule M rather than the total value of the stocks of $385,000.00.	
	Total from continuation schedule(s) (or additional sheet(s)) attached to this schedule	
	Total value of property interests not subject to a QTIP election (enter here and on line 1 of Part 3 on the next page)	277,265.31

(If more space is needed, attach the continuation schedule from the end of this package or additional sheets of the same size.)
(The instructions to Schedule M are in the separate instructions.)

Schedule M—Page 24

EXAMPLE *Form 706, Schedule M and Disclaimer, continued*

Form 706 (Rev. 7-90)

Part 2.—Property Interests Which Are Subject to a QTIP Election

(Note: *Listing terminable interest property on Part 2 of Schedule M constitutes the making of a QTIP election for that property under section 2056(b)(7). A marital deduction will not be allowed for any terminable interest property that is not listed on Part 2. If you use a continuation page for Part 2, be sure that it is clearly labeled as Schedule M, Part 2.)*

Item number	Description of property interests passing to surviving spouse (Describe portion of trust for which allocation is made.)	Value
1	None	
	Total from continuation schedule(s) (or additional sheet(s)) attached to this schedule	
	A. Total value of property interests subject to a QTIP election . . . A	- 0 -

Part 3.—Reconciliation

1	Enter the total from part 1	1	
2	Total interests passing to surviving spouse (add lines A and 1, above)	2	277,265.31
3a	Federal estate taxes (including section 4980A taxes) payable out of property interests listed on Parts 1 and 2 — 3a		
b	Other death taxes payable out of property interests listed on Parts 1 and 2 — 3b		
c	Federal and state GST taxes payable out of property interests listed on Parts 1 and 2 — 3c		
d	Add items a, b, and c	3d	
4	Net value of property interests listed on Schedule M (subtract 3d from 2). Also enter on Part 5, Recapitulation, page 3, at item 18	4	277,265.31

(If more space is needed, attach the continuation schedule from the end of this package or additional sheets of the same size.) **Schedule M—Page 25**

EXAMPLE ***Form 706, Schedule M and Disclaimer, continued***

DISCLAIMER

Sandra Chessman
c/o Michael Scott, Esq.
401 Walnut Street
20th Floor
Philadelphia, PA 19106

Robert Chessman
135 Shoreline Drive
Ocean City, NJ 08224

Re: Estate of Peter Chessman
Date of Death: 5/3/91
Form 706 Schedule A Item 3

Dear Mr. Chessman,

Pursuant to the laws of the Commonwealth of Pennsylvania and according to IRS Code Section 2815 (b), I hereby disclaim all of my right, title, and interest in and to my one-half share, as a beneficiary, of my deceased husband Peter Chessman's share as a tenant in common of the house and lot located at 135 Shoreline Drive, Ocean City, NJ. I understand that said share shall pass to my husband's heirs as if I had predeceased him.

____
Sandra Chessman

____
Dated

charity for tax purposes by searching through the Cumulative List of Organizations, which is published by the Internal Revenue Service. That book which is periodically updated, lists the names of those charities whose tax-exempt status has been passed upon by the Internal Revenue Service. If the bequest is made to an unlisted organization, it is advisable to contact the organization to ascertain the correct corporate designation under which it may be listed in the above book or, if it is not listed, to obtain a copy of the Internal Revenue Service letter granting the tax exemption. When the gift is to an unlisted charity, the exemption letter should be attached to the federal estate tax return as an exhibit.

A charitable bequest need not be made to a particular organization. A trust may be established and the fiduciaries given the obligation and authority to maintain a fund for one or more charitable purposes such as the establishment of scholarships for needy students. A gift in that form will qualify for the charitable deduction provided the purpose is actually charitable. A gift is charitable if it is for a public purpose such as furtherance of religion, science, literature, education, art, and the prevention of cruelty to children and animals (the specific categories of charities mentioned in the Internal Revenue Code).

A bequest to a fraternal society, such as a Masonic Lodge, may be deductible. However, such societies often have both a charitable and noncharitable aspect and the Internal Revenue Service has in some instances taken the position that unless a specific charitable purpose is set forth in the will where a bequest is made to a fraternal organization, the amount so passing is nondeductible. If you are preparing a federal estate tax return for an estate in which such a gift was made, it is important to check with the lawyer in charge to determine whether a deduction is allowable.

Types of Gifts As indicated above, the charitable transfer may be made directly to an organization or the will may establish a charitable trust and give the trustee the power to pick and choose among various charitable recipients. In addition, a charitable deduction is available with regard to any property that is includible in the gross estate because the decedent had a general power of appointment (i.e., property listed on Schedule H of the federal estate tax return) that passes to charity either (1) because the decedent has exercised his power of appointment and directed the distribution of some or all of the property to the charity, or (2) because the decedent failed to exercise the power and the instrument granting the power provides that upon such a failure the property passes to charity.

Gifts in Trust Transfers in trust involving charitable gifts may themselves take a number of forms. As long as there is a reasonable degree of certainty that the charity will receive some property, a charitable deduction equal to the actuarial value of the interest passing to the charity would be allowable. For example, a gift to charity of a remainder interest in a trust would be deductible. The fact that a preceding income interest is distributed to a noncharitable beneficiary affects only the valuation of the deductible interest. Similarly, the gift of an income interest to charity results in a deduction for the present value of that interest even though the charity will not receive the principal of the fund.

Unitrusts and Annuity Trusts Prior to the passage of the Tax Reform Act of 1969, the law imposed no serious limitations on the forms of a charitable trust. As a result of the 1969 act, every will (or trust) drawn (or republished by codicil) after October, 1969, that creates a trust in which interests pass to both charitable and noncharitable beneficiaries must take the form of a *unitrust* or *annuity* trust in order for the charitable interest to be deductible. The new rules also apply, no matter when the will was drawn, if the decedent dies after October 9, 1972. Organizations formed after October 9, 1972 must notify the IRS that they are claiming a tax-exempt status.

A "unitrust" is defined (in § 664 of the Internal Revenue Code) as a trust from which a fixed percentage of the net fair market value of the assets, valued each year, is to be paid either to charity with remainder to noncharitable beneficiaries (a charitable income unitrust), or to individuals, with the remainder passing to qualified charities (a charitable remainder unitrust).

Because of the complexity of the law governing charitable trusts (no matter which law governs) it is extremely important to confer with the lawyer in charge of an estate before making a decision whether, and to what extent, a charitable deduction is available.

Valuation of Charitable Gifts

Outright Gifts Where the testator makes an outright gift to charity, the amount of the deduction is the full amount of the cash value of the gift. If property given to charity is subject to a liability for taxes or otherwise, the amount of the liability will have to be deducted in arriving at the net charitable deduction. If the gift is to be made over a period of years, for example, a gift of $20,000 to be paid in four equal annual installments of $5,000 each, the amount of the deduction available would be reduced to the present discounted value of $20,000 received in such installments. That value can be determined by reference to an actuarial table and should be discussed in detail with the lawyer administering the estate.

Contested Wills Where as a result of a will contest, a compromise agreement is entered into under which the charity receives a gift of a lesser amount than that bequeathed in the will, a charitable deduction is nevertheless allowable for the reduced amount that the charity actually receives.

If, however, the will contains a charitable bequest that is void under local law,[64] a compromise settlement will not give rise to a deductible contribution. On the other hand, if such a statute does no more than make the testamentary transfer voidable, and no positive action is taken to invoke the statute, the transfer would be allowed as a deduction on Schedule O.

Deduction for Death Taxes Where death taxes or any other liabilities are payable out of the amount passing to charity, such amounts must be taken into account in computing the net value of the property available for the deduction. For example, if $50,000 were bequeathed to a charity and there is a state inheritance tax of $5,000 payable out of that sum, only $45,000 would be deductible for federal estate tax purposes. Whether or not any death taxes are, in fact, payable out of the amount passing to charity must be determined either from the will or by reference to the local law governing the apportionment of such taxes. These rules are involved and quite similar to those previously discussed in regard to Schedule M and should be reviewed with the lawyer with whom you are working.

Whenever the reference must be made to the actuarial tables in computing a charitable deduction, all factual information, such as the age of a life tenant, is calculated as of the date of the decedent's death. All calculations and consideration of contingencies should be made as of that date, irrespective of whether the alternate valuation date is elected for reporting the assets of the gross estate. In determining the age to be used, the nearest birthday is used. If the life tenant is 65 and 7 months of age, therefore, his age is deemed to be 66.

Each asset that is specifically bequeathed to charity must be assigned the same value and the same valuation date as was reported on Schedules A to I of the return. Thus, if alternate valuation is used and 100 shares of General Motors is bequeathed to charity, the stock is valued for purposes of completing Schedule O in accordance with its alternate value shown on Schedule B.

Preparation of Schedule O The three questions at the top of Schedule O must be answered whenever there is property passing to

64. In some states charitable bequests made within a short period before death are void. This is a holdover from times when it was feared that the church would benefit inordinately from deathbed gifts.

charity. The first question asks whether an action to contest the charitable bequest has already begun, and the second, whether such an action is contemplated. Even if the will contains a charitable legacy, the Internal Revenue Service must be satisfied that the charity will actually receive that legacy.

The third question asks about qualified disclaimers. The charitable deduction is allowed for amounts that are transferred to charitable organizations as a result of a qualified disclaimer. The disclaimer must meet the requirements of code § 2515. If the property passes to a charity due to a disclaimer, check the "yes" box on line 2 and attach a copy of the written disclaimer.

In filling out the body of the schedule, the name and address of the organization receiving the gift must be given, as well as a brief description of the character of the organization. Thus, a $10,000 gift to the testator's church would be set forth as follows:

Name	Character	Amount
Church of the Holy Grail, Philadelphia, Pennsylvania	Religious	$10,000.00

For each legacy or devise, indicate the paragraph or section of the decedent's will or codicil that applies.

If the computation of the charitable deduction requires reference to actuarial tables, all relevant information concerning the beneficiaries should be set forth, giving dates of birth, etc. Such information should be as complete as possible and should enable the federal estate tax examining agent to follow the computation line by line. Where a residuary portion of the estate passes to charity, a description of all of the preceding interests and legacies, and the computation of the amount constituting the residue of the estate, should be shown in detail on a rider to Schedule O.

At the bottom of Schedule O, as with Schedule M, there is a place to show the amount of the federal and other death taxes that are borne by the property passing to charity. An illustration of a completed Schedule O appears on the next page.

Schedule P—Credit for Foreign Death Taxes

In completing Schedule P, you must list all of the foreign countries in which death taxes have been paid and for which credit is claimed on the federal estate tax return. A separate Schedule P must be attached to the return showing the credit allowable with respect to the tax paid to each such country.

This schedule will not be used unless the estate holds property in a foreign country. The credit is allowable only if the decedent was a U.S. citizen or resident of the U.S. If the decedent is a resident but not a citizen, he or she may qualify for the credit

EXAMPLE *Form 706, Schedule O—Charitable, Public and Similar Gifts and Bequests*

Form 706 (Rev. 7-90)

Estate of: Peter Chessman

SCHEDULE O—Charitable, Public, and Similar Gifts and Bequests

		Yes	No
1a	If the transfer was made by will, has any action been instituted to have interpreted or to contest the will or any of its provisions affecting the charitable deductions claimed in this schedule? If "Yes," full details must be submitted with this schedule.		X
b	According to the information and belief of the person or persons filing the return, is any such action planned? If "Yes," full details must be submitted with this schedule.		X
2	Did any property pass to charity as the result of a qualified disclaimer? If "Yes," attach a copy of the written disclaimer required by section 2518(b).		X

Item number	Name and address of beneficiary	Character of institution	Amount
1	Peter Chessman Parrot Foundation	Educational	10,000.00

	Total from continuation schedule(s) (or additional sheet(s)) attached to this schedule				
3	Total			3	10,000.00
4a	Federal estate tax (including section 4980A taxes) payable out of property interests listed above	4a			
b	Other death taxes payable out of property interests listed above	4b			
c	Federal and state GST taxes payable out of property interests listed above	4c			
d	Add items a, b, and c			4d	
5	Net value of property interests listed above (subtract 4d from 3). Also enter on Part 5, Recapitulation, page 3, at item 19			5	10,000.00

(If more space is needed, attach the continuation schedule from the end of this package or additional sheets of the same size.)
(The instructions to Schedule O are in the separate instructions.)

Schedule O—Page 26

EXAMPLE *Form 706, Schedule P—Credit for Foreign Death Taxes*

Form 706 (Rev. 7-90)

Estate of: Peter Chessman

SCHEDULE P—Credit for Foreign Death Taxes

List all foreign countries to which death taxes have been paid and for which a credit is claimed on this return.

If a credit is claimed for death taxes paid to more than one foreign country, compute the credit for taxes paid to one country on this sheet and attach a separate copy of Schedule P for each of the other countries.

The credit computed on this sheet is for the ____________ (Name of death tax or taxes)

____________ imposed in ____________ (Name of country)

Credit is computed under the ____________ (Insert title of treaty or "statute")

Citizenship (nationality) of decedent at time of death

(All amounts and values must be entered in United States money)

1	Total of estate, inheritance, legacy, and succession taxes imposed in the country named above attributable to property situated in that country, subjected to these taxes, and included in the gross estate (as defined by statute)	
2	Value of the gross estate (adjusted, if necessary, according to the instructions for item 2)	
3	Value of property situated in that country, subjected to death taxes imposed in that country, and included in the gross estate (adjusted, if necessary, according to the instructions for item 3)	
4	Tax imposed by section 2001 reduced by the total credits claimed under sections 2010, 2011, and 2012 (see instructions)	
5	Amount of Federal estate tax attributable to property specified at item 3. (Divide item 3 by item 2 and multiply the result by item 4.)	
6	Credit for death taxes imposed in the country named above (the smaller of item 1 or item 5). Also enter on line 18 of Part 2, Tax Computation	- 0 -

only if the country of which the decedent was a national allows a similar credit to decedents who are citizens of the U.S. and residents in that country. The credit can be no greater than the 706 tax attributable to the foreign property. The foreign tax must be paid and a Form 706 CE must be filed. An example of Schedule P is shown above.

Schedule Q—Credit for Tax on Prior Transfers

If the decedent whose return is being prepared has received property from a transferor who died within ten years before or two years after our decedent's date of death, a credit may be available on Schedule Q for all or a part of the federal estate tax paid by the transferor's estate that is attributable to the property transferred. The calculation of this credit is quite complicated and is beyond the scope of this book. However, the paralegal should be aware of its existence and should refer the intricacies of the calculation to the lawyer who is administering the estate.

It should be noted though that the Schedule Q credit is not dependent on being able to trace the transferor's property and any actuarially determinable interest in property will give rise to the credit, subject to certain limitations. Because so many people fail

EXAMPLE *Form 706, Schedule Q—Credit for Tax on Prior Transfers*

SCHEDULE Q—Credit for Tax on Prior Transfers

Part 1.—Transferor Information

	Name of transferor	Social security number	IRS office where estate tax return was filed	Date of death
A				
B				
C				

Check here ▶ ☐ if section 2013(f) (special valuation of farm, etc., real property) adjustments to the computation of the credit were made (see instructions).

Part 2.—Computation of Credit (see instructions)

Item	Transferor A	Transferor B	Transferor C	Total A, B, & C
1 Transferee's tax as apportioned (from worksheet, (line 7 + line 8) x line 35 for each column) . . .				
2 Transferor's tax (from each column of worksheet, line 20)				
3 Maximum amount before percentage requirement (for each column, enter amount from line 1 or 2, whichever is smaller)				
4 Percentage allowed (each column) (see instructions)	%	%	%	
5 Credit allowable (line 3 x line 4 for each column)				
6 TOTAL credit allowable (add columns A, B, and C of line 5). Enter here and on line 19 of Part 2, Tax Computation				- 0 -

(The instructions to Schedules P and Q are in the separate instructions.) **Schedules P and Q—Page 27**

to take available credits, it should be reiterated that an income interest alone can qualify as "property" for these purposes.

Whenever the decedent is the beneficiary of a testamentary trust the possibility of a credit should be investigated. If other family members have died within ten years, their estates should be investigated since they may have left some legacy to the decedent.

The amount of the credit is all or a part of the 706 tax paid on the transfer of property (including the use of a power of appointment) to the present decedent from a person who died immediately prior to the decedent and up to ten years prior to the decedent. If the first decedent died two years (or less) prior to the second decedent, the second decedent receives 100% of the credit. The credit is reduced by 20% for each two-year period prior to the second death. In other words the credit will be larger if the deaths occur closer together. Schedule Q is shown above.

Schedule R—Generation-Skipping Transfer Tax

It is no longer possible to utilize a series of trusts to pass an individual's assets from one generation to the next, and so on, without incurring federal estate tax liability. Basically, a generation-skipping trust is one that provides for a splitting of the benefits between two or more generations that are younger than the grantor of the trust.

A definition of new terms will be helpful in understanding this concept.

1. A GENERATION-SKIPPING TRANSFER is either a taxable termination or taxable distribution.
2. A TAXABLE TERMINATION is a termination of an interest or power of a younger generation beneficiary. For example, if a trust provided income for life to the grantor's child, with remainder to the grantor's great-grandchild, there would be a "taxable termination" of the child's interest upon his death, because this death would terminate the life income interest of a younger generation beneficiary (the child) who was a member of a generation older than that of any other younger generation beneficiary (the great-grandchild) under the trust.
3. A TAXABLE DISTRIBUTION occurs whenever there is a distribution from the generation-skipping trust, *other than a distribution out of accounting income,* to a younger generation beneficiary of the trust, in cases where there is at least one other younger generation, who is older than the generation receiving the transfer. For example, a discretionary trust is established to benefit the grantor's child and great-grandchild. The trustee exercises his discretion by distributing accounting income to the child, and also makes a distribution out of corpus to the great-grandchild. The distribution to the great-grandchild constitutes a taxable distribution because there would be at least one younger generation beneficiary (the child) who was a member of a generation older than that of the great-grandchild.
4. A DEEMED TRANSFEROR is the person who will be the measuring rod when a generation-skipping transfer is deemed to have been made in order to compute the tax.

These definitions are only a few of the many new concepts discussed in the new chapter. A detailed discussion is beyond the scope of this book. The legal assistant may, however, deal with the estate of a "deemed transferor" and will need to be acquainted with the complex rules regarding generation-skipping transfers.

A new generation-skipping transfer tax was enacted in 1986, effectively repealing the tax established by the 1976 tax reform act.

The new tax applies to transfers after October 22, 1986 (inter vivos transfers after November 25, 1985). The new tax does not apply to any generation-skipping transfer made under a trust that was irrevocable on September 25, 1985. Generation-skipping transfers occurring under wills executed prior to October 22, 1986, are not subject to the new tax if the testator died before January 1, 1987. Any tax paid under the prior law is to be credited (with interest) as an overpayment.

Property transferred to an heir and eventually transferred to the heir's beneficiaries would be subject to two rounds of taxation. To avoid the "double" taxation a testator may create a trust giving the first heir a life interest with remainder interests to subsequent generations. The generation-skipping tax was designed to tax the transfers as if the property had passed outright, thus taking away the advantage of skipping generations. For example, if the decedent (grandfather) created a trust where he gave his son an income interest for life with the remainder to his grandson at his son's death, under the old law the tax would be paid at grandson's death. Thus his son's estate would effectively avoid the federal estate tax at his death even though he enjoyed the use of the property during his life. The new law taxes the transfer of income as well as corpus (principal). The definition of a generation-skipping transfer is a transfer of income or corpus to a beneficiary at least two generations younger than the transferor. The generation-skipping transfer tax is imposed in addition to the federal estate and gift tax.

Exemptions Each grantor is permitted to make transfers up to $1 million during his lifetime. The grantor may also qualify for the $10,000 annual gift tax exclusion (see Chapter Four). In addition, there was an exclusion (that expired 12/21/89) for direct skips (either outright or in trust) to grandchildren of the grantor in the amount of $2 million dollars per grandchild per grantor.

In general, this is a very complex portion of the 706. Because of the severity of the tax, the schedule will not be used very often. The legal assistant should be aware of the terminology and the basic concept of the tax if the situation ever arises in estate planning or estate administration, particularly under old wills and trusts. An example of Schedule R is shown below.

Schedule S—Excise Tax on Excess Pension Distributions

Schedule S that is included on the 706 computes a flat 15% tax if there is a pension distribution of more than $750,000. This tax is in addition to the estate and gift taxes (see pages 262-63).

EXAMPLE *Form 706, Schedule R—Generation-Skipping Transfer Tax*

Form 706 (Rev. 7-90)

Schedule R.—Generation-Skipping Transfer Tax

Note: *To avoid application of the deemed allocation rules, Form 706 and Schedule R should be filed to allocate the GST exemption to trusts which may later have taxable terminations or distributions under section 2612 even if the form is not required to be filed to report estate or GST tax.*

Part 1.— GST Exemption Reconciliation (Section 2631) and Section 2652(a)(3) (Special QTIP) Election

Check box ▶ ☐ if you are making a section 2652(a)(3) (special QTIP) election (see instructions)

1	Maximum allowable GST exemption	1	$1,000,000
2	Total GST exemption allocated by the decedent against decedent's lifetime transfers	2	
3	Total GST exemption allocated by the executor, using Form 709, against decedent's lifetime transfers	3	
4	GST exemption allocated on line 6 of Schedule R, Part 2	4	
5	GST exemption allocated on line 6 of Schedule R, Part 3	5	
6	Total GST exemption allocated on line 4 of Schedule(s) R-1	6	
7	Total GST exemption allocated to intervivos transfers and direct skips (add lines 2–6)	7	
8	GST exemption available to allocate to trusts and section 2032A interests (subtract line 7 from line 1)	8	

9 Allocation of GST exemption to trusts (as defined for GST tax purposes):

A Name of trust	B Trust's EIN (if any)	C GST exemption allocated on lines 2–6, above (see instructions)	D Additional GST exemption allocated (see instructions)	E Trust's inclusion ratio (optional—see instructions)

9D	Total. May not exceed line 8, above	9D	
10	GST exemption available to allocate to section 2032A interests received by individual beneficiaries (subtract line 9D from line 8). You must attach special use allocation schedule (see instructions)	10	– 0 –

(The instructions to Schedule R are in the separate instructions.)

Schedule R—Page 28

EXAMPLE *Form 706, Schedule S—Increased Estate Tax*

Form 706 (Rev. 7-90)

Estate of:

SCHEDULE S—Increased Estate Tax on Excess Retirement Accumulations

(Under section 4980A(d) of the Internal Revenue Code)

Part I Tax Computation

1 Check this box if a section 4980A(d)(5) spousal election is being made . . . . ▶ ☐
You must attach the statement described in the instructions.

2 Enter the name and employer identification number (EIN) of each qualified employer plan and individual retirement account in which the decedent had an interest at the time of death:

	Name	EIN
Plan #1		
Plan #2		
Plan #3		
IRA #1		
IRA #2		
IRA #3		

	A Plan #1	B Plan #2	C Plan #3	D All IRAs
3 Value of decedent's interest				
4 Amounts rolled over after death				
5 Total value (add lines 3 and 4)				
6 Amounts payable to certain alternate payees (see instructions)				
7 Decedent's investment in the contract under section 72(f) .				
8 Excess life insurance amount				
9 Decedent's interest as a beneficiary				
10 Total reductions in value (add lines 6, 7, 8, and 9)				
11 Net value of decedent's interest (subtract line 10 from line 5)				

12 Decedent's aggregate interest in all plans and IRAs (add columns A–D of line 11) . . . . ▶			12	
13 Present value of hypothetical life annuity (from Part III, line 4)	13			
14 Remaining unused grandfather amount (from Part II, line 4)	14			
15 Enter the greater of line 13 or line 14			15	
16 Excess retirement accumulation (subtract line 15 from line 12)			16	
17 Increased estate tax (multiply line 16 by 15%). Enter here and on line 23 of the Tax Computation on page 1.			17	

(The instructions to Schedule S are in the separate instructions.)

Schedule S —Page 33

EXAMPLE ***Form 706, Schedule S—Increased Estate Tax, continued***

Form 706 (Rev. 7-90)

Part II Grandfather Election

1	Was a grandfather election made on a previously filed Form 5329? . . . . . . ▶ ☐ Yes ☐ No If "Yes," complete lines 2–4 below. **You may not make or revoke the grandfather election after the due date (with extensions) for filing the decedent's 1988 income tax return.** If "No," enter "-0-" on line 4 and skip to Part III.		
2	Initial grandfather amount	2	
3	Total amount previously recovered	3	
4	Remaining unused grandfather amount (subtract line 3 from line 2). Enter here and on Part I, line 14, on page 33	4	

Part III Computation of Hypothetical Life Annuity

1	Decedent's attained age at date of death (in whole years, rounded down)	1	
2	Applicable annual annuity amount (see instructions)	2	
3	Present value multiplier (see instructions)	3	
4	Present value of hypothetical life annuity (multiply line 2 by line 3). Enter here and on Part I, line 13, on page 33.	4	

Continuation Schedules

Form 706 has blank continuation schedules located in the back of the form. These can be photocopied and are to be attached to any schedule that requires additional sheets.

Recapitulation Schedule

Completing the Recapitulation Schedule of the federal estate tax return is generally a very mechanical and simple procedure. In most cases it is merely a matter of bringing forward the totals set forth in the preceding schedules. The date-of-death values and the alternate values (if alternate valuation has been chosen) of the assets shown on Schedules A to I are copied on the appropriate columns of the Recapitulation Schedule, and the columns are totaled. By comparing the entire gross value of the estate, as of the date of death and as of the alternate valuation date, one can decide whether to select alternate valuation. That computation must be made early in the preparation of the federal estate tax return because choice of alternate valuation or date-of-death valuation will affect the preparation of many other schedules.

The total of Schedules J and K, which appear in the deduction section, is set forth and if this total does not exceed the date-of-death value (even if alternate valuation has been chosen) of the property owned by the decedent and subject to claims of his creditors under local law (basically, the probate property), the

EXAMPLE *Form 706, Continuation Schedule*

Form 706 (Rev. 7-90) (Make copies of this schedule before completing it if you will need more than one schedule.)

Estate of:

CONTINUATION SCHEDULE

Continuation of Schedule ____________
(Enter letter of schedule you are continuing.)

Item number	Description For securities, give CUSIP number, if available.	Unit value (Sch B or E only)	Alternate valuation date	Alternate value	Value at date of death or amount deductible
1					
TOTAL. (Carry forward to main schedule.)					

See instructions on next page. **Continuation Schedule—Page 35**

EXAMPLE *Form 706, Recapitulation Schedule*

Part 5.—Recapitulation

Item number	Gross estate	Alternate value		Value at date of death	
1	Schedule A—Real Estate	95,075	00	84,735	00
2	Schedule B—Stocks and Bonds	385,000	00	519,941	25
3	Schedule C—Mortgages, Notes, and Cash	85,000	00	85,000	00
4	Schedule D—Insurance on the Decedent's Life (attach Form(s) 712)	100,000	00	100,000	00
5	Schedule E—Jointly Owned Property (attach Form(s) 712 for life insurance)	300,000	00	300,000	00
6	Schedule F—Other Miscellaneous Property (attach Form(s) 712 for life insurance)	30,000	00	30,000	00
7	Schedule G—Transfers During Decedent's Life (attach Form(s) 712 for life insurance)	20,000	00	20,000	00
8	Schedule H—Powers of Appointment	0	00	0	00
9	Schedule I—Annuities	0	00	0	00
10	Total gross estate (add items 1 through 9). Enter here and on line 1 of the Tax Computation.	1,015,075	00	1,139,676	25

Item number	Deductions	Amount	
11	Schedule J—Funeral Expenses and Expenses Incurred in Administering Property Subject to Claims	63,500	00
12	Schedule K—Debts of the Decedent	4,075	00
13	Schedule K—Mortgages and Liens	7,500	00
14	Total of items 11 through 13	75,075	00
15	Allowable amount of deductions from item 14 (see the instructions for item 15 of the Recapitulation)	75,075	00
16	Schedule L—Net Losses During Administration	0	00
17	Schedule L—Expenses Incurred in Administering Property Not Subject to Claims	0	00
18	Schedule M—Bequests, etc., to Surviving Spouse	277,265	31
19	Schedule O—Charitable, Public, and Similar Gifts and Bequests	10,000	00
20	Total allowable deductions (add items 15 through 19). Enter here and on line 2 of the Tax Computation	362,340	31

Page 3

total is entered as the allowable amount of the deductions on the schedule. If the total happens to exceed the date-of-death value of the property subject to claims, the amount allowable is limited to the value of the property on the date of death plus the excess over that amount actually paid prior to the due date of the return for claims listed in Schedules J and K. If the date-of-death value of the property subject to claims is less than the total of the expenses to be incurred, therefore, it is important to make certain that the expenses are actually paid before the due date of the return in order to obtain a deduction for them.

The total of deductions, if any, from Schedule L (for net losses and expenses incurred in administering property not subject to claims) is then entered and the total of all deductions is then set forth.

The value of property passing to the surviving spouse is set forth on line 18.

The charitable bequests from Schedule O are entered on line 19. The totals on line 20 and line 10 will be brought forward to the front page of the return for the tax computation.

Computation of Tax

Page one of the return is the last section of the federal estate tax return to be completed.

Calculation of Taxable Estate The total gross estate, as calculated on the Recapitulation Schedule, is entered and the amount entered would be based on either the date of death or alternate valuation, depending on which has been chosen. The total allowable deduction figure is also brought forward from the Recapitulation Schedule. By subtracting the total allowable deductions from the total gross estate, you are left with the taxable estate.

As taxable gifts other than those reported on Schedule G, which are not in contemplation of death and which were made after December 31, 1976, are requested, the decedent's gift tax returns must be examined and the total amount of taxable gifts entered. No entry will be made for decedents dying before January 1, 1980. These lifetime transfers should be listed at the *date of gift* value.

The taxable estate and the total gifts referred to in the preceding paragraph are then totaled and the tentative tax on this amount is computed using Table A in the instruction book.

If line 5 exceeds $10 million, the additional tax will be added. Otherwise skip to line 8 to continue the tax computation. The gift tax paid on gifts made after December 31, 1976, is added to the taxable estate to compute the gross estate tax.

Table B in the instructions shows the amount of unified credit available for all gifts made during the decedent's lifetime and for his estate. If the decedent made gifts after September 8, 1976, and before January 1, 1977, for which the decedent claimed a specific exemption (it was a maximum of $30,000), the unified credit must be reduced. The reduction is 20% of the specific exemption. If there were no gifts made at this time then enter 0.

The gross estate tax is the tentative tax minus the unified credit. The credit for state death taxes is entered on line 15. Use Table C for this amount. Note $60,000 should be subtracted from the taxable estate when calculating the credit. (This is a carryover from pre-1976 tax law where estates had a flat $60,000 exemption.) Note that the credit allowed for state death taxes is often used by the state of the decedent's domicile to compute the amount of the state inheritance tax.

If federal gift taxes were paid prior to January 1, 1977, § 2012 of the Internal Revenue Code provides a credit for the amount of federal gift tax that the decedent or the decedent's estate has paid with respect to a transfer of property that is subsequently included in the gross estate for federal estate tax purposes. This credit should be entered on line 17. Credits from Schedules P and Q are entered on lines 18 and 19. The total of these three credits is subtracted from line 16 resulting in the net estate tax. Additional taxes from Schedules R and S are added.

Any prior payments of tax should be reflected in the computation of tax. For example, if an extension of time for filing the federal estate tax return had been granted, an estimated payment of federal estate tax might have been paid nine months after the date of death. This amount would be included and a statement explaining this prior payment must be attached to the return pursuant to the instructions.

Any flower bond redemptions would be shown on line 26. As discussed earlier, these bonds will soon cease to exist. However, a few may still be used by the estate. The balance due is entered on line 28.

The return must be signed and dated by the executor/ administrator and the person who prepared the return. Thus in the Peter Chessman estate, Michael Scott would sign as preparer. All questions throughout the return should be answered completely.

Attachments It is important to attach all appraisals, life insurance 712s, disclaimers, etc., to the return when it is filed with the IRS. A complete copy of the return, showing all the appropriate attachments, should be made. A certified copy (raised seal) of the will and the death certificate should also be attached. If tax is owed, a copy of the check should be retained. Receipts and cancelled checks do not have to be attached, but they should be kept carefully in case the return is audited.

Peter Chessman Estate To review the Peter Chessman estate, a complete copy of the 706 prepared for the estate is shown on the following pages. Attachments and schedules not used are not included. In order to show a tax due and thus have a tax computation, Sandra Chessman had to disclaim a large portion of her marital share. Otherwise the entire estate would have passed to her tax free, due to the unlimited marital deduction. Mrs. Chessman also had substantial assets of her own and did not wish to increase her own estate to be taxed at her death. Thus, by disclaiming a portion of her share of the estate, she was able to pass a large amount of property to her two daughters without incurring gift taxes (see Chapter Four), and she never had to include the assets in her estate. Her attorney was able to do some effective "post mortem" (after death) tax planning for Mrs. Chessman after her husband's death.

In reviewing the return, it is recommended that the student start with Schedule A, and review all the schedules showing the assets and deductions. Then turn to page three, the Recapitulation, for a summary of the amounts from each schedule. Finally, review the front page for the tax computation.

RETURN PROCEDURES

Filing the Return with the Internal Revenue Service

Unless an extension of time in which to file the return has been granted, the federal estate tax return is due within nine months following the date of death. The return is filed with the District Director of the Internal Revenue Service in the district in which the decedent was domiciled at the time of death. In the case of a nonresident citizen, as well as in the case of a nonresident alien, the return must be filed with the Director of International Operations, Internal Revenue Service, Washington, D.C. 20225.

Payment of the Tax The federal estate tax is due at the same time the federal estate tax return is due. The check for the federal estate tax should be drawn to the order of the Internal Revenue Service.

As was mentioned above and in the discussion under Schedule B of the federal estate tax return, certain issues of the United States Treasury Bonds may be redeemed by the estate at par value (plus accrued interest) if they are used in payment of the federal estate tax.

Extensions of Time If for some reason it may not be possible to file the return and/or to pay the federal estate tax on the original due date, an extension of time in which to file the federal estate tax return should be requested. This is done by filing Form 4768 that must be submitted in triplicate prior to the due date of the return, and signed by the executors, setting forth the reason the extension is requested (see page 286). The maximum extension allowable is six months, and if for some reason the return cannot be completed by the time the extension has run, it should nevertheless be filed at that time in a form as complete as possible. Any additional information can be supplied later. When an extension has been granted by the District Director, a copy of the approved extension must accompany the return when filed. It should be noted that, as with all tax extensions, the granting of an extension of time does not forgive the requirement to pay the tax. Interest due on the tax will still be charged from the due date (nine months after death). In most cases the extension does prevent the estate from penalty assessment if the return is filed by the extended due date.

EXAMPLE *Form 706 for the Peter Chessman Estate, Page One*

Form **706** (Rev. July 1990) Department of the Treasury Internal Revenue Service

United States Estate (and Generation-Skipping Transfer) Tax Return

Estate of a citizen or resident of the United States (see separate instructions). To be filed for decedents dying after December 31, 1989, and before January 1, 1993.

For Paperwork Reduction Act Notice, see page 1 of the instructions.

OMB No. 1545-0015 Expires 6-30-93

Part 1.—Decedent and Executor

1a Decedent's first name and middle initial (and maiden name, if any): Peter	1b Decedent's last name: Chessman		2 Decedent's social security no.: 045 ⋮ 96 ⋮ 2487
3a Domicile at time of death (county and state): Philadelphia, PA	3b Year domicile established: 1950	4 Date of birth: 8/1/1905	5 Date of death: May 3, 1991
6a Name of executor (see instructions): Sandra Chessman; Michael Scott, Esq.	6b Executor's address (number and street including apartment number or rural route; city, town, or post office; state; and ZIP code): c/o Michael Scott, Esq. 401 Walnut Street, 20th Floor Philadelphia, PA 19106		
6c Executor's social security number (see instructions): 123 ⋮ 45 ⋮ 6789			
7a Name and location of court where will was probated or estate administered: Register of Wills, Philadelphia County, Philadelphia, PA			7b Case number: 15623 of 1991

8 If decedent died testate, check here ▶ [X] and attach a certified copy of the will. 9 If Form 4768 is attached, check here ▶ [ ]

10 If Schedule R-1 is attached, check here ▶ [ ]

Part 2.—Tax Computation

1	Total gross estate (from Part 5, Recapitulation, page 3, item 10)		1	1,015,075 00
2	Total allowable deductions (from Part 5, Recapitulation, page 3, item 20)		2	362,340 31
3	Taxable estate (subtract line 2 from line 1)		3	652,734 69
4	Adjusted taxable gifts (total taxable gifts (within the meaning of section 2503) made by the decedent after December 31, 1976, other than gifts that are includible in decedent's gross estate (section 2001(b))		4	-0-
5	Add lines 3 and 4		5	652,734 69
6	Tentative tax on the amount on line 5 from Table A in the instructions		6	212,311 84
7a	If line 5 exceeds $10,000,000, enter the lesser of line 5 or $21,040,000. If line 5 is $10,000,000 or less, skip lines 7a and 7b and enter zero on line 7c	7a		
b	Subtract $10,000,000 from line 7a	7b		
c	Enter 5% (.05) of line 7b		7c	-0-
8	Total tentative tax (add lines 6 and 7c)		8	212,311 84
9	Total gift tax payable with respect to gifts made by the decedent after December 31, 1976. Include gift taxes paid by the decedent's spouse for such spouse's share of split gifts (section 2513) only if the decedent was the donor of these gifts and they are includible in the decedent's gross estate (see instructions)		9	-0-
10	Gross estate tax (subtract line 9 from line 8)		10	212,311 84
11	Unified credit against estate tax from Table B in the instructions	11: 192,800 00		
12	Adjustment to unified credit. (This adjustment may not exceed $6,000. See instructions.)	12: -0-		
13	Allowable unified credit (subtract line 12 from line 11)		13	192,800 00
14	Subtract line 13 from line 10 (but do not enter less than zero)		14	19,511 84
15	Credit for state death taxes. Do not enter more than line 14. Compute credit by using amount on line 3 less $60,000. See Table C in the instructions and **attach credit evidence** (see instructions)		15	16,109 39
16	Subtract line 15 from line 14		16	3,402 45
17	Credit for Federal gift taxes on pre-1977 gifts (section 2012)(attach computation)	17		
18	Credit for foreign death taxes (from Schedule(s) P). (Attach Form(s) 706CE)	18		
19	Credit for tax on prior transfers (from Schedule Q)	19		
20	Total (add lines 17, 18, and 19)		20	-0-
21	Net estate tax (subtract line 20 from line 16)		21	3,402 45
22	Generation-skipping transfer taxes (from Schedule R, Part 2, line 10)		22	-0-
23	Section 4980A increased estate tax (from Schedule S, Part I, line 17) (see instructions)		23	-0-
24	Total transfer taxes (add lines 21, 22, and 23)		24	3,402 45
25	Prior payments. Explain in an attached statement	25		
26	United States Treasury bonds redeemed in payment of estate tax	26		
27	Total (add lines 25 and 26)		27	-0-
28	Balance due (or overpayment) (subtract line 27 from line 24)		28	3,402 45

Under penalties of perjury, I declare that I have examined this return, including accompanying schedules and statements, and to the best of my knowledge and belief, it is true, correct, and complete. Declaration of preparer other than the executor is based on all information of which preparer has any knowledge.

/s/ Sandra Chessman — 2/3/92

Signature(s) of executor(s) — Date

/s/ Michael Scott, Esq. — 2/3/92

/s/ Michael Scott, Esq. — 401 Walnut Street, 20th Floor Philadelphia, PA 19106 — 2/3/92

Signature of preparer other than executor — Address (and ZIP code) — Date

EXAMPLE *Form 706 for the Peter Chessman Estate, Page Two*

Form 706 (Rev. 7-90)

Estate of: Peter Chessman

Part 3.—Elections by the Executor

Please check the "Yes" or "No" box for each question.	**Yes**	**No**
1 Do you elect alternate valuation?	X	
2 Do you elect special use valuation? If "Yes," you must complete and attach Schedule A-1		X
3 Do you elect to pay the taxes in installments as described in section 6166? If "Yes," you must attach the additional information described in the instructions.		X
4 Do you elect to postpone the part of the taxes attributable to a reversionary or remainder interest as described in section 6163?		X

Part 4.—General Information (Note: *Please attach the necessary supplemental documents.* **You must attach the death certificate.**)

Authorization to receive confidential tax information under Regulations section 601.502(c)(3)(ii), to act as the estate's representative before the Internal Revenue Service, and to make written or oral presentations on behalf of the estate if return prepared by an attorney, accountant, or enrolled agent for the executor:

Name of representative (print or type)	State	Address (number, street, and room or suite no., city, state, and ZIP code)
Michael Scott	PA	401 Walnut Street, 20th Floor Philadelphia, PA 19106

I declare that I am the ☒ attorney ☐ accountant ☐ enrolled agent **(you must check the applicable box)** for the executor and prepared this return for the executor. I am not under suspension or disbarment from practice before the Internal Revenue Service and am qualified to practice in the state shown above.

Signature	CAF number	Date	Telephone number

1 Death certificate number and issuing authority (attach a copy of the death certificate to this return).
#

2 Decedent's business or occupation. If retired, check here ▶ ☐ and state decedent's former business or occupation.
Executive

3 Marital status of the decedent at time of death:
- ☒ Married
- ☐ Widow or widower—Name, SSN and date of death of deceased spouse ▶
- ☐ Single
- ☐ Legally separated
- ☐ Divorced—Date divorce decree became final ▶

4a Surviving spouse's name	4b Social security number	4c Amount received (see instructions)
Sandra Chessman	123 : 45 : 6789	$277,265.31

5 Individuals (other than the surviving spouse), trusts, or other estates who receive benefits from the estate (do not include charitable beneficiaries shown in Schedule O) (see instructions). For Privacy Act Notice (applicable to individual beneficiaries only), see the Instructions for Form 1040.

Name of individual, trust, or estate receiving $5,000 or more	Identifying number	Relationship to decedent	Amount (see instructions)
Linda Chessman	123-67-9177	daughter	22,734.69
		50% Residue of the estate	305,000.00
Laura Chessman	123-67-9778	daughter	20,000.00
		50% Residue of the estate	305,000.00
Peter Chessman Parrot Foundation	54-22179	(None) Charitable Bequest	10,000.00
All unascertainable beneficiaries and those who receive less than $5,000 ▶			
Total			940,000.00

(Continued on next page)

Page 2

EXAMPLE *Form 706 for the Peter Chessman Estate (Recapitulation Schedule), Page Three*

Form 706 (Rev. 7-90)

Part 4.—General Information *(continued)*

Please check the "Yes" or "No" box for each question.	Yes	No
6 Does the gross estate contain any section 2044 property (qualified terminable interest property (QTIP) from a prior gift or estate)(see instructions)?		X
7a Have Federal gift tax returns ever been filed? If "Yes," please attach copies of the returns, if available, and furnish the following information:		X
7b Period(s) covered — **7c** Internal Revenue office(s) where filed		
If you answer "Yes" to any of questions 8–16, you must attach additional information as described in the instructions.		
8a Was there any insurance on the decedent's life that is not included on the return as part of the gross estate?		X
b Did the decedent own any insurance on the life of another that is not included in the gross estate?		X
9 Did the decedent at the time of death own any property as a joint tenant with right of survivorship in which (1) one or more of the other joint tenants was someone other than the decedent's spouse, and (2) less than the full value of the property is included on the return as part of the gross estate? If "Yes," you must complete and attach Schedule E		X
10 Did the decedent, at the time of death, own any interest in a partnership or unincorporated business or any stock in an inactive or closely held corporation?		X
11a Did the decedent make any transfer described in section 2035, 2036, 2037, or 2038 (see the instructions for Schedule G)? If "Yes," you must complete and attach Schedule G	X	
b If "Yes," was it a valuation freeze subject to section 2036(c)?		X
12 Were there in existence at the time of the decedent's death:		
a Any trusts created by the decedent during his or her lifetime?		X
b Any trusts not created by the decedent under which the decedent possessed any power, beneficial interest, or trusteeship?	X	
13 Did the decedent ever possess, exercise, or release any general power of appointment? If "Yes," you must complete and attach Schedule H.		X
14 Was the marital deduction computed under the transitional rule of Public Law 97-34, section 403(e)(3) (Economic Recovery Tax Act of 1981)? If "Yes," attach a separate computation of the marital deduction, enter the amount on item 18 of the Recapitulation, and note on item 18 "computation attached."		X
15 Was the decedent, immediately before death, receiving an annuity described in the "General" paragraph of the instructions for Schedule I? If "Yes," you must complete and attach Schedule I.		X
16 Did the decedent have a total "excess retirement accumulation" (as defined in section 4980A(d)) in qualified employer plans and individual retirement plans? If "Yes," you must complete and attach Schedule S.		X

Part 5.—Recapitulation

Item number	Gross estate	Alternate value	Value at date of death
1	Schedule A—Real Estate	95,075 00	84,735 00
2	Schedule B—Stocks and Bonds	385,000 00	519,941 25
3	Schedule C—Mortgages, Notes, and Cash	85,000 00	85,000 00
4	Schedule D—Insurance on the Decedent's Life (attach Form(s) 712)	100,000 00	100,000 00
5	Schedule E—Jointly Owned Property (attach Form(s) 712 for life insurance)	300,000 00	300,000 00
6	Schedule F—Other Miscellaneous Property (attach Form(s) 712 for life insurance)	30,000 00	30,000 00
7	Schedule G—Transfers During Decedent's Life (attach Form(s) 712 for life insurance)	20,000 00	20,000 00
8	Schedule H—Powers of Appointment	0 00	0 00
9	Schedule I—Annuities	0 00	0 00
10	Total gross estate (add items 1 through 9). Enter here and on line 1 of the Tax Computation	1,015,075 00	1,139,676 25

Item number	Deductions	Amount
11	Schedule J—Funeral Expenses and Expenses Incurred in Administering Property Subject to Claims	63,500 00
12	Schedule K—Debts of the Decedent	4,075 00
13	Schedule K—Mortgages and Liens	7,500 00
14	Total of items 11 through 13	75,075 00
15	Allowable amount of deductions from item 14 (see the instructions for item 15 of the Recapitulation)	75,075 00
16	Schedule L—Net Losses During Administration	0 00
17	Schedule L—Expenses Incurred in Administering Property Not Subject to Claims	0 00
18	Schedule M—Bequests, etc., to Surviving Spouse	277,265 31
19	Schedule O—Charitable, Public, and Similar Gifts and Bequests	10,000 00
20	Total allowable deductions (add items 15 through 19). Enter here and on line 2 of the Tax Computation	362,340 31

Page 3

EXAMPLE *Form 706 for the Peter Chessman Estate, Schedule A*

Form 706 (Rev. 7-90)

Estate of: Peter Chessman

SCHEDULE A—Real Estate

(For jointly owned property that must be disclosed on Schedule E, see the Instructions for Schedule E.)
(Real estate that is part of a sole proprietorship should be shown on Schedule F. Real estate that is included in the gross estate under section 2035, 2036, 2037, or 2038 should be shown on Schedule G. Real estate that is included in the gross estate under section 2041 should be shown on Schedule H.)
(If you elect section 2032A valuation, you must complete Schedule A and Schedule A-1.)

Item number	Description	Alternate valuation date	Alternate value	Value at date of death
1	Apartment building, 1598 Boat Street, Philadelphia, PA, per appraisal of Samuelson Realtors, copy of which is attached			40,000
	Not disposed of within six months following death	11/3/91	50,000	
	Rent payable on first day of each month at $245 per month per tenant Rent due and payable at date of death	11/3/91	735	735
2	Agreement to purchase lot, 1203 Loyola Avenue, Philadelphia, PA. Agreement of sale dated April 20, 1991, by Stanley Brown and the decedent; settlement date May 29, 1991. Valued at purchase price			10,000
	Not disposed of within six months following death	11/3/91	10,000	
3	House and lot, 135 Shoreline Drive, Ocean City, NJ, valued per appraisal of Beach Realty, which is attached. Owned by decedent and his brother, Robert Chessman, as tenants in common, total value $50,000			34,000
	Not disposed of within six months following death	11/3/91	34,340	
	Total from continuation schedule(s) (or additional sheet(s)) attached to this schedule			
	TOTAL. (Also enter on Part 5, Recapitulation, page 3, at item 1.)		95,075	84,735

(If more space is needed, attach the continuation schedule from the end of this package or additional sheets of the same size.)

Schedule A—Page 4

EXAMPLE *Form 706 for the Peter Chessman Estate, Schedule B*

Form 706 (Rev. 7-90)

Estate of: Peter Chessman

SCHEDULE B—Stocks and Bonds

(For jointly owned property that must be disclosed on Schedule E, see the Instructions for Schedule E.)

Item number	Description including face amount of bonds or number of shares and par value where needed for identification. Give CUSIP number if available.	Unit value	Alternate valuation date	Alternate value	Value at date of death
1	1000 shs. Allegheny Ludlum Steel Corp. com NYSE CUSIP 142183-7-2	400.00			400,000.00
	Not disposed of within six months following death	317.03625	11/3/91	317,036.25	
2	200 shs. American Telephone & Telegraph Co. com NYSE CUSIP 030117-10-9	50.6875			10,137.50
	Not disposed of within six months following death	53.65625	11/3/91	10,731.25	
	Dividend declared 3/15 to holders of record 4/1 payable 5/5	.85	11/3/91	170.00	170.00
3	500 shs. Chicago, Milwaukee, St. Paul & Pacific Railroad com NYSE	58.625			29,312.50
	250 shs. received as three-for-two split record date 5/3/91 payable 5/23/91	58.625			14,656.25
	750 shs. not disposed of within six months following death CUSIP 378246-10-3	50.25	11/3/91	37,687.50	
4	100 shs. Continental Bank Com OTC	70.00			7,000.00
	100 shs. distributed CUSIP 235174-09-2	55.75	10/20/91	5,575.00	
	Dividend declared 4/15 to holders of record 5/1 payable 5/20	.50	11/3/91	50.00	50.00
5	200 shs. Crown, Cork & Seal Co., Inc., including $0.45 per share ex-dividend com NYSE CUSIP 107302-40-3	74.15			14,830.00
	Not disposed of within six months following death	68.75	11/3/91	13,750.00	
6	$50,000 Illinois State Toll Highway Commission; 4% due 1/1/95; interest paid semi-annually 1/1 and 7/1	86.25			43,125.00
	Not disposed of within six months following death	84.375	11/3/91	42,187.50	
	Accrued interest 11/15 to 5/3			660.00	660.00
	Total from continuation schedule(s) (or additional sheet(s)) attached to this schedule . . .				
	TOTAL. (Also enter on Part 5, Recapitulation, page 3, at item 2.)			385,000.00	519,941.25

(If more space is needed, attach the continuation schedule from the end of this package or additional sheets of the same size.)
(The instructions to Schedule B are in the separate instructions.)

Schedule B—Page 10

EXAMPLE Form 706 for the Peter Chessman Estate, Schedule C

Form 706 (Rev. 7-90)

Estate of: Peter Chessman

SCHEDULE C—Mortgages, Notes, and Cash

(For jointly owned property that must be disclosed on Schedule E, see the Instructions for Schedule E.)

Item number	Description		Alternate valuation date	Alternate value	Value at date of death
1	Loan of $5,000 to Eva Chessman on June 10, 1983, of which $2,800 remains unpaid.		11/3/91	2,800.00	2,800.00
	Interest, payable at rate of 6%, accrued from 6/10/90 to 5/3/91			149.52	149.52
2	Agreement of Sale for lot, 1010 Cypress Street, Philadelphia, PA, dated 4/30/91; settlement 7/1/91				
	Sale Price	5,000			
	Less payment on account 4/30/91	(500)	11/3/91	4,500.00	4,500.00
3	Cash on hand		11/3/91	200.00	200.00
4	Checking Account No. 1-234-567 Provident National Bank:				
	Date-of-death balance	5,250			
	Less outstanding checks	(400)	11/3/91	4,850.00	4,850.00
5	Savings Account No. AX123,456 Philadelphia Saving Fund Society, including interest accrued to date of death		11/3/91	37,405.00	37,405.00
6	Growth Certificate of Deposit No. 987654, Philadelphia Saving Fund Society, including interest accrued to date of death		11/3/91	35,095.48	35,095.48
	Total from continuation schedule(s) (or additional sheet(s)) attached to this schedule . . .				
	TOTAL. (Also enter on Part 5, Recapitulation, page 3, at item 3.)			85,000.00	85,000.00

(If more space is needed, attach the continuation schedule from the end of this package or additional sheets of the same size.)

Schedule C—Page 11

EXAMPLE *Form 706 for the Peter Chessman Estate, Schedule D*

Form 706 (Rev.7-90)

Estate of: Peter Chessman

SCHEDULE D—Insurance on the Decedent's Life

You must attach a Form 712 for each policy.

Item number	Description		Alternate valuation date	Alternate value	Value at date of death
1	The Equitable Life Assurance Society, Policy No. 9,872,664		11/3/91	5,465.00	5,465.00
	Premium refund			9.71	9.71
2	The Equitable Life Assurance Society, Policy No. 9,625,421		11/3/91	22,568.39	22,568.39
	Accumulated Dividends			107.52	107.52
3	The Equitable Life Assurance Society - Group Insurance, Certificate No. 16405-136A		11/3/91	40,000.00	40,000.00
4	New York Life Insurance Company, Policy No. 13-642-147	20,000.00	11/3/91		
	Termination Dividends	115.00			
	Post-Mortem Dividends	16.08			
	Premium Adjustment Mortuary	141.12			
		20,272.20		20,272.20	20,272.20
5	The Northwestern Mutual Life Insurance Co., Policy No. 2-421-697	16,201.00	11/3/91		
	Less: Outstanding loan	(4,620.50)			
	Less: Interest on loan	(3.32)			
		11,577.18		11,577.18	11,577.18
	The beneficiary of Items 1 to 5 was the decedent's wife, Sandra Chessman				
	The policies listed as Items 6, 7 and 8 were owned by the decedent's wife, Sandra Chessman, and are not includible in his estate.				
6	The Equitable Life Assurance Society, Policy No. 6,842,721				
7	The Travelers Insurance Company, Policy No. 1794267				
8	The Travelers Insurance Company, Policy No. 1942768				
	FORMS 712 SUBMITTED HEREWITH				
	Total from continuation schedule(s) (or additional sheet(s)) attached to this schedule . . .				
	TOTAL (Also enter on Part 5, Recapitulation, page 3, at item 4.)			100,000.00	100,000.00

(If more space is needed, attach the continuation schedule from the end of this package or additional sheets of the same size.)

Schedule D—Page 12

EXAMPLE Form 706 for the Peter Chessman Estate, Schedule E

Form 706 (Rev. 7-90)

Estate of: Peter Chessman

SCHEDULE E—Jointly Owned Property

(If you elect section 2032A valuation, you must complete Schedule E and Schedule A-1.)

PART 1.— Qualified Joint Interests—Interests Held by the Decedent and His or Her Spouse as the Only Joint Tenants (Section 2040(b)(2))

Item number	Description For securities, give CUSIP number, if available.	Alternate valuation date	Alternate value	Value at date of death
1	Checking Account No. 1-234-567 Girard Trust Bank	11/3/91	12,245.04	12,245.04
2	Girard Trust Bank, Income Savings Bonds, Nos. 51555 and 62643	11/3/91	40,000.00	40,000.00
3	Fidelity Bank Savings Certificate No. 01-0444243	11/3/91	20,000.00	20,000.00
4	The First Pennsylvania Banking and Trust Company Savings Certificate No. 9912244	11/3/91	30,000.00	30,000.00
5	House and Lot, located 1201 Loyola Avenue, Philadelphia, PA, value per appraisal attached by Strouse, Greenberg & Co.	11/3/91	439,411.58	439,411.58
6	Contents of home, located 1201 Loyola Avenue, Philadelphia, PA, value per appraisal attached by Samuel T. Freeman & Co.	11/3/91	12,874.00	12,874.00
	Total from continuation schedule(s) (or additional sheet(s)) attached to this schedule			
1a	Totals . . . 1a			554,530.62
1b	Amounts included in gross estate (one-half of line 1a) . . . 1b			277,265.31

PART 2.—All Other Joint Interests

2a State the name and address of each surviving co-tenant. If there are more than three surviving co-tenants, list the additional co-tenants on an attached sheet.

	Name	Address (number and street, city, state, and ZIP code)
A.	Linda Chessman	1201 Loyola Avenue, Philadelphia, PA
B.		
C.		

Item number	Enter letter for co-tenant	Description (including alternate valuation date if any) For securities, give CUSIP number, if available.	Percentage includible	Includible alternate value	Includible value at date of death
1	A	Savings Account No. C-1462 Western Savings Fund Society, including interest accrued to date of death	100%	100%	4,241.23
2	A	Savings Account No. 4-241462 Beneficial Savings Bank, including interest accrued to date of death	100%	100%	2,841.23
3	A	Savings Account No. E241-442 Philadelphia Savings Fund Society, including interest accrued to date of death	100%	100%	15,652.23
		Total from continuation schedule(s) (or additional sheet(s)) attached to this schedule			
2b		Total other joint interests . . . 2b			22,734.69
3		**Total includible joint interests** (add lines 1b and 2b). Also enter on Part 5, Recapitulation, page 3, at item 5			300,000.00

(If more space is needed, attach the continuation schedule from the end of this package or additional sheets of the same size.)

Schedule E—Page 14

EXAMPLE *Form 706 for the Peter Chessman Estate, Schedule F*

Form 706 (Rev. 7-90)

Estate of: Peter Chessman

SCHEDULE F—Other Miscellaneous Property Not Reportable Under Any Other Schedule

(For jointly owned property that must be disclosed on Schedule E, see the Instructions for Schedule E.)
(If you elect section 2032A valuation, you must complete Schedule F and Schedule A-1.)

		Yes	No
1	Did the decedent at the time of death own any articles of artistic or collectible value in excess of $3,000 or any collections whose artistic or collectible value combined at date of death exceeded $10,000? . . . . . If "Yes," full details must be submitted on this schedule.	X	
2	Has the decedent's estate, spouse, or any other person, received (or will receive) any bonus or award as a result of the decedent's employment or death? . . . . . If "Yes," full details must be submitted on this schedule.	X	
3	Did the decedent at the time of death have, or have access to, a safe deposit box?	X	

If "Yes," state location, and if held in joint names of decedent and another, state name and relationship of joint depositor.

Girard Bank, Broad & Chestnut Streets, Philadelphia, PA
held jointly with decedent's wife, Sandra Chessman.

If any of the contents of the safe deposit box are omitted from the schedules in this return, explain fully why omitted.

Property belonging to Sandra Chessman omitted.

Item number	Description For securities, give CUSIP number, if available.	Alternate valuation date	Alternate value	Value at date of death
1	Refund, University of Pennsylvania Hospital	11/3/91	122.50	122.50
2	Pennsylvania Blue Shield, Medicare payment	11/3/91	112.00	112.00
3	Associated Hospital Service of Philadelphia, recovery under Major Medical policy	11/3/91	912.15	912.15
4	Six percent interest in "Chessman Building" Partnership			4,000.00
	Sold in accordance with provisions of Buy-Sell Agreement of December 12, 1970	8/15/91	4,000.00	
5	Account due, Herman F. Drummond -- the amount owed at date of death was $6,000.00 of which $500.00 has been repaid to the date of the filing of this return. Recovery of any portion of the balance is unlikely.	11/3/91	500.00	500.00
	Total from continuation schedule(s) (or additional sheet(s)) attached to this schedule . . .		24,353.35	24,353.35
	TOTAL. (Also enter on Part 5, Recapitulation, page 3, at item 6.)		30,000.00	30,000.00

(If more space is needed, attach the continuation schedule from the end of this package or additional sheets of the same size.)

Schedule F—Page 16

EXAMPLE *Form 706 for the Peter Chessman Estate, Schedule F Rider*

SCHEDULE F - Form 706 cont.

Item No.	Description	Alternate Valuation Date	Alternate Value	Value at Date of Death
6	Reversionary interest under Indenture of Trust established March 15, 1962, by the decedent for his nephew, Milton Chessman, which provides for termination on September 30, 1991, or upon the beneficiary's prior death, at which time the principal of the trust is distributable to the decedent's estate. The actuarial value of this reversionary interest is .94325, calculated in accordance with Example 12 of Actuarial Values for Estate and Gift Tax (Publication No. 11 of the United States Treasury Department). The assets held in the trust consist of a $20,000 Certificate of Deposit, No. 12446, from the First Pennsylvania Banking and Trust Company on which there was no accrued income at the date of death. Copy of Indenture submitted herewith.	11/3/91	17,162.00	17,162.00
7	Aetna Life Insurance Company Policy 8056021-3 insuring life of Sandra Chessman per Form 938 attached.	11/3/91	569.81	569.81
8	Collection of antique watches, valued per net proceeds of auction conducted by Sotheby-Parke-Bernet.	9/26/91	6,001.54	6,001.54
9	Accrued income, Indenture of Trust of Lemuel Chessman.	11/3/91	620.00	620.00
	For Information Purposes Only: On July 1, 1991, the Board of Directors of Chessman Manufacturing Company, Inc., voted to pay a bonus of $10,000 to the decedent's spouse, Sandra Chessman, "in recognition of Peter Chessman's many years of devoted service to the company." This bonus was paid on July 15, 1991.			
	Page Total		24,353.35	24,353.35

EXAMPLE *Form 706 for the Peter Chessman Estate, Schedules G and H*

Form 706 (Rev. 7-90)

Estate of: Peter Chessman

SCHEDULE G—Transfers During Decedent's Life

(If you elect section 2032A valuation, you must complete Schedule G and Schedule A-1.)

Item number	Description For securities, give CUSIP number, if available.	Alternate valuation date	Alternate value	Value at date of death
A.	Gift tax paid by the decedent or the estate for all gifts made by the decedent or his or her spouse within 3 years before the decedent's death (section 2035(c))	X X X X X	- 0 -	- 0 -
B.	Transfers includible under section 2035(a), 2036, 2037, or 2038:			
1	Transfer of Prudential National Bank Account #172-53-967 to Laura Chessman under Uniform Gifts to Minors Act. Lawrence Chessman, guardian. Transfer made 7/2/86. Decedent retained right to receive income. For Information Only Schedule F Item 6 refers to a reversionary interest under indenture of trust dated 3/15/62 for the benefit of Milton Chessman.		20,000	20,000
	Total from continuation schedule(s) (or additional sheet(s)) attached to this schedule			
	TOTAL. (Also enter on Part 5, Recapitulation, page 3, at item 7.)		20,000	20,000

SCHEDULE H—Powers of Appointment

(If you elect section 2032A valuation, you must complete Schedule H and Schedule A-1.)

Item number	Description	Alternate valuation date	Alternate value	Value at date of death
1	For Information Only Under an inter vivos trust created August 3, 1968, by John Chessman, decedent received the income of the trust for life with the power to appoint the remainder to any person other than decedent, his estate, his creditors, or the creditors of his estate.			
	Total from continuation schedule(s) (or additional sheet(s)) attached to this schedule		0.00	0.00
	TOTAL. (Also enter on Part 5, Recapitulation, page 3, at item 8.)			

(If more space is needed, attach the continuation schedule from the end of this package or additional sheets of the same size.)
(The instructions to Schedules G and H are in the separate instructions.)

Schedules G and H—Page 18

EXAMPLE *Form 706 for the Peter Chessman Estate, Schedule J*

Form 706 (Rev. 7-90)

Estate of: Peter Chessman

SCHEDULE J—Funeral Expenses and Expenses Incurred in Administering Property Subject to Claims

Note: *Do not list on this schedule expenses of administering property not subject to claims. For those expenses, see the Instructions for Schedule L.*

If executors' commissions, attorney fees, etc., are claimed and allowed as a deduction for estate tax purposes, they are not allowable as a deduction in computing the taxable income of the estate for Federal income tax purposes. They are allowable as an income tax deduction on Form 1041 if a waiver is filed to waive the deduction on Form 706 (see the Form 1041 instructions).

Item number	Description	Expense amount	Total Amount
	A. Funeral expenses:		
1	J. R. Matthews & Sons, Funeral Bill	2,800.00	
	Pine Haven, Interment	400.00	
	J. J. Kokes, Inc., Memorial Stone	300.00	
	Total funeral expenses		3,500.00
	B. Administration expenses:		
1	Executors' commissions—amount estimated/agreed upon/paid. (Strike out the words that do not apply.)		
2	Attorney fees—amount estimated/~~agreed upon/paid~~. (Strike out the words that do not apply.)		34,000.00
3	Accountant fees—amount estimated/agreed upon/paid. (Strike out the words that do not apply.)		- 0 -
4	Miscellaneous expenses:	Expense amount	
	Register of Wills, Probate Costs	100.00	
	The Legal Intelligencer, Legal Advertising	12.00	
	Wm. J. Mansfield, Legal Advertising	13.00	
	Continental Bank, Safe Deposit Box Rental	12.00	
	Samuel T. Freeman & Co., Appraisal of Personal Property	77.00	
	Strouse, Greenberg & Co., Real Estate Appraisal	536.00	
	Estimated Additional Administration Expenses	250.00	
	Total miscellaneous expenses from continuation schedule(s) (or additional sheet(s)) attached to this schedule		
	Total miscellaneous expenses		1,000.00

TOTAL. (Also enter on Part 5, Recapitulation, page 3, at item 11.) 63,500.00

(If more space is needed, attach the continuation schedule from the end of this package or additional sheets of the same size.)

Schedule J—Page 20

EXAMPLE *Form 706 for the Peter Chessman Estate, Schedule K*

Form 706 (Rev. 7-90)

Estate of: Peter Chessman

SCHEDULE K—Debts of the Decedent, and Mortgages and Liens

Item number	Debts of the Decedent—Creditor and nature of claim, and allowable death taxes	Amount unpaid to date	Amount in contest	Amount claimed as a deduction
1	John Wanamaker, Bill for Merchandise	15.00		15.00
2	Bell Telephone Co., September Bill	8.00		8.00
3	1991 Income Tax	3,987.00		3,987.00
4	1991 School Tax	65.00		65.00
	Total from continuation schedule(s) (or additional sheet(s)) attached to this schedule			
	TOTAL. (Also enter on Part 5, Recapitulation, page 3, at item 12.)			4,075.00

Item number	Mortgages and Liens—Description	Amount
1	First Federal Saving and Loan Association, Mortgage Balance on 1201 Loyola Avenue, Philadelphia, PA (Schedule A, Item 1)	4,350.00
	Interest accrued from 1/1/91 to date of death	50.00
2	Acme Loan Co., Balance due on Collateral Note (collateral listed on Schedule B, Items 3-7)	3,000.00
	Interest accrued from 2/15/91 to date of death at 8½%	100.00
	Total from continuation schedule(s) (or additional sheet(s)) attached to this schedule	
	TOTAL. (Also enter on Part 5, Recapitulation, page 3, at item 13.)	7,500.00

(If more space is needed, attach the continuation schedule from the end of this package or additional sheets of the same size.)

(The instructions to Schedule K are in the separate instructions.) **Schedule K —Page 22**

EXAMPLE Form 706 for the Peter Chessman Estate, Schedule M and Disclaimer

Form 706 (Rev. 7-90)

Estate of: Peter Chessman

SCHEDULE M—Bequests, etc., to Surviving Spouse

Terminable Interest (QTIP) Marital Deduction.—If you elect to claim a marital deduction for qualified terminable interest property (QTIP) under section 2056(b)(7), you MUST list on Part 2 of Schedule M all of the property for which you are making the election. Listing property on Part 2 constitutes the making of the QTIP election. No marital deduction will be allowed for any terminable interest property that is listed on Part 1 of Schedule M.

		Yes	No
1	Did any property pass to the surviving spouse as a result of a qualified disclaimer? *If "Yes," attach a copy of the written disclaimer required by section 2518(b).*		X
2	Is the surviving spouse a U.S. citizen?	X	
3	**Qualified Domestic Trust.**—Do you elect under section 2056A(d) to treat any trusts reported on Schedule M as qualified domestic trusts? (see instructions)		X
4	**Election out of QTIP Treatment of Annuities.**—Do you elect under section 2056(b)(7)(C)(ii) to not treat as qualified terminable interest property any joint and survivor annuities that are included in the gross estate and would otherwise be treated as qualified terminable interest property under section 2056(b)(7)(C)? (see instructions)		X

Part 1.—Property Interests Which Are Not Subject to a QTIP Election

(Note: *A marital deduction will NOT be allowed for any terminable interest property (QTIP) that is listed on Part 1 of Schedule M.)*

Item number	Description of property interests passing to surviving spouse	Value
1	Schedule A, Items 1-3	95,075.00*
2	Schedule B, Items 1-6	375,000.00**
3	Schedule C, Items 1-6	85,000.00*
4	Schedule D, Items 1-5	100,000.00*
5	Schedule E, Items 1-6	277,265.31
6	Schedule F, Items 1-9	30,000.00*
	* Spouse disclaiming all bequests and life insurance. A copy of a signed disclaimer is attached hereto. Jointly owned property is not disclaimed.	
	** Ten thousand dollars from the sale of stock reported on Schedule B was directly bequeathed to the Peter Chessman Parrot Foundation pursuant to Article 5 in the Will. Thus, only $375,000.00 from Schedule B is shown on Schedule M rather than the total value of the stocks of $385,000.00.	
	Total from continuation schedule(s) (or additional sheet(s)) attached to this schedule	
	Total value of property interests not subject to a QTIP election (enter here and on line 1 of Part 3 on the next page)	277,265.31

(If more space is needed, attach the continuation schedule from the end of this package or additional sheets of the same size.)
(The instructions to Schedule M are in the separate instructions.)

Schedule M—Page 24

EXAMPLE *Form 706 for the Peter Chessman Estate, Schedule M and Disclaimer, continued*

Form 706 (Rev. 7-90)

Part 2.—Property Interests Which Are Subject to a QTIP Election

(Note: *Listing terminable interest property on Part 2 of Schedule M constitutes the making of a QTIP election for that property under section 2056(b)(7). A marital deduction will not be allowed for any terminable interest property that is not listed on Part 2. If you use a continuation page for Part 2, be sure that it is clearly labeled as Schedule M, Part 2.)*

Item number	Description of property interests passing to surviving spouse (Describe portion of trust for which allocation is made.)	Value
1	None	
	Total from continuation schedule(s) (or additional sheet(s)) attached to this schedule	
	A. Total value of property interests subject to a QTIP election . . . . **A**	- 0 -

Part 3.—Reconciliation

1	Enter the total from part 1	1	
2	Total interests passing to surviving spouse (add lines A and 1, above)	2	277,265.31
3a	Federal estate taxes (including section 4980A taxes) payable out of property interests listed on Parts 1 and 2 — 3a		
b	Other death taxes payable out of property interests listed on Parts 1 and 2 . . . . — 3b		
c	Federal and state GST taxes payable out of property interests listed on Parts 1 and 2 . . . . . — 3c		
d	Add items a, b, and c	3d	
4	Net value of property interests listed on Schedule M (subtract 3d from 2). Also enter on Part 5, Recapitulation, page 3, at item 18	4	277,265.31

(If more space is needed, attach the continuation schedule from the end of this package or additional sheets of the same size.)

Schedule M—Page 25

EXAMPLE ***Form 706 for the Peter Chessman Estate, Schedule M and Disclaimer, continued***

DISCLAIMER

Sandra Chessman
c/o Michael Scott, Esq.
401 Walnut Street
20th Floor
Philadelphia, PA 19106

Robert Chessman
135 Shoreline Drive
Ocean City, NJ 08224

Re: Estate of Peter Chessman
Date of Death: 5/3/91
Form 706 Schedule A Item 3

Dear Mr. Chessman,

Pursuant to the laws of the Commonwealth of Pennsylvania and according to IRS Code Section 2815 (b), I hereby disclaim all of my right, title, and interest in and to my one-half share, as a beneficiary, of my deceased husband Peter Chessman's share as a tenant in common of the house and lot located at 135 Shoreline Drive, Ocean City, NJ. I understand that said share shall pass to my husband's heirs as if I had predeceased him.

____
Sandra Chessman

____
Dated

EXAMPLE *Form 706 for the Peter Chessman Estate, Schedule O*

Form 706 (Rev. 7-90)

Estate of: Peter Chessman

SCHEDULE O—Charitable, Public, and Similar Gifts and Bequests

	Yes	No
1a If the transfer was made by will, has any action been instituted to have interpreted or to contest the will or any of its provisions affecting the charitable deductions claimed in this schedule? . . . If "Yes," full details must be submitted with this schedule.		X
b According to the information and belief of the person or persons filing the return, is any such action planned? . . . If "Yes," full details must be submitted with this schedule.		X
2 Did any property pass to charity as the result of a qualified disclaimer? . . . If "Yes," attach a copy of the written disclaimer required by section 2518(b).		X

Item number	Name and address of beneficiary	Character of institution	Amount
1	Peter Chessman Parrot Foundation	Educational	10,000.00
Total from continuation schedule(s) (or additional sheet(s)) attached to this schedule. . . .			

3 Total . . .			3	10,000.00
4a Federal estate tax (including section 4980A taxes) payable out of property interests listed above . . .	4a			
b Other death taxes payable out of property interests listed above . . .	4b			
c Federal and state GST taxes payable out of property interests listed above . . .	4c			
d Add items a, b, and c . . .			4d	
5 Net value of property interests listed above (subtract 4d from 3). Also enter on Part 5, Recapitulation, page 3, at item 19			5	10,000.00

(If more space is needed, attach the continuation schedule from the end of this package or additional sheets of the same size.)
(The instructions to Schedule O are in the separate instructions.)

Schedule O—Page 26

EXAMPLE *Treasury Form 4768*

Form **4768** (Rev. August 1990) Department of the Treasury Internal Revenue Service

Application for Extension of Time To File a Return and/or Pay U.S. Estate (and Generation-Skipping Transfer) Taxes

(For filers of Forms 706, 706-A, and 706NA)

OMB No. 1545-0181 Expires 7-31-93

Note: *Use Form 2758 to request an extension for Forms 706GS(D) and 706GS(T).*

Part I Identification

Decedent's first name and middle initial	Decedent's last name	Date of death
Name of application filer		Decedent's social security number
Address of application filer (Number and street)		Estate tax return due date
City, state, and ZIP code		

Part II Extension of Time To File (Sec. 6081)

You must attach your written statement to explain in detail why it is impossible or impractical to file a reasonably complete return within 9 months after the date of the decedent's death.

Extension date requested

Part III Extension of Time To Pay (Sec. 6161)

You must attach your written statement to explain in detail why it is impossible or impractical to pay the full amount of the estate (or GST) tax by the return due date. If the taxes cannot be determined because the size of the gross estate is unascertainable, check here ▶ ☐ and enter "-0-" or other appropriate amount on Part IV, line 3. You must attach an explanation.

Extension date requested

Part IV Payment To Accompany Extension Request

1	Amount of estate and GST taxes estimated to be due	1		
2	Amount of cash shortage (complete Part III)	2		
3	**Balance due (subtract line 2 from line 1) (Pay with this application.)**	3		

Signature and Verification

If filed by executor—Under penalties of perjury, I declare that to the best of my knowledge and belief, the statements made herein and attached are true and correct.

Executor's signature ____ Title ____ Date ____

If filed by someone other than the executor—Under penalties of perjury, I declare that to the best of my knowledge and belief, the statements made herein and attached are true and correct, that I am authorized by the executor to file this application, and that I am (check box(es) that applies):

- ☐ A member in good standing of the bar of the highest court of (specify jurisdiction) ▶ ____
- ☐ A certified public accountant duly qualified to practice in (specify jurisdiction) ▶ ____
- ☐ A person enrolled to practice before the Internal Revenue Service.
- ☐ A duly authorized agent holding a power of attorney. (The power of attorney need not be submitted unless requested.)

Filer's signature (other than the executor) ____ Date ____

Part V Notice to Applicant—To be completed by Internal Revenue Service

1 The application for extension of time to file (Part II) is:
- ☐ Approved
- ☐ Not approved because ____
- ☐ Other ____

2 The application for extension of time to pay (Part III) is:
- ☐ Approved
- ☐ Not approved because ____
- ☐ Other ____

Internal Revenue Service official	Date	Internal Revenue Service official	Date

For Paperwork Reduction Act Notice, see instructions on the back of this form. Form **4768** (Rev. 8-90)

Penalty for Late Filing and/or Late Payment In addition to the annual interest (equal to the short-term federal interest rate plus three points) that is due on any tax not paid at the time the federal estate tax return was originally due, a penalty of ½% per month (up to a maximum of 25%) can be added to the amount due. The interest and penalties are charged the first day the return is late; thus, on a sizable estate the interest and penalties can be severe. It is recommended that if a return with a sizable tax due is close to the due date, the return be hand-delivered to the IRS, and the courier should make certain that a copy of the return is stamped "received" as of that date. The IRS is a large bureaucracy and it is not uncommon for returns to be "misplaced." If it is difficult to send a courier to the IRS, the return can be mailed "certified mail return receipt requested." Of course, you are still taking a chance that the return may be lost in the mail. Having something in writing as evidence that the return was filed on time is very important when there is tax due.

Payment of Tax by Installments Under certain circumstances it is possible to pay the federal estate tax due (or a portion thereof) in installments over a ten- or fifteen-year period. Section 6166 of the IRC provides that in some cases where a decedent held an interest in a "closely held" business (ownership by a small group) that constitutes a significant portion of the estate, the federal estate tax attributable to such a business may be paid in ten equal annual installments, provided that an election is filed by the executors on or before the due date of the return.

An alternate period of fifteen years may be elected with the entire principal being deferred for five years and thereafter payable in equal annual installments over the next ten years. If the estate qualifies for this election and the (IRC § 6166) executor has not elected the fifteen-year extension, the estate will retain the option on the basis of being eligible.

Under the provisions of the Tax Reform Act of 1976 as amended by the Revenue Act of 1978, a new lien procedure is available to both the ten- and fifteen-year installment payouts. Under this provision, an executor can be discharged from personal liability during the extended payment period, and no bond can be required except in cases of inadequate security for the unpaid principal amount.

Signatures on the Return The federal estate tax return should be signed on page one by the executor under penalty of perjury. It should also be signed, under penalty of perjury, by the attorney or other agent of the executors who actually prepared the return. The lawyer in charge of the matter should be consulted in regard to the form of signature appropriate for the preparer.

Exhibits To Be Submitted The following items (in addition to the check) should be submitted to the Internal Revenue Service at the time the return is filed:

a. Copies of all appraisals that were made in connection with the valuation of any of the assets included in the gross estate.

b. Copies of financial statements for any closely held corporations, partnerships, or proprietorships in which the decedent had an interest (including balance sheets and profit-and-loss statements) for the five years preceding the date of death.

c. Copies of settlement sheets, closing statements, contracts, or other evidence of the sale price of assets reflected in the gross estate.

d. United States Treasury Form 712, covering any insurance policies on the decedent's life.

e. United States Treasury Form 938, covering any policies of insurance that the decedent owned at the time of his death on the lives of others.

f. Copies of all trust instruments under which the decedent had either a beneficial interest or under which he was serving as trustee.

g. In connection with any annuity that is includible in Schedule I of the federal estate tax return, a statement from the insurance company or other payer of the annuity indicating the present value as of the date of death or alternate valuation date of the remaining installments due under the contract.

h. If a marital deduction is claimed on Schedule M of the return, a certified copy of the order admitting the will to probate must be submitted with the return. This requirement would also be true if a charitable deduction were taken on Schedule O. If neither of these deductions is claimed, a copy of the will must still be submitted with the return, but most Internal Revenue Service districts will require only that it be certified to be true and correct by the attorney who is counsel for the executors.

i. If any disclaimers have been made affecting the calculation of Schedules M, N, or O, copies are to be filed with the return. If the surviving spouse has elected to take against the will, a certified copy of that election should also be filed.

j. If a foreign death tax credit is claimed, the amount of tax paid to the foreign country must be proven by the submission of Form 706CE. This form should be prepared in triplicate for each country that has levied a tax to which a credit is claimed. Two copies must be forwarded to the foreign government office that administers the tax for certification of the amount paid (and one such certified copy should be forwarded by that government to the Office of the District Director of Internal Revenue). The actual preparation of the form is quite simple and the instructions provided on the form should be self-explanatory.

k. To prove that the amount available for the credit for state death taxes paid did not exceed the amount that was actually paid to the state, some evidence of payment to the state should be submitted with the federal estate tax return (if it is available by that time). Such evidence may take the form of the official receipt of the particular jurisdiction to which the tax has been paid, a copy of the cancelled check, or whatever evidence is demanded by the Internal Revenue Service in your particular district.

State death taxes may not have been paid prior to the filing of the federal estate tax return. They are often paid contemporaneously with that filing. Under such circumstances when the evidence of payment becomes available, it should be submitted to the District Director. It may be best to wait until a specific request for credit evidence has been made by the Internal Revenue Service, either by the examining agent if the return has been audited, or by Treasury Form L–156 if the return has not been audited. Treasury Form L–156 is generally received after the return has been accepted as filed by the Internal Revenue Service and provides notification that upon submission of the credit evidence, an Estate Tax Closing Letter will be issued. It is the practice in most districts that the Internal Revenue Service will not ask the taxpayer to produce credit evidence for the payment of state death taxes (or foreign death taxes) if the amount of credit is less than some minimum figure, generally $400 to $600.

l. A general power of attorney form should be filed with the federal estate tax return. This Treasury Form 2848 authorizes the attorney for the executors to represent the estate in any contest with the Internal Revenue Service (see next page).

m. It will generally not be necessary to file a Notice of Fiduciary Relationship (Treasury Form 56). The Form 56, accompanied by a short certificate, provides the Internal Revenue Service with the requisite notice that the government will be dealing with the fiduciaries.

n. Other exhibits may be required or advisable in accordance with the discussions concerning the various assets,

EXAMPLE *Treasury Form 2848*

Form **2848**
(Rev. March 1991)
Department of the Treasury
Internal Revenue Service

Power of Attorney and Declaration of Representative

► For Paperwork Reduction and Privacy Act Notice, see the instructions.

OMB No. 1545-0150
Expires 5-31-93

Part I **Power of Attorney**

1 Taxpayer Information

Taxpayer name(s) and address **(Please type or print.)**	**Social security number(s)**	**Employer identification number**
		Plan number (if applicable)
	Daytime telephone number ( )	

hereby appoint(s) the following representative(s) as attorney(s)-in-fact:

2 Representative(s) (Please type or print.)

Name and address	CAF No. .... Telephone No. ( ) .... Fax No. ( ) .... Check if new: Address . . . ☐ Telephone No. ☐
Name and address	CAF No. .... Telephone No. ( ) .... Fax No. ( ) .... Check if new: Address . . . ☐ Telephone No. ☐
Name and address	CAF No. .... Telephone No. ( ) .... Fax No. ( ) .... Check if new: Address . . . ☐ Telephone No. ☐

to represent the taxpayer(s) before the Internal Revenue Service for the following tax matters:

3 Tax Matters

Type of Tax (Income, Employment, Excise, etc.)	Tax Form Number (1040, 941, 720, etc.)	Year(s) or Period(s)

4 Specific Use Not Recorded on Centralized Authorization File (CAF).—If the power of attorney is for a specific use not recorded on CAF, please check this box. (See the instructions for *Specific Use Not Recorded on CAF* on page 4.) . . . . ► ☐

5 Acts Authorized.—The representatives are authorized to receive and inspect confidential tax information and to perform any and all acts that I can perform with respect to the tax matters described in line 3, for example, the authority to sign any agreements, consents, or other documents. The authority does not include the power to receive refund checks or the power to sign certain returns. (See instructions.)

List any specific additions or deletions to the acts otherwise authorized in this power of attorney: ....

....

....

Note: *In general, an unenrolled preparer of tax returns cannot sign any document for a taxpayer. See Revenue Procedure 81-38, printed as Pub. 470, for more information.*

Note: *The tax matters partner/person of a partnership or S corporation is not permitted to authorize representatives to perform certain acts. See the instructions for more information.*

6 Receipt of Refund Checks.—If you want to authorize a representative named in line 2 to receive, **BUT NOT TO ENDORSE OR CASH,** refund checks, initial here ________ and list the name of that representative below.

Name of representative to receive refund check(s) ►

Cat. No. 11980J — Form **2848** (Rev. 3-91)

EXAMPLE *Treasury Form 2848, continued*

Form 2848 (Rev. 3-91) Page **2**

7 Notices and Communications.—Notices and other written communications will be sent to the first representative listed in line 2.

a If you want the second representative listed to receive such notices and communications, check this box . . . . ▶ ☐

b If you do not want any notices or communications sent to your representative, check this box . . . . ▶ ☐

8 Retention/Revocation of Prior Power(s) of Attorney.—The filing of this power of attorney automatically revokes all earlier power(s) of attorney on file with the Internal Revenue Service for the **same** tax matters and years or periods covered by this document. If you do not want to revoke a prior power of attorney, check here . . . . ▶ ☐

YOU MUST ATTACH A COPY OF ANY POWER OF ATTORNEY YOU WANT TO REMAIN IN EFFECT.

9 Signature of Taxpayer(s).—If a tax matter concerns a joint return, **both** husband and wife must sign if joint representation is requested, otherwise, see the instructions. If signed by a corporate officer, partner, guardian, tax matters partner/person, executor, receiver, administrator, or trustee on behalf of the taxpayer, I certify that I have the authority to execute this form on behalf of the taxpayer.

▶ **If this power of attorney is not signed, it will be returned.**

.... Signature .... Date .... Title (if applicable)

.... Print Name

.... Signature .... Date .... Title (if applicable)

.... Print Name

Part II Declaration of Representative

Under penalties of perjury, I declare that:

- I am not currently under suspension or disbarment from practice before the Internal Revenue Service;
- I am aware of regulations contained in Treasury Department Circular No. 230 (31 CFR, Part 10), as amended, concerning the practice of attorneys, certified public accountants, enrolled agents, enrolled actuaries, and others;
- I am authorized to represent the taxpayer(s) identified in Part I for the tax matter(s) specified there; and
- I am one of the following:

a Attorney—a member in good standing of the bar of the highest court of the jurisdiction shown below.
b Certified Public Accountant—duly qualified to practice as a certified public accountant in the jurisdiction shown below.
c Enrolled Agent—enrolled as an agent under the requirements of Treasury Department Circular No. 230.
d Officer—a bona fide officer of the taxpayer organization.
e Full-Time Employee—a full-time employee of the taxpayer.
f Family Member—a member of the taxpayer's immediate family (*i.e.*, spouse, parent, child, brother, or sister).
g Enrolled Actuary—enrolled as an actuary by the Joint Board for the Enrollment of Actuaries under 29 U.S.C. 1242 (the authority to practice before the Service is limited by section 10.3(d)(1) of Treasury Department Circular No. 230).
h Unenrolled Return Preparer—an unenrolled return preparer under section 10.7(a)(7) of Treasury Department Circular No. 230.

▶ **If this power of attorney is not signed, it will be returned.**

Designation —Insert above letter (a–h)	Jurisdiction (state) or Enrollment Card No.	Signature	Date

deductions, and credits schedules. Whenever a federal estate tax return is filed, it should be accompanied by a cover letter listing all of the exhibits that are submitted with the return, and a receipt should be requested for the federal estate tax return and exhibits. The receipted cover letter will fix the date on which the federal estate tax return has been filed (to establish the timeliness of the filing) and evidence the documents that have been submitted to the Internal Revenue Service.

EXAMPLE

Cover Letter Accompanying Estate Tax Return

District Director
Internal Revenue Service
600 Arch Street
Philadelphia PA 19106
CERTIFIED MAIL—RETURN RECEIPT REQUESTED

Re: Estate of Peter Chessman, Deceased
Taxpayer I.D. #23-625791

Dear Sir:

Enclosed for filing is the United States Estate (and Generation-Skipping Transfer) Tax Return Form 706 for the above decedent. Also enclosed is a check in the amount of $3,402.45 in full payment of the tax due. We would like to request a prompt determination of the estate tax liability for this estate and would appreciate an estate tax closing letter as soon as possible.

Submitted with the return are the following exhibits:

1. Certified copy of the will.
2. Real estate appraisals covering items A-1 and A-3.
3. Copies of agreements of sale relating to items A-2 and C-2, respectively.
4. Copies of letters from Provident National Bank, Philadelphia Saving Fund Society, Western Savings Bank, Beneficial Savings Bank, Girard Bank, Fidelity Bank, and the First Pennsylvania Bank relating to bank accounts shown on Schedules C and E.
5. Forms 712 relating to insurance policies shown on Schedule D.
6. Balance sheets and profit-and-loss statements for the five years preceding death covering the partnership included as item F-4.
7. Appraisal of tangible personal property included as item F-8.
8. Copy of Indenture of Trust dated March 15, 1962, covering item F-6.

Please stamp the enclosed copy of this letter with the date of receipt and return it to me in the enclosed self-addressed envelope.

Sincerely,
/s/**Mary Whitehead**
Assistant to Michael Scott, Esq.

Filing the Return with the State

In virtually every state a copy of the federal estate tax return and of the Estate Tax Closing Letter must be filed with the state inheritance tax authorities when it is received. In some jurisdictions the amount of the state death tax will depend upon the amount of marital deduction portion that, in turn, can only be established by the federal estate tax return when finally audited. If there is any "slack tax" (tax to make up the maximum federal estate tax credit for state taxes paid) to be paid, the federal estate tax return would be needed to determine the amount of such tax.

Audit of the Federal Estate Tax Return

After the federal estate tax return is filed, it goes through a mathematical check by the Collection Division of the Internal Revenue Service and, assuming that there are no errors in the mathematics that require any communications from the service, the federal estate tax return will then pass physically from the Collection Division to the Audit Division.

The Audit Division will assign the federal estate tax return to one of its examiners who will inspect it, as well as the accompanying documents, in order to determine (1) whether the federal estate tax return should be accepted as filed, (2) whether additional information is needed before a final determination can be made about its acceptance as filed, or (3) whether the federal estate tax return should at that point be selected for examination—i.e., audit.

If the federal estate tax return is to be audited, the executors or their attorney will eventually receive a phone call or letter from the federal estate tax examiner to arrange a meeting for the purpose of reviewing the estate's records. At the meeting, the decedent's income tax returns for the last three years, his bank statements and cancelled checks for the last three years, and other items noted on the form letter will usually be inspected.

After the examiner has met with the estate's representatives and is satisfied that all the relevant information has been reviewed and substantiated, the examiner may either accept the federal estate tax return as filed or else conclude that an additional assessment of tax should be paid or a refund is due. If there is a change to be made in the federal estate tax return, the agent will request the executors to execute a Waiver Form 890 indicating an acceptance of his conclusion. If there is additional credit evidence required to support the payment of state death taxes, the agent will submit the waiver on Form 890-B, which is an identical form except for the fact that the amount of the tax assessment is made contingent upon the receipt of the additional credit evidence.

Post-Audit Review and Litigation

Whenever the agent has either assessed additional tax or has accepted the federal estate tax return as filed, he must write a report to the Review Section of the Internal Revenue Service, detailing all of the items that have been inspected and analyzing all of the assets and deductions set forth on the federal estate tax return. That report may not be seen by the executors or by the attorney. The agent also prepares a brief summary report showing the calculations relevant to the tax assessed. That report will be sent to the estate's representatives. If the Review Section accepts the report (and only a relatively small percentage of reports are not accepted), there will be no further communication with the estate by the examining agent. If the Review Section rejects the agent's report, the agent may be forced to rescind any agreement that has been made with the executors, and he may have to ask for additional tax or additional documents to satisfy the reviewer.

After the audit has been concluded and if a waiver has been executed, the refund check or the bill for the additional tax deficiency, plus interest (and penalty, if that is assessed), will eventually be issued by the Internal Revenue Service. At the same time the Internal Revenue Service will submit an Estate Tax Closing Letter or a counterpart to this form called an Acceptance of Estate Tax Return. The closing letter is proof of the final amount of tax determined to be due the Internal Revenue Service. A bill will be sent separately.

EXAMPLE
Estate Tax Closing Letter

Address any reply to DISTRICT DIRECTOR at office No. 3

Department of the Treasury
District Director
Internal Revenue Service
Date: ______________ In reply refer to
March 5, 1992

____

Trust Company Bank
Executor, et al
8336 Main Street
Norristown, PA 19404

Estate of:
Date of Death: November 11, 1991

ESTATE TAX CLOSING LETTER
(This is not a bill for tax due)

The computation at the bottom of this letter shows the Internal Revenue Service's determination of the Federal estate tax liability for the estate named above. You should keep a copy of this letter as a permanent record, since your attorney may need it to close the probate proceedings for the estate. It, together with proof of payment, is evidence that the Federal estate tax liability for the estate has been settled.

Sincerely yours,

Acting District Director

If there has been no agreement between the agent and the personal representative, after the auditor's report has been considered by the Review Section, the Conference Section of the Internal Revenue Service will issue a "thirty-day letter." The executors, after receiving the thirty-day letter from the Conference Section, may request a hearing with the Conference Section. The hearing will be granted if a written protest to the agent's findings is submitted.

If after meeting with the District Conferee, there is still no agreement as to the amount of tax due, the Conference Section will submit its report and send the case on to the Appellate Division for an appellate hearing, if the taxpayer requests one. At the appellate hearing, for the first time, the taxpayer will encounter a government representative who has the official power to compromise an issue. Neither the examining agent nor the District Conferee has the power to write a report in which he states that, rather than risk going to court over the issue, he will include, for example, property the spouse considered to be his. An Appellate Conferee, on the other hand, has the power to write such a report, subject to approval by his reviewers.

If no agreement is reached with the Appellate Division, the government will issue a "ninety-day letter," which has the effect of requiring the taxpayer either (1) to pay the additional federal estate tax deficiency requested by the government and sue for a refund in one of the federal courts discussed later, or (2) not to pay, in which event the government will sue the taxpayer in the Tax Court.

If the tax is paid and a claim for refund is filed on Treasury Form 843 (see next Example), the taxpayer will have the choice of suing the government either in the Court of Claims or the United States District Court. When the tax is not paid, the suit will be in the Tax Court. Appeals from the Tax Court and the District Court are heard by the Circuit Court of Appeals and appeals from the Court of Claims and from the Court of Appeals are heard by the United States Supreme Court.

EXAMPLE *Refund Claim—Treasury Form 843*

Form **843**
(Rev. August 1990)
Department of the Treasury
Internal Revenue Service

Claim for Refund and Request for Abatement

▶ See separate Instructions.

OMB No. 1545-0024
Expires: 6-30-93

If your claim is for an overpayment of income taxes, do NOT use Form 843. (See Instructions.)
Use Form 843 ONLY if your claim involves one of the taxes shown on line 8a or a refund or abatement of interest or penalties on lines 8b(i)–(iii).

Please type or print

Name of claimant | Telephone number (optional) ( )

Address (number, street, and apt. or suite no. or rural route)(List P.O. box if mail is not delivered to street address.)

City, town, or post office, state, and ZIP code

Fill in applicable items—Use attachments if necessary

1 Your social security number | 2 Spouse's social security number | 3 Employer identification number

4 Name and address shown on return if different from above

5 Period—prepare a separate Form 843 for each tax period
From , 19 , to , 19

6 Amount to be refunded or abated
$

7 Dates of payment

8a Type of tax or penalty
☐ Employment ☐ Estate ☐ Excise ☐ Gift ☐ Penalty IRC section ▶

b Request for abatement, credit, or refund of:
(i) ☐ Interest under Rev. Proc. 87-42.
(ii) ☐ Interest under Rev. Proc. 87-43.
(iii) ☐ A penalty or addition to tax as a result of erroneous advice from IRS.

9 Kind of return filed (see instructions)
☐ 706 ☐ 709 ☐ 720 IRS No. (s) ▶ ☐ 940 ☐ 941 ☐ 990-PF ☐ 2290 ☐ 4720
☐ Other (specify) ▶

10 Explain why you believe this claim should be allowed and show computation of tax refund or abatement of interest or penalty.

Under penalties of perjury, I declare that I have examined this claim, including accompanying schedules and statements, and to the best of my knowledge and belief it is true, correct, and complete.

Director's Stamp
(Date received)

Signature (Title, if applicable. Claims by corporations must be signed by an officer.) Date

Signature Date

For Paperwork Reduction Act Notice, see separate Instructions. ☆U.S. Government Printing Office: 1990-282-002/00192 Form **843** (Rev. 8-90)

CHAPTER SIX

State Taxation of Estates and Trusts

STATE DEATH TAXES

Federal estate taxes will be payable for only relatively large estates. Death taxes imposed by states, on the other hand, affect virtually every estate. All states and the District of Columbia and Puerto Rico impose some form of death tax, and, as a general rule, there are no blanket exclusions or tax credits as there are with the federal estate tax. An estate may be liable for paying both the federal estate tax and a death tax to the state in which the decedent resided at the time of death.[1]

There are three basic types of death taxes. In the majority of the states, the tax is the amount of the state death tax credit shown on the federal estate tax return (706). This is called a "pick up tax." A smaller group of states impose a state inheritance tax and an additional tax for the federal tax credit. A few states impose an estate tax similar to the federal estate tax. The taxes imposed by the various states are shown in the table below, reprinted from the Commerce Clearing House Fiduciary Tax Guide (1990). It should be noted that a number of states impose generation-skipping transfer taxes as well as the estate tax.

Classification of State Laws

State	Inheritance Tax	Additional Estate Tax for Federal Credit	Estate Tax	Estate Tax for Federal Credit Only	Gift Tax
Alabama*				x	
Alaska				x	
Arizona*				x	
Arkansas				x	
California*				x	
Colorado				x	
Connecticut	x	x			
Delaware	x	x			x

1. See Chapter Two, "Decedent's Domicile," for a discussion of which state has a right to tax an estate.

Classification of State Laws, continued

State	Inheritance Tax	Additional Estate Tax for Federal Credit	Estate Tax	Estate Tax for Federal Credit Only	Gift Tax
District of Columbia				x	
Florida*				x	
Georgia				x	
Hawaii				x	
Idaho*				x	
Illinois*				x	
Indiana	x	x			
Iowa*	x	x			
Kansas*	x	x			
Kentucky	x	x			
Louisiana	x	x			x
Maine				x	
Maryland*	x	x			
Massachusetts*			x	x	
Michigan	x	x			
Minnesota				x	
Mississippi				x	
Missouri*				x	
Montana	x	x			
Nebraska	x	x			
Nevada*				x	
New Hampshire	x	x			
New Jersey	x	x			
New Mexico				x	
New York		x	x		x
North Carolina*	x	x			x
North Dakota				x	
Ohio*		x	x		
Oklahoma		x	x		
Oregon				x	
Pennsylvania	x	x			
Puerto Rico			x		x
Rhode Island*				x	
South Carolina*†		x	x		x
South Dakota	x	x			
Tennessee*	x	x			x
Texas*				x	
Utah				x	
Vermont				x	
Virginia*				x	
Washington*				x	
West Virginia				x	
Wisconsin†	x	x			x
Wyoming			x		

*This state also imposes a generation-skipping transfer tax.
†This state is phasing out its inheritance tax to be replaced by an estate tax for federal credit only.
Source: "State Tax Law Survey," paragraph 3302. Commerce Clearing House Inc. Fiduciary Tax Guide, 1990.

Estate versus Inheritance Tax

The federal estate tax is a tax on the transfer of property at death. Technically, the transferor (the estate) is responsible for paying the tax. State death taxes differ from an "estate" tax in that they are technically taxes on the right to receive property rather than on the right to transmit property at death. This type of tax is called an "inheritance" or "succession" tax. For example, assume that two sisters owned some property jointly. One dies, leaving all her other property to a favorite niece. If the death tax to be paid were an "estate" tax, the estate would pay that portion of the tax due from the jointly owned property, even though the sole beneficiary of the estate did not receive it. On the other hand, if the death tax to be paid were an "inheritance" tax, the surviving sister would be responsible for paying it on the jointly owned property and the niece would pay the tax due on the remaining property.

Another practical difference between an "estate" and "inheritance" tax is that the amount of the inheritance tax normally depends upon the relationship of the beneficiaries to the decedent. In an estate tax, family relationships are unimportant (with the exception of the marital deduction as discussed in Chapters Four and Five).[2] Bequests to distant relatives or unrelated persons are taxed at higher rates than bequests to closer relatives. The amount of the inheritance or succession tax in a particular estate will depend upon who is to receive money or property from the estate. Thus, if two estates are of identical size, but property in one is willed to close relatives and in the second is willed to nonrelatives, the first estate will probably pay significantly less tax than the second.

Specific Exemptions

State death taxes generally contain small, specific exemptions as compared with the large marital deduction in the federal estate tax. Most states do, however, exclude from taxation certain property that is subject to the federal estate tax. Life insurance payable to named beneficiaries (i.e., payable to anyone other than the decedent's estate) is a common example of such an exclusion.

Deductions

State death taxes generally permit the same deductions as the federal estate tax: funeral expenses, expenses of the decedent's last illness, probate expenses, claims against the estate, debts of the decedent, income taxes on income up to the time of decedent's

2. See Chapter Five, "Schedule M—Marital Deduction."

death, local property taxes due at decedent's death, executor's commissions, and attorney's fees. The same deductions may be taken on both the federal and state tax returns filed by a particular estate. States may vary on the types of deductions allowable. It is important to check the state laws on deductions when settling a new estate.

Many states permit deductions for small amounts passing to a surviving spouse or children. These deductions are usually called "family allowances" or "homestead rights" and vary widely from state to state. In Pennsylvania the family allowance is $2,000. Many states also allow inheritance taxes paid to other states and foreign countries to be taken as a deduction. A number of states permit the federal estate tax to be taken as a deduction.

Charitable Bequests

All states exempt from death tax, or permit a deduction for, transfers to charities. These usually include religious, educational, charitable, scientific, and literary institutions.

Progressive versus Flat Tax Rates

Some state inheritance taxes are imposed at flat, i.e., nonprogressive, rates. For example, Pennsylvania's inheritance tax is 6% on bequests to a decedent's spouse, parents, grandparents, sons-in-law, daughters-in-law, and lineal descendants (children, grandchildren, etc.) and 15% on bequests to all others.[3] The family exemption ($2,000) is specifically allowed as a deduction. An additional estate tax is imposed to absorb the difference between the inheritance tax and the federal tax credit. The Pennsylvania tax is a flat tax with two classifications of beneficiaries. Many states impose a progressive inheritance tax.

The word "progressive" simply means that as the size of the estate or bequest increases, the rate of tax increases. The federal estate tax and the federal income tax are examples of progressive taxes.

The California inheritance tax is the amount of the federal tax credit. This is also a progressive rate.

New York imposes a state estate tax that is computed differently for state residents and nonresidents. The nonresident tax is computed by using a fraction showing what percentage of the gross estate is New York property. If the property of a nonresident is less than $2,000, then there is no New York tax.

If the computed estate tax results in an amount less than the federal tax credit, an additional tax is computed so that the total

3. Pa.Stat.Ann., Tit. 72, §§ 2485–403 and 404 (Purdon).

amount due will always be the amount of the Federal Estate Tax credit. The additional tax only applies to New York residents. For residents all real property and tangible personal property within the state and all intangible and personal property (wherever it is located) is taxable in New York. For nonresidents only real property and tangible personal property located within the state is taxable. Intangibles not located in New York are not taxable for nonresidents.

New Jersey revised its state death tax rates in July 1988. There is no inheritance tax for spouses, parents, grandparents, children (adopted or natural), stepchildren, or any other issue of the decedent (class A beneficiaries). Class B beneficiaries, religious and charitable institutions, are fully exempt. There is a tax for other family relations, Class C beneficiaries, such as brothers and sisters, sons-in-law and daughters-in-law. Class C beneficiaries have a $25,000 exemption. Class D beneficiaries include anyone not mentioned above. They have a $500 exemption. The rates for any taxable property are progressive, from 11% to 16%. The same rates apply to both residents and nonresidents.

Many states, for simplicity, now impose an estate tax based on the amount of the federal tax credit, designed to absorb the difference between the state inheritance tax and the federal tax credit. A table showing the maximum allowable federal tax credit appears here for quick reference. As mentioned in Chapter Five, the credit is determined by taking the amount of the taxable estate (subtracting the $60,000 exemption) and referring to the table:

State Inheritance, Estate, and Gift Taxes—Maximum Federal Credit

Taxable Estate (After $60,000 Exemption) From	To	Credit =	+	%	Of Excess Over
$ 0	$ 40,000	$ 0		0	$ 0
40,000	90,000	0		0.8	40,000
90,000	140,000	400		1.6	90,000
140,000	240,000	1,200		2.4	140,000
240,000	440,000	3,600		3.2	240,000
440,000	640,000	10,000		4.0	440,000
640,000	840,000	18,000		4.8	640,000
840,000	1,040,000	27,600		5.6	840,000
1,040,000	1,540,000	38,800		6.4	1,040,000
1,540,000	2,040,000	70,800		7.2	1,540,000
2,040,000	2,540,000	106,800		8.0	2,040,000
2,540,000	3,040,000	146,800		8.8	2,540,000
3,040,000	3,540,000	190,800		9.6	3,040,000
3,540,000	4,040,000	238,800		10.4	3,540,000
4,040,000	5,040,000	290,800		11.2	4,040,000
5,040,000	6,040,000	402,800		12.0	5,040,000
6,040,000	7,040,000	522,800		12.8	6,040,000
7,040,000	8,040,000	650,800		13.6	7,040,000

State Inheritance, Estate, and Gift Taxes—Maximum Federal Credit, continued

Taxable Estate (After $60,000 Exemption)					
From	To	Credit =	+	%	Of Excess Over
8,040,000	9,040,000	786,800		14.4	8,040,000
9,040,000	10,040,000	930,800		15.2	9,040,000
10,040,000	...	1,082,800		16.0	10,040,000

Source: Department of the Treasury, Internal Revenue Service, Form 706—United States Estate and Generation Skipping Transfer Tax Return, page 7 of instructions (Revised July 1990).

Residency and Location of Property

State death taxes apply to all property owned by a resident decedent except real and tangible personal property (e.g., furniture, farm machinery, works of art, etc.) permanently located outside the state. Such property is taxed by the state in which it is located.

EXAMPLE
Determining the State(s) Where Decedent May Owe Tax

Hugo Fritz died a resident of Massachusetts. He owned a home in Massachusetts, stocks and bonds located in a safe deposit box in Massachusetts, a summer home together with furnishings in Maine, a small checking account with a Maine bank, and an automobile he customarily garaged at the Maine residence. The Maine house (real estate) and the Maine furnishings and automobile (tangible personal property permanently located in Maine) are subject to the Maine death tax. Everything else (including the intangible Maine bank account) is taxable in Massachusetts.

PROBLEMS

1. L. Priscilla Bowers lived in Illinois at the time of her death. She owned a home, fully furnished, in Chicago. She also had a home in Evanston, Illinois, which she rented out unfurnished. Ms. Bowers kept three bank accounts in Chicago.

   In addition to her properties in Illinois, Ms. Bowers owned a horse farm in Kentucky. At the farm she had $100,000 worth of machinery and equipment and seventy horses. Thirty of the horses were used for racing and, in season, would be taken from one racetrack to another. The thirty race horses are valued at $2.1 million. The other forty horses are valued at $825,000.

   Which states will properly impose death taxes and on which of Ms. Bowers's property?
2. J. Wallingford Turner was the president of Savory Soup Company when he died. Savory's headquarters are in Portland, Oregon. Mr. Turner maintained two homes, one in Portland, and the other in Salmon Creek, Washington. During the course of the year, Mr. Turner and his family divided their time equally between the two homes. Turner had driver's licenses in both Oregon and Washing-

ton, but he was not registered to vote in either state.

Turner's entire estate, except for the two houses and four cars, consists of stocks and bonds worth $1.7 million, bank accounts in Portland totaling $608,000, and bank accounts in Salmon Creek totaling $1,027.

To which state will death taxes be payable, and on what property? Is there any other information you would like to have before deciding?

HINT Refer back to "Determining Place of Domicile" in Chapter Two.

If you had trouble with Problem 2, do not feel badly. The difficult question is "Where was Turner a resident at the time of his death?" In most cases, it will be obvious where the decedent resided. This is not always so, however. A residence for death tax purposes is that place that you consider to be your permanent home. Evidence of residence are such things as owning or renting real estate, voting, being licensed to drive, belonging to civic groups, etc. Even these indicators may not be conclusive, and on a matter such as this it is best to consult your supervising attorney.

Gifts in Contemplation of Death

As discussed in Chapter Four, "Gift Tax" all transfers made from 1976 to 1981 (lifetime gift or death) were automatically included in the decedent's estate both for federal and state death taxes.

Pre-1977 Law Prior to 1977 the gifts were included only if the decedent had made a gift in "contemplation of death." In order to minimize taxes people would try to give away their property prior to death. For example, if they knew that they had terminal cancer, they could give away the bulk of their estate just before their death. The tax authorities thus established certain criteria for these gifts to determine whether a gift given away within three years of death was to be included in the taxable estate. The criteria were such things as the size of the gift in relation to the estate (the larger the gift, the greater the presumption that it was made in contemplation of death); whether the donee was the natural object of the decedent's bounty (if he or she gave it to family it could be presumed that he or she was trying to avoid a testamentary disposition and thus trying to avoid the death taxes); the donee's needs (a gift used to cover basic necessities for a donor thus might not have been a gift made to avoid taxes); the pattern of past gift giving (if the decedent had been making regular gifts to the donee, gifts made within three years of death might not be included); the decedent's health and cause of death (a decedent who died of a heart attack at age 52 with no previous health problems would be in a different position from a decedent who had lived for three years knowing he or she had terminable cancer). Obviously determining whether a gift was in contemplation of death involved a great deal of litigation as the facts in each case could be different. Therefore, the tax authorities determined that any outright transfer made after January 1982 would not be included in the decedent's estate unless the decedent retained any "powers" over the property. As mentions in Chapter Five, there are a few exceptions to this rule.

Jointly Owned Property

Between Husband and Wife Most states do not tax property held by husband and wife due to the unlimited marital deduction. If the state does not have the unlimited marital deduction, they will usually tax one-half of the jointly owned property, because one-half of the property is considered to be owned by each spouse. The jointly owned residence is almost always excluded from taxation.

Other Joint Property Often persons other than spouses own property jointly. For example, two brothers might own stocks jointly with the right of survivorship. In that situation, upon the death of one brother, the property would automatically belong to the surviving brother (regardless of any provisions in the will of the deceased brother).

In this type of situation, many states tax only the percentage share of the property owned by the decedent. In the above example this would be one-half.

Such state laws differ from the federal estate tax that presumes that the first to die owned the entire property and the estate must prove otherwise to escape tax on even a portion of the jointly owned property.

Property may, of course, be owned by more than two people. Any number may be joint tenants.

EXAMPLE
Taxation with Multiple Joint Tenants

Three unmarried sisters, Florence, Louise, and Doris purchase a house, taking title as joint tenants with right of survivorship. Assume they live in a state that taxes only the fractional share of a deceased joint tenant. Florence dies. Louise and Doris now own the property, and Florence's-estate is responsible to pay tax on one-third of the value of the house as of Florence's date of death. Some years later Louise dies. Doris is now the sole owner. Louise's estate must pay tax on one-half the value of the house as of her date of death. When Doris dies, the full value of the house as of her date of death will again be taxed.

Tax Waivers

In Chapter Three waivers were discussed in the context of transferring property from the name of the decedent to the name of the estate.[4] In some states (notably New York), the tax waiver system serves a purpose similar to that served by an Inventory in other states because it places on public record the assets of the estate. The waivers are also an integral part of the death tax scheme because taxing authorities compare the waivers against the return that is filed at a later date. To obtain waivers, the personal representative must first have been duly appointed by the court.

Community Property States

The death tax laws of the eight community property states[5] are not unlike the taxation of jointly owned property in other states. Under the community property system, a husband and wife are considered to contribute equally to the financial success of the marriage. In a case in which one spouse supports the other—for example, the husband works for a salary and the wife does not—this means that half the income earned by the husband is considered as a matter of California property law to have been earned by the wife, on the theory that her work at home and her association with her husband permits him to perform the remunerative work. In states that do not have a community property law, the earnings of a husband are entirely his, subject to his obligation to support his wife and children.

While the laws of the eight community property states differ in their details, in general, earnings of a husband or wife are considered community property and thus belong one-half to each. Gifts and inheritances received by either the husband or wife are generally considered separate property and not community property. Property acquired before marriage is considered separate property. It is frequently important, therefore, to be able to trace the source from which particular funds were derived. Some interesting tracing problems may arise if a couple has moved in and out of community property and non–community property states. Earnings obtained while living outside a community property state are not community property.

The practical effect of the community property doctrine on inheritance taxes is that if a testator dies in a community property state with $100,000 of property that derives from earnings during the marriage, one-half of that amount automatically belongs to the spouse so that the instant before the decedent's death $50,000 was

4. See Chapter Three, "Physical Control," under "Corporate and Governmental Securities."

5. Arizona, California, Idaho, Louisiana, Nevada, New Mexico, Texas, and Washington.

the spouse's property. Accordingly, at the decedent's death only $50,000 of property is transferred from the estate and in such a state there is only $50,000 to tax. As we discussed in Chapter Five, it was determined by the taxing authorities that it was not fair for decedents in community property states to effectively receive a deduction for the value of one-half of the assets in an estate where there was a surviving spouse, while all assets were included and taxed in the non–community property state. Therefore the estates of decedents dying after 1981 have an unlimited marital deduction.

PROBLEM

In this problem assume that Adam French was a resident of your home state and obtain the necessary forms to file the estate death tax return.

Adam French died on March 4, 1991, at the age of 58 years, survived by his wife Ellen, his 23-year-old daughter Sally, and his 28-year-old son William. At the time of his death, he was actively involved in Family Corporation, in which he owned 1,000 shares of common stock. These shares were subject to a binding buy-sell agreement between decedent and the corporation under which the corporation purchased the shares from decedent's estate for $224.87 per share.

Decedent owned a 1989 Oldsmobile F-85, four-door, hard-top Cutlass Supreme automobile at the time of his death. Its date-of-death value was $4,350. Various household furnishings were appraised at $10,000. In a safe deposit box owned jointly with Ellen were found 16 shares of General Motors common stock registered in decedent's name. The General Motors stock was worth $50 per share at the date of death. Decedent had a savings account at Calumet Savings Bank, in his name in trust for Dorothy Jones, his nurse. The balance of this savings account at the decedent's death was $18,150, and interest accrued to the date of his death was $350.

For investment purposes, decedent had purchased a warehouse at 100 E. Broad Street in Hillside that was appraised at his death at $225,000. Decedent and his wife lived in a house at 300 Peach Street, that they owned as tenants by the entireties that they had purchased many years ago. The house was appraised at $177,000. Decedent also had a joint savings account at Calumet Savings Bank with his daughter Sally; the date-of-death balance in this account was $5,000 and the interest accrued to date of death was $100. Decedent owned a joint checking account at Guarantors' Bank, Hillside, account no. 1-1-111, in joint names with his wife. The date-of-death balance in this checking account was $18,000. It was not an interest-bearing account.

On June 10, 1990, decedent opened a second interest-bearing checking account, account no. 0-00, at Guarantors' Bank, in the joint names of himself and his wife. The date-of-death balance in this account was $28,000. The accrued interest was $234.

Decedent owned $250,000 worth of life insurance, payable to his wife and children equally.

Decedent's will left his personal and household effects to his wife, Ellen, and three-quarters of the residue of his estate to his wife. The other one-quarter of the residue is to be divided equally between his son and daughter.

Decedent's funeral cost $3,500. At the time of his death he had unpaid bills with a department store for $750. The balance of his 1990 income tax totaled $5,000. Probate expenses totaled $1,250, and it is estimated that additional administration expenses will total $2,500.

Prepare the state death tax return and all necessary accompanying papers for your home state (the state in which you intend working as a paralegal). In most cases your state will only require that you compute the federal tax credit. However you must check your local tax laws to see if you actually have to compute the inheritance tax return or state estate tax return.

CHAPTER SEVEN

Formal Accounting

An account is a written record of transactions. For example, your bank book shows all deposits and withdrawals to "account" for the balance in the book at any given time. Businesses also keep books of account to record precisely the financial history of the business. In this way a summary of the income and expenses may be made, showing the owners why they have profits (or losses). Similarly, fiduciaries keep accounts to detail all transactions that have occurred in the handling of the estate or trust. The account will show all assets received, the various disbursements made, and the balance left for distribution. The goal of an account is to set forth these items in such a manner that anyone looking at the account will know exactly what was done with every penny that passed through the hands of the fiduciary. Only the assets actually handled by the fiduciary (probate property) are shown in the accounting. Assets such as jointly owned property and life insurance that pass automatically to the beneficiaries are not shown in the accounting because the fiduciary did not control those assets. The fiduciary's only obligation is to collect the assets for the beneficiaries (when necessary) and to value them for tax purposes.

The account serves to protect both the fiduciary and the beneficiaries of the estate or trust. From the point of view of a fiduciary, the account is the opportunity to show all who are interested in the estate or trust, including any court having jurisdiction over it, exactly what assets were received and what was done with them. This is important because a fiduciary who deals improperly with the assets of an estate or trust may, in some circumstances, be forced to repay the estate or trust personally for the losses realized. (This is known as "surcharging" the fiduciary.) If an account is filed in court and approved by the court, the fiduciary will be protected from any liability on the matters set forth in the account.[1]

On the other hand, the account also serves to protect beneficiaries because it allows them to see clearly and succinctly what has happened to the assets prior to the time a distribution is made to them. Claimants against an estate or trust, as well as beneficiaries, may compel a fiduciary to file an account in court if the fiduciary has not done so in a timely fashion. When the account is reviewed (audited) by the court, any persons interested in the estate who have objections to what the fiduciary has done, as shown in the account, may present those objections to the court. In this way persons interested in an estate or trust do not have to search for information in the way other litigants frequently do. Rather, they may compel the fiduciary to tell them exactly what has happened in the estate or trust. If the account is incomplete or improper in any respect, the court will require the fiduciary to file another, proper account.

The end product of the account is the balance available for distribution. This amount may not be too important to a pecuniary legatee who will simply receive a certain dollar sum under the will (assuming there is enough left for distribution to pay all pecuniary bequests). The balance available for distribution is, however, extremely important to the person who is to receive the residue of the estate, or some portion of the residue. If the fiduciary has made an improper investment and a loss has been sustained, the residue of the estate will, of course, be directly affected. In other cases, the assets of the estate may be insufficient to pay all the debts, administration expenses, and death taxes, with the result that there will be no balance available for distribution and some claims against the estate will not be paid in full. The account is the vehicle for showing exactly what is available.

In large estates or trusts, the accounts may run hundreds of pages and cover thousands of items of receipt and disbursement. Under these circumstances, it is clear that rather formalized rules are necessary to govern the method of accounting. These rules are based partly on statute, partly on rules adopted by local courts, and partly on custom.

The forms of fiduciary accounts vary greatly. Each state, and sometimes each county within a state, has its own distinctive form. In most states, guide books (sometimes prepared officially and issued by the courts) are available to answer technical questions about the form of an account. The purpose of this chapter is to provide the background so that a student may understand the

1. Not all accounts are filed in court. Occasionally, the fiduciary will submit an "informal" account to the interested parties. If they all agree, the formality of filing the account with the court may be waived.

general pattern of an account and will know when to seek help from an attorney or a guide book when technical problems arise.

The legal responsibility for preparing an account rests with the fiduciary. As a practical matter, however, accounts are frequently prepared by lawyers, banks, or accountants and then signed by the fiduciary. Practices vary from place to place concerning who is expected to prepare an account. In virtually every location, the attorney for an estate or trust has at least the responsibility to review the account when it has been prepared to determine whether it has complied with all statutory and other rules.

The basic pattern of a fiduciary account is to state the value of assets placed in the account, plus any increase in those assets, less any payments out of the account properly made by the fiduciary. It is sometimes said that the fiduciary is "charged" with responsibility for the assets placed in the account, plus any increase in those assets. Conversely, the fiduciary is "discharged" from responsibility for that portion that has been properly paid out.

ASSEMBLING THE NECESSARY FACTS

Checkbook

One of the first steps in estate administration[2] where there is no corporate fiduciary is to open a checking account for the estate.[3] The fiduciary should ordinarily endeavor to keep sufficient cash in this account to permit the payment of debts, administration expenses, and death taxes. An interest-bearing checking account should be used. Larger sums of cash, not needed for the estate administration expenses, should be placed in other types of accounts that may yield a higher interest rate.

To the extent possible, all disbursements on behalf of the estate should be made through this one estate checking account. Frequently, the attorney for the executor or administrator will keep the checkbook. In this way the attorney will be in a position to determine whether disbursements are proper as they are paid and also record all such disbursements to prepare eventually an account for the fiduciary to sign. While the attorney for the estate keeps the checkbook, the fiduciary is usually required to sign all checks. If the checkbook is carefully kept, there will be a complete record of all income and disbursements in the checking account

2. Frequently in this chapter references are made to estates, rather than trusts, since estate accounting is more common and often more complicated than trust accounting. However, the student should be aware that the same general accounting principles are applicable to both estates and trusts, as well as the even less common guardianship.

3. See Chapter Three for a discussion of the estate checking account.

register. In addition, it is also important to keep a separate ledger sheet in each file showing the income and disbursements. This is useful to have when preparing the tax returns as well as the accounting. It is always a good idea to cross-check your figures. When a corporate fiduciary is involved, that fiduciary will ordinarily be responsible for keeping a complete record of the cash transactions. The attorney then need only to review these records.

Capital Transactions

The checkbook only records cash transactions that go through the checking account. A variety of other financial matters takes place in the course of estate or trust administration that are not reflected by entries in the checkbook. It is therefore essential that a record be kept that will show these other matters.

Among the most important financial matters that may not appear in the checkbook are capital transactions. A capital transaction is the receipt or transfer of principal. For example, if a stock is sold by a broker and he or she immediately uses the proceeds to purchase another security, the estate will not receive a check. Whenever possible it is wise to deposit all cash in the estate checking account and then purchase the new asset. Thus, the checking account acts as a "control account." If the estate is using a broker's account, the cash for purchases and sales would be deposited in the broker's cash account. Other examples of capital transactions are stock dividends and stock splits. These do not involve a cash transaction. These capital transactions will appear on the broker's statement, or the estate will receive the new stock certificates directly if there is no broker involved.

For accounting purposes, the assets of an estate have a basis as of the date of death of the decedent. This is the fair market value of the asset on the date of death. That basis is referred to as the book value or carrying value of the assets. The fiduciary is "charged" with this date-of-death value. If the fiduciary sells an asset during the course of administration, this sale (and the resultant gain or loss) must eventually be reflected in the account. Thus, in order to be able to prepare an account, the fiduciary (or attorney) must keep accurate records of the book value of estate assets and the gains or losses realized upon sales.

One way to keep such a record is by using a "spread" sheet. This is really a ledger showing all principal assets of the estate by description along with their date-of-death values. When a sale takes place, it is noted on the spread sheet and the gain or loss may be recorded as well. When the sale involves brokers' commissions (e.g., stocks or real estate sales) the amount of the commission (which reduces the net proceeds) may also be recorded. A sample page of such a spread sheet is shown in the next Example.

EXAMPLE *Capital Transactions*

Asset	Value (per share) as of 11/19/90*	Total Value	Date of Sale and Sale price per share	Commission and other costs	Net Proceeds	Gain (Loss)
250 shares, common stock, I.B. Meat, Co., Inc. certificate No. 0873429X	high low average 17½ 17 17¼	$ 4,312.50	6/30/91 18¾	$52	$ 4,635.50	$ 323
5 shares, common stock, Fritzel Corporation, certificate No. 000742 (closely held)	per appraisal—$675	$ 3,375.00	4/7/91 $650	—	$ 3,250.00	$(125)
House and lot 192 E. Plush Ave. Corner Ketch	per appraisal—$62,000	$62,000.00	9/2/91 $68,000	$4,080—Commission $ 680—Tax	$63,240.00	$1,240
60—$1,000 Bonds, 7¼%, due 2007, United Kritz Corp.	purchased 9/16/91 at par**	$60,000.00				

*Date of Death
**Meaning, at face value

In addition to sales, it may be that the fiduciary will also purchase assets. For instance, there may be real estate that no beneficiary wants. In this case, the fiduciary may sell the real estate and invest the proceeds in stocks or bonds, or deposit the proceeds in the estate savings account, to assure a proper return. If a new investment is made, the total cost of the purchase (e.g., inclusion of commissions and charges) becomes the basis or carrying value of the asset in the estate. If this asset is later sold, the sale price is compared with this basis in order to determine whether there was a gain or loss. For example, if the proceeds from the house listed on the above spread sheet were used to buy $60,000 worth of a corporate bond, with the balance going into the estate savings account, that transaction might be shown as on the spread sheet in the Example above.[4]

Dividends and Interest

If the estate includes assets that produce income, such as dividends or interest, the fiduciary will eventually have to set forth in the account all such items of income received. Depending on the provisions of the will and the needs of the beneficiaries, the income of the estate during the period of administration may be accumulated by the executor or administrator, or it may be distributed to the appropriate beneficiaries. In any event, precise records must be kept in the checkbook or elsewhere of the exact source, date, and nature of each item of income received.

4. The bank deposit of $3,240 would be reflected in the passbook, not on the spread sheet.

If the checkbook is used as the record-keeping device, a notation should be made for each deposit showing the source of the income. Instead of, or better still, as an additional manner of record keeping, the spread sheet may be utilized by having a separate column (or columns) for dividends or other income, as the following spread sheet illustrates.

EXAMPLE *Capital Transactions, Dividends, and Other Income*

Asset	Value (per share) as of 11/19/90*	Total Value	Date of Sale and Sale price per share	Commission and other costs	Net Proceeds	Gain (Loss)	Income	Income
250 shares, common stock, I.B. Meat, Co., Inc. certificate No. 0873429X	high low average 17½ 17 17¼	$ 4,312.50	6/30/91 18¾	$ 52	$ 4,635.50	$ 323	Dividend 1/3/91— $65 Dividend 4/2/91 $65	
5 shares, common stock, Fritzel Corporation, certificate No. 000742 (closely held)	per appraisal— $675	$ 3,375.00	4/7/91 $650	—	$ 3,250.00	$(125)		
House and lot 192 E. Plush Ave. Corner Ketch	per appraisal— $62,000	$62,000.00	9/2/91 $68,000	$4,080— Commission $ 680—Tax	$63,240.00	$1,240	Monthly rental payments 4/1/91 $350 5/1/91 $350 6/2/91 $350	7/1/91 $350 8/1/91 $350 9/1/91 $350
60—$1,000 Bonds, 7¼%, due 2007, United Kritz Corp.	purchased 9/16/91 at par	$60,000.00					Interest payments 1/5/92 $1,087.50 4/6/92 $1,087.50	

*Date of death.

Obviously, the longer the estate is in administration, the more room will be necessary to record income. This should be considered when initially setting up the spread sheet. It is also possible to have a separate sheet recording nothing but income transactions. This would essentially look like a ledger sheet and might be set up in the following manner:

Income Transactions

Asset	1991	1992
I.B. Meat, Co., Inc.	Jan. 3—$65	
250 shares common stock	Apr. 2—$65	

Asset	1991	1992
Property 192 E. Plush Ave., Corner Ketch	Apr. 1—$350 May 1—$350 June 2—$350 July 1—$350 Aug. 1—$350 Sep. 1—$350	
United Kritz Corp., 7¼% Bonds due 2007 (60 at $1,000)		Jan. 5—$1,087.50 Apr. 6—$1,087.50

Non–Cash Distributions

The fiduciary or the attorney for the estate must keep records pertaining to all distributions from the estate to beneficiaries. If these distributions are in cash, they will be reflected in the checkbook. However, tangible personal property, such as jewelry or automobiles, will frequently be distributed in kind[5] to the beneficiaries immediately after death. This fact must be recorded so that it may later be reported in the account. Since it would be unusual for there to be more than a few items distributed in kind, it is not customary to keep a separate spread sheet for them. They may be included on the regular spread sheet and a notation made of the date of distribution.

A receipt should be obtained from the beneficiary at distribution. The asset should never be distributed before the fiduciary has had the opportunity to value the asset.

PRINCIPAL AND INCOME

The distinction between principal and income is crucial to estate and trust accounting. All accounts must state items of principal and income separately because it is common for beneficiaries to receive either one or the other. Even when a beneficiary receives both, good accounting practice requires that the distinction be indicated.

Principal may be defined generally as the assets owned by a decedent just prior to his death. In the case of a trust, principal would be defined as the total assets transferred by the settlor to the trustee. For example, money left by the decedent in a bank account, stocks owned at the time of death, and such things as an automobile are items of principal. Income is defined as the dividends, interest, rent, or royalties produced by the principal during the course of estate or trust administration.

A distinction between principal and income is particularly important in trust administration. Frequently the beneficiary of

5. An "in kind" distribution is when property is given out in its present state without converting the asset to cash.

income from the trust is different from the person who will ultimately receive the principal of the trust. For instance, a trust may pay the income to A for life, and upon A's death, the principal is to be distributed to B. Upon the death of A, the trustee will be called upon to file an account that must show all distributions of income made to A during life. If the trustee had improperly distributed items of principal to A, a surcharge may be assessed for the improper payments.

The principal of an estate or trust is not a fixed amount but may appreciate or depreciate. For example, under most states' law, capital gains realized from the sale of securities or other assets of a trust or estate are properly credited to principal, not to income. Hence, if a trustee purchases a stock at one price and later sells it at a higher price, the resulting gain is credited to the account of the ultimate remainderman who will receive the principal of the trust. The income beneficiary receives only the cash dividends from the stock.

The distinction between principal and income is important not only in allocating items between the two categories as they are received, but also in charging items of expense to one or the other category. In preparing the account, a trustee will show the income received from the trust assets and the various disbursements that are properly charged against the trust income. For example, the cost of collecting dividends on stock would be chargeable to income, whereas the expenses of selling or purchasing stock would be chargeable to principal. The income beneficiary, therefore, could properly object if the expense of selling stock were charged against income. Similarly, upon the death of the income beneficiary, the remainderman could properly object and surcharge the trustee if ordinary and necessary expenses for collecting dividends were charged against principal. Most expenses are easy to allocate between principal and income, but some require a legal judgment by the lawyer in charge of the case.

The question of allocating income and expense items is generally governed by state statute. However, with regard to difficult allocation problems a lawyer must often review court decisions interpreting a state's statute.

The Commissioners on Uniform State Laws sought to achieve uniformity among the states with regard to many of these problems by proposing the Uniform Principal and Income Act. This act was approved by the commissioners and the American Bar Association in 1931 and revised in 1962. As of the present time, the original act has been adopted by fourteen states,[6] and twenty-six

6. Alabama, Colorado, Illinois, Kentucky, Louisiana, Oklahoma, Pennsylvania, Tennessee, Texas, Utah, Vermont, Virginia, West Virginia, Wisconsin.

have adopted the revised act.[7] As with other so-called "uniform" laws, each state may make changes in the act when adopting it. The Revised Uniform Principal and Income Act is reprinted here. Take the time to read it over several times at least.

Revised Uniform Principal and Income Act

Section 1. Definitions. As used in this Act:

(1) "income beneficiary" means the person to whom income is presently payable or for whom it is accumulated for distribution as income;

(2) "inventory value" means the cost of property purchased by the trustee and the market value of other property at the time it became subject to the trust, but in the case of a testamentary trust the trustee may use any value finally determined for the purposes of an estate or inheritance tax;

(3) "remainderman" means the person entitled to principal, including income which has been accumulated and added to principal;

(4) "trustee" means an original trustee and any successor or added trustee.

Section 2. Duty of Trustee as to Receipts and Expenditure.

(a) A trust shall be administered with due regard to the respective interests of income beneficiaries and remaindermen. A trust is so administered with respect to the allocation of receipts and expenditures if a receipt is credited or an expenditure is charged to income or principal or partly to each—

   (1) in accordance with the terms of the trust instrument, notwithstanding contrary provisions of this Act;

   (2) in the absence of any contrary terms of the trust instrument, in accordance with the provisions of this Act; or

   (3) if neither of the preceding rules of administration is applicable, in accordance with what is reasonable and equitable in view of the interests of those entitled to income as well as of those entitled to principal, and in view of the manner in which men of ordinary prudence, discretion and judgment would act in the management of their own affairs.

(b) If the trust instrument gives the trustee discretion in crediting a receipt or charging an expenditure to income or principal or partly to each, no inference of imprudence or partiality arises from the fact that the trustee has made an allocation contrary to a provision of this Act.

Section 3. Income; Principal; Charges.

(a) Income is the return in money or property derived from the use of principal, including return received as

   (1) rent of real or personal property, including sums received for cancellation or renewal of a lease;

   (2) interest on money lent, including sums received as consideration for the

7. Alaska, Arizona, Arkansas, California, Connecticut, Florida, Hawaii, Idaho, Indiana, Kansas, Maryland, Michigan, Minnesota, Mississippi, Montana, Nevada, New Mexico, New Hampshire, New York, North Carolina, North Dakota, Oregon, South Carolina, South Dakota, Washington, Wyoming.

privilege of prepayment of principal except as provided in section 7 on bond premium and bond discount;

(3) income earned during administration of a decedent's estate as provided in section 5;

(4) corporate distributions as provided in section 6;

(5) accrued increment on bonds or other obligations issued at discount as provided in section 7;

(6) receipts from business and farming operations as provided in section 8;

(7) receipts from disposition of natural resources as provided in sections 9 and 10;

(8) receipts from other principal subject to depletion as provided in section 11;

(9) receipts from disposition of underproductive property as provided in section 12.

(b) Principal is the property which has been set aside by the owner or the person legally empowered so that it is held in trust eventually to be delivered to a remainderman while the return or use of the principal is in the meantime taken or received by or held for accumulation for an income beneficiary. Principal includes

(1) consideration received by the trustee on the sale or other transfer of principal or on repayment of a loan or as a refund or replacement or change in the form of principal;

(2) proceeds of property taken on eminent domain proceedings;

(3) proceeds of insurance upon property forming part of the principal except proceeds of insurance upon a separate interest of an income beneficiary;

(4) stock dividends, receipts on liquidation of a corporation, and other corporate distributions as provided in section 6;

(5) receipts from the disposition of corporate securities as provided in section 7;

(6) royalties and other receipts from disposition of natural resources as provided in sections 9 and 10;

(7) receipts from other principal subject to depletion as provided in section 11;

(8) any profit resulting from any change in the form of principal except as provided in section 12 on underproductive property;

(9) receipts from disposition of underproductive property as provided in section 12;

(10) any allowances for depreciation established under sections 8 and 13(a)(2).

(c) After determining income and principal in accordance with the terms of the trust instrument or of this Act, the trustee shall charge to income or principal expenses and other charges as provided in section 13.

Section 4. When Right to Income Arises; Apportionment of Income.

(a) An income beneficiary is entitled to income from the date specified in the trust instrument, or, if none is specified, from the date an asset becomes subject to the trust. In the case of an asset becoming subject to a trust by reason of a will, it becomes subject to the trust as of the date of the death of the testator even though there is an intervening period of administration of the testator's estate.

(b) In the administration of a decedent's estate or an asset becoming subject to a trust by reason of a will
   (1) receipts due but not paid at the date of death of the testator are principal;
   (2) receipts in the form of periodic payments (other than corporate distributions to stockholders), including rent, interest, or annuities, not due at the date of the death of the testator shall be treated as accruing from day to day. That portion of the receipt accruing before the date of death is principal, and the balance is income.

(c) In all other cases, any receipt from an income producing asset is income even though the receipt was earned or accrued in whole or in part before the date when the asset became subject to the trust.

(d) On termination of an income interest, the income beneficiary whose interest is terminated, or his estate, is entitled to
   (1) income undistributed on the date of termination;
   (2) income due but not paid to the trustee on the date of termination;
   (3) income in the form of periodic payments (other than corporate distributions to stockholders), including rent, interest, or annuities, not due on the date of termination, accrued from day to day.

(e) Corporate distributions to stockholders shall be treated as due on the day fixed by the corporation for determination of stockholders of record entitled to distribution or, if no date is fixed, on the date of declaration of the distribution by the corporation.

Section 5. Income Earned During Administration of a Decedent's Estate.

(a) Unless the will otherwise provides and subject to subsection (b), all expenses incurred in connection with the settlement of a decedent's estate, including debts, funeral expenses, estate taxes, interest and penalties concerning taxes, family allowances, fees of attorneys and personal representatives, and court costs shall be charged against the principal of the estate.

(b) Unless the will otherwise provides, income from the assets of a decedent's estate after the death of the testator and before distribution, including income from property used to discharge liabilities, shall be determined in accordance with the rules applicable to a trustee under this Act and distributed as follows:
   (1) to specific legatees and devisees, the income from the property bequeathed or devised to them respectively, less taxes, ordinary repairs, and other expenses of management and operation of the property, and an appropriate portion of interest accrued since the death of the testator and of taxes imposed on income (excluding taxes on capital gains) which accrue during the period of administration;
   (2) to all other legatees and devisees, except legatees of pecuniary bequests not in trust, the balance of the income, less the balance of taxes, ordinary repairs, and other expenses of management and operation of all property from which the estate is entitled to income, interest ac-

crued since the death of the testator, and taxes imposed on income (excluding taxes on capital gains) which accrue during the period of administration, in proportion to their respective interests in the undistributed assets of the estate computed at times of distribution on the basis of inventory value.

(c) Income received by a trustee under subsection (b) shall be treated as income of the trust.

Section 6. Corporate Distributions.

(a) Corporate distributions of shares of the distributing corporation, including distributions in the form of a stock split or stock dividend, are principal. A right to subscribe to shares or other securities issued by the distributing corporation accruing to stockholders on account of their stock ownership and the proceeds of any sale of the right are principal.

(b) Except to the extent that the corporation indicates that some part of a corporate distribution is a settlement of preferred or guaranteed dividends accrued since the trustee became a stockholder or is in lieu of an ordinary cash dividend, a corporate distribution is principal if the distribution is pursuant to

(1) a call of shares;

(2) a merger, consolidation, reorganization, or other plan by which assets of the corporation are acquired by another corporation; or

(3) a total or partial liquidation of the corporation, including any distribution which the corporation indicates is a distribution in total or partial liquidation or any distribution of assets, other than cash, pursuant to a court decree or final administrative order by a government agency ordering distribution of the particular assets.

(c) Distributions made from ordinary income by a regulated investment company or by a trust qualifying and electing to be taxed under federal law as a real estate investment trust are income. All other distributions made by the company or trust, including distributions from capital gains, depreciation, or depletion, whether in the form of cash or an option to take new stock or cash or an option to purchase additional shares, are principal.

(d) Except as provided in subsections (a), (b), and (c), all corporate distributions are income, including cash dividends, distributions of or rights to subscribe to shares or securities or obligations of corporations other than the distributing corporation, and the proceeds of the rights or property distributions. Except as provided in subsections (b) and (c), if the distributing corporation gives a stockholder an option to receive a distribution either in cash or in its own shares, the distribution chosen is income.

(e) The trustee may rely upon any statement of the distributing corporation as to any fact relevant under any provision of this Act concerning the source or character of dividends or distributions of corporate assets.

Section 7. Bond Premium and Discount.

(a) Bonds or other obligations for the payment of money are principal at their inventory value, except as provided in subsection (b) for discount bonds. No provision shall be made for amortization of bond premiums or for accumulation for discount. The proceeds of sale, redemption, or other disposition of the bonds or obligations are principal.

(b) The increment in value of a bond or other obligation for the payment of money payable at a future time in accordance with a fixed schedule of appreciation in excess of the price at which it was issued is distributable as income. The increment in value is distributable to the beneficiary who was the income beneficiary at the time of increment from the first principal cash available or, if none is available, when realized by sale, redemption, or other disposition. Whenever unrealized increment is distributed as income but out of principal, the principal shall be reimbursed for the increment when realized.

Section 8. Business and Farming Operations.

(a) If a trustee uses any part of the principal in the continuance of a business of which the settlor was a sole proprietor or a partner, the net profits of the business, computed in accordance with generally accepted accounting principles for a comparable business, are income. If a loss results in any fiscal or calendar year, the loss falls on principal and shall not be carried into any other fiscal or calendar year for purposes of calculating net income.

(b) Generally accepted accounting principles shall be used to determine income from an agricultural or farming operation, including the raising of animals or the operation of a nursery.

Section 9. Disposition of Natural Resources.

(a) If any part of the principal consists of a right to receive royalties, overriding or limited royalties, working interests, production payments, net profit interests, or other interests in minerals or other natural resources in, on or under land, the receipts from taking the natural resources from the land shall be allocated as follows:

(1) If received as rent on a lease or extension payments on a lease, the receipts are income.

(2) If received from a production payment, the receipts are income to the extent of any factor for interest or its equivalent provided in the governing instrument. There shall be allocated to principal the fraction of the balance of the receipts which the unrecovered cost of the production payment bears to the balance owed on the production payment, exclusive of any factor for interest or its equivalent. The receipts not allocated to principal are income.

(3) If received as a royalty, overriding or limited royalty, or bonus, or from a working, net profit, or any other interest in minerals or other natural resources, receipts not provided for in the preceding paragraphs of this section shall be apportioned on a yearly basis in accordance with this paragraph whether or not any natural resource was being taken from the land at the time the trust was established. Twenty-seven and one-half per cent of the gross receipts (but not to exceed 50% of the net receipts remaining after payment of all expenses, direct and indirect, computed without allowance for depletion) shall be added to principal as an allowance for depletion. The balance of the gross receipts, after payment therefrom of all expenses, direct and indirect, is income.

(b) If a trustee, on the effective date of this Act, held an item of depletable property of a type specified in this section, he shall allocate receipts from the property in the manner used before the effective date of this Act, but as to all depletable property acquired after the effective date of this Act by an existing or new trust, the method of allocation provided herein shall be used.

(c) This section does not apply to timber, water, soil, sod, dirt, turf, or mosses.

Section 10. Timber. If any part of the principal consists of land from which merchantable timber may be removed, the receipts from taking the timber from the land shall be allocated in accordance with section 2(a)(3).

Section 11. Other Property Subject to Depletion. Except as provided in sections 9 and 10, if the principal consists of property subject to depletion, including leaseholds, patents, copyrights, royalty rights, and rights to receive payments on a contract for deferred compensation, receipts from the property, not in excess of 5% per year of its inventory value, are income, and the balance is principal.

Section 12. Underproductive Property.

(a) Except as otherwise provided in this section, a portion of the net proceeds of sale of any part of principal which has not produced an average net income of at least 1% per year of its inventory value for more than a year (including as income the value of any beneficial use of the property by the income beneficiary) shall be treated as delayed income to which the income beneficiary is entitled as provided in this section. The net proceeds of sale are the gross proceeds received, including the value of any property received in substitution for the property disposed of, less the expenses, including capital gains tax, if any, incurred in disposition and less any carrying charge paid while the property was underproductive.

(b) The sum allocated as delayed income is the difference between the net proceeds and the amount which, had it been invested at simple interest at (4%) per year while the property was underproductive, would have produced the net proceeds. This sum, plus any carrying charges and expenses previously charged against income while the property was underproductive, less any income received by the income beneficiary from the property and less the value of any beneficial use of the property by the income beneficiary, is income, and the balance is principal.

(c) An income beneficiary or his estate is entitled to delayed income under this section as if it accrued from day to day during the time he was a beneficiary.

(d) If principal subject to this section is disposed of by conversion into property which cannot be apportioned easily, including land or mortgages (for example realty acquired by or in lieu of foreclosure), the income beneficiary is entitled to the net income from any property or obligation into which the original principal is converted while the substituted property or obligation is held. If within 5 years after the conversion the substituted property has not been further converted into easily apportionable property, no allocation as provided in this section shall be made.

Section 13. Charges Against Income and Principal.

(a) The following charges shall be made against income:

(1) ordinary expenses incurred in connection with the administration, management, or preservation of the trust property, including regularly recurring taxes assessed against any portion of the principal, water rates, premiums on insurance taken upon the interests of the income beneficiary, remainderman, or trustee, interest paid by the trustee, and ordinary repairs;

(2) a reasonable allowance for depreciation on property subject to depreciation under generally accepted accounting principles, but no allowance shall be made for depreciation of that portion of any real property used by a beneficiary as a residence or for depreciation of any property held by the trustee is not then making an allowance for depreciation;

(3) one-half of court costs, attorney's fees, and other fees on periodic judicial accounting, unless the court directs otherwise;

(4) court costs, attorney's fees, and other fees on other accountings or judicial proceedings if the matter primarily concerns the income interest, unless the court directs otherwise;

(5) one-half of the trustee's regular compensation, whether based on a percentage of principal or income, and all expenses reasonably incurred for current management of principal and application of income;

(6) any tax levied upon receipts defined as income under this Act or the trust instrument and payable by the trustee.

(b) If charges against income are of unusual amount, the trustee may by means of reserves or other reasonable means charge them over a reasonable period of time and withhold from distribution sufficient sums to regularize distributions.

(c) The following charges shall be made against principal:

(1) trustee's compensation not chargeable to income under subsections (a)(4) and (a)(5), special compensation of trustees, expenses reasonably incurred in connection with principal, court costs and attorney's fees primarily concerning matters of principal, and trustee's compensation computed on principal as an acceptance, distribution, or termination fee;

(2) charges not provided for in subsection (a), including the cost of investing and reinvesting principal, the payments on principal of an indebtedness (including a mortgage amortized by periodic payments of principal), expenses for preparation of property for rental or sale, and, unless the court directs otherwise, expenses incurred in maintaining or defending any action to construe the trust or protect it or the property or assure the title of any trust property;

(3) extraordinary repairs or expenses incurred in making a capital improvement to principal, including special assessments, but, a trustee may establish an allowance for depreciation out of income to the extent permitted by subsection (a)(2) and by section 8;

(4) any tax levied upon profit, gain, or other receipts allocated to principal notwithstanding denomination of the tax as an income tax by the taxing authority;

(5) if an estate or inheritance tax is levied in respect of a trust in which both an income beneficiary and a remainderman have an interest, any amount apportioned to the trust, including interest and penalties, even though the income beneficiary also has rights in the principal.

(d) Regularly recurring charges payable from income shall be apportioned to the same extent and in the same manner that income is apportioned under section 4.

Section 14. Application of Act. Except as specifically provided in the trust instrument or the will or in this Act, this Act shall apply to any receipt or expense received or incurred after the effective date of this Act by any trust or decedent's estate whether established before or after the effective date of this Act and whether the asset involved was acquired by the trustee before or after the effective date of this Act.

Section 15. Uniformity of Interpretation. This Act shall be so considered as to effectuate its general purpose to make uniform the law of those states which enact it.

Section 16. Short Title. This Act may be cited as the Revised Uniform Principal and Income Act.

Section 17. Severability. If any provision of this Act or the application thereof to any person or circumstance is held invalid, the invalidity does not affect other provisions or applications of the Act which can be given effect without the invalid provision or application and to this end the provisions of this Act are severable.

Section 18. Repeal. The following acts and parts of acts are repealed:

(1)
(2)
(3)

Section 19. Time of Taking Effect of This Act. This Act shall take effect on __________ .

Problem Areas

Traditionally, there have been numerous areas in trust or estate accounting where directly opposite positions may be equally plausible. It is not unusual, therefore, that courts of different states have established contradictory precedents. The Uniform Principal and Income Act (and the revision of it) may now be said to represent the majority view. It is necessary for the student from a state that has not adopted either act to ascertain what the law is in his state. (Or, if your state has modified the act when adopting it, to learn the local rules.) This may require legal research on your part or the help of your supervising attorney. Bear in mind, however, that the general state law applies only if the will or trust is silent as to allocations between principal and income.

Here are some examples of the kinds of problems that may arise in allocating income and expenses.

Stock Dividends A stock dividend is a distribution of stock by a corporation to its present shareholders instead of, or in addition to, distributions in the customary form of cash.

QUESTION

How are stock dividends to be allocated under the Revised Uniform Principal and Income Act?

Capital Gains Distributions from Mutual Funds Mutual funds are types of companies that diversify their investments in many stocks and/or bonds. A purchaser of shares in a mutual fund then obtains a small, fractional portion of the total investment portfolio of the fund. This is one way to spread risks of loss.

Mutual funds frequently distribute to their shareholders both ordinary income and a portion of the capital gains realized by the fund on the securities it has sold. Regardless of the federal income tax treatment of such payments, state law determines the allocation of capital gain distribution from mutual funds as between principal and income.

QUESTION

How does the Revised Principal and Income Act allocate distributions of capital gains from mutual funds?[8]

Expenses for Repairs to Trust or Estate Assets When a trust or estate owns buildings, problems relating to the allocation of expenses for the repair of the buildings often arise. For instance, if rental property is owned, all the ordinary and necessary expenses (and taxes) incurred in managing, maintaining, insuring, and operating the property are to be charged against the income beneficiary under the Revised Uniform Principal and Income Act.[9]

QUESTION

How does the Revised Uniform Principal and Income Act treat expenses for improvements to property owned by a trust or estate?[10]

---

8. The student should be aware of the fact that a large number of states take the exact opposite position from that of the act.

9. Section 13(a)(1).

10. The student should recognize that the act gives general guidance only. It does not answer the question of what is a "repair" or an "improvement." This is a matter that may require additional research in statutes or previously decided lawsuits.

Depreciation When a trust or estate owns a depreciable asset, the fiduciary must allocate the depreciation expense. If it is all allocated to income, the effect will be to divert a portion of normal income to the capital account. If it is all allocated to principal, the income beneficiary will receive all the normal income without a recognition of the fact that some income should be set aside to replace the depreciable asset as it decreases in value. The Revised Principal and Income Act takes a position between these two extremes. It provides for the allocation of "a reasonable" amount of depreciation as an expense against income.[11] What is reasonable will vary from one situation to another but should be geared to meet the realities of how much the asset is declining in value, its actual useful life, and what the cost of replacing it will be.

DISBURSEMENTS AND DISTRIBUTIONS

One of the requirements of an account is to show all disbursements and distributions properly. The distinction between the two is important. A distribution is a payment to a beneficiary of all or a portion of his share of the estate or trust. Any other payment out of an estate or trust is a disbursement.

Disbursements

Any tax payment, administration expense, fee, commission, or other payment of this kind is a disbursement. Some accounts divide disbursements only between principal disbursements and income disbursements, while others break them down into detailed categories. Generally, disbursements are stated in chronological order within each category.

Frequently, the statement of disbursements will follow the order for priorities of payments under state law when there are insufficient assets to pay all creditors. While state law will vary, we shall review the various types of disbursements that are typically preferred.

Administrative Expenses[12] Administration expenses include filing fees, court costs, legal advertising, rental of a safe deposit box to hold securities or other valuables, notary fees, appraisal fees, storage costs, attorneys' fees, and any other necessary and proper costs or expenses incurred in the administration of the estate or trust.

Generally, the bills for these expenses (like most other expenses) will be paid through the estate or trust checking account.

11. Section 13(a)(2).

12. See Chapters Three and Five, for a further discussion of administration expenses.

This serves to keep records centralized and easy to assemble at the time the account is prepared. In addition, copies of all bills, with receipts of payment, should also be kept in one place to serve as a cross-verification against the checkbook.

Normally, bills for administration expenses will be paid as they are incurred. Counsel fees and commissions to executors are normally paid near the end of the administration of an estate since they are not earned entirely until the estate is closed. Commissions to trustees are generally paid annually, or even less frequently, based on income of the trust for the preceding period.

It is an important job of the estate accountant to keep complete and accurate records of all disbursements, including the date each disbursement is made, the name of the person or entity paid, and the purpose for which the payment was made. Each of these three aspects will eventually have to be stated in the account.

Payments to Family Members Under the law of many states, allowances are made for certain family members. For example, under Pennsylvania law, if the decedent was residing with a spouse, parent, or child at the time of death, that person (or persons) receives $2,000 from the estate. This is not considered a bequest (in which case it would be a "distribution" when paid), but rather a debt of the estate, entitled to be deducted from the gross estate in calculating the state inheritance tax due.

Funeral Expenses The cost of providing a funeral for the decedent, including the funeral director's fee, a grave plot, and grave monument, is typically given a high priority for payment in most states. These expenses may be grouped separately in the account.

Other Debts and Taxes Following the various preferred claims, almost all other debts are grouped in the same category of preference and are shown in the account in the chronological order in which they were paid.

As a general rule, deductions for debts and administration expenses are allowed in computing death taxes.[13] Death taxes will, therefore, normally be payable only if there is a positive balance in the estate after payment of all debts and administration expenses. Death taxes, broken down as to whether they are federal or state, may be shown in the account immediately following all other categories of disbursements.

13. See Chapter Five and Chapter Six.

Distributions

"Distributions" follow "disbursements" in the account. Distributions are payments of money or transfers of property made to the beneficiaries of an estate or trust pursuant to the terms of the will or trust (or under the intestate statute when a decedent dies without a valid will).

While the fiduciary will be bound by the instrument or the law regarding the distributions that are to be made, fiduciaries often have a considerable amount of discretion regarding when distributions are to be made. In exercising this discretion, the fiduciary should consider the tax brackets of the beneficiaries and their needs, the impact of distributions during the period of administration on estate taxes, and the degree of precision with which the fiduciary can identify the eventual beneficiaries of the estate.[14] (For example, if the language of the will is ambiguous, the executor may want to file the account and have the estate formally audited and the will interpreted by the court before actually making any distributions. Usually, however, long before filing the accounts, the fiduciary will know who are to be the beneficiaries of the estate.) Depending on the needs of the beneficiaries and the tax situation, the fiduciary may begin making distributions well in advance of filing the account.

Distributions must be fully recorded in the estate checkbook or other records. A pecuniary legacy will usually be paid by check from the estate account and will, therefore, appear in the checkbook. An item of tangible personal property, on the other hand, will not appear in the checkbook and hence the accountant must note such a distribution in other estate records (such as the spread sheet shown in this chapter). The record will show that such an item of tangible personal property was distributed at its carrying value, with the result that no gain or loss was incurred.

In most states real estate is accounted for separately from tangible personal property. As is true with other aspects of the accounting process, it is necessary to learn the local rules and practices.

Pecuniary and specific legacies will usually be paid early in the period of estate administration. They are charged to principal. If a pecuniary legacy (a cash gift made by the will) remains unpaid for a long period, usually after one year, the laws of most states provide that the estate becomes liable to pay interest on the legacy. The account must show the legacy itself as charged to principal when paid, and it must show any interest paid thereon as charged to income.

14. These are matters to be considered by the supervising attorney.

A specific legacy (a gift of personal property other than cash) or a specific devise (a gift of real estate) on the other hand carries with it all income produced by the specifically bequeathed or devised property from the date of death. Hence, the devisee of real estate gets all income produced by the real estate during the period of estate administration and, consequently, is responsible for all expenses relating to that real estate during the course of estate administration. For this reason, the income and expenses relating to specifically bequeathed or devised property are always separated in an account from those not relating to such property.

Any income from the estate that does not go to particular beneficiaries as outlined above usually passes under the residuary clause of the will to that beneficiary who is entitled to "all the rest of my estate, of whatever kind and wherever situate." This income sometimes will be paid by the executor to the residuary beneficiaries as it accrues during the course of estate administration. Frequently, there will be income tax reasons for accumulating such income rather than distributing it. Such decisions require careful tax planning.

Frequently, the will gives the executor the power to distribute estate assets either in cash or in kind. Normally the fiduciary will consult the beneficiaries in making such choices and not sell any assets (unless needed to pay taxes) without their approval. In the event estate assets are sold during the period of administration, an entry must appear in the estate records showing the proceeds of sale. Eventually the account will show whether there was a gain or loss on the sale.

Upon final distribution of all estate assets, the estate books are closed. This final distribution may take place either prior to the filing of the account or afterward. Usually, the account will show some distributions as having been made, and it will also show the balance yet remaining for distribution. Frequently, the account will show pecuniary legacies and specific legacies and devises as having been distributed. Perhaps some advance distributions of the residuary estate will have been made, but usually there will be a substantial portion of the residuary estate shown as available for distribution but not yet distributed. (In some states such as Virginia the final accounting must show a zero balance prior to court approval.) In reviewing the account and making a determination of its propriety, the court will then award the balance shown as available for distribution to the persons entitled under the will, trust, or intestate law. If the estate is complicated, it may be necessary for the fiduciary, in addition to filing the account, to file a schedule of distribution that will show the court precisely how the various assets listed in the account as available for distribution are actually to be divided for purposes of distribution.

BALANCING AN ACCOUNT AND RECONCILING IT WITH ASSETS ON HAND

As with general business bookkeeping, the account of an estate or trust must be internally consistent, that is, it must balance.[15] Actually, two portions of the account should balance separately; the principal portion and the income portion. Each of these will show certain receipts and certain disbursements, leaving a balance available for distribution. This balance must then reconcile with the actual assets that the executor, administrator, or trustee has on hand. Such assets on hand are generally shown in a separate part of the account entitled "Balance composed of." This item will include the actual assets that the fiduciary controls, plus it will state any distributions that the fiduciary has made. The total of the assets remaining in the hands of the fiduciary and the assets distributed under the terms of the will or trust should equal the balance obtained by subtracting the disbursements made from the receipts.

EXAMPLE
Asset Reconciliation

The executor of an estate has received cash in several bank accounts, totaling $5,127.98, personal property valued at $500, and stocks valued at $2,550 (which have been sold by the executor). The total receipts of principal would then be $8,177.98. Of this sum, assume $4,500 has been spent for things like funeral expenses, debts of the decedent, and administration costs. There would then be a balance left for distribution of $3,677.98 according to the account. (No distributions have yet been made.) This figure should match what is on deposit in the estate checking and/or savings account.

Now, assume that income as produced in the form of interest from banks and stock dividends (received before the stock was sold) and that this income totals $78.05. No expenses have been incurred associated with the income. Adding the income to the balance of principal, the executor should now have $3,756.03 on deposit, available for distribution.

These transactions would be thoroughly detailed in the account. A reconciliation might look like this:

Principal		
Receipts	$8,177.98	
Disbursements	4,500.00	
Balance		$3,677.98
Income		
Receipts	78.05	
Disbursements	0	
Balance		78.05
TOTAL		3,756.03

15. It may be helpful for the student to review at this point the discussion on bookkeeping in Chapter Three.

Balance Composed of Cash on deposit at the Morgan Bank	
Checking Account	556.03
Savings Account	3,200.00
	$3,756.03

WAIVER OF INCOME ACCOUNTING

In some jurisdictions, accountings are required in trusts every year or every two years. In others, accountings are rendered in trusts only when there is some particular reason for doing so, such as the death or resignation of a trustee or death of an income beneficiary. In such an event, the income beneficiary would have the right to require the trustee to file an accounting showing that the trustee in fact paid to the income beneficiary the income properly required under the law. In the jurisdictions that do not require annual accountings, however, the trust may have run for as much as forty or fifty years without an accounting. Under these circumstances, accounting for the income of the trust over this many years produces an extremely bulky account that is a tremendous task to prepare as well as to read. If the income beneficiary has been receiving periodic statements of the trust income and disbursements, although not complete accountings, throughout the period of the trust, he or she may well be satisfied that the trustee has been proceeding properly. In these circumstances, very frequently the income beneficiary will waive the right to an accounting concerning the income of the trust. The trustee may then limit the accounting to principal only—certainly a much more manageable task. A typical form of waiver of an income accounting appears below.

EXAMPLE
Waiver of Income Accounting

I, LYDIA LYONS, widow of LEWIS LYONS, and income beneficiary of this trust, hereby acknowledge receipt of periodic statements of income from the trustee of this trust since October 23, 1959, which was the closing date of the last accounting, and I hereby waive any rights I may have to require an income accounting at this time or at any future time with respect to the period covered by the attached account.

Intending to be legally bound hereby, I have hereunto set my hand and seal this _____ day of ______________, 1992.

/s/ Lydia Lyons
____
[Seal]

Sworn to and subscribed before me this _____ day of 1992.
Notary Public

EXAMINATION OF FIDUCIARY ACCOUNTS

The rules governing the form of accounts are derived from statutes, rules adopted by courts and by tradition. Sometimes it is the part that is governed by tradition that is most difficult to change. The goal is a clear, accurate statement of the administration of an estate. Uniformity of style is imposed to make it easier for a judge to audit an account and know where in each account to find the items of information that are important for review. Nevertheless, virtually all principal accounts will follow this format:

		Disbursements
		+
Assets received by accountant		Distributions
+		+
Appreciation of assets	=	Depreciation of assets
+		+
Income		Assets remaining

The student should study the standard format for principal accounts carefully. When reviewing sample accounts, the student should attempt to fit the various sections of the account into the general headings in the diagram.

The Supreme Court of Pennsylvania adopted an account form as recommended by the Committee of National Fiduciary Accounting Standards effective January 1, 1984. All accounts in Pennsylvania prepared after January 1, 1985, should be prepared in accordance with the National Standard form. (Please note that many other states as well as Pennsylvania use the National Standard accounting form.)

To reflect the basic concept of the National Standards accounting project (prepared in 1983), The Fiduciary Accounting Standards Committee stated the fiduciary accounting principles excerpted here.[16]

1. Accounts should be stated in a manner that is understandable by persons who are not familiar with practices and terminology peculiar to the administration of estates and trusts.
2. A fiduciary account shall begin with a concise summary of its purpose and content.
3. A fiduciary account shall contain sufficient information to put the interested parties on notice as to all significant transactions affecting administration during the accounting period.

16. "The fundamental objective of an account should be to provide essential and useful information in a meaningful form to the parties interested in the accounting process. It is also important that the account should be sufficiently simple to enable its preparation without unreasonable expense to the fund (estate), or undue distraction from the ongoing administration of the estate." It is recommended that the student review the committee report in its entirety when studying the National Standard accounting format. These excerpts are intended to be only a brief overview of the report.

4. A fiduciary account shall include both carrying values—representing the value of assets at acquisition by the fiduciary—and current values at the beginning and end of the accounting period. (Note in the model account the carrying value is referred to as "fiduciary acquisition value." An executor's first account will normally show the date of death value as the fiduciary acquisition value.)
5. Gains and losses incurred during the accounting period shall be shown separately in the same schedule.
6. The account shall show significant transactions that do not affect the amount for which the fiduciary is accountable.[17]

Some transactions such as a stock split, purchase of an investment for the estate, or change of a corporate name do not result in a dollar change. However these events should also be noted in the account on an information schedule incorporated into the account. Two such schedules are typically shown as (1) Investments Made—where the same money may be used for a series of investments, thus the purchases are not totaled; and (2) Changes in Investment Holdings—all changes affecting each individual asset such as IBM stock splits or stock dividends are shown on this schedule.

An example of an account in the National Standards form is provided.[18]

EXAMPLE
Model Executor's Account (National Standards Format)

FIRST AND FINAL ACCOUNT OF
William C. Doe, Executor
For
ESTATE OF John Doe, Deceased

Date of Death:	November 14, 1978
Date of Executor's Appointment:	November 24, 1978
*First Complete Advertisement of Grant of Letters:	December 1, 1978
Accounting for the Period:	November 24, 1978 to November 30, 1979
Gross Estate:	$165,614.16**

Purpose of Account: William C. Doe, Executor, offers this account to

17. Reprinted from *Forms for Use Before the Register of Wills and the Orphans' Court Division in Philadelphia*, Fidelity Bank Financial Management Department (a 1985 revision of the original work of the late David G. Hunter, Judge of the Orphans' Court of Philadelphia County, prepared by the Probate and Trust Law Section of the Philadelphia Bar Association).

18. The exact format of accounts varies. The example given here illustrates the various parts of an account. Do not assume, however, that in your state, or county, for that matter, this same form is followed. The paralegal must check his or her local accounting practices to see if their particular state has adopted the National Standard.

* In Pennsylvania the date of first advertisement of the grant of letters should be shown after the date of the personal representative's appointment.

** Some local rules require inclusion of this item.

acquaint interested parties with the transactions that have occurred during his administration.

The account also indicates the proposed distribution of the estate.

It is important that the account be carefully examined. Requests for additional information or questions or objections can be discussed with:

[Name of Executor, Counsel or other appropriate person]

[address and telephone number]

SUMMARY OF ACCOUNT

	Page	**Current Value**	**Fiduciary Acquisition Value**
*Proposed Distribution to Beneficiaries	10	$102,974.56	$ 90,813.96
Principal			
Receipts	3-4		$160,488.76
Net Gain (or Loss) on Sales or Other Disposition	5		2,662.00
			$163,150.76
Less Disbursements:			
Debts of Decedent	6	$ 485.82	
Funeral Expenses	6	1,375.00	
Administration Expenses	6	194.25	
Federal and State Taxes	6	5,962.09	
Fees and Commissions	6-7	11,689.64	19,706.80
Balance before Distributions			$143,443.96
Distributions to Beneficiaries	8		52,630.00
Principal Balance on Hand	8		$90,813.96
For Information:			
Investments Made	9		
Changes in Investment Holdings	9		
Income			
Receipts	10		$ 2,513.40
Less Disbursements	10		178.67
Balance Before Distributions			$ 2,334.73
Distributions to Beneficiaries	10		2,334.73
Income Balance on Hand			0
Combined Balance on Hand			$90,813.96

* Optional—for use if applicable.

RECEIPTS OF PRINCIPAL

Assets Listed in Inventory (Valued as of Date of Death)		**Fiduciary Acquisition Value**
Cash:		
First National Bank—checking account	$ 516.93	
Prudent Saving Fund Society—savings account	2,518.16	
Cash in possession of decedent	42.54	$ 3,077.63
Tangible Personal Property:		
Jewelry—		
1 pearl necklace		515.00
Furniture—		
1 antique highboy	$ 2,000.00	
1 antique side table	60.00	
1 antique chair	55.00	2,115.00
Stocks:		
200 shs. Home Telephone & Telegraph Co., common	$25,000.00	
50 shs. Best Oil Co., common	5,000.00	
1,000 shs. Central Trust Co., capital	50,850.00	
151 shs. Electric Data Corp., common	1,887.50	
50 shs. Fabulous Mutual Fund	1,833.33	
200 shs. XYZ Corporation, common	6,000.00	90,570.83
Realty:		
Residence—86 Norwood Road West Hartford, CT		50,000.00
Total Inventory		$146,278.46

	Receipts Subsequent to Inventory (Valued When Received)		
2/22/79	Proceeds of Sale—Best Oil Co., rights to subscribe received 2/15/79	$ 50.00**	
3/12/79	Fabulous Mutual Fund, capital gains dividend received in cash	32.50	
5/11/79	Refund of overpayment of 1978 U.S. individual income tax	127.80	
9/25/79	From Richard Roe, Ancillary Administrator, net proceeds on sale of oil and gas leases in Jefferson Parish, Louisiana	10,000.00	$10,210.30

**Proceeds of sale of rights may be treated as an additional receipt, as illustrated here, or may be applied in reduction of carrying value as illustrated on page T-8 [Supplement p. 43] of the Model Trustee's Account. Either method, consistently applied, is acceptable.

Adjustment to Carrying Values

Increased value of 200 shs. XYZ Corporation, common stock upon audit of Federal Estate Tax Return:

Adjusted value upon audit	$10,000.00	
Value per Inventory	6,000.00	$ 4,000.00
Total Receipts of Principal		$160,488.76

Note: To facilitate preparation, the accountant may prefer to detail the starting balance by attaching a copy of the inventory as an exhibit. (This would be inappropriate if the inventory is prepared in a form that includes substantial extraneous material or does not list assets in an orderly manner.) The opening entry would then read:

"Assets Listed in Inventory per copy attached $146,278.46"

GAINS AND LOSSES ON SALES OR OTHER DISPOSITIONS

			Gain	**Loss**
2/7/79	100 shs. Home Telephone & Telegraph Co., common			
	Net Proceeds	$14,025.00		
	Fiduciary Acquisition Value	12,500.00	$1,525.00	
3/15/79	1,000 shs. Central Trust Co., capital			
	Net Proceeds	27,467.00		
	Fiduciary Acquisition Value	25,425.00	2,042.00	
3/15/79	200 shs. XYZ Corporation, common			
	Fiduciary Acquisition Value	10,000.00		
	Net Proceeds	9,000.00		$1,000.00
5/21/79	35 shs. Electric Data Corp., common			
	Net Proceeds	530.00		
	Fiduciary Acquisition Value	437.50	92.50	
7/20/79	$10,000 U.S. Treasury Bonds, 3%, due 7/1/82			
	Net Proceeds	10,000.00		
	Fiduciary Acquisition Value	9,997.50	2.50	
	Total Gains and Losses		$3,662.00	$1,000.00
	Less Loss		1,000.00	
	Net gain		$2,662.00	

DISBURSEMENTS OF PRINCIPAL

Debts of Decedent

1/25/79	John T. Hill, M.D., professional services	$250.00
4/12/79	State Tax Commissioner, 1978 state capital gains tax	156.00
1/25/79	Thomas Pharmacy, prescriptions	23.82

2/1/79	Sanders Hardware, purchases per bill dated 12/15/78		56.00	$ 485.82
	Funeral Expenses			
1/10/79	Smith Funeral Home, services		1,200.00	
2/15/79	Jones Memorials, grave marker		175.00	1,375.00
	Administration Expenses			
11/14/78	Clerk of Court, probate costs		72.00	
2/22/79	Henry Smith, appraisal of jewelry and antiques		50.00	
11/16/79	Arden, Miles & Solomon, disbursements		56.00	
	Various miscellaneous affidavits, registered mail, toll telephone charges and other costs		16.25	194.25
	Federal and State Taxes			
8/13/79	State Tax Commissioner, state death tax		2,501.33	
8/13/79	Internal Revenue Service, federal estate tax		2,663.29	
11/15/79	Internal Revenue Service, U.S. fiduciary income tax for fiscal year ending 7/31/79 (attributable to capital gains)		283.84	
11/23/79	Internal Revenue Service, deficiency in Federal Estate Tax	$505.24		
	interest 8/14/79 to 11/24/79	8.39	513.63	5,962.09
	Fees and Commissions			
11/16/79	Albert Schryver, Esq., fee as Guardian ad litem		375.00	
11/16/79	William C. Doe, Executor's principal commission 5% on $50,000 4% on $50,000 3% on $60,488		6,314.64	
11/16/79	Arden, Miles & Solomon, attorney's fees		5,000.00	11,689.64
				$19,706.80

Note: In Pennsylvania there should be a separate heading for the family exemption.

In all cases fees and commissions shall be shown under a separate heading. Other disbursements, including the family exemption, need not be separated unless the estate is insolvent in which case disbursements shall be classified as provided by Section 3392 of the Probate, Estates and Fiduciaries Code.

DISTRIBUTIONS OF PRINCIPAL TO BENEFICIARIES

	TO: Janet Doe, in satisfaction of gift under Article FIRST of Will		
12/1/78	1 pearl necklace	$ 515.00	
	1 antique highboy	2,000.00	
	1 antique side table	60.00	
	1 antique side chair	55.00	$ 2,630.00
	TO: Janet Doe, in satisfaction of gift under Article SECOND of Will		
12/1/78	Residence—86 Norwood Road West Hartford, CT		50,000.00
	Total Distributions of Principal to Beneficiaries		$52,630.00

PRINCIPAL BALANCE ON HAND*

	Current Value 12/10/79 or as noted	Fiduciary Acquisition Value
Cash	$ 5,305.63	$ 5,305.63
Stocks:		
50 shs. Best Oil Co., common	4,500.00	5,000.00
1,000 shs. Central Trust Co., capital—value at most recent sale, 9/18/79	32,168.76	25,425.00
116 shs. Electric Data Corp., common—not traded, value per company books, 12/29/78	1,684.00	1,450.00
50 shs. Fabulous Mutual Fund	4,016.17	1,833.33
200 shs. Home Telephone & Telegraph Co., common	16,000.00	12,500.00
$40,000 U.S. Treasury Bills due 12/14/79	39,300.00	39,300.00
	$102,974.56	$90,813.96

* The composition of the principal or income balances not in the form of cash could be advanced to follow immediately after "Summary of Account" and thus provide immediately the information of primary interest to all parties reviewing the account.

INFORMATION SCHEDULES—PRINCIPAL

			Cost
	Investments Made		
2/1/79	$10,000 U.S. Treasury Bonds, 3%	$10,022.50	
	Less accrued interest collected 6/29/79	25.00	$ 9,997.50
9/14/79	$40,000 U.S. Treasury Bills, due 12/14/79		39,300.00
	Changes in Investment Holdings Central Trust Co.		
11/14/78	1,000 shs. Capital stock, par $5 inventoried		$50,850.00
1/15/79	1,000 shs. additional received in 2-1 split, ___ par reduced to $2.50		
	2,000 shs. par $2.50 carried at		50,850.00
3/15/78	1,000 shs. sold, carried at		25,425.00
	1,000 shs. remaining, carried at		$25,425.00
	Home Telephone & Telegraph Co.		
11/14/78	200 shs. common par $10, inventoried		$25,000.00
2/7/79	100 shs. sold, carried at		12,500.00
	100 shs. remaining, carried at		12,500.00
3/30/79	100 shs. additional received in 2-1 split, ___ par reduced to $5		
	200 shs. par $5 carried at		$12,500.00

RECEIPTS OF INCOME

Dividends			
Best Oil Co., common			
1/2/79 to 10/2/79—50 shs.		$ 20.00	
Central Trust Co., common			
1/15/79—2,000 shs.	$600.00		
4/13/79 to 10/15/79—1,000 shs.	900.00	1,500.00	
Electric Data Corp., common			
12/29/78 to 3/30/79—151 shs.	30.20		
6/29/79 to 9/28/79—116 shs.	23.20	53.40	
Fabulous Mutual Fund			
3/12/79 to 9/12/79—50 shs.		140.00	
Home Telephone & Telegraph Co., common			
2/1/79—200 shs.	225.00		
5/1/79 to 11/1/79—200 shs. (after stock split)	450.00	675.00	$2,388.40

Interest			
U.S. Treasury Bonds, 3%, due 7/1/82			
6/29/79—$10,000	150.00		
Less: accrued interest paid on purchase 2/1/79	(25.00)	125.00	125.00
	Total		$2,513.40

DISBURSEMENTS OF INCOME

11/15/79	U.S. Fiduciary Income Tax for fiscal year ended 7/31/79 (allocable to income)	$ 53.00
	To be paid:	
	William C. Doe—Executor's income commission 5% on $2,513.40	125.67
		$178.67

DISTRIBUTIONS OF INCOME TO BENEFICIARIES

	TO: William C. Doe, Trustee under Article FOURTH (A) for Walter Doe	
11/16/79	Cash	$1,167.37
	TO: Sharon Doe	
11/16/79	Cash	1,167.36
	Total	$2,334.73

PROPOSED DISTRIBUTIONS TO BENEFICIARIES

	Current Value 12/10/79 or as noted	**Fiduciary Acquisition Value**
Per Article FOURTH (A) of Will:		
TO: William C. Doe, Trustee for Walter Doe		
25 shs. Best Oil Co., common	$ 2,250.00	$ 2,500.00
500 shs. Central Trust Co., capital	16,084.38*	12,712.50
58 shs. Electric Data Corp., common	842.00**	725.00
25 shs. Fabulous Mutual Fund	2,008.09	916.67
100 shs. Home Telephone & Telegraph Co., common	8,000.00	6,250.00
$20,000 U.S. Treasury Bills, due 12/14/79	19,650.00	19,650.00
Cash	2,652.81	2,652.81
	$51,487.28	$45,406.98

* Central Trust Co.—valued at most recent sale, 9/18/79.

** Electric Data Corp.—not traded, valued per company books 12/29/78.

	Current Value 12/10/79 or as noted	Fiduciary Acquisition Value
Per Article FOURTH (B) of Will:		
TO: Sharon Doe		
25 shs. Best Oil Co., common	$ 2,250.00	$ 2,500.00
500 shs. Central Trust Co., capital	16,084.38*	12,712.50
58 shs. Electric Data Corp., common	842.00**	725.00
25 shs. Fabulous Mutual Fund	2,008.09	916.67
100 shs. Home Telephone & Telegraph Co., common	8,000.00	6,250.00
$20,000 U.S. Treasury Bills, due 12/14/79	19,650.00	19,650.00
Cash	2,652.81	2,652.81
	$ 51,487.28	$45,406.98
Total	$102,974.56	$90,813.96

WILLIAM C. DOE, Executor under the Last Will and Testament of JOHN DOE, deceased, hereby declares under oath [penalties of perjury] that he has fully and faithfully discharged the duties of his office; that the foregoing First and Final Account is true and correct and fully discloses all significant transactions occurring during the accounting period; that all known claims against the estate have been paid in full; that, to his knowledge, there are no claims now outstanding against the Estate; and that all taxes presently due from the estate have been paid.

____
WILLIAM C. DOE
Executor

†Subscribed and sworn to
by WILLIAM C. DOE before
me this _____ day of _______________, 19_____

____
Notary Public

*Central Trust Co.—valued at most recent sale, 9/18/79.

**Electric Data Corp.—not traded, valued per company books 12/29/78.

†Execution under oath before a notary or under penalty of perjury is optional, depending on rules of the local jurisdiction.

The above accounting was reprinted from the *Pennsylvania Fiduciary Guide, 1990 Supplement*, Code Section 15.7.

Preparation of an Accounting

Cover Page Various facts relating to the estate, including particularly the dates covered by the account, are shown on the first page, usually called the "cover" page, of the account. The cover page should disclose the name of the executor and of the estate, the date of death, the date of qualification, accounting period, and the purpose. The summary and index make it easy to tell at a glance how much money is involved in each category (e.g., principal receipts, income disbursements) and the page on which the full details appear.

Composition of Net Balances Under this heading are listed all assets held by the accountant at the time of the filing of the account. The principal assets are shown first, followed by those assets that represent the income of the estate.

Here as throughout the account, the items sharing a common factor are grouped together and differentiated from other items in the account. Each class of assets is titled and the title is set off and underlined for the convenience of both the preparer and the reader of the account.

Receipts of Principal Under this heading, reference is usually made to the inventory previously filed in the estate.[19] The first account should detail the items received by the fiduciary. Frequently, the inventory itself will be attached to the account for ready reference.

Following the amount inventoried, subsequent receipts are shown and any adjustments in the inventory values or any "write-offs"[20] of assets are listed. Assets received since the filing of the inventory are also shown. The sum of these two items is the total receipts of principal.

Gains and Losses on Sales or Other Dispositions When the fiduciary has sold assets of the estate (or trust) during its administration, they must be listed. The inventory value and the net amount received from the sale are compared to determine if there was a net gain or net loss. The net gains and net losses are shown in separate columns, and each column is totaled individually. The difference between the totals of the two columns is the net gain or net loss for all conversions. This figure (total net gain of $2,662.00 in our example) is then added in the summary (on the cover page of the account) to principal receipts. The sum of principal receipts and net gain (or net loss) is termed the "adjusted balance in the summary."

Disbursements of Principal As long as there are sufficient funds in the estate to pay all expenses and taxes, the order of preference

19. The inventory of the estate in our example follows the last page of the account.
20. Subtracting worthless assets from the value of the estate.

under law[21] is not important and the account is not set up to reflect such preferences. There is a single list of all disbursements according to the date paid. If several payments have been made to the same recipient, they may be grouped together showing the various dates of distribution. This is not done in our example, but if it were, it would appear as follows:

Register of Wills

7-1-91	Probate and Short Certificates	$ 50.00
8-10-91	Certified Copy of Will	3.00
9-4-91	Inventory filing fee	6.00
10-4-91	Pa. Inheritance Tax-gross $9,473.68 less discount ($473.68)	9,000.00
3-28-92	Balance of Pa. Inheritance Tax	624.04
	Filing fee-Statement of Debts and Deductions	3.00

The list of disbursements shown in our example is typical of those that will ordinarily be encountered in the administration of an estate.

If the estate were insolvent, the accountant would list the various claims according to their priorities under law in general groupings such as administration expenses, preferred debts, taxes, and other debts.

In the example shown, the total of all disbursements ($19,706.80) is subtracted in the summary from the principal receipts and the gains and losses. ($163,150.76). The difference is called the "balance before distributions," representing the amount that is to be distributed to the beneficiaries of the estate.

Principal Distributions to Beneficiaries If distributions have been made prior to the filing of the account, a list is included showing the date, recipient, and amount of each distribution. The listing may be either by date or by beneficiary. The total of distributions prior to the filing of the account in our example is $52,630.00, which is subtracted from the balance before distributions in the summary, to leave a balance of $90,813.96 in principal yet to be distributed.

Principal Balance on Hand This shows an itemized list of all principal assets still held by the executor at the end of the accounting period. All assets should show both the fiduciary acquisition value as well as the value at the end of the accounting period. The beneficiary can thus determine whether the assets have increased or decreased in value during the period of the account.

21. See Chapter Nine for a discussion of preferences in distributions.

Information Schedules—Principal Investments Made Since the fiduciary is charged with the obligation of preserving capital and obtaining a fair return on assets, it is normal that investments of a short-term nature will be made during the administration of the estate. These investments are listed in the account to show how the fiduciary has preserved assets. For each investment, the date, the property acquired, and the money paid for it are recorded. The individual investments are not totaled and shown in the Summary because the same funds are normally invested over and over again. The return on the investments is reflected in that portion of the account showing Income Receipts.

Changes in Investment Holdings—Capital Changes Occasionally, principal assets held in the estate change in form. A capital changes schedule is used to record such changes, e.g., stock splits, stock dividends, or withdrawals from the estate bank account.

Like the investments schedule, the changes in investment holdings is not totaled and carried forward to the cover page. The information shown is, however, necessary to allow the reader of the account to trace and to evaluate the accountant's handling of assets from the date of the decedent's death to the date of the filing of the account.

Receipts of Income On this schedule are listed the various dividends on stocks and interest from bank deposits and treasury bills. Although our example does not contain any income-producing real estate, rental receipts from real property would also be included here.

The accountant may group the income receipts by sources and list each receipt chronologically by source. If the items of income are few in number, the accountant may simply prefer to list the receipts chronologically.

Disbursements of Income Following income receipts, disbursements relating to the production of income are listed. These may include fees and expenses (such as bank charges and broker's commissions) as well as taxes on the income and commissions to the fiduciary.

The total of income disbursements is subtracted from income receipts on the summary to yield the total income available for distribution, shown on the summary as "balance before distributions."

Income Distributions to Beneficiaries Any distributions of income that have been made prior to the filing of the account must be listed just as distributions of principal are. Thus, this schedule shows the dates, persons receiving the distributions, and their amounts. The total of those distributions is subtracted from the balance before distributions on the summary to show the income balance remaining, which will be distributed to the beneficiaries of the estate.

In our example, all income earned during the period of the account was distributed. Therefore there was no income balance on hand. If any income assets remained, they would be shown on another schedule of Income Balance on Hand and itemized.

Proposed Distributions to Beneficiaries A distribution schedule may be included in the account to show how the executor plans to distribute the assets. It should be noted, however, that the executor may wish to retain some cash in case there is an unexpected expense or an audit of the account.

Signature and Affidavit The last item on the account is the signature of the fiduciary. If there is more than one fiduciary, they should all sign the account. The affidavit accompanying the account verifies its accuracy. As a general rule, the affidavit need be signed by only one of the fiduciaries when there are more than one.

PROBLEM

Prepare an account for the estate of Jack Spencer, deceased, using the information given below. If possible, follow the rules of the locale in which you will be working. If not, use the format of the account for the Estate of John Doe.

The executor of the estate is the Morgan Bank. The account should be inclusive from the date of death, February 12, 1991, through February 28, 1992.

Jack Spencer died while a resident of Blueberry County, Pennsylvania. At the time of his death he owned the following assets (each of which has been valued as of the date of death):

1. A home at 272 Pine Street, Rutherford, Pennsylvania, owned by decedent alone. The value was appraised at $236,000. (The home passes as part of the residuary bequest to Jeanne Spencer, decedent's wife.)
2. 200 shares, PDQ Corporation stock (par value $6), having a date-of-death value of $450 per share, and a dividend of $10 per share having been declared on January 20, 1991, payable to shareholders of record February 14, 1991.
3. 300 shares, Danson Oil (par value $5), having a date-of-death value of $80 per share. On February 20, 1991, the executor received a dividend of $2 per share. The dividend had been declared on January 22, 1991, payable to shareholders of record on February 8, 1991.

4. 500 shares, Graball, Incorporated (par value $3), having a date-of-death value of $80 per share.
5. 1,000 shares, Bell Atlantic Company (par value $1), having a date-of-death value of $120 per share.
6. 5,000 shares, E. I. Dupont (par value $10), having a date-of-death value of $200 per share.
7. Personal effects and household items appraised at $95,000.
8. Bank account at the Morgan Bank with a date-of-death balance $5,000; no accrued interest.

The following additional assets were received during the account period:

1. Decedent's final paycheck in the amount of $2,100, received on March 1, 1991.
2. 1990 Federal Income Tax Refund in the amount of $1,080, received on May 22, 1991.

The following items were sold on the dates indicated and at the prices indicated:

1. 50 shares PDQ, March 5, 1991, at $425 per share.
2. 150 shares Danson Oil, April 15, 1991, at $110 per share.
3. 200 shares Graball, June 20, 1991, at $70 per share.
4. 1,000 shares Bell Atlantic, September 20, 1991, at $150 per share.
5. $10,000 U.S. Treasury Bills, 8¾% due October 15, 1991, redeemed on October 15, 1991. (Note: This asset was purchased on March 8, 1991, during the estate administration.)
6. $18,000 Blueberry County Bonds, 6% due December 3, 1998, sold on November 10, 1991, at $15,000 plus $470 accrued interest received upon sale. (Note: This asset was purchased on April 30, 1991, during the estate administration.)

The following disbursements of principal were made:

1. John Merle, funeral bill paid February 25, 1991, $2,200.
2. Real estate taxes on home paid March 1, 1991, $1,000 (debt of the decedent).
3. Ray Roper, payment for installation of new roof on home, December 5, 1991, $1,000 (debt of decedent).
4. Reverend Anderson, $250 for funeral service.
5. Paul Peterson, partial payment of $5,000 of $10,000 total attorney fee paid December 10, 1991.
6. Federal Estate Tax of $160,000 paid on November 12, 1991.
7. Pennsylvania inheritance taxes paid on May 10, 1991, in the amount of $12,000, and on November 12, 1991, in the amount of $3,000.

The following distributions were made to beneficiaries:

1. 100 shares PDQ distributed to John Spencer on March 5, 1991. Distribution value $425.
2. 300 shares Graball distributed to Alan Spencer on June 20, 1991. (Value on date of distribution: $70 per share.)
3. $10,000 Treasury bill (5¾% due October 15, 1991) to Jeane Spencer on September 30, 1991.
4. All personal effects and household items to Jeane Spencer, March 5, 1991.

The following were receipts of income:

1. Dividend of $10 per share on PDQ stock received May 28, August 28, and November 28, 1991, on 50 shares.
2. Dividends of $10 per share on Dupont stock received April 10, July 10, October 10, 1991, and February 10, 1992.
3. Dividend of $5 per share on Bell Atlantic stock paid March 8, June 8, and September 8, 1991. (Sold stock September 20, 1991.)
4. Interest on Morgan bank account for period from date of death through April 15, 1991, when account was closed, $42.
5. Interest on Blueberry County Bonds, $540 on June 3, 1991.
6. Dividend on Danson Oil, $2 a share, March 10, 1991 (300 shares), June 10, September 10, and December 1, 1991 (150 shares).
7. Dividends of $1 a share on Graball stock received on March 20 and June 20, 1991 (500 shares). (Note: Stock was sold June 20, 1991.)
8. Estate checking account interest from February 22, 1991, to February 28, 1992, $7,200 (Morgan Bank).

The following disbursements of income were made:

1. 1991 federal fiduciary income tax for the estate paid on March 27, 1992, $500.
2. No distributions of income were made during the course of the estate's administration.

The following items were purchased by the estate from principal on the dates indicated:

1. $20,000 Treasury bills (5¾% due October 15, 1991), purchased for $19,500 on March 8, 1991. (Each bond valued at $9,750.)
2. $18,000 Blueberry County Bonds (6% due December 3, 1998), purchased for $13,500 plus $450 accrued interest on April 30, 1991.

The following were the values of estate assets as of February 28, 1992, the account date:

1. Home—$238,000 per appraisal.
2. PDQ stock—$400 per share.
3. Danson Oil stock—$85 per share.
4. Dupont stock—$180 per share.
5. Savings account, Morgan Bank—balance $5,000.
6. Cash in the estate's checking account of $159,260. (Note: All sales proceeds, income receipts, and additional cash assets should have been deposited in this account at Morgan Bank. All disbursements, both income and principal, and the bond purchases should have been paid out of the account.)

The accountant, Morgan Bank, seeks court approval of its fee, which you must compute. Fee is based on the following schedule:

Principal—4% up to $100,000
  3% excess over $100,000 up to $500,000
  2% excess over $500,000
Income—2% of income received

PROCEDURES OF NOTICE AND AUDIT

Preparation of the account, while extremely important, is not an end in itself. Interested parties must be given an opportunity to review and to question the facts shown in the account. Further, the probate court that has jurisdiction over the estate or trust must approve the account. The court's review is called the "audit" of the account.

Notice to Interested Parties

When the account is to be filed with the court, the accountant is normally required to give written notice to all parties who may have an interest in it. These would be the beneficiaries and creditors, for the most part, but might also include people who intend to dispute any matter stated in the account.

Upon filing, the account will normally be scheduled to be "heard" before a judge at a particular time and place. The court's audit of the account represents an opportunity for all those with claims to come forward and have the court make a determination on their claims. To do this requires that notice be given sufficiently far enough in advance. Typically, the attorney for the accountant may give notice in simple letter form, although in some states the court itself may send out the notice. Here is an example of a form of notice of the filing of an account.

EXAMPLE
Notice of Filing of Account

[Letterhead]
November 7, 1992

Re: Account of John A. Henderson, Administrator
To the Parties in Interest:

This is to advise you that the Account of John A. Henderson, Administrator of the Estate of Charles Smith, Deceased, has been filed and will be called for audit on Monday, December 1, 1992, at 11:00 A.M. in Room 414, City Hall, East Stratford, Pennsylvania, before Judge Beckett.

At the audit, the Accountant will request the Court to approve the Account as filed, and to award the balance of principal and income as follows:

1/2 to Claire Henderson (sister)
1/14 to Charles S. Naughton (nephew)
1/14 to John L. Naughton (nephew)
1/14 to Lawrence J. Naughton (nephew)
1/14 to Joan Hemple (niece)
1/14 to Rita Mason (niece)
1/14 to Eileen Oliver (niece)
1/14 to Margaret S. Graham (niece)

If you have any questions, kindly notify me as soon as possible, or arrange to be present in the Orphans' Court, either in person or represented by counsel, at the time and place set forth above. If you have no questions, no action is required by this notice. If you do not appear either in person or represented by counsel, the Court will assume that you have no objections.

Sincerely yours,
/s/William R. P. McGonigle
William R. P. McGonigle

When a particular problem exists, such as a dispute to a share in the estate or trust, or a creditor's claim that has been denied by the accountant, special note of the dispute should be made in the notice. The accountant may also state his position on the dispute so that interested parties who have a contrary point of view are advised to be present when the audit is heard.

If none of the interested parties appears at the audit, the auditing judge is at least assured that they have received due notice of the proceedings and have no quarrel with the account.

Court Audit

The auditing judge will already have received the account before the day set for the audit of the account. The attorney for the accountant is normally required to hand up to the judge certain additional documents when the account is called for audit. These may include the original letters testamentary (or letters of administration), a copy of the will or trust instrument, a copy of the inventory, copies of the notices of the audit, and tax receipts for death taxes paid. An important document that may also be presented to the judge is the statement of proposed distribution.[22] This form shows how the accountant will dispose of the assets in his possession. It may also identify questions that have not been resolved, such as disputes over the assets. An Example of such a form is shown on the following pages.

The audit itself may be a relatively informal procedure if the account is routine and there are no questions or objections to the account.

If, on the other hand, certain questions have come to the attention of the accountant, he or she should present these questions orally to the court at the audit even though no other party in interest has appeared to present a position on these questions. In such a case, the accountant (usually through counsel) will simply advise the court of the nature of the questions involved, the position of the accountant on those questions, and request the court to make specific determinations of those questions in its adjudication.[23]

An entirely different situation arises if interested creditors, beneficiaries, heirs, or other parties appear at the audit to make specific objections to the positions taken by the accountant. The objections may be stated orally before the court or the objector may file a formal statement of the objections with the court prior to the audit. The court may take testimony and compel the production of witnesses and documents just as in other lawsuits. Normally, if a hearing is required it will be scheduled for a specific time in the future.

Adjudication

The written opinion of the auditing judge, either approving or disapproving the account as filed and deciding the various questions raised at the audit, is frequently called its adjudication.

The purpose of the adjudication is finally to approve or disapprove the account and resolve all questions raised at the audit. Once the court has adjudicated an account, it also serves to terminate the responsibility and liability of the fiduciary as long as the assets held are distributed in accordance with the court's order.

The account of the Smith estate concluded with the adjudication on page 357.

22. The name of this form varies. It is sometimes referred to as a petition for adjudication.

23. The adjudication is the judge's order regarding the account.

EXAMPLE ***Petition for Adjudication***

ODC-18 (80) -- Petition for Adjudication -- Testacy

Court of Common Pleas of Bucks County, Pennsylvania
Orphans' Court Division

ESTATE OF...DECEASED

Petition for Adjudication

In re..Account of ....

....

Audit List of...................................,19..........,

The Petition of...

..respectfully represents that:

1. Decedent died on.., 19.........,leaving a will dated

..........................,19.........., and codicil dated..., 19.........., probated on

.............................., 19.........., on which the present letters were granted on..................

......................................., 19........, to ....

....

Describe decedent's marital status, whether single, married, widow, widower, divorced, etc. If married state date and place of marriage. If widow or widower, state name of prior spouse(s). State when, where and how such previous marriage(s) was terminated, if termination occurred. If no prior marriage, so state. If marriage terminated by death, attach death certificate. State name of surviving spouse, and whether spouse has elected to take under or against will. State facts of executing, filing, and recording election and submit copy, if any. State facts concerning widow's or children's exemption, and whether or not claimed or paid.

2. Decedent was...

Indicate those, deceased or not sui juris, and explain in Par. 4. Where an interest is taken by representative or substitution, set forth name and date of death of ancestor and any other material facts. Note revocations, lapses or ademptions, if any, with explanation.

3. The legatees, devisees, etc. named or referred to in the will, their relationship to decedent, and the nature of their interests are as follows:

Name & Address	*Relationship*	*Interest*

- 1 -

EXAMPLE *Petition for Adjudication, continued*

- 2 -

State exceptions, if any, giving names, dates of death, and names of executor, administrator, or issue, as material; also names of guardians, and trustees, if any, and how appointed.	**4. All said parties in interest are living, of age, and sui juris**
State whether or not decedent was married or divorced after execution of will or codicil and whether children were born or adopted thereafter. If so, state names, date and reference to records.	**5. Decedent was**
State exceptions, if any, also how and when notice given. Submit copies of notices. See also Pa O.C. Rules 6.3, 6.7, 6.8 and Bucks O.C. Rules 5.4A and 6.3A.	**6. Written notice of the filing of the account and of the time and place of the call thereof for audit was given to all persons to whom notice is required to be given by Pa. O.C.Rule 6.3, by**
State preferred claims first, under heading "Preferred" and in order of preference; then general claims.	**7. The unpaid claims of all creditors, of which accountant....................has......................notice of knowledge, and whether or not admitted to be correct, are as follows:**

Do not write in this space.
Do not attach papers in this space, or on this page.

EXAMPLE Petition for Adjudication, continued

Do not write in this space.
Do not attach papers in this space, or on this page.

State caption of estate in full and status of administration. If none, so state.	**8. Decedent at time of death was a fiduciary of the following estates:**
If none, so state.	**9. Notice of devises and bequests has been given as required by 20 Pa. C.S.A. §3330 to the following corporate bodies:**
State facts as to Pa. Transfer Inheritance Tax and Pa. Additional Estate Tax, and Submit certificate or receipt of Register of Wills showing tax status. If appraisement not filed or tax not settled, so state and give particulars, as material.	**10.**
State here (and include in notice) any questions requiring adjudication, inserting or attaching full statement of facts. Set forth, in detail, the position of accountant.	**11.**
State in full all facts concerning any assignments or attachments of distributive shares and submit copies.	
State here any additional receipts or disbursements since filing account, to be included in adjudication.	
If all executors named in will are not accountants here, explain.	
State here the identity and other material facts as to unknown or nonresident distributees under Pa. O.C. Rules 13.1, 13.2, and 13.3 and Bucks O.C. Rule 13.3A; and 20 Pa. C.S.A. §4111.	

OCD-18 (80) - Petition for Adjudication - Testacy - 3 -

EXAMPLE *Petition for Adjudication, continued*

- 4 -

Fractional shares shall be stated in proportions or in amounts. Agreed "in kind" awards shall be noted as such. Paragraph 3, supra, may be incorporated herein by reference if appropriate and includes all parties presently in interest.
STATE WHETHER THE COURT SHOULD DIRECT A SCHEDULE OF DIS-TRIBUTION BE FILED.

Wherefore petitioner......ask........that distribution of the balance of principal and income be awarded to the persons entitled, and suggests that the distributive shares are as follows:

....

ATTORNEY FOR PETITIONER
ADDRESS..
....
TEL # ....
PA I.D. # ....

State of Pennsylvania :
: **ss.**
County of Bucks :

....

above-named petitioner...,being duly...according to law,

depose(s) and say(s) that the facts set forth in the foregoing petition which are within

...personal knowledge are true, and as to facts based upon information
(her, his, their)

received from others,..believe(s) them to be true.
(she, he, they)

.......................................and subscribed

before me this...................................day ....

of............................., 19.......................

Do not write in this space.
Do not attach papers in this space, or on this page.

EXAMPLE *Petition for Adjudication, continued*

Do not write in this space.

Attach all riders and other papers pertaining to any paragraph of the petition, to this page and to this page only.
Fasten papers IN this space, but so that all writing is below this space.

DO NOT ATTACH PAPERS PROJECTING BEYOND THIS FORM. FOLD IF NECESSARY.

EXAMPLE *Petition for Adjudication, continued*

File No. ....

Audit List of....................................,19........

COURT OF COMMON PLEAS OF BUCKS COUNTY ORPHANS' COURT DIVISION

ESTATE OF

Deceased

Petition for Adjudication

TO BE SUBMITTED HEREWITH:

1. Copy of will, and codicils, if any.
2. Copy of inventory.
3. Copy of election, if any.
4. Proofs of publication of estate notices.
5. Copies of assignments or other instruments.
6. Appearance for parties represented.
7. Certificate or Original Receipt of Register of Wills showing status of Inheritance tax.
8. Copies of notices of audit.

ATTORNEY:
ADDRESS:

TEL #:
PA I.D. #

If spaces provided in this form are insufficient to set forth the necessary and required facts and information, use space provided on page to which papers are to be attached to complete said facts and information.

EXAMPLE
Adjudication of Estate

Orphans' Court Division
Court of Common Pleas of
Wellesley

No. 3371 of 1992

Estate of CHARLES SMITH, DECEASED

Sur account entitled First and Final Account of JOHN A. HENDERSON, ADMINISTRATOR

Before Beckett, J.

This account was called for audit December 1, 1992. Counsel appeared as follows:

William R. P. McGonigle, Esq., for the Accountant

CHARLES SMITH died August 10, 1991, intestate, not survived by a spouse, leaving, as appears from the statement of proposed distribution, as the persons entitled to his estate under the intestate laws, a sister, and seven children of a deceased sister of decedent named in the said statement, all of whom are noted as being sui juris[24] and as having had notice of the audit.

Letters of administration were granted to the accountant on August 16, 1991, and proof of publication of the grant of same is hereto annexed.

Payment of transfer inheritance tax on November 16, 1991, in the sum of $600 less $30 discount, on May 10, 1992, in the sum of $417.53, and on October 16, 1992, in the sum of $4.05, was duly vouched.

There was no objection to the account that shows

a balance of principal, personalty, of	$3,405.22
a balance of principal, proceeds of sale of real estate of	2,737.56
and a balance of income of	22.35
making a total of	$6,165.13

that, composed of cash as indicated in the account, and together with additional income to date of distribution, is awarded as follows:

one-half to Claire Henderson and

one-fourteenth each to Charles S. Naughton, John L. Naughton, Lawrence J. Naughton, Joan Hemple, Rita Mason, Eileen Oliver, and Margaret S. Graham.

Leave is hereby granted the accountant to execute and deliver all necessary transfers and assignments.

AND NOW, December 3, 1992, the account is confirmed.

Beckett, J.

24. A legal term meaning having full legal capabilities. That is, not a minor or incompetent.

CHAPTER EIGHT

Settlement by Agreement

The process described in Chapter Seven for filing an account for audit is somewhat expensive and time consuming. Court costs for simply filing the account may be several hundred dollars. In addition, legal fees to the estate are incurred due to the additional time that must be spent by the attorney who must appear at the audit and prepare the various audit papers with the aid of a paralegal. Furthermore, a court accounting creates a public record of the assets and transactions that some people consider an invasion of privacy.

In estates or trusts where no questions have arisen concerning the interpretation of the will or trust instrument or applicable law, where no creditors' claims have been left unpaid, and where there are no likely objections to the account, it is frequently the practice of attorneys not to file the account for audit in court. This is very often done where the executor, administrator, or trustee is either the only beneficiary or one of the major beneficiaries. In such cases the personal representative or trustee is obviously not going to object to her own account or to her own statement of proposed distribution; hence, it is frequently possible to avoid the expenses of a formal court audit in this situation. It should be noted that in the case where the residuary beneficiary is a charity, the fiduciary is required to file a court accounting. Also some states such as Ohio do not allow a settlement by agreement. In Ohio a court accounting is always required.

When it is decided not to file an account with a court, it is customary to have an agreement among the interested parties. The function of such an agreement is to protect the fiduciary from a later claim that he or she acted improperly. Generally, the signers of such an agreement are all of the major beneficiaries of the estate or trust. People who were entitled only to a specific gift, which has been paid in full, are unlikely to have any later claim against the fiduciary. Therefore, they may safely be omitted from an agreement. A receipt or satisfaction of award should, however, be obtained from them at the time of delivery of the specific gift.

Even if an agreement protects the fiduciary from potential claims by beneficiaries, it will not protect him from claims by unpaid creditors. In some states, however, statute accords the fiduciary some limited protection from creditors in such situations. The normal type of provision would be that unless a claim is presented by the creditors within a certain time (perhaps six months or one year) after advertising the death of the decedent, that creditor will be prohibited from presenting any claim against the estate.

Such provisions (usually statutory in nature) do not govern the claims of beneficiaries of the estate, heirs, next of kin, or any other parties claiming rights as distributees rather than creditors. A fiduciary who makes an improper distribution without confirmation by a court has no statutory protection in regard to such persons claiming rights as distributees rather than as creditors. The procedure, therefore, when a fiduciary wishes to avoid the costs of filing an account for formal court audit in an uncomplicated estate or trust is to obtain an agreement with all potential beneficiaries, under which the fiduciary will be protected.

DRAFTING THE AGREEMENT

The agreement is a composite of various elements designed to overcome the risks that the fiduciary is taking by making distribution without court approval. The style of such agreements varies greatly from place to place and from one attorney to another. Such an agreement may be known as a Family Settlement Agreement; a Receipt, Release, and Indemnification Agreement; an Approval of Account and Receipt and Release; a Receipt, Release and Waiver; or any similar title customary in the locale. Sometimes a separate agreement is prepared for each interested party. Others may prefer a single agreement to which all legatees and beneficiaries will be signatories. If the elements of such an agreement are understood, they can be adapted to any style.

Elements of the Agreement

Caption The first element is the caption of the matter. The caption should include the name of the court, the number of the particular estate, and the name of the estate:

IN THE COURT OF COMMON PLEAS OF
MONTGOMERY COUNTY, PENNSYLVANIA

ORPHANS' COURT DIVISION

WILL NO. 64-69-4321

ESTATE OF J. PIERPONT DuPONT, DECEASED

Title After the caption comes the title. The agreement is a multi-purpose document and this causes difficulty in giving it a title that will be both brief and fully descriptive. The title is mostly a matter of personal preference that is greatly influenced by the legal customs and conventions of the place where it is to be used.

Salutation Since the agreement contains a release, the document often starts with the salutation:

KNOW ALL MEN BY THESE PRESENTS.[1]

Recital of Background The agreement may begin with a recital of the facts concerning the estate or trust, such as the date of death of the decedent and the appointment of executors or trustees.

Account The account itself should be physically attached to the agreement, and the legatee or beneficiary of the trust should certify that he has examined it (Certification of Legatee):

> We, the undersigned, do hereby certify that we have examined the First and Final Account of Morgan DuPont, Executor of the above captioned Estate, a copy of which is attached hereto as Exhibit A.

Approval of Account A legatee or beneficiary should approve the account since that is the basic function of the court audit that is being avoided:

> We do hereby accept and approve said Account with the same force and effect as if it had been duly filed, audited, adjudicated, and confirmed absolutely by the appropriate Court.

Receipt Each legatee or beneficiary should acknowledge receipt of his or her share of the estate. If the agreement is being signed by one party only, then the exact amount or assets received should be noted in the agreement. This is the legal consideration[2] for the agreement:

> I do hereby acknowledge receipt of the sum of $8,481.77 to me in hand paid by the said Executor of the above captioned estate, in full satisfaction of my interest in the said estate.

If the agreement is to be signed by all beneficiaries, then it is helpful to attach an exhibit either to the account or to the

1. This type of wording is a throwback to times when legal documents were required to be much more formal than they are today. Old customs, however, die slowly, especially with lawyers.

2. Consideration is one of the requirements of a contract. It is doing or promising to do something that you are not obliged to do or refraining from doing or promising to refrain from doing something that you have the right to do.

agreement, showing the exact distribution to each party. In that case, the text of the agreement would not show the exact amount or the assets received:

> Each of us hereby acknowledges receipt of the assets as set forth in Exhibit B, attached hereto, to us in hand paid by the said Executor, in full satisfaction of our respective interests in the said Estate.

Release The main purpose of the agreement is protection against claims of the legatees and beneficiaries themselves. This is accomplished by incorporating a general release in the agreement. The release would have the effect of prohibiting a party to the agreement from maintaining after distribution that the fiduciary improperly interpreted the will, or mismanaged the estate or trust assets, or in any other way failed to distribute the proper amount:

> **Beneficiaries' General Release**
> In consideration thereof, We do hereby, jointly and severally, release and forever discharge the said Executor, his heirs, and successors from any and all claims and causes of action that we might have as heirs and legatees of J. Pierpont DuPont, Deceased, or in any other capacity.

> **Individual Beneficiary's General Release**
> I do hereby absolutely and irrevocably release and forever discharge Rodney Cartman and T. Henry Jones as Executors of the Estate of Fisher Cartman, Deceased, and their successors and assigns, of and from any and all actions, suits, payments, reckoning, liabilities, claims, and demands relating in any way to the administration of this Estate.

Waive Filing, Etc. One of the objectives of the agreement is to avoid the filing of the account in order to save time and money. This is accomplished by including in the agreement a waiver of such requirements:

> I do hereby waive the filing, audit, adjudication, and confirmation of that account by the proper court and I desire that distribution be made without such formalities.

Future Audit Many agreements include a provision that permits a court to confirm the account at some later time and discharge the fiduciary without notice to the parties to the agreement:

> We hereby agree that at any time hereafter, any Court having jurisdiction over the above captioned Estate may confirm the said Account and discharge the said Executor without notice to the undersigned.

Indemnification[3] To protect the fiduciary from claims that might arise in the future, those receiving the funds should agree to indemnify the fiduciary for any claims made by others (e.g., creditors) against the fiduciary. If there had been a court-audited account, the fiduciary would have been discharged from such responsibility:

> We do hereby expressly agree, in consideration of the payment to each of us of our respective interests in said Estate and for other good and valuable consideration, receipt of which is hereby acknowledged, to indemnify and forever hold harmless the said Executor, his heirs and successors, against all loss from any and all claims or actions that may hereafter be made against the said Executor in connection with the said Estate.

Refunding Provision As part of the indemnity, the legatees and beneficiaries should agree to give back any amount that may be needed for additional taxes:

> We do hereby agree to refund to the said Executor any amount that may be incurred by him as a result of any taxes, interest, or penalties that any taxing authority may impose hereafter in connection with this estate.

Succession A standard clause in virtually every agreement is a provision making the agreement binding upon those who might succeed to the interest of the signatory to the agreement:

> We agree that this Agreement shall be binding upon our respective heirs, executors, administrators, and assigns.

Governing Law Ordinarily, if the legatee or beneficiary and the fiduciary are residents of the same state, and if the agreement is signed in that state, there is no question regarding the applicable law. However, if the parties live in different states, or if the agreement is signed in another state, the agreement should specify that the law of a particular state shall govern:

> We agree that this Agreement shall be governed by and construed under the law of the Commonwealth of Pennsylvania.

Signing and Sealing The agreement should be dated and signed with the language by which the parties intend to be legally bound. A party may sign in more than one legal capacity (e.g., one person may be both the executor/executrix and a beneficiary under the will):

3. An indemnification is a promise to reimburse someone who has suffered a loss.

IN WITNESS WHEREOF, and intending to be legally bound hereby, we have hereunto set our hands and seals this 22nd day of December, 1992.

Witnesses:

________________________ ________________________ [Seal]
E. I. DuPONT

________________________ ________________________ [Seal]
MORGAN DuPONT

Acknowledgment The agreement should be acknowledged before a notary public. In some states, this is necessary to authenticate an agreement properly.

EXAMPLES OF AGREEMENTS

Three samples of settlement agreements are reproduced next. Note that all of these agreements contain most of the basic elements that were referred to earlier in this chapter.

EXAMPLES
Estate Settlement Agreements

A Separate Agreement for Each of the Interested Parties to an Estate

IN THE COURT OF COMMON PLEAS
OF MONTGOMERY COUNTY, PENNSYLVANIA

ORPHANS' COURT DIVISION

WILL NO. 64-69-4321

ESTATE OF J. PIERPONT DuPONT, DECEASED[4]
RECEIPT, RELEASE, AND INDEMNIFICATION AGREEMENT[5]

KNOW ALL MEN BY THESE PRESENTS:[6]

That I, the undersigned, do hereby certify that I have examined the First and Final Account of Morgan DuPont, Executor of the above captioned Estate, a copy of which is attached hereto as Exhibit A.[7] I do hereby accept and approve said Account with the same force and effect as if it had been duly filed, audited, adjudicated, and confirmed absolutely by the appropriate Court.[8]

4. Caption.
5. Title.
6. Salutation.
7. Attaching account.
8. Approval of account.

I hereby acknowledge receipt of the sum of $53,264.48 to me in hand paid by the said Executor, in full satisfaction of my interest in the said Estate.[9]

In consideration thereof, I do hereby release and forever discharge the said Executor, his heirs, and successors from any and all claims and causes of action that I might have as heir and legatee of J. Pierpoint DuPont, Deceased, or in any other capacity.[10]

I desire that this distribution of the entire estate be made without the formality of the filing, audit, adjudication, and confirmation of the Account in the Court of Common Pleas of Montgomery County or elsewhere.[11] I hereby agree that at any time hereafter, any Court having jurisdiction over the above captioned Estate may confirm the said Account and discharge the said Executor without notice to the undersigned.[12]

And furthermore, I do hereby expressly agree, in consideration of the said payment to me of my respective interest in said Estate and for other good and valuable consideration, receipt of which is hereby acknowledged, to indemnify and forever hold harmless the said Executor, his heirs, and successors, against all loss from any and all claims or actions that may hereafter be made against the said Executor in connection with the said Estate.[13] And furthermore, I do hereby agree to refund to the said Executor any amount that may be incurred by him as a result of any taxes, interest, or penalties that any taxing authority may impose hereafter in connection with this estate.[14]

And furthermore, I agree that this Agreement shall be binding upon my heirs, executors, administrators, and assigns.[15]

I agree that this Agreement shall be governed by and construed under the law of the Commonwealth of Pennsylvania.[16]

IN WITNESS WHEREOF, and intending to be legally bound hereby, I have hereunto set my hand and seal this 22nd day of December, 1992

Witness:

________________________ (Seal)[17]

Morgan DuPont

A Single Agreement for All Interested Parties

IN RE: Estate of FISHER CARTMAN, Deceased

Philadelphia County Will No. 2880 of 1992[18]

9. Receipt.
10. Release.
11. Waiver of filing.
12. Future audit.
13. Indemnification.
14. Refunding provision.
15. Succession provision.
16. Governing law.
17. Signing and sealing.
18. Caption.

APPROVAL OF ACCOUNT
AND
RECEIPT AND RELEASE[19]

THE BACKGROUND of this instrument is as follows:[20]

A. Fisher Cartman, a resident of Philadelphia, Pennsylvania, died testate on July 13, 1991.

B. The Register of Wills for Philadelphia County, Pennsylvania, issued Letters Testamentary to Rodney Cartman and T. Henry Jones on August 13, 1991.

C. The First and Final Account of Rodney Cartman and T. Henry Jones, executors of the Estate of Fisher Cartman, Deceased, is attached hereto.[21]

D. Under the provisions of the will of Fisher Cartman, personal and household effects pass to his wife, Emily Cartman, and the residue passes to Rodney Cartman and T. Henry Jones as testamentary trustees.

E. Under the provisions of the testamentary trust created by article SECOND of the will all income is to be paid to Emily Cartman during her lifetime and thereafter the principal is to be distributed to T. Henry Jones, Elise Jones Bennett, Fisher Cartman, Jr., and Rodney Cartman in specified shares.

F. All of the undersigned parties desire that the distribution of the balance of the Estate's assets be made without the expense and delay of a court accounting and the executors are willing to make distribution upon receipt of an Approval of Account and Receipt and Release signed by all of the undersigned parties.

THEREFORE, WE, the undersigned, do hereby:

1. Declare that we have examined the above-mentioned First and Final Account and that we approve it and accept it in all respects and with the same force and effect as if it had been filed with and confirmed absolutely by a proper court;[22]
2. Waive the filing, audit, adjudication, and confirmation of that account by the proper court;[23]
3. Acknowledge receipt of the Estate's assets as shown in the attached Account and approve the distribution of the balance to Rodney Cartman and T. Henry Jones as trustees of the testamentary trust.[24]
4. Absolutely and irrevocably release and forever discharge Rodney Cartman and T. Henry Jones as executors of the Estate of Fisher Cartman, Deceased, and their successors and assigns, of and from any and all actions, suits, payments, reckoning, liabilities, claims, and demands relating in any way to the administration of this Estate;[25]

19. Title.
20. Background.
21. Attaching account.
22. Approval of account.
23. Waiver of filing.
24. Receipt.
25. Release.

5. Agree that any court having jurisdiction of the Estate of Fisher Cartman, Deceased, may by its decree, confirm the aforesaid account and discharge Rodney Cartman and T. Henry Jones as executors.[26]
6. Agree to indemnify the executors against and save them harmless from any liability, loss, or expense that may hereafter be incurred as a result of this settlement of the account without court approval;[27] and
7. Agree that this instrument should be governed by the law of Pennsylvania,[28] and that it shall be legally binding upon us and upon our heirs, executors, administrators, and assigns.[29]

Executed ______________ ______________________[30]
Rodney Cartman, Executor

Executed ______________ ______________________
T. Henry Jones, Executor

Executed ______________ ______________________
Rodney Cartman, Trustee

Executed ______________ ______________________
T. Henry Jones, Trustee

Executed ______________ ______________________
Beulah Heckman

Executed ______________ ______________________
Craig Cornell

(Note: Each witness should have his or her signature notarized separately. For simplicity the separate notary oaths are not shown here.)

New York State Agreement for Only Interested Party

STATE OF NEW YORK
Surrogate's Court: Queens County

In the Matter of the Judicial Settlement of the Final Account of Proceedings of AARON S. ARNOLD and MICHAEL MARTINS, as Executors under the will of	File No. 9876-1991 RECEIPT, RELEASE, INDEMNITY AGREEMENT AND WAIVER
Robert Martins, Deceased.[31]	with ACCOUNT ATTACHED[32]

26. Future audit.
27. Indemnification.
28. Governing law.
29. Succession provision.
30. Signing.
31. Caption.
32. Title.

KNOW ALL MEN BY THESE PRESENTS:[33]

WHEREAS, Robert Martins died on May 16, 1991, a resident of Queens County, State of New York, leaving a will dated August 31, 1986, and a codicil thereto dated December 10, 1986, which instruments were duly admitted to probate by the Surrogate's Court of said County on November 7, 1991, and letters testamentary were duly issued by said Court on November 7, 1991, to Michael Martins and Aaron S. Arnold, who duly qualified as executors of said will, and have ever since continued to perform their duties as such executors; and

WHEREAS[34] more than seven months have elapsed since the issuance of said letters testamentary; and

WHEREAS[34] the New York estate tax was fixed by an order of the Surrogate's Court of Queens County dated July 12, 1992; and

WHEREAS[34] the will of said decedent dated August 31, 1986, provided for the payment of funeral expenses and debts, and for the payment of various legacies, and thereafter provided for the net residuary estate, after the payment of estate taxes, to be disposed of as follows:

> EIGHTH: All the rest, residue, and remainder of the property, real and personal, and of every kind and description and wheresoever situate, which I shall own at the time of my death, including any and all property over which I have power of disposition or appointment, which power I hereby exercise and appoint (all of which is hereinafter referred to as my "residuary estate"), I give, devise, and bequeath to my brother, MICHAEL MARTINS, of 83-39 99th Avenue, Astoria, Long Island, N.Y., absolutely. In the event that my said brother, MICHAEL MARTINS, shall predecease me, I give, devise, and bequeath my said residuary estate in equal shares to and among the children of my said brother surviving me, the issue of any deceased child of my said brother to take, per stirpes, the share the parent would have taken had he or she survived me.

and

WHEREAS[34] the codicil of said decedent dated December 10, 1986, provided for the payment of an additional preresiduary legacy, but in all other respects confirmed and republished the aforesaid will of said decedent; and

WHEREAS[34] Michael Martins survived the Testator; and

WHEREAS[34] in order to avoid the delay and expense of a judicial accounting, Michael Martins has requested that the executors prepare and present to him for his examination and approval an account of their proceedings as executors as aforesaid; and

WHEREAS[34] pursuant to said request the executors have presented to Michael Martins an account of their proceedings covering the period from November 7, 1991, down to and including August 21, 1992, which account is hereto annexed and made a part hereof.[35]

NOW, THEREFORE, I, MICHAEL MARTINS, do for myself certify that I have examined or caused to be examined on my behalf said account and the schedules thereto annexed, and do in all respects accept and

33. Salutation.
34. Background.
35. Attaching account.

approve the same and ratify and confirm the acts of the said executors as set forth therein.[36]

And I do hereby approve the computation of commissions now due to said executors, as shown by Schedule J of said account, and I do hereby authorize said executors to pay the same to themselves out of the cash balance of said estate remaining in their hands.

And I do hereby approve the reserve and retention by said executors of $2,500.00 in cash out of the balance of said estate remaining in their hands, to pay transfer taxes and fees as well as any other proper charges against said estate, any balance remaining after payment of such taxes, fees, and other charges to be distributed to me.

And I do hereby approve the filing by said executors of a claim for refund of an overpayment of New York estate tax in the amount of $165, which when received by said executors is to be distributed to me.

And I do hereby acknowledge receipt from said executors of the securities and all except $646.63 of the cash shown by Schedule G of said account, being in the aggregate all property belonging to said estate remaining in the hands of said executors after deducting the payment and reserve above mentioned.[37]

And in consideration of the premises and of the payment and reserve herein recited without a judicial accounting and decree, I, MICHAEL MARTINS, do hereby release and discharge said Aaron S. Arnold and said Michael Martins individually and as executors under the aforesaid will and codicil, of and from any and all liabilities, claims, or demands whatsoever in law or in equity that I ever had or now have or that I, my heirs, legal representatives, successors, or assigns ever may have against said Aaron S. Arnold and said Michael Martins as executors as aforesaid by reason of any act, matter, or thing done or omitted to be done by said executors and embraced in said account or in this instrument, and do further release and discharge said executors of and from any obligation to account further to me with respect to said estate or the administration thereof.[38]

And in consideration as aforesaid I, MICHAEL MARTINS, do hereby agree to the extent of the payment made and the property transferred to me as aforesaid to indemnify and hold harmless said executors from and against any and all liabilities, claims, or demands whatsoever that may be made against said estate or the executors thereof, including without limitation the amount of any income or other taxes (including any penalties or interest thereon) that may hereafter be demanded from or assessed against said estate or the executors thereof as the result of any returns heretofore or hereafter filed by said executors or otherwise.[39]

And in consideration as aforesaid I, MICHAEL MARTINS, do hereby waive all rights to a judicial settlement of said account and to the issuance and service of any citation or other process in any action or proceeding brought for the judicial settlement of said account,[40] and I do hereby consent that a judgment or decree may be made and entered at any time in any court of competent jurisdiction without notice to me

36. Approval of account.
37. Receipt.
38. Release.
39. Indemnification.
40. Waiver of filing.

judicially allowing and settling said account and discharging said executors from all liabilities and accountabilities in respect of all matters embraced therein or in this instrument.[41]

And I, MICHAEL MARTINS, do hereby warrant and represent to said executors that I have not assigned, mortgaged, pledged, or otherwise encumbered my interest in said estate or any part thereof and that I have full right to receive the payments made and property transferred to me as above described.

The provisions hereof shall bind and inure to the benefit of my heirs, legal representatives, successors, and assigns and to the benefit of the heirs, legal representatives, successors, and assigns of said executors.[42]

WITNESS my hand and seal this 21st day of August 1992

/s/ Michael Martins [L.S.][43]

STATE OF NEW YORK
County of Queens ss.

On this 21st day of August, 1992, before me personally came MICHAEL MARTINS, to me known and known to me to be the individual described in and who executed the foregoing instrument, and he duly acknowledged to me that he executed the same.

/s/ John Nolan

[*Notary Public*][43]

[*Notary's Stamp*]

QUESTIONS

Which of the elements discussed in "Drafting the Agreement" in this chapter have been omitted from each of the preceding examples? Why do you think these omissions have been made?

PROBLEM

Prepare a settlement agreement for the interested parties in the following fact situation:

Betsy Birkman died on January 23, 1992. Her will, dated June 17, 1985, was duly probated by your local court. Mark Jordan was qualified as executor. The will provided that all of Betsy's estate should be divided between her two nephews Joe and Jack Birkman.

After Betsy's will was admitted for probate, another nephew, Ryan Marshall, filed an objection claiming that the will is invalid. Under the intestate laws if the will is declared to be invalid, all three nephews will get an equal share of the estate.

Joe, Jack, and Ryan reach an agreement providing that Ryan shall receive $6,000 from the estate in return for withdrawing his objections to the will. Mark Jordan makes the $6,000 payment to Ryan and then pays the balance equally to Joe and Jack. Mark now prepares an account. The parties wish to avoid the time delay and expense of the court approving Mark's account.

---

41. Future audit.
42. Succession provision.
43. Signing and sealing.

CHAPTER NINE

Distribution of Assets

This chapter deals primarily with the duties of the personal representative from the time a court approves the account (or the beneficiaries sign a receipt and release) through the complete distribution of the estate. Problems of determining the precise distributive shares under a will or under the intestate laws will be considered. Consideration of the techniques of physical distribution of the assets will be followed by a discussion of the procedures necessary to have a court release the fiduciary from his obligation to continue to serve in that capacity. While the primary focus is on a personal representative, the general principles discussed apply to trustees as well.

DETERMINING THE DISTRIBUTIVE SHARES

Intestate Distribution

All states have laws that govern the distribution of a decedent's estate when there is no valid will. For the most part, these laws attempt to duplicate what the decedent would probably have provided in his will if there had been one. Therefore, a surviving spouse and surviving issue, such as children, grandchildren, and great-grandchildren, are usually given all of the decedent's assets, to the exclusion of all other relatives. The statutory pattern is necessarily imperfect because it does not recognize the fact that a particular decedent may have wanted to favor one child over another, or that a husband and wife may have been estranged (but not divorced) at the time of the death of one of them.

In the typical state intestate law the surviving spouse's intestate share varies depending upon the number of children (or children of deceased children) who survive the decedent. For example, the surviving spouse may be entitled to a fixed sum plus one-half of the estate if there is no surviving issue (descendants) of the decedent. If the decedent is survived by one child, the surviving spouse may be entitled to one-half of the estate. If more descendants survive, the surviving spouse may be entitled to a lesser portion, e.g., one-third of the estate. In some states, if no other relatives survive, the surviving spouse will receive the entire estate.

QUESTION

What is the intestate distribution law in your state? It will probably be found by looking in the index of your state's laws under the heading "Estates; Intestacy."

Normally, the share of the decedent's estate that the surviving spouse is not entitled to (or the entire estate if there is no surviving spouse) is distributable to those who survive the decedent in the following order of priority.

1. Issue of decedent *per stirpes* (see the following paragraph);
2. Parents of decedent if there is no issue;
3. Issue of parents of decedent, if neither issue nor parents of decedent survive;
4. Grandparents of decedent if no issue of the parents survive;
5. Issue of grandparents *per stirpes*, if grandparents, parents, and issue of parents fail to survive; and
6. The state, if no one in the above categories survives the decedent (this is known as "escheat").

Where "issue" are designated as heirs under the intestate law, they take "per stirpes" and not "per capita." "Per stirpes" or "by representation" means that the property is divided into as many equal shares as there are (1) living persons in the nearest degree of relationship to the decedent and (2) persons in the same degree who have died before the decedent but have left issue who survive the decedent. One share then passes to each living person in the degree and one share is divided among the issue of the deceased person in the same degree by representation. An example will help in this difficult area. If it is determined that a particular decedent (a widow) was survived by two of her four children, that one of the dead children had three children (decedent's grandchildren) but one of the grandchildren predeceased the decedent leaving two children (decedent's great-grandchildren) who survived the decedent, and that the fourth child of the decedent predeceased the decedent leaving no issue who survived the decedent, the "per stirpes" rule would require the following pattern of distribution:

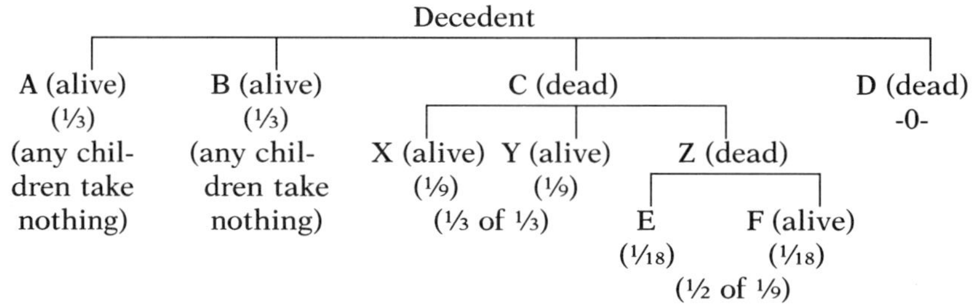

As the pattern suggests, the law is designed to treat the nearest relatives equally but to preserve assets for more remote relatives (e.g., grandchildren) in the same line.

In contrast to this pattern, a testator in a will might choose to benefit all of his surviving issue equally by stating that the estate is to be distributed "per capita" or "by counting the heads" of all surviving issue and dividing the property equally among all. In the above example, A, B, X, Y, E, and F would *each* receive one equal share, one-sixth of the property, if there were a "per capita" distribution. Most testators prefer the "per stirpes" form of distribution to descendants, because it benefits nearer issue to a greater degree than more remote issue.

PROBLEM

Craig Edgerton died intestate. Assume Craig lived in a state that adhered to the same rules on intestate distribution as those enumerated under "Intestate Distribution."

Craig was survived by a sister, Elvira; a son, Errol (who is childless); and the three children of a second son, Edgar, who predeceased Craig. The three grandchildren are Manny, Moe, and Jack. What portion of Craig's estate do each of these surviving relatives receive?

The Typical Patterns of Distribution in a Will

One of the most important reasons for having a will is to vary the pattern of distribution of the estate from the rigid pattern dictated by the intestate laws. A well-drawn will operates to carry out the testator's own preferences. Frequently, the estate planner must take into account property that will pass outside the will, such as life insurance policies or jointly owned property (like a house or bank account), when preparing the estate plan. For instance, if one child is the beneficiary of a life insurance policy or a joint owner on a bank account and the other children are not beneficiaries, the estate planner would want to consider these "automatic" gifts that pass outside of the will when determining if the testator is accomplishing his overall estate planning goals. There are several types of bequests that may be made in a will.

Types of Bequests There are three main ways of making a gift under a will. The first type is known as a "specific legacy." Any gift of a particular item, such as coin collection, an automobile, furniture, jewelry, or a particular piece of land, is a specific legacy. If the testator gives all tangible personal property equally to his children who survive by thirty days, it is a specific legacy. All the tangible personal property is identifiable separately and may be disposed of in this manner.

Another type of gift is a general legacy or general bequest. This ordinarily takes the form of a gift of cash or of a number of shares of a particular stock. A gift of $1,000 to Bob Jones University is a general legacy, as is a gift of $100,000 to be used by a New York City hospital selected by the executors as funding for a program to study and treat those afflicted with Down syndrome. A gift of a certain sum to fund a marital deduction trust is also a general legacy. A general legacy differs from a specific legacy because the general legacy consists of property chosen from tangible property, such as cash or securities, while the specific legacy is of property that has a unique identity.

The third kind of gift that is found in a will is a residuary legacy or residuary bequest. As the name implies, this is the gift of all or a portion of all that remains after the payment of the decedent's debts, taxes, expenses, specific legacies, and general legacies. It may consist of both real and personal property.

The specific legacies are usually made first in a will, followed next by general legacies, and finally by the residuary legacy. Frequently the residue of an estate is given to trustees to hold the assets for the benefit of others. Detailed discussion of will provisions will be delayed until Chapter Ten.

Statutory Modifications of Will Provisions

Several state statutes create the possibility that provisions of a will may be modified. It is sufficient simply to mention some of the more unusual reasons for modification. However, certain reasons must be treated in some depth. Most states have statutes that would modify will provisions if, between the signing of the will and death, the testator marries, is divorced, has a child, or adopts a child. There are usually also statutory provisions to prevent a slayer from sharing in his victim's estate.

Election by Surviving Spouse In many states, but not all, a surviving spouse may elect to receive either the benefits given to him by the decedent's will or a share of the decedent's property fixed by statute. Usually the statutory share that can be obtained by election is the same as the share the surviving spouse would have received if the decedent had died intestate.

The election must be made within nine months of death because the executor must be able to determine the amount of the marital deduction on the federal estate tax return. If the surviving spouse does not elect within the time provided, he or she is required to take whatever property is given by the will, even if this is nothing or less than the spouse would have received if the decedent had died leaving no will.

By the time for distribution, of course, the decision concerning whether or not to elect to take against the will will have been made. The electing spouse must usually deliver to the personal representative written notice of the decision to take against the will. Often the rules also require that the notice must be filed with the probate court. If the spouse does choose to take the elective share rather than the will share, the spouse is then entitled to nothing more under the will. The balance of the decedent's property not needed to satisfy the elective share is distributed in accordance with the terms of the will.

If the testator provided for large specific or general legacies to be given to people other than the spouse and the spouse elects to take against the will, it may be that the property remaining after the spouse's share is paid will be insufficient to pay all legacies in full. The personal representative may then have to cut back the amount of the legacies. If this is done the legacies are said to "abate." This item will be discussed more extensively later because the problem may affect not only an estate where the spouse elects against the will, but also any estate where the testator made specific or general bequests in a total amount that exceeds the amount of the estate after debts, expenses, and taxes have been paid.

Mortmain Many years ago the British Parliament feared that priests would be able to exercise excessive influence at the deathbed. To avoid the possibility that churches would benefit inordinately from such influence, Parliament adopted the Mortmain Statute that invalidated any testamentary provision in favor of a church if that provision was added shortly before death. Most states now allow these deathbed bequests to pass under the will. The circumstances of the gift and the motive of the decedent should be considered because the testator may have a legitimate motive for making the charitable bequest.

Abatement, Ademption, and Lapse If the subject of a specific legacy (such as a piano, a coin collection, or a car) is not part of the decedent's estate at the time of death, the gift is said to be subject to "ademption." This is only a fancy word for saying that the testator cannot give away what he does not own.

If the property exists but the designated recipient has predeceased the decedent, the gift is said to "lapse." The will may provide for an alternate gift of the same property. If there is no such alternate gift, the situation may be governed by an "anti-lapse" statute that would permit distribution to other members of the deceased beneficiary's family. For example, a will provides that

$10,000 is to go to son John. John has died before the testator, leaving two children. In a state with an "anti-lapse" statute, John's two children would share the $10,000 equally, even though they are not mentioned in the will. This may not have been the intention of the testator. Most carefully drafted wills avoid this problem by providing an alternate disposition of a gift in the event a beneficiary fails to survive the testator.

If for any reason the value of the specific and/or general legacies in the will exceeds the property available for distribution, the personal representative will be faced with the problem of reducing the amount of some or all of the legacies. A legacy that is not paid in full is said to have been subject to "abatement." A legacy may abate completely or in part.

The personal representative is obligated generally to enforce the following rules of abatement, subject to variations depending upon state law:

1. Specific legacies abate last, so that all specific legacies are paid in full prior to the payment of any general legacy or residuary legacy;
2. General legacies abate next to last, so that all general legacies are paid in full prior to the payment of any residuary legacy;
3. Residuary legacies abate first;
4. If the fund is insufficient to pay all legacies in a particular class (for example, all general legacies), the legacies in that class abate pro rata. Therefore, if there was a provision for three equal gifts totaling $30,000 ($10,000 each), and only $15,000 was left to distribute, each gift would abate one-half, and each legatee would receive $5,000 rather than $10,000. Using the same figures, if there was a provision for two cash gifts, one of $20,000 and the other of $10,000, the $20,000 gift would abate to $10,000, and the $10,000 to $5,000.
5. The laws of some states provide that if there are specific legacies for a surviving spouse and issue, these abate after other specific legacies.

   In summary, specific legacies are paid first; general legacies are paid next; finally, if there is anything left, the residuary legatee or legatees receive the balance. There is a pro rata abatement within a legacy group, and local law may require that spouse or issue be favored within a group.

The Problem of Whether to Distribute in Cash or in Kind

A personal representative is usually expected to distribute the property of the estate in cash except where there is a specific gift of particular property, such as real estate, an automobile, a coin collection, or "my shares of XYZ Corporation." As you would expect, there are exceptions to the rule and to the exceptions. The will often gives the personal representative the discretion to distribute "in kind." This means to distribute the property itself, where this is more suitable in view of the situation, even though the person entitled to the property is only a general or residuary legatee. Also, where there is no discretion given in the will itself, or where there is an intestacy, state law will often permit the personal representative to petition the probate court to allow an "in kind" distribution if good reasons exist. An interested person may also petition the court for the same reasons.

Typical good reasons might be that the property is somehow unique: real estate not specifically devised and therefore passing to the residuary legatee; a family heirloom that was not specifically devised and that has sentimental value greatly in excess of its monetary value; or a collection that might in the future have value far in excess of its value at the time set for distribution and that again has not been specifically given. Distribution in kind might also be appropriate where an asset has greatly increased in value during the period of administration and a sale by the personal representative would force the estate to realize a large capital gain. The distributee might want to hold the asset for a longer period of time and defer recognition of the gain.

It is often troublesome and risky for the personal representative to hold certain of the decedent's property for the period of time needed until it can be distributed in kind after an adjudication. Houses require care and maintenance; collections may be lost or stolen; securities may decline in value. State law ordinarily protects a personal representative against liability for a decline in the value of assets received from the decedent for a reasonable period of time. That protection lasts only so long as may be reasonably necessary to accomplish an appropriate sale of the property or valuation and distribution of the property. Property held for a long time and distributed in kind must be reappraised as of the date of distribution, adding to the time and expense involved. Therefore, the special procedures necessary for the control and care of property that is to be distributed in kind should be followed from the outset and until the time of actual distribution. This also means that the personal representative must make a decision as early as possible in the administration as to what, if anything, is to be held for distribution in kind, and to check the value of property held in kind regularly to guard against the possibility that it will drastically decrease in value prior to distribution.

If it is clear that the estate will be sufficient in size to meet all claims of creditors, the personal representative may wish to distribute property in kind as soon as the necessary tax waivers and an appropriate indemnity agreement from the person receiving the property may be obtained. In some cases where the property to be distributed in kind early in the administration is income-producing property, it may be necessary to get approval by the residuary legatee of the distribution, since under the laws of many states the residuary legatee is entitled to the income received from all the property during the administration.

OBTAINING COURT APPROVAL OF DISTRIBUTION

The Schedule of Distribution

A schedule of distribution is a supplement to an account prepared to show details of distribution. A schedule of distribution may be included in the account filed with the court or it may be a separate document depending on local law and custom. The discussion that follows primarily considers the schedule of distribution as a separate document, but the general principles are applicable to a schedule of distribution that is incorporated in the account.

The schedule of distribution sets forth all of the transactions in the estate from the date of the account until the date set for distribution. It may be that actual, physical delivery of the assets will take place a few days after the closing of the schedule of distribution reporting period, particularly if state law requires that notice of the filing of the schedule has to be given to the distributees and that they must have an opportunity to lodge objections to the schedule. The assets are revalued in the schedule on the date of distribution.

Deciding Whether or Not a Schedule of Distribution Is Necessary

It is ordinarily good practice for the personal representative to prepare a schedule of distribution and have it approved by the persons interested before actually distributing the property of an estate. Where the account has been filed with the court and an adjudication handed down, the court may or may not require the personal representative to file a schedule of distribution. In an estate where there is a complicated disposition and numerous beneficiaries, or where property is to go to trustees after the estate administration, the court will almost invariably require that a schedule of distribution be filed. In cases where there are few parties and an outright distribution of the property, the court may not require a schedule. There are also states where the law requires that a schedule of distribution be filed for every estate.

Both where there is no formal accounting and where there is one but no schedule is required by the court, the personal representative may nevertheless decide that the preparation of a schedule and its approval are desirable. If the distributees desire a non–pro rata distribution, each one taking different assets but with an equal value, for instance, the property will have to be revalued and an informal schedule approved to provide a memorial of the agreement between the parties. Even if the parties are satisfied to accept a pro rata distribution, the personal representative may think it helpful to provide a schedule of distribution supplementing the account (whether or not either is filed with the court) to show the parties all of the transactions in the estate up to the time of actual distribution.

The schedule sets forth the names of the persons or organizations entitled to the distributions and the respective amount or kind of property to which he, she, or it is entitled. The form of the schedule may be prescribed by the rules of the local probate court. It is usually signed at the end by the personal representative and, if the schedule has been prepared in accordance with the terms of a court adjudication and is to be filed, the personal representative's counsel must certify that the schedule conforms as to parties, amounts, etc., with the requirements set forth in the adjudication. An example of a schedule of distribution follows. The schedule has been prepared and filed to conform with the terms of a court adjudication of the account.

EXAMPLE
Schedule of Distribution

[Caption][1]

Schedule of Distribution in accordance with Adjudication dated January 30, 1992, of J. Smith, upon the First and Final Account of Jane R. Dunn, executrix:

PRINCIPAL		
Balance of principal per Account		$128,028.15
Add:		
Distributions to beneficiaries per Account		28,120.00
		$156,148.15
To which add:		
Increase in value of real estate and securities reappraised as of January 30, 1992, per Schedule A attached:		
Reappraised value	$125,400.00	
Account value	120,000.00	5,400.00
		$161,548.15

1. Reprinted with the permission of the Fidelity Bank, Philadelphia, Pennsylvania, from "Forms for Use Before the Register of Wills and Orphans' Court Division in Philadelphia," 1985. Note: The dates in the example were revised in 1991.

From which deduct:		
January 17, 1992—Jones & Jones advance to Register of Wills, additional fee for filing account		15.00
Balance for distribution as of January 31, 1992		$161,533.15
Which is awarded as follows:		
To: JANE R. DUNN per ITEM 1 of will		
Personal possessions		$ 1,120.00
To: JOSEPH B. DUNN, JR., per ITEM 2 of will		
Cash bequest		1,000.00
To: ELAINE S. DUNN per ITEM 2 of will		
Cash bequest		$ 1,000.00
To: JANE R. DUNN and UPSTANDING TRUST COMPANY, trustees under ITEM 3 of will (marital trust)		
Amount equal to one-half of adjusted gross estate per Federal estate tax return[2]	$94,893.18	
Less value of personal possessions and jointly owned property per Schedule E of said return	20,000.00	74,893.18
Composed of:		
Cash distribution during administration of estate	$25,000.00	
Now distributable:		
350 shs. Alpha Tel. & Tel. Co., com.	19,600.00	
700 shs. Beta Million Uranium Mines, com.	1,680.00	
700 shs. Pure Gold Medical Center Inc., com.	28,000.00	
Cash	613.18	
	$74,893.18	
To: JANE R. DUNN and UPSTANDING TRUST COMPANY, trustees under ITEM 4 of will (residuary trust)		
$20,000 Zephyr Co., 6% due January 15, 1997	$20,000.00	
150 shs. Alpha Tel. & Tel. Co., com.	8,400.00	
300 shs. Beta Million Uranium Mines, com.	720.00	
300 shs. Pure Gold Medical Center Inc., com.	12,000.00	

2. The will was written in 1970. There was no language provided in the will to allow the estate to take advantage of the unlimited marital deduction. Therefore the 1970 law had to be used.

Cash	7,399.97	
	$48,519.97	
and the following Real Property:		
premises known as 47 Main St., Philadelphia, described as follows:	35,000.00	83,519.97
[set forth a legal description of premises]		$161,533.15
INCOME		
Balance of Income per Account		$ 2,077.96
Add:		
Distributions to Jane R. Dunn per Account		5,000.00
		$ 7,077.96
To which add:		
Alpha Telephone & Telegraph Co., com.		
November 15, 1991, Dividend on 500 shs.	$ 535.00	
February 14, 1992, Dividend on 500 shs.	535.00	1,070.00
Safety First Savings Bank		
January 30, 1992, Interest		327.00
$20,000 Zephyr Co. 6% bond due January 15, 1997		
January 15, 1992, Interest		600.00
Balance for Distribution as of January 31, 1992		$ 9,074.96
Which is awarded as follows:		
To: JANE R. DUNN, cash		$ 9,074.96
Composed of		
Distribution per Account	$ 5,000.00	
Now distributable	4,074.96	
	$ 9,074.96	

I hereby certify that the foregoing Schedule of Distribution is correct and in conformity with the adjudication filed, that due notice of the filing thereof was given as required by Rule 72 of the Court, and that I or my agent have examined the last recorded deed or the record thereof and that to the best of my knowledge the description of the property in the Schedule of Distribution is correct.[3]

____

John Jones
Attorney for Accountant

3. The form of this certification is not required at this time by the rules of court but it is under consideration for adoption by the court.

The rules do not require the accountant to sign the schedule of distribution.

Real property is to be described in the same detail and with the same particularity as is commonly required to be included in a deed, including information pertinent to the derivation of title.

Schedule A

Reappraisal of Real Estate and Securities

	Value 1/30/90	Account Value
Real Estate		
47 Main Street, Philadelphia, Pa., conveyed to decedent by deed dated January 14, 1968, recorded in Philadelphia Co. Deed Book 312, p. 73 et seq.	$ 35,000.00	$ 35,000.00
Bonds		
$20,000 Zephyr Co. 6% due January 15, 1997	20,000.00	20,000.00
Stocks		
500 shs. Alpha Tel. & Tel. Co., com.	28,000.00	25,000.00
1000 shs. Beta Million Uranium Mines, com.	2,400.00	4,000.00
1000 shs. Pure Gold Medical Center Inc., com.	40,000.00	38,000.00
	$125,400.00	$120,000.00

Techniques Used in Preparing the Schedule of Distribution

The beginning balances for the schedule are the respective values of principal and income (where the income accounting has not been waived by the parties) shown in the court's adjudication of the account. The personal representative should be careful to see that the adjudication figures agree with those submitted as closing balances in the account.

Accounting for Receipts during the Interim and Reappraisal of Assets Principal transactions, such as the sale or conversion of securities, should be reflected as an addition if the sale resulted in a gain, or as a deduction if the sale resulted in a loss, when compared with the value of the item in the account. The purchase of an item should be reflected as an addition and, to the extent principal cash was used for the purchase, the reduction should be shown as a deduction. Any expenses that are properly principal expenses (such as the fee for filing the account) should be shown as deductions. Where there is a sale or conversion resulting in neither a gain nor a loss, it should be disclosed in the schedule as a "zero" transaction. All of the property held at the distribution date should be reappraised as of that date. If the reappraisal results in a net gain (total gains minus total losses), this should be shown as an addition; any net loss should be shown as a deduction. Principal stock dividends should be shown at zero on the addition side. Cash received in lieu of a fractional share issued pursuant to a stock dividend should be shown as an addition.

A similar procedure should be followed for income. Dividends should be shown, when received, as additions. Stock dividends allocable to income and cash in lieu of fractional shares should be reflected in additions, respectively, at zero or at the dollar amount received. Any fees or expenses properly borne by income should be deducted. Note that income was charged with the amount of the interest portion paid to the Internal Revenue Service for a federal estate tax deficiency at line 18, page 11, of the Peter Chessman Schedule of Distribution because income was earned on the amount of principal later paid to the IRS to make up the principal portion of the estate tax deficiency.

Special Problems If There Is a Marital Deduction Gift or Trust
Chapter Five included a discussion of the computation of the marital deduction for federal estate tax purposes. Bear in mind that a gift will not qualify for the marital deduction unless it is given outright to the spouse or given to the spouse in a marital trust. At the time of distribution, the personal representative must separate out the property available for distribution into the marital deduction gift or trust. While there are hybrids, the two most common types of marital deduction gifts are, as previously mentioned, the pecuniary (or dollar amount) marital gift and the fractional share marital gift.

At the time of distribution, the pecuniary marital gift is easier to handle than the fractional share marital gift. Where the testator provided for a dollar amount marital gift, the amount of the gift is fixed when the final estate tax determination is made. Therefore, once the assets have been reappraised, a representative amount of income-producing property equal to the dollar amount of the gift will be set aside and used to fund it. This division of property must be done with care and with consideration given to investment problems and tax problems, as well as seeing that the provisions of the will are being complied with.

Where there is a fractional share marital deduction (the testator leaves only a percentage of the estate to the spouse, the remainder to a "residuary trust," usually for the benefit of the other family members), the marital portion shares proportionately in either the gains or losses in value of assets until the time of distribution. The value distributed in satisfaction of the marital gift may, therefore, be larger or smaller than the marital deduction allowed on the federal estate tax return. The usual assumption is that the fraction used to calculate the marital deduction will be applied to each separate item for purposes of arriving at the amount to be distributed as the marital portion.

Some wills specify that the fractional marital share need not be satisfied with a porportionate share of each asset. Be aware that most wills today use the unlimited marital deduction, in which case the entire estate will pass to the spouse, either outright or in trust.

Designation of Exact Dollar Amounts and Earmarking of Specific Legacies for Distributees The final step in the preparation of the schedule of distribution is to set forth the names of the distributees, a reference to the provision in the will or trust instrument that states the kind and amount of property each is to receive, and the property to be distributed. The total amount being distributed must equal the value of the property administered by the personal representative as reappraised, minus the expenses, if any, incurred after the account was filed and prior to distribution.

In the event the court has ordered that a fund must be set aside to meet a possible contingent claim, such as additional tax, etc., this fact must be set down in the schedule, together with a statement about the event that will release the fund and the person entitled to it at that time.

Approval of a Schedule of Distribution

If the schedule of distribution is not to be filed with a court, the fiduciary may, for his or her own protection, wish to obtain the approval of the interested parties. If the schedule is filed with a court, it is necessary either to obtain approval of the interested parties or to give them notice of the filing. The schedule of distribution is normally automatically approved by the court if no objections to it are filed within a period specified by the court rules. Upon approval of the schedule of distribution it is appropriate to carry out the physical distribution of the assets.

PHYSICAL DISTRIBUTION

General Problems of Distribution

Distribution to a Minor or Incompetent If the distributee is a minor, the personal representative may not distribute property to that person and be effectively released from further liability for the property unless the will specifically relieves the personal representative of that liability. If a minor were to take property without that waiver in the will and he should squander or waste it, when the minor reached majority he could disavow the distribution and sue to surcharge the personal representative for the value of the property at the time it was distributed. Therefore, the personal representative must insist that a guardian of the property be appointed by the state court having jurisdiction over appointments of guardians. Furthermore, the personal representative must distribute only to the guardian.

It is not the personal representative's responsibility to have a guardian appointed, but the personal representative must require that one be appointed before distributing the property. Similar considerations arise if the distributee is someone who has been declared incompetent by a court or if the personal representative has actual knowledge of incompetency even if there has been no court proceeding.

Distribution to a Foreign Fiduciary Distribution must frequently be made to another fiduciary. The fiduciary receiving the distribution may be a trustee, a guardian, or perhaps the personal representative of a deceased beneficiary. This does not usually present significant problems if the receiving fiduciary is a resident of the same state as the distributing fiduciary. When the fiduciaries are from different states, they are known as "foreign fiduciaries." There are elaborate procedures to insure that the foreign fiduciary has been properly appointed so that the distributing fiduciary is protected from liability when making distribution to such a fiduciary.

Distribution of Real Estate

Distribution When Real Estate Is Listed in a Schedule of Distribution Filed with the Court When real estate is listed by metes and bounds (a surveyor's description) in a schedule of distribution filed with and approved by the court, an excerpt from the schedule, certified by the court to be correct, must be filed with the recorder of deeds for the county in which the real estate is located. The recorder of deeds will index the name of the decedent as "grantor" and the name of the distributee as "grantee." Any fee charged by the recorder of deeds is a proper expense of administration.

In states where there are taxes on the transfer of property from one person to another[4] the transfer from an estate to a distributee is usually exempt from such tax. In order to have the deed recorded without payment of the tax, however, it may be necessary to file applications for a waiver of the tax. The personal representative (or attorney for the estate) should contact the county recorder of deeds or the tax assessor to determine how the exemption should be claimed.

4. Such a tax is normally referred to as a real estate transfer tax.

Distribution of Real Estate Where No Schedule Is Prepared or Where a Schedule of Distribution Is Prepared but Is Not Filed If no schedule of distribution is going to be filed or when no schedule is prepared, real estate may be transferred on the books of the recorder of deeds by filing an executor's deed, showing the personal representative as "grantor" and the distributee as "grantee."

The Problem of Whether or Not to Transfer Real Estate on the Record Where No Schedule Is Filed If real estate is held by the decedent as a tenant by the entireties or a joint tenant with right of survivorship, title passes to the surviving joint tenant automatically, requiring no formal steps by the personal representative. If the surviving joint tenant sells the property, he can document the claim of title by exhibiting a death certificate for the predeceased joint tenant.

Although there is no absolute requirement that a transfer be recorded in the recorder of deeds office if the property was held solely by the decedent or as a tenant in common, complications may arise otherwise. For example, there may be problems later when the claim of title has to be documented for a sale. The personal representative will still have to execute a deed to convey the property, and if a sale occurs years later, the personal representative could be dead or disabled. Also, tax bills will continue to be sent in the name of the decedent. Such notices could be lost or mislaid, or the post office may refuse to forward them to the personal representative after a period of time. Therefore, it should be standard practice to record the transfer in every case, even though a recording fee must be paid and additional paperwork is required.

Cancellation of Fire and Liability Insurance Any liability and fire insurance on the real estate should be cancelled, and a premium refund secured, following distribution. The cancellation value (or refund of premium) is an estate asset.

Distribution of Tangible Personal Property

Tangible personal property is usually the most unwieldy property that a personal representative has to administer. It is bulky in size and often requires special handling and storage. The personal representative may therefore want to distribute tangible personal property prior to the time set for distribution of other property. After the property has been appraised and the decision has been made to distribute, the personal representative must get tax waivers from the Internal Revenue Service if distribution is prior to the filing of the federal estate tax return.

After the waiver is obtained, the personal representative may deliver the property to the distributee. The expenses of delivery (shipping, etc.) are not usually considered a responsibility of the estate, unless the testator has specifically provided for payment of them. The personal representative should get a receipt, release, and agreement of indemnity from the distributee for the property upon delivery. Of course, if distribution is made after a schedule of distribution is filed and approved, the indemnification is not necessary. However, the personal representative should still secure receipts from the distributees.

Following delivery of the tangible personal property, the personal representative should cancel any insurance being carried on it and obtain a rebate of unused premiums.

Distribution of Intangible Personal Property

Distributing Cash The personal representative who wishes to distribute cash needs only to draw a check payable to the distributee and mark the payment on the estate's records. Where there is partial distribution of cash prior to the filing of the schedule of distribution, the personal representative should obtain a receipt, release, and agreement of indemnity. The cancelled check is usually a sufficient receipt at other times.

Distributing Stocks and Bonds The personal representative may take either of two approaches in distributing stocks and bonds: (a) he may deliver to the distributee the certificates for the security registered in the name of the estate together with a stock power in negotiable form (signed) and a short certificate; or (b) he may reregister the security in the name of the distributee and then deliver the new certificates to the distributee. From the standpoint of the distributee, the second alternative is preferable, but it is time consuming for the personal representative. The first alternative is more risky because of increased chances of loss or theft. A broker with a longstanding relationship to the decedent may be willing to make the transfers necessary to permit distribution. Another option may be to put all the estate securities in a broker's account in "street name" when the estate first comes into existence, then at the time of distribution the broker is usually willing to register the certificates in the name of the distributees.

If securities are part of a partial distribution made prior to the filing of a schedule of distribution, the personal representative should again obtain a receipt, release, and agreement of indemnity.

If, after the distribution, the personal representative has no further need for a safe deposit box, the box should be surrendered by delivery of the key or keys. In such a case, a receipt should be obtained for the keys. Normally, a bank will not rebate any portion of the box rental fee. The special requirements to distribute U.S. Savings Bonds are discussed in Chapter Three.

SATISFACTION OF AWARD

Some courts print and make available forms called "satisfaction of award." The purpose of the satisfaction of award is to assure the court that the awards made in its adjudication have been satisfied by proper distribution.

Sometimes a court may require the filing of such forms. At other times, even where no account has been filed with the court, a fiduciary will file satisfactions of award simply to place on public record that distribution of the estate's assets was completed. Where such forms are available, they may be used generally as receipts for distributions.

DISCHARGE OF FIDUCIARY

When a fiduciary has completed all of his or her duties, including a complete distribution of the estate or trust, the fiduciary is entitled to be discharged from fiduciary duties by the court. Although many jurisdictions have such a procedure, it is seldom used. Executors and administrators frequently decide that possible later-discovered assets of the estate will be easier to deal with if they never obtain a formal discharge. This is particularly the case when the fiduciary is a family member. However, if the fiduciary is a corporation (such as a bank trust department) or an unrelated party, they will not wish to continue to be liable for the estate administration. After a reasonable period of time, they will ask the court to discharge them from the responsibility.

One reason a fiduciary may wish to petition the court for a formal discharge is to be relieved of the burden of an annual premium if the fiduciary is bonded. Most well-drafted wills and trusts waive the requirement of a bond, so the problem usually arises in the administration of an intestate estate. Under most circumstances a bonding company will waive payment of future premiums on the bond if the company receives adequate proof that a proper and complete distribution has been accomplished. Forms for that purpose are available from the various bonding companies.

CHAPTER TEN

Estate Planning and Drafting

In today's society, nearly everyone has assets that have been accumulated, unspent, and partially or totally unencumbered that, in the normal course of events, an individual will want to transfer at death. In addition, the proliferation and popularity of life insurance, profit-sharing plans, pension plans, individual retirement accounts, and other types of employee benefit or self-employed retirement-type plans not only provide increased financial security at death, disability, or retirement, but also have the direct result of creating a separate body of estate-related assets that must be planned for. The object of estate planning is to assure, at death, the transmission of a client's assets to those people and organizations the client may choose in a manner that assures the recipient the maximum benefit of the assets. In many cases the primary focus is on finding ways to minimize the tax burdens, while maximizing the objectives and desires, of the client.

Although a lawyer should always be involved, if for no other reason than the fact that legal documents are critical to the estate-planning process, there are many sources of estate-planning advice. Life insurance salesmen frequently give such advice. Most major banks have estate-planning departments. Some accountants and investment advisors also purport to provide estate-planning services. Sometimes the various sources work together for the benefit of a single client. Even when the planning process is begun by nonlawyers, the final steps usually require the services of a lawyer.

Most estate plans involve the writing of a will. The estate plans for some clients may involve one or more deeds of trust in addition to a will. In most parts of the country, such documents are prepared only by lawyers.

The function of a lawyer's assistant in the estate-planning process will vary from employer to employer. With the background provided by this book, the lawyer's assistant should be prepared to obtain the relevant information from a client, participate with the lawyer in making planning judgments based on tax calculations, draft wills and trusts by using forms provided by the lawyer, supervise the proper execution of those documents, and make certain that other planning decisions are carried out.

It should be emphasized that information coming to a lawyer or lawyer's assistant must be treated in strict confidence. Clients are reluctant to disclose to anyone the details of their financial and personal lives, and as this information is of critical importance, full and complete disclosure is essential if an effective estate-planning job is to be done. If a lawyer, bank officer, or member of the staff of either fails to honor the confidentiality of such information, clients who learn of such breach will seek advice from others.

THE INITIAL CLIENT INTERVIEW

A thorough discussion with the client concerning his or her affairs is a crucial first step to good estate planning. The planner must have a complete grasp of all the relevant facts to know how and to whom the client's property is to be transmitted and how to minimize the tax burdens. In addition, information obtained during the client's lifetime is frequently helpful in the settlement of the estate. Facts obtained at the time the estate plan is being discussed can aid immeasurably when the time comes to determine the proper place of probate as well as the location of assets and heirs. Such information can even be of value in disposing of assets promptly at fair prices and in the completion of the federal estate tax return.

An estate-planning interview with the client should, therefore, be lengthy, and the client should be encouraged to be candid. Many lawyers and banks have found it helpful to use an information checklist such as the one presented here. Sometimes a client is given a copy of such a checklist prior to an interview to give him or her an opportunity to gather information in advance. The checklist also serves to protect the lawyer in the event a question arises after death concerning how the estate plan was created.

Information Needed

Careful study of the checklist gives an idea of just how detailed the estate-planning information should be. The client's formal name and any names she has used in her business and personal affairs should be stated. It is also essential to get an accurate family tree with names, birth dates, addresses, and marital status. It may be important to know whether any of the family members listed are illegitimate or adopted. Marriage dates, previous divorces, domicile both present and past, dependents, and the general health of all pertinent individuals should also be listed if possible.

Always obtain copies of any of the client's current wills and trusts as well as those from which she benefits. It may also be necessary to obtain copies of the latest filed gift and income tax returns. Learning the names of the client's accountant, banker, stock broker, insurance agent, doctor, and clergyman can be most helpful both before and after death. The client may resent completing such a detailed checklist; however, it must be explained to the client, that the checklist is detailed only for his or her benefit.

CHECKLIST

Estate Planning Information (Confidential)

Prepared by ____________________
Date ____________________

I. CLIENT

1. Name ____________________
2. Other Names Used ____________________
3. Address ____________________
4. Telephone Numbers ____________________
5. Social Security Number ____________________
6. Birth Date ____________________ Age ____________
7. Place of Birth ____________________
8. Marital Status ____________________
9. Date Married ____________________
10. Prior Marriages ____________________
11. Present Health ____________________
12. Occupation and/or Business ____________________
13. Business Address ____________________
14. Are you and your spouse citizens of the USA? ____________________

II. FAMILY AND DEPENDENTS

	Names	Age or Birth Date	Family Status	Financial Status and/or Occupation	Social Security Number
1. Spouse					
	______	______	______	______	______
	______	______	______	______	______
	______	______	______	______	______
2. Children (Note any adoptions and addresses where appropriate)					
	______	______	______	______	______
	______	______	______	______	______
	______	______	______	______	______
	______	______	______	______	______
3. Grandchildren (Indicate parent)					
	______	______	______	______	______
	______	______	______	______	______
	______	______	______	______	______
4. Parents					
	______	______	______	______	

Father

________ ________ ________ ________

Mother (Maiden Name)
Address: ________

5. Other Dependents (brothers, sisters, and other relatives)

________ ________ ________ ________
________ ________ ________ ________
________ ________ ________ ________

6. Other Beneficiaries

________ ________ ________ ________
________ ________ ________ ________

7. Special facts re persons noted above (i.e., adoptions, disabilities, etc.)

____
____

III. ASSETS

	Description (How title held)	**Estimated Fair Market Value**
1. Real Estate (note name of mortgagee and size of the mortgage)	________	________
2. Cash on Deposit, (Bank account number, note whether savings or checking account)	________	________
3. Stocks (Publicly Held)	________	________
4. Bonds (Publicly Held)	________	________
5. Mortgages and Miscellaneous	________	________
6. Tangible Personal Property	________	________
7. Jointly Held Property	________	________
8. Special Collections (Antiques, Stamp or Coin, etc.)	________	________
9. Safe Deposit Box: Bank	________	Number ________
10. Business Interests (Note here stocks and bonds of closely held corporations and give relevant details)	________	

11. (a) Life Insurance

Company (Policy #)	Beneficiary	Settlement Option	Face Amount
			$
			$
			$

	Company	Type Plan	Benefit(s)
(b) Disability Insurance			
(c) Health and Accident			
(d) Hospitalization			

12. Employment Benefits

Type Plan	Company	Amount Vested, Contributed, or Deferred	Estimated Income or Lump-Sum Payment	Death Benefit
Pension				
Profit Sharing				
Thrift				
Deferred Compensation				
Self-employed retirement fund				

13. Government Benefits (established policy location)

	Description	Account Registration or Serial Number	Retirement Benefit	Death Benefit
Social Security				
Veteran				
—Pension				
—Death Benefit				
—Disability Benefit				

Other ______________________________

____

14. Interest in Estates or Trusts

Name	Fiduciary	Interest and Value

15. Expectancies

____

____

IV. DOCUMENTS REQUIRED

(Checklist for review and/or to establish location.)

Check

_____ 1. Previous Will(s); Spouse's Will; Codicils

_____ 2. Trust agreements or wills under which you are a beneficiary.

_____ 3. Ante-nuptial or other property agreement with spouse; divorce decree

_____ 4. Life Insurance and casualty policies
_____ 5. Business agreements (Partnerships, stockholders' agreements)
_____ 6. Employee Benefit Plans
_____ 7. Deeds to realty, title insurance policy, and title abstract; mortgages and leases; zoning use permits
_____ 8. Cemetery plot deed
_____ 9. Income tax returns, receipts for real estate taxes, water and sewer rents
_____10. Birth and marriage certificates for husband, wife, and children

V. SPOUSE'S ASSETS

____

____

VI. LIABILITIES (Other than mortgage)

1. Notes, Loans, and Judgments ______________________________
2. Agreements ______________________________
3. Support Orders ______________________________
   Other ______________________________

VII. GIFTS

Have any gifts requiring gift tax returns been made? If yes, give dates, amount, and name of donee. Attach copies of returns.

____

____

VIII. PERSONAL REPRESENTATIVES

	Name	**Address/Telephone**
1. Accountant	____________	____________
2. Clergyman/Rabbi	____________	____________
3. Banker	____________	____________
4. Gen. Ins. Broker (Fire, Auto, Liab.)	____________	____________
5. Insurance Agent	____________	____________
6. Stock Broker	____________	____________
7. Member of and/ or attend	____________ Church/Synagogue	____________ Address

Member of Lodges, Fraternal Organizations, etc.

Name (Include chapter name and number)	**Death, Disability or other Benefits**
______________________	____________
______________________	____________

Gifts made

Date ____________

Amount ____________

To whom? ______________________________

PLAN OF DISTRIBUTION

1. Personal effects ______________________________
____
2. Other Specific Legacies ______________________________
____
3. Pecuniary Legacies ______________________________
____
4. Real Estate ______________________________
____
5. Residue:
   (1) ______________________________
   (2) ______________________________
   (3) ______________________________
   (4) ______________________________
   (5) ______________________________
6. Terms of Trust ______________________________
____
7. Trustee Powers:
   (a) Investments ______________________________
   (b) Invasion of Principal ______________________________
   (c) Others ______________________________
8. Spendthrift Clause ______________________________
9. Tax Clause ______________________________
10. Appointments: (Note addresses where appropriate)
   (a) Excecutor (s) (1) ______________________________
   (2) ______________ (3) ______________
   (b) Trustee(s) (1) ______________________________
   (2) ______________ (3) ______________
   (c) Guardians:
   Person (1) ______________ (2) ______________
   Address ______________ ______________
   Estate (1) ______________ (2) ______________
   Address ______________ ______________
11. Fiduciary Compensation letter ______________________________

____

Assets and Liabilities Determining the size, type, location, and nature of ownership of a client's assets is one of the most important aspects of information gathering. Strangely, however, this is often a most difficult task. Much time can be saved if a checklist is sent to the client in advance or if he is advised before the interview that detailed information about his assets will be needed. When all the assets have been finally inventoried, the client will often express surprise at his original underestimate. Few will have difficulty remembering assets such as cash, securities, and real estate, but certain assets, including insurance, are easily overlooked.

It is important to question the client closely about such items as life insurance, both individual and group; pledged assets; receivables; powers of appointment; trusts; employee benefits; patents; and valuable collections. Frequently overlooked is the value of an individual's pension plan; an asset such as a note given or pledged by a family member; accident, health and key-man insurance; and stock options. Sometimes it is important to question a client about "expectancies." An expectancy is an interest under the will of someone who is still living. The nature of the recommended estate plan may be different if, for example, the client is the only grandson of a ninety-year-old millionaire.

An integral part of the asset information obtained should be the nature of ownership. Are all of the insurance policies really owned by the client? Is his real estate in his name alone or does he and his wife hold it as joint tenants? Wherever possible the actual insurance policies and pertinent deeds should be inspected by the lawyer or the lawyer's assistant. Quite often a client's recollection of the actual instrument is imperfect, both as to ownership and special provisions and, sometimes with insurance, even as to amounts. Both tax calculations and the way property will pass at death depend on the answers to these questions. The nature of ownership in community property states can have special significance. Some interesting problems of tracing can arise if the client has passed in and out of community property states during his marriage.

Detailed inquiry into the client's indebtedness is important. The mortgage on his home will be remembered but often a personal note or margin account with his stockbroker will not.

Likely Appraisers and Markets for Sale If the client has an asset with a limited market, like a patent, a trademark, a copyright, a real estate investment, a collection, hobby equipment, or a business interest, he can be quite helpful in estimating its value and in recommending likely appraisers and purchasers. Such information will prove invaluable after the client's death.

Agreements Although the assets may appear ripe for inclusion in the client's estate plan, they may be subject to significant restrictions that can only be discovered by careful inquiry. These restrictions often take the form of agreements voluntarily entered into by the client. If the client has been married more than once, it is appropriate to ask about the existence of a separation agreement made in the process of obtaining a divorce or a prenuptial agreement made with the second spouse. A previously married person should be asked if there is a support order or alimony judgment outstanding against the client in favor of children or a former spouse. As is the case with insurance policies and deeds, the actual separation agreement, prenuptial agreement, or support order should be produced for review by the lawyer or the lawyer's assistant.

If the client is involved in a small business, whether it be a corporation or a partnership, there may be buy-sell agreements, stock purchase agreements, partnership agreements, and options in the hands of others that affect the disposition of his stock or interest. Any agreements made by the client that would affect the transmission or valuation of his wealth after his death should be known by the estate planner, and copies of such agreements should be carefully studied.

Dispositive Wishes An important element of any estate-planning interview is to learn the client's wishes concerning the ultimate disposition of his or her property. Using a checklist that roughly corresponds to the format of a simple will helps both the information-gathering and will-drafting tasks.

The Body Be certain to record in the will all information on what the client wants in regard to funeral arrangements and the disposal of his or her body. The provision can be omitted altogether or it can be very detailed. Although many states may not recognize such instructions as binding, the information can prove useful for those later responsible for funeral plans. Many states have adopted, in whole or with some modification, the Uniform Anatomical Gift Act, in the interest of providing statutory authorization for the gift after death of all or specific parts of the human body. It is recommended that if the client wishes to make an organ donation, the family and personal physician also be given separate letters stating the client's intentions. That way the donation can be made promptly, without having to wait to open the safe deposit box to find the will. If the testator has "unusual" desires and some family members might not otherwise believe that the testator really wanted such arrangements, it helps to have the testator's instructions in the will.

Specific Gifts The client should be questioned about any specific gifts he would like to make of tangible property, cash, or other assets. If tangible property is involved, sufficient information should be recorded to permit identification of the objects at a later time.

Residue Property not disposed of in specific gifts is often treated as part of the residue that may be divided in terms of portions or percentages to be distributed among named individual beneficiaries or charities. If charities are involved, the possibility of a general or restricted gift should be discussed, as well as the erection of a memorial or plaque in the decedent's name or in the name of others. The distribution may be immediate, at the termination of a trust, or some combination of the two. Contingent beneficiaries should be named in the event the primary beneficiaries fail to survive.

Fiduciaries An executor to administer the estate should be named. It must be remembered that bestowing the job of executor frequently is not really a favor. It does entail work. A corporate executive may well be worth the fee and the corporate fee schedule often does not exceed those fees or commissions requested by an individual fiduciary. Thought should also be given to successor executors or even co-executors. The age or ages of the fiduciaries are also of great practical importance. An otherwise capable individual may be too old for a young testator.

If trusts are to be created either in a will or in independent documents, the trustees and their successors should be chosen carefully. The duties of a trustee may extend over many years and pertain to several individual beneficiaries of varying ages. Therefore, it is important to provide for successors if individual trustees are to be used and also to consider carefully the respective ages of the trustees and beneficiaries. Frequently, an individual will be best served by having an individual and corporate fiduciary serving together.

In many states a decedent has the right to name by will a person to raise his minor children (a "guardian of the person") and persons to hold property during the incapacity (minority or illness) of beneficiaries (a "guardian of the estate"). As part of the interview, the client should be encouraged to decide whether or not guardians should be named in the will and, if so, who should act in those capacities. This too is an important decision, and the client should also be encouraged to discuss the potential guardianship with those individuals whom the client is contemplating appointing. Where the children will be raised, whether one household can be retained, and what religion will be practiced, if applicable, should also be discussed as candidly as possible.

Discussion of Fees

The subject of fees for estate-planning services as well as for the ultimate estate administration is likely to be discussed at the initial interviews. Clients are frequently reluctant to ask about fees, but a frank discussion at that point may be helpful. Practices vary significantly from place to place. It has been traditional for lawyers to undercharge for estate-planning services on the theory that they will recover the loss in fees if retained to administer the estate. The recent trend is toward charges that more adequately compensate for estate-planning services, although it is frequently difficult to charge for all of the time that a thorough estate plan entails.

A written agreement should be signed so that the bill (which may be rendered several months later) will be consistent with what the client has been told.

THE TECHNIQUES OF PLANNING

For purposes of analysis, the information-gathering process can be neatly separated from the planning process. In fact, each process affects the other. The type of information gathered and the dispositive wishes of the client may be influenced by planning considerations. As a result of this kind of flow of information and ideas in two directions, it may be necessary to have two or more interviews with a client before the client and the lawyer can be sure that the best possible planning has been done.

Maximizing benefits can generally be achieved by arranging three things: (1) a sufficiently liquid estate, (2) the prompt disposal of assets at the highest prices possible, and (3) the payment of as few tax dollars and administration expenses as possible. These steps take careful planning and the time for such planning is during the client's lifetime.

Liquidity

Simply stated, liquidity is the capability to turn assets into cash quickly. Some degree of liquidity is essential to avoid the potential forced sales, the penalties, and the interest charges incident to the process of settling an estate. The executor with no cash on hand to pay debts, administration costs, funeral expenses, and taxes often finds himself in a real dilemma. If the obligations of the estate (including specific bequests) are not paid within certain time limits, the estate will have to pay interest and even penalties in some cases. Deadlines, which are statutory in nature, and which pertain primarily to the payment of the federal estate tax and the state inheritance tax, as well as the satisfaction of specific bequests, should be met if the estate is to be administered efficiently. On the other hand, raising the cash to avoid those problems may entail the disposal of assets at sacrifice prices. Having cash or a source of cash readily available can actually save the estate money. Most people have sufficient cash, treasury bills, commercial paper, or receivables so that upon their deaths the executors are able to pay immediate obligations. Sufficient time usually remains to sell the more liquid assets such as securities to raise the additional cash needed. Even if this is not the case, heirs sometimes are willing to make loans to the estate if other possible means of raising the cash are not palatable.

Once the planner has an idea of the size of a client's estate, it is a relatively simple matter to predict cash needs. One must merely add the cash necessary to pay funeral expenses, debts, administration expenses, death taxes, and cash bequests. If the client does not possess the cash and securities necessary to meet those needs, various means of assuring liquidity must be considered.

Life Insurance Life insurance, in addition to providing a source of funds to generate the lost income that must be replaced upon the death of the family wage earner, is a vehicle frequently used to improve the liquidity of an estate. Assuming the client is insurable, the uses of insurance can be varied. If the prime concern is the maintenance and support of a spouse and family, they can be named beneficiaries. Not only will this give them needed cash immediately (frequently free of state death taxes and the reach of the client's creditors), but it can also serve as a source of cash loans to those responsible for settling the estate.

Often it is desirable to have insurance for the purpose of "funding" buy-sell agreements related to business interests. Insurance proceeds will enable surviving partners or shareholders or the business itself to buy the client's interest from his or her estate. The ability to dispose of such interests promptly aids immeasurably in the administration of the estate and also provides liquid funds for funeral expenses, debts and obligations of the decedent, and administration expenses.

One popular estate-planning device is the life insurance trust agreement (called LITA for short). It is an inter-vivos (established during the lifetime of the settlor) revocable trust in which the trustees are named as the beneficiary of the settlor's life insurance policies. Immediately upon the death of the insured the trustees can assume the management of the assets for the heirs, and the trust can serve as a source of loans in case the settlor's estate is not sufficiently liquid.

Oddly, the estate itself, which is the entity most likely to be in need of cash subsequent to the decedent's death, frequently should not be named beneficiary of life insurance policies. In many states, payment of the proceeds to be named beneficiary rather than the estate will shield the proceeds from creditors and state death taxes. In addition, payment of life insurance proceeds to the estate will subject them to the costs and delays incident to probate.

Acquiring More Liquid Assets Clients are often quite set in a pattern of investment. It can be most difficult to get them to change the composition of their assets. They are accustomed to having their net worth work for them in a particular manner. If the client will not or cannot obtain insurance, then asset-juggling becomes imperative. The sale of business and real estate interests and the opening of savings accounts and the purchase of marketable widely held stocks, bonds, and commercial paper are advisable. If at all feasible and practical, these steps might be quite beneficial to a client who is heavily indebted during his lifetime and would also preclude the perils of forced sales or unfavorable market conditions often encountered in meeting post-death liquidity needs.

The Internal Revenue Code provides some relief for certain estates that are tied up with closely held business interests that lack liquidity. The Tax Reform Act of 1976 and the Revenue Act of 1978 added additional relief in this area (see Internal Revenue Code §§ 2032A and 6324B for special relief granted certain farms and other real property as well as §§ 6166 and 6166A concerning extensions of time for the payment of the federal estate tax). However, these benefits are somewhat limited in their applicability when the rather widespread problems of lack of liquidity is considered.

Prompt Disposal of Assets

It seems that every estate has its peculiar asset. It may be a Stradivarius violin, amateur radio equipment, a coin collection, a patent, or even a private plane. Such items should command as much attention during the planning stage as the client's closely held business interest or the vacant lot he holds as an investment. Usually much can be done during the client's lifetime to plan for the appraisal of such unusual assets as well as their prompt disposal after death at reasonable prices. It may even be possible to arrange in advance for the sale.

The estate of a client who owns a vacant lot can have much in common with the estates of major real estate investors and developers. Such property frequently proves troublesome. Liquidity problems may exist and estate administration can drag on for years. An estimate of the fair market value of such real estate parcels should be obtained and the client's preferred means of appraisal and disposal must be known. The client may have ideas concerning how the property can be sold quickly. Perhaps zoning changes, subdivision, renovation, or demolition would be logical steps for the client or, ultimately, his or her estate to try. Sometimes it may be possible to encourage the client to dispose of particularly troublesome properties as soon as possible, unless this is totally inconsistent with the client's reasons for holding the property.

Whenever a client owns a business as a sole proprietor or has most of his assets in a business with partners or a few other shareholders, there is a special need for careful estate planning. Planning for the estate and planning for the continued economic health of the business are interrelated. Some of the techniques used are as follows:

- **a.** The client may be encouraged to negotiate a buy-sell agreement or shareholder's agreement that will require another or others to purchase his interest after his death. As part of the agreement, the price should be fixed (or a means to establish the price should be agreed upon with provision for periodic review of the price), and it is helpful if the agreement is couched in terms that will establish death tax values that approximate fair market value as well. This becomes quite important in terms of the audit of the federal estate tax return as the Internal Revenue Service will sometimes accept the submitted value of the decedent's interest if it concludes that the value established by the agreement is representative of fair market value.
- **b.** The parties to a buy-sell agreement may be encouraged to fund the agreement with life insurance. This will assure a prompt buy-out in cash, and supply funds for estate-administration purposes.
- **c.** If negotiation of an agreement is impossible, then at least the client's ideas of valuation, appraisal methods, and prospective buyers should be known.
- **d.** The client should be encouraged to think about who is best suited to manage the property after her death or between her death and a sale.
- **e.** The corporate structure of any closely held corporation may be changed where necessary to solve problems of income for family members who may inherit shares and solve problems of control for those whom the client wishes to run the corporation after her death. The family members may only be interested in a secure source of income, and those who run the corporation may want the freedom to make business decisions independently of family members who do not participate in the business but who share in the income produced.

Lifetime planning may not always result in the prompt disposal of assets after death. Even well-planned estates succumb to some of those problems that exist at the time of death.

Reduction of Tax Bite

Reduction or elimination of the federal estate tax and state death taxes is usually the prime goal of estate planning. As you might expect, many legitimate and widely accepted techniques are utilized in this endeavor. No attempt is made in this chapter to cover all the ways to save on death taxes; however, this chapter will consider the most widely used approaches to the reduction of death taxes:

1. Making lifetime gifts;
2. Taking maximum advantage of the marital deduction;
3. Creating trusts to avoid multiple taxation;
4. Using charitable gifts both during lifetime as well as in the estate; and
5. Selling highly appreciated assets to family members.

Any particular estate-planning situation may demand the use of some or all of these techniques. In this respect the estate-planning process is a peculiarly human and nonmechanical process. It blends human wishes with the rather mechanical restrictions imposed by tax laws. A computer can calculate the tax results of a particular plan, but a computer cannot respond to the subtle but important reactions of the client. A plan that makes excellent tax sense may be repugnant to a particular client because it results in what he feels is unequal treatment of his children. The function of good estate planning is not merely to save taxes; it is to maximize the client's ability to transmit as much of his property as possible to those he wishes to have it.

Lifetime Gifts Prior to the Tax Reform Act of 1976 it could be said that if the client did not own an asset at his death, his estate would not normally be taxed on that asset. Although this was a simplification of a complex body of law, it remained true for the most part so long as the estate plan for gifts did not run afoul of the provisions of the Internal Revenue Code concerning transfers in contemplation of death (§ 2035), transfers with retained life estates (§ 2036), transfers involving reversionary interests (§ 2037), certain revocable transfers (§ 2038), and transfers involving certain types of powers of appointment (§ 2041). The theory as it then existed was that if the client were willing, he could save federal estate taxes and often state death taxes by giving away, during his lifetime, property that would otherwise have passed and would have been distributed under the terms of his will. The federal gift tax rate was three-fourths of the federal estate tax rate and the use of the $3,000 annual exclusion and $30,000 lifetime exemption, in conjunction with the utilization of the same exclusions and exemption available to a donor's spouse, enabled a client to make rather large tax-free or minimally taxable gifts. Even gifts found to have been made in contemplation of death and therefore taxed could result in economic benefit to the estate by way of a possible gift tax credit or the elimination of any tax on the appreciated portion of the property subsequent to the gift.

The Tax Reform Act of 1976 changed all of this. The federal gift tax rate is no longer three-fourths of the federal estate tax rates. There is now one tax rate that applies, on a graduated scale, to a decedent's total estate at death, together with the value of all transfers made during lifetime, subsequent to December 31, 1976, subject to certain credits. In addition, unlike the previous law, all transfers over and above the $10,000 annual gift tax exclusion that were made within three years of a decedent's death may be excludable from the decedent's estate with the exception of life insurance gifted within three years of death. Life insurance proceeds would be included in the estate.

However, all advantages of gifts as an estate-planning technique have not been removed. All gifts (plus the gift tax paid on the amount of the gift) in excess of the $10,000 annual gift tax exclusion are fully includable in the decedent's estate as an adjustment on the federal estate tax return. Any gifts made to a spouse during lifetime or after death qualify for a 100% marital deduction. In addition, a spouse with his donor spouse can still join in the gift to an unlimited number of third persons. (If both spouses wish to give $10,000 to one donee, they may each do so increasing the gift to $20,000.) The cumulative effect of the annual $10,000 per donee gift tax exclusion should not be overlooked in family situations or as an estate-planning technique where there are several potential donees. One other often-overlooked advantage of gifts is the overall reductions in the size of the decedent's probate estate that in turn reduces the probate fees and administration expenses that are characteristically computed as a percentage of the probate estate itself.

Of course, the client does not have to relinquish all his interest in property to make a gift. There are some situations where a donor may retain some interest in the property (particularly when the property is passing to charity). He may wish to make a gift to charity but retain the right to the income during his lifetime. This can be done by using a charitable remainder trust. The gift must be structured carefully so that the gift is not brought back into his estate.

Occasionally a client must be restrained from making gifts. Some clients become so enthusiastic about the prospect of diminishing death taxes that they give away so much of their property that they create a situation where they become dependent on others for their own support. The ultimate welfare and well-being of the client, both financially and otherwise, must always take precedence.

The Marital Deduction In the discussion of the marital deduction in the federal estate tax in Chapter Five, the various forms of gifts and trusts that qualify for the deduction were studied. Prior to the Tax Reform Act of 1976, the maximum marital deduction (whether a gift to the spouse was made outright or in trust) was one-half of the adjusted gross estate. The Tax Reform Act of 1976 changed the law so that the maximum marital deduction was one-half of the adjusted gross estate or $250,000, whichever was greater. For decedents dying after 12/31/81 (and gifts made after that date) Congress made available an unlimited marital deduction for any property passing to the spouse.

Although it is usually to the tax advantage of an estate to make full use of the marital deduction, there are situations where this is not true. Considering the point of view of tax planning for the whole family, there are occasions when a client should be advised to use none or only part of the maximum available marital deduction.

Assume the husband has $500,000 of assets and the wife has $2,000,000 of assets. If the husband uses the full marital deduction in his estate plan, he may add property to the taxable estate of his wife where it will be taxed at a much higher rate. In this situation it may be wise to prevent any of the husband's funds from becoming part of the wife's taxable estate. There would be no tax due in the husband's estate due to the $600,000 exemption.

This example should remind students that one important characteristic of the marital deduction is that to qualify for the deduction, property must be given in a way that makes it subject to federal estate tax at the death of the second spouse.

Similarly, the combined effect of the new unified credit described in the federal estate tax chapter and the new marital deduction provisions often creates a situation in some estates where the maximum marital deductions would not be most desirable. With an adjusted gross estate of $850,000 for a decedent whose death occurred after 1988, the maximum marital deduction would eliminate any federal estate tax on the death of the first spouse. At the death of the surviving spouse with a $200,000 estate plus the $850,000 received from her spouse, $1,050,000 would be subject to federal estate tax. However, if the marital deduction on the death of the first spouse were limited to the difference between the adjusted gross estate and the unified credit ($850,000 less the $600,000 exemption), the second estate would not be subject to tax because the surviving spouse would receive only $250,000 from her husband's estate, that sum when added to her $200,000 would result in her taxable estate being $450,000, less than the $600,000 exemption. The effect is that the marital deduction should never be in excess of that which is required to eliminate all federal estate tax after proper utilization of the unified credit. As an estate plan should always examine the total federal estate taxes paid on both estates, it is always important to consider the federal estate tax consequences of the death of the surviving spouse.

The Use of Trusts to Prevent Repeated Taxation Prior to the enactment of the Tax Reform Act of 1976, property could be left in trust for the benefit of any number of people who survive the client and even for a limited number of succeeding generations without the imposition of additional federal estate taxes at the death of the various beneficiaries. Most state death tax laws provide for the same tax-saving possibilities. If a client were willing to deny her spouse, children, and others all but extremely limited rights to use or control the principal of a trust, the trust device could be quite effective in saving taxes. Without losing the beneficial tax result, each beneficiary could be given the right to receive income and rights in the principal that do not exceed the right to discretionary distributions made by disinterested or adversely interested trustees; the power to appoint the principal to anyone but herself, her estate, or the creditors of either; and the right to obtain for herself up to 5% or $5,000 of the principal (whichever is greater) annually (but noncumulatively) during her lifetime. The right to receive 5% of the value of the trust, or $5,000 annually, results in a slight increase in the beneficiary's tax burden. But if the power is not exercised, there is no gift tax imposed and the maximum federal estate tax liability due to the power is equivalent to the value of the unexercised right for the year of death only.

Irrevocable life insurance trusts may be established during the settlor's lifetime and can be used to exclude the life insurance proceeds from the settlor's estate. The trust would potentially have funds to "loan" the estate money for debts, taxes, and administration expenses. This is advantageous for the entire estate plan because if a beneficiary receives the proceeds directly, he or she may not be inclined to lend the estate the funds. If the trust is funded with "present" interest property, the assets flowing into the trust qualify for the annual gift tax exclusions and will not be subject to the Generation-Skipping Transfer Tax. A present interest requires that the beneficiary have an annual opportunity to withdraw the funds. This can be for a limited period of time, such as 30 days, usually after the assets are deposited in the trust. This is where the family should have a thorough understanding of the overall estate plan so that they can all take advantage of the tax savings. In other words, although they have the right to withdraw the funds, the intention is that the funds stay in the trust so that the trust can grow to benefit everyone in the future.

The provisions of the Tax Reform Act of 1986 (effective for all transfers made after 1985)[1] have also had their impact in this area by imposing a tax on transfers that skip generations. (See Internal Revenue Code §§ 2601–2604, 2611–2613 and 2621–2624.) A generation-skipping transfer refers to " . . . any taxable distribution or taxable termination with respect to a generation-skipping trust or trust equivalent" (Internal Revenue Code § 2611 (a)). A trust that is deemed to be a generation-skipping trust is one with beneficiaries two or more generations younger than the generation of the grantor. Generations are defined along traditional family lines by lineal descendants and also by years for those transfers outside of the family lines (see Internal Revenue Code § 2611 (c)). Thus a trust for the benefit of a grantor's spouse, children, and then grandchildren is a generation-skipping trust, but a trust for the benefit of a grantor's spouse and then grandchildren would not be. Although the generation-skipping tax does remove some of the previously existing incentive for estate planners, the generation-skipping trust is still an effective estate-planning tool as a result of §§ 2631 and 2632 of the Internal Revenue Code. These sections provide that transfers to a grantor's grandchildren are not subject to the generation-skipping tax to the extent the transfers are not in excess of $1,000,000 through what § 2612 of the Internal Revenue Code defines as a "deemed transferor." In this situation the "deemed transferor" would be the grandchild's parent (the child of the grantor as well), and a grantor, by way of the generation-skipping trust, could transfer for the benefit of grandchildren up to $1,000,000 through each of her children who had children of his or her own (the grantor's grandchildren).

It should also be repeated, however, that to save death taxes by the use of trusts, the client must deprive the "natural objects" of his bounty of substantial rights to the property. Many people are not willing to do so.

The most dramatic result of estate planning is achieved by the combination of the marital deduction and the use of a trust, subject to the qualifications above, to prevent repeated taxation. If a wife with an estate of $800,000 wants to minimize the death taxes at her own death, she can do so by making to her spouse an outright gift of the whole estate. That gift would clearly qualify for the maximum marital deduction. At the subsequent death of the husband, however, the whole amount (augmented by whatever he owned prior to the spouse's death) would be subject to taxation. A dramatic saving of taxes is possible by the creation of a trust.

1. The Generation-Skipping Transfer Tax (GST) was originally introduced by the 1976 tax reform act. In 1986, Congress repealed the old generation-skipping tax and enacted the new GST tax with the $1,000,000 exemption per donee.

If the same woman left her spouse only $200,000 outright and placed the residue in a trust that would escape taxation at his death, she can accomplish the result of having no tax at her death. He would have the $600,000 credit at his death and his estate would be taxed on only the amount over $600,000. Most clients who have large combined estates find the tax advantage of such a plan far outweighs their reluctance to tie up money in a trust.

The trust essential to this scheme is a residuary trust that escapes taxation at the death of the surviving spouse. This is sometimes called a "credit shelter" trust or "by pass trust" because the total value of the trust is the same as the federal estate tax unified credit ($600,000). Whether the marital deduction share is given outright or in trust depends entirely on nontax considerations, such as the ability of the surviving spouse to handle investments.

Using Charitable Gifts Charitable gifts can be utilized to reduce death taxes and income taxes if the gift is made during the donor's lifetime. After the family is adequately provided for, then charitable gifts can be used to reduce the estate. The contributions (both made during the donor's lifetime or taking effect after death) can be made in cash or in kind. Often highly appreciated property such as stocks or real estate can be donated to charity, thus saving death taxes as well as capital gains taxes. An outright gift is the simplest gift to make. However, if the gift is planned properly, the donor can take advantage of the tax benefits while retaining some interest in the property. For instance the donor could set up a charitable remainder "Unitrust" or an "Annuity" trust, both defined in IRC § 664 (d).

In a unitrust the property or a certain sum of cash is placed in the trust for the eventual benefit of a "qualified"[2] charity. The trust must provide an annual distribution of the income earned by the trust to a noncharitable beneficiary. The amount of the distribution is a fixed percentage (no less than 5%) based on the fair market value of the assets in the trust, valued annually. Thus the amount of the annual income distribution will depend on the value of the trust. The amount of the federal income tax charitable deduction to which the donor is entitled is based on the life expectancy of the beneficiary[3] and the term (how long it will last) of the trust. Additional contributions can be made to the unitrust.

The annuity trust is set up in the same way. The amount of the annual distributions to the income beneficiaries are either a fixed sum or a percentage of the value of the assets in the trust at the time the trust was established. If the actual income is less than the

2. The charity must be approved by the IRS. It cannot be an individual.

3. To compute the life expectancy of a beneficiary, use the actuarial tables. The computation is based on the age and sex of the beneficiary or the donor (whichever applies).

fixed percentage, the trustee may distribute corpus (principal). No additional contributions can be made to the trust. The amount of the federal income tax deduction is computed by using the rules described in regulations § 1.644-2 (c). This deduction is usually larger than the unitrust deduction.

Both of these trusts are quite complex to set up. The legal assistant will rarely be asked to draft these documents, and therefore we will not show examples of the language for these trusts. However it is important to understand the terms "unitrust" and "annuity trust" and to be aware of different estate-planning schemes that can be used to save estate taxes, while allowing the settlor to continue to receive income during his or her lifetime.

If the client wants to take advantage of these types of "remainder" gifts to charity but doesn't have enough property to set up his own trust, he could contribute to a "pooled income" fund. Most of the larger charities have these funds. All gifts are placed into one fund. Each donor receives income based on the amount he contributed compared to the value of the entire fund. At his death the principal automatically goes to the charity.

Other types of charitable gifts could be a donation of life insurance to a charity. At the donor's death the life insurance would be payable directly to the charity. Also conservation easements can be used to donate valuable open land to a conservation organization. This can save income taxes and property taxes as well as lower the value of the land in the eventual estate. An easement on the land is donated forever and the land can never be developed. Because of this restriction, the land is less valuable. The charitable contribution for federal income taxes is computed by taking the difference between the fair market value before the easement and after the easement. The real property taxes are reduced by giving the land an agricultural value. Obviously this does reduce the marketability of the property and, as stated, the decision is irrevocable.

Estate Planning Computations

To test the liquidity needs of an estate and to compare tax results of alternative dispositive schemes, it is necessary to make estimates of the death taxes that will be imposed. Even when the client provides complete asset and liability information, such estimates must be rough because there is no foolproof way to predict administration expenses or fluctuations in asset values between preparation of the estimate and the time of death. When making estimates it is important to consider all possible orders of death. While it is statistically true that older people die before younger people or that husbands die before wives, there is no assurance that the expected order will occur in a particular case.

When recording estate-planning calculations, it is wise to state the assumptions under which they are prepared. If, for instance, administration expenses are assumed to be 10% of the gross estate, that assumption should be stated.

The computations themselves also represent an excellent analytical tool and basis for additional discussions with the client. Quite often by the utilization of these computations clients can better understand the effect of the potential tax savings and also the complexity of the estate-planning process and the jobs that are being done for them.

EXAMPLE
Estate-Planning Computations

As an example of one set of estate-planning calculations, consider the case of a husband having an estate of $900,000 married to a wife who owns $100,000 of property in her own name. The husband wishes to give $10,000 to his college. Assume that administration expenses are 10% of the gross estate. Further assume that neither spouse has made any gifts and that both deaths take place after 1988. We will show two examples: in one the husband gives his wife an outright gift of his entire estate; in the other, he establishes a "credit shelter" or "by pass" trust for the benefit of his wife and children.

Outright Gift

At husband's death	
Gross estate	$900,000
Admin. exp./debts (−)	<90,000>
Charitable bequest (−)	<10,000>
Marital bequest (−)	<800,000>
Taxable estate	-0-
At wife's subsequent death	
Her assets	$100,000
Inheritance from husband	800,000
Gross estate	900,000
Admin. exp./debts (−)	<100,000>
Taxable estate	800,000
Gross estate tax	267,800
Unified credit (−)	<192,800>
Credit for state death taxes (−)	<25,680>
Net estate tax due	$49,320

Thus if the husband leaves his entire estate to his wife outright (or in trust where she has a power of appointment), the entire amount of his net estate will be taxable in her estate, and her estate will be required to pay $49,320 of federal estate tax. The $600,000 exemption in the husband's estate was not used because all of the assets went to the wife.

If a "credit shelter" or "by pass" trust had been established under the husband's will, you would see a very different tax result. Presume that all the facts in the previous example are the same except the husband establishes a trust in the amount of $300,000 for the benefit of his wife and children. Thus, after the $10,000 bequest is paid to the charity and administration expenses and debts are paid, the spouse will only receive $500,000 that, when added to her $100,000 of assets, will result in a $600,000 estate for her.

Credit Shelter Trust for Family, $500,000 Bequest to Wife

At husband's death	
Gross Estate	$900,000
Admin. exp./debts (−)	<90,000>
Charitable contribution (−)	<10,000>
Bequest to wife (−)	<500,000>
Taxable estate	300,000
Gross estate tax	87,800
Unified credit	<192,800>
Tax Due	0
At wife's death	
Gross estate (Her $100,000 plus the $500,000 inherited from her husband's estate)	$600,000
Administration expenses (−)	<100,000>
Taxable estate	500,000
Tentative tax	155,800
Unified credit (−)	<192,800>
Tax due	0

Therefore with simple planning the husband and the wife can both reduce the tax due in their estates to zero, and their children, in effect, "save" almost $50,000 in estate taxes. The wife can have the right to the income and principal invasions of the $300,000 trust, but because she does not have a power of appointment it would not be included in her taxable estate.

THE ANATOMY OF A WILL

One result of the estate-planning process is the preparation of documents to carry out the chosen plan. A will is likely to be an important part of each estate plan and is frequently the most important single document an individual ever signs. It not only directs the distribution of assets, which in itself may affect the future of many people, but it should also appoint those who are to carry out the terms of the will and hold assets for the benefit of others and in addition select those who will bring up the decedent's minor children where both parents are deceased. Rare is the case that a living person cannot materially benefit his estate by leaving a will. In addition to the tax savings that often accrue, it is always preferable for an individual to select the manner in which his property is to be distributed, rather than leave this to the statutory scheme prescribed by state intestacy laws.

A will can be written on just about anything. So long as it is phrased properly, a will or testamentary writing need not be written on paper. It may appear on anything from tattered clothing to an apartment wall. However due to the importance of the document it should be prepared in the proper format and at least reviewed by a competent estate and trust attorney.

The Component Parts

The discussion that follows will help to identify the corresponding parts of the simple will that appears here. A simple will generally means one by which the husband or wife leaves everything outright to the spouse, their children, or other close relatives. There are usually no trusts involved.

EXAMPLE
Wife's Simple Will

I, MARY MacDONALD JONES, also known as MARY MacD. JONES, of Philadelphia, Pennsylvania, revoke my prior wills and declare this to be my will:

FIRST: *Debts and Funeral Expenses*

My debts and the expenses of my last illness, funeral, and burial shall be paid out of my estate.

SECOND: *Personal and Household Effects*

I give all my automobiles, and all other articles of personal or household use, together with all insurance relating thereto, to my husband, HERMAN R. JONES, if he survives me by thirty days. If he does not so survive me, I give all such property and insurance to such of my children as so survive me, to be divided among them as they may agree or, in the absence of agreement or if any of them is a minor, as my executor may think appropriate; provided that articles that my executor considers unsuitable for my children may be sold and the proceeds thereof added to my residuary estate. My executor may, without further responsibility, distribute property passing to a minor under this article to the minor or to any person to hold for the minor.

THIRD: *Residuary Estate*

I give the residue of my estate, real and personal:

A. To my husband, HERMAN R. JONES, if he survives me by thirty days; or, if he does not so survive me,

B. To such of my issue as so survive me, per stirpes.

FOURTH: *Minor Beneficiaries*

If a minor becomes entitled to a share of my residuary estate, that share shall be retained by my trustee in a separate trust for the minor and as much—even if all—of the net income and the principal of such trust as my trustee may from time to time think desirable for the minor either shall be distributed to the minor or shall be expended on his or her behalf, and all remaining income and principal shall be invested and held and shall be paid to the minor at majority.

FIFTH: *Death Taxes*

All federal, state, and other death taxes payable because of my death on the property forming my gross estate for tax purposes shall be paid out of the principal of my probate estate just as if they were my debts, and none of those taxes shall be charged against any beneficiary.

SIXTH: *Management Provisions*

I authorize my executor and my trustee:

A. To retain and to invest in all forms of real and personal property, regardless of any limitation imposed by law on investments by executors or trustees;
B. To compromise claims;
C. To sell at public or private sale, to exchange or to lease for any period of time, any real or personal property, and to give options for sales or leases;
D. To join in any merger, reorganization, voting trust plan, or other concerted action of security holders, and to delegate discretionary duties with respect thereto:
E. To borrow and to pledge property as security for repayment of any funds borrowed; and
F. To distribute in cash or in kind.

These authorities shall extend to all property at any time held by my executor or my trustee and shall continue in full force until the actual distribution of all such property. All powers, authorities, and discretion granted by this will shall be in addition to those granted by law and shall be exercisable without leave of court.

SEVENTH: *Executor and Trustee*

I appoint my husband, HERMAN R. JONES, executor of this will, but if he for any reason fails to qualify or ceases to act, I appoint GIRARD TRUST BANK executor in his place. I appoint GIRARD TRUST BANK trustee of all trusts hereunder. I direct that:

A. Any corporate executor or trustee shall receive compensation in accordance with its standard schedule of fees in effect at the time its services are performed; and
B. No executor or trustee shall be required to give bond.

EIGHTH: *Adopted Persons*

For the purposes of this will, adopted persons shall be considered as children of their adoptive parents, and they and their descendants shall be considered as issue of their adoptive parents, regardless of the date of the adoption.

NINTH: *Guardian of the Person*

If my husband does not survive me, I appoint my sister, MARGARET MacD. WILSON, guardian of the persons of my children during their minorities.

Executed August 26, 1992

________________________ [*Seal*]
Mary MacDonald Jones

In our presence the above-named testatrix signed this and declared it to be her will, and now at her request, in her presence, and in the presence of each other, we sign as witnesses:

________________________ ________________________
________________________ ________________________
________________________ ________________________

Preamble All wills must appear to be testamentary in nature to be valid. That is, they must appear to operate posthumously in relation to one's estate. If the will is not labeled such, or if it does not otherwise appear to be a testamentary writing, the defect can be most easily cured in the "preamble."

Other helpful information that should appear in the preamble is the testator's name, including all variations that appear on his securities and legal documents, and usually his address. Generally the draftsman will find it desirable to specify the address, including borough, county, and state, to help the executor determine the decedent's domicile for tax and probate purposes. If it appears preferable to remain flexible, however, the draftsman may omit such reference.

The statement that the testator is "of sound and disposing mind and memory" and that "he revokes prior wills and codicils" is also quite common in the preamble. However, the former is frequently of no value because it is self-serving and the latter is often superfluous because the new will automatically supersedes existing wills and codicils anyway.

Sample Clause
I, MARY MacDONALD JONES, also known as MARY MacD. JONES, of Philadelphia, Pennsylvania, revoke my prior wills and declare this to be my will.

Payment of Funeral Expenses and Expenses of Last Illness It is generally the obligation of an executor to see that all debts and funeral expenses are paid with estate funds before distribution is made.

In some states a surviving spouse is responsible for such bills as part of his obligation to support his spouse. The inclusion of a provision directing payment of such debts and expenses from the estate of a married person may be included to assure payment is made from the estate, and that there can be a deduction against death taxes for those payments.

Sample Clause
My debts and the expenses of my last illness, funeral, and burial shall be paid out of my estate.

Funeral and Burial Instructions Funeral and burial instructions are generally helpful when the testator has no one close to her who is aware of her wishes upon her death. The will may not be read until the time for probate, after the funeral. In any case, in many states the desires of the next of kin concerning disposition of the body legally prevail over whatever the testator may have directed in her will.

One exception to this rule is provided by the Uniform Anatomical Gift Act. Adopted in almost all states, the act provides that a person may validly direct by will the disposition of all or part of his or her body for medical or educational purposes. The document used for this direction is called a "Living Will." It is prepared in addition to the will and directs the family to donate organs, or the entire body, to medical research. The document also gives a close family member and the testator's personal physician directions concerning the person's wishes on when he or she should be allowed to die in the case of terminal illness—this is of course in the event that the person cannot make that decision. Most attorneys ask a client at the time a will is being prepared, whether he/she would also like to have a "living will" prepared at the same time.

Preresiduary Gifts Unfortunately, one of the most difficult problems encountered in estate administration is the distribution of tangible personal property. Families can be, and frequently are, torn apart by squabbles over things like furniture and jewelry. To preclude such problems, the thoughtful testator should provide specifically for the items likely to cause problems. Sometimes it is difficult to include a long list of specific tangible personal property bequests in the will. It is also cumbersome to have to revise an entire will if one or two bequests are to be changed. Therefore after the testator has made specific bequests for items of unusual value (sentimental or otherwise), it may be helpful to include a statement in the tangible personal property clause that refers to a separate list given to the executor and directs that the executor use that list as a guide for the disposition of the tangible personal property. That way the list can be updated at any time without changing the entire will. The disadvantage of a separate list is that the executor is not legally bound to the distribution suggested by the list. It is always important in this and similar cases to choose an executor who knows the testator and will abide by her wishes.

Sample Clause

I may from time to time deliver a letter to my executor and successor executors expressing my wishes concerning the disposition of certain items of tangible personal property. Although, the letter may not be legally binding to my executor, it is my wish that he use the letter as a guide to the distribution of some of my tangible personal property and follow my wishes whenever possible.

There are other important reasons for specific gifts. The testator may wish to give certain sums of cash as charitable gifts, as tokens of affection for certain people, or as a source of cash that can be distributed to her family promptly after death. Perhaps a particular institution, friend, or relative outside the immediate family could better use and enjoy certain possessions than the spouse or immediate family. Guns, cameras, amateur radios, and unusual equipment relating to other hobbies may call for special treatment in the will.

Due to a peculiarity in the federal income tax laws, a separate clause dealing with one's personal effects, household furnishings and equipment, is most important. If items are distributed pursuant to specific gift provisions, there are no income tax consequences to the recipients. If, however, the distribution is made out of the general estate or residue, it may under some circumstances be considered a distribution of distributable net income (DNI) that will result in taxable income for the beneficiary. This is so even though no income whatsoever is distributed so long as the estate itself has taxable income. A specific gift of household items or personal effects included in the will avoids the unfavorable tax treatment of recipients of those items.

Sample Clause

I give all my automobiles, and all other articles of personal or household use, together with all insurance relating thereto, to my husband, HERMAN R. JONES, if he survives me by thirty days. If he does not so survive me, I give all such property and insurance to such of my children as so survive me, to be divided among them as they may agree or, in the absence of agreement or if any of them is a minor, as my executor may think appropriate; provided that articles that my executor considers unsuitable for my children may be sold and the proceeds thereof added to my residuary estate. My executor may, without further responsibility, distribute property passing to a minor under this article to the minor or to any person to hold for the minor.

Marital deduction provisions—whether in trust or outright—must be considered as preresiduary gifts.

The estate planner should always consider whether or not the maximum marital deduction is desired or whether the marital deduction clause provides for maximum utilization of the unified credit (so as to avoid using a marital deduction that is larger than is necessary).

EXAMPLE
Outright to Spouse—Contingent Trust for Children

I, HERMAN R. JONES, of Philadelphia, Pennsylvania, revoke my prior wills and declare this to be my will:

FIRST: *Personal and Household Effects*

I give all my automobiles, and all other articles of personal or household use, together with all insurance relating thereto, to my wife, MARY MacDONALD JONES, if she survives me. If she does not, I give all such property and insurance to such of my children as survive me, to be divided among them as they may agree or, in the absence of agreement or if any of them is a minor, as my executor may think appropriate; provided that articles my executor considers unsuitable for my children may be sold and the proceeds thereof added to my residuary estate. My executor may, without further responsibility, distribute property passing to a minor under this article to the minor or to any person to hold for the minor.

SECOND: I direct my personal representative to pay the expenses of my last illness and my funeral expenses, including a suitable marker for my grave from my residuary estate.

THIRD: All inheritance, estate, and other transfer taxes and costs of administration shall be paid from my residuary estate.

FOURTH: *Residuary Estate*

If my wife, MARY MacDONALD JONES, survives me [and she shall be deemed to have survived me if the order of our deaths is not clear], I give my entire estate to her after the payment of all estate expenses.

FIFTH: *Residuary Trust*

If my wife does not survive me, I give the residue of my estate, real and personal, to my trustees, IN TRUST to keep it invested and thereafter for the benefit of my issue.

A. The net income shall be distributed, in quarterly or other convenient instalments, to such one or more of my issue in such amounts or proportions as my trustees may from time to time think appropriate; and also

B. As much of the principal as my trustees may from time to time think desirable for the health, support, maintenance, or education of any of my issue either shall be paid to that person or shall be applied directly for those purposes.

   My primary concern is for the care and education of my children until they become self-supporting and, while my general plan is to treat them alike, I recognize that needs will vary from person to person and from time to time. Accordingly, I direct that all distributees need not be treated equally or proportionally; that one or more of the eligible distributees may be wholly excluded from any or all periodic distributions; that the pattern followed in one distribution need not be followed in others; and that my trustees may give such consideration to the other resources of each of the eligible distributees as they may think appropriate.

C. As soon as there is no living child of mine under twenty-five years of age [or at the death of the survivor of my wife and me if no such child is living at that time], the then-remaining principal shall be paid:

   1. To my then-living issue, per stirpes; or, in default of such issue,
   2. To my heirs under the Pennsylvania intestate law.

SIXTH: *Minor or Disabled Beneficiaries*

If any minor or any person who is, in my trustees' opinion, disabled by advanced age, illness, or other cause becomes entitled to any income or principal of the residuary trust:

A. As much of such income or principal as my trustees may from time to time think desirablc for that beneficiary either shall be paid to him or her or shall be applied for his or her benefit; and
B. The balance of such income and principal shall be held as a separate trust for the beneficiary and, subject to my trustees' power to pay to or to apply for the benefit of the beneficiary both income and principal or such trust, shall—together with any net income therefrom—be kept invested and paid to the minor at majority or to the disabled person when he or she, in my trustees' opinion, becomes free of disability.

Any funds to be applied under this article either shall be applied directly by my trustees or shall be paid to a parent or guardian of the beneficiary or to any person or organization taking care of the beneficiary, and my trustees shall have no further responsibility for any funds so paid.

SEVENTH: *Accelerated Termination*

If my trustees, in their sole discretion, determine that it is impractical to administer any funds held under this will as a trust, my trustees, without further responsibility, may pay the fund to the person then entitled to receive income therefrom or, if there is more than one such person, to them in such amounts or proportions as my corporate trustee may think appropriate. If any person is a minor or is, in my trustees' opinion, disabled by advanced age, illness, or other cause, my trustees may pay the fund [or his or her share of it] to his or her parent or guardian or to any person or organization taking care of him or her or, in the case of a minor, may deposit it in a savings account in the minor's name, payable to him or her at majority. My trustees shall have no further responsibility as to funds so paid or deposited.

EIGHTH: *Undistributed Income*

All income undistributed at a beneficiary's death shall be treated as if it had accrued thereafter.

NINTH: *Protective Provision*

No interest in income or principal shall be assignable by, or available to, anyone having a claim against a beneficiary before actual payment to the beneficiary.

TENTH: *Management Provisions*

I authorize my executors and my trustees:

A. To retain and to invest in all forms of real and personal property regardless of any limitations imposed by law on investments by executors or trustees;
B. To compromise claims;
C. To join in any merger, reorganization, voting-trust plan, or other concerted action of security holders, and to delegate discretionary duties with respect thereto;
D. To sell at public or private sale, to exchange, or to lease for any period of time any real or personal property and to give options for sales or leases;

E. To make loans to, and to buy property from, my wife's executor or administrator;
F. To borrow from anyone, even if the lender is an executor or trustee hereunder, and to pledge property as security for repayment of any funds borrowed;
G. To allocate any property received or charge incurred to principal or income or partly to each, without regard to any law defining principal and income;
H. To use administrative or other expenses as income tax or estate tax deductions and to value my estate for tax purposes by any method permitted by the law in force when I die, without regard to whether the size of the marital gift for my wife will be affected thereby and without requiring adjustments between income and principal for any resulting effect on income or estate taxes, and
I. To distribute in cash or in kind.

These authorities shall extend to all property at any time held by my executors or my trustees and shall continue in full force until the actual distribution of all such property. All powers, authorities, and discretion granted by this will shall be in addition to those granted by law and shall be exercisable without leave of court.

ELEVENTH: *Business Interests*

In dealing with the stock of any close corporation or any other business interest forming a part of my estate or any trust hereunder, I authorize my executors and my trustees:

A. To disregard any principle of investment diversification and to retain any part or all of such interest as long as they consider it advisable to do so;
B. To sell any part or all of such interest at such time or times, for such prices, to such persons [including persons who are fiduciaries or beneficiaries hereunder], and on such terms and conditions as they may think advisable;
C. To do anything that may seem advisable with respect to the operation or liquidation of any such business or any change in the purpose, nature, or structure of any such business;
D. To delegate authority to any director, stockholder, manager, agent, partner, or employee, and to approve payment from the business of adequate compensation to any such person;
E. To cause the business to borrow money from the banking department of my corporate executor and trustee, regardless of any rule of law with respect to conflicts of interest; and
F. To make additional investments in any such business if such action seems in the best interests of the beneficiaries hereunder.

In short, I intend that, in making decisions hereunder, my executors and my trustees shall have the same freedom of action that I would have if living.

TWELFTH: *Additions*

I authorize my trustees to receive as an addition to any of the trustees hereunder (i) the proceeds of any insurance policy on my life or any other death benefit payable to my trustees and (ii) any property added to that trust by my wife's will.

THIRTEENTH: *Executors and Trustees*

I appoint my wife, MARY MacDONALD JONES and GIRARD TRUST BANK executors of this will, and I appoint GIRARD TRUST BANK and my brother STEPHEN JONES, trustees under this will. All personal representatives are to serve without bond. I direct that:

A. No executor or trustee who is also a beneficiary shall participate in (i) the exercise of, or decision not to exercise, any discretion to pay income or principal to, or to apply income or principal for the benefit of, any beneficiary {including discretion to allocate funds among a group of beneficiaries}; (ii) the determination whether a beneficiary is disabled; (iii) a decision to accelerate the termination of any trust hereunder; (iv) the allocation of any receipt or expense to principal or income; (v) the use of expenses as income or estate tax deductions; (vi) the choice of a method of valuation for tax purposes; or (vii) the selection of the property used to satisfy the marital gift to my wife.

B. Except as just stated, the words "my executors" shall refer to all those from time to time acting as such, and the words "my trustees" shall, in their application to each trust, refer to all those from time to time acting as trustees of that trust;

C. My wife may resign as an executor at any time without court approval; and

D. My corporate executor and trustee shall receive compensation in accordance with its schedule of fees in effect from time to time over the period during which its services are performed.

FOURTEENTH: *Adopted Persons*

For the purposes of this will, adopted persons shall be considered as children of their adoptive parents, and they and their descendants shall be considered as issue of their adoptive parents, regardless of the date of the adoption.

FIFTEENTH: *Guardian of Person*

If my wife does not survive me I appoint my sister-in-law, MARGARET M. WILSON, guardian of the persons of my children during their minorities.

Executed August 26, 1992.

________________________ [*Seal*]
Herman R. Jones

In our presence the above-named testator signed this and declared it to be his will, and now at his request, in his presence, and in the presence of each other, we sign as witnesses:

____________________ ____________________
____________________ ____________________
____________________ ____________________

EXAMPLE
Credit Shelter Trust for Children—Marital Trust for Wife

I, RYAN S. MARSHALL III, of Bryn Mawr, Montgomery County, Pennsylvania, revoke my prior wills and declare this to be my will:

FIRST: *Personal and Household Effects*

I give all my automobiles and all other articles of personal or household use, together with all insurance relating thereto, to my wife, ELIZABETH McLENDON MARSHALL, if she survives me by thirty days. If she does not, I give all such property and insurance to such of my children as so survive me, to be divided among them as they may agree or, in the absence of agreement or if any of them is a minor, as my executor may think appropriate; provided that articles my executor considers unsuitable for my children may be sold and the proceeds thereof added to my residuary estate. My executor may, without further responsibility, distribute property passing to a minor under this article to the minor or to any person to hold for the minor.

SECOND: *Marital Trust for Wife*

If my wife, ELIZABETH McLENDON MARSHALL survives me [and she shall be deemed to have survived me if the order of our deaths is not clear], I give an amount exactly sufficient to reduce my taxable estate to the amount of the maximum unified credit computed on my federal estate tax return to my trustees IN TRUST to keep it invested and thereafter:

A. During my wife's lifetime:
   1. The entire net income shall be paid to her, at least quarterly; and
   2. As much of the principal as my corporate trustee may from time to time think desirable for her welfare, comfort, or support shall be paid to her; and in addition
   3. She shall have the noncumulative right in each year to withdraw from the principal up to $5,000 or up to five percent thereof, whichever is the greater amount [the amount subject to withdrawal at any time during a year to be based on the market value of the principal at that time plus the amount of any prior withdrawals during that year and to be reduced by the amount of such prior withdrawals].

B. On my wife's death, any then-remaining principal shall be paid to such one or more persons or organizations, including her estate, on such terms as she may appoint by a will specifically referring to this power of appointment.

C. If my wife does not exhaust her power of appointment under the preceding paragraph, on her death:
   1. Any increase in death taxes or administration expenses in her estate caused by the inclusion of this trust in it for tax purposes shall be paid out of the unappointed principal, and a written statement by her executor or administrator of the amounts thus payable may be accepted as being correct; and
   2. The balance of the unappointed principal shall be added to and thereafter treated as a part of the principal of the residuary trust.

If any property not passing under this article qualifies for the marital deduction or any similar benefit available under the federal estate tax law in force when I die, the value of that property shall be taken into consideration in determining the size of this trust. No property ineligible for the marital deduction or any similar benefit shall be allocated to this trust; any property distributed in kind to it shall be distributed at the lower of (i) its value at the time of distribution and (ii) its adjusted income tax basis; and, subject to the foregoing, my corporate executor shall have absolute discretion in selecting the property to be allocated to this trust, without any duty to make a ratable apportionment of values.

THIRD: *Credit Shelter Trust*

I give the sum of $600,000 (or the amount of the unified credit used on my federal estate tax return) to my trustees, IN TRUST to keep it invested and thereafter:

A. If my wife, ELIZABETH McLENDON MARSHALL, survives me, during her lifetime:
   1. The net income shall be paid to her, in quarterly or other convenient instalments; and also
   2. As much of the principal as my corporate trustee may from time to time think desirable taking into account funds available from other sources for the health, support or maintenance of my wife or any of my children or for the education of any of my children either shall be paid to that person or shall be applied directly for those purposes; provided that none of the principal of this trust shall be paid to or applied for the benefit of my wife unless the principal of the marital trust has been exhausted.

B. After my wife's death [or mine if I survive her] and until there is no living child of mine under twenty-five years of age:
   1. The net income shall be distributed, in quarterly or other convenient instalments, to such one or more of my issue in such amounts or proportions as my corporate trustee may from time to time think appropriate; and also
   2. As much of the principal as my corporate trustee may from time to time think desirable for the health, support, maintenance, or education of any of my issue either shall be paid to that person or shall be applied directly for those purposes.

   My primary concern is for the care and education of my children until they become self-supporting and, while my general plan is to treat them like, I recognize that needs will vary from person to person and from time to time. Accordingly, I direct that all distributees need not be treated equally or proportionally; that one or more of the eligible distributees may be wholly excluded from any or all periodic distributions; that the pattern followed in one distribution need not be followed in others; and that my corporate trustee may give such consideration to the other resources of each of the eligible distributees as it may think appropriate.

C. After my wife's death [or mine if I survive her] and as soon as there is no living child of mine under twenty-five years of age, the then-remaining principal shall be divided into equal shares, so that there will be one share for each child of mine who is then living or then dead, and each such share shall be kept invested as a separate trust and thereafter:
   1. During each child's lifetime:

a. The net income from his or her trust shall be paid to him or her, in quarterly or other convenient instalments; and
b. As much of the principal of his or her trust as my corporate trustee may from time to time think desirable—taking into account funds available from other sources—for that child's health, support, maintenance, or education either shall be paid to him or her or shall be applied directly for those purposes; and in addition
c. Each child shall have the right to withdraw up to one-third of the principal of his or her trust at any time after reaching twenty-five years of age, up to an additional one-third thereof at any time after reaching thirty years of age, and the entire balance thereof at any time reaching thirty-five years of age [the amount that a child may withdraw before reaching thirty-five years of age to be based on the market value of his or her trust at the time of his or her first withdrawal].

2. At each child's death [or at the time for the setting apart of shares in the case of a child who dies before that time], any then-remaining principal of his or her trust shall be paid:
a. To such one or more persons or organizations—excepting only his or her estate, his or her creditors, and the creditors of his or her estate—on such terms as he or she may appoint by a will specifically referring to this power of appointment; or, in default of appointment or insofar as it is not effectual,
b. To his or her then-living issue, per stirpes; or, in default of such issue,
c. To my then-living issue, per stirpes [any portion thus accruing to a child for whom principal is then held in trust hereunder to be added to and thereafter treated as a part of such principal]; or, in default of such issue,
d. To my heirs under the Pennsylvania intestate law.

FOURTH: *Minor or Disabled Beneficiaries*

If any minor or any person who is, in my corporate trustee's opinion, disabled by advanced age, illness, or other cause becomes entitled to any income or principal of the residuary trust:

A. As much of such income or principal as my corporate trustee may from time to time think desirable for that beneficiary either shall be paid to him or her or shall be applied for his or her benefit; and
B. The balance of such income and principal shall be held as a separate trust for the beneficiary and, subject to my corporate trustee's power to pay to, or to apply for the benefit of, the beneficiary both income and principal of such trust, shall—together with any net income therefrom—be kept invested and paid to the minor at majority or to the disabled person when he or she, in my corporate trustee's opinion, becomes free of disability.

Any funds to be applied under this article either shall be applied directly by my trustees or shall be paid to a parent of the beneficiary or to any person or organization taking care of the beneficiary, and my trustees shall have no further responsibility for any funds so paid.

FIFTH: *Accelerated Termination*

If my corporate trustee, in its sole discretion, determines that it is impractical to administer any fund held under this will as a trust, my trustees, without further responsibility, may pay the fund to the person then eligible to receive income therefrom or, if there is more than one such person, to them in such amounts or proportions as my corporate trustee may think appropriate. If any person is a minor or is, in my corporate trustee's opinion, disabled by advanced age, illness, or other cause, my trustees may pay any amount distributable to him or her to his or her parent or guardian or to any person or organization taking care of him or her or, in the case of a minor, may deposit it in a savings account in the minor's name, payable to him or her at majority; provided that funds from the marital trust shall be paid only to my wife or to her legal representative. My trustees shall have no further responsibility as to funds so paid or deposited.

SIXTH: *Undistributed Income*

All income undistributed at a beneficiary's death shall be treated as if it had accrued thereafter.

SEVENTH: *Protective Provision*

No interest in income or principal shall be assignable by, or available to, anyone having a claim against a beneficiary before actual payment to the beneficiary.

EIGHTH: *Death Taxes*

All federal, state, and other death taxes payable because of my death on the property forming my gross estate for tax purposes, whether or not it passes under this will, shall be paid out of the principal of my probate estate just as if they were my debts, and none of those taxes shall be charged against any beneficiary or any outside fund. Any death taxes on future interests may be paid whenever my executors or trustees think best.

NINTH: *Management Provisions*

I authorize my executors and my trustees:

A. To retain and to invest in all forms of real and personal property, regardless of any limitations imposed by law on investments by executors or trustees;
B. To compromise claims;
C. To join in any merger, reorganization, voting-trust plan, or other concerted action of security holders, and to delegate discretionary duties with respect thereto;
D. To sell at public or private sale, to exchange, or to lease for any period of time any real or personal property, and to give options for sales or leases;
E. To make loans to, and to buy property from, my wife's executor or administrator;
F. To borrow from anyone, even if the lender is an executor or trustee hereunder, and to pledge property as security for repayment of any funds borrowed;
G. To apply for my wife's benefit all sums to which she is entitled from the marital trust if she is, in my corporate trustee's opinion, disabled by advanced age, illness, or other cause;
H. To allocate any property received or charge incurred to principal or income or partly to each, without regard to any law defining principal and income; provided that this authority shall not extend to the marital trust for my wife and that all decisions under it shall be made by my corporate executor and trustee alone;

I. To use administrative or other expenses as income tax or estate tax deductions and to value my estate for tax purposes by any method permitted by the law in force when I die, without regard to whether the size of the marital trust for my wife will be affected thereby and without requiring adjustments between income and principal for any resulting effect on income or estate taxes; provided that all decisions under this paragraph shall be made by my corporate executor alone; and

J. To distribute in kind and to allocate specific assets among the beneficiaries [including any trust hereunder] in such proportions as my executors or trustees may think best, so long as the total market value of any beneficiary's share is not affected by such allocation; provided that nothing in this paragraph shall affect the provisions set forth above concerning allocation to the marital trust.

Except as stated in paragraphs G and H, these authorities shall extend to all property at any time held by my executors or my trustees and shall continue in full force until the actual distribution of all such property. All powers, authorities, and discretion granted by this will shall be in addition to those granted by law and shall be exercisable without leave of court.

TENTH: *Additions*

I authorize my trustees to receive as an addition to any of the trusts hereunder (i) the proceeds of any insurance policy on my life or any other death benefit payable to my trustees and (ii) any property added to that trust by my wife's will.

ELEVENTH: *Executors and Trustees*

I appoint my wife, ELIZABETH McLENDON MARSHALL, and GIRARD TRUST BANK executors of and trustees under this will, to serve without bond, and I direct that:

A. My wife may resign as an executor or trustee at any time without court approval; and

B. My corporate executor and trustee shall receive compensation in accordance with its schedule of fees in effect from time to time over the period during which its services are performed.

TWELFTH: *Adopted Persons*

For the purposes of this will, adopted persons shall be considered as children of their adoptive parents, and they and their descendants shall be considered as issue of their adoptive parents, regardless of the date of the adoption.

THIRTEENTH: *Guardian of Person*

If my wife predeceases me, I appoint my sister CATHERINE JOY MARSHALL as guardian of the persons of my minor children.

Executed March 5, 1992.

____
RYAN S. MARSHALL, III

In our presence the above-named testator signed this and declared it to be his will, and now at his request, in his presence, and in the presence of each other, we sign as witnesses:

____________________ ____________________
____________________ ____________________
____________________ ____________________

Residuary Clause The residuary clause is usually the most important clause in the will because it generally disposes of the bulk of the property. As important as it may be, however, it is quite simple to understand.

The clause is a catch-all. By the use of this clause the testator gives away any property that has not been specifically given by other provisions of the will or that the testator may acquire after the execution of the will. Due to this clause the testator makes certain that all the property he owns at his death is governed by his will. The residuary clause literally provides for the disposition of the "rest" of the testator's estate.

The residue has a second important function. It is usually the source for payment of all death taxes, debts, and funeral and administration expenses. To the extent it is insufficient to serve this purpose, the burden will be borne by the specific gifts and perhaps even property that passes outside of the will (i.e., nonprobate property such as life insurance).

The residuary clause can be as simple as a single sentence or as complex as a trust requiring a number of pages. It might provide that all the property be given to one person, to various people in specified percentages, or that it be held in trust for a succession of beneficiaries. The specific scheme of disposition depends on the testator's desires modified somewhat by considerations such as taxes.

Since the clause is responsible for the disposal of the bulk of the testator's assets in most cases, it must be carefully drafted to cover all contingencies and every conceivable sequence of deaths of named beneficiaries.

The residuary clause provides the last chance for avoiding an intestacy situation. If the residuary beneficiaries all predecease the testator or die in an order not covered by the testator, all or part of the residue may then have to be distributed in accordance with the intestate laws. In such case the testator often loses most of the advantages of a properly drafted will.

Sample Clause (Simple Provision)

I give the residue of my estate, real and personal:

A. To my husband, HERMAN R. JONES, if he survives me by thirty days; or, if he does not so survive me,

B. To such of my issue as so survive me, per stirpes.

Sample Clause (Residuary Trust)

I give the residue of my estate, real and personal, to my trustees, IN TRUST to keep it invested and thereafter:

A. If my wife, NANCY JOY JONES, survives me, during her lifetime:

1. The net income shall be paid to her, in quarterly or other convenient instalments; and also
2. As much of the principal as my corporate trustee may from time to time think desirable—taking into account funds available from other sources—for the health, support, or maintenance of my wife or any of my children or for the education of any of my children either shall be paid to that person or shall be applied directly for those purposes; provided that none of the principal of this trust shall be paid to or applied for the benefit of my wife unless the principal of the marital trust has been exhausted.

B. After my wife's death (or mine if I survive her) and until there is no living child of mine under twenty-five years of age:
   1. The net income shall be distributed, in quarterly or other convenient instalments, to such one or more of my issue in such amounts or proportions as my corporate trustee may from time to time think appropriate; and also
   2. As much of the principal as my corporate trustee may from time to time think desirable for the health, support, maintenance, or education of any of my issue either shall be paid to that person or shall be applied directly for those purposes.

   My primary concern is for the care and education of my children until they become self-supporting and, while my general plan is to treat them alike, I recognize that needs will vary from person to person and from time to time. Accordingly, I direct that all distributees need not be treated equally or proportionally; that one or more of the eligible distributees may be wholly excluded from any or all periodic distributions; that the pattern followed in one distribution need not be followed in others; and that my corporate trustee may give such consideration to the other resources of each of the eligible distributees as it may think appropriate.

C. After my wife's death (or mine if I survive her) and as soon as there is no living child of mine under twenty-five years of age, the then-remaining principal shall be divided into equal shares, so that there will be one share for each child of mine who is then living or then dead, and each such share shall be kept invested as a separate trust and thereafter:
   1. During each child's lifetime:
      a. The net income from his or her trust shall be paid to him or her, in quarterly or other convenient installments; and
      b. As much of the principal of his or her trust as my corporate trustee may from time to time think desirable—taking into account funds available from other sources—for that child's health, support, maintenance, or education either shall be paid to him or her or shall be applied directly for those purposes; and in addition
      c. Each child shall have the right to withdraw up to one-third of the principal of his or her trust at any time after reaching twenty-five years of age, up to an additional one-third thereof at any time after reaching thirty years of age, and the entire balance thereof at any time after reaching thirty-five years of age (the amount that a child may

withdraw before reaching thirty-five years of age to be based on the market value of his or her trust at the time of his or her first withdrawal).

2. At each child's death (or at the time for the setting apart of shares in the case of a child who dies before that time), any then-remaining principal of his or her trust shall be paid:
   a. To such one or more persons or organizations—excepting only his or her estate, his or her creditors, and the creditors of his or her estate—on such terms as he or she may appoint by a will specifically referring to this power of appointment; or, in default of appointment or insofar as it is not effectual,
   b. To his or her then-living issue, per stirpes; or, in default of such issue,
   c. To my then-living issue, per stirpes (any portion thus accruing to a child for whom principal is then held in trust hereunder to be added to and thereafter treated as a part of such principal); or, in default of such issue,
   d. To my heirs under the Pennsylvania intestate laws.

One specialized use of the residuary clause is called a "pour-over" provision. It directs that the residue be paid to the trustees of an inter vivos trust to be treated as part of the principal of that trust. An example of a will containing such a provision—and therefore known as a "pour-over will"—follows. This type of will is frequently used with a life insurance trust agreement (LITA) that contains the operative dispositive provisions.

Sample Clause (POUR-OVER PROVISION)
I give the residue of my estate, real and personal, to the trustee or trustees under my deed of trust signed earlier today, under which GIRARD TRUST BANK is named as the trustee, IN TRUST to treat it as an addition to the principal subject to that deed as it exists at my death.

EXAMPLE
"Pour-Over" Will

I, SAMUEL SAGE, of Philadelphia, Pennsylvania, revoke my prior wills and declare this to be my will:

FIRST: *Personal and Household Effects*

I give all my automobiles and all other articles of personal or household use, together with all insurance relating thereto, to my wife, SALLY SAGE, if she survives me by thirty days. If she does not survive me, I give all such property and insurance to such of my children as so survive me, to be divided among them as they may agree or, in the absence of agreement of if any of them is a minor, as my executor may think appropriate; provided that articles that my executor considers unsuitable for my children may be sold and the proceeds thereof added to my residuary estate. My executor may, without further responsibility, distribute property passing to a minor under this article to the minor or to any person to hold for the minor.

SECOND: *Residuary Estate*

I give the residue of my estate, real and personal, to the trustee or trustees under my deed of trust signed earlier today, under which GIRARD TRUST BANK is named as the trustee, IN TRUST to treat it as an addition to the principal subject to that deed as it exists at my death.

THIRD: *Protective Provision*

No interest in income or principal shall be assignable by, or available to anyone having a claim against, a beneficiary before actual payment to the beneficiary.

FOURTH: *Death Taxes*

Except as otherwise provided in the above-mentioned deed of trust, all federal, state, and other death taxes payable because of my death on the property forming my gross estate for tax purposes, whether or not it passes under this will, shall be paid out of the principal of my probate estate just as if they were my debts, and none of those taxes shall be charged against any beneficiary. Any death taxes on future interests may be paid whenever my executors may think best.

FIFTH: *Management Provisions*

I authorize my executors:

A. To retain and to invest in all forms of real and personal property—including stock or other securities of my corporate executor or of a holding company controlling my corporate executor—regardless of any limitations imposed by law on investments by executors;
B. To compromise claims;
C. To borrow from, and to sell property to, the trustee or trustees under my above-mentioned deed of trust or others, and to pledge property as security for repayment of any funds borrowed;
D. To sell at public or private sale, to exchange, or to lease for any period of time any real or personal property, and to give options for sales or leases;
E. To use administrative or other expenses of my estate as income tax or estate tax deductions and to value my estate for tax purposes by any optional method permitted by the law in force when I die, without regard to whether the size of the marital trust for my wife under my above-mentioned deed of trust will be affected thereby and without requiring adjustments between income and principal for any resulting effect on income or estate taxes; provided that all decisions under this paragraph shall be made by my corporate executor alone; and
F. To distribute in cash or in kind.

These authorities shall be in addition to those granted by law and shall be exercisable without leave of court.

SIXTH: *Executors*

I appoint my wife, SALLY SAGE, and GIRARD TRUST BANK executors of this will, to serve without bond. My corporate executor shall receive compensation in accordance with its standard schedule of fees in effect when its services are performed.

SEVENTH: *Adopted Persons*

For the purposes of this will, adopted persons shall be considered as children of their adoptive parents, and they and their descendants shall be considered as issue of their adoptive parents, regardless of the date of the adoption.

EIGHTH: *Guardian of Persons*

If my wife predeceases me I appoint my brother JAMES SAGE as guardian of the persons of my minor children.

Executed June 27, 1992.

____
Samuel Sage

In our presence the above-named testator signed this and declared it to be his will, and now at his request, in his presence, and in the presence of each other, we sign as witnesses:

________________________ ________________________
________________________ ________________________
________________________ ________________________

Standard "Boilerplate" Provisions A well-drafted will should always include more than just the dispositive provisions. Much can happen—and frequently does—between death and distribution so it is important to provide the will with flexibility to deal with such occurrences. Most wills should have variations of the six provisions that follow.

Powers Clause Executors of wills are usually given comprehensive powers by state statute. Often, however, the powers given are not broad enough to deal adequately with the property. Therefore, experienced lawyers make a habit of filling the gaps by specifically enumerating the needed powers in the will.

Because will statutes vary from state to state and even change from time to time in any given state, it is wise to provide certain minimal powers when drafting a will. This provides some measure of certainty with respect to the executor's powers.

Sample Clause

I authorize my executors and my trustees:

A. To retain and invest in all forms of real and personal property, regardless of any limitations imposed by law on investments by executors or trustees;
B. To compromise claims;
C. To join in any merger, reorganization, voting-trust plan, or other concerted action of security holders, and to delegate discretionary duties with respect thereto;
D. To sell at public or private sale, to exchange or to lease for any period of time, any real or personal property, and to give options for sales or leases;

E. To make loans, and to buy property from, my wife's executor or administrator;
F. To borrow from anyone, even if the lender is an executor or trustee hereunder, and to pledge property as security for repayment of any funds borrowed;
G. To apply for my wife's benefit all sums to which she is entitled from the marital trust if she is, in my corporate trustee's opinion, disabled by advanced age, illness, or other cause;
H. To allocate any property received or charge incurred to principal or income or partly to each, without regard to any law defining principal and income; provided that this authority shall not extend to the marital trust for my wife and that all decisions under it shall be made by my corporate executor and trustee alone;
I. To use administrative or other expenses as income tax or estate tax deductions and to value my estate for tax purposes by any method permitted by the law in force when I die, without regard to whether the size of the marital trust for my wife will be affected thereby and without requiring adjustments between income and principal for any resulting effect on income or estate taxes; provided that all decisions under this paragraph shall be made by my corporate executor alone; and
J. To distribute in kind and to allocate specific assets among the beneficiaries (including any trust hereunder) in such proportions as my executors or trustees may think best, so long as the total market value of any beneficiary's share is not affected by such allocation and there is an equitable apportionment of the aggregate appreciation or depreciation from income tax basis; provided that nothing in this paragraph shall affect the provisions set forth above regarding satisfaction of the marital and orphans' deductions.

Except as stated in paragraphs G and H, these authorities shall extend to all property at any time held by my executors or my trustees and shall continue in full force until the actual distribution of all such property. All powers, authorities, and discretion granted by this will shall be in addition to those granted by law and shall be exercisable without leave of court.

It is particularly important that this precaution be taken when a client has an interest in a business. An example of detailed powers given to an executor to deal with business assets appears next.

Sample Clause

In dealing with the stock of any close corporation or any other business interest forming a part of my estate, I authorize my executors:

A. To disregard any principle of investment diversification and to retain any part or all of such interest as long as they consider it advisable to do so;
B. To sell any part or all of such interest at such time or times, for such prices, to such persons (including persons who are fiduciaries or beneficiaries hereunder) and on such terms and conditions as they may think advisable;

C. To do anything that may seem advisable with respect to the operation or liquidation of any such business or any change in the purpose, nature, or structure of any such business;
D. To delegate authority to any director, stockholder, manager, agent, partner, or employee, and to approve payment from the business of adequate compensation to any such person;
E. To cause the business to borrow money from the banking department of my corporate executor, regardless of any rule of law with respect to conflict of interest; and
F. To make additional investments in any such business if such action seems in the best interests of the beneficiaries of my estate.

Payment of Death Taxes Often, the source and time of death tax payments can be important to a client and essential to proper estate planning. Both should be considered carefully and discussed with the client. The will should specify whether such items as specific bequests and taxable but nontestamentary assets such as joint bank accounts are to bear the burden of death taxes or whether the residuary estate or just the nonmarital portion of the residue will pay the taxes. In the case of trusts established by a will, there may also be the possibility of postponing payment of state death taxes until the life beneficiaries die and the fund is finally distributed. Without a proper tax clause, a testator's desires for distribution of his property can be thwarted and flexibility in post-mortem estate planning can be lost.

Sample Clause
All federal, state, and other death taxes payable because of my death on the property forming my gross estate for tax purposes shall be paid out of the principal of my probate estate just as if they were my debts, and none of those taxes shall be charged against any beneficiary.

Minority and Incapacity of Beneficiaries It is not unusual that a decedent leaves property to a minor or to someone with severe mental or physical infirmities. The executors are prohibited by law from making distribution to such beneficiaries unless someone is empowered, usually by court appointment, to hold and manage the property for the beneficiary for the duration of the minority or incapacity. The court appointment of such a guardian can be costly, embarrassing, and time consuming.

A well-drafted will should appoint a guardian or trustee to hold, accumulate, or distribute funds for such beneficiaries so there will be no need for a separate court appointment.

Sample Clause
I appoint LAWRENCE LOFTON guardian of any property passing to a minor by reason of my death with respect to which I am authorized to appoint a guardian and no guardian has previously been appointed. The guardian may pay to, or expend on behalf of, the minor any or all of the minor's property and the income from it without court approval and may retain and invest the balance of the property and income with all the management powers given to my executor by law or by this will. In addition, the guardian shall have the power to exercise on the minor's behalf options available under any insurance policy payable to a minor. If Lawrence Lofton fails or ceases to act as guardian, I appoint GIRARD TRUST BANK guardian in his place. No guardian shall be required to give bond in any jurisdiction.

Common Disaster To prevent needless imposition of administration costs and death taxes on the same assets in two or more estates in quick succession, the will should specify a waiting period between the testator's death and the vesting of a gift to a beneficiary. Unless the beneficiary survives the waiting period, his gift is normally returned to the residue. This is particularly important when a beneficiary is a member of the same household and one with whom the testator may spend a considerable length of time.

The typical waiting period is 30 or 60 days, although some draftsmen use a six-month provision. A waiting-period provision is superior to a more limited common disaster or simultaneous death clause because it covers both the simultaneous death situation and the case of a spouse lingering on for a few hours or days after an accident. Such provisions, rather than being embodied in a separate clause, are often made an integral part of the dispositive clauses.

Spendthrift Provisions A beneficiary in a hurry to receive his inheritance may attempt to sell or assign his interest to another —at a discount—prior to the time the estate is settled. It is also possible that a beneficiary's creditors may attempt to obtain the beneficiary's inheritance from the executor prior to distribution.

In many states beneficiaries can be saved from themselves if a simple spendthrift clause exists in the will. In such states the provision makes void or voidable the beneficiary's attempt to sell his inheritance and prevents a creditor from obtaining the inheritance prior to distribution.

Sample Clause
No interest in income or principal shall be assignable by, or available to, anyone having a claim against a beneficiary before actual payment to the beneficiary.

Adopted Children The laws of most states provide that adopted children are included in the usual or commonly used words of descent such as "children," "issue," "heirs," and "descendants." However, to avoid confusion, a client who wishes to treat adopted children as natural children should include in the will a clause such as the following.

> **Sample Clause**
> For the purposes of this will, any words—such as "child," "children," and "issue"—describing a person or class of persons by relationship to another shall refer not only to persons who are related by blood but shall also include any person whose relationship is derived by adoption.

Appointment of Fiduciaries Of prime importance in a will is the proper selection of the executors, trustees, and guardians who are to manage the client's assets after his death. By carefully exercising the privilege of appointment, the testator can be fairly certain there will always be willing, concerned, and trustworthy fiduciaries assisting in the process of transmitting the estate. The delays, expense, and uncertainties of court appointments of fiduciaries will thereby be avoided.

There are three types of fiduciaries generally appointed by will: executors, trustees, and guardians (both of the minor's property as well as his or her person).

The executor is responsible for the collection of assets, payment of expenses, debts, and taxes; and distribution. In short, the executor is to execute or carry out the terms of the will.

The trustee is normally appointed for a much longer term and is responsible for accepting some assets distributed by the executor and holding them on behalf of a beneficiary under certain specified conditions.

> **Sample Clause**
> I appoint my husband, HERMAN R. JONES, executor of this will, but if he for any reason fails to qualify or ceases to act, I appoint GIRARD TRUST BANK executor in his place. I appoint GIRARD TRUST BANK trustee of all trusts hereunder.
>
> I direct that:
>
> A. Any corporate executor or trustee shall receive compensation in accordance with its standard schedule of fees in effect at the time its services are performed; and
>
> B. No executor or trustee shall be required to give bond.

There can be two types of guardians. A guardian may be appointed with limited powers as guardian of the "estate" (often referred to as "conservator") that is to pass to a minor or incapacitated beneficiary. The same person or another may be directed to serve as the guardian of the "person" of a minor. This type of guardian is concerned with the personal care and upbringing of the beneficiary, rather than with the beneficiary's financial affairs. The following clauses appear in the order that they would appear in the will.

Sample Clause (Guardian of the Estate)
I appoint LAWRENCE LOFTON guardian of any property passing to a minor by reason of my death with respect to which I am authorized to appoint a guardian and no guardian has previously been appointed. The guardian may pay to, or expend on behalf of, the minor any or all of the minor's property and the income from it without court approval and may retain and invest the balance of the property and income with all the management powers given to my executor by law or by this will. In addition, the guardian shall have the power to exercise on the minor's behalf options available under any insurance policy payable to a minor. If Lawrence Lofton fails or ceases to act as guardian, I appoint GIRARD TRUST BANK guardian in his place. No guardian shall be required to give bond in any jurisdiction.

Sample Clause (Guardian of the Person)
If my husband does not survive me, I appoint my sister, MARGARET MacD. WILSON, guardian of the persons of my children during their minorities.

It must be remembered that fiduciary appointments, while flattering, are also burdensome. Generally, the client should consult the prospective appointees prior to their selection. Otherwise, subsequent to his or her death, they may be reluctant to accept the responsibilities.

As an integral part of the appointment, the following may be included:

- **a.** Provision for contingent or successor fiduciaries in the event of the inability or unwillingness of one to qualify or to continue to act. This is extremely important and as a general rule the client should select as many successors as appears reasonable in view of the total estate plan.
- **b.** Provision for co-fiduciaries where it would appear beneficial to have more than one to shoulder the responsibilities. Some states (such as Virginia) require one fiduciary to be a resident of the state. Thus, if your client wishes to name a family member one of his or her fiduciaries, and

that person is an out-of-state resident, a resident will have to be appointed in addition to the family member.

c. Provision for a corporate fiduciary (i.e., a bank) to act, if even as a co-fiduciary, in the case of complicated estates and long-term trusts.

d. Provision for retention of the client's lawyer to represent the fiduciaries.

e. Provision exempting fiduciaries from the filing of fiduciary bonds in jurisdictions in which they must act.

f. Provision determining the compensation of fiduciaries.

Signature of Testator A document cannot qualify or be probated as a will unless the testator's signature or mark appears at the end. Some lawyers also insist that the testator initial or sign each page of a will in the margin. Often, however, the signature alone is insufficient to render a will valid. Certain procedures and the use of witnesses are mandatory in some states.

To remind all interested parties of the procedures that must be followed in the correct execution of the will, additional signature blanks for at least two witnesses and preferably three witnesses should be provided. As it is frequently difficult to locate witnesses many years later, a self-proving clause should be attached to the will. When the will is signed and witnessed, a notary public also signs a statement saying that he/she saw the testator and the witnesses sign the will. The witnesses do not have to be located at the death of the testator. The signature lines should be preceded by a short statement declaring all to have signed as witnesses in front of one another and the testator, and such other language that will serve as a helpful reminder of the proper procedures. A will is customarily signed only on the ribbon original. Other copies may be conformed but not signed.

EXAMPLE
Self-Proving Clause

State of ______________
County of ______________

Before me, the undersigned authority, on this day personally appeared HERMAN R. JONES, GEORGE SMITH, LYNNE SAYLOR, and GERRY BLACK known to me to be the testator and the witnesses, respectively, whose names were signed in my presence to the attached or foregoing instrument and, all of these persons being by me first duly sworn, HERMAN R. JONES, the testator, declared to me and to the witnesses in my presence that said instrument is his last will and testament. He willingly [or willingly directed another to sign for him] executed said last will and testament in the presence of said witnesses as his free and voluntary act for the purposes therein expressed. Said witnesses who, in his presence and at his request, and in the presence of each other, did subscribe their names thereto as attesting witnesses on the date of said last will and testament, and that the testator, at the time of the execution of said last will and testament was over the age of 18 years and of sound and disposing mind and memory and under no constraint or undue influence.

____
Herman R. Jones

____
Witness

____
Witness

____
Witness

Subscribed, sworn, and acknowledged before me by Herman R. Jones, the testator, subscribed and shown before me by __________, __________, and __________ witness, this ________ day of ________, 19____.

____
Notary Public

Commission Expires _______________

Codicils

When marital, financial, or family or other personal factors dictate a change in a will, the change can be effected either through a redraft of the entire document or the addition of an amending document called a codicil. While complete revision is sometimes preferable because of the nature of the change, or because it avoids problems of loss, forgetfulness, bulkiness, and confusion often incident to codicils, the addition of a codicil is far simpler, cheaper, and in some instances advantageous.

In situations where a codicil is desirable, the original will and prior codicils must first be studied to be certain the codicil is drafted to form an integral part of the estate plan. The portions of the will to be revoked or amended should be couched in testamentary terms, and the completed codicil should be executed in the same manner as a will and then placed with the will for safekeeping.

THE ANATOMY OF A TRUST

When a person ("settlor") gives property ("principal" or "corpus") and the legal title thereto to a second party ("trustee") to hold and manage for the benefit of a third person ("beneficiary"), the person has created a trust. The settlor in this case has relinquished his control and ownership of principal to the trustee, who is given specific instructions pertaining to its management and the use of it to benefit (usually by distribution of income) one or more beneficiaries. At the termination of the trust—at a time dictated by the settlor in the trust instrument—the principal remaining is usually turned over by the trustee to yet another party ("remainderman").

Usually the settlor wants to place the property out of his hands altogether and specifically desires a bank or responsible individual to invest the principal and collect and distribute income. Often the settlor's paramount reason for creating the trust is to keep the principal out of the hands of certain beneficiaries and their creditors and from possibly being subject to the generation-skipping transfer tax. Special generation-skipping trusts can be established to prevent succeeding death tax bites as the various beneficiaries die.

By prohibiting the income beneficiaries from withdrawing principal at their discretion, the settlor effectively prevents the beneficiaries (and by state law, their creditors) from depleting the principal. The federal estate tax laws and death tax laws of most states also recognize this limitation on the beneficiaries' right of withdrawal as placing the trust principal outside of their estates and making it nontaxable.

Aside from the management and preservation benefits already mentioned, there is also the possibility the settlor simply wants to control his property as long as possible after his death. By creating a trust he can determine who is to manage his property and who is to benefit from the principal and income for many years.

The duration of his control can be unlimited in the case of trusts established for charity, but it is limited by a legal doctrine known as the "rule against perpetuities" when the trust benefits individuals and noncharitable institutions. Simply stated, the rule against perpetuities means the principal must vest in someone no later than the end of a period measured by the life of a person living at the time the trust becomes irrevocable plus twenty-one years. In other words, a settlor with a great-grandchild living at the creation of the trust can name as the final beneficiary of a long line of succeeding beneficiaries the child of that great-grandchild. So long as the principal must be paid over to that child (the great-great-grandchild) at or before his or her twenty-first birthday, the rule against perpetuities is not violated.

A settlor may also establish a trust for his own benefit. A trust affords the possibility of professional money management and, with it, freedom from the rigors and responsibilities of money management. In addition, the use of a trust that begins during life and continues after death effects a savings in probate costs and the delays incident to the probate process at the death of the settlor and, subject to the provisions of the Tax Reform Act of 1986 pertaining to generation-skipping trusts, again at the death of the beneficiary. Similarly, in spite of the Tax Reform Act of 1986, federal estate tax savings may be achieved through the use of trusts, and during lifetime, income tax savings can be realized.

Often an individual will establish a trust for the benefit of beneficiaries so as to supply the beneficiaries with a capability in dealing with or managing the trust corpus that they would not have if the trust corpus were conveyed to them outright, free of trust. The beneficiaries may be too young; they may lack experience of good judgment or, at least in the opinion of the settlor, lack these capabilities; or they may be under a legal incapacity, whether it be minority or physical or mental incompetency. If the trustee or trustees are carefully selected, their judgment will be substituted for the beneficiaries, and the trust corpus can be even further insulated by shielding it from the claims of the beneficiaries' creditors.

Types of Trusts

Testamentary When the testator creates a trust by the terms of his will, it is called a testamentary trust. This type of trust has the disadvantage of being dependent upon the estate. The will must be probated, the estate must be administered, and the executor must make distribution of the assets to the trustee before the testamentary trust comes alive. Once established, however, it has all the advantages of continued management, preservation, and client control incident to any other trust. Several testamentary trusts are set forth in this chapter.

Perhaps the most popular type of testamentary trust is the nonmarital or residuary trust. Characteristically, this is established for the benefit of a surviving spouse. The surviving spouse receives all of the net income generated by the trust, which trust usually consists of the balance of a decedent's estate after the assets qualifying for the marital deduction have been distributed to the surviving spouse outright or set aside for his or her benefit. The nonmarital or residuary trust will usually provide that the surviving spouse has a somewhat limited right to the principal of the trust, but the limitation is such that the trust corpus is not includable for federal estate tax purposes in the taxable estate of the surviving spouse upon death. Accordingly, the trust corpus may then pass free of federal estate tax to the next specified beneficiaries. As the value of the trust corpus at the death of the surviving spouse is not subject to federal estate tax, this also means that any appreciation in the value of the trust assets will also escape federal estate tax.

Inter Vivos When the settlor establishes a trust in his lifetime to benefit himself or others, the trust is termed an inter vivos (or "living") trust. An inter vivos trust may be designed to continue long after the settlor's death; in fact, it is often drafted with that purpose in mind. The "inter vivos life insurance trust" (LITA) is of this variety. Often a client wishes to establish a trust for the benefit of the family but he or she does not presently have the assets to put into the trust. One way to establish a trust that at death will be substantial enough to support the family is to set up a life insurance trust (LITA). The established trust should be irrevocable. (The settlor cannot change it once it is established). If the trust is properly set up, it will not be part of the settlor's taxable estate. The trust can be used as a source of funds to help pay some of the estate expenses. It can "loan" money to the estate. A beneficiary receiving the proceeds from a life insurance policy might not be as willing to do this. One thing that should be noted however is that the title of the trust should not include the phrase "insurance trust" because gifts of life insurance are brought back into the estate if the settlor dies within three years. This type of trust is a good estate planning tool if it is drafted properly, it is drafted with dispositive provisions usually found in a will and is relatively inactive during the settlor's lifetime. A sample LITA is set forth here.

EXAMPLE
Irrevocable "Insurance" Trust Agreement

Note: do not use the term "insurance" in the actual agreement. It is used here only to serve as a reminder that this is the purpose of this particular agreement.

This Agreement made on February 28, 1992 between THOMAS K. FLYNNE, of Philadelphia, Pa. and GIRARD TRUST BANK hereafter referred to as Trustee, establishes the FLYNNE FAMILY TRUST. Settlor hereby transfers to Trustee $10 in cash and the following life insurance policies: [include list of each policy].

SECTION 1: This Trust Agreement shall be irrevocable.

SECTION 2: Other property, real or personal, may be transferred to the trustee during the lifetime of the settlor.

SECTION 3: Withdrawal Rights

Commencing with the date of the execution of this agreement my spouse may have the right (for 30 days) to withdraw the lesser of $5,000 or the full value of any property transferred to the trust. In addition settlor reserves the right to name other parties who shall have withdrawal rights. These withdrawal rights extend only to the trust principal and not income.

SECTION 4: The beneficiaries of this trust are my spouse and my decedents.

SECTION 5: During settlor's lifetime the trustee shall pay so much of the net income and/or principal as said trustee shall deem necessary in his absolute discretion, for health, education (including college and graduate school) and maintenance in the reasonable comfort of the beneficiary. Any payment may be made without the requirement of equal distributions among beneficiaries. The trustee may, but is not required, to take into account other funds available to the beneficiary.

The trustee may use funds available in the estate to purchase additional insurance on the settlor's life. In all respects said trustee shall possess all incidents of ownership with respect to any such life insurance.

SECTION 6: Upon the death of the settlor, the trustee shall promptly collect any life insurance policies owned on the life of the settlor, which shall then become a part of the principal of the trust. Said trust shall be administered as follows:

The trustee shall pay to the surviving spouse or lineal descendants so much of the net income and/or principal as said trustee shall deem necessary, in his absolute discretion, for health, education (including college and graduate school), and maintenance in the reasonable comfort of the beneficiary. Any payment may be made without the requirement of equal distributions among beneficiaries. The trustee may, but is not required to, take into account other funds available to the beneficiary.

SECTION 7:

A. After my wife's death (or mine if I survive her) and as long as there are any living children under twenty-three years of age:
   1. As much of the net income and the principal as the trustee, in his trustee's sole discretion, may from time to time think desirable shall be distributed to such one or more of my descendants in such amounts or proportions as my trustee may from time to time think appropriate; and
   2. Any net income not so distributed shall from time to time be accumulated and added to the principal.

   My primary concern is for the care and education of my children until they become self-supporting and, while my general plan is to treat them alike, I recognize that needs will vary from person to person and from time to time. Accordingly, I direct that all distributees need not be treated equally or proportionately; that one or more of the eligible distributees may be wholly excluded from any or all periodic distributions; that the pattern followed in one distribution need not be followed in others; that income may be accumulated to whatever extent and in whatever amounts my trustee may think appropriate; and that my trustee may give such consideration to the other resources of each of the eligible distributees as my trustee may think appropriate.
B. After my wife's death (or mine if I survive her) and as soon as there is no living child of mine under twenty-five years of age, the remaining principal shall be divided into equal shares, so that there will be one share for each child of mine who is then living or then dead, and each such share shall be kept invested as a separate trust and thereafter:
   1. During each child's lifetime:
      a. The net income from his or her trust shall be paid to him or her, in quarterly or other convenient instalments;

b. As much of the principal of his or her trust as my trustee may from time to time think desirable taking into account funds available from other sources for the health, support, maintenance, or education of that child or any of his or her descendants either shall be paid to that person or shall be applied directly for those purposes; and

c. Each child shall have the right to withdraw up to one-third of the principal of his or her trust at any time after reaching twenty-five years of age, up to one-half of the balance thereof at any time after reaching thirty years of age, and the entire balance thereof at any time after reaching thirty-five years of age (the maximum amount subject to withdrawal before a child reaches thirty-five years of age to be based on the market value of the principal of that child's trust at the time of his or her first request after reaching each particular age).

2. At each child's death (or at the time for the setting apart of shares in the case of a child who dies before that time), any remaining principal of his or her trust shall be paid:

   a. To such one or more persons or organizations—excepting only his or her estate, his or her creditors, and the creditors of his or her estate—on such terms as he or she may appoint by a will specifically referring to this power of appointment; or, in default of appointment or insofar as it is not effectual,

   b. To his or her then-living descendants, per stirpes; or, in default of such descendants,

   c. To my then-living descendants, per stirpes (any portion thus accruing to a child for whom principal is then held in trust hereunder to be added to and thereafter treated as a part of such principal); or, in default of such descendants,

   d. To the persons who would be entitled to inherit from me under the Pennsylvania intestate laws as if I had then died intestate.

SECTION 8: *Death Taxes*

Any death taxes on any future interests shall be paid from the residuary trust whenever my trustee, in my trustee's sole discretion, thinks best. All federal, state, and other death taxes payable because of my death on any property then held hereunder or on any insurance proceeds or other death benefits payable directly to my trustee shall be paid out of the principal of the residuary trust. No property that would be exempt from federal estate tax if not payable to my executors or administrators shall be used to pay any death taxes under this article.

SECTION 9: *Tax Options*

I authorize my trustee to treat administrative or other expenses of the trusts hereunder as income tax or estate tax deductions or both without regard to whether they were paid from principal or income or whether the size of the marital deduction trust or the orphan's deduction gifts will be affected thereby, and without requiring adjustments between principal and income for any resulting effect on income or estate taxes.

SECTION 10: *Beneficiaries under Twenty-One or Disabled*

If any beneficiary under twenty-one becomes entitled to any income or principal hereunder, or if any beneficiary who is, in my trustee's opinion, disabled by advanced age, illness, or other cause becomes entitled to any income or principal of the residuary trust:

A. As much of such income or principal as my trustee may from time to time think desirable for that beneficiary either shall be paid to him or her or shall be applied for his or her benefit; and

B. The balance of such income and principal shall be held as a separate trust for the beneficiary and, subject to my trustee's power to pay to, or to apply for the benefit of, the beneficiary both income and principal of such trust, shall—together with any net income therefrom—be kept invested and paid, as the case may be, to the beneficiary when he or she reaches twenty-one years of age or becomes, in my trustee's opinion, free of disability.

Any funds to be applied under this article either shall be applied directly by my trustee or shall be paid to a parent or guardian of the beneficiary or to any person or organization taking care of the beneficiary, and my trustee shall have no further responsibility for any funds so applied or paid.

SECTION 11: *Accelerated Termination*

If my trustee, in my trustee's sole discretion, determines that it is desirable to do so, my trustee may, without further responsibility, terminate any trust under this deed and pay the then-remaining principal and income of that trust to the person then eligible to receive income therefrom or, if there is more than one such person, to them in such amounts or proportions as my trustee may think appropriate. If any such person is a minor or is, in my trustee's opinion, disabled by advanced age, illness, or other cause, my trustee may pay any amount distributable to him or her to his or her parent or guardian or to any person or organization taking care of him or her or, in the case of a minor, may deposit it in a savings account in the minor's name, payable to him or her at majority; provided that any amounts attributable to the marital deduction trust or to an orphans' deduction gift shall be paid only to the beneficiary or his or her legal representative. My trustee shall have no further responsibility for funds so paid or deposited.

SECTION 12: *Rights in Income*

Each orphans' deduction gift and each trust hereunder shall be entitled to a proportionate share of income accruing from the event as of which it is to be set apart (e.g., the date of my death in the case of the marital deduction trust), and, pending actual division, distributions of income and principal may be made directly to a trust or, subject to the terms thereof, to the beneficiaries of the trust. All income undistributed at a beneficiary's death shall be treated as if it had accrued thereafter.

SECTION 13: *Protective Provision*

No interest in income or principal shall be assigned by, or available to anyone having a claim against, a beneficiary before actual payment to the beneficiary.

SECTION 14: *Management Provisions*

I authorize my trustee:

A. To retain and to invest in all forms of real and personal property, including common trust funds operated by my corporate trustee, regardless of (i) any limitations imposed by law on investments by trustees, (ii) any principle of law concerning delegation of investment responsibility by trustees, or (iii) any principle of law concerning investment diversification;

B. To compromise claims and to abandon any property that, in my trustee's opinion, is of little or no value;
C. To borrow from anyone, even if the lender is a trustee hereunder, and to pledge property as security for repayment of the funds borrowed;
D. To sell at public or private sale, to exchange, or to lease for any period of time any real or personal property, and to give options for sales or leases;
E. To make loans to, and to buy property from, my or my wife's executors or administrators or the trustee of any generation-skipping trust of which I am a deemed transferor;
F. To join in any merger, reorganization, voting-trust plan, or other concerted action of security holders, and to delegate discretionary duties with respect thereto;
G. To apply directly for my wife's benefit all sums to which she is entitled from the marital deduction trust if she is, in my trustee's opinion, disabled by advanced age, illness, or other cause;
H. To allocate any property received or charge incurred to principal or income or partly to each, without regard to any law defining principal and income; provided that this authority shall not extend to the marital deduction trust; and
I. To distribute in kind and to allocate specific assets among the beneficiaries (including any trust hereunder) in such proportions as my trustee may think best, so long as the total market value of any beneficiary's share is not affected by such allocation and there is an equitable apportionment of the aggregate appreciation or depreciation from income tax bases.

Except as stated in paragraphs G and H, these authorities shall extend to all property at any time held by my trustee and shall continue in full force until the actual distribution of all such property. All powers, authorities, and discretion granted by this deed shall be in addition to those granted by law and shall be exercisable without leave of court.

SECTION 15: *Payments to Aid in Settlement of Estate*

My trustee shall have the power, but not the duty, to make such payments from the principal of the residuary trust as my trustee may think desirable to facilitate the settlement of my estate, and in the exercise of this power my trustee may pay, in whole or in part, any or all of (i) my debts (including debts for which my wife is also liable), (ii) the expenses of my funeral and burial, and (iii) death taxes (except generation-skipping transfer taxes) and administration expenses in connection with my estate, even though they do not relate to property becoming subject to this deed; provided that no property that would be exempt from federal estate tax if not payable to my executors or administrators shall be used to make any payments under this article. Neither my executors or administrators nor any beneficiary of my estate shall be required to reimburse my trustee for any such expenditures.

SECTION 16: *Situs and Governing Law*

The situs of this deed shall be Pennsylvania, and all questions as to the validity or effect of this deed of the administration of the trusts hereunder shall be governed by the law of Pennsylvania.

SECTION 17: *Provisions Regarding My Trustee*

After my death, my wife, HELEN R. FLYNNE, shall become an additional trustee of the trusts hereunder by delivering to the corporate trustee her written acceptance of office. I direct that:

A. No trustee who is a beneficiary hereunder shall ever participate in (i) the exercise of, or decision not to exercise, any discretion to pay income or principal to, or to apply income or principal for the benefit of, any beneficiary (including discretion to allocate funds among a group of beneficiaries and discretion to accumulate income), (ii) the determination whether a beneficiary is disabled, (iii) a decision when to pay death taxes on any future interest, (iv) the decision to terminate any trust hereunder, (v) the exercise of discretion to allocate receipts or expenses between principal and income, (vi) the decision whether to use expenses as income or estate tax deductions, (vii) a decision to make payments to aid in the settlement of my estate, or (viii) the selection of the property to be allocated to the marital deduction trust;
B. Except as just stated, the words "my trustee" shall refer to all those acting as trustees;
C. Any trustee may resign at any time without court approval; and
D. My corporate trustee shall receive compensation in accordance with its standard schedule of fees in effect from time to time over the period during which its services are performed.

Executed May 15, 1992

______________________ [*Seal*]
THOMAS K. FLYNNE

Witnesses:

____

____

STATE OF Pennsylvania
County of Philadelphia ss.

On May 15, 1992, before me, the undersigned notary public, personally appeared THOMAS K. FLYNNE and in due form of law acknowledged the foregoing instrument to be his act and deed and desired the same to be recorded as such.

Witness my hand and notarial seal the day and year aforesaid.

____
Notary Public
My Commission Expires: May 31, 1995

The foregoing deed of trust was delivered, and is hereby accepted, at Philadelphia, Pennsylvania, on May 15, 1992.

GIRARD TRUST BANK

____
By: H. R. Samson
Trust Officer

SCHEDULE OF LIFE INSURANCE POLICIES REFERRED TO IN THE ANNEXED DEED OF TRUST

Dated , 199

From

THOMAS K. FLYNNE, Settlor

to

GIRARD TRUST BANK, Trustee

Policy Company	Face Number	Amount
Metropolitan	AQ4379512	$15,000
Equitable	479-72165	10,000

To satisfy the requirements imposed by most states that the trust not be "dry," i.e., that it hold some property, a nominal amount of principal—sometimes merely life insurance beneficiary designations—is held by the trustee. In states that require a principal of at least a nominal amount, a dollar may be added.

This type of trust can serve as a receptacle ready to receive the proceeds of life insurance and the assets poured into it by the settlor's "pour-over will." The settlor merely designates the trustees the beneficiaries of his insurance and the residuary legatees of his will.

Revocable If the settlor retains the right to revoke, alter, or amend the trust during her lifetime, it is termed revocable. So long as these rights are retained, she has not made a complete gift of the assets to the beneficiaries and cannot be deemed to have placed the assets out of her hands for purposes of avoiding death taxes. Revokable trusts are established for several reasons. Although they are taxed in the estate, the assets in the trust are not part of the probate estate. This can be important in states such as Virginia where the probate fee is based on the size of the probate estate. In addition to saving the probate costs, the nonprobate property does not have to be disclosed to the probate court, and this is not available as public information. Many clients prefer to keep the information private.

Another advantage to the revokable trust is that the settlor can see how the trustee is managing the property. If the settlor becomes disabled or unable to conduct his or her own financial affairs, the trustee is there to manage the property for him or her. If property is placed in trust prior to death, the assets are protected from estate administration problems, such as will contests and spousal renunciation. Therefore if the client has a problem with her spouse or other family member, she can protect some of the assets by placing them in a trust during her lifetime.

Irrevocable A trust that cannot be revoked, altered, or amended by the settlor is irrevocable. An irrevocable decision should never be taken lightly and the client should always understand the full impact of irrevocability. Most states require the settlor to state specifically in the trust that he reserves the right to revoke, alter, or amend or the trust will be deemed irrevocable.

When making a substantial gift or persons or institutions, the settlor may desire to specify in detail the terms of management, benefits, and duration. In such situations, even though the settlor forever relinquishes any rights to revoke, alter, or amend, the desired control can be retained by setting forth detailed management and beneficiary provisions in the trust instrument. Relinquishment of the right to revoke, alter, or amend makes the trust a completed gift and removes the assets from the transferor's estate for death tax purposes. An irrevocable inter vivos trust is set forth next.

EXAMPLE
Irrevocable Inter Vivos Trust

I, PETER CHESSMAN, of Philadelphia, Pennsylvania, hereby transfer the property listed in the annexed schedule to PAUL CHESSMAN and GIRARD TRUST BANK as trustees, IN TRUST to keep it invested and to distribute the net income and the principal as follows:

FIRST: *Term of Trust*

Except as provided below, this trust shall continue until the death of the survivor of SUSAN MAXWELL, GUY GABRIELSON, MARK ROBINSON, AND SALLY GREEN.

SECOND: *Distribution of Income*

The entire net income accruing during the term of this trust shall be applied so that upon the retirement of each of the following persons from employment by me or my family, he or she shall receive, as a monthly payment, the sum indicated next to his or her name:

A. SUSAN MAXWELL	$2,000.00
B. GUY GABRIELSON	1,000.00
C. MARK ROBINSON	1,000.00
D. SALLY GREEN	500.00

Any net income not so applied ("excess income") shall be divided into four shares, pro rata on the basis of the above amounts, and each such living completely retired beneficiary shall receive, at the end of each year, his or her pro rata share of such excess income. The share of such excess income that is allocable to any deceased or nonretired beneficiary shall be accumulated and capitalized.

PROVIDED, HOWEVER, that if MARK ROBINSON dies survived by his wife Catherine Robinson, she shall be entitled, so long as she is alive, to receive the payments that he would have been entitled to receive were he alive; and the termination of this trust shall be postponed until her death, should the other beneficiaries predecease her.

THIRD: *Distribution of Principal*

On the termination of this trust (as it may be extended pursuant to article SECOND) the entire principal (including all accumulated and capitalized income) shall be paid to my then-living issue, per stirpes; or in default thereof the TRUSTEES OF THE UNIVERSITY OF PENNSYLVANIA.

FOURTH: *Protective Provision*

No interest in income shall be assignable by, or available to anyone having a claim against, a beneficiary before actual payment to the beneficiary.

FIFTH: *Management Provisions*

I authorize the trustees:

A. To retain and to invest in all forms of real and personal property regardless of any limitations imposed by law on investments by my trustees;
B. To compromise claims;
C. To apply all income payable to a disabled person directly for that person's benefit without the intervention of a guardian;
D. To sell at public or private sale, to exchange, or to lease for any period of time any real or personal property, and to give options for sales or leases; and
E. To distribute in cash or in kind.

These authorities shall extend to all property at any time held by the trustees and shall continue in full force until the actual distribution of allsuch property. All powers, authorities, and discretion granted by this deed shall be in addition to those granted by law and shall be exercisable without leave of court.

SIXTH: *Accrued Income Provision*

All income accrued but not yet paid on the property transferred to the trustees shall, when received, be treated as income of this trust.

SEVENTH: *Allocation of Certain Distributions*

The following distributions shall be treated as principal:

A. All capital gains distributions by regulated investment companies, whether paid in cash or in additional shares; and
B. All distributions made in shares of stock, regardless of the number or class of shares distributed.

If there is any asset held as part of the principal with respect to which the trust would properly be entitled to an allowance for depreciation or depletion, the trustees shall establish and maintain, out of receipts from that asset, a reserve fund as part of the principal in the amount of the reasonable depreciation or depletion of the asset in question. No part of the reserve fund or the amounts added thereto in each year shall be deemed income.

EIGHTH: *Irrevocability*

This trust shall be irrevocable and I shall not have any right to alter it or revoke it and shall not have any interest in it except as specifically provided.

NINTH: *Compensation*

The corporate trustee shall receive compensation in accordance with an agreement between me and it.

TENTH: *Additions*

I and, with the trustees' approval, anyone else may add to this trust by deed or by will or otherwise.

ELEVENTH: *Governing Law*

All questions as to the validity or effect of this deed or the administration of the trust hereunder shall be governed by the law of Pennsylvania.

Executed October 20, 1992

/s/ ______________________
Peter Chessman

Witnesses:

____

____

STATE OF PENNSYLANIA
County of Philadelphia ss.

On October 20, 1992, before me, the undersigned officer, personally appeared PETER CHESSMAN and in due form of law acknowledged the foregoing instrument to be his act and deed and desired the same to be recorded as such.

Witness my hand and notarial seal the day and year aforesaid.

/s/ ______________________
Mary O. Connors
Notary Public

My Commission Expires: May 31, 1993. The foregoing deed of trust is hereby accepted October 21, 1992.

____
Paul Chessman

____
Girard Trust Bank
By: H. R. Samson
Trust Officer

SCHEDULE OF PROPERTY REFERRED TO IN THE ANNEXED DEED OF TRUST

Dated October 20, 1992
From

PETER CHESSMAN, Settlor

PAUL CHESSMAN and GIRARD TRUST BANK
Trustees

____

$250,000 in cash

After the settlor's death, testamentary trusts and inter vivos trusts are automatically rendered irrevocable. To denominate them as such is superfluous.

Typical Trust Provisions

The terms of trusts can vary considerably but those used for estate-planning purposes contain relatively uniform basic provisions.

Preamble The initial paragraph usually identifies the settlor, trustee, and date of the document. Often the simple but important declaration that the trustee is being given the assets to hold in trust is also included in this paragraph.

> **Sample Clause**
> I, PETER CHESSMAN, of Philadelphia, Pennsylvania, hereby transfer the property listed in the annexed schedule to PAUL CHESSMAN and GIRARD TRUST BANK as trustees, IN TRUST to keep it invested and to distribute the net income and the principal as follows:

Dispositive Provisions The tax consequences of different possible provisions pertaining to the accumulation and distribution of income generally limit the range of such provisions. The more typical provisions follow:

Qualified Terminal Interest Property Trusts Rather than giving his estate to his wife outright, the testator may wish to place it in trust. Of course, consistent with the marital deduction provisions of the Internal Revenue Code (§ 2056), he must at least give her the right to receive the income annually for life and the right to appoint the principal to whomever she pleases.

The client may wish to be quite liberal with the portion of his taxable estate that is placed in a trust qualifying for the marital deduction. He may permit his wife to withdraw all or part of the principal at any time and allow the trustee discretion to make distributions of principal to her for certain specified purposes such as maintenance and support. Any principal that remains undistributed after the wife's death can be added to other assets to be held and distributed in accordance with other trust provisions.

As discussed in the federal estate tax chapter, an estate tax marital deduction will be allowed for property that passes from the decedent to the trust in which the spouse has a qualifying income interest for life. If a QTIP (Qualified Terminal Interest Property) trust is not established in the will, the personal representative can decide, after the testator's death, whether to make the QTIP election on the federal estate tax return.

Although the property qualifies for the marital deduction, the spouse has limited control over the property in the QTIP trust. Thus, the spouse that is first to die can be certain that the property in the trust will pass to his decedents and not (possibly) to the spouse's second husband. The spouse does not have a power of appointment over the trust however; the property in the trust will be included in the second spouse's taxable estate. Thus when the executor of the first estate is making the election, he should consider both taxable estates and decide what is the best overall tax savings. This can be a valuable estate-planning tool.

The QTIP trust is usually incorporated into the will. Following is an example of some language used in establishing the QTIP trust. Please bear in mind that this is only a portion of the will.

EXAMPLE
Establishing the QTIP Trust

> My personal representative shall have the power to make any election required to qualify the marital trust for the federal estate tax marital deduction. If the federal estate tax laws permit a partial election to said property, my personal representative may make such an election to a portion of the marital property. My personal representative shall not be held liable for any decision made prudently and in good faith.

> **Sample Clause**
> If my wife, SUSIE ELIZABETH SMITH survives me (and she shall be deemed to have survived me if the order of our deaths is not clear), I give an amount exactly sufficient to reduce the federal estate tax falling due because of my death to the lowest possible figure to my trustees IN TRUST to keep it invested and thereafter:
>
> A. During my wife's lifetime:
>   1. The entire net income shall be paid to her, at least quarterly; and
>   2. As much of the principal as my corporate trustee may from time to time think desirable for her welfare, comfort, or support shall be paid to her; and in addition
>   3. She shall have the noncumulative right in each year to withdraw from the principal up to $5,000 or up to five percent thereof, whichever is the greater amount (the amount subject to withdrawal at any time during a year to be based on the market value of the principal at that time plus the amount of any prior withdrawals during that year and to be reduced by the amount of such prior withdrawals).
>
> B. On my wife's death, any remaining principal shall be added to and thereafter treated as a part of the principal of my residuary estate.

Residuary Trust Once any preresiduary trusts such as a marital trust have been established, the remaining assets are placed in what is usually termed a residuary trust. Often the widow is the sole beneficiary of this trust during her lifetime and receives the income at least quarterly. Therefore, if she is already benefiting from a marital trust, she is given the right to benefit in terms of income received from all of the assets the deceased client has placed in both his trusts.

Subsequent to the wife's death, the residuary trust usually provides that the principal is to be held for the client's children. If they are minors at the mother's death, the trustee normally can make distributions of principal and income for their health, maintenance, and education in such amounts and at such times as the trustee deems wise. As a minor comes of age the trustees' duties may alter. Perhaps then they need make no distributions from principal but must pay all income on a quarterly basis. Frequently, the principal of the trust is to be paid to the beneficiary in stages as he or she gets older—say, one-half at 25 and the rest at 35. Distributions of principal, as to amounts and dates of distribution, can be structured in any fashion that is satisfactory to the client, although it is not uncommon to provide for periodic distributions over a 10- or 15-year period beginning at age 25. This can provide additional flexibility and avoids the risk that the beneficiary might waste or use the distribution unwisely upon receipt of the distributive share all at once.

To take full advantage of the tax laws, the client may provide for limited principal distributions to his children—or none whatsoever. Although many people feel it unfair to deprive their own children of the principal, when the estate is substantial, the "skipping" of that generation will protect the fund from substantial depletion from death taxes at the death of the children. In fact, if the client's grandchildren are living at the client's death, principal distributions can be deferred until after their death without violating the rule against perpetuities. Subject to the generation-skipping provisions of the Tax Reform Act of 1976, by keeping the assets of the residuary trust out of the estates of his wife, children, and grandchildren while providing for the payment of income and limited principal from the trust to them during their lives, the client can often benefit the "natural objects of his bounty" in a reasonable way and simultaneously preserve the fund for three or more generations.

Sample Clause

The trustee shall hold all of the property not allocated to the marital trust for my wife as a separate trust and shall keep it invested and thereafter:

A. If my wife, HELEN R. FLYNNE, survives me, during her lifetime:
   1. The net income shall be paid to her, in quarterly or other convenient instalments; and
   2. As much of the principal as the trustee may from time to time think desirable—taking into account funds available from other sources—for the health, support, or maintenance of my wife or any of my children or the education of any of my

children either shall be paid to that person or shall be applied directly for those purposes; provided that none of the principal of this trust shall be paid to or applied for the benefit of my wife unless the principal of the marital trust has been exhausted; and in addition

3. In each year following the year in which the marital trust is exhausted, or in each year following my death if no marital trust will be established, my wife shall have the noncumulative right to withdraw from the principal up to $5,000 or up to five per cent thereof, whichever is the greater amount (the amount subject to withdrawal at any one time during a year to be based on the market value of the principal at that time plus the amount of any prior withdrawals during the year and to be reduced by the amount of such prior withdrawals).

B. After my wife's death (or mine if I survive her) and as long as there is any living child of mine who is under twenty-one years of age:

1. The net income shall be distributed in quarterly or other convenient instalments, to such one or more of my issue in such amounts or proportions as the trustee may from time to time think appropriate; and also
2. As much of the principal as the trustees may from time to time think desirable for the health, support, maintenance, or education of any of my issue either shall be paid to that person or shall be applied directly for those purposes.

My primary concern is for the care and education of my children until they become self-supporting and, while my general plan is to treat them alike, I recognize that needs will vary from person to person and from time to time. Accordingly, I direct that all distributees need not be treated equally or proportionally; that one or more of the eligible distributees may be wholly excluded from any or all periodic distributions; that the pattern followed in one distribution need not be followed in others; and that the trustee may give such consideration to the other resources of each of the eligible distributees as it may think appropriate.

C. After my wife's death (or mine if I survive her) and as soon as there is no living child of mine under twenty-one years of age, the then-remaining principal shall be divided into equal shares, so that there will be one share for each child of mine who is then living or then dead, and each such share shall be kept invested as a separate trust and thereafter:

1. During each child's lifetime:
   a. The net income from his or her trust shall be paid to him or her, in quarterly or other convenient instalments; and
   b. As much of the principal of his or her trust as the trustee may from time to time think desirable—taking into account funds available from other sources—for the health, support, maintenance, or education of that child or any of his or her issue either shall be paid to that person or shall be applied directly for those purposes; and in addition
   c. Each child shall have the right to withdraw up to one-third of the principal of his or her trust at any time after reaching twenty-five years of age, up to an additional one-third thereof at any time after reaching thirty years of age, and

the entire balance thereof at any time after reaching thirty-five years of age (the amount that a child may withdraw before reaching thirty-five years of age to be based on the market value of his or her trust at the time of his or her first withdrawal).

2. At each child's death (or at the time for the setting apart of shares in the case of a child who dies before that time), any then-remaining principal of his or her trust shall be paid:
   a. To such one or more persons or organizations—excepting only his or her estate, his or her creditors, and the creditors of his or her estate—on such terms as he or she may appoint by a will specifically referring to this power of appointment; or, in default of appointment or insofar as it is not effectual,
   b. To his or her then-living issue, per stirpes; or, in default of such issue,
   c. To my then-living issue, per stirpes (any portion thus accruing to a child for whom principal is then held in trust hereunder to be added to and thereafter treated as a part of such principal); or, in default of such issue,
   d. To my heirs under the Pennsylvania intestate law.

Powers Trusts frequently include powers of appointment and powers of withdrawal. Each such power may be limited or unlimited.

Income "Sprinkling" and Accumulation The trustees can be given the right to decide who among a given group of beneficiaries is to receive distributions of income; i.e., it is said the trustee can "sprinkle" the income among a group of beneficiaries. Although it does pose a burden on the trustee, such a "sprinkling" provision can be helpful in providing flexibility to minimize income taxes. The trustee should always be given as much in the way of guidelines as is possible and should be someone who is or was familiar with the settlor, her own philosophies, and the needs and personalities of the beneficiaries.

Trustees can also be given the power to accumulate income. Often, however, state law limits the rights to accumulate income except when a charity, minor, or incompetent is the beneficiary. Accumulation provisions are frequently used in the case of minor beneficiaries since their financial requirements are often slight and they have little ability to handle the income.

Sample Clause

As much of the net income or principal or both as the trustees may from time to time think desirable shall be distributed to such one or more of my sons, their issue, and such trusts as may be established for my sons or their issue under article SECOND in such amounts or proportions as the trustees may from time to time think appropriate.

Mandatory and Discretionary Distribution Powers When trustees are given the power to distribute income or principal, such powers are either mandatory or discretionary. It is important to spot the distinction when reading a will or deed of trust. In the case of a marital trust, for instance, the distribution of income to the surviving spouse at least annually must be mandatory. If it were discretionary, an argument could be made that the interest of the spouse is insufficient to qualify for the marital deduction. (See § 2056 of the Internal Revenue Code.)

Standard "Boilerplate" Provisions Like a will, a trust usually contains certain standard clause to guide the fiduciaries responsible for carrying out its provisions.

Power to Revoke, Alter, or Amend An affirmative statement should be included specifying whether or not the settlor has retained the right to revoke, alter, or amend the trust. In most jurisdictions the absence of such a provision means the settlor has given up any right to revoke, alter, or amend. The manner in which the trust can be revoked or changed should be stipulated.

Sample Clause
This trust shall be irrevocable and I shall not have any right to alter it or revoke it and shall not have any interest in it except as specifically provided.

Addition of Property If the settlor anticipates she and others will make periodic additions of assets to the principal, a provision enabling the trustees to accept gifts should be included.

Sample Clause
I authorize my trustees to receive as an addition to any of the trusts hereunder (i) the proceeds of any insurance policy on my life or any other death benefit payable to my trustees and (ii) any property added to that trust by my spouse's will.

Powers State statute gives trustees certain powers to deal with the trust property. Many lawyers find it desirable to expand those powers by provisions included in the trust document. The right to retain assets placed in the trust and broad investment powers ought to be included. Especially in the case of a life insurance trust, the trustees should be empowered to make loans from the trust corpus (i.e., the insurance proceeds) to the estate to facilitate its administration.

Sample Clause

I authorize the trustees:

A. To retain and to invest in all forms of real and personal property, including stock of any corporate trustee, regardless of any limitations imposed by law on investments by trustees;
B. To compromise claims;
C. To hold securities unregistered or in the name of a nominee;
D. To join in any merger, reorganization, voting-trust plan, or other concerted action of security holders, and to delegate discretionary duties with respect thereto;
E. To sell at public or private sale, to exchange, or to lease for any period of time any real or personal property, and to give options for sales or leases;
F. To borrow from anyone, even if the lender is a trustee hereunder, and to pledge property as security for repayment of the fund borrowed;
G. To allocate any property received or charge incurred to principal or income or partly to each, in those case where no rule of law is clearly applicable;
H. To combine the assets of any two or more of the trusts under this deed, or to combine the assets of any trust or trusts hereunder with those of any other trust or trusts heretofore or hereafter created by my wife or me, for purposes of investment and administration, allocating all receipts and expenses ratably among such trusts, so long as such combination does not alter their status as separate trusts;
I. To retain the services of one or more investment advisers or managers and pay reasonable compensation out of the trust for such services, notwithstanding that either a corporate trustee or any individual trustee is fully competent to render such services;
J. To retain the services of a bank or trust company as custodian and pay reasonable compensation out of the trust for such services;
K. To invest in and hold assets that do not produce income—including, but not limited to, life insurance on the life of the settlor or others;
L. To buy property at its fair market value (as reasonably determined by the trustees) from, or loan money to, my or my wife's executors or administrators; and
M. To distribute in cash or in kind.

These authorities shall be exercisable in respect of all real and personal property at any time held by the trustees and shall continue in full force until the actual distribution of all such property. All powers, authorities, and discretion granted by this deed shall be in addition to those granted by law and shall be exercisable without leave of court.

Tax Clause Special care should be used in drafting tax clauses. The trustees may be directed to pay death taxes attributable to trust assets from those assets. Normally, however, the client wants neither his estate nor any beneficiaries to pay death taxes on trust assets, and he particularly desires to protect the marital trust from such burden. In such a case, specific directions should be given to the trustee in the trust instrument.

Certain assets are exempt from federal estate taxation when not received by executors and administrators. Such assets should not be available for the payment of death taxes when in the hands of the trustee. If used for death tax payments, they may be deemed to have been constructively received by the executor or administrator and, therefore, to be includible in the estate.

Sample Clause

All federal, state, and other death taxes payable because of my death on the insurance proceeds or any other death benefits payable directly to the trustee shall be paid out of the principal of the residuary trust, and none of those taxes shall be charged against the marital trust or any beneficiary; provided that no property that would be exempt from federal estate tax if not payable to my executors or administrators shall be used to pay any death taxes under this article. Any death taxes on future interests may be paid whenever the trustee thinks best.

Minority and Incapacity Provisions A special provision relating to payment of income or distribution of principal to a minor or one who is incapacitated should be included in a trust for the same reason it is found in a will.

Sample Clause

If any minor, or any person who is in the trustees' opinion disabled by advanced age, illness, or other cause, becomes entitled to any income or principal of the trusts under articles FIRST or SECOND:

A. As much of such income or principal as the trustees from time to time think desirable for the beneficiary either shall be paid to him or her or shall be expended on his or her behalf; and
B. All remaining income and principal shall be held as a separate trust for the beneficiary and, subject to the right of the trustees to apply both income and principal of such trust for the beneficiary in the same manner as under paragraph A, shall—together with any net income therefrom—be kept invested and paid to the minor at majority or to the disabled person when he or she, in the opinion of the trustees, becomes free of disability.

Any funds to be applied under this article either shall be applied directly by the trustees or shall be paid to the beneficiary, to a parent or guardian of the beneficiary, or to any person or organization taking care of the beneficiary, or in the case of a minor deposited in a savings account in the minor's name, payable to him at majority, and the trustees shall have no further responsibility for any funds so paid or deposited. In making distributions to a minor the trustees may deal with him or her as if he or she were an adult (my intent being that no one shall have the right to disavow any distribution made during minority).

Accelerated Termination To avoid the burdensome and expensive administration of a small fund that turns out to be little more than a nuisance, a termination clause should be provided.

> **Sample Clause**
> If after the death of my son the trustees, in their sole discretion, determine that it is impractical to administer any fund held under article SECOND or article FOURTH as a trust, the trustees, without further responsibility, may pay the fund to the person then eligible to receive income therefrom. If any such person is a minor or is, in the trustees' opinion, disabled by advanced age, illness or other cause, the trustees may pay the fund to him or her, or to his or her parent or guardian or to any person or organization taking care of him or her or, in the case of a minor, may deposit it in a savings account in the minor's name, payable to him or her at majority. The trustees shall have no further responsibility for funds so paid or deposited.

Saving Clause Occasionally a trust is drafted inadvertently or even intentionally in a manner that may violate the rule against perpetuities. A clause is added to some trusts specifying that if the trust does not previously terminate by its own terms, it will terminate upon the expiration of the period permitted by the rule against perpetuities. Such a clause normally specifies the manner of distribution if termination occurs.

> **Sample Clause**
> Any trust under articles FIRST or SECOND that has not previously terminated in accordance with its terms shall terminate twenty-one years after the death of the survivor of myself, my wife, those of my issue now living, and those person or persons now living who are or later become married to my son. At the time of such termination the then-remaining principal of each trust shall be paid, per stirpes, to the persons eligible to receive distributions of income from it; provided that if my son's wife is then living and receiving income from any such trust, she shall receive from the principal of that trust only the then-actuarial value of her income interest and the balance of such principal shall be paid to the then-living persons who would take it if such wife had died at that time, any share of principal that would otherwise remain in trust to be paid, per stirpes, to the then-living persons who would be eligible to receive distributions of income from it.

Spendthrift Provisions As in a will, a spendthrift provision in a trust is frequently quite effective in protecting a beneficiary from himself and his creditors.

Accrued Income Normally, the client desires the income distribution to benefit the income beneficiaries only during their lifetime.

However, state law often provides that income accrued and undistributed at the time of a beneficiary's death must be paid to the deceased beneficiary's estate and heirs. An expression of the settlor's contrary intent will prevent such unexpected results.

Adoption Clause A provision treating adopted children as natural children may be employed in a trust as in a will if desired by the client.

Governing Law Within some limits the settlor can select the state law he desires to be applicable in the event there is some doubt as to the "domicile" or situs of the trust. An expression of the settlor's desires should be included.

> **Sample Clause**
> All questions as to the validity or effect of this deed or the administration of the trust hereunder shall be governed by the law of Pennsylvania.

Trustees Many of the factors applicable to the appointment of the fiduciaries in a will are applicable to the appointment of trustees. A competent person or institution is desired and, because the appointment entails a substantial obligation, the person should be contacted in advance.

Several important considerations in the appointment must be remembered. A trust may exist for generations. In such a case it is wise to consider a corporate fiduciary (i.e., bank) at least as a co-trustee. This will assure continuity of reliable management that can not be assured even by a string of named, succeeding individual trustees.

Because the needs of families and individuals will be important to many distribution decisions, it is wise to have an individual familiar with the family act as a trustee. Ideally, the combination of a corporate trustee and individual trustee should be used.

Finally, the surviving spouse can be named trustee, but his or her powers should not include the right to join in decisions pertaining to discretionary distributions of principal and income to the spouse or spouse's children.

Schedule of Property An asset that can be described should always be included in the trust at the time it is created. A trust cannot exist without a corpus. A schedule or description of the trust corpus should be appended to the trust document, and the existence of the schedule should be referred to in the preamble.

Compensation Agreement To avoid problems, the compensation of trustees should be arranged in advance. The agreement about fees can be incorporated in the trust document. In the case of a corporate trustee, it is helpful to refer to its published fee schedule. The corporate trustee will not want to qualify as trustee if it is restricted by a certain fee as outlined in a will. A fee that was proper when the testator wrote his will in 1960 may not be appropriate in 1990. The corporate trustee's fees are closely scrutinized by the courts.

Execution Trusts usually have the format of an agreement. The trustee agrees to perform services in exchange for certain stipulated considerations. It is a good practice to have both parties execute the document: the settlor declares the trust and the trustee agrees to accept and acknowledges the same. As further protection, the execution should be accomplished in front of disinterested witnesses and a notary public. The existence of the notary's seal will permit recording of the document on the public records if it is later desired. The settlor and each of the trustees should receive executed copies of the trust.

If another document to be signed at the same meeting (such as a pour-over will or insurance beneficiary change) is to refer to or be dependent upon the trust, it is most important that the execution and creation of the trust be the first order of business. In many jurisdictions, if the trust is not created first those acts and documents that are dependent upon its existence are rendered void or voidable.

Amendment and Revocation

Assuming the settlor has reserved the right to revoke or change the trust, the method to be used is normally provided in the trust. For the protection of all interested parties, mere oral or informal written instructions should not be relied upon. The amendment or notice of revocation should be executed in the same manner as the trust itself and executed copies deliveries to all trustees.

In many jurisdictions a change in the trust also entails a reaffirmation of the acts and documents which depend upon it. For example, a change in a pour-over trust may require a codicil to update the pour-over will. A change in a LITA may require a new set of insurance beneficiary forms to be signed. The reason often given for these requirements is that the amended trust is a new trust to which the will and insurance documents do not refer. It is imperative to know and follow the requirements of the governing laws.

PROCEDURES AFTER EXECUTION OF WILLS AND TRUSTS

Location of Originals

Most lawyers maintain a vault in which they store wills and deeds of trusts for clients. The use of such a vault is encouraged because it diminishes the chance that a client will carelessly or incorrectly change the documents. Many lawyers also feel that keeping the document helps to assure that the client will return to the same lawyer when she wants to make changes or her family will consult that lawyer in the event of death. This probably has some validity, but it should be understood that the lawyer holding such documents is obligated to deliver them to the client upon request.

Banks named as a fiduciary in wills and trusts are generally pleased to store the originals without charge. A third possible place of storage is in the hands of the client. The latter should be discouraged because of potential difficulties in locating the documents after her death. The problems increase if the client places the documents in a safe deposit box. Depending upon state law, the formalities of opening the safe deposit box of a decedent may cause several days of delay in obtaining a will for probate.

It is the client who chooses the location of the original and every conformed copy should be marked to indicate the location of the original.

Related Documents

It is essential that all related documents are completed promptly after the execution of a will or trust. Stock may have to be transferred to the name of the trust. Real estate deeds may need to be executed and filed. Frequently, beneficiary changes must be filed to show the names of the trustees of a LITA (life insurance trust). Insurance companies usually have their own forms that they ask the testator to sign designating to whom the life insurance proceeds should be payable. The form is a beneficiary designation form for a new or existing policy. The legal assistant should contact the appropriate insurance company and obtain that company's form prior to the execution of the will or trust, so that the testator can sign it at the same time the other documents are signed. Some bank trust departments have their own beneficiary designation forms available if the proceeds of the life insurance policy are paid to a trust to be administered by the bank. After the execution of the will or trust document, the beneficiary designation form and the original life insurance policy should be sent to the insurance company with a cover letter requesting that the company change the beneficiary designation on the actual policy.

If gifts have been made that necessitate the filing of gift tax returns, the client should be informed of that obligation. He may ask the lawyer to prepare those returns or he may prefer to have an accountant assume that responsibility.

Superseded wills and trusts are treated differently by different lawyers. A lawyer's assistant should ask for guidance on how they should be treated. Some lawyers ask the client to destroy superseded originals in a ceremonial fashion. Others collect them in a file and keep them indexed for future reference.

The lawyer's assistant should take the responsibility to see that all the loose ends are tied up. This responsibility is of critical importance. If documents are to be circulated for signature, it is the responsibility of the lawyer's assistant to see that the documents are forwarded to the right places and that they return within a reasonable time. Elaborate estate plans have occasionally been held to be completely ineffective because the follow-up work was not done adequately. It is important work that deserves full attention and intelligence.

Periodic Review of Estate Plans

Every office should keep a record of wills and trusts for which it is responsible. The book card or computer system should contain at least the name of the client, the nature of the document, the date and location of the documents, and the name of the draftsman. The addition of very basic information about the document's provisions is also helpful. The record system should be established so that every three to five years the draftsman is automatically advised to suggest to the client that the document be reviewed for possible changes.

The reminder system is highly recommended. It not only enhances client contact, but it also assures that changes required because of new laws or the client's circumstances will brought to the draftsman's attention. An office form letter with one or two follow ups might be used for contacting the client.

APPENDIX

Uniform Probate Code*

[The following Appendix is an excerpt from the complete Uniform Probate Code, Ninth Edition (1990). Comments, prefatory notes, footnotes, and historical notes throughout the Code were not included in this appendix due to their length. It is recommended that if students are conducting research and/or referencing the Uniform Probate Code, that they refer to the complete version of the Code.]

AN ACT

Relating to affairs of decedents, missing persons, protected persons, minors, incapacitated persons and certain others and constituting the Uniform Probate Code; consolidating and revising aspects of the law relating to wills and intestacy and the administration and distribution of estates of decedents, missing persons, protected persons, minors, incapacitated persons and certain others; ordering the powers and procedures of the Court concerned with the affairs of decedents and certain others; providing for the validity and effect of certain non-testamentary transfers, contracts and deposits which relate to death and appear to have testamentary effect; providing certain procedures to facilitate enforcement of testamentary and other trusts; making uniform the law with respect to decedents and certain others; and repealing inconsistent legislation.

ARTICLE I. GENERAL PROVISIONS, DEFINITIONS AND PROBATE JURISDICTION OF COURT

PART 1. SHORT TITLE, CONSTRUCTION, GENERAL PROVISIONS

1-101. [Short Title.]
1-102. [Purposes; Rule of Construction.]
1-103. [Supplementary General Principles of Law Applicable.]
1-104. [Severability.]
1-105. [Construction Against Implied Repeal.]
1-106. [Effect of Fraud and Evasion.]
1-107. [Evidence as to Death or Status.]
1-108. [Acts by Holder of General Power.]

PART 2. DEFINITIONS

1-201. [General Definitions.]

PART 3. SCOPE, JURISDICTION AND COURTS

1-301. [Territorial Application.]
1-302. [Subject Matter Jurisdiction.]
1-303. [Venue; Multiple Proceedings; Transfer.]
1-304. [Practice in Court.]

* Official text approved by the National Conference of Commissioners on Uniform State Laws and Joint Editorial Board for Uniform Probate Code.

1-305. [Records and Certified Copies.]
1-306. [Jury Trial.]
1-307. [Registrar; Powers.]
1-308. [Appeals.]
1-309. [Qualifications of Judge.]
1-310. [Oath or Affirmation on Filed Documents.]

PART 4. NOTICE, PARTIES AND REPRESENTATION IN ESTATE LITIGATION AND OTHER MATTERS
1-401. [Notice; Method and Time of Giving.]
1-402. [Notice; Waiver.]
1-403. [Pleadings; When Parties Bound by Others; Notice.]

PART 1. SHORT TITLE, CONSTRUCTION, GENERAL PROVISIONS

Section 1-101. [Short Title.]
This Act shall be known and may be cited as the Uniform Probate Code.

Section 1-102. [Purposes; Rule of Construction.]
(a) This Code shall be liberally construed and applied to promote its underlying purposes and policies.
(b) The underlying purposes and policies of this Code are:

(1) to simplify and clarify the law concerning the affairs of decedents, missing persons, protected persons, minors and incapacitated persons;
(2) to discover and make effective the intent of a decedent in distribution of his property;
(3) to promote a speedy and efficient system for liquidating the estate of the decedent and making distribution to his successors;
(4) to facilitate use and enforcement of certain trusts;
(5) to make uniform the law among the various jurisdictions.

Section 1-103. [Supplementary General Principles of Law Applicable.]
Unless displaced by the particular provisions of this Code, the principles of law and equity supplement its provisions.

Section 1-104. [Severability.]
If any provision of this Code or the application thereof to any person or circumstances is held invalid, the invalidity shall not affect other provisions or applications of the Code which can be given effect without the invalid provision or application, and to this end the provisions of this Code are declared to be severable.

Section 1-105. [Construction Against Implied Repeal.]
This Code is a general act intended as a unified coverage of its subject matter and no part of it shall be deemed impliedly repealed by subsequent legislation if it can reasonably be avoided.

Section 1-106. [Effect of Fraud and Evasion.]
Whenever fraud has been perpetrated in connection with any proceeding or in any statement filed under this Code or if fraud is used to avoid or circumvent the provisions or purposes of this Code, any person injured thereby may obtain appropriate relief against the perpetrator of the fraud or restitution from any person (other than a bona fide purchaser) benefitting from the fraud, whether innocent or not. Any proceeding must be commenced within 2 years after the discovery of the fraud, but no proceeding may be brought against one not a perpetrator of the fraud later than 5 years after the time of commission of the fraud. This section has no bearing on remedies relating to fraud practiced on a decedent during his lifetime which affects the succession of his estate.

Section 1-107. [Evidence as to Death or Status.]
In proceedings under this Code the rules of evidence in courts of general jurisdiction including any relating to simultaneous deaths, are applicable unless specifically displaced by the Code. In addition, the following rules relating to determination of death and status are applicable:

(1) a certified or authenticated copy of a death certificate purporting to be issued by an official or agency of the place where the death purportedly occurred is prima facie proof of the fact, place, date and time of death and the identity of the decedent;
(2) a certified or authenticated copy of any record or report of a governmental agency, domestic or foreign, that a person is missing, detained, dead, or alive is prima facie evidence of the status and of the dates, circumstances and places disclosed by the record or report;
(3) in the absence of prima facie evidence of death under (1) or (2) above, the fact of death may be established by clear and convincing evidence, including circumstantial evidence;
(4) a person whose death is not established under the preceding subparagraphs who is absent for a continuous period of 5 years, during which he has not been heard from, and whose absence is not satisfactorily explained after diligent search or inquiry is presumed to be dead. His death is presumed to have occurred at the end of the period unless there is sufficient evidence for determining that death occurred earlier.

As amended in 1987.

Section 1-108. [Acts by Holder of General Power.]
For the purpose of granting consent or approval with regard to the acts or accounts of a personal representative or trustee, including relief from liability or penalty for failure to post bond, to register a trust, or to perform other duties, and for purposes of consenting to modification or termination of a trust or to deviation from its terms, the sole holder or all co-holders of a presently exercisable general power of appointment, including one in the form of a power of amendment or revocation, are deemed to act for beneficiaries to the extent their interests (as objects, takers in default, or otherwise) are subject to the power.

PART 2. DEFINITIONS

Section 1-201. General Definitions.
The following is the text of section 1-201 as revised in 1990 in conjunction with the approval of Revised Article II of the Code.
Subject to additional definitions contained in the subsequent Articles that are applicable to specific Articles, parts, or sections, and unless the context otherwise requires, in this Code:

(1) "Agent" includes an attorney-in-fact under a durable or nondurable power of attorney, an individual authorized to make decisions concerning another's health care, and an individual authorized to make decisions for another under a natural death act.
(2) "Application" means a written request to the Registrar for an order of informal probate or appointment under Part 3 of Article III.
(3) "Beneficiary," as it relates to a trust beneficiary, includes a person who has any present or future interest, vested or contingent, and also includes the owner of an interest by assignment or other transfer; as it relates to a charitable trust, includes any person entitled to enforce the trust; as it relates to a "beneficiary of a beneficiary designation," refers to a beneficiary of an insurance or annuity policy, of an account with POD designation, of a security registered in beneficiary form (TOD), or of a pension, profit-sharing, retirement, or similar benefit

plan, or other nonprobate transfer at death; and, as it relates to a "beneficiary designated in a governing instrument," includes a grantee of a deed, a devisee, a trust beneficiary, a beneficiary of a beneficiary designation, a donee, appointee, or taker in default of a power of appointment, or a person in whose favor a power of attorney or a power held in any individual, fiduciary, or representative capacity is exercised.

(4) "Beneficiary designation" refers to a governing instrument naming a beneficiary of an insurance or annuity policy, of an account with POD designation, of a security registered in beneficiary form (TOD), or of a pension, profit-sharing, retirement, or similar benefit plan, or other nonprobate transfer at death.

(5) "Child" includes an individual entitled to take as a child under this Code by intestate succession from the parent whose relationship is involved and excludes a person who is only a stepchild, a foster child, a grandchild, or any more remote descendant.

(6) "Claims," in respect to estates of decedents and protected persons, includes liabilities of the decedent or protected person, whether arising in contract, in tort, or otherwise, and liabilities of the estate which arise at or after the death of the decedent or after the appointment of a conservator, including funeral expenses and expenses of administration. The term does not include estate or inheritance taxes, or demands or disputes regarding title of a decedent or protected person to specific assets alleged to be included in the estate.

(7) "Court" means the [. . . . . Court] or branch in this State having jurisdiction in matters relating to the affairs of decedents.

(8) "Conservator" means a person who is appointed by a Court to manage the estate of a protected person.

(9) "Descendant" of an individual means all of his [or her] descendants of all generations, with the relationship of parent and child at each generation being determined by the definition of child and parent contained in this Code.

(10) "Devise," when used as a noun, means a testamentary disposition of real or personal property and, when used as a verb, means to dispose of real or personal property by will.

(11) "Devisee" means a person designated in a will to receive a devise. In the case of a devise to an existing trust or trustee, or to a trustee on trust described by will, the trust or trustee is the devisee and the beneficiaries are not devisees.

(12) "Disability" means cause for a protective order as described in Section 5-401.

(13) "Distributee" means any person who has received property of a decedent from his [or her] personal representative other than as a creditor or purchaser. A testamentary trustee is a distributee only to the extent of distributed assets or increment thereto remaining in his [or her] hands. A beneficiary of a testamentary trust to whom the trustee has distributed property received from a personal representative is a distributee of the personal representative. For the purposes of this provision, "testamentary trustee" includes a trustee to whom assets are transferred by will, to the extent of the devised assets.

(14) "Estate" includes the property of the decedent, trust, or other person whose affairs are subject to this Code as originally constituted and as it exists from time to time during administration.

(15) "Exempt property" means that property of a decedent's estate which is described in Section 2-403.

(16) "Fiduciary" includes a personal representative, guardian, conservator, and trustee.

(17) "Foreign personal representative" means a personal representative appointed by another jurisdiction.

(18) "Formal proceedings" means proceedings conducted before a judge with notice to interested persons.

(19) "Governing instrument" means a deed, will, trust, insurance or annuity policy, account with POD designation, security registered in beneficiary form

(TOD), pension, profit-sharing, retirement, or similar benefit plan, instrument creating or exercising a power of appointment or a power of attorney, or a donative, appointive, or nominative instrument of any other type.

(20) "Guardian" means a person who has qualified as a guardian of a minor or incapacitated person pursuant to testamentary or court appointment, but excludes one who is merely a guardian ad litem.

(21) "Heirs," except as controlled by Section 2-711, means persons, including the surviving spouse and the state, who are entitled under the statutes of intestate succession to the property of a decedent.

(22) "Incapacitated person" means an individual described in Section 5-103.

(23) "Informal proceedings" means those conducted without notice to interested persons by an officer of the Court acting as a registrar for probate of a will or appointment of a personal representative.

(24) "Interested person" includes heirs, devisees, children, spouses, creditors, beneficiaries, and any others having a property right in or claim against a trust estate or the estate of a decedent, ward, or protected person. It also includes persons having priority for appointment as personal representative, and other fiduciaries representing interested persons. The meaning as it relates to particular persons may vary from time to time and must be determined according to the particular purposes of, and matter involved in, any proceeding.

(25) "Issue" of a person means descendant as defined in subsection (9).

(26) "Joint tenants with the right of survivorship" and "community property with the right of survivorship" includes co-owners of property held under circumstances that entitle one or more to the whole of the property on the death of the other or others, but excludes forms of co-ownership registration in which the underlying ownership of each party is in proportion to that party's contribution.

(27) "Lease" includes an oil, gas, or other mineral lease.

(28) "Letters" includes letters testamentary, letters of guardianship, letters of administration, and letters of conservatorship.

(29) "Minor" means a person who is under [21] years of age.

(30) "Mortgage" means any conveyance, agreement, or arrangement in which property is encumbered or used as security.

(31) "Nonresident decedent" means a decedent who was domiciled in another jurisdiction at the time of his [or her] death.

(32) "Organization" means a corporation, business trust, estate, trust, partnership, joint venture, association, government or governmental subdivision or agency, or any other legal or commercial entity.

(33) "Parent" includes any person entitled to take, or who would be entitled to take if the child died without a will, as a parent under this Code by intestate succession from the child whose relationship is in question and excludes any person who is only a stepparent, foster parent, or grandparent.

(34) "Payor" means a trustee, insurer, business entity, employer, government, governmental agency or subdivision, or any other person authorized or obligated by law or a governing instrument to make payments.

(35) "Person" means an individual or an organization.

(36) "Personal representative" includes executor, administrator, successor personal representative, special administrator, and persons who perform substantially the same function under the law governing their status. "General personal representative" excludes special administrator.

(37) "Petition" means a written request to the Court for an order after notice.

(38) "Proceeding" includes action at law and suit in equity.

(39) "Property" includes both real and personal property or any interest therein and means anything that may be the subject of ownership.

(40) "Protected person" is as defined in Section 5-103.

(41) "Protective proceeding" means a proceeding described in Section 5-103.

(42) "Registrar" refers to the official of the Court designated to perform the functions of Registrar as provided in Section 1-307.

(43) "Security" includes any note, stock, treasury stock, bond, debenture, evidence of indebtedness, certificate of interest or participation in an oil, gas, or mining title or lease or in payments out of production under such a title or lease, collateral trust certificate, transferable share, voting trust certificate or, in general, any interest or instrument commonly known as a security, or any certificate of interest or participation, any temporary or interim certificate, receipt, or certificate of deposit for, or any warrant or right to subscribe to or purchase, any of the foregoing.
(44) "Settlement," in reference to a decedent's estate, includes the full process of administration, distribution, and closing.
(45) "Special administrator" means a personal representative as described by Sections 3-614 through 3-618.
(46) "State" means a state of the United States, the District of Columbia, the Commonwealth of Puerto Rico, or any territory or insular possession subject to the jurisdiction of the United States.
(47) "Successor personal representative" means a personal representative, other than a special administrator, who is appointed to succeed a previously appointed personal representative.
(48) "Successors" means persons, other than creditors, who are entitled to property of a decedent under his [or her] will or this Code.
(49) "Supervised administration" refers to the proceedings described in Article III, Part 5.
(50) "Survive," except for purposes of Part 3 of Article VI [Uniform TOD Security Registration Act], means that an individual has neither predeceased an event, including the death of another individual, nor is deemed to have predeceased an event under Section 2-104 or 2-702. The term includes its derivatives, such as "survives," "survived," "survivor," "surviving."
(51) "Testacy proceeding" means a proceeding to establish a will or determine intestacy.
(52) "Testator" includes an individual of either sex.
(53) "Trust" includes an express trust, private or charitable, with additions thereto, wherever and however created. The term also includes a trust created or determined by judgment or decree under which the trust is to be administered in the manner of an express trust. The term excludes other constructive trusts and excludes resulting trusts, conservatorships, personal representatives, trust accounts as defined in Article VI, custodial arrangements pursuant to [each state should list its legislation, including that relating to [gifts] [transfers] to minors, dealing with special custodial situations], business trusts providing for certificates to be issued to beneficiaries, common trust funds, voting trusts, security arrangements, liquidation trusts, and trusts for the primary purpose of paying debts, dividends, interest, salaries, wages, profits, pensions, or employee benefits of any kind, and any arrangement under which a person is nominee or escrowee for another.
(54) "Trustee" includes an original, additional, or successor trustee, whether or not appointed or confirmed by court.
(55) "Ward" means an individual described in Section 5-103.
(56) "Will" includes codicil and any testamentary instrument that merely appoints an executor, revokes or revises another will, nominates a guardian, or expressly excludes or limits the right of an individual or class to succeed to property of the decedent passing by intestate succession.

[FOR ADOPTION IN COMMUNITY PROPERTY STATES]

[(57) "Separate property" (if necessary, to be defined locally in accordance with existing concept in adopting state).
(58) "Community property" (if necessary, to be defined locally in accordance with existing concept in adopting state).]

As revised in 1990.

PART 3. SCOPE, JURISDICTION AND COURTS

Section 1-301. [Territorial Application.]
Except as otherwise provided in this Code, this Code applies to (1) the affairs and estates of decedents, missing persons, and persons to be protected, domiciled in this state, (2) the property of nonresidents located in this state or property coming into the control of a fiduciary who is subject to the laws of this state, (3) incapacitated persons and minors in this state, (4) survivorship and related accounts in this state, and (5) trusts subject to administration in this state.

Section 1-302. [Subject Matter Jurisdiction.]
(a) To the full extent permitted by the constitution, the Court has jurisdiction over all subject matter relating to (1) estates of decedents, including construction of wills and determination of heirs and successors of decedents, and estates of protected persons; (2) protection of minors and incapacitated persons; and (3) trusts.
(b) The Court has full power to make orders, judgments and decrees and take all other action necessary and proper to administer justice in the matters which come before it.
(c) The Court has jurisdiction over protective proceedings and guardianship proceedings.
(d) If both guardianship and protective proceedings as to the same person are commenced or pending in the same court, the proceedings may be consolidated.

Section 1-303. [Venue; Multiple Proceedings; Transfer.]
(a) Where a proceeding under this Code could be maintained in more than one place in this state, the Court in which the proceeding is first commenced has the exclusive right to proceed.
(b) If proceedings concerning the same estate, protected person, ward, or trust are commenced in more than one Court of this state, the Court in which the proceeding was first commenced shall continue to hear the matter, and the other courts shall hold the matter in abeyance until the question of venue is decided, and if the ruling Court determines that venue is properly in another Court, it shall transfer the proceeding to the other Court.
(c) If a Court finds that in the interest of justice a proceeding or a file should be located in another Court of this state, the Court making the finding may transfer the proceeding or file to the other Court.

Section 1-304. [Practice in Court.]
Unless specifically provided to the contrary in this Code or unless inconsistent with its provisions, the rules of civil procedure including the rules concerning vacation of orders and appellate review govern formal proceedings under this Code.

Section 1-305. [Records and Certified Copies.]
The [Clerk of Court] shall keep a record for each decedent, ward, protected person or trust involved in any document which may be filed with the Court under this Code, including petitions and applications, demands for notices or bonds, trust registrations, and of any orders or responses relating thereto by the Registrar or Court, and establish and maintain a system for indexing, filing or recording which is sufficient to enable users of the records to obtain adequate information. Upon payment of the fees required by law the clerk must issue certified copies of any probated wills, letters issued to personal representatives, or any other record or paper filed or recorded. Certificates relating to probated wills must indicate whether the decedent was domiciled in this state and whether the probate was formal or informal. Certificates relating to letters must show the date of appointment.

Section 1-306. [Jury Trial.]
(a) If duly demanded, a party is entitled to trial by jury in [a formal testacy proceeding and] any proceeding in which any controverted question of fact arises as to which any party has a constitutional right to trial by jury.
(b) If there is no right to trial by jury under subsection (a) or the right is waived, the Court in its discretion may call a jury to decide any issue of fact, in which case the verdict is advisory only.

Section 1-307. [Registrar; Powers.]
The acts and orders which this Code specifies as performable by the Registrar may be performed either by a judge of the Court or by a person, including the clerk, designated by the Court by a written order filed and recorded in the office of the Court.

Section 1-308. [Appeals.]
Appellate review, including the right to appellate review, interlocutory appeal, provisions as to time, manner, notice, appeal bond, stays, scope of review, record on appeal, briefs, arguments and power of the appellate court, is governed by the rules applicable to the appeals to the [Supreme Court] in equity cases from the [court of general jurisdiction], except that in proceedings where jury trial has been had as a matter of right, the rules applicable to the scope of review in jury cases apply.

Section 1-309. [Qualifications of Judge.]
A judge of the Court must have the same qualifications as a judge of the [court of general jurisdiction.]

Section 1-310. [Oath or Affirmation on Filed Documents.]
Except as otherwise specifically provided in this Code or by rule, every document filed with the Court under this Code including applications, petitions, and demands for notice, shall be deemed to include an oath, affirmation, or statement to the effect that its representations are true as far as the person executing or filing it knows or is informed, and penalties for perjury may follow deliberate falsification therein.

PART 4. NOTICE, PARTIES AND REPRESENTATION IN ESTATE LITIGATION AND OTHER MATTERS

Section 1-401. [Notice; Method and Time of Giving.]
(a) If notice of a hearing on any petition is required and except for specific notice requirements as otherwise provided, the petitioner shall cause notice of the time and place of hearing of any petition to be given to any interested person or his attorney if he has appeared by attorney or requested that notice be sent to his attorney. Notice shall be given:

(1) by mailing a copy thereof at least 14 days before the time set for the hearing by certified, registered or ordinary first class mail addressed to the person being notified at the post office address given in his demand for notice, if any, or at his office or place of residence, if known;
(2) by delivering a copy thereof to the person being notified personally at least 14 days before the time set for the hearing; or
(3) if the address, or identity of any person is not known and cannot be ascertained with reasonable diligence, by publishing at least once a week for 3 consecutive weeks, a copy thereof in a newspaper having general circulation in the county where the hearing is to be held, the last publication of which is to be at least 10 days before the time set for the hearing.

(b) The Court for good cause shown may provide for a different method or time of giving notice for any hearing.

(c) Proof of the giving of notice shall be made on or before the hearing and filed in the proceeding.

Section 1-402. [Notice; Waiver.]
A person, including a guardian ad litem, conservator, or other fiduciary, may waive notice by a writing signed by him or his attorney and filed in the proceeding. A person for whom a guardianship or other protective order is sought, a ward, or a protected person may not waive notice.

Section 1-403. [Pleadings; When Parties Bound by Others; Notice.]
In formal proceedings involving trusts or estates of decedents, minors, protected persons, or incapacitated persons, and in judicially supervised settlements, the following apply:

(1) Interests to be affected shall be described in pleadings which give reasonable information to owners by name or class, by reference to the instrument creating the interests, or in other appropriate manner.
(2) Persons are bound by orders binding others in the following cases:
(i) Orders binding the sole holder or all co-holders of a power of revocation or a presently exercisable general power of appointment, including one in the form of a power of amendment, bind other persons to the extent their interests (as objects, takers in default, or otherwise) are subject to the power.
(ii) To the extent there is no conflict of interest between them or among persons represented, orders binding a conservator bind the person whose estate he controls; orders binding a guardian bind the ward if no conservator of his estate has been appointed; orders binding a trustee bind beneficiaries of the trust in proceedings to probate a will establishing or adding to a trust, to review the acts or accounts of a prior fiduciary and in proceedings involving creditors or other third parties; and orders binding a personal representative bind persons interested in the undistributed assets of a decedent's estate in actions or proceedings by or against the estate. If there is no conflict of interest and no conservator or guardian has been appointed, a parent may represent his minor child.
(iii) An unborn or unascertained person who is not otherwise represented is bound by an order to the extent his interest is adequately represented by another party having a substantially identical interest in the proceeding.
(3) Notice is required as follows:
(i) Notice as prescribed by Section 1-401 shall be given to every interested person or to one who can bind an interested person as described in (2)(i) or (2)(ii) above. Notice may be given both to a person and to another who may bind him.
(ii) Notice is given to unborn or unascertained persons, who are not represented under (2)(i) or (2)(ii) above, by giving notice to all known persons whose interests in the proceedings are substantially identical to those of the unborn or unascertained persons.
(4) At any point in a proceeding, a court may appoint a guardian ad litem to represent the interest of a minor, an incapacitated, unborn, or unascertained person, or a person whose identity or address is unknown, if the Court determines that representation of the interest otherwise would be inadequate. If not precluded by conflict of interests, a guardian ad litem may be appointed to represent several persons or interests. The Court shall set out its reasons for appointing a guardian ad litem as a part of the record of the proceeding.

ARTICLE II. INTESTACY, WILLS, AND DONATIVE TRANSFERS (1990)

PART 1. INTESTATE SUCCESSION

2-101. Intestate Estate.
2-102. Share of Spouse.

2-102A. Share of Spouse.
2-103. Share of Heirs Other Than Surviving Spouse.
2-104. Requirement That Heir Survive Decedent For 120 Hours.
2-105. No Taker.
2-106. Representation.
2-107. Kindred of Half Blood.
2-108. Afterborn Heirs.
2-109. Advancements.
2-110. Debts to Decedent.
2-111. Alienage.
2-112. Dower and Curtesy Abolished.
2-113. Individuals Related to Decedent Through Two Lines.
2-114. Parent and Child Relationship.

PART 2. ELECTIVE SHARE OF SURVIVING SPOUSE

2-201. Elective Share.
2-202. Augmented Estate.
2-203. Right of Election Personal to Surviving Spouse.
2-204. Waiver of Right to Elect and of Other Rights.
2-205. Proceeding for Elective Share; Time Limit.
2-206. Effect of Election on Statutory Benefits.
2-207. Charging Spouse With Owned Assets and Gifts Received; Liability of Others For Balance of Elective Share.

PART 3. SPOUSE AND CHILDREN UNPROVIDED FOR IN WILLS

2-301. Entitlement of Spouse; Premarital Will.
2-302. Omitted Children.

PART 4. EXEMPT PROPERTY AND ALLOWANCES

2-401. Applicable Law.
2-402. Homestead Allowance.
2-402A. Constitutional Homestead.
2-403. Exempt Property.
2-404. Family Allowance.
2-405. Source, Determination, and Documentation.

PART 5. WILLS, WILL CONTRACTS, AND CUSTODY AND DEPOSIT OF WILLS

2-501. Who May Make Will.
2-502. Execution; Witnessed Wills; Holographic Wills.
2-503. Writings Intended as Wills, Etc.
2-504. Self-proved Will.
2-505. Who May Witness.
2-506. Choice of Law as to Execution.
2-507. Revocation by Writing or by Act.
2-508. Revocation by Change of Circumstances.
2-509. Revival of Revoked Will.
2-510. Incorporation by Reference.
2-511. Testamentary Additions to Trusts.
2-512. Events of Independent Significance.
2-513. Separate Writing Identifying Devise of Certain Types of Tangible Personal Property.
2-514. Contracts Concerning Succession.
2-515. Deposit of Will With Court in Testator's Lifetime.
2-516. Duty of Custodian of Will; Liability.
2-517. Penalty Clause for Contest.

PART 6. RULES OF CONSTRUCTION APPLICABLE ONLY TO WILLS

2-601. Scope.
2-602. Will May Pass All Property and After-acquired Property.
2-603. Anti-lapse; Deceased Devisee; Class Gifts.
2-604. Failure of Testamentary Provision.
2-605. Increase in Devised Securities; Accessions.
2-606. Nonademption of Specific Devises; Unpaid Proceeds of Sale, Condemnation, or Insurance; Sale by Conservator or Agent.
2-607. Nonexoneration.
2-608. Exercise of Power of Appointment.
2-609. Ademption by Satisfaction.

PART 7. RULES OF CONSTRUCTION APPLICABLE TO DONATIVE DISPOSITIONS IN WILLS AND OTHER GOVERNING INSTRUMENTS

2-701. Scope.
2-702. Requirement of Survival by 120 Hours.
2-703. Choice of Law as to Meaning and Effect of Donative Dispositions.
2-704. Power of Appointment; Meaning of Specific Reference Requirement.
2-705. Class Gifts Construed to Accord with Intestate Succession.
2-706. Life Insurance; Retirement Plan; Account With POD Designation; Transfer-on-Death Registration; Deceased Beneficiary.
2-707. Survivorship With Respect to Future Interests Under Terms of Trust; Substitute Takers.
2-708. Class Gifts to "Descendants," "Issue," or "Heirs of the Body"; Form of Distribution If None Specified.
2-709. Representation; Per Capita at Each Generation; Per Stirpes.
2-710. Worthier-Title Doctrine Abolished.
2-711. Future Interests in "Heirs" and Like.

PART 8. GENERAL PROVISIONS CONCERNING PROBATE AND NONPROBATE TRANSFERS

2-801. Disclaimer of Property Interests.
2-802. Effect of Divorce, Annulment, and Decree of Separation.
2-803. Effect of Homicide on Intestate Succession, Wills, Trusts, Joint Assets, Life Insurance, and Beneficiary Designations.
2-804. Revocation of Probate and Nonprobate Transfers by Divorce; No Revocation by Other Changes of Circumstances.

PART 9. STATUTORY RULE AGAINST PERPETUITIES; HONORARY TRUSTS

Subpart 1. Statutory Rule Against Perpetuities

2-901. Statutory Rule Against Perpetuities.
2-902. When Nonvested Property Interest or Power of Appointment Created.
2-903. Reformation.
2-904. Exclusions From Statutory Rule Against Perpetuities.
2-905. Prospective Application.
2-906. [Supersession] [Repeal].

Subpart 2. [Honorary Trusts].

2-907. [Honorary Trusts; Trusts for Pets.]

PART 10. UNIFORM INTERNATIONAL WILLS ACT [INTERNATIONAL WILL; INFORMATION REGISTRATION]

1 [2-1001]. [Definitions.]
2 [2-1002]. [International Will; Validity.]
3 [2-1003]. [International Will; Requirements.]
4 [2-1004]. [International Will; Other Points of Form.]
5 [2-1005]. [International Will; Certificate.]
6 [2-1006]. [International Will; Effect of Certificate.]

7 [2-1007]. [International Will; Revocation.]
8 [2-1008]. [Source and Construction.]
9 [2-1009]. [Persons Authorized to Act in Relation to International Will; Eligibility; Recognition by Authorizing Agency.]
10 [2-1010]. [International Will Information Registration.]

PART 1. INTESTATE SUCCESSION

Section 2-101. Intestate Estate.
(a) Any part of a decedent's estate not effectively disposed of by will passes by intestate succession to the decedent's heirs as prescribed in this Code, except as modified by the decedent's will.
(b) A decedent by will may expressly exclude or limit the right of an individual or class to succeed to property of the decedent passing by intestate succession. If that individual or a member of that class survives the decedent, the share of the decedent's intestate estate to which that individual or class would have succeeded passes as if that individual or each member of that class had disclaimed his [or her] intestate share.

Section 2-102. Share of Spouse.
The intestate share of a decedent's surviving spouse is:

(1) the entire intestate estate if:
(i) no descendant or parent of the decedent survives the decedent; or
(ii) all of the decedent's surviving descendants are also descendants of the surviving spouse and there is no other descendant of the surviving spouse who survives the decedent;
(2) the first [$200,000], plus three-fourths of any balance of the intestate estate, if no descendant of the decedent survives the decedent, but a parent of the decedent survives the decedent;
(3) the first [$150,000], plus one-half of any balance of the intestate estate, if all of the decedent's surviving descendants are also descendants of the surviving spouse and the surviving spouse has one or more surviving descendants who are not descendants of the decedent;
(4) the first [$100,000], plus one-half of any balance of the intestate estate, if one or more of the decedent's surviving descendants are not descendants of the surviving spouse.

[ALTERNATIVE PROVISION FOR COMMUNITY PROPERTY STATES]

[Section 2-102A. Share of Spouse.
(a) The intestate share of a surviving spouse in separate property is:

(1) the entire intestate estate if:
(i) no descendant or parent of the decedent survives the decedent; or
(ii) all of the decedent's surviving descendants are also descendants of the surviving spouse and there is no other descendant of the surviving spouse who survives the decedent;
(2) the first [$200,000], plus three-fourths of any balance of the intestate estate, if no descendant of the decedent survives the decedent, but a parent of the decedent survives the decedent;
(3) the first [$150,000], plus one-half of any balance of the intestate estate, if all of the decedent's surviving descendants are also descendants of the surviving spouse and the surviving spouse has one or more surviving descendants who are not descendants of the decedent;
(4) the first [$100,000], plus one-half of any balance of the intestate estate, if one or more of the decedent's surviving descendants are not descendants of the surviving spouse.

(b) The one-half of community property belonging to the decedent passes to the [surviving spouse] as the intestate share.]

Section 2-103. Share of Heirs other than Surviving Spouse.
Any part of the intestate estate not passing to the decedent's surviving spouse under Section 2-102, or the entire intestate estate if there is no surviving spouse, passes in the following order to the individuals designated below who survive the decedent:

(1) to the decedent's descendants by representation;
(2) if there is no surviving descendant, to the decedent's parents equally if both survive, or to the surviving parent;
(3) if there is no surviving descendant or parent, to the descendants of the decedent's parents or either of them by representation;
(4) if there is no surviving descendant, parent, or descendant of a parent, but the decedent is survived by one or more grandparents or descendants of grandparents, half of the estate passes to the decedent's paternal grandparents equally if both survive, or to the surviving paternal grandparent, or to the descendants of the decedent's paternal grandparents or either of them if both are deceased, the descendants taking by representation; and the other half passes to the decedent's maternal relatives in the same manner; but if there is no surviving grandparent or descendant of a grandparent on either the paternal or the maternal side, the entire estate passes to the decedent's relatives on the other side in the same manner as the half.

Section 2-104. Requirement that Heir Survive Decedent for 120 Hours.
An individual who fails to survive the decedent by 120 hours is deemed to have predeceased the decedent for purposes of homestead allowance, exempt property, and intestate succession, and the decedent's heirs are determined accordingly. If it is not established by clear and convincing evidence that an individual who would otherwise be an heir survived the decedent by 120 hours, it is deemed that the individual failed to survive for the required period. This section is not to be applied if its application would result in a taking of intestate estate by the state under Section 2-105.

Section 2-105. No Taker.
If there is no taker under the provisions of this Article, the intestate estate passes to the [state].

Section 2-106. Representation.
(a) [Definitions.] In this section:

(1) "Deceased descendant," "deceased parent," or "deceased grandparent" means a descendant, parent, or grandparent who either predeceased the decedent or is deemed to have predeceased the decedent under Section 2-104.
(2) "Surviving descendant" means a descendant who neither predeceased the decedent nor is deemed to have predeceased the decedent under Section 2-104.

(b) [Decedent's Descendants.] If, under Section 2-103(1), a decedent's intestate estate or a part thereof passes "by representation" to the decedent's descendants, the estate or part thereof is divided into as many equal shares as there are (i) surviving descendants in the generation nearest to the decedent which contains one or more surviving descendants and (ii) deceased descendants in the same generation who left surviving descendants, if any. Each surviving descendant in the nearest generation is allocated one share. The remaining shares, if any, are combined and then divided in the same manner among the surviving descendants of the deceased descendants as if the surviving descendants who were allocated a share and their surviving descendants had predeceased the decedent.
(c) [Descendants of Parents or Grandparents.] If, under Section 2-103(3) or (4), a decedent's intestate estate or a part thereof passes "by representation" to the

descendants of the decedent's deceased parents or either of them or to the descendants of the decedent's deceased paternal or maternal grandparents or either of them, the estate or part thereof is divided into as many equal shares as there are (i) surviving descendants in the generation nearest the deceased parents or either of them, or the deceased grandparents or either of them, that contains one or more surviving descendants and (ii) deceased descendants in the same generation who left surviving descendants, if any. Each surviving descendant in the nearest generation is allocated one share. The remaining shares, if any, are combined and then divided in the same manner among the surviving descendants of the deceased descendants as if the surviving descendants who were allocated a share and their surviving descendants had predeceased the decedent.

Section 2-107. Kindred of Half Blood.
Relatives of the half blood inherit the same share they would inherit if they were of the whole blood.

Section 2-108. Afterborn Heirs.
An individual in gestation at a particular time is treated as living at that time if the individual lives 120 hours or more after birth.

Section 2-109. Advancements.
(a) If an individual dies intestate as to all or a portion of his [or her] estate, property the decedent gave during the decedent's lifetime to an individual who, at the decedent's death, is an heir is treated as an advancement against the heir's intestate share only if (i) the decedent declared in a contemporaneous writing or the heir acknowledged in writing that the gift is an advancement or (ii) the decedent's contemporaneous writing or the heir's written acknowledgment otherwise indicates that the gift is to be taken into account in computing the division and distribution of the decedent's intestate estate.
(b) For purposes of subsection (a), property advanced is valued as of the time the heir came into possession or enjoyment of the property or as of the time of the decedent's death, whichever first occurs.
(c) If the recipient of the property fails to survive the decedent, the property is not taken into account in computing the division and distribution of the decedent's intestate estate, unless the decedent's contemporaneous writing provides otherwise.

Section 2-110. Debts to Decedent.
A debt owed to a decedent is not charged against the intestate share of any individual except the debtor. If the debtor fails to survive the decedent, the debt is not taken into account in computing the intestate share of the debtor's descendants.

Section 2-111. Alienage.
No individual is disqualified to take as an heir because the individual or an individual through whom he [or she] claims is or has been an alien.

[Section 2-112. Dower and Curtesy Abolished.
The estates of dower and curtesy are abolished.]

Section 2-113. Individuals Related to Decedent Through Two Lines.
An individual who is related to the decedent through two lines of relationship is entitled to only a single share based on the relationship that would entitle the individual to the larger share.

Section 2-114. Parent and Child Relationship.
(a) Except as provided in subsections (b) and (c), for purposes of intestate succession by, through, or from a person, an individual is the child of his [or her] natural

parents, regardless of their marital status. The parent and child relationship may be established under [the Uniform Parentage Act] [applicable state law] [insert appropriate statutory reference].
(b) An adopted individual is the child of his [or her] adopting parent or parents and not of his [or her] natural parents, but adoption of a child by the spouse of either natural parent has no effect on (i) the relationship between the child and that natural parent or (ii) the right of the child or a descendant of the child to inherit from or through the other natural parent.
(c) Inheritance from or through a child by either natural parent or his [or her] kindred is precluded unless that natural parent has openly treated the child as his [or hers], and has not refused to support the child.

PART 2. ELECTIVE SHARE OF SURVIVING SPOUSE

Section 2-201. Elective Share.
(a) [Elective-Share Amount.] The surviving spouse of a decedent who dies domiciled in this State has a right of election, under the limitations and conditions stated in this Part, to take an elective-share amount equal to the value of the elective-share percentage of the augmented estate, determined by the length of time the spouse and the decedent were married to each other, in accordance with the following schedule:

If the decedent and the spouse were married to each other:	The elective-share percentage is:
Less than 1 year	Supplemental Amount Only.
1 year but less than 2 years	3% of the augmented estate.
2 years but less than 3 years	6% of the augmented estate.
3 years but less than 4 years	9% of the augmented estate.
4 years but less than 5 years	12% of the augmented estate.
5 years but less than 6 years	15% of the augmented estate.
6 years but less than 7 years	18% of the augmented estate.
7 years but less than 8 years	21% of the augmented estate.
8 years but less than 9 years	24% of the augmented estate.
9 years but less than 10 years	27% of the augmented estate.
10 years but less than 11 years	30% of the augmented estate.
11 years but less than 12 years	34% of the augmented estate.
12 years but less than 13 years	38% of the augmented estate.
13 years but less than 14 years	42% of the augmented estate.
14 years but less than 15 years	46% of the augmented estate.
15 years or more	50% of the augmented estate.

(b) [Supplemental Elective-Share Amount.] If the sum of the amounts described in Sections 2-202(b)(3) and (4), 2-207(a)(1) and (3), and that part of the elective-share amount payable from the decedent's probate and reclaimable estates under Sections 2-207(b) and (c) is less than [$50,000], the surviving spouse is entitled to a supplemental elective-share amount equal to [$50,000], minus the sum of the amounts described in those sections. The supplemental elective-share amount is payable from the decedent's probate estate and from recipients of the decedent's reclaimable estate in the order of priority set forth in Sections 2-207(b) and (c).
(c) [Non-Domiciliary.] The right, if any, of the surviving spouse of a decedent who dies domiciled outside this State to take an elective share in property in this State is governed by the law of the decedent's domicile at death.

Section 2-202. Augmented Estate.
(a) [Definitions.]

(1) In this section:

(i) "Bona fide purchaser" means a purchaser for value in good faith and without notice of an adverse claim. The notation of a state documentary fee on a recorded instrument pursuant to [insert appropriate reference] is prima facie evidence that the transfer described therein was made to a bona fide purchaser.
(ii) "Nonadverse party" means a person who does not have a substantial beneficial interest in the trust or other property arrangement that would be adversely affected by the exercise or nonexercise of the power that he [or she] possesses respecting the trust or other property arrangement. A person having a general power of appointment over property is deemed to have a beneficial interest in the property.
(iii) "Presently exercisable general power of appointment" means a power of appointment under which, at the time in question, the decedent by an exercise of the power could have created an interest, present or future, in himself [or herself] or his [or her] creditors.
(iv) "Probate estate" means property, whether real or personal, movable or immovable, wherever situated, that would pass by intestate succession if the decedent died without a valid will.
(v) "Right to income" includes a right to payments under an annuity or similar contractual arrangement.
(vi) "Value of property owned by the surviving spouse at the decedent's death" and "value of property to which the surviving spouse succeeds by reason of the decedent's death" include the commuted value of any present or future interest then held by the surviving spouse and the commuted value of amounts payable to the surviving spouse after the decedent's death under any trust, life insurance settlement option, annuity contract, public or private pension, disability compensation, death benefit or retirement plan, or any similar arrangement, exclusive of the federal Social Security system.

(2) In subsections (b)(2)(iii) and (iv), "transfer" includes an exercise or release of a power of appointment, but does not include a lapse of a power of appointment.

(b) [Property Included in Augmented Estate.] The augmented estate consists of the sum of:

(1) the value of the decedent's probate estate, reduced by funeral and administration expenses, homestead allowance, family allowances and exemptions, and enforceable claims;
(2) the value of the decedent's reclaimable estate. The decedent's reclaimable estate is composed of all property, whether real or personal, movable or immovable, wherever situated, not including in the decedent's probate estate, of any of the following types:

(i) property to the extent the passing of the principal thereof to or for the benefit of any person, other than the decedent's surviving spouse, was subject to a presently exercisable general power of appointment held by the decedent alone, if the decedent held that power immediately before his [or her] death or if and to the extent the decedent, while married to his [or her] surviving spouse and during the two-year period next preceding the decedent's death, released that power or exercised that power in favor of any person other than the decedent or the decedent's estate, spouse, or surviving spouse;
(ii) property, to the extent of the decedent's unilaterally severable interest therein, held by the decedent and any other person, except the decedent's surviving spouse, with right of survivorship, if the decedent held that interest immediately before his [or her] death or if and to the extent the decedent, while married to his [or her] surviving spouse and during the two-year period preceding the decedent's death, transferred that interest to any person other than the decedent's surviving spouse;

(iii) proceeds of insurance, including accidental death benefits, on the life of the decedent payable to any person other than the decedent's surviving spouse, if the decedent owned the insurance policy, had the power to change the beneficiary of the insurance policy, or the insurance policy was subject to a presently exercisable general power of appointment held by the decedent alone immediately before his [or her] death or if and to the extent the decedent, while married to his [or her] surviving spouse and during the two-year period next preceding the decedent's death, transferred that policy to any person other than the decedent's surviving spouse; and
(iv) property transferred by the decedent to any person other than a bona fide purchaser at any time during the decedent's marriage to the surviving spouse, to or for the benefit or any person, other than the decedent's surviving spouse, if the transfer is of any of the following types:

(A) any transfer to the extent that the decedent retained at the time of or during the two-year period next preceding his [or her] death the possession or enjoyment of, or right to income from, the property;
(B) any transfer to the extent that, at the time of or during the two-year period next preceding the decedent's death, the income or principal was subject to a power, exercisable by the decedent alone or in conjunction with any other person or exercisable by a nonadverse party, for the benefit of the decedent or the decedent's estate;
(C) any transfer of property, to the extent the decedent's contribution to it, as a percentage of the whole, was made within two years before the decedent's death, by which the property is held, at the time of or during the two-year period next preceding the decedent's death, by the decedent and another, other than the decedent's surviving spouse, with right of survivorship; or
(D) any transfer made to a donee within two years before the decedent's death to the extent that the aggregate transfers to any one donee in either of the years exceed $10,000.00;

(3) the value of property to which the surviving spouse succeeds by reason of the decedent's death, other than by homestead allowance, exempt property, family allowance, testate succession, or intestate succession, including the proceeds of insurance, including accidental death benefits, on the life of the decedent and benefits payable under a retirement plan in which the decedent was a participant, exclusive of the federal Social Security system; and
(4) the value of property owned by the surviving spouse at the decedent's death, reduced by enforceable claims against that property or that spouse, plus the value of amounts that would have been includible in the surviving spouse's reclaimable estate had the spouse predeceased the decedent. But amounts that would have been includible in the surviving spouse's reclaimable estate under subsection (b)(2)(iii) are not valued as if he [or she] were deceased.

(c) [Exclusions.] Any transfer or exercise or release of a power of appointment is excluded from the decedent's reclaimable estate (i) to the extent the decedent received adequate and full consideration in money or money's worth for the transfer, exercise, or release or (ii) if irrevocably made with the written consent or joinder of the surviving spouse.
(d) [Valuation.] Property is valued as of the decedent's death, but property irrevocably transferred during the two-year period next preceding the decedent's death which is included in the decedent's reclaimable estate under subsection (b)(2)(i), (ii), and (iv) is valued as of the time of the transfer. If the terms of more than one of the subparagraphs or sub-subparagraphs of subsection (b)(2) apply, the property is included in the augmented estate under the subparagraph or sub-subparagraph that yields the highest value. For the purposes of this subsection, an

"irrevocable transfer of property" includes an irrevocable exercise or release of a power of appointment.

(e) [Protection of Payors and Other Third Parties.]

(1) Although under this section a payment, item of property, or other benefit is included in the decedent's reclaimable estate, a payor or other third party is not liable for having made a payment or transferred an item of property or other benefit to a beneficiary designated in a governing instrument, or for having taken any other action in good faith reliance on the validity of a governing instrument, upon request and satisfactory proof of the decedent's death, before the payor or other third party received written notice from the surviving spouse or spouse's representative of an intention to file a petition for the elective share or that a petition for the elective share has been filed. A payor or other third party is liable for payments made or other actions taken after the payor or other third party received written notice of an intention to file a petition for the elective share or that a petition for the elective share has been filed.

(2) The written notice of intention to file a petition for the elective share or that a petition for the elective share has been filed must be mailed to the payor's or other third party's main office or home by registered or certified mail, return receipt requested, or served upon the payor or other third party in the same manner as a summons in a civil action. Upon receipt of written notice of intention to file a petition for the elective share or that a petition for the elective share has been filed, a payor or other third party may pay any amount owed or transfer or deposit any item of property held by it to or with the court having jurisdiction of the probate proceedings relating to the decedent's estate, or if no proceedings have been commenced, to or with the court having jurisdiction of probate proceedings relating to decedents' estates located in the county of the decedent's residence. The court shall hold the funds or item of property and, upon its determination under Section 2-205(d), shall order disbursement in accordance with the determination. If no petition is filed in the court within the specified time under Section 2-205(a) or, if filed, the demand for an elective share is withdrawn under Section 2-205(c), the court shall order disbursement to the designated beneficiary. Payments, transfers, or deposits made to or with the court discharge the payor or other third party from all claims for the value of amounts paid to or items of property transferred to or deposited with the Court.

(3) Upon petition to the probate court by the beneficiary designated in a governing instrument, the court may order that all or part of the property be paid to the beneficiary in an amount and subject to conditions consistent with this section.

(f) [Protection of Bona Fide Purchasers; Personal Liability of Recipient.]

(1) A person who purchases property from a recipient for value and without notice, or who receives a payment or other item of property in partial or full satisfaction of a legally enforceable obligation, is neither obligated under this Part to return the payment, item of property, or benefit nor is liable under this Part for the amount of the payment or the value of the item of property or benefit. But a person who, not for value, receives a payment, item of property, or any other benefit included in the decedent's reclaimable estate is obligated to return the payment, item of property, or benefit, or is personally liable for the amount of the payment or the value of the item of property or benefit, as provided in Section 2-207.

(2) If any section or part of any section of this Part is preempted by federal law with respect to a payment, an item of property, or any other benefit included in the decedent's reclaimable estate, a person who, not for value, receives the payment, item of property, or any other benefit is obligated to return that payment, item of property, or benefit, or is personally liable for the amount of that payment or the value of that item of property or benefit, as provided in

Section 2-207, to the person who would have been entitled to it were that section or part of that section not preempted.

Section 2-203. Right of Election Personal to Surviving Spouse.
(a) [Surviving Spouse Must Be Living at Time of Election.] The right of election may be exercised only by a surviving spouse who is living when the petition for the elective share is filed in the court under Section 2-205(a). If the election is not exercised by the surviving spouse personally, it may be exercised on the surviving spouse's behalf by his [or her] conservator, guardian, or agent under the authority of a power of attorney.
(b) [Incapacitated Surviving Spouse.] If the election is exercised on behalf of a surviving spouse who is an incapacitated person, that portion of the elective-share and supplemental elective-share amounts due from the decedent's probate estate and recipients of the decedent's reclaimable estate under Sections 2-207(b) and (c) must be placed in a custodial trust for the benefit of the surviving spouse under the provisions of the [Enacting state] Uniform Custodial Trust Act, except as modified below. For the purposes of this subsection, an election on behalf of a surviving spouse by an agent under a durable power of attorney is presumed to be on behalf of a surviving spouse who is an incapacitated person. For purposes of the custodial trust established by this subsection, (i) the electing guardian, conservator, or agent is the custodial trustee, (ii) the surviving spouse is the beneficiary, (iii) the custodial trust is deemed to have been created by the decedent spouse by written transfer that takes effect at the decedent spouse's death and that directs the custodial trustee to administer the custodial trust as for an incapacitated beneficiary.
(c) [Custodial Trust.] For the purposes of subsection (b), the [Enacting state] Uniform Custodial Trust Act must be applied as if Section 6(b) thereof were repealed and Sections 2(e), 9(b), and 17(a) were amended to read as follows:

(1) Neither an incapacitated beneficiary nor anyone acting on behalf of an incapacitated beneficiary has a power to terminate the custodial trust; but if the beneficiary regains capacity, the beneficiary then acquires the power to terminate the custodial trust by delivering to the custodial trustee a writing signed by the beneficiary declaring the termination. If not previously terminated, the custodial trust terminates on the death of the beneficiary.
(2) If the beneficiary is incapacitated, the custodial trustee shall expend so much or all of the custodial trust property as the custodial trustee considers advisable for the use and benefit of the beneficiary and individuals who were supported by the beneficiary when the beneficiary became incapacitated, or who are legally entitled to support by the beneficiary. Expenditures may be made in the manner, when, and to the extent that the custodial trustee determines suitable and proper, without court order but with regard to other support, income, and property of the beneficiary [exclusive of] [and] benefits of medical or other forms of assistance from any state or federal government or governmental agency for which the beneficiary must qualify on the basis of need.
(3) Upon the beneficiary's death, the remaining custodial trust property, in the following order: (i) under the residuary clause, if any, of the will of the beneficiary's predeceased spouse against whom the elective share was taken, as if that predeceased spouse died immediately after the beneficiary; or (ii) to that predeceased spouse's heirs under Section 2-711 of [this State's] Uniform Probate Code.

[STATES THAT HAVE NOT ADOPTED THE UNIFORM CUSTODIAL TRUST ACT SHOULD ADOPT THE FOLLOWING ALTERNATIVE SUBSECTION (B) AND NOT ADOPT SUBSECTION (B) OR (C) ABOVE]
[**(b) [Incapacitated Surviving Spouse.]** If the election is exercised on behalf of a surviving spouse who is an incapacitated person, the court must set aside that portion of the elective-share and supplemental elective-share amounts due from the decedent's probate estate and recipients of the decedent's reclaimable estate under

Section 2-207(b) and (c) and must appoint a trustee to administer that property for the support of the surviving spouse. For the purposes of this subsection, an election on behalf of a surviving spouse by an agent under a durable power of attorney is presumed to be on behalf of a surviving spouse who is an incapacitated person. The trustee must administer the trust in accordance with the following terms and such additional terms as the court determines appropriate:

(1) Expenditures of income and principal may be made in the manner, when, and to the extent that the trustee determines suitable and proper for the surviving spouse's support, without court order but with regard to other support, income, and property of the surviving spouse [exclusive of] [and] benefits of medical or other forms of assistance from any state or federal government or governmental agency for which the surviving spouse must qualify on the basis of need.
(2) During the surviving spouse's incapacity, neither the surviving spouse nor anyone acting on behalf of the surviving spouse has a power to terminate the trust; but if the surviving spouse regains capacity, the surviving spouse then acquires the power to terminate the trust and acquire full ownership of the trust property free of trust, by delivering to the trustee a writing signed by the surviving spouse declaring the termination.
(3) Upon the surviving spouse's death, the trustee shall transfer the unexpended trust property in the following order: (i) under the residuary clause, if any, of the will of the predeceased spouse against whom the elective share was taken, as if that predeceased spouse died immediately after the surviving spouse; or (ii) to that predeceased spouse's heirs under Section 2-711.]

Section 2-204. Waiver of Right to Elect and of Other Rights.
(a) The right of election of a surviving spouse and the rights of the surviving spouse to homestead allowance, exempt property, and family allowance, or any of them, may be waived, wholly or partially, before or after marriage, by a written contract, agreement, or waiver signed by the surviving spouse.
(b) A surviving spouse's waiver is not enforceable if the surviving spouse proves that:

(1) he [or she] did not execute the waiver voluntarily;
(2) the waiver was unconscionable when it was executed and, before execution of the waiver, he [or she]:

(i) was not provided a fair and reasonable disclosure of the property or financial obligations of the decedent;
(ii) did not voluntarily and expressly waive, in writing, any right to disclosure of the property or financial obligations of the decedent beyond the disclosure provided; and
(iii) did not have, or reasonably could not have had, an adequate knowledge of the property or financial obligations of the decedent.

(c) An issue of unconscionability of a waiver is for decision by the court as a matter of law.
(d) Unless it provides to the contrary, a waiver of "all rights," or equivalent language, in the property or estate of a present or prospective spouse or a complete property settlement entered into after or in anticipation of separation or divorce is a waiver of all rights of elective share, homestead allowance, exempt property, and family allowance by each spouse in the property of the other and a renunciation by each of all benefits that would otherwise pass to him [or her] from the other by intestate succession or by virtue of any will executed before the waiver or property settlement.

Section 2-205. Proceeding for Elective Share; Time Limit.
(a) Except as provided in subsection (b), the election must be made by filing in the court and mailing or delivering to the personal representative, if any, a petition for the elective share within nine months after the date of the decedent's death, or within six months after the probate of the decedent's will, whichever limitation later expires. The surviving spouse must give notice of the time and place set for hearing to persons interested in the estate and to the distributees and recipients of portions of the augmented estate whose interests will be adversely affected by the taking of the elective share. Except as provided in subsection (b), the decedent's reclaimable estate, described in Section 2-202(b)(2), is not included within the augmented estate for the purpose of computing the elective share, if the petition is filed more than nine months after the decedent's death.
(b) Within nine months after the decedent's death, the surviving spouse may petition the court for an extension of time for making an election. If, within nine months after the decedent's death, the spouse gives notice of the petition to all persons interested in the decedent's reclaimable estate, the court for cause shown by the surviving spouse may extend the time for election. If the court grants the spouse's petition for an extension, the decedent's reclaimable estate, described in Section 2-202(b)(2), is not excluded from the augmented estate for the purpose of computing the elective-share and supplemental elective-share amounts, if the spouse makes an election by filing in the court and mailing or delivering to the personal representative, if any, a petition for the elective share within the time allowed by the extension.
(c) The surviving spouse may withdraw his [or her] demand for an elective share at any time before entry of a final determination by the court.
(d) After notice and hearing, the court shall determine the elective-share and supplemental elective-share amounts, and shall order its payment from the assets of the augmented estate or by contribution as appears appropriate under Section 2-207. If it appears that a fund or property included in the augmented estate has not come into the possession of the personal representative, or has been distributed by the personal representative, the court nevertheless shall fix the liability of any person who has any interest in the fund or property or who has possession thereof, whether as trustee or otherwise. The proceeding may be maintained against fewer than all persons against whom relief could be sought, but no person is subject to contribution in any greater amount than he [or she] would have been under Section 2-207 had relief been secured against all persons subject to contribution.
(e) An order or judgment of the court may be enforced as necessary in suit for contribution or payment in other courts of this State or other jurisdictions.

Section 2-206. Effect of Election on Statutory Benefits.
If the right of election is exercised by or on behalf of the surviving spouse, the surviving spouse's homestead allowance, exempt property, and family allowance, if any, are not charged against but are in addition to the elective-share and supplemental elective-share amounts.

Section 2-207. Charging Spouse with Owned Assets and Gifts Received; Liability of Others for Balance of Elective Share.
(a) [Elective-Share Amount Only.] In a proceeding for an elective share, the following are applied first to satisfy the elective-share amount and to reduce or eliminate any contributions due from the decedent's probate estate and recipients of the decedent's reclaimable estate:

(1) amounts included in the augmented estate which pass or have passed to the surviving spouse by testate or intestate succession;
(2) amounts included in the augmented estate under Section 2-202(b)(3);
(3) amounts included in the augmented estate which would have passed to the spouse but were disclaimed; and

(4) amounts included in the augmented estate under Section 2-202(b)(4) up to the applicable percentage thereof. For the purposes of this subsection, the "applicable percentage" is twice the elective-share percentage set forth in the schedule in Section 2-201(a) appropriate to the length of time the spouse and the decedent were married to each other.

(b) [Unsatisfied Balance of Elective-Share Amount; Supplemental Elective-Share Amount.] If, after the application of subsection (a), the elective-share amount is not fully satisfied or the surviving spouse is entitled to a supplemental elective-share amount, amounts included in the decedent's probate estate and that portion of the decedent's reclaimable estate other than amounts irrevocably transferred within two years before the decedent's death are applied first to satisfy the unsatisfied balance of the elective-share amount or the supplemental elective-share amount. The decedent's probate estate and that portion of the decedent's reclaimable estate are so applied that liability for the unsatisfied balance of the elective-share amount or for the supplemental elective-share amount is equitably apportioned among the recipients of the decedent's probate estate and that portion of the decedent's reclaimable estate in proportion to the value of their interests therein.

(c) [Unsatisfied Balance of Elective-Share and Supplemental Elective-Share Amounts.] If, after the application of subsections (a) and (b), the elective-share or supplemental elective-share amount is not fully satisfied, the remaining portion of the decedent's reclaimable estate is so applied that liability for the unsatisfied balance of the elective-share or supplemental elective-share amount is equitably apportioned among the recipients of that portion of the decedent's reclaimable estate in proportion to the value of their interests therein.

(d) [Liability of Recipients of Reclaimable Estate and Their Donees.] Only original recipients of the reclaimable estate described in Section 2-202(b)(2), and the donees of the recipients of the reclaimable estate to the extent the donees have the property or its proceeds, are liable to make a proportional contribution toward satisfaction of the surviving spouse's elective-share or supplemental elective-share amount. A person liable to make contribution may choose to give up the proportional part of the reclaimable estate or to pay the value of the amount for which he [or she] is liable.

PART 3. SPOUSE AND CHILDREN UNPROVIDED FOR IN WILLS

Section 2-301. Entitlement of Spouse; Premarital Will.

(a) If a testator's surviving spouse married the testator after the testator executed his [or her] will, the surviving spouse is entitled to receive, as an intestate share, no less than the value of the share of the estate he [or she] would have received if the testator had died intestate as to that portion of the testator's estate, if any, that neither is devised to a child of the testator who was born before the testator married the surviving spouse and who is not a child of the surviving spouse nor is devised or passes under Sections 2-603 or 2-604 to a descendant of such a child, unless:

(1) it appears from the will or other evidence that the will was made in contemplation of the testator's marriage to the surviving spouse;
(2) the will expresses the intention that it is to be effective notwithstanding any subsequent marriage; or
(3) the testator provided for the spouse by transfer outside the will and the intent that the transfer be in lieu of a testamentary provision is shown by the testator's statements or is reasonably inferred from the amount of the transfer or other evidence.

(b) In satisfying the share provided by this section, devises made by the will to the testator's surviving spouse, if any, are applied first, and other devises, other than a devise to a child of the testator who was born before the testator married the surviving spouse and who is not a child of the surviving spouse or a devise or substitute gift under Section 2-603 or 2-604 to a descendant of such a child, abate as provided in Section 3-902.

Section 2-302. Omitted Children.
(a) Except as provided in subsection (b), if a testator fails to provide in his [or her] will for any of his [or her] children born or adopted after the execution of the will, the omitted after-born or after-adopted child receives a share in the estate as follows:

(1) If the testator had no child living when he [or she] executed the will, an omitted after-born or after-adopted child receives a share in the estate equal in value to that which the child would have received had the testator died intestate, unless the will devised all or substantially all the estate to the other parent of the omitted child and that other parent survives the testator and is entitled to take under the will.
(2) If the testator had one or more children living when he [or she] executed the will, and the will devised property or an interest in property to one or more of the then-living children, an omitted after-born or after-adopted child is entitled to share in the testator's estate as follows:

(i) The portion of the testator's estate in which the omitted after-born or after-adopted child is entitled to share is limited to devises made to the testator's then-living children under the will.
(ii) The omitted after-born or after-adopted child is entitled to receive the share of the testator's estate, as limited in subparagraph (i), that the child would have received had the testator included all omitted after-born and after-adopted children with the children to whom devises were made under the will and had given an equal share of the estate to each child.
(iii) To the extent feasible, the interest granted an omitted after-born or after-adopted child under this section must be of the same character, whether equitable or legal, present or future, as that devised to the testator's then-living children under the will.
(iv) In satisfying a share provided by this paragraph, devises to the testator's children who were living when the will was executed abate ratably. In abating the devises of the then-living children, the court shall preserve to the maximum extent possible the character of the testamentary plan adopted by the testator.

(b) Neither subsection (a)(1) nor subsection (a)(2) applies if:

(1) it appears from the will that the omission was intentional; or
(2) the testator provided for the omitted after-born or after-adopted child by transfer outside the will and the intent that the transfer be in lieu of a testamentary provision is shown by the testator's statements or is reasonably inferred from the amount of the transfer or other evidence.

(c) If at the time of execution of the will the testator fails to provide in his [or her] will for a living child solely because he [or she] believes the child to be dead, the child receives a share in the estate equal in value to that which the child would have received had the testator died intestate.
(d) In satisfying a share provided by subsection (a)(1) or (c), devises made by the will abate under Section 3-902.

PART 4. EXEMPT PROPERTY AND ALLOWANCES

Section 2-401. Applicable Law.
This Part applies to the estate of a decedent who dies domiciled in this State. Rights to homestead allowance, exempt property, and family allowance for a decedent who dies not domiciled in this State are governed by the law of the decedent's domicile at death.

Section 2-402. Homestead Allowance.
A decedent's surviving spouse is entitled to a homestead allowance of [$15,000]. If there is no surviving spouse, each minor child and each dependent child of the decedent is entitled to a homestead allowance amounting to [$15,000] divided by the number of minor and dependent children of the decedent. The homestead allowance is exempt from and has priority over all claims against the estate. Homestead allowance is in addition to any share passing to the surviving spouse or minor or dependent child by the will of the decedent, unless otherwise provided, by intestate succession, or by way of elective share.

[Section 2-402A. Constitutional Homestead.
The value of any constitutional right of homestead in the family home received by a surviving spouse or child must be charged against the spouse or child's homestead allowance to the extent the family home is part of the decedent's estate or would have been but for the homestead provision of the constitution.]

Section 2-403. Exempt Property.
In addition to the homestead allowance, the decedent's surviving spouse is entitled from the estate to a value, not exceeding $10,000 in excess of any security interests therein, in household furniture, automobiles, furnishings, appliances, and personal effects. If there is no surviving spouse, the decedent's children are entitled jointly to the same value. If encumbered chattels are selected and the value in excess of security interests, plus that of other exempt property, is less than $10,000, or if there is not $10,000 worth of exempt property in the estate, the spouse or children are entitled to other assets of the estate, if any, to the extent necessary to make up the $10,000 value. Rights to exempt property and assets needed to make up a deficiency of exempt property have priority over all claims against the estate, but the right to any assets to make up a deficiency of exempt property abates as necessary to permit earlier payment of homestead allowance and family allowance. These rights are in addition to any benefit or share passing to the surviving spouse or children by the decedent's will, unless otherwise provided, by intestate succession, or by way of elective share.

Section 2-404. Family Allowance.
(a) In addition to the right to homestead allowance and exempt property, the decedent's surviving spouse and minor children whom the decedent was obligated to support and children who were in fact being supported by the decedent are entitled to a reasonable allowance in money out of the estate for their maintenance during the period of administration, which allowance may not continue for longer than one year if the estate is inadequate to discharge allowed claims. The allowance may be paid as a lump sum or in periodic installments. It is payable to the surviving spouse, if living, for the use of the surviving spouse and minor and dependent children; otherwise to the children, or persons having their care and custody. If a minor child or dependent child is not living with the surviving spouse, the allowance may be made partially to the child or his [or her] guardian or other person having the child's care and custody, and partially to the spouse, as their needs may appear. The family allowance is exempt from and has priority over all claims except the homestead allowance.
(b) The family allowance is not chargeable against any benefit or share passing to the surviving spouse or children by the will of the decedent, unless otherwise

provided, by intestate succession or by way of elective share. The death of any person entitled to family allowance terminates the right to allowances not yet paid.

Section 2-405. Source, Determination, and Documentation.
(a) If the estate is otherwise sufficient, property specifically devised may not be used to satisfy rights to homestead allowance or exempt property. Subject to this restriction, the surviving spouse, guardians of minor children, or children who are adults may select property of the estate as homestead allowance and exempt property. The personal representative may make those selections if the surviving spouse, the children, or the guardians of the minor children are unable or fail to do so within a reasonable time or there is no guardian of a minor child. The personal representative may execute an instrument or deed of distribution to establish the ownership of property taken as homestead allowance or exempt property. The personal representative may determine the family allowance in a lump sum not exceeding $18,000 or periodic installments not exceeding $1,500 per month for one year, and may disburse funds of the estate in payment of the family allowance and any part of the homestead allowance payable in cash. The personal representative or an interested person aggrieved by any selection, determination, payment, proposed payment, or failure to act under this section may petition the court for appropriate relief, which may include a family allowance other than that which the personal representative determined or could have determined.
(b) If the right to an elective share is exercised on behalf of a surviving spouse who is an incapacitated person, the personal representative may add any unexpended portions payable under the homestead allowance, exempt property, and family allowance to the trust established under Section 2-203(b).

PART 5. WILLS, WILL CONTRACTS, AND CUSTODY AND DEPOSIT OF WILLS

Section 2-501. Who May Make Will.
An individual 18 or more years of age who is of sound mind may make a will.

Section 2-502. Execution; Witnessed Wills; Holographic Wills.
(a) Except as provided in subsection (b) and in Sections 2-503, 2-506, and 2-513, a will must be:

(1) in writing;
(2) signed by the testator or in the testator's name by some other individual in the testator's conscious presence and by the testator's direction; and
(3) signed by at least two individuals, each of whom signed within a reasonable time after he [or she] witnessed either the signing of the will as described in paragraph (2) or the testator's acknowledgment of that signature or acknowledgment of the will.

(b) A will that does not comply with subsection (a) is valid as a holographic will, whether or not witnessed, if the signature and material portions of the document are in the testator's handwriting.
(c) Intent that the document constitute the testator's will can be established by extrinsic evidence, including, for holographic wills, portions of the document that are not in the testator's handwriting.

Section 2-503. Writings Intended as Wills, etc.
Although a document or writing added upon a document was not executed in compliance with Section 2-502, the document or writing is treated as if it had been executed in compliance with that section if the proponent of the document or writing establishes by clear and convincing evidence that the decedent intended the document or writing to constitute (i) the decedent's will, (ii) a partial or complete revocation of the will, (iii) an addition to or an alteration of the will, or (iv) a partial

or complete revival of his [or her] formerly revoked will or of a formerly revoked portion of the will.

Section 2-504. Self-Proved Will.
(a) A will may be simultaneously executed, attested, and made self-proved, by acknowledgment thereof by the testator and affidavits of the witnesses, each made before an officer authorized to administer oaths under the laws of the state in which execution occurs and evidenced by the officer's certificate, under official seal, in substantially the following form:

I, ___________, the testator, sign my name to this instrument this ________ day of ___________, and being first duly sworn, do hereby declare to the undersigned authority that I sign and execute this instrument as my will and that I sign it willingly (or willingly direct another to sign for me), that I execute it as my free and voluntary act for the purposes therein expressed, and that I am eighteen years of age or older, of sound mind, and under no constraint or undue influence.

____
Testator

We, ___________, ___________, the witnesses, sign our names to this instrument, being first duly sworn, and do hereby declare to the undersigned authority that the testator signs and executes this instrument as [his] [her] will and that [he] [she] signs it willingly (or willingly directs another to sign for [him] [her]), and that each of us, in the presence and hearing of the testator, hereby signs this will as witness to the testator's signing, and that to the best of our knowledge the testator is eighteen years of age or older, of sound mind, and under no constraint or undue influence.

____
Witness

____
Witness

The State of ________________
County of ________________
Subscribed, sworn to and acknowledged before me by ___________, the testator, and subscribed and sworn to before me by ___________, and ___________, witness, this ___________ day of ___________.
(Seal)

(Signed) ________________________

____
(Official capacity of officer)

(b) An attested will may be made self-proved at any time after its execution by the acknowledgment thereof by the testator and the affidavits of the witnesses, each made before an officer authorized to administer oaths under the laws of the state in which the acknowledgment occurs and evidenced by the officer's certificate, under the official seal, attached or annexed to the will in substantially the following form:

The State of ______________
County of ______________
We, ___________, ___________, and ___________, the testator and the witnesses, respectively, whose names are signed to the attached or foregoing instrument, being first duly sworn, do hereby declare to the undersigned authority that the testator signed and executed the instrument as the testator's will and that [he] [she] had signed willingly (or willingly directed another to sign for [him] [her]), and that [he] [she] executed it as [his] [her] free and voluntary act for the purposes therein expressed, and that each of the witnesses,

in the presence and hearing of the testator, signed the will as witness and that to the best of [his] [her] knowledge the testator was at that time eighteen years of age or older, of sound mind, and under no constraint or undue influence.

____
Testator

____
Witness

____
Witness

Subscribed, sworn to and acknowledged before me by __________, the testator, and subscribed and sworn to before me by __________, and __________, witnesses, this __________ of __________.
(Seal)

(Signed) ____________________

____
(Official capacity of officer)

(c) A signature affixed to a self-proving affidavit attached to a will is considered a signature affixed to the will, if necessary to prove the will's due execution.

Section 2-505. Who May Witness.
(a) An individual generally competent to be a witness may act as a witness to a will.
(b) The signing of a will by an interested witness does not invalidate the will or any provision of it.

Section 2-506. Choice of Law as to Execution.
A written will is valid if executed in compliance with Section 2-502 or 2-503 or if its execution complies with the law at the time of execution of the place where the will is executed, or of the law of the place where at the time of execution or at the time of death the testator is domiciled, has a place of abode, or is a national.

Section 2-507. Revocation by Writing or by Act.
(a) A will or any part thereof is revoked:

(1) by executing a subsequent will that revokes the previous will or part expressly or by inconsistency; or
(2) by performing a revocatory act on the will, if the testator performed the act with the intent and for the purpose of revoking the will or part or if another individual performed the act in the testator's conscious presence and by the testator's direction. For purposes of this paragraph, "revocatory act on the will" includes burning , tearing, canceling, obliterating, or destroying the will or any part of it. A burning, tearing, or canceling is a "revocatory act on the will," whether or not the burn, tear, or cancellation touched any of the words on the will.

(b) If a subsequent will does not expressly revoke a previous will, the execution of the subsequent will wholly revokes the previous will by inconsistency if the testator intended the subsequent will to replace rather than supplement the previous will.
(c) The testator is presumed to have intended a subsequent will to replace rather than supplement a previous will if the subsequent will makes a complete disposition of the testator's estate. If this presumption arises and is not rebutted by clear and convincing evidence, the previous will is revoked; only the subsequent will is operative on the testator's death.
(d) The testator is presumed to have intended a subsequent will to supplement rather than replace a previous will if the subsequent will does not make a complete disposition of the testator's estate. If this presumption arises and is not rebutted by clear and convincing evidence, the subsequent will revokes the previous will only to

the extent the subsequent will is inconsistent with the previous will; each will is fully operative on the testator's death to the extent they are not inconsistent.

Section 2-508. Revocation by Change of Circumstances.
Except as provided in Sections 2-803 and 2-804, a change of circumstances does not revoke a will or any part of it.

Section 2-509. Revival of Revoked Will.
(a) If a subsequent will that wholly revoked a previous will is thereafter revoked by a revocatory act under Section 2-507(a)(2), the previous will remains revoked unless it is revived. The previous will is revived if it is evident from the circumstances of the revocation of the subsequent will or from the testator's contemporary or subsequent declarations that the testator intended the previous will to take effect as executed.
(b) If a subsequent will that partly revoked a previous will is thereafter revoked by a revocatory act under Section 2-507(a)(2), a revoked part of the previous will is revived unless it is evident from the circumstances of the revocation of the subsequent will or from the testator's contemporary or subsequent declarations that the testator did not intend the revoked part to take effect as executed.
(c) If a subsequent will that revoked a previous will in whole or in part is thereafter revoked by another, later, will, the previous will remains revoked in whole or in part, unless it or its revoked part is revived. The previous will or its revoked part is revived to the extent it appears from the terms of the later will that the testator intended the previous will to take effect.

Section 2-510. Incorporation by Reference.
A writing in existence when a will is executed may be incorporated by reference if the language of the will manifests this intent and describes the writing sufficiently to permit its identification.

Section 2-511. Testamentary Additions to Trusts.
(a) A will may validly devise property to the trustee of a trust established or to be established (i) during the testator's lifetime by the testator, by the testator and some other person, or by some other person, including a funded or unfunded life insurance trust, although the settlor has reserved any or all rights of ownership of the insurance contracts, or (ii) at the testator's death by the testator's devise to the trustee, if the trust is identified in the testator's will and its terms are set forth in a written instrument, other than a will, executed before, concurrently with, or after the execution of the testator's will or in another individual's will if that other individual has predeceased the testator, regardless of the existence, size, or character of the corpus of the trust. The devise is not invalid because the trust is amendable or revocable, or because the trust was amended after the execution of the will or the testator's death.
(b) Unless the testator's will provides otherwise, property devised to a trust described in subsection (a) is not held under a testamentary trust of the testator, but it becomes a part of the trust to which it is devised, and must be administered and disposed of in accordance with the provisions of the governing instrument setting forth the terms of the trust, including any amendments thereto made before or after the testator's death.
(c) Unless the testator's will provides otherwise, a revocation or termination of the trust before the testator's death causes the devise to lapse.

Section 2-512. Events of Independent Significance.
A will may dispose of property by reference to acts and events that have significance apart from their effect upon the dispositions made by the will, whether they occur before or after the execution of the will or before or after the testator's death. The execution or revocation of another individual's will is such an event.

Section 2-513. Separate Writing Identifying Devise of Certain Types of Tangible Personal Property.
Whether or not the provisions relating to holographic wills apply, a will may refer to a written statement or list to dispose of items of tangible personal property not otherwise specifically disposed of by the will, other than money. To be admissible under this section as evidence of the intended disposition, the writing must be signed by the testator and must describe the items and the devisees with reasonable certainty. The writing may be referred to as one to be in existence at the time of the testator's death; it may be prepared before or after the execution of the will; it may be altered by the testator after its preparation; and it may be a writing that has no significance apart from its effect on the dispositions made by the will.

Section 2-514. Contracts Concerning Succession.
A contract to make a will or devise, or not to revoke a will or devise, or to die intestate, if executed after the effective date of this Article, may be established only by (i) provisions of a will stating material provisions of the contract, (ii) an express reference in a will to a contract and extrinsic evidence proving the terms of the contract, or (iii) a writing signed by the decedent evidencing the contract. The execution of a joint will or mutual wills does not create a presumption of a contract not to revoke the will or wills.

Section 2-515. Deposit of Will with Court in Testator's Lifetime.
A will may be deposited by the testator or the testator's agent with any court for safekeeping, under rules of the court. The will must be sealed and kept confidential. During the testator's lifetime, a deposited will must be delivered only to the testator or to a person authorized in writing signed by the testator to receive the will. A conservator may be allowed to examine a deposited will of a protected testator under procedures designed to maintain the confidential character of the document to the extent possible, and to ensure that it will be resealed and kept on deposit after the examination. Upon being informed of the testator's death, the court shall notify any person designated to receive the will and deliver it to that person on request; or the court may deliver the will to the appropriate court.

Section 2-516. Duty of Custodian of Will; Liability.
After the death of a testator and on request of an interested person, a person having custody of a will of the testator shall deliver it with reasonable promptness to a person able to secure its probate and if none is known, to an appropriate court. A person who wilfully fails to deliver a will is liable to any person aggrieved for any damages that may be sustained by the failure. A person who wilfully refuses or fails to deliver a will after being ordered by the court in a proceeding brought for the purpose of compelling delivery is subject to penalty for contempt of court.

Section 2-517. Penalty Clause for Contest.
A provision in a will purporting to penalize an interested person for contesting the will or instituting other proceedings relating to the estate is unenforceable if probable cause exists for instituting proceedings.

PART 6. RULES OF CONSTRUCTION APPLICABLE ONLY TO WILLS

Section 2-601. Scope.
In the absence of a finding of a contrary intention, the rules of construction in this Part control the construction of a will.

Section 2-602. Will May Pass All Property and After-Acquired Property.
A will may provide for the passage of all property the testator owns at death and all property acquired by the estate after the testator's death.

Section 2-603. Antilapse; Deceased Devisee; Class Gifts.
(a) [Definitions.] In this section:

(1) "Alternative devise" means a devise that is expressly created by the will and, under the terms of the will, can take effect instead of another devise on the happening of one or more events, including survival of the testator or failure to survive the testator, whether an event is expressed in condition-precedent, condition-subsequent, or any other form. A residuary clause constitutes an alternative devise with respect to a nonresiduary devise only if the will specifically provides that, upon lapse or failure, the nonresiduary devise, or nonresiduary devises in general, pass under the residuary clause.
(2) "Class member" includes an individual who fails to survive the testator but who would have taken under a devise in the form of a class gift had he [or she] survived the testator.
(3) "Devise" includes an alternative devise, a devise in the form of a class gift, and an exercise of a power of appointment.
(4) "Devisee" includes (i) a class member if the devise is in the form of a class gift, (ii) the beneficiary of a trust but not the trustee, (iii) an individual or class member who was deceased at the time the testator executed his [or her] will as well as an individual or class member who was then living but who failed to survive the testator, and (iv) an appointee under a power of appointment exercised by the testator's will.
(5) "Stepchild" means a child of the surviving, deceased, or former spouse of the testator or of the donor of a power of appointment, and not of the testator or donor.
(6) "Surviving devisee" or "surviving descendant" means a devisee or a descendant who neither predeceased the testator nor is deemed to have predeceased the testator under Section 2-702.
(7) "Testator" includes the donee of a power of appointment if the power is exercised in the testator's will.

(b) [Substitute Gift.] If a devisee fails to survive the testator and is a grandparent, a descendant of a grandparent, or a stepchild of either the testator or the donor of a power of appointment exercised by the testator's will, the following apply:

(1) Except as provided in paragraph (4), if the devise is not in the form of a class gift and the deceased devisee leaves surviving descendants, a substitute gift is created in the devisee's surviving descendants. They take by representation the property to which the devisee would have been entitled had the devisee survived the testator.
(2) Except as provided in paragraph (4), if the devise is in the form of a class gift, other than a devise to "issue," "descendants," "heirs of the body," "heirs," "next of kin," "relatives," or "family," or a class described by language of similar import, a substitute gift is created in the deceased devisee or devisee's surviving descendants. The property to which the devisees would have been entitled had all of them survived the testator passes to the surviving devisees and the surviving descendants of the deceased devisees. Each surviving devisee takes the share to which he [or she] would have been entitled had the deceased devisees survived the testator. Each deceased devisee's surviving descendants who are substituted for the deceased devisee take by representation the share to which the deceased devisee would have been entitled had the deceased devisee survived the testator. For the purposes of this paragraph, "deceased devisee" means a class member who failed to survive the testator and left one or more surviving descendants.
(3) For the purposes of Section 2-601, words of survivorship, such as in a devise to an individual "if he survives me," or in a devise to "my surviving children," are not, in the absence of additional evidence, a sufficient indication of an intent contrary to the application of this section.

(4) If the will creates an alternative devise with respect to a devise for which a substitute gift is created by paragraph (1) or (2), the substitute gift is superseded by the alternative devise only if an expressly designated devisee of the alternative devise is entitled to take under the will.
(5) Unless the language creating a power of appointment expressly excludes the substitution of the descendants of an appointee for the appointee, a surviving descendant of a deceased appointee of a power of appointment can be substituted for the appointee under this section, whether or not the descendant is an object of the power.

(c) [More Than One Substitute Gift; Which One Takes.] If, under subsection (b), substitute gifts are created and not superseded with respect to more than one devise and the devises are alternative devises, one to the other, the determination of which of the substitute gifts takes effect is resolved as follows:

(1) Except as provided in paragraph (2), the devised property passes under the primary substitute gift.
(2) If there is a younger-generation devise, the devised property passes under the younger-generation substitute gift and not under the primary substitute gift.
(3) In this subsection:

(i) "Primary devise" means the devise that would have taken effect had all the deceased devisees of the alternative devises who left surviving descendants survived the testator.
(ii) "Primary substitute gift" means the substitute gift created with respect to the primary devise.
(iii) "Younger-generation devise" means a devise that (A) is to a descendant of a devisee of the primary devise, (B) is an alternative devise with respect to the primary devise, (C) is a devise for which a substitute gift is created, and (D) would have taken effect had all the deceased devisees who left surviving descendants survived the testator except the deceased devisee or devisees of the primary devise.
(iv) "Younger-generation substitute gift" means the substitute gift created with respect to the younger-generation devise.

Section 2-604. Failure of Testamentary Provision.
(a) Except as provided in Section 2-603, a devise, other than a residuary devise, that fails for any reason becomes a part of the residue.
(b) Except as provided in Section 2-603, if the residue is devised to two or more persons, the share of a residuary devisee that fails for any reason passes to the other residuary devisee, or to other residuary devisees in proportion to the interest of each in the remaining part of the residue.

Section 2-605. Increase in Securities; Accessions.
(a) If a testator executes a will that devises securities and the testator then owned securities that meet the description in the will, the devise includes additional securities owned by the testator at death to the extent the additional securities were acquired by the testator after the will was executed as a result of the testator's ownership of the described securities and are securities of any of the following types:

(1) securities of the same organization acquired by reason of action initiated by the organization or any successor, related, or acquiring organization, excluding any acquired by exercise of purchase options;
(2) securities of another organization acquired as a result of a merger, consolidation, reorganization, or other distribution by the organization or any successor, related, or acquiring organization; or

(3) securities of the same organization acquired as a result of a plan of reinvestment.

(b) Distributions in cash before death with respect to a described security are not part of the devise.

Section 2-606. Nonademption of Specific Devises; Unpaid Proceeds of Sale, Condemnation, or Insurance; Sale by Conservator or Agent.
(a) A specific devisee has a right to the specifically devised property in the testator's estate at death and:

(1) any balance of the purchase price, together with any security agreement, owing from a purchaser to the testator at death by reason of sale of the property;
(2) any amount of a condemnation award for the taking of the property unpaid at death;
(3) any proceeds unpaid at death on fire or casualty insurance on or other recovery for injury to the property;
(4) property owned by the testator at death and acquired as a result of foreclosure, or obtained in lieu of foreclosure, of the security interest for a specifically devised obligation;
(5) real or tangible personal property owned by the testator at death which the testator acquired as a replacement for specifically devised real or tangible personal property; and
(6) unless the facts and circumstances indicate that ademption of the devise was intended by the testator or ademption of the devise is consistent with the testator's manifested plan of distribution, the value of the specifically devised property to the extent the specifically devised property is not in the testator's estate at death and its value or its replacement is not covered by paragraphs (1) through (5).

(b) If specifically devised property is sold or mortgaged by a conservator or by an agent acting within the authority of a durable power of attorney for an incapacitated principal, or if a condemnation award, insurance proceeds, or recovery for injury to the property are paid to a conservator or to an agent acting within the authority of a durable power of attorney for an incapacitated principal, the specific devisee has the right to a general pecuniary devise equal to the net sale price, the amount of the unpaid loan, the condemnation award, the insurance proceeds, or the recovery.
(c) The right of a specific devisee under subsection (b) is reduced by any right the devisee has under subsection (a).
(d) For the purposes of the references in subsection (b) to a conservator, subsection (b) does not apply if after the sale, mortgage, condemnation, casualty, or recovery, it was adjudicated that the testator's incapacity ceased and the testator survived the adjudication by one year.
(e) For the purposes of the references in subsection (b) to an agent acting within the authority of a durable power of attorney for an incapacitated principal, (i) "incapacitated principal" means a principal who is an incapacitated person, (ii) no adjudication of incapacity before death is necessary, and (iii) the acts of an agent within the authority of a durable power of attorney are presumed to be for an incapacitated principal.

Section 2-607. Nonexoneration.
A specific devise passes subject to any mortgage interest existing at the date of death, without right of exoneration, regardless of a general directive in the will to pay debts.

Section 2-608. Exercise of Power of Appointment.
In the absence of a requirement that a power of appointment be exercised by a reference, or by an express or specific reference, to the power, a general residuary clause in a will, or a will making general disposition of all of the testator's property, expresses an intention to exercise a power of appointment held by the testator only if (i) the power is a general power and the creating instrument does not contain a gift if the power is not exercised or (ii) the testator's will manifests an intention to include the property subject to the power.

Section 2-609. Ademption by Satisfaction.
(a) Property a testator gave in his [or her] lifetime to a person is treated as a satisfaction of a devise in whole or in part, only if (i) the will provides for deduction of the gift, (ii) the testator declared in a contemporaneous writing that the gift is in satisfaction of the devise or that its value is to be deducted from the value of the devise, or (iii) the devisee acknowledged in writing that the gift is in satisfaction of the devise or that its value is to be deducted from the value of the devise.
(b) For purposes of partial satisfaction, property given during lifetime is valued as of the time the devisee came into possession or enjoyment of the property or at the testator's death, whichever occurs first.
(c) If the devisee fails to survive the testator, the gift is treated as a full or partial satisfaction of the devise, as appropriate, in applying Sections 2-603 and 2-604, unless the testator's contemporaneous writing provides otherwise.

PART 7. RULES OF CONSTRUCTION APPLICABLE TO DONATIVE DISPOSITIONS IN WILLS AND OTHER GOVERNING INSTRUMENTS

Section 2-701. Scope.
In the absence of a finding of a contrary intention, the rules of construction in this Part control the construction of a governing instrument. The rules of construction in this Part apply to a governing instrument of any type, except as the application of a particular section is limited by its terms to a specific type or types of donative disposition or governing instrument.

Section 2-702. Requirement of Survival by 120 Hours.
(a) [Requirement of Survival by 120 Hours Under Probate Code.] For the purposes of this Code, except for purposes of Part 3 of Article VI [Uniform TOD Security Registration Act] and except as provided in subsection (d), an individual who is not established by clear and convincing evidence to have survived an event, including the death of another individual, by 120 hours is deemed to have predeceased the event.
(b) [Requirement of Survival by 120 Hours under Donative Provision of Governing Instrument.] Except as provided in subsection (d) and except for a security registered in beneficiary form (TOD) under Part 3 of Article VI [Uniform TOD Security Registration Act], for purposes of a donative provision of a governing instrument, an individual who is not established by clear and convincing evidence to have survived an event, including the death of another individual, by 120 hours is deemed to have predeceased the event.
(c) [Co-owners With Right of Survivorship; Requirement of Survival by 120 Hours.] Except as provided in subsection (d), if (i) it is not established by clear and convincing evidence that one of two co-owners with right of survivorship survived the other co-owner by 120 hours, one-half of the property passes as if one had survived by 120 hours and one-half as if the other had survived by 120 hours and (ii) there are more than two co-owners and it is not established by clear and convincing evidence that at least one of them survived the others by 120 hours, the property passes in the proportion that one bears to the whole number of co-owners. For the purposes of this subsection, "co-owners with right of survivorship" includes joint tenants, tenants by the entireties, and other co-owners of property or accounts held

under circumstances that entitle one or more to the whole of the property or account on the death of the other or others.

(d) [Exceptions.] This section does not apply if:

(1) the governing instrument contains language dealing explicitly with simultaneous deaths or deaths in a common disaster and that language is operable under the facts of the case;
(2) the governing instrument expressly indicates that an individual is not required to survive an event, including the death of another individual, by any specified period or expressly requires the individual to survive the event by a specified period;
(3) the imposition of a 120-hour requirement of survival would cause a nonvested property interest or a power of appointment to fail to qualify for validity under Section 2-901(a)(1), (b)(1), or (c)(1) or to become invalid under Section 2-901(a)(2), (b)(2), or (c)(2); or
(4) the application of this section to multiple governing instruments would result in an unintended failure or duplication of a disposition.

(e) [Protection of Payors and Other Third Parties.]

(1) A payor or other third party is not liable for having made a payment or transferred an item of property or any other benefit to a beneficiary designated in a governing instrument who, under this section, is not entitled to the payment or item of property, or for having taken any other action in good faith reliance on the beneficiary's apparent entitlement under the terms of the governing instrument, before the payor or other third party received written notice of a claimed lack of entitlement under this section. A payor or other third party is liable for a payment made or other action taken after the payor or other third party received written notice of a claimed lack of entitlement under this section.
(2) Written notice of a claimed lack of entitlement under paragraph (1) must be mailed to the payor's or other third party's main office or home by registered or certified mail, return receipt requested, or served upon the payor or other third party in the same manner as a summons in a civil action. Upon receipt of written notice of a claimed lack of entitlement under this section, a payor or other third party may pay any amount owed or transfer or deposit any item of property held by it to or with the court having jurisdiction of the probate proceedings relating to the decedent's estate, or if no proceedings have been commenced, to or with the court having jurisdiction of probate proceedings relating to decedents' estates located in the county of the decedent's residence. The court shall hold the funds or item of property and, upon its determination under this section, shall order disbursement in accordance with the determination. Payments, transfers, or deposits made to or with the court discharge the payor or other third party from all claims for the value of amounts paid to or items of property transferred to or deposited with the court.

(f) [Protection of Bona Fide Purchasers; Personal Liability of Recipient.]

(1) A person who purchases property for value and without notice, or who receives a payment or other item of property in partial or full satisfaction of a legally enforceable obligation, is neither obligated under this section to return the payment, item of property, or benefit nor is liable under this section for the amount of the payment or the value of the item of property or benefit. But a person who, not for value, receives a payment, item of property, or any other benefit to which the person is not entitled under this section is obligated to return the payment, item of property, or benefit, or is personally liable for the amount of the payment or the value of the item of property or benefit, to the person who is entitled to it under this section.

(2) If this section or any part of this section is preempted by federal law with respect to a payment, an item of property, or any other benefit covered by this section, a person who, not for value, receives the payment, item of property, or any other benefit to which the person is not entitled under this section is obligated to return the payment, item of property, or benefit, or is personally liable for the amount of the payment or the value of the item of property or benefit, to the person who would have been entitled to it were this section or part of this section not preempted.

Section 2-703. Choice of Law as to Meaning and Effect of Donative Dispositions.
The meaning and legal effect of a donative disposition is determined by the local law of the state selected by the transferor in the governing instrument, unless the application of that law is contrary to the provisions relating to the elective share described in Part 2, the provisions relating to exempt property and allowances described in Part 4, or any other public policy of this State otherwise applicable to the disposition.

Section 2-704. Power of Appointment; Meaning of Specific Reference Requirement.
If a governing instrument creating a power of appointment expressly requires that the power be exercised by a reference, an express reference, or a specific reference, to the power or its source, it is presumed that the donor's intention, in requiring that the donee exercise the power by making reference to the particular power or to the creating instrument, was to prevent an inadvertent exercise of the power.

Section 2-705. Class Gifts Construed to Accord With Intestate Succession.
(a) Adopted individuals and individuals born out of wedlock, and their respective descendants if appropriate to the class, are included in class gifts and other terms of relationship in accordance with the rules for intestate succession. Terms of relationship that do not differentiate relationships by blood from those by affinity, such as "uncles," "aunts," "nieces," or "nephews," are construed to exclude relatives by affinity. Terms of relationship that do not differentiate relationships by the half blood from those by the whole blood, such as "brothers," "sisters," "nieces," or "nephews," are construed to include both types of relationships.
(b) In addition to the requirements of subsection (a), in construing a donative disposition by a transferor who is not the natural parent, an individual born to the natural parent is not considered the child of that parent unless the individual lived while a minor as a regular member of the household of that natural parent or of that parent's parent, brother, sister, spouse, or surviving spouse.
(c) In addition to the requirements of subsection (a), in construing a donative disposition by a transferor who is not the adopting parent, an adopted individual is not considered the child of the adopting parent unless the adopted individual lived while a minor, either before or after the adoption, as a regular member of the household of the adopting parent.

Section 2-706. Life Insurance; Retirement Plan; Account With POD Designation; Transfer-on-Death Registration; Deceased Beneficiary.
(a) [Definitions.] In this section:

(1) "Alternative beneficiary designation" means a beneficiary designation that is expressly created by the governing instrument and, under the terms of the governing instrument, can take effect instead of another beneficiary designation on the happening of one or more events, including survival of the decedent or failure to survive the decedent, whether an event is expressed in condition-precedent, condition-subsequent, or any other form.
(2) "Beneficiary" means the beneficiary of a beneficiary designation and includes (i) a class member if the beneficiary designation is in the form of a class

gift and (ii) an individual or class member who was deceased at the time the beneficiary designation was executed as well as an individual or class member who was then living but who failed to survive the decedent.
(3) "Beneficiary designation" includes an alternative beneficiary designation and a beneficiary designation in the form of a class gift.
(4) "Class member" includes an individual who fails to survive the decedent but who would have taken under a beneficiary designation in the form of a class gift had he [or she] survived the decedent.
(5) "Stepchild" means a child of the decedent's surviving, deceased, or former spouse, and not of the decedent.
(6) "Surviving beneficiary" or "surviving descendant" means a beneficiary or a descendant who neither predeceased the decedent nor is deemed to have predeceased the decedent under Section 2-702.

(b) [Substitute Gift.] If a beneficiary fails to survive the decedent and is a grandparent, a descendant of a grandparent, or a stepchild of the decedent, the following apply:

(1) Except as provided in paragraph (4), if the beneficiary designation is not in the form of a class gift and the deceased beneficiary leaves surviving descendants, a substitute gift is created in the beneficiary's surviving descendants. They take by representation the property to which the beneficiary would have been entitled had the beneficiary survived the decedent.
(2) Except as provided in paragraph (4), if the beneficiary designation is in the form of a class gift, other than a beneficiary designation to "issue," "descendants," "heirs of the body," "heirs," "next of kin," "relatives," or "family," or a class described by language of similar import, a substitute gift is created in the deceased beneficiary or beneficiaries' surviving descendants. The property to which the beneficiaries would have been entitled had all of them survived the decedent passes to the surviving beneficiaries and the surviving descendants of the deceased beneficiaries. Each surviving beneficiary takes the share to which he [or she] would have been entitled had the deceased beneficiaries survived the decedent. Each deceased beneficiary's surviving descendants who are substituted for the deceased beneficiary take by representation the share to which the deceased beneficiary would have been entitled had the deceased beneficiary survived the decedent. For the purposes of this paragraph, "deceased beneficiary" means a class member who failed to survive the decedent and left one or more surviving descendants.
(3) For the purposes of Section 2-701, words of survivorship, such as in a beneficiary designation to an individual "if he survives me," or in a beneficiary designation to "my surviving children," are not, in the absence of additional evidence, a sufficient indication of an intent contrary to the application of this section.
(4) If a governing instrument creates an alternative beneficiary designation with respect to a beneficiary designation for which a substitute gift is created by paragraph (1) or (2), the substitute gift is superseded by the alternative beneficiary designation only if an expressly designated beneficiary of the alternative beneficiary designation is entitled to take.

(c) [More Than One Substitute Gift; Which One Takes.] If, under subsection (b), substitute gifts are created and not superseded with respect to more than one beneficiary designation and the beneficiary designations are alternative beneficiary designations, one to the other, the determination of which of the substitute gifts takes effect is resolved as follows:

(1) Except as provided in paragraph (2), the property passes under the primary substitute gift.
(2) If there is a younger-generation beneficiary designation, the property passes under the younger-generation substitute gift and not under the primary substitute gift.
(3) In this subsection:

(i) "Primary beneficiary designation" means the beneficiary designation that would have taken effect had all the deceased beneficiaries of the alternative beneficiary designations who left surviving descendants survived the decedent.
(ii) "Primary substitute gift" means the substitute gift created with respect to the primary beneficiary designation.
(iii) "Younger-generation beneficiary designation" means a beneficiary designation that (A) is to a descendant of a beneficiary of the primary beneficiary designation, (B) is an alternative beneficiary designation with respect to the primary beneficiary designation, (C) is a beneficiary designation for which a substitute gift is created, and (D) would have taken effect had all the deceased beneficiaries who left surviving descendants survived the decedent except the deceased beneficiary or beneficiaries of the primary beneficiary designation.
(iv) "Younger-generation substitute gift" means the substitute gift created with respect to the younger-generation beneficiary designation.

(d) [Protection of Payors.]

(1) A payor is protected from liability in making payments under the terms of the beneficiary designation until the payor has received written notice of a claim to a substitute gift under this section. Payment made before the receipt of written notice of a claim to a substitute gift under this section discharges the payor, but not the recipient, from all claims for the amounts paid. A payor is liable for a payment made after the payor has received written notice of the claim. A recipient is liable for a payment received, whether or not written notice of the claim is given.
(2) The written notice of the claim must be mailed to the payor's main office or home by registered or certified mail, return receipt requested, or served upon the payor in the same manner as a summons in a civil action. Upon receipt of written notice of the claim, a payor may pay any amount owed by it to the court having jurisdiction of the probate proceedings relating to the decedent's estate or, if no proceedings have been commenced, to the court having jurisdiction of probate proceedings relating to decedents' estates located in the county of the decedent's residence. The court shall hold the funds and, upon its determination under this section, shall order disbursement in accordance with the determination. Payment made to the court discharges the payor from all claims for the amounts paid.

(e) [Protection of Bona Fide Purchasers; Personal Liability of Recipient.]

(1) A person who purchases property for value and without notice, or who receives a payment or other item of property in partial or full satisfaction of a legally enforceable obligation, is neither obligated under this section to return the payment, item of property, or benefit nor is liable under this section for the amount of the payment or the value of the item of property or benefit. But a person who, not for value, receives a payment, item of property, or any other benefit to which the person is not entitled under this section is obligated to return the payment, item of property, or benefit, or is personally liable for the amount of the payment or the value of the item of property or benefit, to the person who is entitled to it under this section.

(2) If this section or any part of this section is preempted by federal law with respect to a payment, an item of property, or any other benefit covered by this section, a person who, not for value, receives the payment, item of property, or any other benefit to which the person is not entitled under this section is obligated to return the payment, item of property, or benefit, or is personally liable for the amount of the payment or the value of the item of property or benefit, to the person who would have been entitled to it were this section or part of this section not preempted.

Section 2-707. Survivorship with Respect to Future Interests under Terms of Trust; Substitute Takers.
(a) [Definitions.] In this section:

(1) "Alternative future interest" means an expressly created future interest that can take effect in possession or enjoyment instead of another future interest on the happening of one or more events, including survival of an event or failure to survive an event, whether an event is expressed in condition-precedent, condition-subsequent, or any other form. A residuary clause in a will does not create an alternative future interest with respect to a future interest created in a nonresiduary devise in the will, whether or not the will specifically provides that lapsed or failed devises are to pass under the residuary clause.
(2) "Beneficiary" means the beneficiary of a future interest and includes a class member if the future interest is in the form of a class gift.
(3) "Class member" includes an individual who fails to survive the distribution date but who would have taken under a future interest in the form of a class gift had he [or she] survived the distribution date.
(4) "Distribution date," with respect to a future interest, means the time when the future interest is to take effect in possession or enjoyment. The distribution date need not occur at the beginning or end of a calendar day, but can occur at a time during the course of a day.
(5) "Future interest" includes an alternative future interest and a future interest in the form of a class gift.
(6) "Future interest under the terms of a trust" means a future interest that was created by a transfer creating a trust or to an existing trust or by an exercise of a power of appointment to an existing trust, directing the continuance of an existing trust, designating a beneficiary of an existing trust, or creating a trust.
(7) "Surviving beneficiary" or "surviving descendant" means a beneficiary or a descendant who neither predeceased the distribution date nor is deemed to have predeceased the distribution date under Section 2-702.

(b) [Survivorship Required; Substitute Gift.] A future interest under the terms of a trust is contingent on the beneficiary's surviving the distribution date. If a beneficiary of a future interest under the terms of a trust fails to survive the distribution date, the following apply:

(1) Except as provided in paragraph (4), if the future interest is not in the form of a class gift and the deceased beneficiary leaves surviving descendants, a substitute gift is created in the beneficiary's surviving descendants. They take by representation the property to which the beneficiary would have been entitled had the beneficiary survived the distribution date.
(2) Except as provided in paragraph (4), if the future interest is in the form of a class gift, other than a future interest to "issue," "descendants," "heirs of the body," "heirs," "next of kin," "relatives," or "family," or a class described by language of similar import, a substitute gift is created in the deceased beneficiary or beneficiaries' surviving descendants. The property to which the beneficiaries would have been entitled had all of them survived the distribution date passes to the surviving beneficiaries and the surviving descendants of the deceased beneficiaries. Each surviving beneficiary takes the share to which he

[or she] would have been entitled had the deceased beneficiaries survived the distribution date. Each deceased beneficiary's surviving descendants who are substituted for the deceased beneficiary take by representation the share to which the deceased beneficiary would have been entitled had the deceased beneficiary survived the distribution date. For the purposes of this paragraph, "deceased beneficiary" means a class member who failed to survive the distribution date and left one or more surviving descendants.

(3) For the purposes of Section 2-701, words of survivorship attached to a future interest are not, in the absence of additional evidence, a sufficient indication of an intent contrary to the application of this section. Words of survivorship include words of survivorship that relate to the distribution date or to an earlier or an unspecified time, whether those words of survivorship are expressed in condition-precedent, condition-subsequent, or any other form.

(4) If a governing instrument creates an alternative future interest with respect to a future interest for which a substitute gift is created by paragraph (1) or (2), the substitute gift is superseded by the alternative future interest only if an expressly designated beneficiary of the alternative future interest is entitled to take in possession or enjoyment.

(c) [More Than One Substitute Gift; Which One Takes.] If, under subsection (b), substitute gifts are created and not superseded with respect to more than one future interest and the future interests are alternative future interests, one to the other, the determination of which of the substitute gifts takes effect is resolved as follows:

(1) Except as provided in paragraph (2), the property passes under the primary substitute gift.

(2) If there is a younger-generation future interest, the property passes under the younger-generation substitute gift and not under the primary substitute gift.

(3) In this subsection:

(i) "Primary future interest" means the future interest that would have taken effect had all the deceased beneficiaries of the alternative future interests who left surviving descendants survived the distribution date.

(ii) "Primary substitute gift" means the substitute gift created with respect to the primary future interest.

(iii) "Younger-generation future interest" means a future interest that (A) is to a descendant of a beneficiary of the primary future interest, (B) is an alternative future interest with respect to the primary future interest, (C) is a future interest for which a substitute gift is created, and (D) would have taken effect had all the deceased beneficiaries who left surviving descendants survived the distribution date except the deceased beneficiary or beneficiaries of the primary future interest.

(iv) "Younger-generation substitute gift" means the substitute gift created with respect to the younger-generation future interest.

(d) [If No Other Takers, Property Passes Under Residuary Clause or to Transferor's Heirs.] If, after the application of subsections (b) and (c), there is no surviving taker, the property passes in the following order:

(1) if the trust was created in a nonresiduary devise in the transferor's will or in a codicil to the transferor's will, the property passes under the residuary clause in the transferor's will; for purposes of this section, the residuary clause is treated as creating a future interest under the terms of a trust.

(2) if no taker is produced by the application of paragraph (1), the property passes to the transferor's heirs under Section 2-711.

Section 2-708. Class Gifts to "Descendants," "Issue," or "Heirs of the Body"; Form of Distribution if None Specified.
If a class gift in favor of "descendants," "issue," or "heirs of the body" does not specify the manner in which the property is to be distributed among the class members, the property is distributed among the class members who are living when the interest is to take effect in possession or enjoyment, in such shares as they would receive, under the applicable law of intestate succession, if the designated ancestor had then died intestate owning the subject matter of the class gift.

Section 2-709. Representation; Per Capita at Each Generation; Per Stirpes.
(a) [Definitions.] In this section:

(1) "Deceased child" or "deceased descendant" means a child or a descendant who either predeceased the distribution date or is deemed to have predeceased the distribution date under Section 2-702.
(2) "Distribution date," with respect to an interest, means the time when the interest is to take effect in possession or enjoyment. The distribution date need not occur at the beginning or end of a calendar day, but can occur at a time during the course of a day.
(3) "Surviving ancestor," "surviving child," or "surviving descendant" means an ancestor, a child, or a descendant who neither predeceased the distribution date nor is deemed to have predeceased the distribution date under Section 2-702.

(b) [Representation; Per Capita at Each Generation.] If an applicable statute or a governing instrument calls for property to be distributed "by representation" or "per capita at each generation," the property is divided into as many equal shares as there are (i) surviving descendants in the generation nearest to the designated ancestor which contains one or more surviving descendants (ii) and deceased descendants in the same generation who left surviving descendants, if any. Each surviving descendant in the nearest generation is allocated one share. The remaining shares, if any, are combined and then divided in the same manner among the surviving descendants of the deceased descendants as if the surviving descendants who were allocated a share and their surviving descendants had predeceased the distribution date.
(c) [Per Stirpes.] If a governing instrument calls for property to be distributed "per stripes," the property is divided into as many equal shares as there are (i) surviving children of the designated ancestor and (ii) deceased children who left surviving descendants. Each surviving child is allocated one share. The share of each deceased child with surviving descendants is divided in the same manner, with subdivision repeating at each succeeding generation until the property is fully allocated among surviving descendants.
(d) [Deceased Descendant With No Surviving Descendant Disregarded.] For the purposes of subsections (b) and (c), an individual who is deceased and left no surviving descendant is disregarded, and an individual who leaves a surviving ancestor who is a descendant of the designated ancestor is not entitled to a share.

Section 2-710. Worthier-Title Doctrine Abolished.
The doctrine of worthier title is abolished as a rule of law and as a rule of construction. Language in a governing instrument describing the beneficiaries of a donative disposition as the transferor's "heirs," "heirs at law," "next of kin," "distributees," "relatives," or "family," or language of similar import, does not create or presumptively create a reversionary interest in the transferor.

Section 2-711. Future Interests in "Heirs" and Like.
If an applicable statute or a governing instrument calls for a future distribution to or creates a future interest in a designated individual's "heirs," "heirs at law," "next of kin," "relatives," or "family," or language of similar import, the property passes

to those persons, including the state under Section 2-105, and in such shares as would succeed to the designated individual's intestate estate under the intestate succession law of the designated individual's domicile if the designated individual died when the donative disposition is to take effect in possession or enjoyment. If the designated individual's surviving spouse is living but is remarried at the time the interest is to take effect in possession or enjoyment, the surviving spouse is not an heir of the designated individual.

PART 8. GENERAL PROVISIONS CONCERNING PROBATE AND NONPROBATE TRANSFERS

Section 2-801. Disclaimer of Property Interests.

(a) [Right to Disclaim Interest in Property.] A person, or the representative of a person, to whom an interest in or with respect to property or an interest therein devolves by whatever means may disclaim it in whole or in part by delivering or filing a written disclaimer under this section. The right to disclaim exists notwithstanding (i) any limitation on the interest of the disclaimant in the nature of a spendthrift provision or similar restriction or (ii) any restriction or limitation on the right to disclaim contained in the governing instrument. For purposes of this subsection, the "representative of a person" includes a personal representative of a decedent, a conservator of a disabled person, a guardian of a minor or incapacitated person, and an agent acting on behalf of the person within the authority of a power of attorney.

(b) [Time of Disclaimer.] The following rules govern the time when a disclaimer must be filed or delivered:

(1) If the property or interest has devolved to the disclaimant under a testamentary instrument or by the laws of intestacy, the disclaimer must be filed, if of a present interest, not later than [nine] months after the death of the deceased owner or deceased donee of a power of appointment and, if of a future interest, not later than [nine] months after the event determining that the taker of the property or interest is finally ascertained and his [or her] interest is indefeasibly vested. The disclaimer must be filed in the [probate] court of the county in which proceedings for the administration of the estate of the deceased owner or deceased donee of the power have been commenced. A copy of the disclaimer must be delivered in person or mailed by registered or certified mail, return receipt requested, to any personal representative or other fiduciary of the decedent or donee of the power.

(2) If a property or interest has devolved to the disclaimant under a nontestamentary instrument or contract, the disclaimer must be delivered or filed, if of a present interest, not later than [nine] months after the effective date of the nontestamentary instrument or contract and, if of a future interest, not later than [nine] months after the event determining that the taker of the property or interest is finally ascertained and his [or her] interest is indefeasibly vested. If the person entitled to disclaim does not know of the existence of the interest, the disclaimer must be delivered or filed not later than [nine] months after the person learns of the existence of the interest. The effective date of a revocable instrument or contract is the date on which the maker no longer has power to revoke it or to transfer to himself [or herself] or another the entire legal and equitable ownership of the interest. The disclaimer or a copy thereof must be delivered in person or mailed by registered or certified mail, return receipt requested, to the person who has legal title to or possession of the interest disclaimed.

(3) A surviving joint tenant [or tenant by the entireties] may disclaim as a separate interest any property or interest therein devolving to him [or her] by right of survivorship. A surviving joint tenant [or tenant by the entireties] may disclaim the entire interest in any property or interest therein that is the subject of a joint tenancy [or tenancy by the entireties] devolving to him [or her], if the

joint tenancy [or tenancy by the entireties] was created by act of a deceased joint tenant [or tenant by the entireties], the survivor did not join in creating the joint tenancy [or tenancy by the entireties], and has not accepted a benefit under it.
(4) If real property or an interest therein is disclaimed, a copy of the disclaimer may be recorded in the office of the [Recorder of Deeds] of the county in which the property or interest disclaimed is located.*

(c) [Form of Disclaimer.] The disclaimer must (i) describe the property or interest disclaimed, (ii) declare the disclaimer and extent thereof, and (iii) be signed by the disclaimant.
(d) [Effect of Disclaimer.] The effects of a disclaimer are:

(1) If property or an interest therein devolves to a disclaimant under a testamentary instrument, under a power of appointment exercised by a testamentary instrument, or under the laws of intestacy, and the decedent has not provided for another disposition of that interest, should it be disclaimed, or of disclaimed, or failed interests in general, the disclaimed interest devolves as if the disclaimant had predeceased the decedent, but if by law or under the testamentary instrument the descendants of the disclaimant would take the disclaimant's share by representation were the disclaimant to predecease the decedent, then the disclaimed interest passes by representation to the descendants of the disclaimant who survive the decedent. A future interest that takes effect in possession or enjoyment after the termination of the estate or interest disclaimed takes effect as if the disclaimant had predeceased the decedent. A disclaimer relates back for all purposes to the date of death of the decedent.
(2) If property or an interest therein devolves to a disclaimant under a nontestamentary instrument or contract and the instrument or contract does not provide for another disposition of that interest, should it be disclaimed, or of disclaimed or failed interests in general, the disclaimed interest devolves as if the disclaimant has predeceased the effective date of the instrument or contract, but if by law or under the nontestamentary instrument or contract the descendants of the disclaimant would take the disclaimant's share by representation were the disclaimant to predecease the effective date of the instrument, then the disclaimed interest passes by representation to the descendants of the disclaimant who survive the effective date of the instrument. A disclaimer relates back for all purposes to that date. A future interest that takes effect in possession or enjoyment at or after the termination of the disclaimed interest takes effect as if the disclaimant had died before the effective date of the instrument or contract that transferred the disclaimed interest.
(3) The disclaimer or the written waiver of the right to disclaim is binding upon the disclaimant or person waiving and all persons claiming through or under either of them.

(e) [Waiver and Bar.] The right to disclaim property or an interest therein is barred by (i) an assignment, conveyance, encumbrance, pledge, or transfer of the property or interest, or a contract therefor, (ii) a written waiver of the right to disclaim, (iii) an acceptance of the property or interest or a benefit under it or (iv) a sale of the property or interest under judicial sale made before the disclaimer is made.
(f) [Remedy Not Exclusive.] This section does not abridge the right of a person to waive, release, disclaim, or renounce property or an interest therein under any other statute.
(g) [Application.] An interest in property that exists on the effective date of this section as to which, if a present interest, the time for filing a disclaimer under this section has not expired or, if a future interest, the interest has not become indefeasibly vested or the taker finally ascertained, may be disclaimed within [nine] months after the effective date of this section.

* If Torrens system is in effect, add provisions to comply with local law.

Section 2-802. Effect of Divorce, Annulment, and Decree of Separation.
(a) An individual who is divorced from the decedent or whose marriage to the decedent has been annulled is not a surviving spouse unless, by virtue of a subsequent marriage, he [or she] is married to the decedent at the time of death. A decree of separation that does not terminate the status of husband and wife is not a divorce for purposes of this section.
(b) For purposes of Parts 1, 2, 3, and 4 of this Article, and of Section 3-203, a surviving spouse does not include:

(1) an individual who obtains or consents to a final decree or judgment of divorce from the decedent or an annulment of their marriage, which decree or judgment is not recognized as valid in this State, unless subsequently they participate in a marriage ceremony purporting to marry each to the other or live together as husband and wife;
(2) an individual who, following an invalid decree or judgment of divorce or annulment obtained by the decedent, participates in a marriage ceremony with a third individual; or
(3) an individual who was a party to a valid proceeding concluded by an order purporting to terminate all marital property rights.

Section 2-803. Effect of Homicide on Intestate Succession, Wills, Trusts, Joint Assets, Life Insurance, and Beneficiary Designations.
(a) [Definitions.] In this section:

(1) "Disposition or appointment of property" includes a transfer of an item of property or any other benefit to a beneficiary designated in a governing instrument.
(2) "Governing instrument" means a governing instrument executed by the decedent.
(3) "Revocable," with respect to a disposition, appointment, provision, or nomination, means one under which the decedent, at the time of or immediately before death, was alone empowered, by law or under the governing instrument, to cancel the designation, in favor of the killer, whether or not the decedent was then empowered to designate himself [or herself] in place of his [or her] killer and or the decedent then had capacity to exercise the power.

(b) [Forfeiture of Statutory Benefits.] An individual who feloniously and intentionally kills the decedent forfeits all benefits under this Article with respect to the decedent's estate, including an intestate share, an elective share, an omitted spouse's or child's share, a homestead allowance, exempt property, and a family allowance. If the decedent died intestate, the decedent's intestate estate passes as if the killer disclaimed his [or her] intestate share.
(c) [Revocation of Benefits Under Governing Instruments.] The felonious and intentional killing of the decedent:

(1) revokes any revocable (i) disposition or appointment of property made by the decedent to the killer in a governing instrument, (ii) provision in a governing instrument conferring a general or nongeneral power of appointment on the killer, and (iii) nomination of the killer in a governing instrument, nominating or appointing the killer to serve in any fiduciary or representative capacity, including a personal representative, executor, trustee, or agent; and
(2) severs the interests of the decedent and killer in property held by them at the time of the killing as joint tenants with the right of survivorship [or as community property with the right of survivorship], transforming the interests of the decedent and killer into tenancies in common.

(d) [Effect of Severance.] A severance under subsection (c)(2) does not affect any third-party interest in property acquired for value and in good faith reliance on an apparent title by survivorship in the killer unless a writing declaring the severance has been noted, registered, filed, or recorded in records appropriate to the kind and location of the property which are relied upon, in the ordinary course of transactions involving such property, as evidence of ownership.

(e) [Effect of Revocation.] Provisions of a governing instrument that are not revoked by this section are given effect as if the killer disclaimed all revoked provisions or, in the case of a revoked nomination in a fiduciary or representative capacity, as if the killer predeceased the decedent.

(f) [Wrongful Acquisition of Property.] A wrongful acquisition of property or interest by a killer not covered by this section must be treated in accordance with the principle that a killer cannot profit from his [or her] wrong.

(g) [Felonious and Intentional Killing; How Determined.] After all right to appeal has been exhausted, a judgment of conviction establishing criminal accountability for the felonious and intentional killing of the decedent conclusively establishes the convicted individual as the decedent's killer for purposes of this section. In the absence of a conviction, the court, upon the petition of an interested person, must determine whether, under the preponderance of evidence standard, the individual would be found criminally accountable for the felonious and intentional killing of the decedent. If the court determines that, under that standard, the individual would be found criminally accountable for the felonious and intentional killing of the decedent, the determination conclusively establishes that individual as the decedent's killer for purposes of this section.

(h) [Protection of Payors and Other Third Parties.]

(1) A payor or other third party is not liable for having made a payment or transferred an item of property or any other benefit to a beneficiary designated in a governing instrument affected by an intentional and felonious killing, or for having taken any other action in good faith reliance on the validity of the governing instrument, upon request and satisfactory proof of the decedent's death, before the payor or other third party received written notice of a claimed forfeiture or revocation under this section. A payor or other third party is liable for a payment made or other action taken after the payor or other third party received written notice of a claimed forfeiture or revocation under this section.

(2) Written notice of a claimed forfeiture or revocation under paragraph (1) must be mailed to the payor's or other third party's main office or home by registered or certified mail, return receipt requested, or served upon the payor or other third party in the same manner as a summons in a civil action. Upon receipt of written notice of a claimed forfeiture or revocation under this section, a payor or other third party may pay any amount owed or transfer or deposit any item of property held by it to or with the court having jurisdiction of the probate proceedings relating to the decedent's estate, or if no proceedings have been commenced, to or with the court having jurisdiction of probate proceedings relating to decedents' estates located in the county of the decedent's residence. The court shall hold the funds or item of property and, upon its determination under this section, shall order disbursement in accordance with the determination. Payments, transfers, or deposits made to or with the court discharge the payor or other third party from all claims for the value of amounts paid to or items of property transferred to or deposited with the court.

(i) [Protection of Bona Fide Purchasers; Personal Liability of Recipient.]

(1) A person who purchases property for value and without notice, or who receives a payment or other item of property in partial or full satisfaction of a legally enforceable obligation, is neither obligated under this section to return the payment, item of property, or benefit nor is liable under this section for the amount of the payment or the value of the item of property or benefit. But a person who, not for value, receives a payment, item of property, or any other benefit to which the person is not entitled under this section is obligated to

return the payment, item of property, or benefit, or is personally liable for the amount of the payment or the value of the item of property or benefit, to the person who is entitled to it under this section.
(2) If this section or any part of this section is preempted by federal law with respect to a payment, an item of property, or any other benefit covered by this section, a person who, not for value, receives the payment, item of property, or any other benefit to which the person is not entitled under this section is obligated to return the payment, item of property, or benefit, or is personally liable for the amount of the payment or the value of the item of property or benefit, to the person who would have been entitled to it were this section or part of this section not preempted.

Section 2-804. Revocation of Probate and Nonprobate Transfers by Divorce; No Revocation by other Changes of Circumstances.
(a) [Definitions.] In this section:

(1) "Disposition or appointment of property" includes a transfer of an item of property or any other benefit to a beneficiary designated in a governing instrument.
(2) "Divorce or annulment" means any divorce or annulment, or any dissolution or declaration of invalidity of a marriage, that would exclude the spouse as a surviving spouse within the meaning of Section 2-802. A decree of separation that does not terminate the status of husband and wife is not a divorce for purposes of this section.
(3) "Divorced individual" includes an individual whose marriage has been annulled.
(4) "Governing instrument" means a governing instrument executed by the divorced individual before the divorce or annulment of his [or her] marriage to his [or her] former spouse.
(5) "Relative of the divorced individual's former spouse" means an individual who is related to the divorced individual's former spouse by blood, adoption, or affinity and who, after the divorce or annulment, is not related to the divorced individual by blood, adoption, or affinity.
(6) "Revocable," with respect to a disposition, appointment, provision, or nomination, means one under which the divorced individual, at the time of the divorce or annulment, was alone empowered, by law or under the governing instrument, to cancel the designation in favor of his [or her] former spouse or former spouse's relative, whether or not the divorced individual was then empowered to designate himself [or herself] in place of his [or her] former spouse or in place of his [or her] former spouse's relative and whether or not the divorced individual then had the capacity to exercise the power.

(b) [Revocation Upon Divorce.] Except as provided by the express terms of a governing instrument, a court order, or a contract relating to the division of the marital estate made between the divorced individuals before or after the marriage, divorce, or annulment, the divorce or annulment of a marriage:

(1) revokes any revocable (i) disposition or appointment of property made by a divorced individual to his [or her] former spouse in a governing instrument and any disposition or appointment created by law or in a governing instrument to a relative of the divorced individual's former spouse, (ii) provision in a governing instrument conferring a general or nongeneral power of appointment on the divorced individual's former spouse or on a relative of the divorced individual's former spouse, and (iii) nomination in a governing instrument, nominating a divorced individual's former spouse or a relative of the divorced individual's former spouse to serve in any fiduciary or representative capacity, including a personal representative, executor, trustee, conservator, agent, or guardian; and

(2) severs the interests of the former spouses in property held by them at the time of the divorce or annulment as joint tenants with the right of survivorship [or as community property with the right of survivorship], transforming the interests of the former spouses into tenancies in common.

(c) [Effect of Severance.] A severance under subsection (b)(2) does not affect any third-party interest in property acquired for value and in good faith reliance on an apparent title by survivorship in the survivor of the former spouses unless a writing declaring the severance has been noted, registered, filed, or recorded in records appropriate to the kind and location of the property which are relied upon, in the ordinary course of transactions involving such property, as evidence of ownership.

(d) [Effect of Revocation.] Provisions of a governing instrument that are not revoked by this section are given effect as if the former spouse and relatives of the former spouse disclaimed the revoked provisions or, in the case of a revoked nomination in a fiduciary or representative capacity, as if the former spouse and relatives of the former spouse died immediately before the divorce or annulment.

(e) [Revival if Divorce Nullified.] Provisions revoked solely by this section are revived by the divorced individual's remarriage to the former spouse or by a nullification of the divorce or annulment.

(f) [No Revocation for Other Change of Circumstances.] No change of circumstances other than as described in this section and in Section 2-803 effects a revocation.

(g) [Protection of Payors and Other Third Parties.]

(1) A payor or other third party is not liable for having made a payment or transferred an item of property or any other benefit to a beneficiary designated in a governing instrument affected by a divorce, annulment, or remarriage, or for having taken any other action in good faith reliance on the validity of the governing instrument, before the payor or other third party received written notice of the divorce, annulment, or remarriage. A payor or other third party is liable for a payment made or other action taken after the payor or other third party received written notice of a claimed forfeiture or revocation under this section.

(2) Written notice of the divorce, annulment, or remarriage under subsection (g)(2) must be mailed to the payor's or other third party's main office or home by registered or certified mail, return receipt requested, or served upon the payor or other third party in the same manner as a summons in a civil action. Upon receipt of written notice of the divorce, annulment, or remarriage, a payor or other third party may pay any amount owed or transfer or deposit any item of property held by it to or with the court having jurisdiction of the probate proceedings relating to the decedent's estate or, if no proceedings have been commenced, to or with the court having jurisdiction of probate proceedings relating to decedents' estates located in the county of the decedent's residence. The court shall hold the funds or item of property and, upon its determination under this section, shall order disbursement or transfer in accordance with the determination. Payments, transfers, or deposits made to or with the court discharge the payor or other third party from all claims for the value of amounts paid to or items of property transferred to or deposited with the court.

(h) [Protection of Bona Fide Purchasers; Personal Liability of Recipient.]

(1) A person who purchases property from a former spouse, relative of a former spouse, or any other person for value and without notice, or who receives from a former spouse, relative of a former spouse, or any other person a payment or other item of property in partial or full satisfaction of a legally enforceable obligation, is neither obligated under this section to return the payment, item of property, or benefit nor is liable under this section for the amount of the payment or the value of the item of property or benefit. But a former spouse,

relative of a former spouse, or other person who, not for value, received a payment, item of property, or any other benefit to which that person is not entitled under this section is obligated to return the payment, item of property, or benefit, or is personally liable for the amount of the payment or the value of the item of property or benefit, to the person who is entitled to it under this section.
(2) If this section or any part of this section is preempted by federal law with respect to a payment, an item of property, or any other benefit covered by this section, a former spouse, relative of the former spouse, or any other person who, not for value, received a payment, item of property, or any other benefit to which that person is not entitled under this section is obligated to return that payment, item of property, or benefit, or is personally liable for the amount of the payment or the value of the item of property or benefit, to the person who would have been entitled to it were this section or part of this section not preempted.

PART 9. STATUTORY RULE AGAINST PERPETUITIES; HONORARY TRUSTS

Subpart 1. Statutory Rule Against Perpetuities

Section 2-901. Statutory Rule Against Perpetuities.
(a) [Validity of Nonvested Property Interest.] A nonvested property interest is invalid unless:

(1) when the interest is created, it is certain to vest or terminate no later than 21 years after the death of an individual then alive; or
(2) the interest either vests or terminates within 90 years after its creation.

(b) [Validity of General Power of Appointment Subject to a Condition Precedent.] A general power of appointment not presently exercisable because of a condition precedent is invalid unless:

(1) when the power is created, the condition precedent is certain to be satisfied or becomes impossible to satisfy no later than 21 years after the death of an individual then alive; or
(2) the condition precedent either is satisfied or becomes impossible to satisfy within 90 years after its creation.

(c) [Validity of Nongeneral or Testamentary Power of Appointment.] A nongeneral power of appointment or a general testamentary power of appointment is invalid unless:

(1) when the power is created, it is certain to be irrevocably exercised or otherwise to terminate no later than 21 years after the death of an individual then alive; or
(2) the power is irrevocably exercised or otherwise terminates within 90 years after its creation.

(d) [Possibility of Post-death Child Disregarded.] In determining whether a nonvested property interest or a power of appointment is valid under subsection (a)(1), (b)(1), or (c)(1), the possibility that a child will be born to an individual after the individual's death is disregarded.
(e) [Effect of Certain "Later-of" Type Language.] If, in measuring a period from the creation of a trust or other property arrangement, language in a governing instrument (i) seeks to disallow the vesting or termination of any interest or trust beyond, (ii) seeks to postpone the vesting or termination of any interest or trust until, or (iii) seeks to operate in effect in any similar fashion upon, the later of (A) the expiration of a period of time not exceeding 21 years after the death of the

survivor of specified lives in being at the creation of the trust or other property arrangement or (B) the expiration of a period of time that exceeds or might exceed 21 years after the death of the survivor of lives in being at the creation of the trust or other property arrangement, that language is inoperative to the extent it produces a period of time that exceeds 21 years after the death of the survivor of the specified lives.

Section 2-902. When Nonvested Property Interest or Power of Appointment Created.
(a) Except as provided in subsections (b) and (c) and in Section 2-905(a), the time of creation of a nonvested property interest or a power of appointment is determined under general principles of property law.
(b) For purposes of Subpart 1 of this Part, if there is a person who alone can exercise a power created by a governing instrument to become the unqualified beneficial owner of (i) a nonvested property interest or (ii) a property interest subject to a power of appointment described in Section 2-901(b) or (c), the nonvested property interest or power of appointment is created when the power to become the unqualified beneficial owner terminates. [For purposes of Subpart 1 of this Part, a joint power with respect to community property or to marital property under the Uniform Marital Property Act held by individuals married to each other is a power exercisable by one person alone.]
(c) For purposes of Subpart 1 of this Part, a nonvested property interest or a power of appointment arising from a transfer of property to a previously funded trust or other existing property arrangement is created when the nonvested property interest or power of appointment in the original contribution was created.

Section 2-903. Reformation.
Upon the petition of an interested person, a court shall reform a disposition in the manner that most closely approximates the transferor's manifested plan of distribution and is within the 90 years allowed by Section 2-901(a)(2), 2-901(b)(2), or 2-901(c)(2) if:

(1) a nonvested property interest or a power of appointment becomes invalid under Section 2-901 (statutory rule against perpetuities);
(2) a class gift is not but might become invalid under Section 2-901 (statutory rule against perpetuities) and the time has arrived when the share of any class member is to take effect in possession or enjoyment; or
(3) a nonvested property interest that is not validated by Section 2-901(a)(1) can vest but not within 90 years after its creation.

Section 2-904. Exclusions from Statutory Rule Against Perpetuities.
Section 2-901 (statutory rule against perpetuities) does not apply to:

(1) a nonvested property interest or a power of appointment arising out of a nondonative transfer, except a nonvested property interest or a power of appointment arising out of (i) a premarital or postmarital agreement, (ii) a separation or divorce settlement, (iii) a spouse's election, (iv) a similar arrangement arising out of a prospective, existing, or previous marital relationship between the parties, (v) a contract to make or not to revoke a will or trust, (vi) a contract to exercise or not to exercise a power of appointment, (vii) a transfer in satisfaction of a duty of support, or (viii) a reciprocal transfer;
(2) a fiduciary's power relating to the administration or management of assets, including the power of a fiduciary to sell, lease, or mortgage property, and the power of a fiduciary to determine principal and income;
(3) a power to appoint a fiduciary;
(4) a discretionary power of a trustee to distribute principal before termination of a trust to a beneficiary having an indefeasibly vested interest in the income and principal;

(5) a nonvested property interest held by a charity, government, or governmental agency or subdivision, if the nonvested property interest is preceded by an interest held by another charity, government, or governmental agency or subdivision;
(6) a nonvested property interest in or a power of appointment with respect to a trust or other property arrangement forming part of a pension, profit-sharing, stock bonus, health, disability, death benefit, income deferral, or other current or deferred benefit plan for one or more employees, independent contractors, or their beneficiaries or spouses, to which contributions are made for the purpose of distributing to or for the benefit of the participants or their beneficiaries or spouses the property, income, or principal in the trust or other property arrangement, except a nonvested property interest or a power of appointment that is created by an election of a participant or a beneficiary or spouse; or
(7) a property interest, power of appointment, or arrangement that was not subject to the common-law rule against perpetuities or is excluded by another statute of this State.

Section 2-905. Prospective Application.
(a) Except as extended by subsection (b), Subpart 1 of this Part applies to a nonvested property interest or a power of appointment that is created on or after the effective date of Subpart 1 of this Part. For purposes of this section, a nonvested property interest or a power of appointment created by the exercise of a power of appointment is created when the power is irrevocably exercised or when a revocable exercise becomes irrevocable.
(b) If a nonvested property interest or a power of appointment was created before the effective date of Subpart 1 of this Part and is determined in a judicial proceeding, commenced on or after the effective date of Subpart 1 of this Part, to violate this State's rule against perpetuities as that rule existed before the effective date of Subpart 1 of this Part, a court upon the petition of an interested person may reform the disposition in the manner that most closely approximates the transferor's manifested plan of distribution and is within the limits of the rule against perpetuities applicable when the nonvested property interest or power of appointment was created.

Section 2-906. [Supersession][Repeal].
Subpart 1 of this Part [supersedes the rule of the common law known as the rule against perpetuities][repeals (list statutes to be repealed)].

SUBPART 2. [HONORARY TRUSTS]
[Optional provision for validating and limiting the duration of so-called honorary trusts and trusts for pets.]

[Section 2-907. Honorary Trusts; Trusts for Pets.
(a) [Honorary Trust.] A trust for a noncharitable corporation or unincorporated society or for a lawful noncharitable purpose may be performed by the trustee for [21] years but no longer, whether or not there is a beneficiary who can seek the trust's enforcement or termination and whether or not the terms of the trust contemplate a longer duration.
(b) [Trust for Pets.] Subject to this subsection, a trust for the care of a designated domestic or pet animal and the animal's offspring is valid. Except as expressly provided otherwise in the trust instrument:

(1) No portion of the principal or income may be converted to the use of the trustee or to any use other than for the benefit of a covered animal.
(2) The trust terminates at the earlier of [21] years after the trust was created or when no living animal is covered by the trust.
(3) Upon termination, the trustee shall transfer the unexpended trust property in the following order:

(i) as directed in the trust instrument;
(ii) if the trust was created in a nonresiduary clause in the transferor's will or in a codicil to the transferor's will, under the residuary clause in the transferor's will; and
(iii) if no taker is produced by the application of subparagraph (i) or (ii), to the transferor's heirs under Section 2-711.

(4) For the purposes of Section 2-707, the residuary clause is treated as creating a future interest under the terms of a trust.
(5) The intended use of the principal or income can be enforced by an individual designated for that purpose in the trust instrument or, if none, by an individual appointed by a court upon application to it by an individual.
(6) Except as ordered by the court or required by the trust instrument, no filing, report, registration, periodic accounting, separate maintenance of funds, appointment, or fee is required by reason of the existence of the fiduciary relationship of the trustee.
(7) A governing instrument must be liberally construed to bring the transfer within this section, to presume against the merely precatory or honorary nature of the disposition, and to carry out the general intent of the transferor. Extrinsic evidence is admissible in determining the transferor's intent.
(8) A court may reduce the amount of the property transferred, if it determines that that amount substantially exceeds the amount required for the intended use. The amount of the reduction, if any, passes as unexpended trust property under subsection (b)(3).
(9) If no trustee is designated or no designated trustee is willing or able to serve, a court shall name a trustee. A court may order the transfer of the property to another trustee, if required to assure that the intended use is carried out and if no successor trustee is designated in the trust instrument or if no designated successor trustee agrees to serve or is able to serve. A court may also make such other orders and determinations as shall be advisable to carry out the intent of the transferor and the purpose of this section.]

PART 10. UNIFORM INTERNATIONAL WILLS ACT [INTERNATIONAL WILL; INFORMATION REGISTRATION]

NUMBERING SECTIONS OF ACT

The Uniform International Wills Act may be adopted as a separate act or as part of the Uniform Probate Code. If adopted as a separate act, the unbracketed section numbers would govern. If adopted as part of the Probate Code, i.e., as Part 10 of Article 2, the section numbers in brackets would govern.

Section 1. [2-1001.] [Definitions.]

In this Act: [Part:]

(1) "International will" means a will executed in conformity with sections 2 [2-1002] through 5 [2-1005].
(2) "Authorized person" and "person authorized to act in connection with international wills" mean a person who by section 9 [2-1009], or by the laws of the United States including members of the diplomatic and consular service of the United States designated by Foreign Service Regulations, is empowered to supervise the execution of international wills.

Section 2. [2-1002.] [International Will; Validity.]

(a) A will shall be valid as regards form, irrespective particularly of the place where it is made, of the location of the assets and of the nationality, domicile, or residence of the testator, if it is made in the form of an international will complying with the requirements of this Act. [Part.]

(b) The invalidity of the will as an international will shall not affect its formal validity as a will of another kind.
(c) This Act [Part] shall not apply to the form of testamentary dispositions made by two or more persons in one instrument.

Section 3. [2-1003.] [International Will; Requirements.]
(a) The will shall be made in writing. It need not be written by the testator himself. It may be written in any language, by hand or by any other means.
(b) The testator shall declare in the presence of two witnesses and of a person authorized to act in connection with international wills that the document is his will and that he knows the contents thereof. The testator need not inform the witnesses, or the authorized person, of the contents of the will.
(c) In the presence of the witnesses, and of the authorized person, the testator shall sign the will or, if he has previously signed it, shall acknowledge his signature.
(d) When the testator is unable to sign, the absence of his signature does not affect the validity of the international will if the testator indicates the reason for his inability to sign and the authorized person makes note thereof on the will. In these cases, it is permissible for any other person present, including the authorized person or one of the witnesses, at the direction of the testator to sign the testator's name for him, if the authorized person makes note of this also on the will, but it is not required that any person sign the testator's name for him.
(e) The witnesses and the authorized person shall there and then attest the will by signing in the presence of the testator.

Section 4. [2-1004.] [International Will; Other Points of Form.]
(a) The signatures shall be placed at the end of the will. If the will consists of several sheets, each sheet will be signed by the testator or, if he is unable to sign, by the person signing on his behalf or, if there is no such person, by the authorized person. In addition, each sheet shall be numbered.
(b) The date of the will shall be the date of its signature by the authorized person. That date shall be noted at the end of the will by the authorized person.
(c) The authorized person shall ask the testator whether he wishes to make a declaration concerning the safekeeping of his will. If so and at the express request of the testator the place where he intends to have his will kept shall be mentioned in the certificate provided for in Section 5.
(d) A will executed in compliance with Section 3 shall not be invalid merely because it does not comply with this section.

Section 5. [2-1005.] [International Will; Certificate.]
The authorized person shall attach to the will a certificate to be signed by him establishing that the requirements of this Act [Part] for valid execution of an international will have been complied with. The authorized person shall keep a copy of the certificate and deliver another to the testator. The certificate shall be substantially in the following form:

CERTIFICATE
(Convention of October 26, 1973)

1. I, ________________ (name, address and capacity), a person authorized to act in connection with international wills
2. Certify that on __________ (date) at __________ (place)
3. (testator ______________________________
(name, address, date and place of birth) in my presence and that of the witnesses
4. (a) __________ (name, address, date and place of birth)
(b) __________ (name, address, date and place of birth)
has declared that the attached document is his will and that he knows the contents thereof.
5. I furthermore certify that:

6. (a) in my presence and in that of the witnesses
   (1) the testator has signed the will or has acknowledged his signature previously affixed.
   * following a declaration of the testator stating that he
   (2) was unable to sign his will for the following reason ______________,
   I have mentioned this declaration on the will
   * and the signature has been affixed by ______________ (name and address)
7. (b) the witnesses and I have signed the will;
8. *(c) each page of the will has been signed by __________ and numbered;
9. (d) I have satisfied myself as to the identity of the testator and of the witnesses as designated above;
10. (e) the witnesses met the conditions requisite to act as such according to the law under which I am acting;
11. *(f) the testator has requested me to include the following statement concerning the safekeeping of his will:
12. PLACE OF EXECUTION
13. DATE
14. SIGNATURE and, if necessary, SEAL

* to be completed if appropriate

Section 6. [2-1006.] [International Will; Effect of Certificate.]
In the absence of evidence to the contrary, the certificate of the authorized person shall be conclusive of the formal validity of the instrument as a will under this Act. [Part.] The absence or irregularity of a certificate shall not affect the formal validity of a will under this Act. [Part.]

Section 7. [2-1007.] [International Will; Revocation.]
The international will shall be subject to the ordinary rules of revocation of wills.

Section 8. [2-1008.] [Source and Construction.]
Sections 1 [2-1001] through 7 [2-1007] derive from Annex to Convention of October 26, 1973, Providing a Uniform Law on the Form of an International Will. In interpreting and applying this Act [Part], regard shall be had to its international origin and to the need for uniformity in its interpretation.

Section 9. [2-1009.] [Persons Authorized to Act in Relation to International Will; Eligibility; Recognition by Authorizing Agency.]
Individuals who have been admitted to practice law before the courts of this state and who are in good standing as active law practitioners in this state, are hereby declared to be authorized persons in relation to international wills.

[Section 10. [2-1010.] [International Will Information Registration.]
The [Secretary of State] shall establish a registry system by which authorized persons may register in a central information center, information regarding the execution of international wills, keeping that information in strictest confidence until the death of the maker and then making it available to any person desiring information about any will who presents a death certificate or other satisfactory evidence of the testator's death to the center. Information that may be received, preserved in confidence until death, and reported as indicated is limited to the name, social-security or any other individual-identifying number established by law, address, and date and place of birth of the testator, and the intended place of deposit or safekeeping of the instrument pending the death of the maker. The [Secretary of State], at the request of the authorized person, may cause the information it receives about execution of any international will to be transmitted to the registry system of another jurisdiction as identified by the testator, if that other system adheres to rules protecting the confidentiality of the information similar to those established in this state.]

ARTICLE III. PROBATE OF WILLS AND ADMINISTRATION

PART 1. GENERAL PROVISIONS

3-101. [Devolution of Estate at Death; Restrictions.]
[3-101A. [Devolution of Estate at Death; Restrictions.]]
3-102. [Necessity of Order of Probate For Will.]
3-103. [Necessity of Appointment For Administration.]
3-104. [Claims Against Decedent; Necessity of Administration.]
3-105. [Proceedings Affecting Devolution and Administration; Jurisdiction of Subject Matter.]
3-106. [Proceedings Within the Exclusive Jurisdiction of Court; Service; Jurisdiction Over Persons.]
3-107. [Scope of Proceedings; Proceedings Independent; Exception.]
3-108. [Probate, Testacy and Appointment Proceedings; Ultimate Time Limit.]
3-109. [Statutes of Limitation on Decedent's Cause of Action.]

PART 2. VENUE FOR PROBATE AND ADMINISTRATION; PRIORITY TO ADMINISTER; DEMAND FOR NOTICE

3-201. [Venue for First and Subsequent Estate Proceedings; Location of Property.]
3-202. [Appointment or Testacy Proceedings; Conflicting Claim of Domicile in Another State.]
3-203. [Priority Among Persons Seeking Appointment as Personal Representative.]
3-204. [Demand for Notice of Order or Filing Concerning Decedent's Estate.]

PART 3. INFORMAL PROBATE AND APPOINTMENT PROCEEDINGS; SUCCESSION WITHOUT ADMINISTRATION

3-301. [Informal Probate or Appointment Proceedings; Application; Contents.]
3-302. [Informal Probate; Duty of Registrar; Effect of Informal Probate.]
3-303. [Informal Probate; Proof and Findings Required.]
3-304. [Informal Probate; Unavailable in Certain Cases.]
3-305. [Informal Probate; Registrar Not Satisfied.]
3-306. [Informal Probate; Notice Requirements.]
3-307. [Informal Appointment Proceedings; Delay in Order; Duty of Registrar; Effect of Appointment.]
3-308. [Informal Appointment Proceedings; Proof and Findings Required.]
3-309. [Informal Appointment Proceedings; Registrar Not Satisfied.]
3-310. [Informal Appointment Proceedings; Notice Requirements.]
3-311. [Informal Appointment Unavailable in Certain Cases.]

SUCCESSION WITHOUT ADMINISTRATION

3-312. [Universal Succession; In General.]
3-313. [Universal Succession; Application; Contents.]
3-314. [Universal Succession; Proof and Findings Required.]
3-315. [Universal Succession; Duty of Registrar; Effect of Statement of Universal Succession.]
3-316. [Universal Succession; Universal Successors' Powers.]
3-317. [Universal Succession; Universal Successors' Liability to Creditors, Other Heirs, Devisees and Persons Entitled to Decedent's Property; Liability of Other Persons Entitled to Property.]
3-318. [Universal Succession; Universal Successors' Submission to Jurisdiction; When Heirs or Devisees May Not Seek Administration.]
3-319. [Universal Succession; Duty of Universal Successors; Information to Heirs and Devisees.]
3-320. [Universal Succession; Universal Successors' Liability For Restitution to Estate.]
3-321. [Universal Succession; Liability of Universal Successors for Claims, Expenses, Intestate Shares and Devises.]

3-322. [Universal Succession; Remedies of Creditors, Other Heirs, Devisees or Persons Entitled to Decedent's Property.]

PART 4. FORMAL TESTACY AND APPOINTMENT PROCEEDINGS

3-401. [Formal Testacy Proceedings; Nature; When Commenced.]
3-402. [Formal Testacy or Appointment Proceedings; Petition; Contents.]
3-403. [Formal Testacy Proceedings; Notice of Hearing on Petition.]
3-404. [Formal Testacy Proceedings; Written Objections to Probate.]
3-405. [Formal Testacy Proceedings; Uncontested Cases; Hearings and Proof.]
3-406. [Formal Testacy Proceedings; Contested Cases; Testimony of Attesting Witnesses.]
3-407. [Formal Testacy Proceedings; Burdens in Contested Cases.]
3-408. [Formal Testacy Proceedings; Will Construction; Effect of Final Order in Another Jurisdiction.]
3-409. [Formal Testacy Proceedings; Order; Foreign Will.]
3-410. [Formal Testacy Proceedings; Probate of More Than One Instrument.]
3-411. [Formal Testacy Proceedings; Partial Intestacy.]
3-412. [Formal Testacy Proceedings; Effect of Order; Vacation.]
3-413. [Formal Testacy Proceedings; Vacation of Order For Other Cause.]
3-414. [Formal Proceedings Concerning Appointment of Personal Representative.]

PART 5. SUPERVISED ADMINISTRATION

3-501. [Supervised Administration; Nature of Proceeding.]
3-502. [Supervised Administration; Petition; Order.]
3-503. [Supervised Administration; Effect on Other Proceedings.]
3-504. [Supervised Administration; Powers of Personal Representative.]
3-505. [Supervised Administration; Interim Orders; Distribution and Closing Orders.]

PART 6. PERSONAL REPRESENTATIVE; APPOINTMENT, CONTROL AND TERMINATION OF AUTHORITY

3-601. [Qualification.]
3-602. [Acceptance of Appointment; Consent to Jurisdiction.]
3-603. [Bond Not Required Without Court Order, Exceptions.]
3-604. [Bond Amount; Security; Procedure; Reduction.]
3-605. [Demand For Bond by Interested Person.]
3-606. [Terms and Conditions of Bonds.]
3-607. [Order Restraining Personal Representative.]
3-608. [Termination of Appointment; General.]
3-609. [Termination of Appointment; Death or Disability.]
3-610. [Termination of Appointment; Voluntary.]
3-611. [Termination of Appointment by Removal; Cause; Procedure.]
3-612. [Termination of Appointment; Change of Testacy Status.]
3-613. [Successor Personal Representative.]
3-614. [Special Administrator; Appointment.]
3-615. [Special Administrator; Who May Be Appointed.]
3-616. [Special Administrator; Appointed Informally; Powers and Duties.]
3-617. [Special Administrator; Formal Proceedings; Power and Duties.]
3-618. [Termination of Appointment; Special Administrator.]

PART 7. DUTIES AND POWERS OF PERSONAL REPRESENTATIVES

3-701. [Time of Accrual of Duties and Powers.]
3-702. [Priority Among Different Letters.]
3-703. [General Duties; Relation and Liability to Persons Interested in Estate; Standing to Sue.]
3-704. [Personal Representative to Proceed Without Court Order; Exception.]
3-705. [Duty of Personal Representative; Information to Heirs and Devisees.]
3-706. [Duty of Personal Representative; Inventory and Appraisement.]
3-707. [Employment of Appraisers.]

3-708. [Duty of Personal Representative; Supplementary Inventory.]
3-709. [Duty of Personal Representative; Possession of Estate.]
3-710. [Power to Avoid Transfers.]
3-711. [Powers of Personal Representatives; In General.]
3-712. [Improper Exercise of Power; Breach of Fiduciary Duty.]
3-713. [Sale, Encumbrance or Transaction Involving Conflict of Interest; Voidable; Exceptions.]
3-714. [Persons Dealing with Personal Representative; Protection.]
3-715. [Transactions Authorized for Personal Representatives; Exceptions.]
3-716. [Powers and Duties of Successor Personal Representative.]
3-717. [Co-representatives; When Joint Action Required.]
3-718. [Powers of Surviving Personal Representative.]
3-719. [Compensation of Personal Representative.]
3-720. [Expenses in Estate Litigation.]
3-721. [Proceedings for Review of Employment of Agents and Compensation of Personal Representatives and Employees of Estate.]

PART 8. CREDITORS' CLAIMS

3-801. [Notice to Creditors.]
3-802. [Statutes of Limitations.]
3-803. [Limitations on Presentation of Claims.]
3-804. [Manner of Presentation of Claims.]
3-805. [Classification of Claims.]
3-806. [Allowance of Claims.]
3-807. [Payment of Claims.]
3-808. [Individual Liability of Personal Representative.]
3-809. [Secured Claims.]
3-810. [Claims Not Due and Contingent or Unliquidated Claims.]
3-811. [Counterclaims.]
3-812. [Execution and Levies Prohibited.]
3-813. [Compromise of Claims.]
3-814. [Encumbered Assets.]
3-815. [Administration in More Than One State; Duty of Personal Representative.]
3-816. [Final Distribution to Domiciliary Representative.]

PART 9. SPECIAL PROVISIONS RELATING TO DISTRIBUTION

3-901. [Successors' Rights if No Administration.]
3-902. [Distribution; Order in Which Assets Appropriated; Abatement.]
[3-902A. [Distribution; Order in Which Assets Appropriated; Abatement.]]
3-903. [Right of Retainer.]
3-904. [Interest on General Pecuniary Devise.]
3-905. [Penalty Clause for Contest.]
3-906. [Distribution in Kind; Valuation; Method.]
3-907. [Distribution in Kind; Evidence.]
3-908. [Distribution; Right or Title of Distributee.]
3-909. [Improper Distribution; Liability of Distributee.]
3-910. [Purchasers from Distributees Protected.]
3-911. [Partition for Purpose of Distribution.]
3-912. [Private Agreements Among Successors to Decedent Binding on Personal Representative.]
3-913. [Distributions to Trustee.]
3-914. [Disposition of Unclaimed Assets.]
3-915. [Distribution to Person Under Disability.]
3-916. [Apportionment of Estate Taxes.]

PART 10. CLOSING ESTATES

3-1001. [Formal Proceedings Terminating Administration; Testate or Intestate; Order of General Protection.]

3-1002. [Formal Proceedings Terminating Testate Administration; Order Construing Will Without Adjudicating Testacy.]
3-1003. [Closing Estates; By Sworn Statement of Personal Representative.]
3-1004. [Liability of Distributees to Claimants.]
3-1005. [Limitations on Proceedings Against Personal Representative.]
3-1006. [Limitations on Actions and Proceedings Against Distributees.]
3-1007. [Certificate Discharging Liens Securing Fiduciary Performance.]
3-1008. [Subsequent Administration.]

PART 11. COMPROMISE OF CONTROVERSIES
3-1101. [Effect of Approval of Agreements Involving Trusts, Inalienable Interests, or Interests of Third Persons.]
3-1102. [Procedure for Securing Court Approval of Compromise.]

PART 12. COLLECTION OF PERSONAL PROPERTY BY AFFIDAVIT AND SUMMARY ADMINISTRATION PROCEDURE FOR SMALL ESTATES
3-1201. [Collection of Personal Property by Affidavit.]
3-1202. [Effect of Affidavit.]
3-1203. [Small Estates; Summary Administration Procedure.]
3-1204. [Small Estates; Closing by Sworn Statement of Personal Representative.]

PART 1. GENERAL PROVISIONS

Section 3-101. [Devolution of Estate at Death; Restrictions.]
The power of a person to leave property by will, and the rights of creditors, devisees, and heirs to his property are subject to the restrictions and limitations contained in this Code to facilitate the prompt settlement of estates. Upon the death of a person, his real and personal property devolves to the persons to whom it is devised by his last will or to those indicated as substitutes for them in cases involving lapse, renunciation, or other circumstances affecting the devolution of testate estate, or in the absence of testamentary disposition, to his heirs, or to those indicated as substitutes for them in cases involving renunciation or other circumstances affecting devolution of intestate estates, subject to homestead allowance, exempt property and family allowance, to rights of creditors, elective share of the surviving spouse, and to administration.

ALTERNATIVE SECTION FOR COMMUNITY PROPERTY STATES

[Section 3-101A. [Devolution of Estate at Death; Restrictions.]
The power of a person to leave property by will, and the rights of creditors, devisees, and heirs to his property are subject to the restrictions and limitations contained in this Code to facilitate the prompt settlement of estates. Upon the death of a person, his separate property devolves to the persons to whom it is devised by his last will, or to those indicated as substitutes for them in cases involving lapse, renunciation or other circumstances affecting the devolution of testate estates, or in the absence of testamentary disposition to his heirs, or to those indicated as substitutes for them in cases involving renunciation or other circumstances affecting the devolution of intestate estates, and upon the death of a husband or wife, the decedent's share of their community property devolves to the persons to whom it is devised by his last will, or in the absence of testamentary disposition, to his heirs, but all of their community property which is under the management and control of the decedent is subject to his debts and administration, and that portion of their community property which is not under the management and control of the decedent but which is necessary to carry out the provisions of his will is subject to administration; but the devolution of all the above described property is subject to rights to homestead allowance, exempt property and family allowances, to renunciation, to rights of creditors, [elective share of the surviving spouse] and to administration.]

Section 3-102. [Necessity of Order of Probate For Will.]
Except as provided in Section 3-1201, to be effective to prove the transfer of any property or to nominate an executor, a will must be declared to be valid by an order of informal probate by the Registrar, or an adjudication of probate by the Court, except that a duly executed and unrevoked will which has not been probated may be admitted as evidence of a devise if (1) no Court proceeding concerning the succession or administration of the estate has occurred, and (2) either the devisee or his successors and assigns possessed the property devised in accordance with the provisions of the will, or the property devised was not possessed or claimed by anyone by virtue of the decedent's title during the time period for testacy proceedings.

Section 3-103. [Necessity of Appointment For Administration.]
Except as otherwise provided in Article IV, to acquire the powers and undertake the duties and liabilities of a personal representative of a decedent, a person must be appointed by order of the Court or Registrar, qualify and be issued letters. Administration of an estate is commenced by the issuance of letters.

Section 3-104. [Claims Against Decedent; Necessity of Administration.]
No proceeding to enforce a claim against the estate of a decedent or his successors may be revived or commenced before the appointment of a personal representative. After the appointment and until distribution, all proceedings and actions to enforce a claim against the estate are governed by the procedure prescribed by this Article. After distribution a creditor whose claim has not been barred may recover from the distributees as provided in Section 3-1004 or from a former personal representative individually liable as provided in Section 3-1005. This section has no application to a proceeding by a secured creditor of the decedent to enforce his right to his security except as to any deficiency judgment which might be sought therein.

Section 3-105. [Proceedings Affecting Devolution and Administration; Jurisdiction of Subject Matter.]
Persons interested in decedents' estates may apply to the Registrar for determination in the informal proceedings provided in this Article, and may petition the Court for orders in formal proceedings within the Court's jurisdiction including but not limited to those described in this Article. The Court has exclusive jurisdiction of formal proceedings to determine how decedents' estates subject to the laws of this state are to be administered, expended and distributed. The Court has concurrent jurisdiction of any other action or proceeding concerning a succession or to which an estate, through a personal representative, may be a party, including actions to determine title to property alleged to belong to the estate, and of any action or proceeding in which property distributed by a personal representative or its value is sought to be subjected to rights of creditors or successors of the decedent.

Section 3-106. [Proceedings Within the Exclusive Jurisdiction of Court; Service; Jurisdiction Over Persons.]
In proceedings within the exclusive jurisdiction of the Court where notice is required by this Code or by rule, and in proceedings to construe probated wills or determine heirs which concern estates that have not been and cannot now be open for administration, interested persons may be bound by the orders of the Court in respect to property in or subject to the laws of this state by notice in conformity with Section 1-401. An order is binding as to all who are given notice of the proceeding though less than all interested persons are notified.

Section 3-107. [Scope of Proceedings; Proceedings Independent; Exception.]
Unless supervised administration as described in Part 5 is involved, (1) each proceeding before the Court or Registrar is independent of any other proceeding involving the same estate; (2) petitions for formal orders of the Court may combine various requests for relief in a single proceeding if the orders sought may be finally granted without delay. Except as required for proceedings which are particularly

described by other sections of this Article, no petition is defective because it fails to embrace all matters which might then be the subject of a final order; (3) proceedings for probate of wills or adjudications of no will may be combined with proceedings for appointment of personal representatives; and (4) a proceeding for appointment of a personal representative is concluded by an order making or declining the appointment.

Section 3-108. [Probate, Testacy and Appointment Proceedings; Ultimate Time Limit.]
No informal probate or appointment proceeding or formal testacy or appointment proceeding, other than a proceeding to probate a will previously probated at the testator's domicile and appointment proceedings relating to an estate in which there has been a prior appointment, may be commenced more than 3 years after the decedent's death, except (1) if a previous proceeding was dismissed because of doubt about the fact of the decedent's death, appropriate probate, appointment or testacy proceedings may be maintained at any time thereafter upon a finding that the decedent's death occurred prior to the initiation of the previous proceeding and the applicant or petitioner has not delayed unduly in initiating the subsequent proceeding; (2) appropriate probate, appointment or testacy proceedings may be maintained in relation to the estate of an absent, disappeared or missing person for whose estate a conservator has been appointed, at any time within three years after the conservator becomes able to establish the death of the protected person; and (3) a proceeding to contest an informally probated will and to secure appointment of the person with legal priority for appointment in the event the contest is successful, may be commenced within the later of twelve months from the informal probate or three years from the decedent's death; and (4) if no proceeding concerning the succession or administration of the estate has occurred within 3 years after decedent's death, a formal testacy proceeding may be commenced at any time thereafter for the sole purpose of establishing a devise of property which the devisee or his successors and assigns possessed in accordance with the will or property which was not possessed or claimed by anyone by virtue of the decedent's title during the 3-year period, and the order of the Court shall be limited to that property. These limitations do not apply to proceedings to construe probated wills or determine heirs of an intestate. In cases under (1) or (2) above, the date on which a testacy or appointment proceeding is properly commenced shall be deemed to be the date of the decedent's death for purposes of other limitations provisions of this Code which relate to the date of death.
As amended in 1987.

Section 3-109. [Statutes of Limitation on Decedent's Cause of Action.]
No statute of limitation running on a cause of action belonging to a decedent which had not been barred as of the date of his death, shall apply to bar a cause of action surviving the decedent's death sooner than four months after death. A cause of action which, but for this section, would have been barred less than four months after death, is barred after four months unless tolled.

PART 2. VENUE FOR PROBATE AND ADMINISTRATION; PRIORITY TO ADMINISTER; DEMAND FOR NOTICE

Section 3-201. [Venue for First and Subsequent Estate Proceedings; Location of Property.]
(a) Venue for the first informal or formal testacy or appointment proceedings after a decedent's death is:

(1) in the [county] where the decedent had his domicile at the time of his death; or
(2) if the decedent was not domiciled in this state, in any [county] where property of the decedent was located at the time of his death.

(b) Venue for all subsequent proceedings within the exclusive jurisdiction of the Court is in the place where the initial proceeding occurred, unless the initial proceeding has been transferred as provided in Section 1-303 or (c) of this section.
(c) If the first proceeding was informal, on application of an interested person and after notice to the proponent in the first proceeding, the Court, upon finding that venue is elsewhere, may transfer the proceeding and the file to the other court.
(d) For the purpose of aiding determinations concerning location of assets which may be relevant in cases involving non-domiciliaries, a debt, other than one evidenced by investment or commercial paper or other instrument in favor of a non-domiciliary is located where the debtor resides or, if the debtor is a person other than an individual, at the place where it has its principal office. Commercial paper, investment paper and other instruments are located where the instrument is. An interest in property held in trust is located where the trustee may be sued.

Section 3-202. [Appointment or Testacy Proceedings; Conflicting Claim of Domicile in Another State.]
If conflicting claims as to the domicile of a decedent are made in a formal testacy or appointment proceeding commenced in this state, and in a testacy or appointment proceeding after notice pending at the same time in another state, the Court of this state must stay, dismiss, or permit suitable amendment in, the proceeding here unless it is determined that the local proceeding was commenced before the proceeding elsewhere. The determination of domicile in the proceeding first commenced must be accepted as determinative in the proceeding in this state.

Section 3-203. [Priority Among Persons Seeking Appointment as Personal Representative.]
(a) Whether the proceedings are formal or informal, persons who are not disqualified have priority for appointment in the following order:

(1) the person with priority as determined by a probated will including a person nominated by a power conferred in a will;
(2) the surviving spouse of the decedent who is a devisee of the decedent;
(3) other devisees of the decedent;
(4) the surviving spouse of the decedent;
(5) other heirs of the decedent;
(6) 45 days after the death of the decedent, any creditor.

(b) An objection to an appointment can be made only in formal proceedings. In case of objection the priorities stated in (a) apply except that

(1) if the estate appears to be more than adequate to meet exemptions and costs of administration but inadequate to discharge anticipated unsecured claims, the Court, on petition of creditors, may appoint any qualified person;
(2) in case of objection to appointment of a person other than one whose priority is determined by will by an heir or devisee appearing to have a substantial interest in the estate, the Court may appoint a person who is acceptable to heirs and devisees whose interests in the estate appear to be worth in total more than half of the probable distributable value, or, in default of this accord any suitable person.

(c) A person entitled to letters under (2) through (5) of (a) above, and a person aged [18] and over who would be entitled to letters but for his age, may nominate a qualified person to act as personal representative. Any person aged [18] and over may renounce his right to nominate or to an appointment by appropriate writing filed with the Court. When two or more persons share a priority, those of them who do not renounce must concur in nominating another to act for them, or in applying for appointment.
(d) Conservators of the estates of protected persons, or if there is no conservator, any

guardian except a guardian ad litem of a minor or incapacitated person, may exercise the same right to nominate, to object to another's appointment, or to participate in determining the preference of a majority in interest of the heirs and devisees that the protected person or ward would have if qualified for appointment.
(e) Appointment of one who does not have priority, including priority resulting from renunciation or nomination determined pursuant to this section, may be made only in formal proceedings. Before appointing one without priority, the Court must determine that those having priority, although given notice of the proceedings, have failed to request appointment or to nominate another for appointment, and that administration is necessary.
(f) No person is qualified to serve as a personal representative who is:

(1) under the age of [21];
(2) a person whom the Court finds unsuitable in formal proceedings.

(g) A personal representative appointed by a court of the decedent's domicile has priority over all other persons except where the decedent's will nominates different persons to be personal representative in this state and in the state of domicile. The domiciliary personal representative may nominate another, who shall have the same priority as the domiciliary personal representative.
(h) This section governs priority for appointment of a successor personal representative but does not apply to the selection of a special administrator.

Section 3-204. [Demand for Notice of Order or Filing Concerning Decedent's Estate.]
Any person desiring notice of any order or filing pertaining to a decedent's estate in which he has a financial or property interest, may file a demand for notice with the Court at any time after the death of the decedent stating the name of the decedent, the nature of his interest in the estate, and the demandant's address or that of his attorney. The clerk shall mail a copy of the demand to the personal representative if one has been appointed. After filing of a demand, no order or filing to which the demand relates shall be made or accepted without notice as prescribed in Section 1-401 to the demandant or his attorney. The validity of an order which is issued or filing which is accepted without compliance with this requirement shall not be affected by the error, but the petitioner receiving the order or the person making the filing may be liable for any damage caused by the absence of notice. The requirement of notice arising from a demand under this provision may be waived in writing by the demandant and shall cease upon the termination of his interest in the estate.

PART 3. INFORMAL PROBATE AND APPOINTMENT PROCEEDINGS; SUCCESSION WITHOUT ADMINISTRATION

Section 3-301. [Informal Probate or Appointment Proceedings; Application; Contents.]
(a) Applications for informal probate or informal appointment shall be directed to the Registrar, and verified by the applicant to be accurate and complete to the best of his knowledge and belief as to the following information:

(1) Every application for informal probate of a will or for informal appointment of a personal representative, other than a special or successor representative, shall contain the following:

(i) a statement of the interest of the applicant;
(ii) the name, and date of death of the decedent, his age, and the county and state of his domicile at the time of death, and the names and addresses of the spouse, children, heirs and devisees and the ages of any who are minors so far as known or ascertainable with reasonable diligence by the applicant;

(iii) if the decedent was not domiciled in the state at the time of his death, a statement showing venue;
(iv) a statement identifying and indicating the address of any personal representative of the decedent appointed in this state or elsewhere whose appointment has not been terminated;
(v) a statement indicating whether the applicant has received a demand for notice, or is aware of any demand for notice of any probate or appointment proceeding concerning the decedent that may have been filed in this state or elsewhere; and
(vi) that the time limit for informal probate or appointment as provided in this Article has not expired either because 3 years or less have passed since the decedent's death, or, if more than 3 years from death have passed, circumstances as described by Section 3-108 authorizing tardy probate or appointment have occurred.

(2) An application for informal probate of a will shall state the following in addition to the statements required by (1):

(i) that the original of the decedent's last will is in the possession of the court, or accompanies the application, or that an authenticated copy of a will probated in another jurisdiction accompanies the application;
(ii) that the applicant, to the best of his knowledge, believes the will to have been validly executed;
(iii) that after the exercise of reasonable diligence, the applicant is unaware of any instrument revoking the will, and that the applicant believes that the instrument which is the subject of the application is the decedent's last will.

(3) An application for informal appointment of a personal representative to administer an estate under a will shall describe the will by date of execution and state the time and place of probate or the pending application or petition for probate. The application for appointment shall adopt the statements in the application or petition for probate and state the name, address and priority for appointment of the person whose appointment is sought.
(4) An application for informal appointment of an administrator in intestacy shall state in addition to the statements required by (1):

(i) that after the exercise of reasonable diligence, the applicant is unaware of any unrevoked testamentary instrument relating to property having a situs in this state under Section 1-301, or, a statement why any such instrument of which he may be aware is not being probated;
(ii) the priority of the person whose appointment is sought and the names of any other persons having a prior or equal right to the appointment under Section 3-203.

(5) An application for appointment of a personal representative to succeed a personal representative appointed under a different testacy status shall refer to the order in the most recent testacy proceeding, state the name and address of the person whose appointment is sought and of the person whose appointment will be terminated if the application is granted, and describe the priority of the applicant.
(6) An application for appointment of a personal representative to succeed a personal representative who has tendered a resignation as provided in 3-610(c), or whose appointment has been terminated by death or removal, shall adopt the statements in the application or petition which led to the appointment of the person being succeeded except as specifically changed or corrected, state the name and address of the person who seeks appointment as successor, and describe the priority of the applicant.

(b) By verifying an application for informal probate, or informal appointment, the applicant submits personally to the jurisdiction of the court in any proceeding for relief from fraud relating to the application, or for perjury, that may be instituted against him.

Section 3-302. [Informal Probate; Duty of Registrar; Effect of Informal Probate.] Upon receipt of an application requesting informal probate of a will, the Registrar, upon making the findings required by Section 3-303 shall issue a written statement of informal probate if at least 120 hours have elapsed since the decedent's death. Informal probate is conclusive as to all persons until superseded by an order in a formal testacy proceeding. No defect in the application or procedure relating thereto which leads to informal probate of a will renders the probate void.

Section 3-303. [Informal Probate; Proof and Findings Required.]
(a) In an informal proceeding for original probate of a will, the Registrar shall determine whether:

(1) the application is complete;
(2) the applicant has made oath or affirmation that the statements contained in the application are true to the best of his knowledge and belief;
(3) the applicant appears from the application to be an interested person as defined in Section 1-201(20);
(4) on the basis of the statements in the application, venue is proper;
(5) an original, duly executed and apparently unrevoked will is in the Registrar's possession;
(6) any notice required by Section 3-204 has been given and that the application is not within Section 3-304; and
(7) it appears from the application that the time limit for original probate has not expired.

(b) The application shall be denied if it indicates that a personal representative has been appointed in another [county] of this state or except as provided in subsection (d) below, if it appears that this or another will of the decedent has been the subject of a previous probate order.
(c) A will which appears to have the required signatures and which contains an attestation clause showing that requirements of execution under Section 2-502, 2-503 or 2-506 have been met shall be probated without further proof. In other cases, the Registrar may assume execution if the will appears to have been properly executed, or he may accept a sworn statement or affidavit of any person having knowledge of the circumstances of execution, whether or not the person was a witness to the will.
(d) Informal probate of a will which has been previously probated elsewhere may be granted at any time upon written application by any interested person, together with deposit of an authenticated copy of the will and of the statement probating it from the office or court where it was first probated.
(e) A will from a place which does not provide for probate of a will after death and which is not eligible for probate under subsection (a) above, may be probated in this state upon receipt by the Registrar of a duly authenticated copy of the will and a duly authenticated certificate of its legal custodian that the copy filed is a true copy and that the will has become operative under the law of the other place.

Section 3-304. [Informal Probate; Unavailable in Certain Cases.]
Applications for informal probate which relate to one or more of a known series of testamentary instruments (other than a will and one or more codicils thereto), the latest of which does not expressly revoke the earlier, shall be declined.
As amended in 1987.

Section 3-305. [Informal Probate; Registrar Not Satisfied.]
If the Registrar is not satisfied that a will is entitled to be probated in informal

proceedings because of failure to meet the requirements of Sections 3-303 and 3-304 or any other reason, he may decline the application. A declination of informal probate is not an adjudication and does not preclude formal probate proceedings.

Section 3-306. [Informal Probate; Notice Requirements.]
[*] The moving party must give notice as described by Section 1-401 of his application for informal probate to any person demanding it pursuant to Section 3-204, and to any personal representative of the decedent whose appointment has not been terminated. No other notice of informal probate is required.
[(b) If an informal probate is granted, within 30 days thereafter the applicant shall give written information of the probate to the heirs and devisees. The information shall include the name and address of the applicant, the name and location of the court granting the informal probate, and the date of the probate. The information shall be delivered or sent by ordinary mail to each of the heirs and devisees whose address is reasonably available to the applicant. No duty to give information is incurred if a personal representative is appointed who is required to give the written information required by Section 3-705. An applicant's failure to give information as required by this section is a breach of his duty to the heirs and devisees but does not affect the validity of the probate.]

Section 3-307. [Informal Appointment Proceedings; Delay in Order; Duty of Registrar; Effect of Appointment.]
(a) Upon receipt of an application for informal appointment of a personal representative other than a special administrator as provided in Section 3-614, if at least 120 hours have elapsed since the decedent's death, the Registrar, after making the findings required by Section 3-308, shall appoint the applicant subject to qualification and acceptance; provided, that if the decedent was a non-resident, the Registrar shall delay the order of appointment until 30 days have elapsed since death unless the personal representative appointed at the decedent's domicile is the applicant, or unless the decedent's will directs that his estate be subject to the laws of this state.
(b) The status of personal representative and the powers and duties pertaining to the office are fully established by informal appointment. An appointment, and the office of personal representative created thereby, is subject to termination as provided in Sections 3-608 through 3-612, but is not subject to retroactive vacation.

Section 3-308. [Informal Appointment Proceedings; Proof and Findings Required.]
(a) In informal appointment proceedings, the Registrar must determine whether:

(1) the application for informal appointment of a personal representative is complete;
(2) the applicant has made oath or affirmation that the statements contained in the application are true to the best of his knowledge and belief;
(3) the applicant appears from the application to be an interested person as defined in Section 1-201(20);
(4) on the basis of the statements in the application, venue is proper;
(5) any will to which the requested appointment relates has been formally or informally probated; but this requirement does not apply to the appointment of a special administrator;
(6) any notice required by Section 3-204 has been given;
(7) from the statements in the application, the person whose appointment is sought has priority entitling him to the appointment.

(b) Unless Section 3-612 controls, the application must be denied if it indicates that a personal representative who has not filed a written statement of resignation as provided in Section 3-610(c) has been appointed in this or another [county] of this

* This paragraph becomes (a) if optional subsection (b) is accepted.

state, that (unless the applicant is the domiciliary personal representative or his nominee) the decedent was not domiciled in this state and that a personal representative whose appointment has not been terminated has been appointed by a Court in the state of domicile, or that other requirements of this section have not been met.

Section 3-309. [Informal Appointment Proceedings; Registrar Not Satisfied.]
If the Registrar is not satisfied that a requested informal appointment of a personal representative should be made because of failure to meet the requirements of Sections 3-307 and 3-308, or for any other reason, he may decline the application. A declination of informal appointment is not an adjudication and does not preclude appointment in formal proceedings.

Section 3-310. [Informal Appointment Proceedings; Notice Requirements.]
The moving party must give notice as described by Section 1-401 of his intention to seek an appointment informally: (1) to any person demanding it pursuant to Section 3-204; and (2) to any person having a prior or equal right to appointment not waived in writing and filed with the Court. No other notice of an informal appointment proceeding is required.

Section 3-311. [Informal Appointment Unavailable in Certain Cases.]
If an application for informal appointment indicates the existence of a possible unrevoked testamentary instrument which may relate to property subject to the laws of this state, and which is not filed for probate in this court, the Registrar shall decline the application.

Section 3-312. [Universal Succession; In General.]
The heirs of an intestate or the residuary devisees under a will, excluding minors and incapacitated, protected, or unascertained persons, may become universal successors to the decedent's estate by assuming personal liability for (1) taxes, (2) debts of the decedent, (3) claims against the decedent or the estate, and (4) distributions due other heirs, devisees, and persons entitled to property of the decedent as provided in Sections 3-313 through 3-322.

Section 3-313. [Universal Succession; Application; Contents.]
(a) An application to become universal successors by the heirs of an intestate or the residuary devisees under a will must be directed to the [Registrar], signed by each applicant, and verified to be accurate and complete to the best of the applicant's knowledge and belief as follows:

(1) An application by heirs of an intestate must contain the statements required by Section 3-301(a)(1) and (4)(i) and state that the applicants constitute all the heirs other than minors and incapacitated, protected, or unascertained persons.
(2) An application by residuary devisees under a will must be combined with a petition for informal probate if the will has not been admitted to probate in this State and must contain the statements required by Section 3-301(a)(1) and (2). If the will has been probated in this State, an application by residuary devisees must contain the statements required by Section 3-301(a)(2)(iii). An application by residuary devisees must state that the applicants constitute the residuary devisees of the decedent other than any minors and incapacitated, protected, or unascertained persons. If the estate is partially intestate, all of the heirs other than minors and incapacitated, protected, or unascertained persons must join as applicants.

(b) The application must state whether letters of administration are outstanding, whether a petition for appointment of a personal representative of the decedent is pending in any court of this State, and that the applicants waive their right to seek appointment of a personal representative.

(c) The application may describe in general terms the assets of the estate and must state that the applicants accept responsibility for the estate and assume personal liability for (1) taxes, (2) debts of the decedent, (3) claims against the decedent or the estate and (4) distributions due other heirs, devisees, and persons entitled to property of the decedent as provided in Sections 3-316 through 3-322.

Section 3-314. [Universal Succession; Proof and Findings Required.]
(a) The [Registrar] shall grant the application if:

(1) the application is complete in accordance with Section 3-313;
(2) all necessary persons have joined and have verified that the statements contained therein are true, to the best knowledge and belief of each;
(3) venue is proper;
(4) any notice required by Section 3-204 has been given or waived;
(5) the time limit for original probate or appointment proceedings has not expired and the applicants claim under a will;
(6) the application requests informal probate of a will, the application and findings conform with Sections 3-301(a)(2) and 3-303(a)(c)(d) and (e) so the will is admitted to probate; and
(7) none of the applicants is a minor or an incapacitated or protected person.

(b) The [Registrar] shall deny the application if letters of administration are outstanding.
(c) Except as provided in Section 3-322, the [Registrar] shall deny the application if any creditor, heir, or devisee who is qualified by Section 3-605 to demand bond files an objection.

Section 3-315. [Universal Succession; Duty of Registrar; Effect of Statement of Universal Succession.]
Upon receipt of an application under Section 3-313, if at least 120 hours have elapsed since the decedent's death, the [Registrar], upon granting the application, shall issue a written statement of universal succession describing the estate as set forth in the application and stating that the applicants (i) are the universal successors to the assets of the estate as provided in Section 3-312, (ii) have assumed liability for the obligations of the decedent, and (iii) have acquired the powers and liabilities of universal successors. The statement of universal succession is evidence of the universal successors' title to the assets of the estate. Upon its issuance, the powers and liabilities of universal successors provided in Sections 3-316 through 3-322 attach and are assumed by the applicants.

Section 3-316. [Universal Succession; Universal Successors' Powers.]
Upon the [Registrar's] issuance of a statement of universal succession:

(1) Universal successors have full power of ownership to deal with the assets of the estate subject to the limitations and liabilities in this [Act]. The universal successors shall proceed expeditiously to settle and distribute the estate without adjudication but if necessary may invoke the jurisdiction of the court to resolve questions concerning the estate.
(2) Universal successors have the same powers as distributees from a personal representative under Sections 3-908 and 3-909 and third persons with whom they deal are protected as provided in Section 3-910.
(3) For purposes of collecting assets in another state whose law does not provide for universal succession, universal successors have the same standing and power as personal representatives or distributees in this State.

Section 3-317. [Universal Succession; Universal Successors' Liability to Creditors, Other Heirs, Devisees and Persons Entitled to Decedent's Property; Liability of Other Persons Entitled to Property.]

(a) In the proportions and subject to limits expressed in Section 3-321, universal successors assume all liabilities of the decedent that were not discharged by reason of death and liability for all taxes, claims against the decedent or the estate, and charges properly incurred after death for the preservation of the estate, to the extent those items, if duly presented, would be valid claims against the decedent's estate.

(b) In the proportions and subject to the limits expressed in Section 3-321, universal successors are personally liable to other heirs, devisees, and persons entitled to property of the decedent for the assets or amounts that would be due those heirs, were the estate administered, but no allowance having priority over devisees may be claimed for attorney's fees or charges for preservation of the estate in excess of reasonable amounts properly incurred.

(c) Universal successors are entitled to their interests in the estate as heirs or devisees subject to priority and abatement pursuant to Section 3-902 and to agreement pursuant to Section 3-912.

(d) Other heirs, devisees, and persons to whom assets have been distributed have the same powers and liabilities as distributees under Sections 3-908, 3-909, and 3-910.

(e) Absent breach of fiduciary obligations or express undertaking, a fiduciary's liability is limited to the assets received by the fiduciary.

Section 3-318. [Universal Succession; Universal Successors' Submission to Jurisdiction; When Heirs or Devisees May Not Seek Administration.]

(a) Upon issuance of the statement of universal succession, the universal successors become subject to the personal jurisdiction of the courts of this state in any proceeding that may be instituted relating to the estate or to any liability assumed by them.

(b) Any heir or devisee who voluntarily joins in an application under Section 3-313 may not subsequently seek appointment of a personal representative.

Section 3-319. [Universal Succession; Duty of Universal Successors; Information to Heirs and Devisees.]

Not later than thirty days after issuance of the statement of universal succession, each universal successor shall inform the heirs and devisees who did not join in the application of the succession without administration. The information must be delivered or be sent by ordinary mail to each of the heirs and devisees whose address is reasonably available to the universal successors. The information must include the names and addresses of the universal successors, indicate that it is being sent to persons who have or may have some interest in the estate, and describe the court where the application and statement of universal succession has been filed. The failure of a universal successor to give this information is a breach of duty to the persons concerned but does not affect the validity of the approval of succession without administration or the powers or liabilities of the universal successors. A universal successor may inform other persons of the succession without administration by delivery or by ordinary first class mail.

Section 3-320. [Universal Succession; Universal Successors' Liability For Restitution to Estate.]

If a personal representative is subsequently appointed, universal successors are personally liable for restitution of any property of the estate to which they are not entitled as heirs or devisees of the decedent and their liability is the same as a distributee under Section 3-909, subject to the provisions of Sections 3-317 and 3-321 and the limitations of Section 3-1006.

Section 3-321. [Universal Succession; Liability of Universal Successors for Claims, Expenses, Intestate Shares and Devises.]

The liability of universal successors is subject to any defenses that would have been available to the decedent. Other than liability arising from fraud, conversion, or other wrongful conduct of a universal successor, the personal liability of each universal successor to any creditor, claimant, other heir, devisee, or person entitled to decedent's property may not exceed the proportion of the claim that the universal successor's share bears to the share of all heirs and residuary devisees.

Section 3-322. [Universal Succession; Remedies of Creditors, Other Heirs, Devisees or Persons Entitled to Decedent's Property.]
In addition to remedies otherwise provided by law, any creditor, heir, devisee, or person entitled to decedent's property qualified under Section 3-605, may demand bond of universal successors. If the demand for bond precedes the granting of an application for universal succession, it must be treated as an objection under Section 3-314(c) unless it is withdrawn, the claim satisfied, or the applicants post bond in an amount sufficient to protect the demandant. If the demand for bond follows the granting of an application for universal succession, the universal successors, within 10 days after notice of the demand, upon satisfying the claim or posting bond sufficient to protect the demandant, may disqualify the demandant from seeking administration of the estate.

PART 4. FORMAL TESTACY AND APPOINTMENT PROCEEDINGS

Section 3-401. [Formal Testacy Proceedings; Nature; When Commenced.]
A formal testacy proceeding is litigation to determine whether a decedent left a valid will. A formal testacy proceeding may be commenced by an interested person filing a petition as described in Section 3-402(a) in which he requests that the Court, after notice and hearing, enter an order probating a will, or a petition to set aside an informal probate of a will or to prevent informal probate of a will which is the subject of a pending application, or a petition in accordance with Section 3-402(b) for an order that the decedent died intestate.
A petition may seek formal probate of a will without regard to whether the same or a conflicting will has been informally probated. A formal testacy proceeding may, but need not, involve a request for appointment of a personal representative.
During the pendency of a formal testacy proceeding, the Registrar shall not act upon any application for informal probate of any will of the decedent or any application for informal appointment of a personal representative of the decedent. Unless a petition in a formal testacy proceeding also requests confirmation of the previous informal appointment, a previously appointed personal representative, after receipt of notice of the commencement of a formal probate proceeding, must refrain from exercising his power to make any further distribution of the estate during the pendency of the formal proceeding. A petitioner who seeks the appointment of a different personal representative in a formal proceeding also may request an order restraining the acting personal representative from exercising any of the powers of his office and requesting the appointment of a special administrator. In the absence of a request, or if the request is denied, the commencement of a formal proceeding has no effect on the powers and duties of a previously appointed personal representative other than those relating to distribution.

Section 3-402. [Formal Testacy or Appointment Proceedings; Petition; Contents.]
(a) Petitions for formal probate of a will, or for adjudication of intestacy with or without request for appointment of a personal representative, must be directed to the Court, request a judicial order after notice and hearing and contain further statements as indicated in this section. A petition for formal probate of a will

(1) requests an order as to the testacy of the decedent in relation to a particular instrument which may or may not have been informally probated and determining the heirs,

(2) contains the statements required for informal applications as stated in the six subparagraphs under Section 3-301(a)(1), the statements required by subparagraphs (ii) and (iii) of Section 3-301(a)(2), and
(3) states whether the original of the last will of the decedent is in the possession of the Court or accompanies the petition.

If the original will is neither in the possession of the Court nor accompanies the petition and no authenticated copy of a will probated in another jurisdiction accompanies the petition, the petition also must state the contents of the will, and indicate that it is lost, destroyed, or otherwise unavailable.
(b) A petition for adjudication of intestacy and appointment of an administrator in intestacy must request a judicial finding and order that the decedent left no will and determining the heirs, contain the statements required by (1) and (4) of Section 3-301(a) and indicate whether supervised administration is sought. A petition may request an order determining intestacy and heirs without requesting the appointment of an administrator, in which case, the statements required by subparagraph (ii) of Section 3-301(a)(4) above may be omitted.

Section 3-403. [Formal Testacy Proceedings; Notice of Hearing on Petition.]
(a) Upon commencement of a formal testacy proceeding, the Court shall fix a time and place of hearing. Notice shall be given in the manner prescribed by Section 1-401 by the petitioner to the persons herein enumerated and to any additional person who has filed a demand for notice under Section 3-204 of this Code.
Notice shall be given to the following persons: the surviving spouse, children, and other heirs of the decedent, the devisees and executors named in any will that is being, or has been, probated, or offered for informal or formal probate in the [county,] or that is known by the petitioner to have been probated, or offered for informal or formal probate elsewhere, and any personal representative of the decedent whose appointment has not been terminated. Notice may be given to other persons. In addition, the petitioner shall give notice by publication to all unknown persons and to all known persons whose addresses are unknown who have any interest in the matters being litigated.
(b) If it appears by the petition or otherwise that the fact of the death of the alleged decedent may be in doubt, or on the written demand of any interested person, a copy of the notice of the hearing on said petition shall be sent by registered mail to the alleged decedent at his last known address. The Court shall direct the petitioner to report the results of, or make and report back concerning, a reasonably diligent search for the alleged decedent in any manner that may seem advisable, including any or all of the following methods:

(1) by inserting in one or more suitable periodicals a notice requesting information from any person having knowledge of the whereabouts of the alleged decedent;
(2) by notifying law enforcement officials and public welfare agencies in appropriate locations of the disappearance of the alleged decedent;
(3) by engaging the services of an investigator.

The costs of any search so directed shall be paid by the petitioner if there is no administration or by the estate of the decedent in case there is administration.

Section 3-404. [Formal Testacy Proceedings; Written Objections to Probate.]
Any party to a formal proceeding who opposes the probate of a will for any reason shall state in his pleadings his objections to probate of the will.

Section 3-405. [Formal Testacy Proceedings; Uncontested Cases; Hearings and Proof.]
If a petition in a testacy proceeding is unopposed, the Court may order probate or intestacy on the strength of the pleadings if satisfied that the conditions of Section

3-409 have been met, or conduct a hearing in open court and require proof of the matters necessary to support the order sought. If evidence concerning execution of the will is necessary, the affidavit or testimony of one of any attesting witnesses to the instrument is sufficient. If the affidavit or testimony of an attesting witness is not available, execution of the will may be proved by other evidence or affidavit.

Section 3-406. [Formal Testacy Proceedings; Contested Cases; Testimony of Attesting Witnesses.]

(a) If evidence concerning execution of an attested will which is not self-proved is necessary in contested cases, the testimony of at least one of the attesting witnesses, if within the state, competent and able to testify, is required. Due execution of an attested or unattested will may be proved by other evidence.

(b) If the will is self-proved, compliance with signature requirements for execution is conclusively presumed and other requirements of execution are presumed subject to rebuttal without the testimony of any witness upon filing the will and the acknowledgment and affidavits annexed or attached thereto, unless there is proof of fraud or forgery affecting the acknowledgment or affidavit.

Section 3-407. [Formal Testacy Proceedings; Burdens in Contested Cases.]

In contested cases, petitioners who seek to establish intestacy have the burden of establishing prima facie proof of death, venue, and heirship. Proponents of a will have the burden of establishing prima facie proof of due execution in all cases, and, if they are also petitioners, prima facie proof of death and venue. Contestants of a will have the burden of establishing lack of testamentary intent or capacity, undue influence, fraud, duress, mistake or revocation. Parties have the ultimate burden of persuasion as to matters with respect to which they have the initial burden of proof. If a will is opposed by the petition for probate of a later will revoking the former, it shall be determined first whether the later will is entitled to probate, and if a will is opposed by a petition for a declaration of intestacy, it shall be determined first whether the will is entitled to probate.

Section 3-408. [Formal Testacy Proceedings; Will Construction; Effect of Final Order in Another Jurisdiction.]

A final order of a court of another state determining testacy, the validity or construction of a will, made in a proceeding involving notice to and an opportunity for contest by all interested persons must be accepted as determinative by the courts of this state if it includes, or is based upon, a finding that the decedent was domiciled at his death in the state where the order was made.

Section 3-409. [Formal Testacy Proceedings; Order; Foreign Will.]

After the time required for any notice has expired, upon proof of notice, and after any hearing that may be necessary, if the Court finds that the testator is dead, venue is proper and that the proceeding was commenced within the limitation prescribed by Section 3-108, it shall determine the decedent's domicile at death, his heirs and his state of testacy. Any will found to be valid and unrevoked shall be formally probated. Termination of any previous informal appointment of a personal representative, which may be appropriate in view of the relief requested and findings, is governed by Section 3-612. The petition shall be dismissed or appropriate amendment allowed if the court is not satisfied that the alleged decedent is dead. A will from a place which does not provide for probate of a will after death, may be proved for probate in this state by a duly authenticated certificate of its legal custodian that the copy introduced is a true copy and that the will has become effective under the law of the other place.

Section 3-410. [Formal Testacy Proceedings; Probate of More Than One Instrument.]

If two or more instruments are offered for probate before a final order is entered in a formal testacy proceeding, more than one instrument may be probated if neither expressly revokes the other or contains provisions which work a total revocation by implication. If more than one instrument is probated, the order shall indicate what provisions control in respect to the nomination of an executor, if any. The order may, but need not, indicate how any provisions of a particular instrument are affected by the other instrument. After a final order in a testacy proceeding has been entered, no petition for probate of any other instrument of the decedent may be entertained, except incident to a petition to vacate or modify a previous probate order and subject to the time limits of Section 3-412.

Section 3-411. [Formal Testacy Proceedings; Partial Intestacy.]
If it becomes evident in the course of a formal testacy proceeding that, though one or more instruments are entitled to be probated, the decedent's estate is or may be partially intestate, the Court shall enter an order to that effect.

Section 3-412. [Formal Testacy Proceedings; Effect of Order; Vacation.]
Subject to appeal and subject to vacation as provided herein and in Section 3-413, a formal testacy order under Sections 3-409 to 3-411, including an order that the decedent left no valid will and determining heirs, is final as to all persons with respect to all issues concerning the decedent's estate that the court considered or might have considered incident to its rendition relevant to the question of whether the decedent left a valid will, and to the determination of heirs, except that:

(1) The court shall entertain a petition for modification or vacation of its order and probate of another will of the decedent if it is shown that the proponents of the later-offered will were unaware of its existence at the time of the earlier proceeding or were unaware of the earlier proceeding and were given no notice thereof, except by publication.
(2) If intestacy of all or part of the estate has been ordered, the determination of heirs of the decedent may be reconsidered if it is shown that one or more persons were omitted from the determination and it is also shown that the persons were unaware of their relationship to the decedent, were unaware of his death or were given no notice of any proceeding concerning his estate, except by publication.
(3) A petition for vacation under either (1) or (2) above must be filed prior to the earlier of the following time limits:

(i) If a personal representative has been appointed for the estate, the time of entry of any order approving final distribution of the estate, or, if the estate is closed by statement, 6 months after the filing of the closing statement.
(ii) Whether or not a personal representative has been appointed for the estate of the decedent, the time prescribed by Section 3-108 when it is no longer possible to initiate an original proceeding to probate a will of the decedent.
(iii) 12 months after the entry of the order sought to be vacated.

(4) The order originally rendered in the testacy proceeding may be modified or vacated, if appropriate under the circumstances, by the order of probate of the later-offered will or the order redetermining heirs.
(5) The finding of the fact of death is conclusive as to the alleged decedent only if notice of the hearing on the petition in the formal testacy proceeding was sent by registered or certified mail addressed to the alleged decedent at his last known address and the court finds that a search under Section 3-403(b) was made.

If the alleged decedent is not dead, even if notice was sent and search was made, he may recover estate assets in the hands of the personal representative. In addition to any remedies available to the alleged decedent by reason of any fraud or intentional wrongdoing, the alleged decedent may recover any estate or its proceeds from distributees that is in their hands, or the value of distributions received by them, to the extent that any recovery from distributees is equitable in view of all of the circumstances.

Section 3-413. [Formal Testacy Proceedings; Vacation of Order For Other Cause.]
For good cause shown, an order in a formal testacy proceeding may be modified or vacated within the time allowed for appeal.

Section 3-414. [Formal Proceedings Concerning Appointment of Personal Representative.]
(a) A formal proceeding for adjudication regarding the priority or qualification of one who is an applicant for appointment as personal representative, or of one who previously has been appointed personal representative in informal proceedings, if an issue concerning the testacy of the decedent is or may be involved, is governed by Section 3-402, as well as by this section. In other cases, the petition shall contain or adopt the statements required by Section 3-301(1) and describe the question relating to priority or qualification of the personal representative which is to be resolved. If the proceeding precedes any appointment of a personal representative, it shall stay any pending informal appointment proceedings as well as any commenced thereafter. If the proceeding is commenced after appointment, the previously appointed personal representative, after receipt of notice thereof, shall refrain from exercising any power of administration except as necessary to preserve the estate or unless the Court orders otherwise.
(b) After notice to interested persons, including all persons interested in the administration of the estate as successors under the applicable assumption concerning testacy, any previously appointed personal representative and any person having or claiming priority for appointment as personal representative, the Court shall determine who is entitled to appointment under Section 3-203, make a proper appointment and, if appropriate, terminate any prior appointment found to have been improper as provided in cases of removal under Section 3-611.

PART 5. SUPERVISED ADMINISTRATION

Section 3-501. [Supervised Administration; Nature of Proceeding.]
Supervised administration is a single in rem proceeding to secure complete administration and settlement of a decedent's estate under the continuing authority of the Court which extends until entry of an order approving distribution of the estate and discharging the personal representative or other order terminating the proceeding. A supervised personal representative is responsible to the Court, as well as to the interested parties, and is subject to directions concerning the estate made by the Court on its own motion or on the motion of any interested party. Except as otherwise provided in this Part, or as otherwise ordered by the Court, a supervised personal representative has the same duties and powers as a personal representative who is not supervised.

Section 3-502. [Supervised Administration; Petition; Order.]
A petition for supervised administration may be filed by any interested person or by a personal representative at any time or the prayer for supervised administration may be joined with a petition in a testacy or appointment proceeding. If the testacy of the decedent and the priority and qualification of any personal representative have not been adjudicated previously, the petition for supervised administration shall include the matters required of a petition in a formal testacy proceeding and the notice requirements and procedures applicable to a formal testacy proceeding apply. If not previously adjudicated, the Court shall adjudicate the testacy of the decedent and questions relating to the priority and qualifications of the personal representative in any case involving a request for supervised administration, even though the request for supervised administration may be denied. After notice to interested persons, the Court shall order supervised administration of a decedent's estate: (1) if the decedent's will directs supervised administration, it shall be

ordered unless the Court finds that circumstances bearing on the need for supervised administration have changed since the execution of the will and that there is no necessity for supervised administration; (2) if the decedent's will directs unsupervised administration, supervised administration shall be ordered only upon a finding that it is necessary for protection of persons interested in the estate; or (3) in other cases if the Court finds that supervised administration is necessary under the circumstances.

Section 3-503. [Supervised Administration; Effect on Other Proceedings.]
(a) The pendency of a proceeding for supervised administration of a decedent's estate stays action on any informal application then pending or thereafter filed.
(b) If a will has been previously probated in informal proceedings, the effect of the filing of a petition for supervised administration is as provided for formal testacy proceedings by Section 3-401.
(c) After he has received notice of the filing of a petition for supervised administration, a personal representative who has been appointed previously shall not exercise his power to distribute any estate. The filing of the petition does not affect his other powers and duties unless the Court restricts the exercise of any of them pending full hearing on the petition.

Section 3-504. [Supervised Administration; Powers of Personal Representative.]
Unless restricted by the Court, a supervised personal representative has, without interim orders approving exercise of a power, all powers of personal representatives under this Code, but he shall not exercise his power to make any distribution of the estate without prior order of the Court. Any other restriction on the power of a personal representative which may be ordered by the Court must be endorsed on his letters of appointment and, unless so endorsed, is ineffective as to persons dealing in good faith with the personal representative.

Section 3-505. [Supervised Administration; Interim Orders; Distribution and Closing Orders.]
Unless otherwise ordered by the Court, supervised administration is terminated by order in accordance with time restrictions, notices and contents of orders prescribed for proceedings under Section 3-1001. Interim orders approving or directing partial distributions or granting other relief may be issued by the Court at any time during the pendency of a supervised administration on the application of the personal representative or any interested person.

PART 6. PERSONAL REPRESENTATIVE; APPOINTMENT, CONTROL AND TERMINATION OF AUTHORITY

Section 3-601. [Qualification.]
Prior to receiving letters, a personal representative shall qualify by filing with the appointing Court any required bond and a statement of acceptance of the duties of the office.

Section 3-602. [Acceptance of Appointment; Consent to Jurisdiction.]
By accepting appointment, a personal representative submits personally to the jurisdiction of the Court in any proceeding relating to the estate that may be instituted by any interested person. Notice of any proceeding shall be delivered to the personal representative, or mailed to him by ordinary first class mail at his address as listed in the application or petition for appointment or as thereafter reported to the Court and to his address as then known to the petitioner.

Section 3-603. [Bond Not Required Without Court Order, Exceptions.]
No bond is required of a personal representative appointed in informal proceedings, except (1) upon the appointment of a special administrator; (2) when an executor or other personal representative is appointed to administer an estate under a will

containing an express requirement of bond or (3) when bond is required under Section 3-605. Bond may be required by court order at the time of appointment of a personal representative appointed in any formal proceeding except that bond is not required of a personal representative appointed in formal proceedings if the will relieves the personal representative of bond, unless bond has been requested by an interested party and the Court is satisfied that it is desirable. Bond required by any will may be dispensed with in formal proceedings upon determination by the Court that it is not necessary. No bond is required of any personal representative who, pursuant to statute, has deposited cash or collateral with an agency of this state to secure performance of his duties.

Section 3-604. [Bond Amount; Security; Procedure; Reduction.]
If bond is required and the provisions of the will or order do not specify the amount, unless stated in his application or petition, the person qualifying shall file a statement under oath with the Registrar indicating his best estimate of the value of the personal estate of the decedent and of the income expected from the personal and real estate during the next year, and he shall execute and file a bond with the Registrar, or give other suitable security, in an amount not less than the estimate. The Registrar shall determine that the bond is duly executed by a corporate surety, or one or more individual sureties whose performance is secured by pledge of personal property, mortgage on real property or other adequate security. The Registrar may permit the amount of the bond to be reduced by the value of assets of the estate deposited with a domestic financial institution (as defined in Section 6-101) in a manner that prevents their unauthorized disposition. On petition of the personal representative or another interested person the Court may excuse a requirement of bond, increase or reduce the amount of the bond, release sureties, or permit the substitution of another bond with the same or different sureties.

Section 3-605. [Demand For Bond by Interested Person.]
Any person apparently having an interest in the estate worth in excess of [$1000], or any creditor having a claim in excess of [$1000], may make a written demand that a personal representative give bond. The demand must be filed with the Registrar and a copy mailed to the personal representative, if appointment and qualification have occurred. Thereupon, bond is required, but the requirement ceases if the person demanding bond ceases to be interested in the estate, or if bond is excused as provided in Section 3-603 or 3-604. After he has received notice and until the filing of the bond or cessation of the requirement of bond, the personal representative shall refrain from exercising any powers of his office except as necessary to preserve the estate. Failure of the personal representative to meet a requirement of bond by giving suitable bond within 30 days after receipt of notice is cause for his removal and appointment of a successor personal representative.

Section 3-606. [Terms and Conditions of Bonds.]
(a) The following requirements and provisions apply to any bond required by this Part:

(1) Bonds shall name the [state] as obligee for the benefit of the persons interested in the estate and shall be conditioned upon the faithful discharge by the fiduciary of all duties according to law.
(2) Unless otherwise provided by the terms of the approved bond, sureties are jointly and severally liable with the personal representative and with each other. The address of sureties shall be stated in the bond.
(3) By executing an approved bond of a personal representative, the surety consents to the jurisdiction of the probate court which issued letters to the primary obligor in any proceedings pertaining to the fiduciary duties of the personal representative and naming the surety as a party. Notice of any proceeding shall be delivered to the surety or mailed to him by registered or

certified mail at his address as listed with the court where the bond is filed and to his address as then known to the petitioner.
(4) On petition of a successor personal representative, any other personal representative of the same decedent, or any interested person, a proceeding in the Court may be initiated against a surety for breach of the obligation of the bond of the personal representative.
(5) The bond of the personal representative is not void after the first recovery but may be proceeded against from time to time until the whole penalty is exhausted.

(b) No action or proceeding may be commenced against the surety on any matter as to which an action or proceeding against the primary obligor is barred by adjudication or limitation.

Section 3-607. [Order Restraining Personal Representative.]
(a) On petition of any person who appears to have an interest in the estate, the Court by temporary order may restrain a personal representative from performing specified acts of administration, disbursement, or distribution, or exercise of any powers or discharge of any duties of his office, or make any other order to secure proper performance of his duty, if it appears to the Court that the personal representative otherwise may take some action which would jeopardize unreasonably the interest of the applicant or of some other interested person. Persons with whom the personal representative may transact business may be made parties.
(b) The matter shall be set for hearing within 10 days unless the parties otherwise agree. Notice as the Court directs shall be given to the personal representative and his attorney of record, if any, and to any other parties named defendant in the petition.

Section 3-608. [Termination of Appointment; General.]
Termination of appointment of a personal representative occurs as indicated in Sections 3-609 to 3-612, inclusive. Termination ends the right and power pertaining to the office of personal representative as conferred by this Code or any will, except that a personal representative, at any time prior to distribution or until restrained or enjoined by court order, may perform acts necessary to protect the estate and may deliver the assets to a successor representative. Termination does not discharge a personal representative from liability for transactions or omissions occurring before termination, or relieve him of the duty to preserve assets subject to his control, to account therefor and to deliver the assets. Termination does not affect the jurisdiction of the Court over the personal representative, but terminates his authority to represent the estate in any pending or future proceeding.

Section 3-609. [Termination of Appointment; Death or Disability.]
The death of a personal representative or the appointment of a conservator for the estate of a personal representative, terminates his appointment. Until appointment and qualification of a successor or special representative to replace the deceased or protected representative, the representative of the estate of the deceased or protected personal representative, if any, has the duty to protect the estate possessed and being administered by his decedent or ward at the time his appointment terminates, has the power to perform acts necessary for protection and shall account for and deliver the estate assets to a successor or special personal representative upon his appointment and qualification.

Section 3-610. [Termination of Appointment; Voluntary.]
(a) An appointment of a personal representative terminates as provided in Section 3-1003, one year after the filing of a closing statement.
(b) An order closing an estate as provided in Section 3-1001 or 3-1002 terminates an appointment of a personal representative.
(c) A personal representative may resign his position by filing a written statement

of resignation with the Registrar after he has given at least 15 days written notice to the persons known to be interested in the estate. If no one applies or petitions for appointment of a successor representative within the time indicated in the notice, the filed statement of resignation is ineffective as a termination of appointment and in any event is effective only upon the appointment and qualification of a successor representative and delivery of the assets to him.

Section 3-611. [Termination of Appointment by Removal; Cause; Procedure.]
(a) A person interested in the estate may petition for removal of a personal representative for cause at any time. Upon filing of the petition, the Court shall fix a time and place for hearing. Notice shall be given by the petitioner to the personal representative, and to other persons as the Court may order. Except as otherwise ordered as provided in Section 3-607, after receipt of notice of removal proceedings, the personal representative shall not act except to account, to correct maladministration or preserve the estate. If removal is ordered, the Court also shall direct by order the disposition of the assets remaining in the name of, or under the control of, the personal representative being removed.
(b) Cause for removal exists when removal would be in the best interests of the estate, or if it is shown that a personal representative or the person seeking his appointment intentionally misrepresented material facts in the proceedings leading to his appointment, or that the personal representative has disregarded an order of the Court, has become incapable of discharging the duties of his office, or has mismanaged the estate or failed to perform any duty pertaining to the office. Unless the decedent's will directs otherwise, a personal representative appointed at the decedent's domicile, incident to securing appointment of himself or his nominee as ancillary personal representative, may obtain removal of another who was appointed personal representative in this state to administer local assets.

Section 3-612. [Termination of Appointment; Change of Testacy Status.]
Except as otherwise ordered in formal proceedings, the probate of a will subsequent to the appointment of a personal representative in intestacy or under a will which is superseded by formal probate of another will, or the vacation of an informal probate of a will subsequent to the appointment of the personal representative thereunder, does not terminate the appointment of the personal representative although his powers may be reduced as provided in Section 3-401. Termination occurs upon appointment in informal or formal appointment proceedings of a person entitled to appointment under the later assumption concerning testacy. If no request for new appointment is made within 30 days after expiration of time for appeal from the order in formal testacy proceedings, or from the informal probate, changing the assumption concerning testacy, the previously appointed personal representative upon request may be appointed personal representative under the subsequently probated will, or as in intestacy as the case may be.

Section 3-613. [Successor Personal Representative.]
Parts 3 and 4 of this Article govern proceedings for appointment of a personal representative to succeed one whose appointment has been terminated. After appointment and qualification, a successor personal representative may be substituted in all actions and proceedings to which the former personal representative was a party, and no notice, process or claim which was given or served upon the former personal representative need be given to or served upon the successor in order to preserve any position or right the person giving the notice or filing the claim may thereby have obtained or preserved with reference to the former personal representative. Except as otherwise ordered by the Court, the successor personal representative has the powers and duties in respect to the continued administration which the former personal representative would have had if his appointment had not been terminated.

Section 3-614. [Special Administrator; Appointment.]
A special administrator may be appointed:

(1) informally by the Registrar on the application of any interested person when necessary to protect the estate of a decedent prior to the appointment of a general personal representative or if a prior appointment has been terminated as provided in Section 3-609;
(2) in a formal proceeding by order of the Court on the petition of any interested person and finding, after notice and hearing, that appointment is necessary to preserve the estate or to secure its proper administration including its administration in circumstances where a general personal representative cannot or should not act. If it appears to the Court that an emergency exists, appointment may be ordered without notice.

Section 3-615. [Special Administrator; Who May Be Appointed.]
(a) If a special administrator is to be appointed pending the probate of a will which is the subject of a pending application or petition for probate, the person named executor in the will shall be appointed if available, and qualified.
(b) In other cases, any proper person may be appointed special administrator.

Section 3-616. [Special Administrator; Appointed Informally; Powers and Duties.]
A special administrator appointed by the Registrar in informal proceedings pursuant to Section 3-614(1) has the duty to collect and manage the assets of the estate, to preserve them, to account therefor and to deliver them to the general personal representative upon his qualification. The special administrator has the power of a personal representative under the Code necessary to perform his duties.

Section 3-617. [Special Administrator; Formal Proceedings; Power and Duties.]
A special administrator appointed by order of the Court in any formal proceeding has the power of a general personal representative except as limited in the appointment and duties as prescribed in the order. The appointment may be for a specified time, to perform particular acts or on other terms as the Court may direct.

Section 3-618. [Termination of Appointment; Special Administrator.]
The appointment of a special administrator terminates in accordance with the provisions of the order of appointment or on the appointment of a general personal representative. In other cases, the appointment of a special administrator is subject to termination as provided in Sections 3-608 through 3-611.

PART 7. DUTIES AND POWERS OF PERSONAL REPRESENTATIVES

Section 3-701. [Time of Accrual of Duties and Powers.]
The duties and powers of a personal representative commence upon his appointment. The powers of a personal representative relate back in time to give acts by the person appointed which are beneficial to the estate occurring prior to appointment the same effect as those occurring thereafter. Prior to appointment, a person named executor in a will may carry out written instructions of the decedent relating to his body, funeral and burial arrangements. A personal representative may ratify and accept acts on behalf of the estate done by others where the acts would have been proper for a personal representative.

Section 3-702. [Priority Among Different Letters.]
A person to whom general letters are issued first has exclusive authority under the letters until his appointment is terminated or modified. If, through error, general letters are afterwards issued to another, the first appointed representative may recover any property of the estate in the hands of the representative subsequently appointed, but the acts of the latter done in good faith before notice of the first letters are not void for want of validity of appointment.

Section 3-703. [General Duties; Relation and Liability to Persons Interested in Estate; Standing to Sue.]
(a) A personal representative is a fiduciary who shall observe the standards of care

applicable to trustees as described by Section 7-302. A personal representative is under a duty to settle and distribute the estate of the decedent in accordance with the terms of any probated and effective will and this Code, and as expeditiously and efficiently as is consistent with the best interests of the estate. He shall use the authority conferred upon him by this Code, the terms of the will, if any, and any order in proceedings to which he is party for the best interests of successors to the estate.

(b) A personal representative shall not be surcharged for acts of administration or distribution if the conduct in question was authorized at the time. Subject to other obligations of administration, an informally probated will is authority to administer and distribute the estate according to its terms. An order of appointment of a personal representative, whether issued in informal or formal proceedings, is authority to distribute apparently intestate assets to the heirs of the decedent if, at the time of distribution, the personal representative is not aware of a pending testacy proceeding, a proceeding to vacate an order entered in an earlier testacy proceeding, a formal proceeding questioning his appointment or fitness to continue, or a supervised administration proceeding. Nothing in this section affects the duty of the personal representative to administer and distribute the estate in accordance with the rights of claimants, the surviving spouse, any minor and dependent children and any pretermitted child of the decedent as described elsewhere in this Code.

(c) Except as to proceedings which do not survive the death of the decedent, a personal representative of a decedent domiciled in this state at his death has the same standing to sue and be sued in the courts of this state and the courts of any other jurisdiction as his decedent had immediately prior to death.

Section 3-704. [Personal Representative to Proceed Without Court Order; Exception.]

A personal representative shall proceed expeditiously with the settlement and distribution of a decedent's estate and, except as otherwise specified or ordered in regard to a supervised personal representative, do so without adjudication, order, or direction of the Court, but he may invoke the jurisdiction of the Court, in proceedings authorized by this Code, to resolve questions concerning the estate or its administration.

Section 3-705. [Duty of Personal Representative; Information to Heirs and Devisees.]

Not later than 30 days after his appointment every personal representative, except any special administrator, shall give information of his appointment to the heirs and devisees, including, if there has been no formal testacy proceeding and if the personal representative was appointed on the assumption that the decedent died intestate, the devisees in any will mentioned in the application for appointment of a personal representative. The information shall be delivered or sent by ordinary mail to each of the heirs and devisees whose address is reasonably available to the personal representative. The duty does not extend to require information to persons who have been adjudicated in a prior formal testacy proceeding to have no interest in the estate. The information shall include the name and address of the personal representative, indicate that it is being sent to persons who have or may have some interest in the estate being administered, indicate whether bond has been filed, and describe the court where papers relating to the estate are on file. The information shall state that the estate is being administered by the personal representative under the [State] Probate Code without supervision by the Court but that recipients are entitled to information regarding the administration from the personal representative and can petition the Court in any matter relating to the estate, including distribution of assets and expenses of administration. The personal representative's failure to give this information is a breach of his duty to the persons concerned but does not affect the validity of his appointment, his powers or other duties. A

personal representative may inform other persons of his appointment by delivery or ordinary first class mail.
As amended in 1987.

Section 3-706. [Duty of Personal Representative; Inventory and Appraisement.]
Within 3 months after his appointment, a personal representative, who is not a special administrator or a successor to another representative who has previously discharged this duty, shall prepare and file or mail an inventory of property owned by the decedent at the time of his death, listing it with reasonable detail, and indicating as to each listed item, its fair market value as of the date of the decedent's death, and the type and amount of any encumbrance that may exist with reference to any item.
The personal representative shall send a copy of the inventory to interested persons who request it. He may also file the original of the inventory with the court.

Section 3-707. [Employment of Appraisers.]
The personal representative may employ a qualified and disinterested appraiser to assist him in ascertaining the fair market value as of the date of the decedent's death of any asset the value of which may be subject to reasonable doubt. Different persons may be employed to appraise different kinds of assets included in the estate. The names and addresses of any appraiser shall be indicated on the inventory with the item or items he appraised.

Section 3-708. [Duty of Personal Representative; Supplementary Inventory.]
If any property not included in the original inventory comes to the knowledge of a personal representative or if the personal representative learns that the value or description indicated in the original inventory for any item is erroneous or misleading, he shall make a supplementary inventory or appraisement showing the market value as of the date of the decedent's death of the new item or the revised market value or descriptions, and the appraisers or other data relied upon, if any, and file it with the Court if the original inventory was filed, or furnish copies thereof or information thereof to persons interested in the new information.

Section 3-709. [Duty of Personal Representative; Possession of Estate.]
Except as otherwise provided by a decedent's will, every personal representative has a right to, and shall take possession or control of, the decedent's property, except that any real property or tangible personal property may be left with or surrendered to the person presumptively entitled thereto unless or until, in the judgment of the personal representative, possession of the property by him will be necessary for purposes of administration. The request by a personal representative for delivery of any property possessed by an heir or devisee is conclusive evidence, in any action against the heir or devisee for possession thereof, that the possession of the property by the personal representative is necessary for purposes of administration. The personal representative shall pay taxes on, and take all steps reasonably necessary for the management, protection and preservation of, the estate in his possession. He may maintain an action to recover possession of property or to determine the title thereto.

Section 3-710. [Power to Avoid Transfers.]
The property liable for the payment of unsecured debts of a decedent includes all property transferred by him by any means which is in law void or voidable as against his creditors, and subject to prior liens, the right to recover this property, so far as necessary for the payment of unsecured debts of the decedent, is exclusively in the personal representative.

Section 3-711. [Powers of Personal Representatives; In General.]
Until termination of his appointment a personal representative has the same power over the title to property of the estate that an absolute owner would have, in trust

however, for the benefit of the creditors and others interested in the estate. This power may be exercised without notice, hearing, or order of court.

Section 3-712. [Improper Exercise of Power; Breach of Fiduciary Duty.]
If the exercise of power concerning the estate is improper, the personal representative is liable to interested persons for damage or loss resulting from breach of his fiduciary duty to the same extent as a trustee of an express trust. The rights of purchasers and others dealing with a personal representative shall be determined as provided in Sections 3-713 and 3-714.

Section 3-713. [Sale, Encumbrance or Transaction Involving Conflict of Interest; Voidable; Exceptions.]
Any sale or encumbrance to the personal representative, his spouse, agent or attorney, or any corporation or trust in which he has a substantial beneficial interest, or any transaction which is affected by a substantial conflict of interest on the part of the personal representative, is voidable by any person interested in the estate except one who has consented after fair disclosure, unless

(1) the will or a contract entered into by the decedent expressly authorized the transaction; or
(2) the transaction is approved by the Court after notice to interested persons.

Section 3-714. [Persons Dealing with Personal Representative; Protection.]
A person who in good faith either assists a personal representative or deals with him for value is protected as if the personal representative properly exercised his power. The fact that a person knowingly deals with a personal representative does not alone require the person to inquire into the existence of a power or the propriety of its exercise. Except for restrictions on powers of supervised personal representatives which are endorsed on letters as provided in Section 3-504, no provision in any will or order of court purporting to limit the power of a personal representative is effective except as to persons with actual knowledge thereof. A person is not bound to see to the proper application of estate assets paid or delivered to a personal representative. The protection here expressed extends to instances in which some procedural irregularity or jurisdictional defect occurred in proceedings leading to the issuance of letters, including a case in which the alleged decedent is found to be alive. The protection here expressed is not by substitution for that provided by comparable provisions of the laws relating to commercial transactions and laws simplifying transfers of securities by fiduciaries.

Section 3-715. [Transactions Authorized for Personal Representatives; Exceptions.]
Except as restricted or otherwise provided by the will or by an order in a formal proceeding and subject to the priorities stated in Section 3-902, a personal representative, acting reasonably for the benefit of the interested persons, may properly:

(1) retain assets owned by the decedent pending distribution or liquidation including those in which the representative is personally interested or which are otherwise improper for trust investment;
(2) receive assets from fiduciaries, or other sources;
(3) perform, compromise or refuse performance of the decedent's contracts that continue as obligations of the estate, as he may determine under the circumstances. In performing enforceable contracts by the decedent to convey or lease land, the personal representative, among other possible courses of action, may:

(i) execute and deliver a deed of conveyance for cash payment of all sums remaining due or the purchaser's note for the sum remaining due secured by a mortgage or deed of trust on the land; or

(ii) deliver a deed in escrow with directions that the proceeds, when paid in accordance with the escrow agreement, be paid to the successors of the decedent, as designated in the escrow agreement;

(4) satisfy written charitable pledges of the decedent irrespective of whether the pledges constituted binding obligations of the decedent or were properly presented as claims, if in the judgment of the personal representative the decedent would have wanted the pledges completed under the circumstances;
(5) if funds are not needed to meet debts and expenses currently payable and are not immediately distributable, deposit or invest liquid assets of the estate, including moneys received from the sale of other assets, in federally insured interest-bearing accounts, readily marketable secured loan arrangements or other prudent investments which would be reasonable for use by trustees generally;
(6) acquire or dispose of an asset, including land in this or another state, for cash or on credit, at public or private sale; and manage, develop, improve, exchange, partition, change the character of, or abandon an estate asset;
(7) make ordinary or extraordinary repairs or alterations in buildings or other structures, demolish any improvements, raze existing or erect new party walls or buildings;
(8) subdivide, develop or dedicate land to public use; make or obtain the vacation of plats and adjust boundaries; or adjust differences in valuation on exchange or partition by giving or receiving considerations; or dedicate easements to public use without consideration;
(9) enter for any purpose into a lease as lessor or lessee, with or without option to purchase or renew, for a term within or extending beyond the period of administration;
(10) enter into a lease or arrangement for exploration and removal of minerals or other natural resources or enter into a pooling or unitization agreement;
(11) abandon property when, in the opinion of the personal representative, it is valueless, or is so encumbered, or is in condition that it is of no benefit to the state;
(12) vote stocks or other securities in person or by general or limited proxy;
(13) pay calls, assessments, and other sums chargeable or accruing against or on account of securities, unless barred by the provisions relating to claims;
(14) hold a security in the name of a nominee or in other form without disclosure of the interest of the estate but the personal representative is liable for any act of the nominee in connection with the security so held;
(15) insure the assets of the estate against damage, loss and liability and himself against liability as to third persons;
(16) borrow money with or without security to be repaid from the estate assets or otherwise; and advance money for the protection of the estate;
(17) effect a fair and reasonable compromise with any debtor or obligor, or extend, renew or in any manner modify the terms of any obligation owing to the estate. If the personal representative holds a mortgage, pledge or other lien upon property of another person, he may, in lieu of foreclosure, accept a conveyance or transfer of encumbered assets from the owner thereof in satisfaction of the indebtedness secured by lien;
(18) pay taxes, assessments, compensation of the personal representative, and other expenses incident to the administration of the estate;
(19) sell or exercise stock subscription or conversion rights; consent, directly or through a committee or other agent, to the reorganization, consolidation, merger, dissolution, or liquidation of a corporation or other business enterprise;
(20) allocate items of income or expense to either estate income or principal, as permitted or provided by law;
(21) employ persons, including attorneys, auditors, investment advisors, or agents, even if they are associated with the personal representative, to advise or assist the personal representative in the performance of his administrative

duties; act without independent investigation upon their recommendations; and instead of acting personally, employ one or more agents to perform any act of administration, whether or not discretionary;
(22) prosecute or defend claims, or proceedings in any jurisdiction for the protection of the estate and of the personal representative in the performance of his duties;
(23) sell, mortgage, or lease any real or personal property of the estate or any interest therein for cash, credit, or for part cash and part credit, and with or without security for unpaid balances;
(24) continue any unincorporated business or venture in which the decedent was engaged at the time of his death (i) in the same business form for a period of not more than 4 months from the date of appointment of a general personal representative if continuation is a reasonable means of preserving the value of the business including good will, (ii) in the same business form for any additional period of time that may be approved by order of the Court in a formal proceeding to which the persons interested in the estate are parties; or (iii) throughout the period of administration if the business is incorporated by the personal representative and if none of the probable distributees of the business who are competent adults object to its incorporation and retention in the estate;
(25) incorporate any business or venture in which the decedent was engaged at the time of his death;
(26) provide for exoneration of the personal representative from personal liability in any contract entered into on behalf of the estate;
(27) satisfy and settle claims and distribute the estate as provided in this Code.

Section 3-716. [Powers and Duties of Successor Personal Representative.]
A successor personal representative has the same power and duty as the original personal representative to complete the administration and distribution of the estate, as expeditiously as possible, but he shall not exercise any power expressly made personal to the executor named in the will.

Section 3-717. [Co-representatives; When Joint Action Required.]
If two or more persons are appointed co-representatives and unless the will provides otherwise, the concurrence of all is required on all acts connected with the administration and distribution of the estate. This restriction does not apply when any co-representative receives and receipts for property due the estate, when the concurrence of all cannot readily be obtained in the time reasonably available for emergency action necessary to preserve the estate, or when a co-representative has been delegated to act for the others. Persons dealing with a co-representative if actually unaware that another has been appointed to serve with him or if advised by the personal representative with whom they deal that he has authority to act alone for any of the reasons mentioned herein, are as fully protected as if the person with whom they dealt had been the sole personal representative.

Section 3-718. [Powers of Surviving Personal Representative.]
Unless the terms of the will otherwise provide, every power exercisable by personal co-representatives may be exercised by the one or more remaining after the appointment of one or more is terminated, and if one of 2 or more nominated as co-executors is not appointed, those appointed may exercise all the powers incident to the office.

Section 3-719. [Compensation of Personal Representative.]
A personal representative is entitled to reasonable compensation for his services. If a will provides for compensation of the personal representative and there is no contract with the decedent regarding compensation, he may renounce the provision before qualifying and be entitled to reasonable compensation. A personal representative also may renounce his right to all or any part of the compensation. A written renunciation of fee may be filed with the Court.

Section 3-720. [Expenses in Estate Litigation.]
If any personal representative or person nominated as personal representative defends or prosecutes any proceeding in good faith, whether successful or not he is entitled to receive from the estate his necessary expenses and disbursements including reasonable attorneys' fees incurred.

Section 3-721. [Proceedings for Review of Employment of Agents and Compensation of Personal Representatives and Employees of Estate.]
After notice to all interested persons or on petition of an interested person or on appropriate motion if administration is supervised, the propriety of employment of any person by a personal representative including any attorney, auditor, investment advisor or other specialized agent or assistant, the reasonableness of the compensation of any person so employed, or the reasonableness of the compensation determined by the personal representative for his own services, may be reviewed by the Court. Any person who has received excessive compensation from an estate for services rendered may be ordered to make appropriate refunds.

PART 8. CREDITORS' CLAIMS

Section 3-801. [Notice to Creditors.]
(a) Unless notice has already been given under this section, a personal representative upon appointment [may] [shall] publish a notice to creditors once a week for three successive weeks in a newspaper of general circulation in the [county] announcing the appointment and the personal representative's address and notifying creditors of the estate to present their claims within four months after the date of the first publication of the notice or be forever barred.
(b) A personal representative may give written notice by mail or other delivery to a creditor, notifying the creditor to present his [or her] claim within four months after the published notice, if given as provided in subsection (a), or within 60 days after the mailing or other delivery of the notice, whichever is later, or be forever barred. Written notice must be the notice described in subsection (a) above or a similar notice.
(c) The personal representative is not liable to a creditor or to a successor of the decedent for giving or failing to give notice under this section.

As amended in 1989.

Section 3-802. [Statutes of Limitations.]
(a) Unless an estate is insolvent, the personal representative, with the consent of all successors whose interests would be affected, may waive any defense of limitations available to the estate. If the defense is not waived, no claim barred by a statute of limitations at the time of the decedent's death may be allowed or paid.
(b) The running of a statute of limitations measured from an event other than death or the giving of notice to creditors is suspended for four months after the decedent's death, but resumes thereafter as to claims not barred by other sections.
(c) For purposes of a statute of limitations, the presentation of a claim pursuant to Section 3-804 is equivalent to commencement of a proceeding on the claim.

As amended in 1989.

Section 3-803. [Limitations on Presentation of Claims.]
(a) All claims against a decedent's estate which arose before the death of the decedent, including claims of the state and any subdivision thereof, whether due or to become due, absolute or contingent, liquidated or unliquidated, founded on contract, tort, or other legal basis, if not barred earlier by another statute of limitations or non-claim statute, are barred against the estate, the personal representative, and the heirs and devisees of the decedent, unless presented within the earlier of the following:

(1) one year after the decedent's death; or
(2) the time provided by Section 3-801(b) for creditors who are given actual notice, and within the time provided in 3-801(a) for all creditors barred by publication.

(b) A claim described in subsection (a) which is barred by the non-claim statute of the decedent's domicile before the giving of notice to creditors in this State is barred in this State.
(c) All claims against a decedent's estate which arise at or after the death of the decedent, including claims of the state and any subdivision thereof, whether due or to become due, absolute or contingent, liquidated or unliquidated, founded on contract, tort, or other legal basis, are barred against the estate, the personal representative, and the heirs and devisees of the decedent, unless presented as follows:

(1) a claim based on a contract with the personal representative, within four months after performance by the personal representative is due; or
(2) any other claim, within the later of four months after it arises, or the time specified in subsection (a)(1).

(d) Nothing in this section affects or prevents:

(1) any proceeding to enforce any mortgage, pledge, or other lien upon property of the estate;
(2) to the limits of the insurance protection only, any proceeding to establish liability of the decedent or the personal representative for which he is protected by liability insurance; or
(3) collection of compensation for services rendered and reimbursement for expenses advanced by the personal representative or by the attorney or accountant for the personal representative of the estate.

As amended in 1989.

Section 3-804. [Manner of Presentation of Claims.]
Claims against a decedent's estate may be presented as follows:

(1) The claimant may deliver or mail to the personal representative a written statement of the claim indicating its basis, the name and address of the claimant, and the amount claimed, or may file a written statement of the claim, in the form prescribed by rule, with the clerk of the Court. The claim is deemed presented on the first to occur of receipt of the written statement of claim by the personal representative, or the filing of the claim with the Court. If a claim is not yet due, the date when it will become due shall be stated. If the claim is contingent or unliquidated, the nature of the uncertainty shall be stated. If the claim is secured, the security shall be described. Failure to describe correctly the security, the nature of any uncertainty, and the due date of a claim not yet due does not invalidate the presentation made.
(2) The claimant may commence a proceeding against the personal representative in any Court where the personal representative may be subjected to jurisdiction, to obtain payment of his claim against the estate, but the commencement of the proceeding must occur within the time limited for presenting the claim. No presentation of claim is required in regard to matters claimed in proceedings against the decedent which were pending at the time of his death.
(3) If a claim is presented under subsection (1), no proceeding thereon may be commenced more than 60 days after the personal representative has failed a notice of disallowance; but, in the case of a claim which is not presently due or which is contingent or unliquidated, the personal representative may consent to an extension of the 60-day period, or to avoid injustice the Court, on petition,

may order an extension of the 60-day period, but in no event shall the extension run beyond the applicable statute of limitations.

Section 3-805. [Classification of Claims.]
(a) If the applicable assets of the estate are insufficient to pay all claims in full, the personal representative shall make payment in the following order:

(1) costs and expenses of administration;
(2) reasonable funeral expenses;
(3) debts and taxes with preference under federal law;
(4) reasonable and necessary medical and hospital expenses of the last illness of the decedent, including compensation of persons attending him;
(5) debts and taxes with preference under other laws of this state;
(6) all other claims.

(b) No preference shall be given in the payment of any claim over any other claim of the same class, and a claim due and payable shall not be entitled to a preference over claims not due.

Section 3-806. [Allowance of Claims.]
(a) As to claims presented in the manner described in Section 3-804 within the time limit prescribed in 3-803, the personal representative may mail a notice to any claimant stating that the claim has been disallowed. If, after allowing or disallowing a claim, the personal representative changes his decision concerning the claim, he shall notify the claimant. The personal representative may not change a disallowance of a claim after the time for the claimant to file a petition for allowance or to commence a proceeding on the claim has run and the claim has been barred. Every claim which is disallowed in whole or in part by the personal representative is barred so far as not allowed unless the claimant files a petition for allowance in the Court or commences a proceeding against the personal representative not later than 60 days after the mailing of the notice of disallowance or partial allowance if the notice warns the claimant of the impending bar. Failure of the personal representative to mail notice to a claimant of action on his claim for 60 days after the time for original presentation of the claim has expired has the effect of a notice of allowance.
(b) After allowing or disallowing a claim the personal representative may change the allowance or disallowance as hereafter provided. The personal representative may prior to payment change the allowance to a disallowance in whole or in part, but not after allowance by a court order or judgment or an order directing payment of the claim. He shall notify the claimant of the change to disallowance, and the disallowed claim is then subject to bar as provided in subsection (a). The personal representative may change a disallowance to an allowance, in whole or in part, until it is barred under subsection (a); after it is barred, it may be allowed and paid only if the estate is solvent and all successors whose interests would be affected consent.
(c) Upon the petition of the personal representative or of a claimant in a proceeding for the purpose, the Court may allow in whole or in part any claim or claims presented to the personal representative or filed with the clerk of the Court in due time and not barred by subsection (a) of this section. Notice in this proceeding shall be given to the claimant, the personal representative and those other persons interested in the estate as the Court may direct by order entered at the time the proceeding is commenced.
(d) A judgment in a proceeding in another court against a personal representative to enforce a claim against a decedent's estate is an allowance of the claim.
(e) Unless otherwise provided in any judgment in another court entered against the personal representative, allowed claims bear interest at the legal rate for the period commencing 60 days after the time for original presentation of the claim has

expired unless based on a contract making a provision for interest, in which case they bear interest in accordance with that provision.

As amended in 1987.

Section 3-807. [Payment of Claims.]
(a) Upon the expiration of the earlier of the time limitations provided in Section 3-803 for the presentation of claims, the personal representative shall proceed to pay the claims allowed against the estate in the order of priority prescribed, after making provision for homestead, family and support allowances, for claims already presented that have not yet been allowed or whose allowance has been appealed, and for unbarred claims that may yet be presented, including costs and expenses of administration. By petition to the Court in a proceeding for the purpose, or by appropriate motion if the administration is supervised, a claimant whose claim has been allowed but not paid may secure an order directing the personal representative to pay the claim to the extent funds of the estate are available to pay it.
(b) The personal representative at any time may pay any just claim that has not been barred, with or without formal presentation, but is personally liable to any other claimant whose claim is allowed and who is injured by its payment if:

(1) payment was made before the expiration of the time limit stated in subsection (a) and the personal representative failed to require the payee to give adequate security for the refund of any of the payment necessary to pay other claimants; or
(2) payment was made, due to negligence or willful fault of the personal representative, in such manner as to deprive the injured claimant of priority.

As amended in 1989.

Section 3-808. [Individual Liability of Personal Representative.]
(a) Unless otherwise provided in the contract, a personal representative is not individually liable on a contract properly entered into in his fiduciary capacity in the course of administration of the estate unless he fails to reveal his representative capacity and identify the estate in the contract.
(b) A personal representative is individually liable for obligations arising from ownership or control of the estate or for torts committed in the course of administration of the estate only if he is personally at fault.
(c) Claims based on contracts entered into by a personal representative in his fiduciary capacity, on obligations arising from ownership or control of the estate or on torts committed in the course of estate administration may be asserted against the estate by proceeding against the personal representative in his fiduciary capacity, whether or not the personal representative is individually liable therefor.
(d) Issues of liability as between the estate and the personal representative individually may be determined in a proceeding for accounting, surcharge or indemnification or other appropriate proceeding.

Section 3-809. [Secured Claims.]
Payment of a secured claim is upon the basis of the amount allowed if the creditor surrenders his security; otherwise payment is upon the basis of one of the following:

(1) if the creditor exhausts his security before receiving payment, [unless precluded by other law] upon the amount of the claim allowed less the fair value of the security; or
(2) if the creditor does not have the right to exhaust his security or has not done so, upon the amount of the claim allowed less the value of the security determined by converting it into money according to the terms of the agreement pursuant to which the security was delivered to the creditor, or by the creditor and personal representative by agreement, arbitration, compromise or litigation.

Section 3-810. [Claims Not Due and Contingent or Unliquidated Claims.]
(a) If a claim which will become due at a future time or a contingent or unliquidated claim becomes due or certain before the distribution of the estate, and if the claim has been allowed or established by a proceeding, it is paid in the same manner as presently due and absolute claims of the same class.
(b) In other cases the personal representative or, on petition of the personal representative or the claimant in a special proceeding for the purpose, the Court may provide for payment as follows:

(1) if the claimant consents, he may be paid the present or agreed value of the claim, taking any uncertainty into account;
(2) arrangement for future payment, or possible payment, on the happening of the contingency or on liquidation may be made by creating a trust, giving a mortgage, obtaining a bond or security from a distributee, or otherwise.

Section 3-811. [Counterclaims.]
In allowing a claim the personal representative may deduct any counterclaim which the estate has against the claimant. In determining a claim against an estate a Court shall reduce the amount allowed by the amount of any counterclaims and, if the counterclaims exceed the claim, render a judgment against the claimant in the amount of the excess. A counterclaim, liquidated or unliquidated, may arise from a transaction other than that upon which the claim is based. A counterclaim may give rise to relief exceeding in amount or different in kind from that sought in the claim.

Section 3-812. [Execution and Levies Prohibited.]
No execution may issue upon nor may any levy be made against any property of the estate under any judgment against a decedent or a personal representative, but this section shall not be construed to prevent the enforcement of mortgages, pledges or liens upon real or personal property in an appropriate proceeding.

Section 3-813. [Compromise of Claims.]
When a claim against the estate has been presented in any manner, the personal representative may, if it appears for the best interest of the estate, compromise the claim, whether due or not due, absolute or contingent, liquidated or unliquidated.

Section 3-814. [Encumbered Assets.]
If any assets of the estate are encumbered by mortgage, pledge, lien, or other security interest, the personal representative may pay the encumbrance or any part thereof, renew or extend any obligation secured by the encumbrance or convey or transfer the assets to the creditor in satisfaction of his lien, in whole or in part, whether or not the holder of the encumbrance has presented a claim, if it appears to be for the best interest of the estate. Payment of an encumbrance does not increase the share of the distributee entitled to the encumbered assets unless the distributee is entitled to exoneration.

Section 3-815. [Administration in More Than One State; Duty of Personal Representative.]
(a) All assets of estates being administered in this state are subject to all claims, allowances and charges existing or established against the personal representative wherever appointed.
(b) If the estate either in this state or as a whole is insufficient to cover all family exemptions and allowances determined by the law of the decedent's domicile, prior charges and claims, after satisfaction of the exemptions, allowances and charges, each claimant whose claim has been allowed either in this state or elsewhere in administrations of which the personal representative is aware, is entitled to receive payment of an equal proportion of his claim. If a preference or security in regard to a claim is allowed in another jurisdiction but not in this state, the creditor so

benefited is to receive dividends from local assets only upon the balance of his claim after deducting the amount of the benefit.
(c) In case the family exemptions and allowances, prior charges and claims of the entire estate exceed the total value of the portions of the estate being administered separately and this state is not the state of the decedent's last domicile, the claims allowed in this state shall be paid their proportion if local assets are adequate for the purpose, and the balance of local assets shall be transferred to the domiciliary personal representative. If local assets are not sufficient to pay all claims allowed in this state the amount to which they are entitled, local assets shall be marshalled so that each claim allowed in this state is paid its proportion as far as possible, after taking into account all dividends on claims allowed in this state from assets in other jurisdictions.

Section 3-816. [Final Distribution to Domiciliary Representative.]
The estate of a non-resident decedent being administered by a personal representative appointed in this state shall, if there is a personal representative of the decedent's domicile willing to receive it, be distributed to the domiciliary personal representative for the benefit of the successors of the decedent unless (1) by virtue of the decedent's will, if any, and applicable choice of law rules, the successors are identified pursuant to the local law of this state without reference to the local law of the decedent's domicile; (2) the personal representative of this state, after reasonable inquiry, is unaware of the existence or identity of a domiciliary personal representative; or (3) the Court orders otherwise in a proceeding for a closing order under Section 3-1001 or incident to the closing of a supervised administration. In other cases, distribution of the estate of a decedent shall be made in accordance with the other Parts of this Article.

PART 9. SPECIAL PROVISIONS RELATING TO DISTRIBUTION

Section 3-901. [Successors' Rights if No Administration.]
In the absence of administration, the heirs and devisees are entitled to the estate in accordance with the terms of a probated will or the laws of intestate succession. Devisees may establish title by the probated will to devised property. Persons entitled to property by homestead allowance, exemption or intestacy may establish title thereto by proof of the decedent's ownership, his death, and their relationship to the decedent. Successors take subject to all charges incident to administration, including the claims of creditors and allowances of surviving spouse and dependent children, and subject to the rights of others resulting from abatement, retainer, advancement, and ademption.

Section 3-902. [Distribution; Order in Which Assets Appropriated; Abatement.]
(a) Except as provided in subsection (b) and except as provided in connection with the share of the surviving spouse who elects to take an elective share, shares of distributees abate, without any preference or priority as between real and personal property, in the following order: (1) property not disposed of by the will; (2) residuary devises; (3) general devises; (4) specific devises. For purposes of abatement, a general devise charged on any specific property or fund is a specific devise to the extent of the value of the property on which it is charged, and upon the failure or insufficiency of the property on which it is charged, a general devise to the extent of the failure or insufficiency. Abatement within each classification is in proportion to the amounts of property each of the beneficiaries would have received if full distribution of the property had been made in accordance with the terms of the will.
(b) If the will expresses an order of abatement, or if the testamentary plan or the express or implied purpose of the devise would be defeated by the order of abatement stated in subsection (a), the shares of the distributees abate as may be found necessary to give effect to the intention of the testator.
(c) If the subject of a preferred devise is sold or used incident to administration,

abatement shall be achieved by appropriate adjustments in, or contribution from, other interests in the remaining assets.

[Section 3-902A. [Distribution; Order in Which Assets Appropriated; Abatement.]
(addendum for adoption in community property states)
[(a) and (b) as above.]
(c) If an estate of a decedent consists partly of separate property and partly of community property, the debts and expenses of administration shall be apportioned and charged against the different kinds of property in proportion to the relative value thereof.
[(d) same as (c) in common law state.]]

Section 3-903. [Right of Retainer.]
The amount of a non-contingent indebtedness of a successor to the estate if due, or its present value if not due, shall be offset against the successor's interest; but the successor has the benefit of any defense which would be available to him in a direct proceeding for recovery of the debt.

Section 3-904. [Interest on General Pecuniary Devise.]
General pecuniary devises bear interest at the legal rate beginning one year after the first appointment of a personal representative until payment, unless a contrary intent is indicated by the will.

Section 3-905. [Penalty Clause for Contest.]
A provision in a will purporting to penalize any interested person for contesting the will or instituting other proceedings relating to the estate is unenforceable if probable cause exists for instituting proceedings.

Section 3-906. [Distribution in Kind; Valuation; Method.]
(a) Unless a contrary intention is indicated by the will, the distributable assets of a decedent's estate shall be distributed in kind to the extent possible through application of the following provisions:

(1) A specific devisee is entitled to distribution of the thing devised to him, and a spouse or child who has selected particular assets of an estate as provided in Section 2-402 shall receive the items selected.
(2) Any homestead or family allowance or devise of a stated sum of money may be satisfied in kind provided

(i) the person entitled to the payment has not demanded payment in cash;
(ii) the property distributed in kind is valued at fair market value as of the date of its distribution, and
(iii) no residuary devisee has requested that the asset in question remain a part of the residue of the estate.

(3) For the purpose of valuation under paragraph (2) securities regularly traded on recognized exchanges, if distributed in kind, are valued at the price for the last sale of like securities traded on the business day prior to distribution, or if there was no sale on that day, at the median between amounts bid and offered at the close of that day. Assets consisting of sums owed the decedent or the estate by solvent debtors as to which there is no known dispute or defense are valued at the sum due with accrued interest or discounted to the date of distribution. For assets which do not have readily ascertainable values, a valuation as of a date not more than 30 days prior to the date of distribution, if otherwise reasonable, controls. For purposes of facilitating distribution, the personal representative may ascertain the value of the assets as of the time of the proposed distribution in any reasonable way, including the employment of qualified appraisers, even if the assets may have been previously appraised.

(4) The residuary estate shall be distributed in any equitable manner.

(b) After the probable charges against the estate are known, the personal representative may mail or deliver a proposal for distribution to all persons who have a right to object to the proposed distribution. The right of any distributee to object to the proposed distribution on the basis of the kind or value of asset he is to receive, if not waived earlier in writing, terminates if he fails to object in writing received by the personal representative within 30 days after mailing or delivery of the proposal.

As amended in 1987.

Section 3-907. [Distribution in Kind; Evidence.]
If distribution in kind is made, the personal representative shall execute an instrument or deed of distribution assigning, transferring or releasing the assets to the distributee as evidence of the distributee's title to the property.

Section 3-908. [Distribution; Right or Title of Distributee.]
Proof that a distributee has received an instrument or deed of distribution of assets in kind, or payment in distribution, from a personal representative, is conclusive evidence that the distributee has succeeded to the interest of the estate in the distributed assets, as against all persons interested in the estate, except that the personal representative may recover the assets or their value if the distribution was improper.

Section 3-909. [Improper Distribution; Liability of Distributee.]
Unless the distribution or payment no longer can be questioned because of adjudication, estoppel, or limitation, a distributee of property improperly distributed or paid, or a claimant who was improperly paid, is liable to return the property improperly received and its income since distribution if he has the property. If he does not have the property, then he is liable to return the value as of the date of disposition of the property improperly received and its income and gain received by him.

Section 3-910. [Purchasers from Distributees Protected.]
If property distributed in kind or a security interest therein is acquired for value by a purchaser from or lender to a distributee who has received an instrument or deed of distribution from the personal representative, or is so acquired by a purchaser from or lender to a transferee from such distributee, the purchaser or lender takes title free of rights of any interested person in the estate and incurs no personal liability to the estate, or to any interested person, whether or not the distribution was proper or supported by court order or the authority of the personal representative was terminated before execution of the instrument or deed. This section protects a purchaser from or lender to a distributee who, as personal representative, has executed a deed of distribution to himself, as well as a purchaser from or lender to any other distributee or his transferee. To be protected under this provision, a purchaser or lender need not inquire whether a personal representative acted properly in making the distribution in kind, even if the personal representative and the distributee are the same person, or whether the authority of the personal representative had terminated before the distribution. Any recorded instrument described in this section on which a state documentary fee is noted pursuant to [insert appropriate reference] shall be prima facie evidence that such transfer was made for value.

Section 3-911. [Partition for Purpose of Distribution.]
When two or more heirs or devisees are entitled to distribution of undivided interests in any real or personal property of the estate, the personal representative or one or more of the heirs or devisees may petition the Court prior to the formal or

informal closing of the estate, to make partition. After notice to the interested heirs or devisees, the Court shall partition the property in the same manner as provided by the law for civil actions of partition. The Court may direct the personal representative to sell any property which cannot be partitioned without prejudice to the owners and which cannot conveniently be allotted to any one party.

Section 3-912. [Private Agreements Among Successors to Decedent Binding on Personal Representative.]
Subject to the rights of creditors and taxing authorities, competent successors may agree among themselves to alter the interests, shares, or amounts to which they are entitled under the will of the decedent, or under the laws of intestacy, in any way that they provide in a written contract executed by all who are affected by its provisions. The personal representative shall abide by the terms of the agreement subject to his obligation to administer the estate for the benefit of creditors, to pay all taxes and costs of administration, and to carry out the responsibilities of his office for the benefit of any successors of the decedent who are not parties. Personal representatives of decedents' estates are not required to see to the performance of trusts if the trustee thereof is another person who is willing to accept the trust. Accordingly, trustees of a testamentary trust are successors for the purposes of this section. Nothing herein relieves trustees of any duties owed to beneficiaries of trusts.

Section 3-913. [Distributions to Trustee.]
(a) Before distributing to a trustee, the personal representative may require that the trust be registered if the state in which it is to be administered provides for registration and that the trustee inform the beneficiaries as provided in Section 7-303.
(b) If the trust instrument does not excuse the trustee from giving bond, the personal representative may petition the appropriate Court to require that the trustee post bond if he apprehends that distribution might jeopardize the interests of persons who are not able to protect themselves, and he may withhold distribution until the Court has acted.
(c) No inference of negligence on the part of the personal representative shall be drawn from his failure to exercise the authority conferred by subsections (a) and (b).

[Section 3-914. [Disposition of Unclaimed Assets.]
(a) If an heir, devisee or claimant cannot be found, the personal representative shall distribute the share of the missing person to his conservator, if any, otherwise to the [state treasurer] to become a part of the [state escheat fund].
(b) The money received by [state treasurer] shall be paid to the person entitled on proof of his right thereto or, if the [state treasurer] refuses or fails to pay, the person may petition the Court which appointed the personal representative, whereupon the Court upon notice to the [state treasurer] may determine the person entitled to the money and order the [treasurer] to pay it to him. No interest is allowed thereon and the heir, devisee or claimant shall pay all costs and expenses incident to the proceeding. If no petition is made to the [court] within 8 years after payment to the [state treasurer], the right of recovery is barred.]

Section 3-915. [Distribution to Person Under Disability.]
(a) A personal representative may discharge his obligation to distribute to any person under legal disability by distributing in a manner expressly provided in the will.
(b) Unless contrary to an express provision in the will, the personal representative may discharge his obligation to distribute to a minor or person under other disability as authorized by Section 5-101 or any other statute. If the personal representative knows that a conservator has been appointed or that a proceeding for appointment of a conservator is pending, the personal representative is authorized to distribute only to the conservator.

(c) If the heir or devisee is under disability other than minority, the personal representative is authorized to distribute to:

(1) an attorney in fact who has authority under a power of attorney to receive property for that person; or
(2) the spouse, parent or other close relative with whom the person under disability resides if the distribution is of amounts not exceeding [$10,000] a year, or property not exceeding [$10,000] in value, unless the court authorizes a larger amount or greater value.

Persons receiving money or property for the disabled person are obligated to apply the money or property to the support of that person, but may not pay themselves except by way of reimbursement for out-of-pocket expenses for goods and services necessary for the support of the disabled person. Excess sums must be preserved for future support of the disabled person. The personal representative is not responsible for the proper application of money or property distributed pursuant to this subsection.

As amended in 1987.

Section 3-916. [Apportionment of Estate Taxes.]
(a) For purposes of this section:

(1) "estate" means the gross estate of a decedent as determined for the purpose of federal estate tax and the estate tax payable to this state;
(2) "person" means any individual, partnership, association, joint stock company, corporation, government, political subdivision, governmental agency, or local governmental agency;
(3) "person interested in the estate" means any person entitled to receive, or who has received, from a decedent or by reason of the death of a decedent any property or interest therein included in the decedent's estate. It includes a personal representative, conservator, and trustee;
(4) "state" means any state, territory, or possession of the United States, the District of Columbia, and the Commonwealth of Puerto Rico;
(5) "tax" means the federal estate tax and the additional inheritance tax imposed by _______ and interest and penalties imposed in addition to the tax;
(6) "fiduciary" means personal representative or trustee.

(b) Except as provided in subsection (i) and, unless the will otherwise provides, the tax shall be apportioned among all persons interested in the estate. The apportionment is to be made in the proportion that the value of the interest of each person interested in the estate bears to the total value of the interests of all persons interested in the estate. The values used in determining the tax are to be used for that purpose. If the decedent's will directs a method of apportionment of tax different from the method described in this Code, the method described in the will controls.
(c)(1) The Court in which venue lies for the administration of the estate of a decedent, on petition for the purpose may determine the apportionment of the tax.

(2) If the Court finds that it is inequitable to apportion interest and penalties in the manner provided in subsection (b), because of special circumstances, it may direct apportionment thereof in the manner it finds equitable.
(3) If the Court finds that the assessment of penalties and interest assessed in relation to the tax is due to delay caused by the negligence of the fiduciary, the Court may charge him with the amount of the assessed penalties and interest.
(4) In any action to recover from any person interested in the estate the amount of the tax apportioned to the person in accordance with this Code the determination of the Court in respect thereto shall be prima facie correct.

(d)(1) The personal representative or other person in possession of the property of the decedent required to pay the tax may withhold from any property distributable to any person interested in the estate, upon its distribution to him, the amount of tax attributable to his interest. If the property in possession of the personal representative or other person required to pay the tax and distributable to any person interested in the estate is insufficient to satisfy the proportionate amount of the tax determined to be due from the person, the personal representative or other person required to pay the tax may recover the deficiency from the person interested in the estate. If the property is not in the possession of the personal representative or the other person required to pay the tax, the personal representative or the other person required to pay the tax may recover from any person interested in the estate the amount of the tax apportioned to the person in accordance with this Act.

(2) If property held by the personal representative is distributed prior to final apportionment of the tax, the distributee shall provide a bond or other security for the apportionment liability in the form and amount prescribed by the personal representative.

(e)(1) In making an apportionment, allowances shall be made for any exemptions granted, any classification made of persons interested in the estate and for any deductions and credits allowed by the law imposing the tax.

(2) Any exemption or deduction allowed by reason of the relationship of any person to the decedent or by reason of the purposes of the gift inures to the benefit of the person bearing such relationship or receiving the gift; but if an interest is subject to a prior present interest which is not allowable as a deduction, the tax apportionable against the present interest shall be paid from principal.

(3) Any deduction for property previously taxed and any credit for gift taxes or death taxes of a foreign country paid by the decedent or his estate inures to the proportionate benefit of all persons liable to apportionment.

(4) Any credit for inheritance, succession or estate taxes or taxes in the nature thereof applicable to property or interests includable in the estate, inures to the benefit of the persons or interests chargeable with the payment thereof to the extent proportionately that the credit reduces the tax.

(5) To the extent that property passing to or in trust for a surviving spouse or any charitable, public or similar purpose is not an allowable deduction for purposes of the tax solely by reason of an inheritance tax or other death tax imposed upon and deductible from the property, the property is not included in the computation provided for in subsection (b) hereof, and to that extent no apportionment is made against the property. The sentence immediately preceding does not apply to any case if the result would be to deprive the estate of a deduction otherwise allowable under Section 2053(d) of the Internal Revenue Code of 1954, as amended, of the United States, relating to deduction for state death taxes on transfers for public, charitable, or religious uses.

(f) No interest in income and no estate for years or for life or other temporary interest in any property or fund is subject to apportionment as between the temporary interest and the remainder. The tax on the temporary interest and the tax, if any, on the remainder is chargeable against the corpus of the property or funds subject to the temporary interest and remainder.

(g) Neither the personal representative nor other person required to pay the tax is under any duty to institute any action to recover from any person interested in the estate the amount of the tax apportioned to the person until the expiration of the 3 months next following final determination of the tax. A personal representative or other person required to pay the tax who institutes the action within a reasonable time after the 3 months' period is not subject to any liability or surcharge because any portion of the tax apportioned to any person interested in the estate was collectible at a time following the death of the decedent but thereafter became uncollectible. If the personal representative or other person required to pay the tax cannot collect from any person interested in the estate the amount of the tax apportioned to the person, the amount not recoverable shall be equitably apportioned among the other persons interested in the estate who are subject to apportionment.

(h) A personal representative acting in another state or a person required to pay the tax domiciled in another state may institute an action in the courts of this state and may recover a proportionate amount of the federal estate tax, of an estate tax payable to another state or of a death duty due by a decedent's estate to another state, from a person interested in the estate who is either domiciled in this state or who owns property in this state subject to attachment or execution. For the purposes of the action the determination of apportionment by the Court having jurisdiction of the administration of the decedent's estate in the other state is prima facie correct.

(i) If the liabilities of persons interested in the estate as prescribed by this act differ from those which result under the Federal Estate tax law, the liabilities imposed by the federal law will control and the balance of this Section shall apply as if the resulting liabilities had been prescribed herein.

PART 10. CLOSING ESTATES

Section 3-1001. [Formal Proceedings Terminating Administration; Testate or Intestate; Order of General Protection.]

(a) A personal representative or any interested person may petition for an order of complete settlement of the estate. The personal representative may petition at any time, and any other interested person may petition after one year from the appointment of the original personal representative except that no petition under this section may be entertained until the time for presenting claims which arose prior to the death of the decedent has expired. The petition may request the Court to determine testacy, if not previously determined, to consider the final account or compel or approve an accounting and distribution, to construe any will or determine heirs and adjudicate the final settlement and distribution of the estate. After notice to all interested persons and hearing the Court may enter an order or orders, on appropriate conditions, determining the persons entitled to distribution of the estate, and, as circumstances require, approving settlement and directing or approving distribution of the estate and discharging the personal representative from further claim or demand of any interested person.

(b) If one or more heirs or devisees were omitted as parties in, or were not given notice of, a previous formal testacy proceeding, the Court, on proper petition for an order of complete settlement of the estate under this section, and after notice to the omitted or unnotified persons and other interested parties determined to be interested on the assumption that the previous order concerning testacy is conclusive as to those given notice of the earlier proceeding, may determine testacy as it affects the omitted persons and confirm or alter the previous order of testacy as it affects all interested persons as appropriate in the light of the new proofs. In the absence of objection by an omitted or unnotified person, evidence received in the original testacy proceeding shall constitute prima facie proof of due execution of any will previously admitted to probate, or of the fact that the decedent left no valid will if the prior proceedings determined this fact.

Section 3-1002. [Formal Proceedings Terminating Testate Administration; Order Construing Will Without Adjudicating Testacy.]

A personal representative administering an estate under an informally probated will or any devisee under an informally probated will may petition for an order of settlement of the estate which will not adjudicate the testacy status of the decedent. The personal representative may petition at any time, and a devisee may petition after one year, from the appointment of the original personal representative, except that no petition under this section may be entertained until the time for presenting claims which arose prior to the death of the decedent has expired. The petition may request the Court to consider the final account or compel or approve an accounting and distribution, to construe the will and adjudicate final settlement and distribution of the estate. After notice to all devisees and the personal representative and hearing, the Court may enter an order or orders, on appropriate conditions, determining the persons entitled to distribution of the estate under the will, and, as circumstances require, approving settlement and directing or approving distribution of the estate and discharging the personal representative from further claim or demand of any devisee who is a party to the proceeding and those he represents. If it appears that a part of the estate is intestate, the proceedings shall be dismissed or amendments made to meet the provisions of Section 3-1001.

Section 3-1003. [Closing Estates; By Sworn Statement of Personal Representative.]
(a) Unless prohibited by order of the Court and except for estates being administered in supervised administration proceedings, a personal representative may close an estate by filing with the court no earlier than six months after the date of original appointment of a general personal representative for the estate, a verified statement stating that the personal representatives or a previous personal representative, has:

(1) determined that the time limited for presentation of creditors' claims has expired.
(2) fully administered the estate of the decedent by making payment, settlement, or other disposition of all claims that were presented, expenses of administration and estate, inheritance and other death taxes, except as specified in the statement, and that the assets of the estate have been distributed to the persons entitled. If any claims remain undischarged, the statement must state whether the personal representative has distributed the estate subject to possible liability with the agreement of the distributees or state in detail other arrangements that have been made to accommodate outstanding liabilities; and
(3) sent a copy of the statement to all distributees of the estate and to all creditors or other claimants of whom the personal representative is aware whose claims are neither paid nor barred and has furnished a full account in writing of the personal representative's administration to the distributees whose interests are affected thereby.

(b) If no proceedings involving the personal representative are pending in the Court one year after the closing statement is filed, the appointment of the personal representative terminates.
As amended in 1989.

Section 3-1004. [Liability of Distributees to Claimants.]
After assets of an estate have been distributed and subject to Section 3-1006, an undischarged claim not barred may be prosecuted in a proceeding against one or more distributees. No distributee shall be liable to claimants for amounts received as exempt property, homestead or family allowances, or for amounts in excess of the value of his distribution as of the time of distribution. As between distributees, each shall bear the cost of satisfaction of unbarred claims as if the claim had been satisfied in the course of administration. Any distributee who shall have failed to notify other distributees of the demand made upon him by the claimant in sufficient time to permit them to join in any proceeding in which the claim was asserted against him loses his right of contribution against other distributees.

Section 3-1005. [Limitations on Proceedings Against Personal Representative.]
Unless previously barred by adjudication and except as provided in the closing statement, the rights of successors and of creditors whose claims have not otherwise

been barred against the personal representative for breach of fiduciary duty are barred unless a proceeding to assert the same is commenced within 6 months after the filing of the closing statement. The rights thus barred do not include rights to recover from a personal representative for fraud, misrepresentation, or inadequate disclosure related to the settlement of the decedent's estate.

Section 3-1006. [Limitations on Actions and Proceedings Against Distributees.]
Unless previously adjudicated in a formal testacy proceeding or in a proceeding settling the accounts of a personal representative or otherwise barred, the claim of a claimant to recover from a distributee who is liable to pay the claim, and the right of an heir or devisee, or of a successor personal representative acting in their behalf, to recover property improperly distributed or its value from any distributee is forever barred at the later of three years after the decedent's death or one year after the time of its distribution thereof, but all claims of creditors of the decedent, are barred one year after the decedent's death. This section does not bar an action to recover property or value received as a result of fraud.
Amended in 1989.

Section 3-1007. [Certificate Discharging Liens Securing Fiduciary Performance.]
After his appointment has terminated, the personal representative, his sureties, or any successor of either, upon the filing of a verified application showing, so far as is known by the applicant, that no action concerning the estate is pending in any court, is entitled to receive a certificate from the Registrar that the personal representative appears to have fully administered the estate in question. The certificate evidences discharge of any lien on any property given to secure the obligation of the personal representative in lieu of bond or any surety, but does not preclude action against the personal representative or the surety.

Section 3-1008. [Subsequent Administration.]
If other property of the estate is discovered after an estate has been settled and the personal representative discharged or after one year after a closing statement has been filed, the Court upon petition of any interested person and upon notice as it directs may appoint the same or a successor personal representative to administer the subsequently discovered estate. If a new appointment is made, unless the Court orders otherwise, the provisions of this Code apply as appropriate; but no claim previously barred may be asserted in the subsequent administration.

PART 11. COMPROMISE OF CONTROVERSIES

Section 3-1101. [Effect of Approval of Agreements Involving Trusts, Inalienable Interests, or Interests of Third Persons.]
A compromise of any controversy as to admission to probate of any instrument offered for formal probate as the will of a decedent, the construction, validity, or effect of any probated will, the rights or interests in the estate of the decedent, of any successor, or the administration of the estate, if approved in a formal proceeding in the Court for that purpose, is binding on all the parties thereto including those unborn, unascertained or who could not be located. An approved compromise is binding even though it may affect a trust or an inalienable interest. A compromise does not impair the rights of creditors or of taxing authorities who are not parties to it.

Section 3-1102. [Procedure for Securing Court Approval of Compromise.]
The procedure for securing court approval of a compromise is as follows:

(1) The terms of the compromise shall be set forth in an agreement in writing which shall be executed by all competent persons and parents acting for any minor child having beneficial interests or having claims which will or may be affected by the compromise. Execution is not required by any person whose

identity cannot be ascertained or whose whereabouts is unknown and cannot reasonably be ascertained.

(2) Any interested person, including the personal representative or a trustee, then may submit the agreement to the Court for its approval and for execution by the personal representative, the trustee of every affected testamentary trust, and other fiduciaries and representatives.

(3) After notice to all interested persons or their representatives, including the personal representative of the estate and all affected trustees of trusts, the Court, if it finds that the contest or controversy is in good faith and that the effect of the agreement upon the interests of persons represented by fiduciaries or other representatives is just and reasonable, shall make an order approving the agreement and directing all fiduciaries subject to its jurisdiction to execute the agreement. Minor children represented only by their parents may be bound only if their parents join with other competent persons in execution of the compromise. Upon the making of the order and the execution of the agreement, all further disposition of the estate is in accordance with the terms of the agreement.

PART 12. COLLECTION OF PERSONAL PROPERTY BY AFFIDAVIT AND SUMMARY ADMINISTRATION PROCEDURE FOR SMALL ESTATES

Section 3-1201. [Collection of Personal Property by Affidavit.]

(a) Thirty days after the death of a decedent, any person indebted to the decedent or having possession of tangible personal property or an instrument evidencing a debt, obligation, stock or chose in action belonging to the decedent shall make payment of the indebtedness or deliver the tangible personal property or an instrument evidencing a debt, obligation, stock or chose in action to a person claiming to be the successor of the decedent upon being presented an affidavit made by or on behalf of the successor stating that:

(1) the value of the entire estate, wherever located, less liens and encumbrances, does not exceed $5,000;

(2) 30 days have elapsed since the death of the decedent;

(3) no application or petition for the appointment of a personal representative is pending or has been granted in any jurisdiction; and

(4) the claiming successor is entitled to payment or delivery of the property.

(b) A transfer agent of any security shall change the registered ownership on the books of a corporation from the decedent to the successor or successors upon the presentation of an affidavit as provided in subsection (a).

Section 3-1202. [Effect of Affidavit.]

The person paying, delivering, transferring, or issuing personal property or the evidence thereof pursuant to affidavit is discharged and released to the same extent as if he dealt with a personal representative of the decedent. He is not required to see to the application of the personal property or evidence thereof or to inquire into the truth of any statement in the affidavit. If any person to whom an affidavit is delivered refuses to pay, deliver, transfer, or issue any personal property or evidence thereof, it may be recovered or its payment, delivery, transfer, or issuance compelled upon proof of their right in a proceeding brought for the purpose by or on behalf of the persons entitled thereto. Any person to whom payment, delivery, transfer or issuance is made is answerable and accountable therefor to any personal representative of the estate or to any other person having a superior right.

Section 3-1203. [Small Estates; Summary Administration Procedure.]

If it appears from the inventory and appraisal that the value of the entire estate, less liens and encumbrances, does not exceed homestead allowance, exempt property, family allowance, costs and expenses of administration, reasonable funeral expenses, and reasonable and necessary medical and hospital expenses of the last illness of the decedent, the personal representative, without giving notice to creditors, may immediately disburse and distribute the estate to the persons entitled thereto and file a closing statement as provided in Section 3-1204.

Section 3-1204. [Small Estates; Closing by Sworn Statement of Personal Representative.]

(a) Unless prohibited by order of the Court and except for estates being administered by supervised personal representatives, a personal representative may close an estate administered under the summary procedures of Section 3-1203 by filing with the Court, at any time after disbursement and distribution of the estate, a verified statement stating that:

(1) to the best knowledge of the personal representative, the value of the entire estate, less liens and encumbrances, did not exceed homestead allowance, exempt property, family allowance, costs and expenses of administration, reasonable funeral expenses, and reasonable, necessary medical and hospital expenses of the last illness of the decedent;

(2) the personal representative has fully administered the estate by disbursing and distributing it to the persons entitled thereto; and

(3) the personal representative has sent a copy of the closing statement to all distributees of the estate and to all creditors or other claimants of whom he is aware whose claims are neither paid nor barred and has furnished a full account in writing of his administration to the distributees whose interests are affected.

(b) If no actions or proceedings involving the personal representative are pending in the Court one year after the closing statement is filed, the appointment of the personal representative terminates.

(c) A closing statement filed under this section has the same effect as one filed under Section 3-1003.

ARTICLE IV. FOREIGN PERSONAL REPRESENTATIVES; ANCILLARY ADMINISTRATION

PART 1. DEFINITIONS

4-101. [Definitions.]

PART 2. POWERS OF FOREIGN PERSONAL REPRESENTATIVES

4-201. [Payment of Debt and Delivery of Property to Domiciliary Foreign Personal Representative Without Local Administration.]
4-202. [Payment or Delivery Discharges.]
4-203. [Resident Creditor Notice.]
4-204. [Proof of Authority—Bond.]
4-205. [Powers.]
4-206. [Power of Representatives in Transition.]
4-207. [Ancillary and Other Local Administrations; Provisions Governing.]

PART 3. JURISDICTION OVER FOREIGN REPRESENTATIVES

4-301. [Jurisdiction by Act of Foreign Personal Representative.]
4-302. [Jurisdiction by Act of Decedent.]
4-303. [Service on Foreign Personal Representative.]

PART 4. JUDGMENTS AND PERSONAL REPRESENTATIVE

4-401. [Effect of Adjudication For or Against Personal Representative.]

PART 1. DEFINITIONS

Section 4-101. [Definitions.]
In this Article

(1) "local administration" means administration by a personal representative appointed in this state pursuant to appointment proceedings described in Article III.
(2) "local personal representative" includes any personal representative appointed in this state pursuant to appointment proceedings described in Article III and excludes foreign personal representatives who acquire the power of a local personal representative pursuant to Section 4-205.
(3) "resident creditor" means a person domiciled in, or doing business in this state, who is, or could be, a claimant against an estate of a non-resident decedent.

PART 2. POWERS OF FOREIGN PERSONAL REPRESENTATIVES

Section 4-201. [Payment of Debt and Delivery of Property to Domiciliary Foreign Personal Representative Without Local Administration.]
At any time after the expiration of sixty days from the death of a nonresident decedent, any person indebted to the estate of the nonresident decedent or having possession or control of personal property, or of an instrument evidencing a debt, obligation, stock or chose in action belonging to the estate of the nonresident decedent may pay the debt, deliver the personal property, or the instrument evidencing the debt, obligation, stock or chose in action, to the domiciliary foreign personal representative of the nonresident decedent upon being presented with proof of his appointment and an affidavit made by or on behalf of the representative stating:

(1) the date of the death of the nonresident decedent,
(2) that no local administration, or application or petition therefor, is pending in this state,
(3) that the domiciliary foreign personal representative is entitled to payment or delivery.

Section 4-202. [Payment or Delivery Discharges.]
Payment or delivery made in good faith on the basis of the proof of authority and affidavit releases the debtor or person having possession of the personal property to the same extent as if payment or delivery had been made to a local personal representative.

Section 4-203. [Resident Creditor Notice.]
Payment or delivery under Section 4-201 may not be made if a resident creditor of the nonresident decedent has notified the debtor of the nonresident decedent or the person having possession of the personal property belonging to the nonresident decedent that the debt should not be paid nor the property delivered to the domiciliary foreign personal representative.

Section 4-204. [Proof of Authority—Bond.]
If no local administration or application or petition therefor is pending in this state, a domiciliary foreign personal representative may file with a Court in this State in a [county] in which property belonging to the decedent is located, authenticated copies of his appointment and of any official bond he has given.

Section 4-205. [Powers.]
A domiciliary foreign personal representative who has complied with Section 4-204 may exercise as to assets in this state all powers of a local personal representative

and may maintain actions and proceedings in this state subject to any conditions imposed upon nonresident parties generally.

Section 4-206. [Power of Representatives in Transition.]
The power of a domiciliary foreign personal representative under Section 4-201 or 4-205 shall be exercised only if there is no administration or application therefor pending in this state. An application or petition for local administration of the estate terminates the power of the foreign personal representative to act under Section 4-205, but the local Court may allow the foreign personal representative to exercise limited powers to preserve the estate. No person who, before receiving actual notice of a pending local administration, has changed his position in reliance upon the powers of a foreign personal representative shall be prejudiced by reason of the application or petition for, or grant of, local administration. The local personal representative is subject to all duties and obligations which have accrued by virtue of the exercise of the powers by the foreign personal representative and may be substituted for him in any action or proceedings in this state.

Section 4-207. [Ancillary and Other Local Administrations; Provisions Governing.]
In respect to a nonresident decedent, the provisions of Article III of this Code govern (1) proceedings, if any, in a Court of this state for probate of the will, appointment, removal, supervision, and discharge of the local personal representative, and any other order concerning the estate; and (2) the status, powers, duties and liabilities of any local personal representative and the rights of claimants, purchasers, distributees and others in regard to a local administration.

PART 3. JURISDICTION OVER FOREIGN REPRESENTATIVES

Section 4-301. [Jurisdiction by Act of Foreign Personal Representative.]
A foreign personal representative submits personally to the jurisdiction of the Courts of this state in any proceeding relating to the estate by (1) filing authenticated copies of his appointment as provided in Section 4-204, (2) receiving payment of money or taking delivery of personal property under Section 4-201, or (3) doing any act as a personal representative in this state which would have given the state jurisdiction over him as an individual. Jurisdiction under (2) is limited to the money or value of personal property collected.

Section 4-302. [Jurisdiction by Act of Decedent.]
In addition to jurisdiction conferred by Section 4-301, a foreign personal representative is subject to the jurisdiction of the courts of this state to the same extent that his decedent was subject to jurisdiction immediately prior to death.

Section 4-303. [Service on Foreign Personal Representative.]
(a) Service of process may be made upon the foreign personal representative by registered or certified mail, addressed to his last reasonably ascertainable address, requesting a return receipt signed by addressee only. Notice by ordinary first class mail is sufficient if registered or certified mail service to the addressee is unavailable. Service may be made upon a foreign personal representative in the manner in which service could have been made under other laws of this state on either the foreign personal representative or his decedent immediately prior to death.
(b) If service is made upon a foreign personal representative as provided in subsection (a), he shall be allowed at least [30] days within which to appear or respond.

PART 4. JUDGMENTS AND PERSONAL REPRESENTATIVE

Section 4-401. [Effect of Adjudication For or Against Personal Representative.]
An adjudication rendered in any jurisdiction in favor of or against any personal

representative of the estate is as binding on the local personal representative as if he were a party to the adjudication.

ARTICLE V. PROTECTION OF PERSONS UNDER DISABILITY AND THEIR PROPERTY

PART 1. GENERAL PROVISIONS AND DEFINITIONS

5-101. [Facility of Payment or Delivery.]
5-102. [Delegation of Powers by Parent or Guardian.]
5-103. [General Definitions.]
5-104. [Request for Notice; Interested Person.]

PART 2. GUARDIANS OF MINORS

5-201. [Appointment and Status of Guardian of Minor.]
5-202. [Parental Appointment of Guardian for Minor.]
5-203. [Objection by Minor of Fourteen or Older to Parental Appointment.]
5-204. [Court Appointment of Guardian of Minor; Conditions for Appointment.]
5-205. [Venue.]
5-206. [Procedure for Court-appointment of Guardian of Minor.]
5-207. [Court Appointment of Guardian of Minor; Qualifications; Priority of Minor's Nominee.]
5-208. [Consent to Service by Acceptance of Appointment; Notice.]
5-209. [Powers and Duties of Guardian of Minor.]
5-210. [Termination of Appointment of Guardian; General.]
5-211. [Proceedings Subsequent to Appointment; Venue.]
5-212. [Resignation, Removal, and Other Post-appointment Proceedings.]

PART 3. GUARDIANS OF INCAPACITATED PERSONS

5-301. [Appointment of Guardian for Incapacitated Person by Will or Other Writing.]
5-302. [Venue.]
5-303. [Procedure for Court-appointment of a Guardian of an Incapacitated Person.]
5-304. [Notice in Guardianship Proceeding.]
5-305. [Who May Be Guardian; Priorities.]
5-306. [Findings; Order of Appointment.]
5-307. [Acceptance of Appointment; Consent to Jurisdiction.]
5-308. [Emergency Orders; Temporary Guardians.]
5-309. [General Powers and Duties of Guardian.]
5-310. [Termination of Guardianship for Incapacitated Person.]
5-311. [Removal or Resignation of Guardian; Termination of Incapacity.]
5-312. [Proceedings Subsequent to Appointment; Venue.]

PART 4. PROTECTION OF PROPERTY OF PERSONS UNDER DISABILITY AND MINORS

5-401. [Protective Proceedings.]
5-402. [Protective Proceedings; Jurisdiction of Business Affairs of Protected Persons.]
5-403. [Venue.]
5-404. [Original Petition for Appointment or Protective Order.]
5-405. [Notice.]
5-406. [Procedure Concerning Hearing and Order on Original Petition.]
5-407. [Permissible Court Orders.]
5-408. [Protective Arrangements and Single Transactions Authorized.]
5-409. [Who May Be Appointed Conservator; Priorities.]
5-410. [Bond.]
5-411. [Terms and Requirements of Bonds.]
5-412. [Effect of Acceptance of Appointment.]

5-413. [Compensation and Expenses.]
5-414. [Death, Resignation, or Removal of Conservator.]
5-415. [Petitions for Orders Subsequent to Appointment.]
5-416. [General Duty of Conservator.]
5-417. [Inventory and Records.]
5-418. [Accounts.]
5-419. [Conservators; Title By Appointment.]
5-420. [Recording of Conservator's Letters.]
5-421. [Sale, Encumbrance, or Transaction Involving Conflict of Interest; Voidable; Exceptions.]
5-422. [Persons Dealing With Conservators; Protection.]
5-423. [Powers of Conservator in Administration.]
5-424. [Distributive Duties and Powers of Conservator.]
5-425. [Enlargement or Limitation of Powers of Conservator.]
5-426. [Preservation of Estate Plan; Right to Examine.]
5-427. [Claims Against Protected Person; Enforcement.]
5-428. [Personal Liability of Conservator.]
5-429. [Termination of Proceedings.]
5-430. [Payment of Debt and Delivery of Property to Foreign Conservator without Local Proceedings.]
5-431. [Foreign Conservator; Proof of Authority; Bond; Powers.]

PART 5. DURABLE POWER OF ATTORNEY
5-501. [Definition.]
5-502. [Durable Power of Attorney Not Affected By Disability or Incapacity.]
5-503. [Relation of Attorney in Fact to Court-appointed Fiduciary.]
5-504. [Power of Attorney Not Revoked Until Notice.]
5-505. [Proof of Continuance of Durable and Other Powers of Attorney by Affidavit.]

PART 1. GENERAL PROVISIONS AND DEFINITIONS

Section 5-101. [Facility of Payment or Delivery.]
(a) Any person under a duty to pay or deliver money or personal property to a minor may perform the duty, in amounts not exceeding $5,000 a year, by paying or delivering the money or property to:

(1) the minor if 18 or more years of age or married;
(2) any person having the care and custody of the minor with whom the minor resides;
(3) a guardian of the minor; or
(4) a financial institution incident to a deposit in a state or federally insured savings account or certificate in the sole name of the minor with notice of the deposit to the minor.

(b) This section does not apply if the person making payment or delivery knows that a conservator has been appointed or proceedings for appointment of a conservator of the estate of the minor are pending.
(c) Persons, other than the minor or any financial institution, receiving money or property for a minor, are obligated to apply the money to the support and education of the minor, but may not pay themselves except by way of reimbursement for out-of-pocket expenses for goods and services necessary for the minor's support. Any excess sums must be preserved for future support and education of the minor and any balance not so used and any property received for the minor must be turned over to the minor when majority is attained. A person who pays or delivers money or property in accordance with provisions of this section is not responsible for the proper application thereof.

Section 5-102. [Delegation of Powers by Parent or Guardian.]
A parent or guardian of a minor or incapacitated person, by a properly executed power of attorney, may delegate to another person, for a period not exceeding 6 months, any power regarding care, custody or property of the minor child or ward, except the power to consent to marriage or adoption of a minor ward.

Section 5-103. [General Definitions.]
As used in Parts 1, 2, 3 and 4 of this Article:

(1) "Claims," in respect to a protected person, includes liabilities of the protected person, whether arising in contract, tort, or otherwise, and liabilities of the estate which arise at or after the appointment of a conservator, including expenses of administration.
(2) "Court" means the [________] court.
(3) "Conservator" means a person who is appointed by a Court to manage the estate of a protected person and includes a limited conservator described in Section 5-419(a).
(4) "Disability" means cause for a protective order as described in Section 5-401.
(5) "Estate" includes the property of the person whose affairs are subject to this Article.
(6) "Guardian" means a person who has qualified as a guardian of a minor or incapacitated person pursuant to parental or spousal nomination or court appointment and includes a limited guardian as described in Sections 5-209(e) and 5-306(c), but excludes one who is merely a guardian ad litem.
(7) "Incapacitated person" means any person who is impaired by reason of mental illness, mental deficiency, physical illness or disability, advanced age, chronic use of drugs, chronic intoxication, or other cause (except minority) to the extent of lacking sufficient understanding or capacity to make or communicate responsible decisions.
(8) "Lease" includes an oil, gas, or other mineral lease.
(9) "Letters" includes letters of guardianship and letters of conservatorship.
(10) "Minor" means a person who is under [21] years of age.
(11) "Mortgage" means any conveyance, agreement, or arrangement in which property is used as collateral.
(12) "Organization" includes a corporation, business trust, estate, trust, partnership, association, 2 or more persons having a joint or common interest, government, governmental subdivision or agency, or any other legal entity.
(13) "Parent" includes any person entitled to take, or who would be entitled to take if the child died without a will, as a parent by intestate succession from the child whose relationship is in question and excludes any person who is only a stepparent, foster parent, or grandparent.
(14) "Person" means an individual or an organization.
(15) "Petition" means a written request to the Court for an order after notice.
(16) "Proceeding" includes action at law and suit in equity.
(17) "Property" includes both real and personal property or any interest therein and means anything that may be the subject of ownership.
(18) "Protected person" means a minor or other person for whom a conservator has been appointed or other protective order has been made as provided in Sections 5-407 and 5-408.
(19) "Protective proceeding" means a proceeding under the provisions of Part 4 of this Article.
(20) "Security" includes any note, stock, treasury stock, bond, debenture, evidence of indebtedness, certificate of interest or participation in an oil, gas, or mining title or lease or in payments out of production under such a title or lease, collateral trust certificate, transferable share, voting trust certificate or, in general, any interest or instrument commonly known as a security, or any certificate of interest or participation, any temporary or interim certificate,

receipt or certificate of deposit for, or any warrant or right to subscribe to or purchase any of the foregoing.
(21) "Visitor" means a person appointed in a guardianship or protective proceeding who is trained in law, nursing, or social work, is an officer, employee, or special appointee of the Court, and has no personal interest in the proceeding.
(22) "Ward" means a person for whom a guardian has been appointed. A "minor ward" is a minor for whom a guardian has been appointed solely because of minority.

Section 5-104. [Request for Notice; Interested Person.]
Upon payment of any required fee, an interested person who desires to be notified before any order is made in a guardianship proceeding, including any proceeding subsequent to the appointment of a guardian under Section 5-312, or in a protective proceeding under Section 5-401, may file a request for notice with the clerk of the court in which the proceeding is pending. The clerk shall mail a copy of the request to the guardian and to the conservator if one has been appointed. A request is not effective unless it contains a statement showing the interest of the person making it and the address of that person or an attorney to whom notice is to be given. The request is effective only as to proceedings occurring after the filing. Any governmental agency paying or planning to pay benefits to the person to be protected is an interested person in protective proceedings.

PART 2. GUARDIANS OF MINORS

Section 5-201. [Appointment and Status of Guardian of Minor.]
A person may become a guardian of a minor by parental appointment or upon appointment by the Court. The guardianship status continues until terminated, without regard to the location from time to time of the guardian or minor ward.

Section 5-202. [Parental Appointment of Guardian for Minor.]
(a) The parent of an unmarried minor may appoint a guardian for the minor by will, or other writing signed by the parent and attested by at least 2 witnesses.
(b) Subject to the right of the minor under Section 5-203, if both parents are dead or incapacitated or the surviving parent has no parental rights or has been adjudged to be incapacitated, a parental appointment becomes effective when the guardian's acceptance is filed in the Court in which a nominating instrument is probated, or, in the case of a non-testamentary nominating instrument, in the Court at the place where the minor resides or is present. If both parents are dead, an effective appointment by the parent who died later has priority.
(c) A parental appointment effected by filing the guardian's acceptance under a will probated in the state of the testator's domicile is effective in this State.
(d) Upon acceptance of appointment, the guardian shall give written notice of acceptance to the minor and to the person having the minor's care or the minor's nearest adult relative.

Section 5-203. [Objection by Minor of Fourteen or Older to Parental Appointment.]
A minor 14 or more years of age who is the subject of a parental appointment may prevent the appointment or cause it to terminate by filing in the Court in which the nominating instrument is filed a written objection to the appointment before it is accepted or within 30 days after receiving notice of its acceptance. An objection may be withdrawn. An objection does not preclude appointment by the Court in a proper proceeding of the parental nominee or any other suitable person.

Section 5-204. [Court Appointment of Guardian of Minor; Conditions for Appointment.]
(a) The Court may appoint a guardian for an unmarried minor if all parental rights have been terminated or suspended by circumstances or prior Court order. A guardian appointed pursuant to Section 5-202 whose appointment has not been

prevented or nullified under Section 5-203 has priority over any guardian who may be appointed by the Court, but the Court may proceed with another appointment upon a finding that the parental nominee has failed to accept the appointment within 30 days after notice of the guardianship proceeding.
(b) If necessary, and on appropriate petition or application, the Court may appoint a temporary guardian who shall have the full authority of a general guardian of a minor, but the authority of a temporary guardian may not last longer than 6 months. The appointment of a temporary guardian for a minor may occur even though the conditions described in subsection (a) have not been established.

Section 5-205. [Venue.]
The venue for guardianship proceedings for a minor is in the court at the place where the minor resides or is present at the time the proceedings are commenced.

Section 5-206. [Procedure for Court-appointment of Guardian of Minor.]
(a) A minor or any person interested in the welfare of the minor may petition for appointment of a guardian.
(b) After the filing of a petition, the Court shall set a date for hearing, and the petitioner shall give notice of the time and place of hearing the petition in the manner prescribed by Section 1-401 to:

(1) the minor, if 14 or more years of age and not the petitioner;
(2) any person alleged to have had the principal care and custody of the minor during the 60 days preceding the filing of the petition; and
(3) any living parent of the minor.

(c) Upon hearing, if the Court finds that a qualified person seeks appointment, venue is proper, the required notices have been given, the conditions of Section 5-204(a) have been met, and the welfare and best interest of the minor will be served by the requested appointment, it shall make the appointment and issue letters. In other cases, the Court may dismiss the proceedings or make any other disposition of the matter that will serve the best interest of the minor.
(d) If the Court determines at any time in the proceeding that the interests of the minor are or may be inadequately represented, it may appoint an attorney to represent the minor, giving consideration to the preference of the minor if the minor is 14 or more years of age.

Section 5-207. [Court Appointment of Guardian of Minor; Qualifications; Priority of Minor's Nominee.]
The Court may appoint as guardian any person whose appointment would be in the best interest of the minor. The Court shall appoint a person nominated by the minor, if the minor is 14 or more years of age, unless the Court finds the appointment contrary to the best interest of the minor.

Section 5-208. [Consent to Service by Acceptance of Appointment; Notice.]
By accepting a parental or court appointment as guardian, a guardian submits personally to the jurisdiction of the Court in any proceeding relating to the guardianship that may be instituted by any interested person. The petitioner shall cause notice of any proceeding to be delivered or mailed to the guardian at the guardian's address listed in the Court records and to the address then known to the petitioner. Letters of guardianship must indicate whether the guardian was appointed by court order or parental nomination.

Section 5-209. [Powers and Duties of Guardian of Minor.]
(a) A guardian of a minor ward has the powers and responsibilities of a parent regarding the ward's support, care, and education, but a guardian is not personally liable for the ward's expenses and is not liable to third persons by reason of the relationship for acts of the ward.

(b) In particular and without qualifying the foregoing, a guardian shall:

(1) become or remain personally acquainted with the ward and maintain sufficient contact with the ward to know of the ward's capacities, limitations, needs, opportunities, and physical and mental health;
(2) take reasonable care of the ward's personal effects and commence protective proceedings if necessary to protect other property of the ward;
(3) apply any available money of the ward to the ward's current needs for support, care, and education;
(4) conserve any excess money of the ward for the ward's future needs, but if a conservator has been appointed for the estate of the ward, the guardian, at least quarterly, shall pay to the conservator money of the ward to be conserved for the ward's future needs; and
(5) report the condition of the ward and of the ward's estate that has been subject to the guardian's possession or control, as ordered by the Court on petition of any person interested in the ward's welfare or as required by Court rule.

(c) A guardian may:

(1) receive money payable for the support of the ward to the ward's parent, guardian, or custodian under the terms of any statutory benefit or insurance system or any private contract, devise, trust, conservatorship, or custodianship, and money or property of the ward paid or delivered pursuant to Section 5-101;
(2) if consistent with the terms of any order by a court of competent jurisdiction relating to detention or commitment of the ward, take custody of the person of the ward and establish the ward's place of abode within or without this State;
(3) if no conservator for the estate of the ward has been appointed, institute proceedings, including administrative proceedings, or take other appropriate action to compel the performance by any person of a duty to support the ward or to pay sums for the welfare of the ward;
(4) consent to medical or other professional care, treatment, or advice for the ward without liability by reason of the consent for injury to the ward resulting from the negligence or acts of third persons unless a parent would have been liable in the circumstances;
(5) consent to the marriage or adoption of the ward; and
(6) if reasonable under all of the circumstances, delegate to the ward certain responsibilities for decisions affecting the ward's well-being.

(d) A guardian is entitled to reasonable compensation for services as guardian and to reimbursement for room, board and clothing personally provided to the ward, but only as approved by order of the Court. If a conservator, other than the guardian or one who is affiliated with the guardian, has been appointed for the estate of the ward, reasonable compensation and reimbursement to the guardian may be approved and paid by the conservator without order of the Court controlling the guardian.
(e) In the interest of developing self-reliance on the part of a ward or for other good cause, the Court, at the time of appointment or later, on its own motion or on appropriate petition or motion of the minor or other interested person, may limit the powers of a guardian otherwise conferred by this section and thereby create a limited guardianship. Any limitation on the statutory power of a guardian of a minor must be endorsed on the guardian's letters or, in the case of a guardian by parental appointment, must be reflected in letters that are issued at the time any limitation is imposed. Following the same procedure, a limitation may be removed and appropriate letters issued.

Section 5-210. [Termination of Appointment of Guardian; General.]
A guardian's authority and responsibility terminates upon the death, resignation,

or removal of the guardian or upon the minor's death, adoption, marriage, or attainment of majority, but termination does not affect the guardian's liability for prior acts or the obligation to account for funds and assets of the ward. Resignation of a guardian does not terminate the guardianship until it has been approved by the Court. A parental appointment under an informally probated will terminates if the will is later denied probate in a formal proceeding.

Section 5-211. [Proceedings Subsequent to Appointment; Venue.]
(a) The Court at the place where the ward resides has concurrent jurisdiction with the Court that appointed the guardian or in which acceptance of a parental appointment was filed over resignation, removal, accounting, and other proceedings relating to the guardianship.
(b) If the Court at the place where the ward resides is neither the appointing court nor the court in which acceptance of appointment is filed, the court in which proceedings subsequent to appointment are commenced in all appropriate cases shall notify the other court, in this or another state, and after consultation with that court determine whether to retain jurisdiction or transfer the proceedings to the other court, whichever is in the best interest of the ward. A copy of any order accepting a resignation or removing a guardian must be sent to the appointing court or the court in which acceptance of appointment is filed.

Section 5-212. [Resignation, Removal, and Other Post-appointment Proceedings.]
(a) Any person interested in the welfare of a ward or the ward, if 14 or more years of age, may petition for removal of a guardian on the ground that removal would be in the best interest of the ward or for any other order that is in the best interest of the ward. A guardian may petition for permission to resign. A petition for removal or for permission to resign may, but need not, include a request for appointment of a successor guardian.
(b) Notice of hearing on a petition for an order subsequent to appointment of a guardian must be given to the ward, the guardian, and any other person as ordered by the court.
(c) After notice and hearing on a petition for removal or for permission to resign, the Court may terminate the guardianship and make any further order that may be appropriate.
(d) If the Court determines at any time in the proceeding that the interest of the ward is or may be inadequately represented, it may appoint an attorney to represent the minor, giving consideration to the preference of the minor if the minor is 14 or more years of age.

PART 3. GUARDIANS OF INCAPACITATED PERSONS

Section 5-301. [Appointment of Guardian for Incapacitated Person by Will or Other Writing.]
(a) The parent of an unmarried incapacitated person may appoint by will, or other writing signed by the parent and attested by at least 2 witnesses, a guardian of the incapacitated person. If both parents are dead or the surviving parent is adjudged incapacitated, a parental appointment becomes effective when, after having given 7 days prior written notice of intention to do so to the incapacitated person and to the person having the care of the person or to the nearest adult relative, the guardian files acceptance of appointment in the court in which the will is [informally or formally] probated, or in the case of a non-testamentary nominating instrument, in the Court at the place where the incapacitated person resides or is present. The notice shall state that the appointment may be terminated by filing a written objection in the Court, as provided by subsection (d). If both parents are dead, an effective appointment by the parent who died later has priority.
(b) The spouse of a married incapacitated person may appoint by will, or other writing signed by the spouse and attested by at least 2 witnesses, a guardian of the incapacitated person. The appointment becomes effective when, after having given

7 days prior written notice of intention to do so to the incapacitated person and to the person having care of the incapacitated person or to the nearest adult relative, the guardian files acceptance of appointment in the Court in which the will is informally or formally probated or, in the case of non-testamentary nominating instrument, in the Court at the place where the incapacitated person resides or is present. The notice shall state that the appointment may be terminated by filing a written objection in the Court, as provided by subsection (d). An effective appointment by a spouse has priority over an appointment by a parent.
(c) An appointment effected by filing the guardian's acceptance under a will probated in the state of the decedent's domicile is effective in this State.
(d) Upon the filing in the Court in which the will was probated or, in the case of a non-testamentary nominating instrument, in the Court at the place where the incapacitated person resides or is present, of written objection to the appointment by the incapacitated person for whom a parental or spousal appointment of guardian has been made, the appointment is terminated. An objection does not prevent appointment by the Court in a proper proceeding of the parental or spousal nominee or any other suitable person upon an adjudication of incapacity in proceedings under the succeeding sections of this Part.
As amended in 1987.

Section 5-302. [Venue.]
The venue for guardianship proceedings for an incapacitated person is in the place where the incapacitated person resides or is present at the time the proceedings are commenced. If the incapacitated person is admitted to an institution pursuant to order of a court of competent jurisdiction, venue is also in the [county] in which that court is located.

Section 5-303. [Procedure for Court-appointment of a Guardian of an Incapacitated Person.]
(a) An incapacitated person or any person interested in the welfare of the incapacitated person may petition for appointment of a guardian, limited or general.
(b) After the filing of a petition, the Court shall set a date for hearing on the issue of incapacity so that notices may be given as required by Section 5-304, and, unless the allegedly incapacitated person is represented by counsel, appoint an attorney to represent the person in the proceeding. The person so appointed may be granted the powers and duties of a guardian ad litem. The person alleged to be incapacitated must be examined by a physician or other qualified person appointed by the Court who shall submit a report in writing to the Court. The person alleged to be incapacitated also must be interviewed by a visitor sent by the Court. The visitor also shall interview the person who appears to have caused the petition to be filed and any person who is nominated to serve as guardian and visit the present place of abode of the person alleged to be incapacitated and the place it is proposed that the person will be detained or reside if the appointment is made and submit a report in writing to the Court. The Court may utilize the service of any public or charitable agency as an additional visitor to evaluate the condition of the allegedly incapacitated person and to make appropriate recommendations to the Court.
(c) A person alleged to be incapacitated is entitled to be present at the hearing in person. The person is entitled to be represented by counsel, to present evidence, to cross-examine witnesses, including the Court-appointed physician or other qualified person and any visitor [, and to trial by jury]. The issue may be determined at a closed hearing [or without a jury] if the person alleged to be incapacitated or counsel for the person so requests.
(d) Any person may apply for permission to participate in the proceeding, and the Court may grant the request, with or without hearing, upon determining that the best interest of the alleged incapacitated person will be served thereby. The Court may attach appropriate conditions to the permission.

Section 5-304. [Notice in Guardianship Proceeding.]
(a) In a proceeding for the appointment of a guardian of an incapacitated person, and, if notice is required in a proceeding for appointment of a temporary guardian, notice of hearing must be given to each of the following:

(1) the person alleged to be incapacitated and spouse, or, if none, adult children, or if none, parents;
(2) any person who is serving as guardian, conservator, or who has the care and custody of the person alleged to be incapacitated;
(3) in case no other person is notified under paragraph (1), at least one of the nearest adult relatives, if any can be found; and
(4) any other person as directed by the Court.

(b) Notice of hearing on a petition for an order subsequent to appointment of a guardian must be given to the ward, the guardian and any other person as ordered by the Court.
(c) Notice must be served personally on the alleged incapacitated person. Notices to other persons as required by subsection (a)(1) must be served personally if the person to be notified can be found within the state. In all other cases, required notices must be given as provided in Section 1-401.
(d) The person alleged to be incapacitated may not waive notice.

Section 5-305. [Who May Be Guardian; Priorities.]
(a) Any qualified person may be appointed guardian of an incapacitated person.
(b) Unless lack of qualification or other good cause dictates the contrary, the Court shall appoint a guardian in accordance with the incapacitated person's most recent nomination in a durable power of attorney.
(c) Except as provided in subsection (b), the following are entitled to consideration for appointment in the order listed:

(1) the spouse of the incapacitated person or a person nominated by will of a deceased spouse or by other writing signed by the spouse and attested by at least 2 witnesses;
(2) an adult child of the incapacitated person;
(3) a parent of the incapacitated person, or a person nominated by will of a deceased parent or by other writing signed by a parent and attested by at least two witnesses;
(4) any relative of the incapacitated person with whom the person has resided for more than 6 months prior to the filing of the petition; and
(5) a person nominated by the person who is caring for or paying for the care of the incapacitated person.

(d) With respect to persons having equal priority, the Court shall select the one it deems best qualified to serve. The Court, acting in the best interest of the incapacitated person, may pass over a person having priority and appoint a person having a lower priority or no priority.

Section 5-306. [Findings; Order of Appointment.]
(a) The Court shall exercise the authority conferred in this Part so as to encourage the development of maximum self-reliance and independence of the incapacitated person and make appointive and other orders only to the extent necessitated by the incapacitated person's mental and adaptive limitations or other conditions warranting the procedure.
(b) The Court may appoint a guardian as requested if it is satisfied that the person for whom a guardian is sought is incapacitated and that the appointment is necessary or desirable as a means of providing continuing care and supervision of the person of the incapacitated person. The Court, on appropriate findings, may (i)

treat the petition as one for a protective order under Section 5-401 and proceed accordingly, (ii) enter any other appropriate order, or (iii) dismiss the proceedings.
(c) The Court, at the time of appointment or later, on its own motion or on appropriate petition or motion of the incapacitated person or other interested person, may limit the powers of a guardian otherwise conferred by Parts 1, 2, 3 and 4 of this Article and thereby create a limited guardianship. Any limitation on the statutory power of a guardian of an incapacitated person must be endorsed on the guardian's letters or, in the case of a guardian by parental or spousal appointment, must be reflected in letters issued at the time any limitation is imposed. Following the same procedure, a limitation may be removed or modified and appropriate letters issued.

Section 5-307. [Acceptance of Appointment; Consent to Jurisdiction.]
By accepting appointment, a guardian submits personally to the jurisdiction of the Court in any proceeding relating to the guardianship that may be instituted by any interested person. Notice of any proceeding must be delivered or mailed to the guardian at the address listed in the Court records and at the address as then known to the petitioner.

Section 5-308. [Emergency Orders; Temporary Guardians.]
(a) If an incapacitated person has no guardian, an emergency exists, and no other person appears to have authority to act in the circumstances, on appropriate petition the Court may appoint a temporary guardian whose authority may not extend beyond [15 days] [the period of effectiveness of ex parte restraining orders], and who may exercise those powers granted in the order.
(b) If an appointed guardian is not effectively performing duties and the Court further finds that the welfare of the incapacitated person requires immediate action, it may appoint, with or without notice, a temporary guardian for the incapacitated person having the powers of a general guardian for a specified period not to exceed 6 months. The authority of any permanent guardian previously appointed by the Court is suspended as long as a temporary guardian has authority.
(c) The Court may remove a temporary guardian at any time. A temporary guardian shall make any report the Court requires. In other respects the provisions of Parts 1, 2, 3 and 4 of this Article concerning guardians apply to temporary guardians.

Section 5-309. [General Powers and Duties of Guardian.]
Except as limited pursuant to Section 5-306(c), a guardian of an incapacitated person is responsible for care, custody, and control of the ward, but is not liable to third persons by reason of that responsibility for acts of the ward. In particular and without qualifying the foregoing, a guardian has the same duties, powers and responsibilities as a guardian for a minor as described in Section 5-209(b), (c) and (d).

Section 5-310. [Termination of Guardianship for Incapacitated Person.]
The authority and responsibility of a guardian of an incapacitated person terminates upon the death of the guardian or ward, the determination of incapacity of the guardian, or upon removal or resignation as provided in Section 5-311. Testamentary appointment under an informally probated will terminates if the will is later denied probate in a formal proceeding. Termination does not affect a guardian's liability for prior acts or the obligation to account for funds and assets of the ward.

Section 5-311. [Removal or Resignation of Guardian; Termination of Incapacity.]
(a) On petition of the ward or any person interested in the ward's welfare, the Court, after hearing, may remove a guardian if in the best interest of the ward. On petition of the guardian, the Court, after hearing, may accept a resignation.
(b) An order adjudicating incapacity may specify a minimum period, not exceeding six months, during which a petition for an adjudication that the ward is no longer incapacitated may not be filed without special leave. Subject to that restriction, the

ward or any person interested in the welfare of the ward may petition for an order that the ward is no longer incapacitated and for termination of the guardianship. A request for an order may also be made informally to the Court and any person who knowingly interferes with transmission of the request may be adjudged guilty of contempt of court.
(c) Upon removal, resignation, or death of the guardian, or if the guardian is determined to be incapacitated, the Court may appoint a successor guardian and make any other appropriate order. Before appointing a successor guardian, or ordering that a ward's incapacity has terminated, the Court shall follow the same procedures to safeguard the rights of the ward that apply to a petition for appointment of a guardian.
As amended in 1987.

Section 5-312. [Proceedings Subsequent to Appointment; Venue.]
(a) The Court at the place where the ward resides has concurrent jurisdiction with the Court that appointed the guardian or in which acceptance of a parental or spousal appointment was filed over resignation, removal, accounting, and other proceedings relating to the guardianship, including proceedings to limit the authority previously conferred on a guardian or to remove limitations previously imposed.
(b) If the Court at the place where the ward resides is not the Court in which acceptance of appointment is filed, the Court in which proceedings subsequent to appointment are commenced, in all appropriate cases, shall notify the other Court, in this or another state, and after consultation with that Court determine whether to retain jurisdiction or transfer the proceedings to the other Court, whichever may be in the best interest of the ward. A copy of any order accepting a resignation, removing a guardian, or altering authority must be sent to the Court in which acceptance of appointment is filed.

PART 4. PROTECTION OF PROPERTY OF PERSONS UNDER DISABILITY AND MINORS

Section 5-401. [Protective Proceedings.]
(a) Upon petition and after notice and hearing in accordance with the provisions of this Part, the Court may appoint a conservator or make any other protective order for cause as provided in this section.
(b) Appointment of a conservator or other protective order may be made in relation to the estate and affairs of a minor if the Court determines that a minor owns money or property requiring management or protection that cannot otherwise be provided or has or may have business affairs that may be jeopardized or prevented by minority, or that funds are needed for support and education and that protection is necessary or desirable to obtain or provide funds.
(c) Appointment of a conservator or other protective order may be made in relation to the estate and affairs of a person if the Court determines that (i) the person is unable to manage property and business affairs effectively for such reasons as mental illness, mental deficiency, physical illness or disability, chronic use of drugs, chronic intoxication, confinement, detention by a foreign power, or disappearance; and (ii) the person has property that will be wasted or dissipated unless property management is provided or money is needed for the support, care, and welfare of the person or those entitled to the person's support and that protection is necessary or desirable to obtain or provide money.
As amended in 1988.

Section 5-402. [Protective Proceedings; Jurisdiction of Business Affairs of Protected Persons.]
After the service of notice in a proceeding seeking the appointment of a conservator or other protective order and until termination of the proceeding, the Court in which the petition is filed has:

(1) exclusive jurisdiction to determine the need for a conservator or other protective order until the proceedings are terminated;
(2) exclusive jurisdiction to determine how the estate of the protected person which is subject to the laws of this State must be managed, expended, or distributed to or for the use of the protected person, the protected person's dependents, or other claimants; and
(3) concurrent jurisdiction to determine the validity of claims against the person or estate of the protected person and questions of title concerning any estate asset.

Section 5-403. [Venue.]
Venue for proceedings under this Part is:

(1) in the Court at the place in this State where the person to be protected resides whether or not a guardian has been appointed in another place; or
(2) if the person to be protected does not reside in this State, in the Court at any place where property of the person is located.

Section 5-404. [Original Petition for Appointment or Protective Order.]
(a) The person to be protected or any person who is interested in the estate, affairs, or welfare of the person, including a parent, guardian, custodian, or any person who would be adversely affected by lack of effective management of the person's property and business affairs may petition for the appointment of a conservator or for other appropriate protective order.
(b) The petition must set forth to the extent known the interest of the petitioner; the name, age, residence, and address of the person to be protected; the name and address of the guardian, if any; the name and address of the nearest relative known to the petitioner; a general statement of the person's property with an estimate of the value thereof, including any compensation, insurance, pension, or allowance to which the person is entitled; and the reason why appointment of a conservator or other protective order is necessary. If the appointment of a conservator is requested, the petition must also set forth the name and address of the person whose appointment is sought and the basis of the claim to priority for appointment.

Section 5-405. [Notice.]
(a) On a petition for appointment of a conservator or other protective order, the requirements for notice described in Section 5-304 apply, but (i) if the person to be protected has disappeared or is otherwise situated so as to make personal service of notice impracticable, notice to the person must be given by publication as provided in Section 1-401, and (ii) if the person to be protected is a minor, the provisions of Section 5-206 also apply.
(b) Notice of hearing on a petition for an order subsequent to appointment of a conservator or other protective order must be given to the protected person, any conservator of the protected person's estate, and any other person as ordered by the Court.

Section 5-406. [Procedure Concerning Hearing and Order on Original Petition.]
(a) Upon receipt of a petition for appointment of a conservator or other protective order because of minority, the Court shall set a date for hearing. If the Court determines at any time in the proceeding that the interests of the minor are or may be inadequately represented, it may appoint an attorney to represent the minor, giving consideration to the choice of the minor if 14 or more years of age. An attorney appointed by the Court to represent a minor may be granted the powers and duties of a guardian ad litem.
(b) Upon receipt of a petition for appointment of a conservator or other protective order for reasons other than minority, the Court shall set a date for hearing. Unless the person to be protected has chosen counsel, the Court shall appoint an attorney to represent the person who may be granted the powers and duties of a guardian ad

litem. If the alleged disability is mental illness, mental deficiency, physical illness or disability, chronic use of drugs, or chronic intoxication, the Court may direct that the person to be protected be examined by a physician designated by the Court, preferably a physician who is not connected with any institution in which the person is a patient or is detained. The Court may send a visitor to interview the person to be protected. The visitor may be a guardian ad litem or an officer or employee of the Court.
(c) The Court may utilize, as an additional visitor, the service of any public or charitable agency to evaluate the condition of the person to be protected and make appropriate recommendations to the Court.
(d) The person to be protected is entitled to be present at the hearing in person. The person is entitled to be represented by counsel, to present evidence, to cross-examine witnesses, including any Court-appointed physician or other qualified person and any visitor [, and to trial by jury]. The issue may be determined at a closed hearing [or without a jury] if the person to be protected or counsel for the person so requests.
(e) Any person may apply for permission to participate in the proceeding and the Court may grant the request, with or without hearing, upon determining that the best interest of the person to be protected will be served thereby. The Court may attach appropriate conditions to the permission.
(f) After hearing, upon finding that a basis for the appointment of a conservator or other protective order has been established, the Court shall make an appointment or other appropriate protective order.
As amended in 1988.

Section 5-407. [Permissible Court Orders.]
(a) The Court shall exercise the authority conferred in this Part to encourage the development of maximum self-reliance and independence of a protected person and make protective orders only to the extent necessitated by the protected person's mental and adaptive limitations and other conditions warranting the procedure.
(b) The Court has the following powers that may be exercised directly or through a conservator in respect to the estate and business affairs of a protected person:

(1) While a petition for appointment of a conservator or other protective order is pending and after preliminary hearing and without notice to others, the Court may preserve and apply the property of the person to be protected as may be required for the support of the person or dependents of the person.
(2) After hearing and upon determining that a basis for an appointment or other protective order exists with respect to a minor without other disability, the Court has all those powers over the estate and business affairs of the minor which are or may be necessary for the best interest of the minor and members of the minor's immediate family.
(3) After hearing and upon determining that a basis for an appointment or other protective order exists with respect to a person for reasons other than minority, the Court, for the benefit of the person and members of the person's immediate family, has all the powers over the estate and business affairs which the person could exercise if present and not under disability, except the power to make a will. Those powers include, but are not limited to, power to make gifts; to convey or release contingent and expectant interests in property, including marital property rights and any right of survivorship incident to joint tenancy or tenancy by the entirety; to exercise or release powers held by the protected person as trustee, personal representative, custodian for minors, conservator, or donee of a power of appointment; to enter into contracts; to create revocable or irrevocable trusts of property of the estate which may extend beyond the disability or life of the protected person; to exercise options of the protected person to purchase securities or other property; to exercise rights to elect options and change beneficiaries under insurance and annuity policies and to surrender the policies for their cash value; to exercise any right to an elective

share in the estate of the person's deceased spouse and to renounce or disclaim any interest by testate or intestate succession or by inter vivos transfer.

(c) The Court may exercise or direct the exercise of the following powers only if satisfied, after notice and hearing, that it is in the best interest of the protected person, and that the person either is incapable of consenting or has consented to the proposed exercise of power:

(1) to exercise or release powers of appointment of which the protected person is donee;
(2) to renounce or disclaim interests;
(3) to make gifts in trust or otherwise exceeding 20 percent of any year's income of the estate; and
(4) to change beneficiaries under insurance and annuity policies.

(d) A determination that a basis for appointment of a conservator or other protective order exists has no effect on the capacity of the protected person.

Section 5-408. [Protective Arrangements and Single Transactions Authorized.]
(a) If it is established in a proper proceeding that a basis exists as described in Section 5-401 for affecting the property and business affairs of a person, the Court, without appointing a conservator, may authorize, direct or ratify any transaction necessary or desirable to achieve any security, service, or care arrangement meeting the foreseeable needs of the protected person. Protective arrangements include payment, delivery, deposit, or retention of funds or property; sale, mortgage, lease, or other transfer of property; entry into an annuity contract, a contract for life care, a deposit contract, or a contract for training and education; or addition to or establishment of a suitable trust.
(b) If it is established in a proper proceeding that a basis exists as described in Section 5-401 for affecting the property and business affairs of a person, the Court, without appointing a conservator, may authorize, direct, or ratify any contract, trust, or other transaction relating to the protected person's property and business affairs if the Court determines that the transaction is in the best interest of the protected person.
(c) Before approving a protective arrangement or other transaction under this section, the Court shall consider the interests of creditors and dependents of the protected person and, in view of the disability, whether the protected person needs the continuing protection of a conservator. The Court may appoint a special conservator to assist in the accomplishment of any protective arrangement or other transaction authorized under this section who shall have the authority conferred by the order and serve until discharged by order after report to the Court of all matters done pursuant to the order of appointment.

Section 5-409. [Who May Be Appointed Conservator; Priorities.]
(a) The Court may appoint an individual or a corporation with general power to serve as trustee or conservator of the estate of a protected person. The following are entitled to consideration for appointment in the order listed:

(1) a conservator, guardian of property, or other like fiduciary appointed or recognized by an appropriate court of any other jurisdiction in which the protected person resides;
(2) an individual or corporation nominated by the protected person 14 or more years of age and of sufficient mental capacity to make an intelligent choice;
(3) the spouse of the protected person;
(4) an adult child of the protected person;
(5) a parent of the protected person, or a person nominated by the will of a deceased parent;

(6) any relative of the protected person who has resided with the protected person for more than 6 months before the filing of the petition; and
(7) a person nominated by one who is caring for or paying benefits to the protected person.

(b) A person in priorities (1), (3), (4), (5), or (6) may designate in writing a substitute to serve instead and thereby transfer the priority to the substitute. With respect to persons having equal priority, the Court shall select the one it deems best qualified to serve. The Court, acting in the best interest of the protected person, may pass over a person having priority and appoint a person having a lower priority or no priority.

Section 5-410. [Bond.]
The Court may require a conservator to furnish a bond conditioned upon faithful discharge of all duties of the trust according to law, with sureties as it shall specify. Unless otherwise directed, the bond must be in the amount of the aggregate capital value of the property of the estate in the conservator's control, plus one year's estimated income, and minus the value of securities deposited under arrangements requiring an order of the Court for their removal and the value of any land which the fiduciary, by express limitation of power, lacks power to sell or convey without Court authorization. The Court, in lieu of sureties on a bond, may accept other collateral for the performance of the bond, including a pledge of securities or a mortgage of land.

Section 5-411. [Terms and Requirements of Bonds.]
(a) The following requirements and provisions apply to any bond required under Section 5-410.

(1) Unless otherwise provided by the terms of the approved bond, sureties are jointly and severally liable with the conservator and with each other.
(2) By executing an approved bond of a conservator, the surety consents to the jurisdiction of the Court that issued letters to the primary obligor in any proceeding pertaining to the fiduciary duties of the conservator and naming the surety as a party respondent. Notice of any proceeding must be delivered to the surety or mailed by registered or certified mail to the address listed with the Court at the place where the bond is filed and to the address as then known to the petitioner.
(3) On petition of a successor conservator or any interested person, a proceeding may be initiated against a surety for breach of the obligation of the bond of the conservator.
(4) The bond of the conservator is not void after the first recovery but may be proceeded against from time to time until the whole penalty is exhausted.

(b) No proceeding may be commenced against the surety on any matter as to which an action or proceeding against the primary obligor is barred by adjudication or limitation.

Section 5-412. [Effect of Acceptance of Appointment.]
By accepting appointment, a conservator submits personally to the jurisdiction of the Court in any proceeding relating to the estate which may be instituted by any interested person. Notice of any proceeding must be delivered to the conservator or mailed by registered or certified mail to the address as listed in the petition for appointment or as thereafter reported to the Court and to the address as then known to the petitioner.

Section 5-413. [Compensation and Expenses.]
If not otherwise compensated for services rendered, any visitor, attorney, physician, conservator, or special conservator appointed in a protective proceeding and any attorney whose services resulted in a protective order or in an order that was

beneficial to a protected person's estate is entitled to reasonable compensation from the estate.

Section 5-414. [Death, Resignation, or Removal of Conservator.]
The Court may remove a conservator for good cause, upon notice and hearing, or accept the resignation of a conservator. Upon the conservator's death, resignation, or removal, the Court may appoint another conservator. A conservator so appointed succeeds to the title and powers of the predecessor.

Section 5-415. [Petitions for Orders Subsequent to Appointment.]
(a) Any person interested in the welfare of a person for whom a conservator has been appointed may file a petition in the appointing court for an order:

(1) requiring bond or collateral or additional bond or collateral, or reducing bond;
(2) requiring an accounting for the administration of the trust;
(3) directing distribution;
(4) removing the conservator and appointing a temporary or successor conservator; or
(5) granting other appropriate relief.

(b) A conservator may petition the appointing court for instructions concerning fiduciary responsibility.
(c) Upon notice and hearing, the Court may give appropriate instructions or make any appropriate order.

Section 5-416. [General Duty of Conservator.]
A conservator, in relation to powers conferred by this Part, or implicit in the title acquired by virtue of the proceeding, shall act as a fiduciary and observe the standards of care applicable to trustees.

Section 5-417. [Inventory and Records.]
(a) Within 90 days after appointment, each conservator shall prepare and file with the appointing Court a complete inventory of the estate subject to the conservatorship together with an oath or affirmation that the inventory is believed to be complete and accurate as far as information permits. The conservator shall provide a copy thereof to the protected person if practicable and the person has attained the age of 14 years and has sufficient mental capacity to understand the arrangement. A copy also shall be provided to any guardian or parent with whom the protected person resides.
(b) The conservator shall keep suitable records of the administration and exhibit the same on request of any interested person.

Section 5-418. [Accounts.]
Each conservator shall account to the Court for administration of the trust not less than annually unless the Court directs otherwise, upon resignation or removal and at other times as the Court may direct. On termination of the protected person's minority or disability, a conservator shall account to the Court or to the formerly protected person or the successors of that person. Subject to appeal or vacation within the time permitted, an order after notice and hearing allowing an intermediate account of a conservator adjudicates as to liabilities concerning the matters considered in connection therewith; and an order, following notice and hearing, allowing a final account adjudicates as to all previously unsettled liabilities of the conservator to the protected person or the protected person's successors relating to the conservatorship. In connection with any account, the Court may require a conservator to submit to a physical check of the estate, to be made in any manner the Court specifies.
As amended in 1987.

Section 5-419. [Conservators; Title By Appointment.]
(a) The appointment of a conservator vests in the conservator title as trustee to all property, or to the part thereof specified in the order, of the protected person, presently held or thereafter acquired, including title to any property theretofore held for the protected person by custodians or attorneys-in-fact. An order specifying that only a part of the property of the protected person vests in the conservator creates a limited conservatorship.
(b) Except as otherwise provided herein, the interest of the protected person in property vested in a conservator by this section is not transferrable or assignable by the protected person. An attempted transfer or assignment by the protected person, though ineffective to affect property rights, may generate a claim for restitution or damages which, subject to presentation and allowance, may be satisfied as provided in Section 5-427.
(c) Neither property vested in a conservator by this section nor the interest of the protected person in that property is subject to levy, garnishment, or similar process other than an order issued in the protective proceeding made as provided in Section 5-427.

Section 5-420. [Recording of Conservator's Letters.]
(a) Letters of conservatorship are evidence of transfer of all assets, or the part thereof specified in the letters, of a protected person to the conservator. An order terminating a conservatorship is evidence of transfer of all assets subjected to the conservatorship from the conservator to the protected person, or to successors of the person.
(b) Subject to the requirements of general statutes governing the filing or recordation of documents of title to land or other property, letters of conservatorship and orders terminating conservatorships, may be filed or recorded to give record notice of title as between the conservator and the protected person.

Section 5-421. [Sale, Encumbrance, or Transaction Involving Conflict of Interest; Voidable; Exceptions.]
Any sale or encumbrance to a conservator, the spouse, agent, attorney of a conservator, or any corporation, trust, or other organization in which the conservator has a substantial beneficial interest, or any other transaction involving the estate being administered by the conservator which is affected by a substantial conflict between fiduciary and personal interests is voidable unless the transaction is approved by the Court after notice as directed by the Court.

Section 5-422. [Persons Dealing With Conservators; Protection.]
(a) A person who in good faith either assists or deals with a conservator for value in any transaction other than those requiring a Court order as provided in Section 5-407 is protected as if the conservator properly exercised the power. The fact that a person knowingly deals with a conservator does not alone require the person to inquire into the existence of a power or the propriety of its exercise, but restrictions on powers of conservators which are endorsed on letters as provided in Section 5-425 are effective as to third persons. A person is not bound to see to the proper application of estate assets paid or delivered to a conservator.
(b) The protection expressed in this section extends to any procedural irregularity or jurisdictional defect occurred in proceedings leading to the issuance of letters and is not a substitution for protection provided by comparable provisions of the law relating to commercial transactions or to simplifying transfers of securities by fiduciaries.

Section 5-423. [Powers of Conservator in Administration.]
(a) Subject to limitation provided in Section 5-425, a conservator has all of the powers conferred in this section and any additional powers conferred by law on trustees in this State. In addition, a conservator of the estate of an unmarried minor [under the age of 18 years], as to whom no one has parental rights, has the duties

and powers of a guardian of a minor described in Section 5-209 until the minor attains [the age of 18 years] or marries, but the parental rights so conferred on a conservator do not preclude appointment of a guardian as provided in Part 2.
(b) A conservator without Court authorization or confirmation, may invest and reinvest funds of the estate as would a trustee.
(c) A conservator, acting reasonably in efforts to accomplish the purpose of the appointment, may act without Court authorization or confirmation, to

(1) collect, hold, and retain assets of the estate including land in another state, until judging that disposition of the assets should be made, and the assets may be retained even though they include an asset in which the conservator is personally interested;
(2) receive additions to the estate;
(3) continue or participate in the operation of any business or other enterprise;
(4) acquire an undivided interest in an estate asset in which the conservator, in any fiduciary capacity, holds an undivided interest;
(5) invest and reinvest estate assets in accordance with subsection (b);
(6) deposit estate funds in a state or federally insured financial institution, including one operated by the conservator;
(7) acquire or dispose of an estate asset, including land in another state, for cash or on credit, at public or private sale, and manage, develop, improve, exchange, partition, change the character of, or abandon an estate asset;
(8) make ordinary or extraordinary repairs or alterations in buildings or other structures; demolish any improvements; and raze existing or erect new party walls or buildings;
(9) subdivide, develop, or dedicate land to public use; make or obtain the vacation of plats and adjust boundaries; adjust differences in valuation or exchange or partition by giving or receiving considerations; and dedicate easements to public use without consideration;
(10) enter for any purpose into a lease as lessor or lessee with or without option to purchase or renew for a term within or extending beyond the term of the conservatorship;
(11) enter into a lease or arrangement for exploration and removal of minerals or other natural resources or enter into a pooling or unitization agreement;
(12) grant an option involving disposition of an estate asset and take an option for the acquisition of any asset;
(13) vote a security, in person or by general or limited proxy;
(14) pay calls, assessments, and any other sums chargeable or accruing against or on account of securities;
(15) sell or exercise stock-subscription or conversion rights;
(16) consent, directly or through a committee or other agent, to the reorganization, consolidation, merger, dissolution, or liquidation of a corporation or other business enterprise;
(17) hold a security in the name of a nominee or in other form without disclosure of the conservatorship so that title to the security may pass by delivery, but the conservator is liable for any act of the nominee in connection with the stock so held;
(18) insure the assets of the estate against damage or loss and the conservator against liability with respect to third persons;
(19) borrow money to be repaid from estate assets or otherwise; advance money for the protection of the estate or the protected person and for all expenses, losses, and liability sustained in the administration of the estate or because of the holding or ownership of any estate assets, for which the conservator has a lien on the estate as against the protected person for advances so made;
(20) pay or contest any claim; settle a claim by or against the estate or the protected person by compromise, arbitration, or otherwise; and release, in whole or in part, any claim belonging to the estate to the extent the claim is uncollectible;

(21) pay taxes, assessments, compensation of the conservator, and other expenses incurred in the collection, care, administration, and protection of the estate;
(22) allocate items of income or expense to either estate income or principal, as provided by law, including creation of reserves out of income for depreciation, obsolescence, or amortization, or for depletion in mineral or timber properties;
(23) pay any sum distributable to a protected person or dependent of the protected person by paying the sum to the distributee or by paying the sum for the use of the distributee to the guardian of the distributee, or, if none, to a relative or other person having custody of the distributee;
(24) employ persons, including attorneys, auditors, investment advisors, or agents, even though they are associated with the conservator, to advise or assist in the performance of administrative duties; act upon their recommendation without independent investigation; and instead of acting personally, employ one or more agents to perform any act of administration, whether or not discretionary;
(25) prosecute or defend actions, claims, or proceedings in any jurisdiction for the protection of estate assets and of the conservator in the performance of fiduciary duties; and
(26) execute and deliver all instruments that will accomplish or facilitate the exercise of the powers vested in the conservator.

Section 5-424. [Distributive Duties and Powers of Conservator.]
(a) A conservator may expend or distribute income or principal of the estate without Court authorization or confirmation for the support, education, care, or benefit of the protected person and dependents in accordance with the following principles:

(1) The conservator shall consider recommendations relating to the appropriate standard of support, education, and benefit for the protected person or dependent made by a parent or guardian, if any. The conservator may not be surcharged for sums paid to persons or organizations furnishing support, education, or care to the protected person or a dependent pursuant to the recommendations of a parent or guardian of the protected person unless the conservator knows that the parent or guardian derives personal financial benefit therefrom, including relief from any personal duty of support or the recommendations are clearly not in the best interest of the protected person.
(2) The conservator shall expend or distribute sums reasonably necessary for the support, education, care, or benefit of the protected person and dependents with due regard to (i) the size of the estate, the probable duration of the conservatorship, and the likelihood that the protected person, at some future time, may be fully able to be wholly self-sufficient and able to manage business affairs and the estate; (ii) the accustomed standard of living of the protected person and dependents; and (iii) other funds or sources used for the support of the protected person.
(3) The conservator may expend funds of the estate for the support of persons legally dependent on the protected person and others who are members of the protected person's household who are unable to support themselves, and who are in need of support.
(4) Funds expended under this subsection may be paid by the conservator to any person, including the protected person, to reimburse for expenditures that the conservator might have made, or in advance for services to be rendered to the protected person if it is reasonable to expect the services will be performed and advance payments are customary or reasonably necessary under the circumstances.
(5) A conservator, in discharging the responsibilities conferred by Court order and this Part, shall implement the principles described in Section 5-407(a), to the extent possible.

(b) If the estate is ample to provide for the purposes implicit in the distributions

authorized by the preceding subsections, a conservator for a protected person other than a minor has power to make gifts to charity and other objects as the protected person might have been expected to make, in amounts that do not exceed in total for any year 20 percent of the income from the estate.
(c) When a minor who has not been adjudged disabled under Section 5-401(c) attains majority, the conservator, after meeting all claims and expenses of administration, shall pay over and distribute all funds and properties to the formerly protected person as soon as possible.
(d) If satisfied that a protected person's disability, other than minority, has ceased, the conservator, after meeting all claims and expenses of administration, shall pay over and distribute all funds and properties to the formerly protected person as soon as possible.
(e) If a protected person dies, the conservator shall deliver to the Court for safekeeping any will of the deceased protected person which may have come into the conservator's possession, inform the executor or beneficiary named therein of the delivery, and retain the estate for delivery to a duly appointed personal representative of the decedent or other persons entitled thereto. If, 40 days after the death of the protected person, no other person has been appointed personal representative and no application or petition for appointment is before the Court, the conservator may apply to exercise the powers and duties of a personal representative in order to be able to proceed to administer and distribute the decedent's estate. Upon application for an order granting the powers of a personal representative to a conservator, after notice to any person nominated personal representative by any will of which the applicant is aware, the Court may grant the application upon determining that there is no objection and endorse the letters of the conservator to note that the formerly protected person is deceased and that the conservator has acquired all of the powers and duties of a personal representative. The making and entry of an order under this section has the effect of an order of appointment of a personal representative [as provided in Section 3-308 and Parts 6 through 10 of Article III], but the estate in the name of the conservator, after administration, may be distributed to the decedent's successors without prior re-transfer to the conservator as personal representative.

Section 5-425. [Enlargement or Limitation of Powers of Conservator.]
Subject to the restrictions in Section 5-407(c), the Court may confer on a conservator at the time of appointment or later, in addition to the powers conferred by Sections 5-423 and 5-424, any power that the Court itself could exercise under Sections 5-407(b)(2) and 5-407(b)(3). The Court, at the time of appointment or later, may limit the powers of a conservator otherwise conferred by Sections 5-423 and 5-424 or previously conferred by the Court and may at any time remove or modify any limitation. If the Court limits any power conferred on the conservator by Section 5-423 or Section 5-424, or specifies, as provided in Section 5-419(a), that title to some but not all assets of the protected person vest in the conservator, the limitation or specification of assets subject to the conservatorship must be endorsed upon the letters of appointment.

Section 5-426. [Preservation of Estate Plan; Right to Examine.]
In (i) investing the estate, (ii) selecting assets of the estate for distribution under subsections (a) and (b) of Section 5-424, and (iii) utilizing powers of revocation or withdrawal available for the support of the protected person and exercisable by the conservator or the Court, the conservator and the Court shall take into account any estate plan of the protected person known to them, including a will, any revocable trust of which the person is settlor, and any contract, transfer, or joint ownership arrangement originated by the protected person with provisions for payment or transfer of benefits or interests at the person's death to another or others. The conservator may examine the will of the protected person.

Section 5-427. [Claims Against Protected Person; Enforcement.]
(a) A conservator may pay or secure from the estate claims against the estate or against the protected person arising before or after the conservatorship upon their presentation and allowance in accordance with the priorities stated in subsection (c). A claim may be presented by either of the following methods:

(1) The claimant may deliver or mail to the conservator a written statement of the claim indicating its basis, the name and mailing address of the claimant, and the amount claimed; or
(2) The claimant may file a written statement of the claim, in the form prescribed by rule, with the clerk of Court and deliver or mail a copy of the statement to the conservator.

(b) A claim is deemed presented on the first to occur of receipt of the written statement of claim by the conservator or the filing of the claim with the Court. A presented claim is allowed if it is not disallowed by written statement mailed by the conservator to the claimant within 60 days after its presentation. The presentation of a claim tolls any statute of limitation relating to the claim until 30 days after its disallowance.
(c) A claimant whose claim has not been paid may petition the [appropriate] Court for determination of the claim at any time before it is barred by the applicable statute of limitation and, upon due proof, procure an order for its allowance, payment, or security from the estate. If a proceeding is pending against a protected person at the time of appointment of a conservator or is initiated against the protected person thereafter, the moving party shall give notice of the proceeding to the conservator if the proceeding could result in creating a claim against the estate.
(d) If it appears that the estate in conservatorship is likely to be exhausted before all existing claims are paid, the conservator shall distribute the estate in money or in kind in payment of claims in the following order:

(1) costs and expenses of administration;
(2) claims of the federal or state government having priority under other laws;
(3) claims incurred by the conservator for care, maintenance, and education, previously provided to the protected person or the protected person's dependents;
(4) claims arising prior to the conservatorship;
(5) all other claims.

(e) No preference may be given in the payment of any claim over any other claim of the same class, and a claim due and payable is not entitled to a preference over claims not due; but if it appears that the assets of the conservatorship are adequate to meet all existing claims, the Court, acting in the best interest of the protected person, may order the conservator to give a mortgage or other security on the conservatorship estate to secure payment at some future date of any or all claims in class 5.

Section 5-428. [Personal Liability of Conservator.]
(a) Unless otherwise provided in the contract, a conservator is not personally liable on a contract properly entered into in fiduciary capacity in the course of administration of the estate unless the conservator fails to reveal the representative capacity and identify the estate in the contract.
(b) The conservator is personally liable for obligations arising from ownership or control of property of the estate or for torts committed in the course of administration of the estate only if personally at fault.
(c) Claims based on (i) contracts entered into by a conservator in fiduciary capacity, (ii) obligations arising from ownership or control of the estate, or (iii) torts committed in the course of administration of the estate, may be asserted against the

estate by proceeding against the conservator in fiduciary capacity, whether or not the conservator is personally liable therefor.
(d) Any question of liability between the estate and the conservator personally may be determined in a proceeding for accounting, surcharge, or indemnification, or other appropriate proceeding or action.

Section 5-429. [Termination of Proceedings.]
The protected person, conservator, or any other interested person, may petition the Court to terminate the conservatorship. A protected person seeking termination is entitled to the same rights and procedures as in an original proceeding for a protective order. The Court, upon determining after notice and hearing that the minority or disability of the protected person has ceased, shall terminate the conservatorship. Upon termination, title to assets of the estate passes to the formerly protected person or to successors. The order of termination must provide for expenses of administration and direct the conservator to execute appropriate instruments to evidence the transfer.

Section 5-430. [Payment of Debt and Delivery of Property to Foreign Conservator without Local Proceedings.]
(a) Any person indebted to a protected person or having possession of property or of an instrument evidencing a debt, stock, or chose in action belonging to a protected person may pay or deliver it to a conservator, guardian of the estate, or other like fiduciary appointed by a court of the state of residence of the protected person upon being presented with proof of appointment and an affidavit made by or on behalf of the fiduciary stating:

(1) that no protective proceeding relating to the protected person is pending in this State; and
(2) that the foreign fiduciary is entitled to payment or to receive delivery.

(b) If the person to whom the affidavit is presented is not aware of any protective proceeding pending in this State, payment or delivery in response to the demand and affidavit discharges the debtor or possessor.

Section 5-431. [Foreign Conservator; Proof of Authority; Bond; Powers.]
If a conservator has not been appointed in this State and no petition in a protective proceeding is pending in this State, a conservator appointed in the state in which the protected person resides may file in a Court of this State in a [county] in which property belonging to the protected person is located, authenticated copies of letters of appointment and of any bond. Thereafter, the domiciliary foreign conservator may exercise as to assets in this State all powers of a conservator appointed in this State and may maintain actions and proceedings in this State subject to any conditions imposed upon non-resident parties generally.

PART 5. DURABLE POWER OF ATTORNEY

Adoption of Uniform Durable Power of Attorney Act

Part 5 of Article V of the Uniform Probate Code was amended by the National Conference of Commissioners on Uniform State Laws in 1979. Sections 5-501 to 5-505, as enacted in 1979, are identical to sections 1 to 5 of the Uniform Durable Power of Attorney Act, also approved by the National Conference in 1979 as an alternative to Part 5 of Article V of the Uniform Probate Code. See Prefatory Note, infra.

Section 5-501. [Definition.]
A durable power of attorney is a power of attorney by which a principal designates another his attorney in fact in writing and the writing contains the words "This power of attorney shall not be affected by subsequent disability or incapacity of the

principal, or lapse of time," or "This power of attorney shall become effective upon the disability or incapacity of the principal," or similar words showing the intent of the principal that the authority conferred shall be exercisable notwithstanding the principal's subsequent disability or incapacity, and, unless it states a time of termination, notwithstanding the lapse of time since the execution of the instrument.

As amended in 1984.

Section 5-502. [Durable Power of Attorney Not Affected By Lapse of Time, Disability or Incapacity.]

All acts done by an attorney in fact pursuant to a durable power of attorney during any period of disability or incapacity of the principal have the same effect and inure to the benefit of and bind the principal and his successors in interest as if the principal were competent and not disabled. Unless the instrument states a time of termination, the power is exercisable notwithstanding the lapse of time since the execution of the instrument.

As amended in 1987.

Section 5-503. [Relation of Attorney in Fact to Court-appointed Fiduciary.]

(a) If, following execution of a durable power of attorney, a court of the principal's domicile appoints a conservator, guardian of the estate, or other fiduciary charged with the management of all of the principal's property or all of his property except specified exclusions, the attorney in fact is accountable to the fiduciary as well as to the principal. The fiduciary has the same power to revoke or amend the power of attorney that the principal would have had if he were not disabled or incapacitated.

(b) A principal may nominate, by a durable power of attorney, the conservator, guardian of his estate, or guardian of his person for consideration by the court if protective proceedings for the principal's person or estate are thereafter commenced. The court shall make its appointment in accordance with the principal's most recent nomination in a durable power of attorney except for good cause or disqualification.

Section 5-504. [Power of Attorney Not Revoked Until Notice.]

(a) The death of a principal who has executed a written power of attorney, durable or otherwise, does not revoke or terminate the agency as to the attorney in fact or other person, who, without actual knowledge of the death of the principal, acts in good faith under the power. Any action so taken, unless otherwise invalid or unenforceable, binds successors in interest of the principal.

(b) The disability or incapacity of a principal who has previously executed a written power of attorney that is not a durable power does not revoke or terminate the agency as to the attorney in fact or other person, who, without actual knowledge of the disability or incapacity of the principal, acts in good faith under the power. Any action so taken, unless otherwise invalid or unenforceable, binds the principal and his successors in interest.

Section 5-505. [Proof of Continuance of Durable and Other Powers of Attorney by Affidavit.]

As to acts undertaken in good faith reliance thereon, an affidavit executed by the attorney in fact under a power of attorney, durable or otherwise, stating that he did not have at the time of exercise of the power actual knowledge of the termination of the power by revocation or of the principal's death, disability, or incapacity is conclusive proof of the nonrevocation or nontermination of the power at that time. If the exercise of the power of attorney requires execution and delivery of any instrument that is recordable, the affidavit when authenticated for record is likewise recordable. This section does not affect any provision in a power of attorney for its termination by expiration of time or occurrence of an event other than express revocation or a change in the principal's capacity.

ARTICLE VI. NONPROBATE TRANSFERS ON DEATH (1989)

PART 1. PROVISIONS RELATING TO EFFECT OF DEATH
6-101. Nonprobate Transfers on Death.

PART 2. MULTIPLE-PERSON ACCOUNTS

SUBPART 1. DEFINITIONS AND GENERAL PROVISIONS
6-201. Definitions.
6-202. Limitation on Scope of Part.
6-203. Types of Account; Existing Accounts.
6-204. Forms.
6-205. Designation of Agent.
6-206. Applicability of Part.

SUBPART 2. OWNERSHIP AS BETWEEN PARTIES AND OTHERS
6-211. Ownership During Lifetime.
6-212. Rights at Death.
6-213. Alteration of Rights.
6-214. Accounts and Transfers Nontestamentary.
6-215. Rights of Creditors and Others.
6-216. Community Property and Tenancy by the Entireties.

SUBPART 3. PROTECTION OF FINANCIAL INSTITUTIONS
6-221. Authority of Financial Institution.
6-222. Payment on Multiple-Party Account.
6-223. Payment on POD Designation.
6-224. Payment to Designated Agent.
6-225. Payment to Minor.
6-226. Discharge.
6-227. Set-off.

PART 3. UNIFORM TOD SECURITY REGISTRATION ACT
6-301. Definitions.
6-302. Registration in Beneficiary Form; Sole or Joint Tenancy Ownership.
6-303. Registration in Beneficiary Form; Applicable Law.
6-304. Origination of Registration in Beneficiary Form.
6-305. Form of Registration in Beneficiary Form.
6-306. Effect of Registration in Beneficiary Form.
6-307. Ownership on Death of Owner.
6-308. Protection of Registering Entity.
6-309. Nontestamentary Transfer on Death.
6-310. Terms, Conditions, and Forms for Registration.
[6-311. Application of Part].

PART 1. PROVISIONS RELATING TO EFFECT OF DEATH

§ 6-101. Nonprobate Transfers on Death.
(a) A provision for a nonprobate transfer on death in an insurance policy, contract of employment, bond, mortgage, promissory note, certificated or uncertificated security, account agreement, custodial agreement, deposit agreement, compensation plan, pension plan, individual retirement plan, employee benefit plan, trust, conveyance, deed of gift, marital property agreement, or other written instrument of a similar nature is nontestamentary. This subsection includes a written provision that:

(1) money or other benefits due to, controlled by, or owned by a decedent before death must be paid after the decedent's death to a person whom the decedent designates either in the instrument or in a separate writing, including a will, executed either before or at the same time as the instrument, or later;

(2) money due or to become due under the instrument ceases to be payable in the event of death of the promisee or the promisor before payment or demand; or
(3) any property controlled by or owned by the decedent before death which is the subject of the instrument passes to a person the decedent designates either in the instrument or in a separate writing, including a will, executed either before or at the same time as the instrument, or later.

(b) This section does not limit rights of creditors under other laws of this State.

PART 2. MULTIPLE-PERSON ACCOUNTS

SUBPART 1. DEFINITIONS AND GENERAL PROVISIONS

§ 6-201. Definitions.
In this part:

(1) "Account" means a contract of deposit between a depositor and a financial institution, and includes a checking account, savings account, certificate of deposit, and share account.
(2) "Agent" means a person authorized to make account transactions for a party.
(3) "Beneficiary" means a person named as one to whom sums on deposit in an account are payable on request after death of all parties or for whom a party is named as trustee.
(4) "Financial institution" means an organization authorized to do business under state or federal laws relating to financial institutions, and includes a bank, trust company, savings bank, building and loan association, savings and loan company or association, and credit union.
(5) "Multiple-party account" means an account payable on request to one or more of two or more parties, whether or not a right of survivorship is mentioned.
(6) "Party" means a person who, by the terms of an account, has a present right, subject to request, to payment from the account other than as a beneficiary or agent.
(7) "Payment" of sums on deposit includes withdrawal, payment to a party or third person pursuant to check or other request, and a pledge of sums on deposit by a party, or a set-off, reduction, or other disposition of all or part of an account pursuant to a pledge.
(8) "POD designation" means the designation of (i) a beneficiary in an account payable on request to one party during the party's lifetime and on the party's death to one or more beneficiaries, or to one or more parties during their lifetimes and on death of all of them to one or more beneficiaries, or (ii) a beneficiary in an account in the name of one or more parties as trustee for one or more beneficiaries if the relationship is established by the terms of the account and there is no subject of the trust other than the sums on deposit in the account, whether or not payment to the beneficiary is mentioned.
(9) "Receive," as it relates to notice to a financial institution, means receipt in the office or branch office of the financial institution in which the account is established, but if the terms of the account require notice at a particular place, in the place required.
(10) "Request" means a request for payment complying with all terms of the account, including special requirements concerning necessary signatures and regulations of the financial institution; but, for purposes of this part, if terms of the account condition payment on advance notice, a request for payment is treated as immediately effective and a notice of intent to withdraw is treated as a request for payment.
(11) "Sums on deposit" means the balance payable on an account, including interest and dividends earned, whether or not included in the current balance, and any deposit life insurance proceeds added to the account by reason of death of a party.

(12) "Terms of the account" includes the deposit agreement and other terms and conditions, including the form, of the contract of deposit.

§ 6-202. Limitation on Scope of Part.
This part does not apply to (i) an account established for a partnership, joint venture, or other organization for a business purpose, (ii) an account controlled by one or more persons as an agent or trustee for a corporation, unincorporated association, or charitable or civic organization, or (iii) a fiduciary or trust account in which the relationship is established other than by the terms of the account.

§ 6-203. Types of Account; Existing Accounts.
(a) An account may be for a single party or multiple parties. A multiple-party account may be with or without a right of survivorship between the parties. Subject to Section 6-212(c), either a single-party account or a multiple-party account may have a POD designation, an agency designation, or both.
(b) An account established before, on, or after the effective date of this part, whether in the form prescribed in Section 6-204 or in any other form, is either a single-party account or a multiple-party account, with or without right of survivorship, and with or without a POD designation or an agency designation, within the meaning of this part, and is governed by this part.

§ 6-204. Forms.
(a) A contract of deposit that contains provisions in substantially the following form establishes the type of account provided, and the account is governed by the provisions of this part applicable to an account of that type:

UNIFORM SINGLE-OR MULTIPLE-PARTY ACCOUNT FORM

PARTIES [Name One or More Parties]:

____________________ ____________________

OWNERSHIP [Select One And Initial]:
________ SINGLE-PARTY ACCOUNT
________ MULTIPLE-PARTY ACCOUNT
Parties own account in proportion to net contributions unless there is clear and convincing evidence of a different intent.
RIGHTS AT DEATH [Select One And Initial]:
________ SINGLE-PARTY ACCOUNT
At death of party, ownership passes as part of party's estate.
________ SINGLE-PARTY ACCOUNT WITH POD (PAY ON DEATH) DESIGNATION
[Name One Or More Beneficiaries]:

____________________ ____________________

At death of party, ownership passes to POD beneficiaries and is not part of party's estate.
________ MULTIPLE-PARTY ACCOUNT WITH RIGHT OF SURVIVORSHIP
At death of party, ownership passes to surviving parties.
________ MULTIPLE-PARTY ACCOUNT WITH RIGHT OF SURVIVORSHIP AND POD (PAY ON DEATH) DESIGNATION
[Name One Or More Beneficiaries]:

____________________ ____________________

At death of last surviving party, ownership passes to POD beneficiaries and is not part of last surviving party's estate.
________ MULTIPLE-PARTY ACCOUNT WITHOUT RIGHT OF SURVIVORSHIP
At death of party, deceased party's ownership passes as part of deceased party's estate.
AGENCY (POWER OF ATTORNEY) DESIGNATION [Optional]
Agents may make account transactions for parties but have no ownership or rights at death unless named as POD beneficiaries.

[To Add Agency Designation To Account, Name One Or More Agents]:

________________________ ________________________

[Select One And Initial]:

________ AGENCY DESIGNATION SURVIVES DISABILITY OR INCAPACITY OF PARTIES

________ AGENCY DESIGNATION TERMINATES ON DISABILITY OR INCAPACITY OF PARTIES

(b) A contract of deposit that does not contain provisions in substantially the form provided in subsection (a) is governed by the provisions of this part applicable to the type of account that most nearly conforms to the depositor's intent.

§ 6-205. Designation of Agent.

(a) By a writing signed by all parties, the parties may designate as agent of all parties on an account a person other than a party.

(b) Unless the terms of an agency designation provide that the authority of the agent terminates on disability or incapacity of a party, the agent's authority survives disability and incapacity. The agent may act for a disabled or incapacitated party until the authority of the agent is terminated.

(c) Death of the sole party or last surviving party terminates the authority of an agent.

§ 6-206. Applicability of Part.

The provisions of Subpart 2 concerning beneficial ownership as between parties or as between parties and beneficiaries apply only to controversies between those persons and their creditors and other successors, and do not apply to the right of those persons to payment as determined by the terms of the account. Subpart 3 governs the liability and set-off rights of financial institutions that make payments pursuant to it.

SUBPART 2. OWNERSHIP AS BETWEEN PARTIES AND OTHERS

§ 6-211. Ownership During Lifetime.

(a) In this section, "net contribution" of a party means the sum of all deposits to an account made by or for the party, less all payments from the account made to or for the party which have not been paid to or applied to the use of another party and a proportionate share of any charges deducted from the account, plus a proportionate share of any interest or dividends earned, whether or not included in the current balance. The term includes deposit life insurance proceeds added to the account by reason of death of the party whose net contribution is in question.

(b) During the lifetime of all parties, an account belongs to the parties in proportion to the net contribution of each to the sums on deposit, unless there is clear and convincing evidence of a different intent. As between parties married to each other, in the absence of proof otherwise, the net contribution of each is presumed to be an equal amount.

(c) A beneficiary in an account having a POD designation has no right to sums on deposit during the lifetime of any party.

(d) An agent in an account with an agency designation has no beneficial right to sums on deposit.

§ 6-212. Rights at Death.

(a) Except as otherwise provided in this section, on death of a party sums on deposit in a multiple-party account belong to the surviving party or parties. If two or more parties survive and one is the surviving spouse of the decedent, the amount to which the decedent, immediately before death, was beneficially entitled under Section 6-211 belongs to the surviving spouse. If two or more parties survive and none is the surviving spouse of the decedent, the amount to which the decedent, immediately before death, was beneficially entitled under Section 6-211 belongs to the surviving

parties in equal shares, and augments the proportion to which each survivor, immediately before the decedent's death, was beneficially entitled under Section 6-211, and the right of survivorship continues between the surviving parties.
(b) In an account with a POD designation:

(1) On death of one of two or more parties, the rights in sums on deposit are governed by subsection (a).
(2) On death of the sole party or the last survivor of two or more parties, sums on deposit belong to the surviving beneficiary or beneficiaries. If two or more beneficiaries survive, sums on deposit belong to them in equal and undivided shares, and there is no right of survivorship in the event of death of a beneficiary thereafter. If no beneficiary survives, sums on deposit belong to the estate of the last surviving party.

(c) Sums on deposit in a single-party account without a POD designation, or in a multiple-party account that, by the terms of the account, is without right of survivorship, are not affected by death of a party, but the amount to which the decedent, immediately before death, was beneficially entitled under Section 6-211 is transferred as part of the decedent's estate. A POD designation in a multiple-party account without right of survivorship is ineffective. For purposes of this section, designation of an account as a tenancy in common establishes that the account is without right of survivorship.
(d) The ownership right of a surviving party or beneficiary, or of the decedent's estate, in sums on deposit is subject to requests for payment made by a party before the party's death, whether paid by the financial institution before or after death, or unpaid. The surviving party or beneficiary, or the decedent's estate, is liable to the payee of an unpaid request for payment. The liability is limited to a proportionate share of the amount transferred under this section, to the extent necessary to discharge the request for payment.

§ 6-213. Alteration of Rights.
(a) Rights at death under Section 6-212 are determined by the type of account at the death of a party. The type of account may be altered by written notice given by a party to the financial institution to change the type of account or to stop or vary payment under the terms of the account. The notice must be signed by a party and received by the financial institution during the party's lifetime.
(b) A right of survivorship arising from the express terms of the account, Section 6-212, or a POD designation, may not be altered by will.

§ 6-214. Accounts and Transfers Nontestamentary.
Except as provided in Part 2 of Article II (elective share of surviving spouse) or as a consequence of, and to the extent directed by, Section 6-215, a transfer resulting from the application of Section 6-212 is effective by reason of the terms of the account involved and this part and is not testamentary or subject to Articles I through IV (estate administration).

§ 6-215. Rights of Creditors and Others.
(a) If other assets of the estate are insufficient, a transfer resulting from a right of survivorship or POD designation under this part is not effective against the estate of a deceased party to the extent needed to pay claims against the estate and statutory allowances to the surviving spouse and children.
(b) A surviving party or beneficiary who receives payment from an account after death of a party is liable to account to the personal representative of the decedent for a proportionate share of the amount received to the extent necessary to discharge the claims and allowances described in subsection (a) remaining unpaid after application of the decedent's estate. A proceeding to assert the liability may not be commenced unless the personal representative has received a written demand by the surviving spouse, a creditor, a child, or a person acting for a child

of the decedent. The proceeding must be commenced within one year after death of the decedent.
(c) A surviving party or beneficiary against whom a proceeding to account is brought may join as a party to the proceeding a surviving party or beneficiary of any other account of the decedent.
(d) Sums recovered by the personal representative must be administered as part of the decedent's estate. This section does not affect the protection from claims of the personal representative or estate of a deceased party provided in Section 6-226 for a financial institution that makes payment in accordance with the terms of the account.

§ 6-216. Community Property and Tenancy by the Entireties.
(a) A deposit of community property in an account does not alter the community character of the property or community rights in the property, but a right of survivorship between parties married to each other arising from the express terms of the account or Section 6-212 may not be altered by will.
(b) This part does not affect the law governing tenancy by the entireties.

SUBPART 3. PROTECTION OF FINANCIAL INSTITUTIONS

§ 6-221. Authority of Financial Institution.
A financial institution may enter into a contract of deposit for a multiple-party account to the same extent it may enter into a contract of deposit for a single-party account, and may provide for a POD designation and an agency designation in either a single-party account or a multiple-party account. A financial institution need not inquire as to the source of a deposit to an account or as to the proposed application of a payment from an account.

§ 6-222. Payment on Multiple-Party Account.
A financial institution, on request, may pay sums on deposit in a multiple-party account to:

(1) one or more of the parties, whether or not another party is disabled, incapacitated, or deceased when payment is requested and whether or not the party making the request survives another party; or
(2) the personal representative, if any, or, if there is none, the heirs or devisees of a deceased party if proof of death is presented to the financial institution showing that the deceased party was the survivor of all other persons named on the account either as a party or beneficiary, unless the account is without right of survivorship under Section 6-212.

§ 6-223. Payment on POD Destination.
A financial institution, on request, may pay sums on deposit in an account with a POD designation to:

(1) one or more of the parties, whether or not another party is disabled, incapacitated, or deceased when the payment is requested and whether or not a party survives another party;
(2) the beneficiary or beneficiaries, if proof of death is presented to the financial institution showing that the beneficiary or beneficiaries survived all persons named as parties; or
(3) the personal representative, if any, or, if there is none, the heirs or devisees of a deceased party, if proof of death is presented to the financial institution showing that the deceased party was the survivor of all other persons named on the account either as a party or beneficiary.

§ 6-224. Payment to Designated Agent.
A financial institution, on request of an agent under an agency designation for an

account, may pay to the agent sums on deposit in the account, whether or not a party is disabled, incapacitated, or deceased when the request is made or received, and whether or not the authority of the agent terminates on the disability or incapacity of a party.

§ 6-225. Payment to Minor.
If a financial institution is required or permitted to make payment pursuant to this part to a minor designated as a beneficiary, payment may be made pursuant to the Uniform Transfers to Minors Act.

§ 6-226. Discharge.
(a) Payment made pursuant to this part in accordance with the type of account discharges the financial institution from all claims for amounts so paid, whether or not the payment is consistent with the beneficial ownership of the account as between parties, beneficiaries, or their successors. Payment may be made whether or not a party, beneficiary, or agent is disabled, incapacitated, or deceased when payment is requested, received, or made.
(b) Protection under this section does not extend to payments made after a financial institution has received written notice from a party, or from the personal representative, surviving spouse, or heir or devisee of a deceased party, to the effect that payments in accordance with the terms of the account, including one having an agency designation, should not be permitted, and the financial institution has had a reasonable opportunity to act on it when the payment is made. Unless the notice is withdrawn by the person giving it, the successor of any deceased party must concur in a request for payment if the financial institution is to be protected under this section. Unless a financial institution has been served with process in an action or proceeding, no other notice or other information shown to have been available to the financial institution affects its right to protection under this section.
(c) A financial institution that receives written notice pursuant to this section or otherwise has reason to believe that a dispute exists as to the rights of the parties may refuse, without liability, to make payments in accordance with the terms of the account.
(d) Protection of a financial institution under this section does not affect the rights of parties in disputes between themselves or their successors concerning the beneficial ownership of sums on deposit in accounts or payments made from accounts.

§ 6-227. Set-Off.
Without qualifying any other statutory right to set-off or lien and subject to any contractual provision, if a party is indebted to a financial institution, the financial institution has a right to set-off against the account. The amount of the account subject to set-off is the proportion to which the party is, or immediately before death was, beneficially entitled under Section 6-211 or, in the absence of proof of that proportion, an equal share with all parties.

PART 3. UNIFORM TOD SECURITY REGISTRATION ACT

§ 6-301. Definitions.
In this part:

(1) "Beneficiary form" means a registration of a security which indicates the present owner of the security and the intention of the owner regarding the person who will become the owner of the security upon the death of the owner.
(2) "Register," including its derivatives, means to issue a certificate showing the ownership of a certificated security or, in the case of an uncertificated security, to initiate or transfer an account showing ownership of securities.
(3) "Registering entity" means a person who originates or transfers a security title by registration, and includes a broker maintaining security accounts for

customers and a transfer agent or other person acting for or as an issuer of securities.

(4) "Security" means a share, participation, or other interest in property, in a business, or in an obligation of an enterprise or other issuer, and includes a certificated security, an uncertificated security, and a security account.

(5) "Security account" means (i) a reinvestment account associated with a security, a securities account with a broker, a cash balance in a brokerage account, cash, interest, earnings, or dividends earned or declared on a security in an account, a reinvestment account, or a brokerage account, whether or not credited to the account before the owner's death, or (ii) a cash balance or other property held for or due to the owner of a security as a replacement for or product of an account security, whether or not credited to the account before the owner's death.

§ 6-302. Registration in Beneficiary Form; Sole or Joint Tenancy Ownership.
Only individuals whose registration of a security shows sole ownership by one individual or multiple ownership by two or more with right of survivorship, rather than as tenants in common, may obtain registration in beneficiary form. Multiple owners of a security registered in beneficiary form hold as joint tenants with right of survivorship, as tenants by the entireties, or as owners of community property held in survivorship form, and not as tenants in common.

§ 6-303. Registration in Beneficiary Form; Applicable Law.
A security may be registered in beneficiary form if the form is authorized by this or a similar statute of the state of organization of the issuer or registering entity, the location of the registering entity's principal office, the office of its transfer agent or its office making the registration, or by this or a similar statute of the law of the state listed as the owner's address at the time of registration. A registration governed by the law of a jurisdiction in which this or similar legislation is not in force or was not in force when a registration in beneficiary form was made is nevertheless presumed to be valid and authorized as a matter of contract law.

§ 6-304. Origination of Registration in Beneficiary Form.
A security, whether evidenced by certificate or account, is registered in beneficiary form when the registration includes a designation of a beneficiary to take the ownership at the death of the owner or the deaths of all multiple owners.

§ 6-305. Form of Registration in Beneficiary Form.
Registration in beneficiary form may be shown by the words "transfer on death" or the abbreviation "TOD," or by the words "pay on death" or the abbreviation "POD," after the name of the registered owner and before the name of a beneficiary.

§ 6-306. Effect of Registration in Beneficiary Form.
The designation of a TOD beneficiary on a registration in beneficiary form has no effect on ownership until the owner's death. A registration of a security in beneficiary form may be canceled or changed at any time by the sole owner or all then surviving owners without the consent of the beneficiary.

§ 6-307. Ownership on Death of Owner.
On death of a sole owner or the last to die of all multiple owners, ownership of securities registered in beneficiary form passes to the beneficiary or beneficiaries who survive all owners. On proof of death of all owners and compliance with any applicable requirements of the registering entity, a security registered in beneficiary form may be reregistered in the name of the beneficiary or beneficiaries who survive the death of all owners. Until division of the security after the death of all owners, multiple beneficiaries surviving the death of all owners hold their interests as tenants in common. If no beneficiary survives the death of all owners, the

security belongs to the estate of the deceased sole owner or the estate of the last to die of all multiple owners.

§ 6-308. Protection of Registering Entity.
(a) A registering entity is not required to offer or to accept a request for security registration in beneficiary form. If a registration in beneficiary form is offered by a registering entity, the owner requesting registration in beneficiary form assents to the protections given to the registering entity by this part.
(b) By accepting a request for registration of a security in beneficiary form, the registering entity agrees that the registration will be implemented on death of the deceased owner as provided in this part.
(c) A registering entity is discharged from all claims to a security by the estate, creditors, heirs, or devisees of a deceased owner if it registers a transfer of the security in accordance with Section 6-307 and does so in good faith reliance (i) on the registration, (ii) on this part, and (iii) on information provided to it by affidavit of the personal representative of the deceased owner, or by the surviving beneficiary or by the surviving beneficiary's representatives, or other information available to the registering entity. The protections of this part do not extend to a reregistration or payment made after a registering entity has received written notice from any claimant to any interest in the security objecting to implementation of a registration in beneficiary form. No other notice or other information available to the registering entity affects its right to protection under this part.
(d) The protection provided by this part to the registering entity of a security does not affect the rights of beneficiaries in disputes between themselves and other claimants to ownership of the security transferred or its value or proceeds.

§ 6-309. Nontestamentary Transfer on Death.
(a) A transfer on death resulting from a registration in beneficiary form is effective by reason of the contract regarding the registration between the owner and the registering entity and this part and is not testamentary.
(b) This part does not limit the rights of creditors of security owners against beneficiaries and other transferees under other laws of this State.

§ 6-310. Terms, Conditions, and Forms for Registration.
(a) A registering entity offering to accept registrations in beneficiary form may establish the terms and conditions under which it will receive requests (i) for registrations in beneficiary form, and (ii) for implementation of registrations in beneficiary form, including requests for cancellation of previously registered TOD beneficiary designations and requests for reregistration to effect a change of beneficiary. The terms and conditions so established may provide for proving death, avoiding or resolving any problems concerning fractional shares, designating primary and contingent beneficiaries, and substituting a named beneficiary's descendants to take in the place of the named beneficiary in the event of the beneficiary's death. Substitution may be indicated by appending to the name of the primary beneficiary the letters LDPS, standing for "lineal descendants per stripes." This designation substitutes a deceased beneficiary's descendants who survive the owner for a beneficiary who fails to so survive, the descendants to be identified and to share in accordance with the law of the beneficiary's domicile at the owner's death governing inheritance by descendants of an intestate. Other forms of identifying beneficiaries who are to take on one or more contingencies, and rules for providing proofs and assurances needed to satisfy reasonable concerns by registering entities regarding conditions and identities relevant to accurate implementation of registrations in beneficiary form, may be contained in a registering entity's terms and conditions.
(b) The following are illustrations of registrations in beneficiary form which a registering entity may authorize:

(1) Sole owner-sole beneficiary: John S Brown TOD (or POD) John S Brown Jr.

(2) Multiple owners-sole beneficiary: John S Brown Mary B Brown JT TEN TOD John S Brown Jr.
(3) Multiple owners-primary and secondary (substituted) beneficiaries: John S Brown Mary B Brown JT TEN TOD John S Brown Jr SUB BENE Peter Q Brown *or* John S Brown Mary B Brown JT TEN TOD John S Brown Jr LDPS.

[§ 6-311. Application of Part.
This part applies to registrations of securities in beneficiary form made before or after [effective date], by decedents dying on or after [effective date].

ARTICLE VII. TRUST ADMINISTRATION

PART 1. TRUST REGISTRATION
7-101. [Duty to Register Trusts.]
7-102. [Registration Procedures.]
7-103. [Effect of Registration.]
7-104. [Effect of Failure to Register.]
7-105. [Registration, Qualification of Foreign Trustee.]

PART 2. JURISDICTION OF COURT CONCERNING TRUSTS
7-201. [Court; Exclusive Jurisdiction of Trusts.]
7-202. [Trust Proceedings; Venue.]
7-203. [Trust Proceedings; Dismissal of Matters Relating to Foreign Trusts.]
7-204. [Court; Concurrent Jurisdiction of Litigation Involving Trusts and Third Parties.]
7-205. [Proceedings for Review of Employment of Agents and Review of Compensation of Trustee and Employees of Trust.]
7-206. [Trust Proceedings; Initiation by Notice; Necessary Parties.]

PART 3. DUTIES AND LIABILITIES OF TRUSTEES
7-301. [General Duties Not Limited.]
7-302. [Trustee's Standard of Care and Performance.]
7-303. [Duty to Inform and Account to Beneficiaries.]
7-304. [Duty to Provide Bond.]
7-305. [Trustee's Duties; Appropriate Place of Administration; Deviation.]
7-306. [Personal Liability of Trustee to Third Parties.]
7-307. [Limitations on Proceedings Against Trustees After Final Account.]

PART 4. POWERS OF TRUSTEES
[GENERAL COMMENT ONLY]

PART 1. TRUST REGISTRATION

Section 7-101. [Duty to Register Trusts.]
The trustee of a trust having its principal place of administration in this state shall register the trust in the Court of this state at the principal place of administration. Unless otherwise designated in the trust instrument, the principal place of administration of a trust is the trustee's usual place of business where the records pertaining to the trust are kept, or at the trustee's residence if he has no such place of business. In the case of co-trustees, the principal place of administration, if not otherwise designated in the trust instrument, is (1) the usual place of business of the corporate trustee if there is but one corporate co-trustee, or (2) the usual place of business or residence of the individual trustee who is a professional fiduciary if there is but one such person and no corporate co-trustee, and otherwise (3) the usual place of business or residence of any of the co-trustees as agreed upon by them. The duty to register under this Part does not apply to the trustee of a trust if registration would be inconsistent with the retained jurisdiction of a foreign court from which the trustee cannot obtain release.

Section 7-102. [Registration Procedures.]
Registration shall be accomplished by filing a statement indicating the name and address of the trustee in which it acknowledges the trusteeship. The statement shall indicate whether the trust has been registered elsewhere. The statement shall identify the trust: (1) in the case of a testamentary trust, by the name of the testator and the date and place of domiciliary probate; (2) in the case of a written inter vivos trust, by the name of each settlor and the original trustee and the date of the trust instrument; or (3) in the case of an oral trust, by information identifying the settlor or other source of funds and describing the time and manner of the trust's creation and the terms of the trust, including the subject matter, beneficiaries and time of performance. If a trust has been registered elsewhere, registration in this state is ineffective until the earlier registration is released by order of the Court where prior registration occurred, or an instrument executed by the trustee and all beneficiaries, filed with the registration in this state.

Section 7-103. [Effect of Registration.]
(a) By registering a trust, or accepting the trusteeship of a registered trust, the trustee submits personally to the jurisdiction of the Court in any proceeding under Section 7-201 of this Code relating to the trust that may be initiated by any interested person while the trust remains registered. Notice of any proceeding shall be delivered to the trustee, or mailed to him by ordinary first class mail at his address as listed in the registration or as thereafter reported to the Court and to his address as then known to the petitioner.
(b) To the extent of their interests in the trust, all beneficiaries of a trust properly registered in this state are subject to the jurisdiction of the court of registration for the purposes of proceedings under Section 7-201, provided notice is given pursuant to Section 1-401.

Section 7-104. [Effect of Failure to Register.]
A trustee who fails to register a trust in a proper place as required by this Part, for purposes of any proceedings initiated by a beneficiary of the trust prior to registration, is subject to the personal jurisdiction of any Court in which the trust could have been registered. In addition, any trustee who, within 30 days after receipt of a written demand by a settlor or beneficiary of the trust, fails to register a trust as required by this Part is subject to removal and denial of compensation or to surcharge as the Court may direct. A provision in the terms of the trust purporting to excuse the trustee from the duty to register, or directing that the trust or trustee shall not be subject to the jurisdiction of the Court, is ineffective.

Section 7-105. [Registration, Qualification of Foreign Trustee.]
A foreign corporate trustee is required to qualify as a foreign corporation doing business in this state if it maintains the principal place of administration of any trust within the state. A foreign co-trustee is not required to qualify in this state solely because its co-trustee maintains the principal place of administration in this state. Unless otherwise doing business in this state, local qualification by a foreign trustee, corporate or individual, is not required in order for the trustee to receive distribution from a local estate or to hold, invest in, manage or acquire property located in this state, or maintain litigation. Nothing in this section affects a determination of what other acts require qualification as doing business in this state.

PART 2. JURISDICTION OF COURT CONCERNING TRUSTS

Section 7-201. [Court; Exclusive Jurisdiction of Trusts.]
(a) The Court has exclusive jurisdiction of proceedings initiated by interested parties concerning the internal affairs of trusts. Proceedings which may be maintained under this section are those concerning the administration and distribution of trusts, the declaration of rights and the determination of other matters

involving trustees and beneficiaries of trusts. These include, but are not limited to, proceedings to:

(1) appoint or remove a trustee;
(2) review trustees' fees and to review and settle interim or final accounts;
(3) ascertain beneficiaries, determine any question arising in the administration or distribution of any trust including questions of construction of trust instruments, to instruct trustees, and determine the existence or nonexistence of any immunity, power, privilege, duty or right; and
(4) release registration of a trust.

(b) Neither registration of a trust nor a proceeding under this section result in continuing supervisory proceedings. The management and distribution of a trust estate, submission of accounts and reports to beneficiaries, payment of trustee's fees and other obligations of a trust, acceptance and change of trusteeship, and other aspects of the administration of a trust shall proceed expeditiously consistent with the terms of the trust, free of judicial intervention and without order, approval or other action of any court, subject to the jurisdiction of the Court as invoked by interested parties or as otherwise exercised as provided by law.

Section 7-202. [Trust Proceedings; Venue.]
Venue for proceedings under Section 7-201 involving registered trusts is in the place of registration. Venue for proceedings under Section 7-201 involving trusts not registered in this state is in any place where the trust properly could have been registered, and otherwise by the rules of civil procedure.

Section 7-203. [Trust Proceedings; Dismissal of Matters Relating to Foreign Trusts.]
The Court will not, over the objection of a party, entertain proceedings under Section 7-201 involving a trust registered or having its principal place of administration in another state, unless (1) when all appropriate parties could not be bound by litigation in the courts of the state where the trust is registered or has its principal place of administration or (2) when the interests of justice otherwise would seriously be impaired. The Court may condition a stay or dismissal of a proceeding under this section on the consent of any party to jurisdiction of the state in which the trust is registered or has its principal place of business, or the Court may grant a continuance or enter any other appropriate order.

Section 7-204. [Court; Concurrent Jurisdiction of Litigation Involving Trusts and Third Parties.]
The Court of the place in which the trust is registered has concurrent jurisdiction with other courts of this state of actions and proceedings to determine the existence or nonexistence of trusts created other than by will, of actions by or against creditors or debtors of trusts, and of other actions and proceedings involving trustees and third parties. Venue is determined by the rules generally applicable to civil actions.

Section 7-205. [Proceedings for Review of Employment of Agents and Review of Compensation of Trustee and Employees of Trust.]
On petition of an interested person, after notice to all interested persons, the Court may review the propriety of employment of any person by a trustee including any attorney, auditor, investment advisor or other specialized agent or assistant, and the reasonableness of the compensation of any person so employed, and the reasonableness of the compensation determined by the trustee for his own services. Any person who has received excessive compensation from a trust may be ordered to make appropriate refunds.

Section 7-206. [Trust Proceedings; Initiation by Notice; Necessary Parties.]
Proceedings under Section 7-201 are initiated by filing a petition in the Court and giving notice pursuant to Section 1-401 to interested parties. The Court may order notification of additional persons. A decree is valid as to all who are given notice of the proceeding though fewer than all interested parties are notified.

PART 3. DUTIES AND LIABILITIES OF TRUSTEES

Section 7-301. [General Duties Not Limited.]
Except as specifically provided, the general duty of the trustee to administer a trust expeditiously for the benefit of the beneficiaries is not altered by this Code.

Section 7-302. [Trustee's Standard of Care and Performance.]
Except as otherwise provided by the terms of the trust, the trustee shall observe the standards in dealing with the trust assets that would be observed by a prudent man dealing with the property of another, and if the trustee has special skills or is named trustee on the basis of representations of special skills or expertise, he is under a duty to use those skills.

Section 7-303. [Duty to Inform and Account to Beneficiaries.]
The trustee shall keep the beneficiaries of the trust reasonably informed of the trust and its administration. In addition:

(a) Within 30 days after his acceptance of the trust, the trustee shall inform in writing the current beneficiaries and if possible, one or more persons who under Section 1-403 may represent beneficiaries with future interests, of the Court in which the trust is registered and of his name and address.
(b) Upon reasonable request, the trustee shall provide the beneficiary with a copy of the terms of the trust which describe or affect his interest and with relevant information about the assets of the trust and the particulars relating to the administration.
(c) Upon reasonable request, a beneficiary is entitled to a statement of the accounts of the trust annually and on termination of the trust or change of the trustee.

Section 7-304. [Duty to Provide Bond.]
A trustee need not provide bond to secure performance of his duties unless required by the terms of the trust, reasonably requested by a beneficiary or found by the Court to be necessary to protect the interests of the beneficiaries who are not able to protect themselves and whose interests otherwise are not adequately represented. On petition of the trustee or other interested person the Court may excuse a requirement of bond, reduce the amount of the bond, release the surety, or permit the substitution of another bond with the same or different sureties. If bond is required, it shall be filed in the Court of registration or other appropriate Court in amounts and with sureties and liabilities as provided in Sections 3-604 and 3-606 relating to bonds of personal representatives.

Section 7-305. [Trustee's Duties; Appropriate Place of Administration; Deviation.]
A trustee is under a continuing duty to administer the trust at a place appropriate to the purposes of the trust and to its sound, efficient management. If the principal place of administration becomes inappropriate for any reason, the Court may enter any order furthering efficient administration and the interests of beneficiaries, including, if appropriate, release of registration, removal of the trustee and appointment of a trustee in another state. Trust provisions relating to the place of administration and to changes in the place of administration or of trustee control unless compliance would be contrary to efficient administration or the purposes of the trust. Views of adult beneficiaries shall be given weight in determining the suitability of the trustee and the place of administration.

Section 7-306. [Personal Liability of Trustee to Third Parties.]
(a) Unless otherwise provided in the contract, a trustee is not personally liable on contracts properly entered into in his fiduciary capacity in the course of administration of the trust estate unless he fails to reveal his representative capacity and identify the trust estate in the contract.
(b) A trustee is personally liable for obligations arising from ownership or control of property of the trust estate or for torts committed in the course of administration of the trust estate only if he is personally at fault.
(c) Claims based on contracts entered into by a trustee in his fiduciary capacity, on obligations arising from ownership or control of the trust estate, or on torts committed in the course of trust administration may be asserted against the trust estate by proceeding against the trustee in his fiduciary capacity, whether or not the trustee is personally liable therefor.
(d) The question of liability as between the trust estate and the trustee individually may be determined in a proceeding for accounting, surcharge or indemnification or other appropriate proceeding.

Section 7-307. [Limitations on Proceedings Against Trustees After Final Account.]
Unless previously barred by adjudication, consent or limitation, any claim against a trustee for breach of trust is barred as to any beneficiary who has received a final account or other statement fully disclosing the matter and showing termination of the trust relationship between the trustee and the beneficiary unless a proceeding to assert the claim is commenced within [6 months] after receipt of the final account or statement. In any event and notwithstanding lack of full disclosure a trustee who has issued a final account or statement received by the beneficiary and has informed the beneficiary of the location and availability of records for his examination is protected after 3 years. A beneficiary is deemed to have received a final account or statement if, being an adult, it is received by him personally or if, being a minor or disabled person, it is received by his representative as described in Section 1-403(1) and (2).

PART 4. POWERS OF TRUSTEES

ARTICLE VIII. EFFECTIVE DATE AND REPEALER

8-101. [Time of Taking Effect; Provisions for Transition.]
8-102. [Specific Repealer and Amendments.]

Section 8-101. [Time of Taking Effect; Provisions for Transition.]
(a) This Code takes effect on January 1, 19______.
(b) Except as provided elsewhere in this Code, on the effective date of this Code:

(1) the Code applies to any wills of decedents dying thereafter;
(2) the Code applies to any proceedings in Court then pending or thereafter commenced regardless of the time of the death of decedent except to the extent that in the opinion of the Court the former procedure should be made applicable in a particular case in the interest of justice or because of infeasibility of application of the procedure of this Code;
(3) every personal representative including a person administering an estate of a minor or incompetent holding an appointment on that date, continues to hold the appointment but has only the powers conferred by this Code and is subject to the duties imposed with respect to any act occurring or done thereafter;
(4) an act done before the effective date in any proceeding and any accrued right is not impaired by this Code. If a right is acquired, extinguished or barred upon the expiration of a prescribed period of time which has commenced to run by the provisions of any statute before the effective date, the provisions shall remain in force with respect to that right;

(5) any rule of construction or presumption provided in this Code applies to instruments executed and multiple party accounts opened before the effective date unless there is a clear indication of a contrary intent;
(6) a person holding office as judge of the Court on the effective date of this Act may continue the office of judge of this Court and may be selected for additional terms after the effective date of this Act even though he does not meet the qualifications of a judge as provided in Article I.

Section 8-102. [Specific Repealer and Amendments.]
(a) The following Acts and parts of Acts are repealed:

(1)
(2)
(3)

(b) The following Acts and parts of Acts are amended:

(1)
(2)
(3)

GLOSSARY

Abate, Abatement The reduction (or elimination) of a bequest made under a will because there are insufficient assets in the estate to satisfy the amount of the bequest.

Account, Accounting The formal document showing the assets received by a fiduciary, all income received on the assets, and all disbursements made. Anyone reviewing an account is able to see exactly what happened to all the assets in an estate or trust.

Accountant The person preparing an Account for the Court or beneficiaries of the estate or trust. Usually, the fiduciary is referred to as "the accountant" when the account is prepared. A C.P.A., Certified Public Accountant, can also be hired by the estate.

Accrue The coming due of a debt or the maturing of the right to receive an asset. In both cases, by showing the debt or asset has "accrued" the indication is that it has not yet been paid or received (as the case may be).

Accumulate 1. To retain income in a trust rather than distributing it. 2. To increase the amount of dividends due a stockholder by not paying them out until some time after they were originally due.

Ademption The inability to satisfy a bequest made in a will because the property, which is the subject of the bequest, was not owned by the decedent at the time of death.

Adjudication The confirmation by a court that the account filed by a fiduciary is in proper form.

Administration The handling of the assets of an estate by collecting them, valuing them and paying the debts of the decedent from the assets.

Administrator, Administratrix The person who administers an estate when the decedent either left no will or did not name an executor for the estate in the will.

Affidavit of Domicile An assurance given in writing to a corporation confirming the permanent place of residence of the decedent prior to death.

Agreement of Sale The written contract for the sale of real estate.

Alternate Valuation Date For federal estate tax purposes, assets may be valued as of six months after death rather than as of the date of death, which would be the normal valuation date.

Ancillary Letters The right given to the personal representative of an estate to act in a state other than that in which the original letters (testamentary or of administration) were granted. Ancillary letters are granted in the case where the decedent owned property in a state other than his/her state of domicile.

Annuity A series of regular payments of money over a period of time which may be fixed or paid for the lifetime of the recipient (known as an annuitant). There are private and commercial annuities.

Appraisal A valuation placed on property by a recognized expert.

Appreciation Increase in value of an asset by the mere passing of time (normally due to market conditions).

Asset Property or anything of value.

Audit The review of financial records by an outside party, e.g. the court or a governmental agency, such as the Internal Revenue Service.

Basis The value given to an asset for tax purposes to determine the gain or loss in value of the asset.

Beneficiaries Those people or organizations who benefit by the terms of a will or trust.

Bequest A gift of personal property or money through a will.

Boilerplate Provisions of a will, trust or other legal document which are used in most standard wills or trusts, such as the Powers Clause, the Tax Clause, etc.

Bona Fides In good faith. Honest.

Bond Security given to assure proper performance. With an estate this usually takes the form of a guarantee by an insurance company to reimburse the estate (up to a fixed dollar amount) for any misconduct by the personal representative causing loss to the estate (sometimes referred to as a fidelity bond).

Bonds Obligations of a corporation or government acknowledging that the holder of the bond has the right to receive a certain fixed sum at a given time, and interest on that sum in the interim. The bond is a debt of the corporation or government and an asset to the holder of the bond.

Book Value The date of death value of an asset held by an estate or the value of an asset on the date of creation of a trust.

Buy-Sell Agreement An agreement among owners of a business (incorporated or not) concerning the disposition of the interest of each owner in the case of death, retirement, disability or other circumstances.

Capital Gains Increase in value of property which has been held for investment purposes (e.g. stocks, a share in a partnership, etc.).

Caption The names of the parties and designation of the court in which a certain legal proceeding is taking place. The caption appears at the top of each document filed with the court.

Carrying Value The value of assets held by an estate or trust as of the date of death of the decedent or the date of the creation of the trust.

Cash Value The savings feature of whole life insurance. Each year, part of the premium on the policy is put aside by the insurance company and is saved for the insured. The insured may borrow against this amount or cash in the policy and receive its cash value.

Casualty Insurance Insurance to protect against casualty losses.

Casualty Loss The complete or partial destruction of property resulting from a sudden, unexpected or unusual destructive force (e.g. flood, fire, hurricane, vandalism, etc.).

Certificates of Deposit An interest bearing obligation of a bank usually not redeemable until some fixed time, or at periodic times, in the future.

Closely Held Corporation A corporation whose stock is owned by a small group of people and is not freely transferable outside that group.

Closing The date on which a transaction is concluded. For example, in the sale of real estate the date the deed is given to the purchaser and the check is received by the seller, is called the closing date.

Codicil An amendment to a will changing certain portions of the will or making additions to the will. The codicil should be physically attached to the will.

Collateral Descendants One's surviving brothers, sisters, nieces, nephews, aunts, uncles, cousins, etc., as distinguished from lineal descendants.

Commercial Paper Debt obligations of corporations which may be purchased and held as an investment. Usually such debts are in the form of promissory notes paying a relatively high rate of interest compared to what a bank may offer.

Common Stock Documents representing a share of the ownership of a corporation. The value of such shares is proportionate with the value of the corporation.

Common Trust Fund The commingling of money from numerous trusts held by a bank into a private mutual fund, owned and operated by the bank.

Community Property Community property states are states where the husband and wife are said to own all property accumulated during the marriage equally.

Consideration Something of value given in return for a performance or a promise of performance by another, for the purpose of forming a contract.

Contemplation of Death Disposing of property to avoid death taxes at a time when one believes he or she is about to die or when that presumption is imputed by law.

Convenience Accounts Joint accounts established at a bank for the purpose of paying bills or receiving income for a person unable to perform these functions for themselves. The balance is not automatically distributed to the surviving joint owner at the time of death.

Convertible Securities A corporate security which may be changed from one form to another. For example, convertible preferred stock would be exchangeable for common stock in the corporation at a certain fixed ratio.

Corpus Property which has been placed into a trust. Also a term used for the principal of a trust as opposed to income.

Creditor One who is owned money by another. A *secured* creditor is one who has an interest in property of the debtor to secure the payment. An *unsecured* creditor is one who has no such interest and relies solely on the promise of the debtor to pay.

Curtesy Rights A right which a husband has (or may have had under prior law) to receive certain property from the estate of his wife.

Custodian One who holds an asset for another person. With a bank account under the Uniform Gifts to Minors Act, the person who is the holder of the account (for the benefit of the minor) is called the custodian.

Death Certificate A document signed by a physician evidencing the death of an individual. This document is filed either with a local or state office, or both, as a permanent record.

Death Taxes Taxes imposed by a state or federal government on the transfer of assets from a decedent to his or her beneficiaries. Death taxes may be referred to as estate or inheritance taxes depending upon who bears the burden of payment—the estate (estate taxes) or the beneficiaries (inheritance taxes).

Debt Obligation A duty to repay a sum of money owed to another. This is frequently represented by documentary evidence of the debt, such as a promissory note.

Debenture A debt security of a corporation which is not secured by a mortgage on any property of the corporation.

Decedent Someone who has died.

Deed A written document conveying an interest in property to another. Most commonly, the document used to transfer ownership of real estate from one person to another.

Deed of Gift A writing transferring property as a gift from one person to another.

Deed of Trust The written document transferring property into a trust.

Depreciation A decline in value of an asset, usually due to its increase in age. This decrease in value is shown on books of account to properly reflect the current value of the asset. Depreciation can be taken as a deduction on income tax returns.

Devise, Devisee The gift of property to someone by a will. The recipient of the gift under the will is known as the devisee.

Disclaimer When a person refuses to accept a bequest under the will. The bequest will pass to the next beneficiary named in the will as if the first beneficiary had predeceased the decedent. The disclaimer must be in writing.

Distribution The transfer of property to the beneficiaries of an estate or trust.

Distribution "in kind" The transfer of assets to a beneficiary in their present state. For example, furniture might be given to a beneficiary rather than selling it and then distributing the cash to the beneficiary.

Dividend A payment by a corporation to its shareholders representing some portion of the earnings of the company. The payment is typically in cash (cash dividend). It may however, be in additional shares of stock of the corporation (stock dividends).

Domicile The place where a person has his or her primary residence.

Donee The recipient of a gift.

Donor The person who makes a gift.

Dower Rights A right which a wife has (or may have had under prior law) to receive certain property from the estate of her husband.

Duress Unlawful pressure put on a person to do something that the person would not otherwise have done of their own free will.

Equity Security The documentary evidence of ownership of a portion of a corporation. The most common would be a stock certificate.

Escheat The passing of property of a decedent to the state when there are no legally recognizable heirs of the decedent. This usually occurs when there is no will.

Escrow Property held by one person for another pending the performance of an obligation by the person whose property is being held.

Estate The total assets owned by the decedent at the time of death. The term can also be used to define all assets owned by a living person.

Estate Plan An arrangement for the disposition of a person's assets during life and at death by the use of trusts and a will.

Estate Tax A tax paid by a decedent's estate on the value of assets of the estate.

Execution The signing of a document.

Executor, Executrix The person (or corporation) charged with handling the affairs of a decedent. The decedent appoints this person by naming him or her in the will.

Expectancy An interest a living person may have under a will or trust which has not yet been received because the will or trust is not yet in effect. The term is also used in reference to life estates. An individual has a certain life expectancy.

Fair Market Value The price which a willing buyer will pay a willing seller for an asset at any given time.

Face Value The dollar amount appearing on a document, presumptively representing its value.

Family Allowance A deduction allowed on a state death tax return for property which is to go to a surviving family member. The amount of the deduction is usually relatively small. For example, the Pennsylvania family allowance is $2,000.

Federal Employer Identification Number A number that must be obtained from the Internal Revenue Service for each individual estate or trust. It is the same as a Social Security number for an individual.

Fiduciary One who acts in a position of utmost trust and may do so only in the best interests of the person who has placed that trust in the fiduciary. Examples would be the executor/trix or administrator/trix of an estate and a trustee of a trust. Lawyers, stockbrokers or bankers, acting in those capacities, may also be fiduciaries.

Foreclosure The act of taking real estate from the owner of the property as a means of enforcing the obligation to pay a debt owed on the property, usually represented by a mortgage.

Fraud Any kind of trickery used by one person to cheat another.

Fungible Goods or Property Things which are interchangeable. For example, one bushel of a certain grade of wheat is fungible in the sense that it can be replaced by another similarly graded bushel of wheat.

Future Interest The right to receive property in the future but this right may be contingent on the occurrence of certain events.

General Creditor One to whom a debt is owed but the debt is not secured by any property.

Gift A transfer of property without payment and without the expectation of receiving anything in return for it.

Gift Tax A tax imposed by the federal government on the donor of a gift, based on the value of the property transferred.

Guardian A person charged with overseeing another's person or property. Frequently, guardians are appointed to care for children or to take possession of assets of an incompetent person.

Heir A person who has a right to inherit property from a decedent under a state's intestacy law.

Homestead Rights A deduction allowed on a state death tax return for property passing to a surviving family member (the amount is usually relatively small).

Income Interest, dividends, or other return from money which has been invested.

Indemnify To reimburse someone for money which they have paid out. Usually this is a matter of contract, as when an insurance company agrees to bear the burden of paying (indemnifying) a policyholder.

Inherit To receive property from the estate of a decedent by reason of being related to that decedent.

Inheritance Tax A tax imposed by a state on the right to receive property from the estate of a decedent.

Inheritance Tax Waiver A notice from a taxing authority indicating that either no inheritance tax is due on certain property (so that ownership to it may be transferred) or that the tax on the property has been paid.

Intangible Personal Property Property which is, of itself, not worth anything but is valuable because of the rights it represents; e.g. bonds or stock certificates.

Inter Vivos Trust A trust created during the lifetime of the person who is placing the property into trust.

Intestacy, Intestate To die without leaving a valid will. An "intestate" is a decedent without a valid will.

Invade To pay principal from a trust as distinguished from paying the income.

Inventory A statement filed with a court showing the assets in a decedent's estate. This is usually filed four months after the date of death.

Irrevocable Trust A trust whose provisions may not be changed after its creation.

Issue A person's lineal decedents: children, grandchildren, great-grandchildren, etc.

Joint Ownership When two or more people own property. See tenants in common, tenants by the entireties, and joint tenants with right of survivorship.

Joint Tenants The people who own real estate jointly.

Joint Tenants with Right of Survivorship When property is titled in this manner, the property automatically passes to the surviving joint tenant at the time of the death of the first tenant.

Journal A book which regularly records cash and capital transactions.

Judgment A final order of a court deciding the rights and claims presented in a lawsuit.

Jurisdiction The authority by which a particular court may hear a case and make a decision which will be binding on the parties.

Lapse The failure of a gift made in a will because the named beneficiary has died before the decedent.

Lease A contract for the use of real estate, but not representing any ownership in it.

Ledger A book of account, categorizing various monetary transactions according to each individual asset.

Legacy A gift made in a will. There are general and specific legacies.

Legal Descripton The written designation of the exact location of a piece of real estate.

Legatee The person who is named as a beneficiary of personal property in a will.

Lessee The person who is named as being allowed to use real estate pursuant to a lease.

Lessor The owner of real estate who leases it to another.

Letters (Testamentary or Administration) The official designation by a court that a person has the authority to act for a decedent's estate. When that person has been named in the decedent's will, they are called *letters testamentary*. When there is no will, or the will does not name such a person to act for the estate, they are called *letters of administration*.

Liability Insurance Insurance to protect against the possibility that the policyholder will be held liable for consequences suffered by another and will have to pay damages to that other person. Instead, the insurance company pays the damages.

Lien An interest in property held by a creditor which would allow the creditor to have the property sold in order to provide funds to pay the debt owed to the creditor.

Life Insurance A contract with an insurance company to pay a specific amount of money to a named beneficiary when a person dies: There are various types of such contracts. Term Life—the insurance is for a specified period, the premiums increasing as the insured gets older. Whole Life—the same premium is paid annually and the insurance may continue throughout a person's life. This type of insurance also provides for forced savings—not all of the premium goes to pay for insurance but instead adds to the "cash value". Endowment—the face amount of this type of insurance is payable at a specific age to the insured, or at death if the insured dies before reaching that age.

Life Interest A right to receive a benefit from property only during one's life—without the right to give the property to another or sell it. For example, the right to receive income for life from $1,000,000 placed in trust is a life estate.

Life Tenant The person who holds a life estate in property.

Lineal Descendants One's children, grandchildren, great-grandchildren, etc.; as distinguished from collateral descendants.

Liquidate, Liquidity To turn assets into cash by their sale and the ability to do so.

Litigant A party to litigation.

Litigation Lawsuits. The use of the legal process to settle disputes between people.

Marital Deduction A deduction allowed on the federal estate tax and gift tax returns (and the death taxes of some states) for property given by the decedent to a surviving spouse. All spouses of U.S. citizens have an unlimited marital deduction. Non–U.S. spouses have a $100,000 exemption.

Marketable The possibility of selling an asset on the open market to some other person, usually unknown to the seller.

Minority Reference to a person who has not yet reached the age of legal competence (in most states this is now age eighteen). Also refers to a minority interest in a business, owning less than a controlling interest.

Mortgage A security interest in real estate granted by the owner of the real estate to guarantee the payment of a debt.

Mortgagee The person who receives the security interest in real estate by means of a mortgage.

Mortgagor The person who owns real estate and gives a secured interest in it to another.

Mortmain A law prohibiting gifts to charities by wills made within a short time prior to death.

Motion A request, either written or oral, made to a court that the judge make some ruling or take some action.

Mutual Funds Companies which pool the money of their investors and buy a variety of securities. The investors in the mutual fund then own a fractional interest in the holdings of the mutual fund according to the amount of shares they own of the mutual fund.

Nominee Name Also referred to as "street name." Stock brokers often put stocks and other securities in their nominee name so that the security can be sold or transferred quickly. It avoids the delay of re-registering the security from the buyer's name to the seller's name.

Par Value With *stocks*—the face value, usually having nothing to do with the real value of the stock. With *bonds*—the face value, representing the full value of the bond which, however, may be sold at a discount below par or a premium above it.

Partnership *General*—an agreement between two or more people to do business together and share profits and losses. *Limited*—a partnership in which some partners losses (and/or profits) may be fixed in amount.

Pecuniary Bequest, Pecuniary Legatee A bequest of money. The recipient of a pecuniary bequest is a pecuniary legatee.

Per Capita A distribution of property based on giving equal shares to all those entitled to the estate.

Per Stirpes A distribution of property in accordance with the relationship to another. All those within the same relationship take equally but beneficiaries in different generations may take different amounts.

Personal Property All those items of wealth other than real estate. For example, jewelry and stocks are all personal property.

Personal Representative The person appointed by a court to act on behalf of a decedent's estate. This person may be an executor/trix or administrator/trix and is also known as a fiduciary.

Pledge The grant of a security interest in something to guarantee the repayment of a debt.

Pour-Over Generally used to refer to the funding of a previous existing trust by assets which are to come from a decedent's estate: as in "pour-over will."

Power of Appointment The right to designate the person who shall enjoy the use of property in the future. Frequently, this is a right given to a beneficiary of a trust to designate future beneficiaries.

Power of Attorney The right to act legally on behalf of another. The power of attorney must be granted in writing by the person on whose behalf the "attorney in fact" is permitted to act. A power of attorney granted during life expires at the moment of death.

Preamble The introductory portion of a will or trust.

Predecease To die before another.

Preferred Stock Shares in a corporation which receive first payments of dividends and usually do not have voting rights.

Premium The amount above the face value of a security which is necessary to pay to acquire the security. The term may also refer to the monthly, quarterly or annual amount paid for a life insurance policy.

Prenuptial Agreement An agreement entered into before marriage in which the prospective bride and groom divulge to each other all the assets they hold and provide for how they are to be divided after marriage. Such an agreement may preclude rights of one of the spouse's in the other's property.

Presumption A conclusion or inference made as a result of a situation. For example, in some states, gifts made within a certain time prior to death are *presumed* to have been made in contemplation of death.

Principal The capital value of an asset not including income earned on that asset.

Probate To offer a will to a court for confirmation of its validity. To "prove" the will.

Probate Estate The amount of money and other assets which are subject to the provisions of a will and under the control of the personal representative.

Progressive Tax A tax in which the rates increase as the amount of money involved increases.

Promissory Note A contract to pay money to another person or company.

Proof of Advertising The forms provided by a newspaper to prove that a certain notice has appeared in that newspaper. Most of the time, advertising is used in an estate to notify creditors of the qualified, personal representative of the estate.

Property Anything which is subject to ownership.

Proponent The person who offers a will for probate.

Publicly Owned Corporation A corporation whose stock may be traded on the open market to the public.

Qualified Terminable Interest Property (QTIP) This is property that passes to the spouse from the decedent. The property must "qualify" for the marital deduction, and the interest in the property must "terminate" at the death of the spouse.

Re:, In re: "With regard to" or "concerning", "In the matter of."

Real Property, Real Estate, Realty Land and the buildings and other permanent things on it.

Reconcile To balance a statement of account.

Redemption The repurchase of an item. Turning something in in return for a payment. Redemption of bonds is the submitting of the bonds to the issuer for money.

Registrar A court official charged with overseeing probate of wills and otherwise administering decedent's estates on behalf of the court.

Release A written document by which one party relinquishes a legal claim against another party.

Remainder 1. An interest in property which comes into being when a prior interest terminates. 2. What is left of an estate after specific bequests have been paid out.

Remainderman The person named to receive the remainder interest.

Renunciation The relinquishing of the right to administer the estate of a decedent. The term also means to "turn down" or refuse to accept a bequest in a will.

Residue, Residuary The part of an estate which is left over after all other bequests have been paid out.

Reversion, Reversionary Interest The possibility that property placed in trust may return to the settlor of the trust if certain things occur in the future.

Revocable Trust A trust which may be changed or even invalidated by the person who created the trust.

Rider A separate sheet of paper attached to a form or document to give additional information which may not fit on the form or document.

Safe Deposit Box A locked box kept in a bank vault to which only the renter of the box has access.

Saving Clause A provision of a legal document which provides that if one of its terms is found to be invalid it will not invalidate the entire document.

Schedule of Distribution A form filed with the court showing to whom the assets of the estate are to be distributed.

Secured Creditor One who is owed a debt and has an interest in certain property of the debtor to assure payment of the debt. A mortgagee is a secured creditor. The security for the debt is the real estate on which the mortgage is held.

Securities Stocks, bonds and similar documents issued by corporations. They evidence either ownership in the corporation (stocks) or debts of the corporation (bonds).

Self Proving Clause An affidavit attached to the end of a will that shows the will was properly witnessed at the time of execution. A notary public signs the affidavit, and witnesses do not have to be located at the time of death.

Settlement *Sale of Real Estate*—The occasion on which the ownership is transferred and money paid for the property. Also referred to as the closing. *Of Lawsuit*—The agreement of parties to a dispute to amicably resolve their differences without a final decision of a court.

Settlor The person who creates a trust by executing an agreement with a trustee, and transfers property into the trust.

Short Certificate A document (in abbreviated form) issued by a court to show that a particular person has qualified to act as the personal representative of an estate. It summaries the information in the Letters Testamentary.

Situs Location. The place where a thing exists.

Slack Tax A form of state death tax which is calculated to make up the difference between the amount of state death tax paid and the savings on the federal estate tax by reason of the credit given for state death tax.

Sole Proprietor Someone who owns a business individually.

Solvent Having at least enough assets to pay all one's debts.

Sprinkle In a trust, the ability of the trustee to make discretionary distributions among a group of beneficiaries.

Stock Certificate A document issued by a corporation to show that someone is the owner of a certain number of shares of stock in that corporation.

Stock Power, Bond Power A form granting the authority to a corporation to transfer ownership of the stock or bond.

Stock Split The issuance of additional shares of stock by a corporation to its existing stockholders by multiplying the number of shares held by a factor. For example, a three for one stock split triples the number of shares of stock held by each stockholder. The value of each share would then be only one-third of what it was prior to the stock split.

Stocks Fractional shares of the ownership of a corporation.

Succession Tax A tax imposed by a state on the receipt of property from a decedent's estate.

Sui Juris "Of his or her own right." As used in the law denotes that one has full capacity to manage his or her own affairs.

Supercede To be replaced by a new document.

Surcharge A fine imposed by a court for failure of a fiduciary to act in accordance with law or for acting in a grossly negligent fashion.

Surety The person or company who guarantees payment on a fidelity bond.

Taking Against Will The election by a surviving spouse to forego any gift made under the deceased spouse's will and to receive instead his or her intestate portion of the estate.

Tangible Personal Property Things that can be touched; having a value in and of themselves such as furniture, jewelry, cars, etc.

Tenants by the Entireties Ownership of real estate by husband and wife in such form that when one dies the other automatically receives the property. During the lifetime of both spouses, such property may not be reached by the creditors of only one spouse.

Tenants in Common Ownership of real or personal property by two or more people giving each a fractional share of the whole with no rights of survivorship as in a joint tenancy with right of survivorship. A tenant may devise his or her share of the property to a third party.

Tentative Trust A trust which will not become effective until the death of the settlor. Commonly refers to "bank book trusts" in which X holds in trust for Y. X may withdraw the money at any time up until death. At X's death the money in the account goes to Y.

Terminable Interest A right in property (usually pursuant to a trust), which will expire if certain contingencies occur; the property then passing to another person. For example, a trust which gives income of certain property to A until age 50 and then to A's children creates a terminable interest in the income to A.

Testamentary Trust A trust created by a will. This trust only comes into existence after the death of the testator.

Testate To die leaving a valid will.

Testator, Testatrix The person who has executed the will. That is, the decedent who has left a valid will.

Title Legal ownership of an asset. This term also refers to a section in a legal document that describes the matter.

Title Insurance Insurance guaranteeing one's ownership of real estate.

Totten Trust A tentative, bank-book trust.

Transfer Agent That entity (usually a bank) which keeps the list of stockholders of a publicly owned corporation and records changes in the ownership of the stock.

Treasury Bills Obligations of the federal government much like a certificate of deposit in a bank. Usually Treasury bills are redeemable in a relatively short period of time.

Trust A transfer of property from one person (settlor) to another for the benefit of a third person (beneficiary).

Trustee The person who holds legal ownership of property in a trust and is charged with acting for the benefit of the beneficiary of the trust.

Undue Influence Using a position of trust to persuade someone to do something which that person would not otherwise have done.

Unified Credit Credit given against the federal estate tax after death, or credit against the gift tax for certain transfers prior to death.

Unified Tax The method by which the federal estate tax and gift taxes are determined, taking into account lifetime as well as testamentary transfers.

Uniform Probate Code A uniform probate procedure developed by the National Conference of Commissioners on Uniform State Laws. Its purpose is to try to unify the probate procedures in all of the states. Not all states have adopted the Uniform Probate Code to date.

Unsecured Creditor One who is owed money but has no interest in any property of the debtor to guarantee payment.

Waiver Relinquishing a right which one may have.

Warrant A right issued by a corporation to buy its stock at a fixed price.

Will A written document disposing of one's assets at death.

Write-Off When an asset becomes worthless, its value is subtracted from the total value of the estate or trust. This subtraction is known as "writing-off."

SUBJECT INDEX

ABATEMENT, 375, 376

ACCEPTANCE (OF GIFT), 102

ACCOUNTS/ACCOUNTING, 309–57
Adjudication of, 350, 351–57
Assembling facts for, 311–15
Audit of, 348, 349–50, 359
Balancing and reconciliation of, 330–31
Capital transactions in, 312–13
Checking account in, 311–12
Disbursements, 326–27
Distributions, 327, 328–29
Dividends and interest, 313–15
Form of, 332–41
National Standards format, 332, 333–41
Non-cash distributions, 315
Notice to interested parties, 348–49
Parts of, 341–45
Principal and income, 315–26
Purpose of, 309–10
Receipts during the interim, 382–83
Schedule of distributions and, 378
Settlement by agreement as alternative to court audit, 359. See also, Settlement by agreement
Waiver of income accounting, 331

ACCRUED CASH DIVIDENDS, 167–69

ACCRUED INCOME (TRUSTS), 458–59

ACCRUED INTEREST
Bonds, 159–60, 167
Certificates of deposit, 178
Owed by decedent, 232, 233

ACCRUED RENT, 144

ACCUMULATION PROVISIONS (TRUSTS), 454

ADEMPTION, 375

ADMINISTRATION EXPENSES, 398, 400, 404
Accountants' fees, 223
Attorneys' fees, 223
Community property considerations, 228
Deductibility of, 132, 221, 222, 223, 224
Disbursements for, 326–27
Election to deduct on fiduciary income tax return, 224, 226
Executors' commissions, 221–23
Expenses relating to income in respect of decedent, 226–27
Expenses relating to tax-exempt income, 227–28
Incurred in administering property not subject to claims, 237
Miscellaneous expenses, 223–24

ADMINISTRATOR/ ADMINISTRATRIX, 5
See also, Fiduciary; Personal representative
Appointment of, 16–17
Bond, posting of, 18–19
Petition of Administration, 17
Renunciation of right to be, 17–18
Short certificate, 19

ADMINISTRATOR C.T.A., 21

ADMINISTRATOR D.B.N., 18

ADMINISTRATOR D.B.N.C.T.A., 21

ADOPTED CHILDREN
Trust, provisions concerning, 459
Will, provisions concerning, 434

AGREEMENT, SETTLEMENT BY
See Settlement by agreement

ALIMONY, 396

ALLOWANCES (TO FAMILY MEMBERS), 327

ALTERNATE VALUATION, 136, 139, 170–73, 234
Casualty or theft loss and, 236–37
Charitable bequests and, 254
Deciding whether to elect, 173
Recapitulation Schedule and, 263

ANCILLARY LETTERS, 26

ANNUAL EXCLUSION
Federal gift tax, 102, 106–8, 111, 260, 404

ANNUITY(IES), 213–20
Federal estate tax and, 217
Form 712, 218
Payments under approved plans, 217–18, 220
Statement with federal estate tax return, 288
Types of, 215–17

ANNUITY TRUST, 253, 408–9

APPRAISAL
Of commercial real estate, 145, 146–50
Lifetime, of unusal assets, 401
Likely appraisers as part of estate planning, 396
Of real estate, 76, 78–79, 144–50
Reappraisal of assets at distribution date, 382–83
Of residential real estate, 145–46
Submitted with federal estate tax return, 288
Of tangible personal property, 72, 196–97

ASSETS
See also, specific types of assets, e.g., Real estate
Acquiring possession without letters, 96–97
Acquiring, valuing, and liquidating, 34–84
Ascertaining for estate planning, 395–96
Basis, 312
Depreciation on, 326
Discovery of, 30, 31–34
Distribution of. See Distribution
Initial inquiry into, 15
Intangible personal property, 35–66, 68–71
Inventory of, 93–95
Investment of, 91–93
Liquidity of, and estate planning, 399–401
Obligation of personal representative for, 29–30
Ownership registered by name, 11
Prompt disposal of, planning for, 401–2
Real estate, 73–84, 141–50
Reconciliation of, 330–31
Repairs to, 325
Short certificate needed for transfer, 19
Tangible personal property, 67, 72–73
Transferring, methods of, 1–4

AUCTION
Of real estate, 79
Of tangible personal property, 72

AUDIT
Of account, 348, 349–50, 362
Of federal estate tax return, 293
Post-audit review and litigation, 294–95

BANK ACCOUNTS, 171
Checking (estate), 25, 30, 36, 85–90. See also, Checking account
Estate tax and, 177–78
Interest-bearing (estate), 85–86, 91
Joint, 101
In name of decedent and another person, 38
In name of decedent "in trust" for another, 38–39
In name of decedent only, 36–38
Under Uniform Gifts to Minors Act, 39

BANK COMMON TRUST FUNDS, 166

BASIS (OF ESTATE ASSETS), 312

BENEFICIARY(IES)
See also, Heir
Contingent, naming, 398
Estate, 5
Minority and incapacity of, provisions concerning, 432–33, 457

Notification of, 25–26
Trust, 2, 437

BEQUEST(S)
Charitable. See Charitable bequest
General, 374
Residuary, 374

BLUE BOOK (VALUES OF AUTOMOBILES), 73, 196

BODY, DISPOSITION OF, 397, 415

BOND (FIDELITY)
Distribution of assets and, 388
Posting by administrator, 18–19
Usually not required of executor, 21–22

BONDS (CORPORATE AND GOVERNMENTAL), 43, 46, 189, 267
See also, Securities
Accrued interest on, 159–60, 167
Alternate valuation of, 170–71
Corporate, 163–64
Distributions of, 387–88
Flower, 160, 267
Government, 158–60, 164
Power, 51
Transfer of, 47, 50–53
U.S. Savings, 53, 54–55, 97, 160, 161
U.S. Treasury, 160–62
Valuation of, 151–57

BOOK VALUE, 312

BUY-SELL AGREEMENTS, 397, 402

BY PASS TRUST, 408

CAPITAL CHANGES SCHEDULE, 344

CAPITAL GAINS, 316
Distributions from mutual funds, 325

CAPITAL TRANSACTIONS, 312–13

CASH, 35–36, 400
Distributions of, 328, 329, 387
On estate tax return, 179
Versus in kind distributions, 376–78
Specific gifts of, 397

CASH-REFUND ANNUITY, 216, 217

CASUALTY LOSSES, 234, 236–37

CERTIFICATES OF DEPOSIT, 171
On estate tax return, 178–79
Growth, 178–79
Investing estate assets in, 92

CHARITABLE BEQUEST(S), 248, 252–5, 256, 288
Contested wills and, 254
Deductibility of, 248, 252, 300
Deduction of death taxes and, 254
Estate planning and, 397–98
Mortmain and, 375
Qualified recipients, 248
Schedule O of federal estate tax return, 254–55, 256
In trust, 252–53
Types of, 252
Valuation of, 253–54

CHARITABLE GIFTS
Estate planning and, 408–9

CHARITABLE PLEDGES, 232

CHARITABLE REMAINDER TRUST, 404, 408

CHECKING ACCOUNT(S), 25, 30, 36, 189, 229
See also, Bank accounts
Accounting, role of estate account in, 311–12
Balancing estate account, 86–88
Decedent's and estate tax return, 177–78, 204
Disbursements and, 326–27
Journal system for estate account, 88–90, 177

CLAIMS BASED UPON PROMISE OR AGREEMENT (VS. DECEDENT), 231–32

CLOSED END MUTUAL FUNDS, 165, 166

CLOSELY HELD CORPORATIONS
Estate planning and, 402
Valuation of stock of, 193–94

CLOSING (SETTLEMENT), 80, 81–84

CODICIL, 3, 437

COMMERCIAL PAPER
Investing estate assets in, 92–93

COMMON DISASTER (PROVISION FOR IN WILLS), 433
See also, Simultaneous death

COMMON STOCK
See Stock

COMMUNITY PROPERTY, 105–6, 185
Considerations in deducting funeral and administration expenses, 228
On estate tax return, 185, 186
State death taxes and, 305–6

CONSERVATION EASEMENT, 409

CONSERVATOR, 435

CONSIDERATION, 99

CONTINGENT LIABILITIES, 232–33

CONVERTIBLE SECURITIES, 165

CORPUS, 437
See also, Principal

CREDIT SHELTER TRUST, 408, 421–25

CUMULATIVE LIST OF ORGANIZATIONS, 252

CURTESY, 132, 232, 239
Exercise of rights, 243

DEATH BENEFITS, 198–99
Social Security, 56–57, 220–21
Veterans', 221

DEATH CERTIFICATE, 12–13

DEATH TAXES, 400
Charitable bequests and, 254, 255
Disbursements for, 327
Foreign, 255, 257
Payment of, provision in will, 432
State. See State death taxes

DEBENTURES, 163, 164

DEBTS
Bona fide claims, 85
Decedent's, payment of, 30, 84–85, 400
Disbursements for, 327
Doubtful claims, treatment of, 85
On estate tax return, 228–32
Home equity loan, 77
Mortgage, 77, 177, 179, 233–34, 246
Priority of payment, 84–85

DEED OF GIFT, 100

DEEMED TRANSFEROR (GENERATION-SKIPPING TRANSFER TAX), 259, 407

DEFERRED COMPENSATION PLAN
Benefits under, 64

DELIVERY (OF GIFT), 100–101

DEPRECIATION, 326

DEVISEE, 25

DISBURSEMENTS, 89–90
Accounting for, 326–27
Of income, 344
Of principal, 342–43

DISCLAIMER
Property disclaimed not treated as a gift, 106

DISCOVERY
Of estate assets, 30, 31–34
Safe deposit boxes, 33–34

DISCRETIONARY DISTRIBUTION POWERS (TRUSTS), 455

DISTRIBUTABLE NET INCOME (DNI), 416

DISTRIBUTION(S), 371–88
Accounting for, 328–29
Cash, 387
Cash vs. in kind, 376–78
Discharge of fiduciary, 388
Distributive shares, determining, 371–78
To a foreign fiduciary, 385
Of income, 344–45
Of intangible personal property, 387–88
Intestate, 371–73
Mandatory and discretionary powers of, 455
To a minor or incompetent, 384–85
Non-cash, accounting for, 315
Obtaining court approval of, 378–84
Per stirpes vs. per capita, 372–73
Of principal, 343
Proposed, 345
Of real estate, 328, 329, 385–86
Satisfaction of award, 388
Schedule of, 378–84. See also Schedule of distribution
Statutory modifications of will provisions and, 374–76
Of stocks and bonds, 387–88
Of tangible personal property, 328, 329, 386–87
Typical patterns under wills, 373–74

DIVIDENDS
Accounting for, 313–15
Accrued cash, 167–69
On common and preferred stock, 162, 163
Declaration date, 167
On life insurance policies, 42–43
Of mutual insurance companies, 182
Payment date, 167, 168
Record date, 167, 168
Stock, 169, 170, 325, 383

DOMICILE
Of decedent, determining, 14–15

DONATIVE INTENT, 99–100

DOWER, 132, 232, 239
Exercise of rights, 243

DURESS, 3

EASEMENT, 409

ELECTION BY SURVIVING SPOUSE, 374–75

ELECTIONS BY EXECUTOR, 136, 138
Alternate valuation, 136, 139. See also, Alternate valuation
Deferred/installment payments, 139
Liability for employee stock-ownership plans, transferring, 139
Reversions/remainders, postponing tax on, 139
Special-use valuation, 139. See also, Special-use valuation

EMPLOYEE BENEFITS, 198–99
See also, Retirement plans

EMPLOYEE CREDIT UNIONS
Benefits under, 64

EMPLOYEE STOCK-OWNERSHIP PLANS, 139

EMPLOYER ANNUITY, 217

ENDOWMENT LIFE INSURANCE, 182

ESCHEAT, 372

ESTATE(S)
Accounting, 6, 309–57. See also, Accounts/accounting
Acquiring possession of assets without letters, 96–97
Assets. See Assets
Bank accounts, 25, 30, 85–90. See also, Bank accounts; Checking account
Collection of, 5–6
Definition of, 5
Disbursements from, 89–90, 326–27. See also, Disbursements
Distributions from, 326, 328–29, 371–88. See also, Distribution
Filing system for documents, 23–24, 135
Identification number, 26
Intestacy and, 3–4. See also, Intestacy

Inventory, 93–95
Investment of assets, 91–93
Payment of debts, 30, 84–85
Plan, 6
Planning. See Estate planning
Principal vs. income, 315–16
Reminder system for deadlines, 24–25
Settlement by agreement. See Settlement by agreement
Taxable, 266–67
Taxation of. See Death taxes; Estate tax; Estate tax (federal); State death taxes
Total gross, 131–32

ESTATE AND GIFT TAX REFORM ACT OF 1976, 131

ESTATE BINDER, 13–14
Filing system 23–24
Index, 13

ESTATE PLANNING, 389–462
Agreements restricting assets, 396–97
Assets and liabilities, determining, 395–96
Charitable gifts and, 408–9
Computations, 409–11
Dispositive wishes of client, learning, 397–99
Estate and death taxes, reducing, 403–9
Fees for, 398–99
Information needed for, 390–95
Initial client interview, 390–99
Lifetime gifts and, 403–5
Likely appraisers and markets for assets, 396
Liquidity of estate and, 399–401
Marital deduction and, 405–6
Procedures of execution of wills and trusts, 460–62
Prompt disposal of assets, preparing for, 401–2
Techniques of, 399–411
Trust drafting, 437–60. See also, Trust
Trusts and, 406–8
Will drafting, 411–37. See also, Will

ESTATE TAX
Federal. See Estate tax (federal)
Versus inheritance tax, 299

ESTATE TAX (FEDERAL), 131–296, 402
Alternate valuation. See Alternate valuation
Annuities, 213–20
Application for employer identification number, 133–34
Assembling facts for, 134–35
Bank accounts, 177–79
Cash, 179
Charitable bequests, 248, 252–55, 256
Charitable gifts, 408–9
Computation of, 266–68
Credit, and state death taxes, 301–2
Debts, mortgages, and liens of decedent, 228–34
Deferred/installment payments of, 139, 150, 287
Due date, 133
Employee stock-ownership plans, 139
Estate planning and, 403–9
Excess pension distributions, excise tax on, 260, 262–63
Exemption, 132–33
Expenses in administering property not subject to claims, 237
Foreign death taxes, credit for, 255, 257
Funeral and administration expenses, 220–28
Generation-skipping transfer tax and, 258–60, 261
Gift tax and, 102, 110, 266
Insurance on the life of another, 199
Jointly owned property, 185, 187–92
Life insurance, proceeds of, 179, 181–85, 186
Lifetime gifts and, 403–5
Marital deduction, 237–48, 249–51, 405–6
Miscellaneous property, 199
Net losses during administration, 234, 236–37
Noncorporate business interests, 192–95, 402
Notes and mortgages, 179
Payment of, 268, 287
Penalties for late filing or late payment, 268, 287
Pensions and death benefits, 198–99
Powers of appointment, 205–11

Qualified ESOP sales, 248
Rates, 133
Real estate, 141–50
Refund, 295–96
Return. See Estate tax return (federal)
Reversions/remainders, postponing tax, 139
Special-use valuation. See Special-use valuation
Tangible personal property, 195–97
Taxable estate, computing, 132, 266–67
Tax on prior transfers, credit for, 257–58
Total gross estate, computing, 131–32
Transfers during decedent's life, 201–5, 403–5
Trusts and, 406–8
Trusts, interests in, 197–98
Unified credit, 132–33, 266
U.S. Treasury bonds, redeeming at par in payment of, 160, 162, 268

ESTATE TAX RETURN (FEDERAL)
Attachments to, 267
Audit of, 293
Continuation schedules, 263, 264
Elections by the executor, 136, 138, 139
Exhibits with, 288–92
Extensions of time for filing, 268, 285
Filing, 268, 287–93
Form 706, 137–38, 140, 173, 269–71
General information section, 139–41
Post-audit review and litigation, 294–95
Preparing, 135–50
Recapitulation Schedule, 140, 141, 263, 265, 266, 271
Refund claim, 295, 296
Schedule A, 141–50, 272
Schedule A–1, 150–51, 152–54, 170, 233
Schedule B, 151, 159, 160, 163, 164, 166, 173, 194, 273
Schedule C, 177–79, 180, 274
Schedule D, 179, 181–85, 186, 275
Schedule E, 143, 144, 185, 189–91, 276
Schedule F, 192–201, 215, 229, 277–78
Schedule G, 201–5, 206, 266, 279
Schedule H, 205–13, 252, 279
Schedule I, 213–20, 288
Schedule J, 220–28, 263, 265, 280
Schedule K, 228–34, 235, 263, 265, 281
Schedule L, 234, 236–37, 238, 265
Schedule M, 237, 239–48, 249–51, 282–84, 288
Schedule N, 248, 288
Schedule O, 248, 252–5, 256, 265, 285, 288
Schedule P, 255, 257, 266
Schedule Q, 257–58, 266
Schedule R, 258–60, 261
Schedule S, 260, 262–63
Section 2032, 150, 151, 155, 170–72
Signatures on, 287

EX-DIVIDEND, 168

EXECUTOR/EXECUTRIX, 5
See also, Fiduciary; Personal representative
Accounting by, 6, 309–57. See also, Accounts/accounting
Appointment of, 20–21, 434
Bond usually not required of, 21–22
Commissions, 221–23
Distributions by. See Distribution
Elections by, on tax returns, 136, 138, 139
Powers clause in will and, 430–32

EXPECTANCY, 396

FAMILY EXEMPTIONS (HOMESTEAD RIGHTS), 85

FEDERAL EMPLOYER IDENTIFICATION NUMBER, 133–34

FIDUCIARY, 5
See also, Administrator/administratix; Executor/executrix; Personal representative; Trustee
Accounting by. See Accounts/accounting

Appointment of, in will, 434–36
Choosing, in estate planning, 398
Discharge of, 388
Foreign, distribution to, 385
Notice of (Form 56), 289

FOREIGN DEATH TAXES, 255, 257
Form 706CE, 288–89

FORMAL ACCOUNTING
See Accounts/accounting

FORMAL PROBATE, 10

FRACTIONAL SHARE MARITAL GIFT, 383–84

FRAUD, 3

FUNERAL/BURIAL EXPENSES, 84, 400
Deductibility of, 132, 220, 228
Deductions from, 220–21
Disbursements for, 327
Provisions for in will, 414

FUTURE INTEREST
Annual exclusion from gift tax and, 106, 107–8

GENERAL LEGACY/BEQUEST, 374
Abatement and, 376

GENERATION-SKIPPING TRANSFER (GST) TAX, 123–25, 297, 406, 407, 438, 452
Estate tax and, 258–60, 261

GIFT(S)
Charitable, 248, 252–55, 408–9
Upon death, 2–4
After December 31, 1976, in computing taxable estate, 132
Estate planning and, 397, 403–5, 408–9
Of future interest, 107–8
Legal elements of, 99–102
Lifetime, and estate planning, 403–5
Marital deduction and, 240
Outright, 1
Pecuniary marital vs. fractional share, 383–84
Preresiduary, 415–16
Specific, 397
Splitting, 105–6, 122, 404
Taxation of, 102–25. See also, Gift tax
Within three years of death, 132, 203, 204, 303–4
In trust, 1–2, 252–53
Valuation of charitable, 253–54
Under a will, 373–76. See also, Beneficiary; Legacy; Will

GIFT TAX (FEDERAL), 99–129
Annual exclusion, 102, 106–8, 260, 404
Charitable and educational exclusion, 109
Cumulative and progressive nature of, 102, 109–10
Deductions, 111
Federal estate tax and, 110, 132–33, 202–3, 204, 266, 404
Generation-skipping transfer tax and, 123–25, 259–60, 406
Gift splitting between spouses, 105–6, 122
Introduction to, 102–3
Nontaxable transfers, 102, 103–5
Prior laws, 103, 105, 108, 403–4
Return, preparing, 111–12
Taxable transfers, 102, 103–5
Unified credit, 102, 103, 108–9, 132–33

GOOD WILL, 194

GROUP LIFE INSURANCE, 182

GUARDIAN(S)
Appointing in will, 432, 434–35
Of the estate vs. of the person, 398, 434–35
For minors, 385, 398

HEIR(S), 5
See also, Beneficiary
Under intestate law, 372–73

HOMESTEAD RIGHTS (FAMILY EXEMPTION), 85

INCAPACITY
Trust, provision for, 457
Will, provision for, 432

INCIDENTS OF OWNERSHIP (LIFE INSURANCE), 182, 183–84

INCOME (ESTATE OR TRUST)
Accrued, 458–59
Disbursements and distributions of, 344–45
Mandatory and discretionary distribution, powers of, 455
Versus principal, 315–16, 325–26
Receipt of, 344
Schedule of distribution and, 383
Sprinkling and accumulation, power to, 454
Uniform Principal and Income Act, 316, 317–24
Waiver of income accounting, 331

INCOME IN RESPECT OF DECEDENT, 226–27

INCOME TAX
Owed by decedent, 230–31

INCOME TAX RETURN (FIDUCIARY)
Casualty or theft losses on, 236
Election to deduct administration expenses on, 224, 226
Expenses relating to income in respect of decedent and, 226–27
Expenses relating to tax-exempt income and, 227–28
Medical expenses of decedent and, 229–30

INCOMPETENT PERSONS
Distributions to, 384–85

INDEMNIFICATION, 363, 387

INFORMAL PROBATE, 10

INHERITANCE TAX
Versus estate tax, 299
State. See State death taxes

INSTALLMENT PAYMENTS (OF ESTATE TAX), 139, 150, 287

INSURANCE
Accident, health, and key-man, 396
Casualty, on tangible personal property, 72, 76
Casualty and liability, on real estate, 75–76, 386
Form 938, 197, 288
Group, 64
Life insurance proceeds in estate, 40–43, 171, 179, 181–85. See also, Life insurance
On the life of others, 199
For losses during administration, 234, 236
Renewal commissions, 195
Veterans' claim for, 64, 67

INTANGIBLE PERSONAL PROPERTY
Bank accounts, 36–39
Business interests, 56–57
Cash, 35–36. See also, Cash
Claims and contracts, 57–67
Company benefits, 64
Corporate and governmental securities, 43, 46–56. See also, Securities
Distributions of, 387–88
Life insurance, 40–43. See also Life insurance
Social Security benefits, 57–58
Veterans' benefits, 58, 64

INTEREST
Accounting for, 313–15
Accrued. See Accrued interest

INTERNAL REVENUE SERVICE, 133, 134, 139, 171, 184, 195, 196, 197, 231, 252, 268, 287, 289, 383, 386
Audit and review of federal estate tax return, 293, 294–95

INTER VIVOS TRUST, 2, 428, 440
Irrevocable, 447–49
Powers of appointment and, 209–10

INTESTACY, 3–4
Administrator, appointment of, 16–17
Administrator D.B.N., 18
Distribution of estate in cases of, 371–73
Marital deduction and, 237, 239
Probate in cases of, 16–19

INVENTORY (ESTATE), 29

INVESTMENT COMPANY SHARES, 165–66

INVESTMENTS SCHEDULE, 344

IRREVOCABLE TRUST, 104, 107, 440–46, 447
Gift of future interest to, 107–8
Inter vivos trust, 447–49

JOINT AND SURVIVOR ANNUITY, 216

JOINTLY OWNED PROPERTY, 185
Estate tax treatment of, 187–91
Marital deduction and, 239, 240
Simultaneous death of spouses and, 245
State death taxes and, 304

JOINT TENANCY, 73, 74, 239, 386, 396
Estate tax and, 143, 185
Gifts and, 103–4

JOURNAL SYSTEMS (ESTATE CHECKING ACCOUNT), 88–90, 135

LAPSE (OF GIFT), 375–76

LEASES
Of property leased by decedent to others, 77
Of property rented by decedent from others, 77–78

LEGACY(IES)
Abatement, ademption, and lapse and, 375–76
Earmarking specific legacies for distribution, 384
General, 374
Residuary, 374
Specific, 373–74

LETTERS OF ADMINISTRATION
Advertising of, 23
Disposition of estate assets without, 96–97
Petition for, 17

LETTERS TESTAMENTARY
Advertising of, 23
Disposition of estate assets without, 96–97
Petition for probate and, 20

LIENS, 233

LIFE ESTATE, 241

LIFE INSURANCE, 239, 373, 396
Amount of proceeds payable, 41–43
Charitable gifts of, 409
Collection of proceeds, 40–41, 96
Estate tax and, 179, 181–85
Form 712, 40, 43, 183, 288
Group, provided by employer, 64
Liquidity of, and estate planning, 400
Marital deduction and, 239, 240, 241–42
Mortgage, 77
Policy as gift, valuation of, 104–5
Proceeds payable to beneficiaries other than estate, 183–85
Proceeds payable to decedent's estate, 182–83
Types of, 181–82
Valuation of, 43
Veterans' claim for, 64, 67

LIFE INSURANCE TRUST AGREEMENT (LITA), 400, 406, 428, 455, 461
Inter vivos, 440
Irrevocable, 440–46

LIFETIME TRANSFERS, 1–2

LIQUIDATION (ESTATE ASSETS), 30

LIQUIDITY
Estate planning and, 399–401

LIVING WILL, 415

LOSSES (DURING ADMINISTRATION), 234, 236–37

MANDATORY DISTRIBUTION POWERS (TRUSTS), 455

MARITAL DEDUCTION, 106, 132, 237–48, 249–51, 288, 306
Disclaimer of interest under will, 243–44, 246–47, 249, 251
Election against will, 243
Estate planning and, 405–6, 407, 408
Exercise of dower or curtesy rights and, 243
Form of marital share, 240–42
Gift tax and, 105–6, 111

Pecuniary marital gift vs. fractional share marital gift, 383–84
QTIP trust and, 450–51
Schedule M of federal estate tax return, 245–48, 249–51
Schedule of distribution and, 383–84
Simultaneous death of spouses and, 244–45
Size of marital share, 242–43
State death taxes and, 304
Unlimited, 239–40
Wills, provisions in, 416

MEDICAL EXPENSES (DECEDENT), 224, 226, 229–30

MINORS, 452
Distributions to, 384–85
Guardians for, naming, 398, 432–33, 434–35
Trust, provision for, 457
Will, provision for, 432

MORTGAGES, 177, 179, 233–34, 246

MORTMAIN, 375

MUTUAL COMPANY (INSURANCE), 182

MUTUAL FUNDS, 165–66
Capital gains distributions from, 325

NATIONAL STANDARDS FORMAT FOR ACCOUNTING, 332, 333–41

NON-CASH DISTRIBUTIONS, 315

NONMARITAL TRUST, 439

NOTES, 177, 179, 234

OPEN END MUTUAL FUNDS, 165–66

ORGAN DONATIONS, 397

PARALEGALS
Checklists and procedures for, 7–8
Clients, dealing with, 8
Confidentiality, 8
Letters, 8
Role of, 6–8

PARTNERSHIP, INTEREST IN, 56–57, 171, 193
Agreements, 397
Estate planning and, 402
Valuation for estate tax, 193–95

PECUNIARY LEGACY, 328, 329

PECUNIARY MARITAL GIFT, 383

PENSIONS
See Retirement plans

PER CAPITA DISTRIBUTION, 372, 373

PERSONAL PROPERTY, 34
See also, Intangible personal property; Tangible personal property; and specific types
Intangible, collecting, valuing and liquidating, 35–67
Tangible, collecting, valuing, and liquidating, 67, 72–73

PERSONAL REPRESENTATIVE
See also, Administrator/administratrix; Executor/executrix; Fiduciary
Accounting by, 6, 309–57. See also, Accounts/accounting
Ancillary letters issued to, 26
Appointment of, 5
Collection of estate, 5–6
Distributions by. See Distribution
Domicile of decedent and, 14
Duties of, 29–30
Liability for decline in value of assets, 377
Probate, role in, 9–10

PER STIRPES DISTRIBUTION, 4, 372–73

PETITION FOR ADMINISTRATION, 17
Advertising of, 23

PETITION FOR PROBATE AND LETTERS TESTAMENTARY, 20
Advertising of, 23

PICK UP TAX, 297

POOLED INCOME FUNDS, 409

POUR-OVER PROVISIONS (WILLS), 428–30, 446

POWER OF ATTORNEY, 101
Filing Form 2848 with IRS, 136, 289, 290–91

POWERS CLAUSE (WILLS), 430–32

POWERS OF APPOINTMENT, 239, 396
Charitable deduction and, 252
General, created after October 21, 1942, 211–12
General, created before October 22, 1942, 209–11
General vs. special (limited), 207–9
Schedule H of federal estate tax return and, 205–13
Trust, 241, 454

PREAMBLE
Trust, 450
Will, 414

PREFERRED STOCK
See Stock

PRENUPTIAL AGREEMENT, 396, 397

PRERESIDUARY GIFTS, 415–16

PRESENT INTEREST, 107
Annual gift tax exclusion available for, 106

PRINCIPAL
Balance on hand, 343
Disbursements of, 342–43
Distributions of, 343
Versus income, 315–16, 325–26
Receipts of, 342
Schedule of distribution and, 382–83
Trust, 437
Uniform Principal and Income Act, 316, 317–24

PRIVATE ANNUITY, 215, 218

PROBATE
After appointment of personal representative, 23–26
Assets, listing, 15
Death, information about, 12–13
Definition of, 9
Disposition of assets without, 96
Domicile of decedent, determining, 14–15
Formal, 10
Informal, 10
Intestacy, in cases of, 16–20
Name of decedent, determining, 10–11
With a will, 20–22
Will, search for, 15–16

PROPERTY TAXES
Owed by decedent, 230

QUALIFIED TERMINABLE INTEREST PROPERTY (QTIP), 111, 199, 239, 241
Election on Schedule M of federal estate tax return, 247–48, 250
Trusts, provisions for, 450–51

REAL ESTATE
Alternate valuation, 170, 171
Casualty and liability insurance on, 75–76, 386
Charitable gifts and, 409
Distributions of, 328, 329, 385–86
Estate planning and, 401
Forms of ownership in, 141, 143–44
Interests in, 73–74
Maintenance of, 76–7
Mortgage payments on, 77
Property leased to others, 77
Property rented by decedent, 77–78
Sale of, 79–84, 313
Schedule A of federal estate tax return, 141, 142, 144
Schedule E of federal estate tax return, 143, 144
Security of, 74
Valuation of, 78–79, 144–50

REAL PROPERTY, 34
See also, Real estate

REFUND ANNUITY, 216

REGISTRATION
Of assets by name, 11–12

REMAINDERMAN, 438

RENEWAL COMMISSIONS (INSURANCE AGENTS), 195

RENT
Accrued, 144
Obligation of estate, 229

RENUNCIATION
By administrator, 17–18
By executor, 21

REPAIRS TO TRUST OR ESTATE ASSETS, 325

RESIDUARY CLAUSE (WILLS), 426–30

RESIDUARY LEGACY/BEQUEST, 374
Abatement and, 376

RESIDUARY TRUST, 383, 408, 439, 451–54

RESIDUE
Estate planning and, 397–98

RETIREMENT PLANS
Benefits under, 64, 96, 198
Excess pension distributions, excise tax on, 260, 262–63

REVENUE ACT OF 1978, 150, 244, 287, 401

REVERSIONS/REMAINDERS, TAX ON, 139

REVISED UNIFORM PRINCIPAL AND INCOME ACT, 317–24, 325, 326

REVOCABLE TRUST, 104, 446

RIGHTS (CORPORATE), 164–65

ROYALTIES, 195, 199

RULE AGAINST PERPETUITIES, 438

SAFE DEPOSIT BOX
Joint owners, potential confusion from, 101
Locating assets in, 33–34
Short certificate needed for opening, 19, 34
Wills in, 16, 461

SATISFACTION OF AWARD, 388

SAVING CLAUSE (TRUSTS), 458

SAVINGS ACCOUNT
See also, Bank accounts
Decedent's and estate tax return, 178, 204
Estate, 85–86, 91

SCHEDULE OF DISTRIBUTION, 378–84
Account for receipts during the interim and reappraisal of assets, 382–83
Approval, 384
Earmarking specific legacies, 384
Marital deduction gift or trust, 383–84
When necessary, 378–79

SCHEDULES (TAX)
See Estate tax return (federal)

SECURITIES, 204
Alternate valuation, 170–71, 172–73
Bonds, 46, 158–62, 163–64. See also, Bonds (corporate and governmental)
Convertible, 165
Corporate, 162–64
Debentures, 163, 164
Definition of, 43
Distributions of, 387–88
Government, 158–60
Mutual funds and, 165–66
Physical control, obtaining, 46–47
Registration of, 47, 50–53
Sale of, 53, 56
Stocks, 43, 46, 162–63. See also, Stock
Valuation of, 151–57
Warrants and rights, 164–65
Worthless, 173

SELF-PROVING CLAUSE (WILLS), 10, 436–37

SEPARATION AGREEMENT, 396, 397

SETTLEMENT (CLOSING), 80, 81–84
Sheets, inclusion with federal estate tax return, 288

SETTLEMENT BY AGREEMENT, 359–71
Advantages and disadvantages of, 359–60
Elements of the agreement, 360–64
Examples of, 364–70

SETTLOR, 2, 437, 438

SHAREHOLDER'S AGREEMENT, 402

SHORT CERTIFICATE
Closing decedent's bank accounts, 36
Intestacy and, 19
Opening safe deposit box and, 19, 34
Selling real estate and, 82
Transferring securities and, 50, 53
With a will, 22

SIMULTANEOUS DEATH, 244–45, 433
See also, Common disaster

SOCIAL SECURITY BENEFITS, 56–57
As deduction from funeral expenses, 220–21

SOCIAL SECURITY NUMBER (DECEDENT), 136

SOLE PROPRIETORSHIP, 56, 171, 192–93
Estate planning and, 402
Valuation of, 193–95

SPECIAL-USE VALUATION, 139
Schedule A–1, 150–51, 152–54

SPECIFIC LEGACY, 373–74
Abatement and, 375

SPENDTHRIFT PROVISIONS
Trust, 458
Will, 433

SPOUSE(S)
See also, Marital deduction
In community property states, 105–6
Disclaimer of interest under will, 243–44
Dower and curtesy rights, 132, 232, 239, 243
Election against will by, 243
Election to receive statutory share, 374–75
Estate tax marital deduction, 237, 239–48, 249–51
Gift splitting between, 106–7, 122, 404
Gifts to, 404
Marital deduction for gifts and, 105–6, 111
Rights in real estate, 74
Share of survivor under intestate law, 371
Simultaneous death of, 244–45, 433
Social Security benefits for surviving, 58

SPREAD SHEET, 312
Capital transactions on, 313–14
Dividends and interest on, 314
Non-cash distributions, 315

SPRINKLING PROVISION (TRUSTS), 454

STATE DEATH TAXES, 131, 297–307
Charitable bequests and, 300
Classification of state laws, 297–98
In community property states, 305–6
Credit for, 132, 266
Deductions, 299–300
Estate and inheritance tax distinguished, 299
Estate planning and, 403, 406
Exemptions, 299
Filing of federal estate tax return and, 289
Gifts in contemplation of death and, 303–4
Jointly owned property and, 187
Life insurance proceeds and, 185

Rates, 300–302
Residency and location of property and, 302–3
Waivers, 305

STOCK(S), 189, 204
See also, Dividends; Securities
Accrued cash dividends on, 167–69
Alternate valuation of, 170–71, 172–73
In capital transactions, accounting for, 312
Certificate, 48
Of closely held corporations, valuation of, 193–94
Common, 43, 46, 162–63, 164
Cumulative preferred, 163
Distributions of, 387–88
Dividends, 169, 170, 325, 383
Options, 396
Power, 51, 52
Preferred, 46, 163
Splits, 169–70
Transfer of, 47, 50–53
Valuation of, 151–57, 160, 161, 175–76
Warrants and rights and, 164–65

STOCK COMPANY (INSURANCE), 182

STOCK PURCHASE AGREEMENT, 397

STRAIGHT LIFE ANNUITY, 215–16

STREET NAME (NOMINEE NAME), 52–53, 387

SUPPORT ORDER, 396, 397

SURCHARGE/SURCHARGING, 309, 316, 384

TANGIBLE PERSONAL PROPERTY
Distinguished from intangible personal property, 34–35
Distributions of, 328, 329, 386–87
On estate tax return, 195–97
Examples of, 67
Sale of, 72–73
Security of, 67, 72, 76
Specific gifts of, 397
Valuation of, 72, 196–97
In wills, 415–16

TAX(ES)/TAXATION
Federal estate, 131–296. See also, Estate tax (federal)
Federal gift tax, 102–25. See also, Gift tax
Generation-skipping tax. See Generation-skipping tax
Pick up tax, 297
Returns of decedent, reviewing, 135
State death, 131, 132, 185, 187, 297–307. See also, State death taxes
On transfers of property, 385
Waiver, 386–87

TAXABLE DISTRIBUTION (GENERATION-SKIPPING TRANSFER), 124, 259

TAXABLE TERMINATION (GENERATION-SKIPPING TRANSFERS), 123, 124, 259

TAX CLAUSE (TRUSTS), 456–57

TAX REFORM ACT OF 1969, 253

TAX REFORM ACT OF 1976, 108, 110, 123, 131, 150, 184, 188, 243, 244, 259, 287, 401, 403, 404, 405, 406, 452

TAX REFORM ACT OF 1986, 407, 439

TENANCY BY THE ENTIRETIES, 143–44, 386
On estate tax return, 185, 189

TENANTS/TENANCY IN COMMON, 73–74, 185
On estate tax return, 185, 186
Gifts and, 103
Reporting on Schedule A, 141, 143

TENTATIVE TRUST, 38

TERM CERTAIN ANNUITY, 217

TERMINABLE INTEREST, 241

TERMINATION CLAUSE (TRUSTS), 458

TERM LIFE INSURANCE, 181

TESTAMENTARY CAPACITY, 3

TESTAMENTARY TRUST, 2, 258, 439–40, 449

THEFT, LOSSES FROM 234, 236–37

THRIFT PLANS
Benefits under, 64

TOTAL GROSS ESTATE, 131–32

TOTTEN TRUST, 38

TRANSFER AGENT (SECURITIES), 50

TRANSFEROR (SETTLOR), 2

TRUST(S), 135, 396, 437–60
Accelerated termination, provision for, 458
Accounting for. See Accounts/accounting
Accrued income, 458–59
Addition of property, provision for, 455
Adopted children, provision concerning, 459
Amendment and revocation, 460
Anatomy of, 437–60
Annuity, 253, 408–9
Appointment and compensation of trustees, 459, 460
Charitable remainder, 404, 408
Contingent, in will, 417–20
Credit shelter/by pass, 408, 421–25
Definition of, 2
Estate planning and, 406–8
Estate tax and, 203–4
Execution, 460
Generation-skipping, 259, 407, 438
Gifts in, 1–2, 104, 252–53
Governing law, 459
Income sprinkling and accumulation, powers of, 454
Instruments, inclusion with federal estate tax return, 288
Interests in, on federal estate tax return, 197–98
Inter vivos, 2, 209–10, 428, 440, 447–49
Irrevocable, 104, 107, 440–46, 447–49
Life insurance trust agreement, 400, 440–46, 455
Mandatory and discretionary distribution powers, 455
Marital, 241, 421–25
Marital deduction and, 383–84
Minority and incapacity, provision for, 457
Nonmarital, 439
Powers of appointment and, 205, 206, 207, 208, 209–10, 241
Powers of trustees, 455–56
Power to revoke, alter, or amend, 455
Preamble, 450
Principal vs. income, 315–16
Reasons for establishing, 437–39
Related documents, 461–62
Residuary, 383, 408, 439, 451–54
Revocable, 104, 446
Saving clause, 458
Schedule of property, 459
Spendthrift provisions, 458
Storage of, 461
Tax clause, 456–57
Tentative (Totten), 38
Testamentary, 2, 258, 439–40, 449
Trustees, choosing, 398
Types of, 439–49
Unitrusts, 253, 408, 409

TRUSTEE(S), 2, 434, 438
Appointment of, 459
Compensation of, 459, 60

UNIFIED CREDIT, 102, 103, 108–9, 242–43, 266
Phase-in, 132–33

UNIFIED TAX SYSTEM, 132

UNIFORM ANATOMICAL GIFT ACT, 397, 415

UNIFORM GIFTS TO MINORS ACT
Bank accounts under, 39
Gifts of future interest and annual gift tax exclusion, 108

UNIFORM PRINCIPAL AND INCOME ACT, 316–17, 324
See also, Revised Uniform Principal and Income Act

UNIFORM PROBATE CODE (U.P.C.), 10

UNIFORM SIMULTANEOUS DEATH ACT, 244, 245

UNITED STATES SAVINGS BONDS, 33, 54–55, 97, 160, 161, 171

UNITED STATES TREASURY BILLS
Investing estate assets in, 92

UNITED STATES TREASURY BONDS
Redeeming at par in payment of federal estate tax, 160, 162, 268

UNITRUST, 253, 408, 409

VALUATION, 30
Accrued cash dividends, 167–69
Accrued interest, 159–60, 167
Alternate. See Alternate valuation
Annuities, 217, 218
Automobiles, 73
Bank common trust funds, 166
Charitable gifts, 253–54
Closely held corporations, 193–94
Gift made by transfer into joint tenancy, 103–4
For gift tax, 104–5
Government securities, 159–60
Life insurance, 43, 183
Marital deduction assets, 246
Mutual fund shares, 165–66
Partnership interest, 193–95
Real estate, 76, 78–79, 144–50
Sole proprietorship, 193–95
Special-use. See Special-use valuation
Stock dividends and splits, 169–70
Stock and bonds, 151–57, 160, 161
Tangible personal property, 72, 196–97
Warrants and rights, 96–97

VETERANS' BENEFITS, 58, 64

WAIVER FORM 890/890–B, 293

WARRANTS (CORPORATE), 164–65

WHOLE LIFE INSURANCE, 181

WILL(S), 411–37
Adopted children, provisions concerning, 434
Anatomy of, 411–37
Appointment of fiduciaries, 434–36
Characteristics of, 2–3
Codicils, 3, 437
Common disaster, provision for, 433
Contested, and charitable bequests, 254, 255
Contingent trust for children, 417–20
Credit shelter and marital trusts in, 421–25
Disclaimer of interest under, by spouse, 243–44
Election against, by spouse, 239, 243
Election to take against, 6
Funeral arrangements and disposal of body, provisions for, 397, 414–15
Funeral expenses, payment of, 414
Guardians named in, 398
Living, 415
Minority or incapacity of beneficiaries, provisions for, 432–33
Payment of death taxes, provision for, 432
Pour-over provision, 428–30
Powers clause, 430–32
Powers of appointment and, 205, 206, 207, 208, 209
Preamble, 414
Preresiduary gifts in, 415–16
Probate of, 6, 9–12, 20–22
QTIP trust in, 451
Related documents, 461–62
Residuary clause, 426–30
Search, 15–16
Self-proving clause, 10, 436–37
Signature of testator, 436
Simple, 412–13
Spendthrift provisions, 433
Statutory modifications of provisions, 374–76
Storage of, 461
Types of bequests under, 373–74
Wishes of testator and, 397–98
Witnesses to, 22

FORMS INDEX

ACCOUNTS/ACCOUNTING
Adjudication, 357
Asset reconciliation, 330–31
Capital transactions. See Capital transactions
Model account (National Standards format), 333–41
Notice of filing account, 349
Petition for adjudication, 351–56
Waiver of income accounting, 331

ALTERNATE VALUATION
Form 706, Schedule B—Stocks and Bonds, 174
Stocks, 172–73

ANNUITIES
Form 706, Schedule I, 219

APPRAISAL
Affidavit of executor for, 197
Commercial, 146–50
Residential, 145–46

ASSETS
See Assets, locating; Assets, organizing information; specific types, e.g., Bonds

ASSETS, LOCATING (LETTERS FOR)
Of authorization, 31
Bank account information, 37
Insurance proceeds, 41
Safe deposit box information, 33
Savings account information, 37–38

ASSETS, ORGANIZING INFORMATION
Estate check and stub, 87
Inventory, 94
Journal system, 88–89
Ledger sheet, 39
Spread-sheet securities, 47

BANK ACCOUNT
Estate check and stub, 87
Ledger sheet for account information, 39
Letter requesting information on, 37

BONDS
Accrued interest on, determining, 159–60
Corporate, 49–50
Form 706, Schedule B, 174, 273
Redemption chart for U.S. Series EE Savings Bonds, 161
Transactions involving, 313, 314
Treasury Form PD 1787 (Reissue of U.S. Savings Bonds), 54–55
U.S. Treasury redeemable at par in payment of federal estate tax, 162
Valuation of, 156–57

BURIAL BENEFITS
Application for, 65–66

CAPITAL TRANSACTIONS
Spread sheet for, 313
With dividends and other income, spread sheet for, 314

CASH
Form 706, Schedule M, 180, 274

CHARITABLE BEQUESTS
Form 706, Schedule O, 256, 285

DEBTS
Form 706, Schedule K, 235, 281

EMPLOYER IDENTIFICATION NUMBER
Application for (Form SS-4), 27
Cover letter with application, 134

ESTATE
Inventory, 94
Name of, procedure for determining, 12
Settlement, checklist for, 26

ESTATE BINDER INDEX, 13

ESTATE CHECKING ACCOUNT
Check and stub, 87
Journal system, 88–89

ESTATE PLANNING
Computations, 410–11
Information checklist, 391–95

ESTATE TAX RETURN (FEDERAL)—FORM 706 AND SCHEDULES
Continuation Schedule, 264
Estate (and Generation-Skipping Transfer) Tax Return (pp. 1–3), 137–38, 140, 269–71
Recapitulation Schedule, 264
Schedule A—Real Estate, 142, 272
Schedule A–1—Section 2032A Valuation, 152–54
Schedule B—Stocks and Bonds, 174, 273
Schedule C—Mortgages, Notes, and Cash, 180, 274
Schedule D—Insurance on the Decedent's Life, 186, 275
Schedule E—Jointly Owned Property, 190, 276
Schedule F—Other Miscellaneous Property, 200, 277
Schedule F—Rider, 201, 278
Schedule G—Transfers during Decedent's Life, 206, 279
Schedule H—Powers of Appointment, 212, 279
Schedule H—Powers of Appointment and Riders, 213, 214
Schedule I—Annuities, 219
Schedule J—Funeral Expenses and Expenses Incurred, 225, 280
Schedule K—Debts of the Decedent, 235, 281
Schedule L—Net Losses, 238
Schedule M—Bequests, etc. to Surviving Spouses and Disclaimer, 249–51, 282–84
Schedule O—Charitable, Public and Similar Gifts and Bequests, 256, 285
Schedule P—Credit for Foreign Death Taxes, 257
Schedule Q—Credit for Prior Transfers, 257–58
Schedule R—Generation-Skipping Transfer Tax, 261

ESTATE TAX RETURN (FEDERAL)—LETTERS WITH
Closing letter, 294–95
Cover letter for documents filed with Internal Revenue Service, 134
Cover letter with, 292

ESTATE TAX RETURN (FEDERAL)—OTHER FORMS
Treasury Form 4768—Application for Extension of Time, 286
Treasury Form 8431—Refund Claim, 296

EXECUTOR/ADMINISTRATOR
Commissions, affidavit for, 222–23

FOREIGN DEATH TAXES
Form 706, Schedule P, 257

FUNERAL EXPENSES
Form 706, Schedule J, 225, 280

GENERATION-SKIPPING TRANSFER TAX
Computing, 124
Computing inclusion rate, 124–25
Form 706, Schedule R, 261
Grandparent's gift to grandchildren (Form 709), 126–29

GIFTS
Deed of gift, 100
Letter informing donee of gift, 100–101
Present and future interests, 107
Symbolic delivery of, 100–101

GIFT TAX
Cumulative rates on taxable gifts, 109–10
Federal gift tax return (Short Form 709–A), 121
Husband's federal gift tax return (Form 709), 113–16
Law prior to 1977, 105
Rate table under Tax Reform Act of 1986, 110
Requirement to file return (with gift splitting), 122
Wife's federal gift tax return (Form 709), 117–20

INSURANCE
Applicaton for veterans', 67
Form 706, Schedule D, 186, 275
Letter notice of death of homeowner, 76
Letter requesting proceeds, 41

Treasury Form 712 (Life Insurance Statement), 44–45

INTESTACY
Father's, 4

INVENTORY (ESTATE), 94

JOINTLY OWNED PROPERTY
Form 706, Schedule E, 190, 276

JOINT TENANCY, 104

JOURNAL SYSTEM, 88–89

LIFE INSURANCE
See Insurance

MORTGAGES
Form 706, Schedule C, 180, 274

NET LOSSES
Form 706, Schedule L, 238

PENSION DISTRIBUTION
Form 706, Schedule S, 262–63

POWER OF ATTORNEY
Treasury Form 2848, 290–91

POWERS OF APPOINTMENT
Form 706, Schedule H, 212, 213, 214, 279

QUALIFIED TERMINABLE INTEREST PROPERTY (QTIP)
Election on Schedule M, 250
Trust, establishing, 451

REAL ESTATE
Agreement of sale, 80, 81, 82, 83
Commercial appraisal, 146–50
Form 706, Schedule A, 142, 272
Residential appraisal, 145–46

SAFE DEPOSIT BOX
Letter requesting information about, 33

SAVINGS ACCOUNT
Letter requesting information about, 37–38

SCHEDULE OF DISTRIBUTION, 379–82

SECURITIES
See also, Bonds; Stock
Affidavit of individual executrix (for transfer), 51
Capital transactions involving. See Capital transactions
Corporate bond, 49–50
Spread sheet, 47
Stock certificate, 48

SETTLEMENT AGREEMENTS
New York State agreement for only interested party, 367–70
Separate agreement for each interested party, 364–65
Single agreement for all interested parties, 365–67

SOCIAL SECURITY
Form SSA–8–F4—Application for Lump-Sum Death Payment, 59–62
Form SSA–24—Application for Survivors Benefits, 63

SPREAD SHEET
Capital transactions, 313, 314
Securities, 47

STATE DEATH TAXES
Determining state where decedent may owe taxes, 302
With multiple joint tenants, 304

STOCK
Alternate valuation of, 172–73
Certificate, 48
Form 706, Schedule B, 174, 273
Power, 52
Transactions involving, 313, 314
Valuation of, 156–57

SURVIVING SPOUSE
Form 706, Schedule M, 249–51, 282–84

TANGIBLE PERSONAL PROPERTY
Affidavit of executor for appaisal of, 197
Preliminaries to distribution of, 197

TRUSTS
Contingent trust in will, 417–20
Credit shelter trust and marital trust in will, 421–25

Irrevocable "insurance" trust agreement, 440–46
Irrevocable inter vivos trust, 447–49
Powers of trustees, 456
QTIP trust, establishing, 451
Residuary trust, 426–28, 452–54

VETERANS' BENEFITS
Burial benefits, application for, 65–66
Dependency and indemnity compensation or death pension, application for, 68–71
Life insurance, claim for, 67

WILLS
Credit shelter trust for children—marital trust for wife, 421–25
Outright to spouse—contingent trust to children, 417–20
Pour-over will, 428–30
Powers clause, 430–31
Powers clause involving business asset, 431–32
Residuary trust in, 426–28
Self-proving clause, 436–37
Wife's simple will, 412–13